HISTORICAL ESSAYS

EDWARD D. DUVALL

Also by Edward D. Duvall

The Federalist Companion: A Guide to Understanding *The Federalist Papers*

This book contains a direct account of the historical events of the Revolutionary era from 1760 to 1788, emphasizing the causes of the war, its conduct, and the failures of the Articles of Confederation following the peace. It also shows the structure of the arguments presented by Jay, Hamilton, and Madison in their defense of the Constitution as contained in *The Federalist Papers*, and a cross-reference between the Federalist essays and provisions of the Constitution.

Can You Afford That Student Loan?
How To Avoid Excessive Student Loan Indebtedness

This book describes the basics of the student loan programs as well as the risks and benefits of student loans. It then provides a clear method by which the student can determine the affordability of a student loan. This is done using an extensive table of occupations and their starting salaries from the Bureau of Labor Statistics. Using some common rules for debt repayment, the book contains a unique nomographic method for determining the affordability of a loan when the payments come due, given starting salaries and repayment terms. It concludes with several examples that illustrate the most common issues regarding the affordability of student loans.

Real World Graduation
The Entrance Exam for Adulthood

This book contains 101 questions and answers that will help young people adjust from school to the real world. Warning: the real world does not function in the neat, organized fashion as represented in the school textbooks. The real world operates entirely differently.

The Control and Manipulation of Money
Basic economics, and a financial and economic history of the U. S.

Part 1 discusses basic economics, including labor, capital, rent, money, and the banking system. Part 2 is a complete financial and economic history of the U. S. from 1775 to 2020. It is divided into 12 chapters; one describes the National Banking system (1862-1914), and one describes the Federal Reserve (1914-present). Each of the other chapters cover a certain period in U. S. monetary history, mostly aligned along the lines of the banking system in force. Each chapter includes data regarding: U. S. government revenues and expenditures, national debt, condition statements of the banking system, money supply, and consumer price / income indices.

https://fremontvalleybooks.com

Historical Essays

Edward D. Duvall

Fremont Valley Books, LLC
Queen Creek, AZ

1 May 2023

ISBN: 978-0-9845773-5-4

For further information, contact edward.d.duvall@gmail.com

Published by Fremont Valley Books, LLC
https://fremontvalleybooks.com

Edward Duvall's blog: http://edduvall.com

CONTENTS

Preface ---------- vii

1 The Revolutionary Period to the U. S. Constitution ---------- 1
- History of the American Revolution 3
- The Defects of the Articles of Confederation 83
- Washington's Circular Letter (8 Jun 1783) 123
- Benjamin Franklin Asks for Prayer (28 Jun 1787) 125
- Regarding the "Three-Fifths Rule" 127
- On the General Welfare Clause 173
- Why the House Originates Revenue Bills 175
- The False Claim for a "Living Constitution" 177
- Phrases from the U. S. Constitution 179

2 Economics and Finances ---------- 181
- The Origin of the Bank of England 183
- History of the "Continental Currency" During the American Revolution 187
- History of the Assignats of the French Revolution 211
- Facts Concerning the National Debt 223
- The Financial Status of Social Security 225
- On Bail-outs and Bail-ins 237
- The Nature of U. S. Currency 239

3 Recent Issues ---------- 241
- Operation "Fast and Furious" 243
- The Practical Aspects of Gun Control 247
- Dealing with Anti-Gay Activists 277
- The Prospects for Immigration Reform 279
- The Politics of Dependency 283
- A Review of the IRS Scandal 287
- Why Hillary Clinton Cannot Be Indicted 289
- Donald Trump's Two Crimes 293
- How "Black Lives Matter" Will Fail 297
- The Nature of ANTIFA 299

The Biden Inaugural Address, Translated 301
The Open-Border Policy Rationale 305
Fourscore and Seven (Thousand New IRS Agents) 307
President Zelenskyy's Speech Before Congress, Americanized 309
What Politicians Fear Most 315
4 Looking Ahead -- 317
The Differences Between Islam, Humanism, and Christianity 319
Ninety-Four Things You Don't Have To Do 323

Preface

The aim of this book is to assemble in one place a variety of my previous studies and analyses that, in my opinion, are important for the average educated American to know. Much of what is detailed here is not taught in the schools. Length, complexity, and the reliance on facts generally preclude any discussion in the modern media. These are not easy subjects, but I believe they are important if we, as Americans, are to retain our liberties. The errors of the past seem to recur shortly after they are forgotten.

The first objective in chapter one is to present accurate details on important historical events in early U. S. history. It begins with a detailed chronology of the Revolutionary War period from 1761 to 1788, including a catalog of the defects of the Articles of Confederation (showing why a different system was required). Next comes two short essays citing George Washington's observation that a better union of the states was necessary, and Benjamin Franklin's call for prayer during the Constitutional Convention.

The second objective in chapter one is to address some provisions of the U. S. Constitution that are currently either being distorted or misunderstood. The first of these is an extended recounting of the debates and compromises during the conventions that led to the Articles of Confederation and the Federal Constitution, resulting in the famous "three-fifths rule". The next three consider the meaning of the general welfare clause, why the House of Representatives originates revenue bills, and the claims regarding a "living Constitution".

Chapter two is devoted to economic and financial topics. First is a description of how the Bank of England came into being. Next is a recounting of the disastrous effects caused by issuing large quantities of paper money by Congress during the American Revolution ("Continentals") and later by the Revolutionary Government during the French Revolution ("assignats" and "mandats"). The chapter closes out with essays on the U. S. national debt, the financial situation of Social Security, a comment on bank bailouts, and a clarification on the nature of the U. S. dollar.

Chapter three contains essays on recent issues: a) federal agencies (BATFE and IRS); b) famous people (Hillary Clinton, Donald Trump, Joe Biden, and Volodymyr Zelenskyy); c) famous organizations (ANTIFA and Black Lives Matter); and d) relevant issues of the day (gun control and immigration).

Chapter four reminds all of us of the most important issue; far more important than history, economic conditions, or political situations.

Some of the essays in this book are from past blog posts at https://edduvall.com.

A few of them are sections extracted from my books, including the *Federalist Companion: A Guide to Understanding The Federalist Papers, The Control and Manipulation of Money,* and *Real World Graduation.* All my books can be downloaded free in pdf format at: https://fremontvalleybooks.com. Many of the historical documents cited herein are in the public domain, including *Elliot's Debates on the Federal Constitution*, and *The Federalist Papers*.

1

The Revolutionary Period to the U. S. Constitution

Introduction

This chapter contains nine essays devoted to early American history and some elements of the U. S. Constitution.

The first one is a history of the major events of the American Revolutionary period: a) from 1761-1775, when the first agitation against Britain's tyranny began; b) the Revolutionary War (1775-1781); c) the troubled times after the war (1781-1787); and d) the adoption of the U. S. Constitution (1788). The main emphasis is on the political and military events of the period, showing the problems encountered by the Congress and George Washington as the commander of the army. (A significant problem was funding the war by issuing paper money called "Continentals", which is discussed more fully in an essay in chapter 2.) The description of those problems leads directly to the second essay, which addresses the problems of governing the nation under the Articles of Confederation, and how the subsequent Constitution resolved them.

The third essay is taken directly from a letter by George Washington in 1783, in which he urges the states to establish a better governing system than the Articles of Confederation. The fourth essay is a call for prayer by Benjamin Franklin during the Constitutional Convention in 1787.

The fifth essay concerns the "three-fifths rule" of apportionment of representation in Congress under the original Constitution. It is in two parts: a) an extract from Thomas Jefferson's notes taken during the debate on the provisions of the Articles of Confederation; and b) a long extract from the debates in the Constitutional Convention, taken directly from *Elliot's Debates on the Federal Constitution*. Both of these together give an accurate picture of how the famous "three-fifths rule" was adopted at the 1787 Federal Constitutional Convention. You will see from the original debates that this compromise position came about because of money, not race.

The next three essays contain some comments on particular provisions in the U. S. Constitution. The sixth essay discusses the real meaning of the "general welfare" clause; the seventh explains why the House of Representatives originates revenue bills, and the eighth addresses the false claim the Constitution should be treated as a "living document" to be changed and re-interpreted per the latest political fad.

The ninth essay presents a "multiple-guess" question on provisions of the U. S. Constitution, along with an explanation of the correct answer.

History of the American Revolution

Note: This essay is derived from chapter 2 of the book *The Federalist Companion.* It shows the historical context of the *Federalist Papers* (1787), which were issued by Hamilton, Madison, and Jay to promote the ratification by New York of the proposed Constitution. In order to appreciate the difficulties faced by the newly independent states after the Revolution, it is necessary to examine the events dating back prior to the Revolution. This essay describes briefly: a) the general attitudes of the Americans during this period; b) prominent persons; c) the types of money in use; and d) a chronology of events. These illustrate the overall ineffectiveness of Congress in the management of both the war and the peace.

1 General Attitudes of the People in the Colonial Era

The American colonists had endured plenty of abuse from the English crown and were reluctant to convey powers to a government beyond that of their own state. It was obvious that some sort of central direction of the war was necessary, and the states consented to the operation of Congress under the Articles of Confederation, but gave it very few powers. Even these powers were mostly dependent on the goodwill of individual states for their operation.

The people were not particularly enamored of the prospect of a union. First, they retained intense local and state loyalties since the familiar state governments generally operated in accordance with local needs. Secondly, the people did not perceive a need for a union, especially since the apparent danger from England had passed. Third, many people harbored a fear that any central government would become as tyrannical as had the British Crown.

The people did not appreciate the benefits of trade; mostly they adhered to the old mercantile concept, in which it was believed one party gained at the expense of the other in every transaction. In modern times, common experience dictates that both parties gain in most transactions, otherwise transactions would simply stop. But this was a new concept in colonial times, having just been explained by Adam Smith in his 1776 *Wealth of Nations*. The state governments therefore took the narrow-minded view that restrictions on trade, if properly managed, would accrue advantages to each state. This attitude was no doubt an outgrowth of how England had treated the colonies: as captive customers for the produce of England. English policy had been to prohibit the colonies from trading elsewhere. In effect, the colonies were required to buy from manufacturers in England while selling raw materials to the English at fixed prices. It was implemented partly through the activities of authorized monopolies. In other words, the colonists paid enough to ensure a profit for the English, but sold to the English at just above subsistence prices. These policies had another pernicious effect, which was to inhibit commercial development in the colonies, since the total market was more or less fixed. The only antidote for this situation was smuggling. Although the Revolution was partly over unfair trade restrictions imposed by England, most people in the states did not perceive the big picture after the peace, namely that internecine economic warfare between the states would have the same negative effects on the newly independent states as had existed while they had been English colonies.

But America also had several advantages. First, the institutions of all thirteen states were more or less homogeneous, either being English in character or heavily influenced by English practices. Secondly, they had been successful against a common enemy and had maintained friendly relations before the Revolution. Third, the numerous immigrants had assimilated English customs and the English language.

The population of the thirteen colonies prior to the war was about 2,750,000, of which about 395,000 were slaves; and by the end of the war, had increased to about 3,250,000, of which about 465,000 were slaves. The 1790 census totaled 3,929,214, but that figure included the new state of Kentucky. Vermont had also become a state by that time, but its population would have been included under either New York or New Hampshire during the war period.

2 Prominent Persons

Adams, John, early patriot in Massachusetts; envoy to France, Great Britain, and Holland; later second President of the United States

Adams, Samuel, early patriot instigator in Massachusetts

Alexander, William, American general, also known as Lord Stirling, from his claim to an expired Scottish earldom

Arnold, Benedict, American general until his betrayal in 1780; thereafter a British officer

Bernard, Sir Francis, royal governor of Massachusetts, Aug 1760–Jul 1769

Botetourt, Lord, (Norborne Berkeley), royal governor of Virginia, 1769–1770

Bourbon, King Louis XVI, king of France

Burgoyne, John, British general

Burke, Edmund, member of House of Lords, generally sympathetic to America

Bute, Lord (John Stuart), Prime Minister of Great Britain, May 1762–Apr 1763

Camden, Lord (Charles Pratt), British cabinet officer, generally sympathetic to America

Carleton, Sir Guy, royal governor of Canada, Nov 1768–Jun 1778, became a British general and commander of all British forces Nov 1781

Clinton, George, American general (from New York), later governor of New York

Clinton, Henry, British general, commander of all British forces May 1778–Nov 1781

Conway, Henry Seymour, British cabinet officer, generally sympathetic to America

Cornwallis, Lord Charles, British general

Dartmouth, Lord (William Legge), British cabinet officer, hostile to America

De Grasse, Count Francois Joseph Paul, French admiral

Dickinson, John, legislator from New Jersey, probable author of the Articles of Confederation

Donop, Count Carl von, Hessian general fighting on the British side

Dunmore, Lord, (John Murray), royal governor of Virginia, Sep 1771–Dec 1776

Fox, Charles, British cabinet member, generally sympathetic to America

Franklin, Benjamin, American scientist and diplomat

Fraser, Simon, British general, killed at Freeman's Farm

Gage, Thomas, British general, commander of all British forces until Dec 1774

Gates, Horatio, American general (a retired English officer)

Germain, Lord George Sackville, Secretary for American affairs, Nov 1775–Nov 1781; hostile to America; was the British civilian in overall charge of the conduct of the war

Grant, James, British general

Grafton, Duke of, (Augustus FitzRoy), nominal leader of ministry during Pitt's illness, Jul 1766–Jan 1770

Greene, Nathanael, American general (from Rhode Island)

Grenville, George, Prime Minister of Great Britain, May 1763–Jul 1765

Hamilton, Alexander, Washington's military aide and later colonel; wrote some of *The Federalist Papers*, afterward became first Secretary of the Treasury

Hancock, John, early patriot instigator in Massachusetts, later governor of Massachusetts

Hanover, King George III, king of Great Britain

Henry, Patrick, preacher and patriot in Virginia, later governor of Virginia

Hillsborough, Lord (Wills Hill), British cabinet officer, hostile to America

Howe, Lord Richard, British admiral

Howe, Robert, American general

Howe, Sir William, British general, commander of all British forces, Oct 1774 –May 1778

Hutchinson, Thomas, royal governor of Massachusetts, Jul 1769–Apr 1774

Jay, John, American diplomat, wrote part of *The Federalist Papers*

Jefferson, Thomas, American legislator and diplomat, governor of Virginia; later third President of the United States

Johnson, Sir John, British general

Johnson, Sir William, British general and leader of Britain's Indian allies

de Kalb, Baron Johann, German general fighting on American side, killed at Camden

Knox, Henry, American general

von Knyphausen, Baron Wilhelm, Hessian general fighting on British side

de Lafayette, Marquis, (Marie-Joseph Paul Yves Roch Gilbert du Motier), French adventurer, general on American side

Lee, Charles, American general (an Englishman by birth); traitor to both sides

Lee, Henry "Lighthorse Harry", American cavalry officer

Lee, Richard Henry, legislator from Virginia

Lincoln, Benjamin, American general

de la Luzerne, Chevalier, French diplomat in America

Madison, James, American legislator, a driving force behind Constitution, wrote some of *The Federalist Papers*, fourth President of the United States

Marion, Francis, American militia leader

Maxwell, William, American general

Mercer, Hugh, American general, killed at Princeton

Montgomery, Richard, American general (from New York), killed at Quebec

Morgan, Daniel, American general (from Virginia, although a native of New Jersey)

Morris, Gouverneur, American legislator and finance officer

Morris, Robert, American financier; instrumental in keeping forces in the field

North, Lord Frederick, Prime Minister of Great Britain, Jan 1770–Mar 1782

Otis, James, early patriot and legislator in Massachusetts assembly

Paine, Thomas, American pamphleteer

Parker, Sir Peter, British admiral

Percy, Lord Hugh, British general

Phillips, William, British general

Pitt, Sr., William (Earl of Chatham), Prime Minister of Great Britain, Jul 1766–Jul 1769

Pitt, Jr., William, Prime Minister of Great Britain, May 1784 - Mar 1801

Prevost, Augustine, British general

Pulaski, Count Casimir, Polish engineer on the American side, killed at Savannah

Putman, Israel, American general

von Riedesel, Baron Friedrich Adolf, Hessian general fighting on the British side

Rochambeau, Count de, (Jean Baptiste Donatien de Vimeur), French general, fighting on the American side

Rodney, Sir George, British admiral

Rockingham, Marquis of, (Charles Watson-Wentworth), Prime Minister of Great Britain, Jul 1765–Jul 1766

St. Clair, Arthur, American general

Sandwich, Earl of, (John Montagu), British cabinet officer, hostile to America

Shelburne, Earl of, (William Petty), British cabinet officer, generally sympathetic to America

Schuyler, Philip, American general (from New York)

Stark, John, American general (from New Hampshire)

Stephen, Adam, American general

von Steuben, Baron Friedrich, German general aiding the American side

Stevens, Edward, American general

Stirling, Lord, American general (see William Alexander)

Sullivan, John, American general (from New Hampshire)

Sumter, Thomas, American general

Tarleton, Banastre, British general, conducted the reign of terror in the southern states

Thomas, John, American general, died of smallpox in Quebec

Townshend, Charles, chancellor of the exchequer 1766–1767; author of the "Intolerable Acts"

Tryon, William, royal governor of North Carolina and New York, later a British general

de Vergennes, Count, (Charles Gravier), foreign minister of France

Warren, Joseph, early patriot in Massachusetts and American general, killed at Bunker Hill

Wayne, Anthony, American general

Washington, George, American general (from Virginia), commander of the Continental Army, Jun 1775-Dec 1783; later first President of the United States

Weymouth, Lord, (Thomas Thynne), British cabinet officer, hostile to America

Whately, Thomas, private secretary to George Grenville

Wooster, David, American general, killed at Ridgefield

3 Coinage and Money

The British pound sterling was originally defined in the early medieval era under King Alfred as one pound of pure silver, which contains 5760 troy grains. Thus a shilling (20 to a pound) was 288 grains, and a penny (12 to a shilling) was 24 grains of silver. The penny was the standard coinage, and was improved under Henry II, who introduced a sterling standard of 0.925 pure, making the coins more durable. The actual silver content was reduced over the centuries (debased) until it stabilized in 1601 under Elizabeth I, with the silver content of the penny fixed at 7 and 23/31 grains pure silver. The physical coinage contained about two-thirds copper for weight and durability. At 7.74193 grains of silver per penny (abbreviated as d.), the shilling (abbreviated as s.) contained 92.9031 grains of silver, and the British pound sterling therefore contained 1,858.0632 grains of silver. By this convention a physical pound of silver (5,760 grains) yielded 62 shillings of coin. A later act of George III in 1816 reduced the silver content in a penny to 7 and 3/11 grains, which remained in effect until the twentieth century, but such does not concern us here. It should be noted however, that the formal exchange rate with London during this period was 4.44 Spanish milled dollars per pound sterling, a ratio often quoted when discussing conversion rates of this era. This exchange rate was fixed by statute of Parliament, and does not correlate with the ratio of actual silver content of the coinage.

The Spanish milled dollar (also known as a "piece of 8," meaning 8 *reales*) was defined as 550.209 Spanish grains of silver at 0.93055 fine, which is equivalent to 423.9 troy grains at 0.93055 fine. This equates to 394.46 grains of pure silver. However, the Spanish mint had occasionally altered the standard and some of the coins were of inferior quality; therefore, people in the colonies were accustomed to evaluating the Spanish milled dollar as a certain quantity of shillings and pence in their currency, which turned out to be only an approximation of the true weight value of the Spanish milled dollar. In other words, the Spanish milled dollar was reckoned in terms of the local currency and was, therefore, reckoned as having a different weight than the Spanish mint had decreed. This ratio, on average, resulted in the Spanish milled dollar being commonly reckoned at the equivalent of 386.7 grains of pure silver by the various colonies during the course of the Revolution and afterward.

There were two standards of coinage used in every colony: the colony pound and the Spanish milled dollar. But the colonies had adopted different standards for their own pound; none of them were equivalent to the British pound sterling. The colony pounds were subdivided into 20 shillings and 240 pence, just as in Great Britain. In Georgia and South Carolina, the pound was defined as 1547 grains of silver; in Virginia, Massachusetts, Rhode Island, Connecticut, and New Hampshire as 1289 grains; in New Jersey, Delaware, Pennsylvania, and Maryland as 1,031.25 grains; and in New York and North Carolina as 966 grains. Therefore, the Spanish milled dollar, reckoned at 386.7 grains of silver, was worth different amounts of local currency in the various colonies and was a source of great confusion in trade. For example, in Virginia, a Spanish milled dollar was reckoned at 6 s., but was 8 s. in North Carolina, 5 s. in Georgia, and 7 s. 6 d. in New Jersey. Conversion of currency from state to state was likewise inconvenient owing to a lack of a fixed standard.

The French *livre tournois*, hereafter called simply a *livre*, consisted of 20 *sous*, each *sou* consisting of 12 *deniers*. In 1726, the French government fixed the denomination at 740 *livres*, 9 *sous* per 8 troy ounces (1 mark) of pure gold, or 92.5562 *livres* per troy ounce of gold. Also, eight troy ounces of silver contained 51 *livres*, 2 *sous* and 3 *deniers*, or 6.389 *livres* per troy ounce of silver. A troy ounce consists of 480 grains, so one *livre* equaled 5.186 grains of gold or 75.129 grains of silver. The ratio of gold to silver in French coinage was therefore one to 14.487. Using the 386.7 grains of silver as the nominal reckoned value of a Spanish milled dollar, the French *livre* was worth 0.194 Spanish milled dollars. But compared to the official Spanish standard, in which the milled dollar contained 394.46 grains of silver, the French *livre* was worth 0.190 Spanish milled dollars. In the following, the former (reckoned) values are used for conversion.

The Dutch *guilder*, or *gulder*, also called a *florin*, consisted of 0.60561 grams of fine gold, or 9.615 grams of fine silver. There are 15.4323 grains per gram (31.103 grams per troy ounce), so the gold *guilder* contained 9.345 grains of fine gold or 148.38 grains of fine silver. Using the reckoned value of the Spanish milled dollar of 386.7 grains of silver, the *guilder* was worth 0.38 milled dollars. The *guilder* was thus worth 1.97 French *livres* at 75.129 grains of silver. However, the French typically valued the Dutch *guilder* at twice the value of a French *livre* [1], and that conversion is used here (*guilder* = 0.388 Spanish milled dollar).

Under the Confederation, the United States in 1786 adopted a silver coinage system in which the dollar was defined to contain 375.64 grains of pure silver, but dividing it into 100 pennies. In 1792, Congress altered the definition of a U. S. dollar to 371.245 grains of pure silver, which is 24.1 grams pure, or 416 grains (27 grams) of standard silver at 0.89259 pure. This later revision was based on an estimate the average content of Spanish coins then in circulation.

In the narrative that follows, the colony currency amounts are given in their native pounds, followed by the equivalent in Spanish milled dollars. Conversion to U. S. dollars per the 1792 standard is accomplished by multiplying the number of reckoned Spanish milled dollars by 1.0416; for the 1786 standard, multiply by 1.0294. Many of the older authors used the 1792 dollar for these conversions. Continental currency is called out per its face value in dollars ($), and afterwards summarized as to its true reckoned value in Spanish milled dollars (SM$) after depreciation.

Converting all the various coinages to Spanish milled dollars as a common reference leads to the following ratios. The British pound sterling by weight was equal to 4.71 SM$ per the Spanish mint definition. But by the reckoned value of 386.7 grains per SM$, the pound sterling was equivalent to 4.80 SM$. However, the official exchange rate with England was fixed by Parliament at 4.44 SM$. Based on the definition of the colonial pounds in grains of silver, the pound of Georgia and South Carolina were reckoned as worth 4.0 SM$; that of Virginia, Massachusetts, Rhode Island, Connecticut, and New Hampshire reckoned as 3.333 SM$; that of New Jersey, Delaware, Pennsylvania, and Maryland reckoned as 2.666 SM$, and that of North Carolina and New York reckoned as 2.5 SM$. The French *livre* equated to 0.194 SM$, and the Dutch *guilder* equated to 0.388 SM$.

One-sixth of a Spanish milled dollar was called a *picayune* in the Spanish-controlled Louisiana territory. There was also a common gold coin called a *Johanes*, or *joe*; it was worth 16 Spanish milled dollars.

Most of the paper currency issued by the states and by Congress was in the form of "bills of credit," which circulated like money, and commonly called "Continentals". The two terms are used interchangeably in the following narrative.

4 Chronology of Events in America from 1761 to 1787

Feb 1761: The British decided to enforce the Navigation Acts, which required all trade with the colonies to be conducted on British ships. In order to suppress smuggling, a revenue agent in Boston could request a general search warrant, known as a "writ of assistance," which would allow him to conduct an arbitrary search of any warehouse or private home without having to give a justification, or to announce what he was searching for. These were a bad idea, held over from the reign of Charles II and were used from time to time in Britain. They were, however, unknown in the colonies, and were contrary to the established constitutions. James Otis, John Adams, and Oxenbridge Thatcher argued against them. The writs were granted by Chief Justice Hutchinson of Boston, the king's highest-ranking judicial officer in the colony, after he had traded messages with legal experts back in Great Britain.

May 1761: The legislature of Virginia voted to gradually reduce slavery in Virginia by imposing a tax on it, but was vetoed by Parliament.

9 Dec 1761: The chief justice of the colony of New York had always been removable by the colonial assembly. But on 9 Dec 1761, continuation in office was made dependent only on the wishes of the king, thus removing popular control over the highest judicial officer. The net effect was to make the local judiciary subservient directly to the king.

Jun 1762: The New York assembly responded to the edict regarding judges by refusing to vote a salary for the chief justice, but that action was nullified when the king directed that the salaries of all judges in the colonies would be paid directly from royal revenue. Now the people of the colonies had no control over the judiciary.

Sep 1762: The royal governor of Massachusetts, Sir Francis Bernard, sent an expedition against the French to protect some fishing rights, for which he presented a bill to the assembly for payment of 400 pounds (SM$1,332). The assembly refused to pay it on the grounds that the expense had been incurred without their authorization. James Otis led the movement to refuse payment, writing in his "Vindication" that colonial assemblies had the same power over expenses as Parliament did in England.

3 Nov 1762: Preliminary articles of peace were signed between France (allied with Spain) and Great Britain (allied with Portugal), ending the Seven Years War (called the French and Indian War in North America). Under the terms: a) Spain ceded the Florida territories to Great Britain; b) France

ceded Canada, Acadia, Cape Breton, and all the islands in the West Indies except St. Pierre and Miquelon to Great Britain; c) France and Great Britain to share the fisheries off Newfoundland; d) France ceded New Orleans and territory west of the Mississippi to Spain; d) Great Britain received Senegal in Africa and all of the slave trade; e) France ceded Minorca to Great Britain; f) France retained the islands in the East Indies that it had held in 1749. During the negotiations, the French foreign minister predicted that ceding Canada to Great Britain would lead to independence of colonies in North America.

Jan 1763: The king issued an edict in which a standing army of 20 battalions were to be retained in the colonies after the return of peace, which were to be paid by the colonies.

10 Feb 1763: The peace treaty ending the Seven Years War was ratified by Parliament.

Mar 1763: Parliament passed an act in which the British navy was authorized to search and seize any ship in the Atlantic traveling to the colonies. The intent of the law was to enlist the aid of the navy in enforcing the customs duties, and naval officers were awarded part of the proceeds in the case of confiscations. The navy was thus directed to act as spies, informers, and agents for the customs house.

May - Sep 1763: Pontiac's War: The Indians in the west (what is now western New York, western Pennsylvania, Ohio, Michigan, Indiana, and Illinois) conducted a series of attacks and massacres upon English settlements in those areas. The Indians did not harm any of the French settlers.

17 Mar 1764: Parliament passed the Declaratory Resolves, promoted by George Grenville, Prime Minister of Great Britain, which announced that Parliament intended to impose taxes on the American colonies through a tax on newspapers and legal documents. The revenue was to be collected by requiring the affected documents to bear a stamp, which could be purchased only from the local British revenue officer. The tax was to take effect in 1765. The Americans were opposed to it because the notion that a tax could be imposed without their consent was contrary to established custom in the colonies.

Apr 1764: France transferred New Orleans and all of Louisiana to Spain per the treaty with Great Britain, fearing that it would cost too much to maintain those territories.

5 Apr 1764: Parliament passed a series of trade restrictions and taxes on the colonies: a) import duties on wines; b) a new duty on molasses; c) increased duty on sugar; d) some protection measures to benefit English manufacturers; e) a prohibition on trade between the colonies and the West Indies islands of St. Pierre and Miquelon; and f) expanded means to enforce the trade regulations.

25 Jun 1764: Town hall meetings were held in Boston throughout June to discuss the proposed revenue measure. Samuel Adams led the opposition, issuing a series of resolutions in which he declared that Parliament had no legitimate power to impose a tax on the colonists unless the colony were represented in Parliament. A circular letter was sent on 25 Jun 1764 to all the other colonies, asking them to take a stand on the issue.

Aug 1764: In July, militias from New Jersey, New York, and Connecticut, organized by General Gage and commanded by Colonel John Bradstreet, had advanced to central New York to deal with the marauding Indian tribes. In August, the Indians settled on peaceable terms at a meeting at Niagara, knowing their villages would all be destroyed if they didn't.

Sep 1764: King George III had issued an edict in which the western half of New Hampshire (the present-day state of Vermont) was to be annexed to New York. It was done because the royal officers of New York, greedy to obtain a profit on the sale of a land grant, managed to mislead the king about the state of the territory. The king made a new grant of land that he had already been paid for; and the current owners under the old grant had to either buy it again from the new grantees, or be evicted. The notices arrived in the colonies throughout September.

Sep 1764: The assemblies in New York, South Carolina, Pennsylvania, and Connecticut passed resolutions agreeing with the resolution from Massachusetts opposing the new taxes and duties; Connecticut, South Carolina, and New York sent petitions to Parliament.

7 Sep 1764: Bradstreet concluded a peace treaty with the Indians of Michigan and the Ohio Valley at a meeting in Detroit; these territories came under British rule, and the British promised to protect the Indians from their enemies.

12 Oct 1764: The governor of Rhode Island, popularly elected by the people, declared that Parliament had no power to regulate trade in the colonies. On 12 Oct 1764, a committee of correspondence issued a circular letter to the other colonies asking for their opinion on the trade acts. It also sent a petition to Parliament asking for reconsideration.

26 Oct 1764: The colonists sent a notice to Parliament through their agent in London, Benjamin Franklin, that they would contribute to the royal treasury if asked, but did not support a general tax imposed by Parliament.

31 Oct 1764: The legislature of North Carolina rejected the principle of taxation by Parliament.

3 Nov 1764: The Massachusetts assembly issued a petition to Parliament opposing the revenue acts of 5 Apr 1764 on the grounds that their implementation would ruin commerce in the colony. They also complained about the lack of money in the colony owing to the constant drainage of it by the monopoly position of Great Britain with respect to the colony.

14 Nov 1764: The legislature in Virginia issued a document called a Remonstrance, outlining the history of the colonies, the relations between them and Great Britain, and rejecting Parliament's power to enact a tax on them without their consent. It also warned Britain that the colonies may decide to stop importing from Britain and begin to do its own manufacturing. It was sent to the House of Commons along with a petition against the new taxes.

11 Dec 1764: The British board of trade wrote to the king that the resolutions of Massachusetts and New York had shown disrespect to Parliament, and urged the king to take some action to restrain the colonies.

18 Dec 1764: The Virginia House of Burgesses wrote a petition to Parliament opposing the Declaratory Resolves of 17 Mar 1764 on the grounds that a stamp act amounted to taxation without representation, unknown in the colonies up to that time.

10 Jan 1765: King George III opened Parliament with a statement that the central question regarding the colonies was their "obedience to the laws and respect for the legislative authority of the kingdom."

15 Feb 1765: Parliament rejected the petitions that had been sent from Rhode Island, New York, Massachusetts, Virginia, South Carolina, and Connecticut. Parliament had decided that it had a right to tax the colonies.

22 Mar 1765: Parliament passed the Stamp Act, requiring stamps on marriage certificates, loan documents, lawsuits, real estate sales, wills, and newspapers. Legal documents without the required stamp would be regarded as null and void. It was widely denounced in the colonies. It was to go into effect on 1 Nov 1765.

24 Mar 1765: Parliament extended the Mutiny Act to the colonies: a) soldiers could be quartered in inns, taverns, barns, and empty houses at the colonist's expense; and b) people were required to provide some items upon demand from the military. It also modified some trade regulations, under which colonies were allowed to export lumber, iron, and rice to England. But the colonies were still constrained to export their most valuable products, namely sugar, indigo, tobacco, cotton, pelts, tar, turpentine, copper, pitch, molasses, ships rigging, silk, or hides only to ports in Great Britain. The colonists were also prohibited from carrying wool or hats across colonial boundaries; wool had to be imported from Great Britain. Bibles could not be printed in the colonies; foundries, forges, and steel-making were prohibited.

30 May 1765: Patrick Henry of Virginia introduced a resolution in the Virginia assembly condemning the Stamp Act on several grounds: a) colonists had the same rights as the king's subjects in Britain; b) taxes could only be imposed by the consent of the people or of people representing them; c) that any attempt by Parliament to impose a tax on the colonists threatened the liberty of the colonists and the people in Britain alike; d) the people of Virginia were not obligated to obey the Stamp Act since it violated these principles, and e) those who did obey it should be considered public enemies. The royal governor of Virginia dissolved the assembly before a vote could be taken on it; but the resolution was published throughout the colonies and met with widespread approval.

Summer 1765: The colonists staged a general rejection of the Stamp Act throughout the colonies: a) boxes of stamps were seized and tossed overboard from the ships; b) stamp officers were forced to resign; and c) merchants reduced or stopped importation of British products. It became clear to Parliament, once it heard of these, that enforcement of the Stamp Act would likely prove impossible.

6 Jun 1765: The assembly in Massachusetts, on a recommendation by James Otis, sent a circular letter to the assemblies in the other colonies, calling for a general meeting to discuss how to respond to the Stamp Act.

25 Jul 1765: The assembly of South Carolina became the first colony to endorse a general meeting, per the recommendation from Massachusetts.

14 Aug 1765: Throughout the summer, men in Massachusetts had formed themselves into small groups calling themselves "Sons of Liberty" which were devoted to resisting the Stamp Act. On 14 Aug 1765, the Sons of Liberty burned effigies of the stamp-officer Oliver and the former Prime Minister Lord Bute, and destroyed the stamp house (still under construction).

26 Aug 1765: The Sons of Liberty invaded and ruined the home of Chief Justice Hutchinson. This invasion did not make much sense, since Hutchinson had done his best to prevent the imposition of the Stamp Act.

28 Aug 1765: Patriots in Providence, Rhode Island, ruined the houses of two people who had written in support of the Stamp Act, and forced the stamp officer to resign his commission.

Sep 1765: The assemblies of Pennsylvania, Rhode Island, Delaware, Maryland, and Connecticut agreed to send delegates to a general meeting of the colonies.

2 Sep 1765: The assembly of Georgia agreed to send delegates to a general meeting of the colonies.

2 Sep 1765: The stamp officer in Maryland, afraid for his life due to the unrest, fled to New York.

3 Sep 1765: The stamp officer for New Jersey resigned.

9 Sep 1765: The stamp officer for New Hampshire, arriving by sea at Boston, resigned his commission before leaving the ship.

~20 Sep 1765: The stamp officer in Connecticut was forced to resign by a large number of men who followed him on a trip to Wethersfield.

21 Sep 1765: The Pennsylvania assembly issued a resolution opposing the Stamp Act: a) the colony had always supported the king's requests for money and men; b) money is to be raised in a constitutional way; c) the only constitutional way is taxation with representation; and d) since the colonists were not represented in Parliament, the Stamp Act was destructive to happiness.

3 Oct 1765: The stamp officer in Pennsylvania resigned his office.

~5 Oct 1765: The Massachusetts assembly passed a resolution against the Stamp Act, authored by Samuel Adams. It declared that the Stamp Act was contrary to long-standing traditions, would serve to reduce confidence in the royal government, and was viewed in America as a revision of the fundamental rules by which the colonies had always been governed.

7 Oct-25 Oct 1765: The first meeting of delegates from the colonies met as a congress at New York. Only nine colonies were represented: Connecticut, Delaware, Maryland, Massachusetts, New York, Pennsylvania, Rhode Island, Georgia, and South Carolina. Virginia could not send delegates be-

cause the governor dissolved the assembly before delegates could be chosen. On 19 Oct, the congress issued a letter to the king and Parliament expressing their common sentiments: a) opposition to the Stamp Act; b) that trial by the admiralty in cases of suspected smuggling was contrary to their rights as Englishmen; c) that the colonies could only be taxed by colonial legislatures; d) colonies could not be represented in Parliament due to local circumstances; e) all revenues from the colonies to the crown were to be regarded as gifts; and f) Parliament's alleged power to take property from any colonist was contrary to established constitutional principles.

31 Oct 1765: About 200 merchants of New York pledged to each other not to buy anything from British merchants in response to the Stamp Act. They pledged: a) not to import anything from Great Britain until the Stamp Act was repealed; b) cancellation of existing orders at the earliest opportunity; and c) products received from Great Britain after 1 Jan 1766 would not be sold. It is known as the New York Non-Importation Agreement.

1 Nov 1765: On the day the Stamp Act was to take effect, many people in all the colonies staged public demonstrations against it, vowing they would never buy a stamp. Newspapers were published without the required stamp, and many contained editorials denouncing it.

1-2 Nov 1765: Several men staged a riot in New York over the Stamp Act. A group of men, intent on seizing the stamps, broke into the governor's stable, stole one of his carriages, rode it around town, and then burned it. Lieutenant-Governor Colden threatened to set the army on the mob, but he was warned that he would be hanged if he did so. General Gage, commander of the royal army in the colonies, did not interfere, as he did not have sufficient troops to deal with the situation. The stamps were handed over by Colden to the New York common council, and secured.

Jan-May 1766: The colonies were united in opposition to the Stamp Act; no one bought them, people refused to buy imports from Great Britain, and women took to spinning their own cloth. Several of the legislatures declared that the Stamp Act was null and void in the colonies.

8 Jan 1766: The Sons of Liberty in New York searched an incoming ship from Great Britain, and found ten packages of stamps intended for New York and Connecticut. The stamps were removed and burned.

13 Feb 1766: George Grenville and Charles Townshend had an interview with Benjamin Franklin, Pennsylvania's agent in London. They asked him if the Americans would ever submit to the Stamp Act, or any other internal tax or any tax levied without their consent, and how the colonists would behave if an army were sent to enforce it. Franklin replied that the Americans would never submit to any internal taxes; and, if an army were sent, they would find nothing to do because the Americans would do for themselves, make all their own manufactures, and find a way to peacefully avoid the taxes. Franklin warned them that the colonists may start to believe that Parliament had no right to levy external taxes either. In this context, an "internal tax" is any type of tax that is not in the form of an import duty. Import duties were popularly known as "external taxes," and the Americans had not objected to them.

18 Mar 1766: Parliament repealed the Stamp Act and the authorization for general search warrants. But Parliament also passed a Declaratory Act in which it asserted arbitrary power to pass any laws for the colonies. The repeal of the Stamp Act was celebrated in the colonies. The Declaratory Act was ignored; it was regarded as little more than a means for Parliament to save face.

Jul 1766: A significant political change occurred in Great Britain. William Pitt Sr. succeeded Rockingham as Prime Minister. But Pitt was in poor health, so he took a position in the House of Lords as the Earl of Chatham, and the office of Prime Minister passed to the Duke of Grafton. His cabinet consisted of Conway, Camden, Shelburne, and Townshend. The first three were sympathetic to America's views on the power of Parliament; but Townshend, as Chancellor of the Exchequer (finance officer), was hostile to America. Townshend would become the most powerful person in the cabinet.

29 Jun 1767: Parliament passed the Townshend Acts, a series of measures for obtaining revenue from the American colonies through port duties. Townshend was attempting to capitalize on the sentiment expressed previously by the Americans, namely that they were amenable to "external" taxation, but opposed to "internal" taxation. In this they were referring to direct taxes as internal, and taxes related to trade as external. Therefore, the revenue portion of the Townshend Acts contained only import duties. The Townshend Acts consisted of: a) import duties on wine, oil, fruits, glass, paper, lead, paints, and tea; b) establishment of a central board of commissioners at Boston charged with administration of the duties for all the colonies; c) powers of writs of assistance for enforcement; d) power given to the crown to appoint all civil offices in all the colonies and to pay their salaries; and e) annulment of the New York assembly until it agreed to fund the royal army at New York. The duty revenue was to be used to pay salaries and pensions to the royal administrators and civil servants in the colonies. These acts were denounced in the colonies because they meant a removal of all political freedom. King George III was in a peculiar position: if he conceded the colonists the notion of "no taxation without representation," he would be adopting in the colonies the opposite of what prevailed in Britain itself. It would mean unrelenting calls for Parliament to be reformed such that every part of Britain was represented. If that happened, the king would lose the ability to buy and sell seats in Parliament from which much of his power derived. So, George III believed it necessary to impose arbitrary rule on the colonies in order to consolidate and continue to legitimize his manner of ruling in Britain.

4 Sep 1767: Chancellor of Exchequer Townshend died, and was succeeded by Lord North, who was competent but indolent, devoted to the king, and opposed to popular government. This was accompanied by a general change in the ministry by replacement of Shelburne, Conway, and Camden with Lord Hillsborough, Lord Weymouth, and the Earl of Sandwich, all of whom were hostile to the Americans.

Oct 1767: John Dickinson, writing under the pen name of The Farmer, issued a series of essays showing that the recent laws by Parliament were a "dangerous innovation"; especially those that prohibited manufacturing in the colonies, since a duty on items the colonists were prohibited to manufacture would spell the end of liberty. He urged the colonists to attempt to find some peaceful way to obtain redress; otherwise, he reminded his readers, that English history had shown the way to resist intrusions upon liberty were by force. “The Farmer's Letters” were widely distributed in the colonies, and kept the issue in the forefront of political debate.

28 Oct 1767: A town meeting was held in Boston, and the people resolved to not buy or use any of the items that were subject to an import duty; they also sent a circular letter to the other towns in Massachusetts and the other colonies. This was the colonists' method of depriving the Townshend Acts of any benefit to the crown or to the local royal officers.

11 Feb 1768: Samuel Adams and the Massachusetts assembly wrote a series of letters to the ministry, the king, and a circular letter to all the other colonies. He outlined his opposition to the Townshend Acts on the ground they were unconstitutional: a) legislatures have limited powers derived from the constitution; b) allegiance to government is forfeited if the government oversteps its powers; c) colonists had the right of property by natural law regardless of the interpretation of colonial charters; d) Parliament had no constitutional authority to tax the colonists, since the colonists were not represented; e) there was no practical method for the colonists to be represented in Parliament (because it could not be done proportional to population, and it was common knowledge that seats were bought and sold in Parliament); f) there was no means to appeal Parliament's taxes; g) the colonists had equal rights with all Englishmen; h) the colonists could not be prohibited from manufacturing because people in Britain were not so prohibited; i) using duty revenues to pay royal officers would lead to a corrupt government because it was outside the control of the people; j) Parliament had no power to suspend the legislature of New York; and k) Parliament had no power to impose quartering on the people. He urged that they be repealed, and relations restored as before. Meanwhile, the general public refused to buy British goods as a means of protesting the import duties.

Spring 1768: Impressments of citizens as seamen on the frigate *Romney* in Boston caused popular resentment, but no violence.

21 Apr 1768: Lord Hillsborough ordered the assembly at Massachusetts to rescind the circular letter of 11 Feb 1768, and ordered all the other colonial legislatures to ignore it. The penalty for refusing was that the legislature would be dissolved. This was a case of a royal officer promoting himself to dictatorial powers over all the legislatures in all the colonies. The letter arrived in Boston on 18 Jun 1768.

8 Jun 1768: Hillsborough ordered General Gage to send troops and five ships to Boston as a show of force, although no violence had occurred there.

10 Jun 1768: A ship owned by John Hancock was seized in Boston harbor on suspicion of violating the customs laws, and was searched without a warrant. It led to a small riot on the waterfront in Boston. A few days later, assurance was given by Governor Bernard that there would be no further impressments of citizens, but he refused to order the removal of the frigate *Romney*.

21 Jun 1768: The Massachusetts assembly refused to rescind its circular letter of 11 Feb 1768, and was dissolved by Governor Bernard. The legislatures of the other colonies followed suit, and they were also dissolved. The colonists now began to believe that a break with Great Britain was both desirable and likely.

27 Jul 1768: Parliament restored the "Treason Abroad" statutes of Henry VIII in response to the disturbances in Boston. Under that statute, a person accused of treason while in a foreign country was to be brought back to England for trial before the King's Bench. It had not been used for several centuries. In reality, the riots in Boston had been minor affairs, but the reports of the governor contained such exaggerations that the people in Britain began to believe that the people of Boston were pirates, mobsters, and traitors, and that only recourse to martial law could restore order. Hillsborough ordered two regiments of 500 men each to Boston to keep order, and adopted measures to outlaw the town hall meeting.

1 Aug 1768: The merchants of Boston pledged to each other not to buy anything from British merchants except for a few necessities, and not to import any items upon which there was an import duty (tea, glass, paper, and painter's colors). It is known as the Boston Non-Importation Agreement.

28 Sep 1768: The British forces landed at Boston, but could not be stationed in Boston owing to a previous act that required the troops to fully occupy the barracks at Castle William before they could be quartered in Boston. Bernard refused to convene the assembly to decide how to allocate the military. The people used their own initiative to send delegates to Boston to decide in their place. Bernard ordered the delegates to disperse, but the delegates simply voted that the existing law had to be observed. The British initially stayed in tents on the common, and then moved into old warehouses, which had to be rented at high rates. The interaction between the people and the military was tense, as the soldiers liked to get drunk and fight, and to antagonize the people.

6 Dec 1768: Parliament resolved to isolate the people of Boston for their rejection of Parliament's authority, and make it an example such that the other colonies would not imitate their actions.

26 Jan 1769: Parliament passed a set of resolutions which condemned the assembly at Massachusetts and approved the sending of a military force to bring the colony under military rule. It authorized the governor of Massachusetts to obtain evidence and order arrests for treason, which were to be prosecuted by trial in England under the statute of Henry VIII. The objective was to try and hang the ringleaders in Boston, especially Samuel Adams, John Hancock, and James Otis.

Apr 1779: The American tactic of boycotting British goods began to affect British merchants. Under pressure from London businessmen, Parliament debated repeal of the Townshend Acts.

2 May 1769: The Virginia House of Burgesses, whose members included George Washington, Patrick Henry, and Thomas Jefferson, met at Williamsburg. It passed a series of resolutions condemning the Townshend Acts on the following grounds: a) people of Virginia could only be taxed by their own

representatives; b) it was the duty of all Americans to defend the rights of the colonists (thus supporting Massachusetts); and c) warned the king of the high risk he was taking if any Americans were sent to England for trial. Lord Botetourt, royal governor of Virginia, dissolved the House for passing them. But they were circulated a few days later to the other legislatures as the "Virginia Resolutions" and were endorsed by all the legislatures of the southern colonies.

22 Jul 1769: The assembly at Charleston, SC passed a non-importation agreement in response to the Townshend Acts: a) to promote manufactures in the colony; b) no importation of slaves after 1 Jan 1770; and c) agreed not to import anything from Great Britain, except coal and salt. It is known as the Charleston Non-Importation Agreement.

31 Jul 1769: The ministry replaced Massachusetts royal governor Sir Francis Bernard with Thomas Hutchinson, a native of Massachusetts. Bernard was known to be corrupt, greedy, and conniving; he had engaged in smuggling when profitable, but aggressively enforced the Navigation Acts and obtained large revenues from fines and forfeitures. He had exaggerated the discontent in Boston, portraying minor disturbances as riots, revolution, and treason. He was regarded by the British military as a coward and a liar.

Aug 1769 ff: There was a great deal of tension between the people of Boston and the soldiers; the men of the 29th regiment were very rowdy, and routinely insulted the women and children. The soldiers were anxious for a chance to attack the people, but the people were careful not to provoke them. The soldiers frequently broke the law, and the people made many complaints to the local judges.

Sep 1769: James Otis of Boston, who had been in declining mental health, was attacked by a British customs officer, and suffered permanent injury.

17 Oct 1769: The people of Boston agreed to extend the voluntary refusal to import any British goods after being requested to do so by the assembly of New York.

18 Oct 1769: The town assembly of Boston, led by Samuel Adams, issued an "Appeal to the World," ridiculing General Gage, Governor Hutchinson, and the revenue collectors. The appeal informed the British that: a) the removal of the duties on tea, glass, and paper alone would not be sufficient to bring the people back into the British fold; and b) because Parliament had violated their rights, it would be necessary for the duties to be repealed and the military evacuated before the people would consider their complaints to have been addressed.

Nov 1769: The legislature of Virginia passed a bill to end the traditional higher taxes imposed on black people; Jefferson added to it a section that would emancipate all the slaves in the colony, with a prohibition on further importation. It was sent to Parliament for approval.

31 Jan 1770: Lord North became the Prime Minister of Great Britain. He was generally sympathetic to the colonies, but was weak, and easily dominated by the king, who wanted above all to establish an autocratic personal government in both the colonies and Great Britain.

22 Feb 1770: A British informer in Boston, harassed by rock-throwing boys, opened fire into a crowd from his house, killing a boy. He was convicted of murder, but was pardoned by the governor.

5-6 Mar 1770: A confrontation between some Boston men and the British soldiers ended when the soldiers fired on the crowd on 5 Mar 1770. Five people were killed, including Crispus Attucks, a black freeman who was one of the first to respond to insults and provocations by the soldiers upon some boys in the square. This became known as the "Boston Massacre." The people armed themselves, but did not fight the soldiers; they demanded justice from the governor. The governor ordered the commanding officer, Capt. Preston, and several of his men arrested. But Samuel Adams and the rest of the assembly, backed by about three thousand people, intimidated the royal officers into removing the soldiers from Boston on 6 Mar 1770.

7 Apr 1770: Parliament voted on a resolution to repeal the Townshend Acts, except for the duty on tea. The other duties were repealed because of complaints from London merchants about the loss of business owing to the boycott by the colonists. The duty on tea remained as a matter of principle; by

leaving the tea duty intact, Parliament asserted it had a legitimate power to levy it. Tea thus became the central issue between Great Britain and the colonies; it was the symbol by which the king and Parliament claimed arbitrary power. It put Great Britain in a good position, since trade would resume on all the other articles, and the duty on tea was so small that a continued boycott would not affect the financial condition of the colonists.

Jul 1770: New York merchants broke the non-importation agreement by ordering a large amount of merchandise from Britain. This angered some of the other colonies, since holding together on the non-importation policy had been the driving force that got the Townshend Acts repealed. New York had been most steadfast in adhering to the agreement. Some of the other colonies (Pennsylvania, Maryland, Virginia, North Carolina, and Georgia) had been slowly increasing their imports, mostly out of necessity.

6 Jul 1770: King George III violated the Massachusetts charter by issuing an order imposing martial law in Massachusetts. The military was concentrated in Boston, commanded by General Gage. Hutchinson handed power to Gage, and went to the fortress at Castle William for his safety.

Oct 1770: Governor Hutchinson proposed a series of measures designed to bring the people into line: a) abolish the assembly altogether, and make all offices dependent on the king; b) impose greater restrictions on commerce and fishing; and c) permit the military to act on its own without oversight by civilians. These were sent as recommendations to Parliament.

10 Dec 1770: King George III rejected the Nov 1769 Virginia bill to reduce taxation on free black people and the emancipation of slaves; there was too much profit in the slave trade for officers commissioned by the government. George III issued an order to the governor of Virginia prohibiting him from concurring with any of the numerous bills passed against slavery in Virginia.

Mar 1771: The people of western North Carolina had suffered for several years under corrupt local government: a) farmers could not obtain land titles; b) tax revenues were routinely stolen by the officials, who then attempted to extort the amount missing from the people; c) very high expenses for lawsuits and official clerical services; d) refusal of the judges to hear their cases or to decide them fairly; and e) arbitrary confiscations of property and some executions on false charges against those who opposed the government. The rural people of North Carolina had relied on local posses, known as "Regulators" to maintain nominal law and order. On 11 Mar 1771, royal Governor Tryon fraudulently obtained felony indictments against several leaders of the Regulators. Under another of the corrupt laws, a person who did not answer an indictment in 60 days, regardless of how far he had to travel, was judged guilty, his property confiscated, and he was sentenced to death. Tryon led a force of 1,800 men to Orange County, burning homes and farms on the way, to catch the Regulators. He met the Regulators on 16 Mar 1771 at Great Alamance, and told them to surrender. The Regulators refused, and Tryon attacked and defeated them. About one hundred of the Regulators were killed or wounded, and seven survivors were hanged for treason. Tryon then confiscated most of the lands held by the Regulators.

Jul 1771: The customs officers in Boston had demanded to be made exempt from income taxes, which the ministry had approved, and ordered the Massachusetts assembly to comply with it. But the assembly passed a tax law in July that required all to pay, same as usual. Samuel Adams led the opposition to the exemption, writing that selective taxation was a symptom of tyranny. The assembly's refusal to exempt the customs officers led to increased scrutiny of Boston by the military.

Jan-Jun 1772: The British schooner *Gaspee*, under command of Lt. Duddington, enforced the customs duty arbitrarily all along the Rhode Island coastline, searching and seizing whatever he chose without regard to the actual law. He also made a habit of landing troops and harassing local farmers. The people complained in Mar 1772, but were told that Lt. Duddington was only doing his duty. On 9 Jun 1772, the *Gaspee* ran aground, and was subsequently attacked by a band of men. The ship was burned and the crew placed on shore. A large reward was offered for information leading to the arrest of the attackers, but no one came forward.

Apr 1772: Parliament passed an act by which any destruction of property belonging to the British navy, no matter how trivial, was to be punished with death, and that any accused in the colonies were to be transported to Great Britain for trial.

7 Aug 1772: King George III issued a decree in which all judges in Massachusetts would hold their offices at the king's pleasure, and that their salaries would be paid out of royal revenues. This was regarded by the people of Massachusetts as an attack on the independence of the judicial system. It provoked the prominent people of Massachusetts to set up local delegations known as Committees of Correspondence to discuss what action should be taken.

Oct-Dec 1772: Lord North, Prime Minister of Great Britain, conceived a plan to aid the East India Tea Company. The Company had incurred large debts, and had warehouses full of tea in England, but could not find a market for them. It could not pay its debts or dividends, and its stock price had fallen by 50%. It also could not pay the £400,000 sterling due annually to the government. North's plan was to refund the entire import duty imposed at British ports (instead of the usual 60%), and permit the Company to re-export to America on its own. This was known as a drawback of the duties. By eliminating the duty on tea for re-export in Britain, the East India Company would be able to afford to export a great amount of tea to the colonies, and the colonists would be able to buy it cheaper than before the present colonial duty had been enacted. Politically, tempting the Americans to buy the English tea would amount to an admission on their part that Parliament did in fact have a power to impose the import duties in America, and by extension, to pass any other law for the colonies. The amount of duty on tea was not the real issue in America (the 3d. per pound was not considered unreasonable); the main issue was the principle of taxation. North's plan was intended to solve both problems: the financial problem of the East India Company and the political problem of the boycott in the colonies over a tax question. There was a suggestion of repealing the tea duty in America altogether, as it would also solve the problem, but North would not consider it.

28 Oct-2 Nov 1772: The people of Massachusetts desired to know if the order on judges was to be carried out. They appointed a committee to pose this question, and presented a petition to allow a public debate in assembly. Governor Hutchinson told the committee to stay out of the government's affairs and denied the petition for the Massachusetts assembly to meet.

3 Nov-Dec 1772: The Committees of Correspondence organized assemblies in most of the towns in Massachusetts to debate political conditions and to correspond with the people of other colonies. They became informal legislatures, and although they had no real power, were also outside the power of the governor to dissolve or abolish them.

20 Nov 1772: A town meeting in Boston reviewed and endorsed a report by its Committee of Correspondence, which claimed that people: a) have natural rights to life, liberty, and property; b) are free to alter their allegiance to oppressive government; and c) have a right to preserve their liberties by force if necessary. It set out the various complaints against the British government: a) its claim of absolute power on all topics; b) raising of taxes without the consent of the people; c) grants of arbitrary power to people tasked with collecting the revenue; d) maintaining an occupying army in peacetime; e) maintaining the civil service by the unconstitutional revenue, thus bypassing the local assembly; f) extension of the power of the admiralty courts; g) prohibitions and restrictions on manufacturing, which affected their livelihoods; h) allowing people to be sent to Great Britain for trial; i) alteration of the boundaries of colonies and re-granting of lands, which required people to purchase their property again from royal officers; and j) Parliament's claim that it could establish bishoprics and religious courts without consent of the people. It was sent to all the towns in Massachusetts.

Dec 1772: Several town meetings were held in Massachusetts, and all of them came to the conclusion that the situation with Great Britain was becoming intolerable. The towns concluded that there should be a union of the colonies to defend their rights against the king and Parliament, by force if necessary.

31 Dec 1772: An accounting of the finances of the colonies showed that the expenses and salaries for collection of the stamp office while the Stamp Act was in force were 12,000 pounds sterling, but the revenue collected was about 1,500 pounds, mostly from Canada and the West Indies. For 1772, the total revenues from the import duties on tea, wine, and paper amounted to 85 pounds, whereas the cost of collection and the army to assist them was 100,000 pounds. Meanwhile, the East India Company had lost sales revenue of about 550,000 pounds sterling annually due to the boycott by the colonists.

6-8 Jan 1773: Governor Hutchinson convened the Massachusetts assembly, and gave a speech in which he ordered them either to concede to or to disprove the supremacy of Parliament. His objective was either: a) to get the assembly sitting at Boston to endorse the legitimacy of Parliament in all cases, which would contradict the opinions lately expressed by the other towns; or b) to get the assembly to deny Parliament's powers, in which case he would have the excuse he needed to impose an autocratic regime and prosecute the leaders for treason. But Samuel Adams, in his reply, noted that if the supreme authority of Parliament and independence of the colonies were mutually exclusive, then the compact establishing the colonies must have intended independence, since the colonists would not have entered an agreement contrary to their interests. Therefore, either the colonies are independent from Parliament, or Parliament has only limited powers.

Jan-Mar 1773: Local assemblies of the people grew to importance in Virginia as they had in Massachusetts.

Feb 1773: There had been some correspondence between Thomas Hutchinson, royal Governor of Massachusetts, his Lieutenant Governor Andrew Oliver, and Thomas Whately, who had been Prime Minister George Grenville's private secretary. These letters openly discussed negative opinions about the liberties of the colonists, and laid out a conspiracy by which the colonies may be brought under total subjection. When Whately died in Dec 1772, his letters were stolen and were shown to Benjamin Franklin by a member of Parliament. Franklin was at this time the agent for Massachusetts in London. Franklin sent the letters to the Massachusetts assembly, ostensibly for secret discussion as requested by the person who had obtained the letters. They were received in April.

12 Mar 1773: The assembly in Virginia sent out a circular letter to all the other colonies urging them to establish committees of correspondence in order to debate political issues outside the control of the royal colonial governments. It also recommended the establishment of a union of the councils throughout the colonies. These were received favorably in all the colonies, but especially in Massachusetts, where the worst problems had been festering.

10 May 1773: Parliament passed the Tea Act, which implemented Lord North's plan to aid the East India Tea Company, while offering tea for sale in the colonies at a cheaper price than before. It retained the import duty on tea in the colonies.

2-9 Jun 1773: In a secret session of the Massachusetts assembly, Samuel Adams read the letters between Hutchinson, Oliver, and Whately that Franklin had sent. They had been circulating secretly for about two months at this time. The letters revealed a conspiracy between the governor, the military, and the customs officers to remove all the liberties of the colony by essentially abolishing the traditional constitution: a) imposition of martial law; b) restrictions on commerce and fishing; and c) abolition of the charter of Rhode Island. The assembly asked Hutchinson for copies of the letters of certain dates (which they already had in their possession), along with any others he might think appropriate, which he refused. On 9 Jun 1773, the assembly then published the letters they had received.

Summer-Fall 1773: The letters between Whately and Hutchinson were denounced throughout the colonies as evidence of a conspiracy to deprive the colonies of all their liberties as Englishmen. The dissemination of the letters, combined with the tea tax, provoked widespread animosity in the colonies, and the anger was directed at the most available target, the incoming ships of tea.

23 Jun 1773: The assembly at Massachusetts drew up a petition and forwarded it to the king's Privy Council, demanding the removal of Hutchinson and Oliver based on the contents of their letters.

16 Oct 1773: The assembly of Philadelphia passed resolutions condemning the tea duty, rejected Parliament's right to tax the colonists at all, and requested the local agents for the East India Company to resign.

2-29 Nov 1773: On 2, 5, and 18 Nov 1773, attempts were made in Boston to intimidate the tea agents to resign, but they refused, and Boston then became the central point in the contest over the tea duty. Governor Hutchinson and his two sons were among the local tea agents. The local committees of correspondence around Boston passed resolutions: a) emulating the one at Philadelphia, and b) that the tea should not be landed. It was endorsed by the other towns. The first tea ship arrived in Boston on 28 Nov, but they obtained an assurance from the owner that he would stay outside the customs house until 30 Nov. A public meeting was held in Boston on 29 Nov 1773, in which delegates representing many surrounding towns voted to have the tea sent back to England, despite Hutchinson's order that the meeting be dispersed. A resolution was passed proclaiming anyone who imported tea to be an enemy of the country. The committees of correspondence organized patrols to keep a watch on the ships to make sure none were unloaded; volunteers armed themselves and communicated the status every half-hour.

5-8 Nov 1773: The people of New York resolved not to allow the tea from Great Britain to be landed. On the 8th, the commissioners and agents for the Tea Company resigned. The local Sons of Liberty maintained a watch on the harbor to ensure the tea remained on the ships.

26 Nov 1773: The local assembly at Charleston, SC, resolved that the tea should not be landed.

16 Dec 1773: In order to prevent the Boston revenue officers from unloading the tea, about 200 men, some disguised as Indians, boarded the ships in Boston harbor on 16 Dec 1773 and tossed the cargo of 340 chests of tea overboard; the loss was calculated at 18,000 pounds sterling. This became known as the Boston Tea Party. The news was sent the next day to Philadelphia and New York by Paul Revere.

22 Dec 1773: In Charleston, the tea was unloaded, but was not received because the local brokers were intimidated by the people. The tea ended up in unsuitable warehouses, where it spoiled due to dampness.

25-28 Dec 1773: A ship of tea arrived in Philadelphia on 25 Dec. But the agent for it, who was a passenger on the ship, was forced to resign on 27 Dec by a group of 5,000 men assembled in opposition to the tea, and the ship's captain set sail back to Great Britain on 28 Dec.

29 Jan-7 Feb 1774: The king's Privy Council heard the 23 Jun 1773 petition from Massachusetts on 29 Jan, brought to the Council by Benjamin Franklin, the agent for Massachusetts in Great Britain. Franklin pointed out that the petition to have Hutchinson removed was political in nature, and was not asking for a criminal indictment. But Wedderburn, representing Hutchinson, delivered an attack upon Franklin's reputation and honor. On 7 Feb, the Privy Council rejected the petition, claiming that it was "groundless, vexatious, and scandalous."

Feb-Mar 1774: At this point, the king decided that he was going to resolve the American issue first by imposing more severe restrictions until the Americans capitulated, and secondly by force if necessary. The consensus in Parliament was that the colonies must be convinced that Parliament had legitimate power to pass any laws it desired. Because of exaggerated claims made by royal officials, the people in England believed that the colonists were a crazed mob, and that it was necessary for Parliament to establish its supremacy. At the same time, the colonies were united in the attitude that they must resist tyranny now or never. Although the colonies were still willing to remain part of Great Britain, they would require a repeal of all the unconstitutional measures taken by Parliament.

31 Mar-22 Jun 1774: Parliament debated the conditions in the colonies, and passed five acts in response to the Boston Tea Party as a general display of policy. The British were confident both that the Americans would not be willing to fight it out, and that Massachusetts would not be supported by the other colonies.

31 Mar 1774: Parliament passed the first of the five acts, called the Boston Port Act: a) the port of Boston would be closed until the towns had compensated the East India Tea Company for the losses incurred in the Tea Party; b) all commerce was to pass through the port at Marblehead; and c) the seat of government was moved from Boston to Salem. The Boston Port Act was to be enforced starting on 1 Jun 1774.

12 May 1774: News of the Boston Port Act had reached Boston on 10 May 1774. The committees of correspondence met in Boston on 12 May, and issued a circular letter to all the other colonies asking their assistance in opposing it. The other colonies responded by sending supplies to Boston.

16 May-1 Jun 1774: Within a few weeks, most of the colonies endorsed the idea of a united congress: New York (16 May), Connecticut, (17 May), Rhode Island (17 May), Pennsylvania (21 May), Virginia (24 May), Maryland (~ 25 May), New Hampshire (28 May), New Jersey (31 May), and South Carolina (~ 1 Jun).

20 May 1774: Parliament passed the second and third of the five acts. The second was called the Regulating Act: a) the Massachusetts charter was revoked; b) the assembly was abolished, to be replaced by a council appointed by the king; c) the governor obtained power to appoint all judges and court officers; d) all officers were to serve at the pleasure of the king; e) town hall meetings were outlawed except for the election of local town offices; and f) sheriffs acquired the sole power to select jurors. Its effect was to destroy popular government and transfer all the power into the hands of the governor. In retrospect, the Regulating Act, which abolished free government in Massachusetts, was the underlying cause of the Revolution. It was insisted upon by George III, and passed through Parliament by votes from seats that were bought and paid for by the king (known as "rotten boroughs"). The third act was the Administrative Justice Act, by which any charge of murder against any royal officer was to be tried in England, not in Massachusetts. Its effect, although unintentional, was to make the British soldiers less cautious about killing colonists.

1 Jun 1774: The port of Boston was closed, putting many men out of work. It was enforced very strictly: even small boats from local areas were not allowed to dock at Boston. Fishermen were required to unload their catch at Marblehead and transport it from there to Boston by wagon.

2 Jun 1774: Parliament passed the fourth of the five acts, called the Quartering Act, which required residents of all the towns in Massachusetts to quarter British troops when demanded.

14-15 Jun 1774: Boston was occupied by two regiments and two artillery companies; these were supplemented by more troops in the next few weeks.

17 Jun 1774: The Massachusetts assembly was convened by the new governor of Massachusetts, General Gage, on 7 Jun 1774. Samuel Adams desired to have a regular bill passed in the assembly calling for a convention of the colonies, but he knew full well that Gage would dissolve the assembly if such a subject were brought up. Adams arranged to have the door locked on 17 Jun by prior coordination with some members, then brought up a resolution to call for a congress of the colonies. Some of the members managed to leave, and notified Gage, who promptly issued a writ to dissolve the assembly. But the messenger was unable to obtain entry into the assembly hall, and the resolution was passed with a large majority. It elected Thomas Cushing, Robert T. Paine, Samuel Adams, and John Adams to be delegates to a convention at Philadelphia in Sep 1774. A circular letter was authorized to be sent to all the other colonies to join in the meeting.

22 Jun 1774: Parliament passed the fifth act, called the Quebec Act: it a) permitted the Roman Catholic religion to be practiced in Quebec, b) extended the boundary of Canada as far south as the Ohio River, contradicting the claims of some colonies, especially Virginia, Massachusetts, New York, and Connecticut; and c) directed that this entire region, including the Ohio Valley, be ruled solely by the king's officers.

Summer 1774: All the other colonies except Georgia accepted the invitation to a congress in Philadelphia. Also, the towns in Massachusetts organized their men into fighting units, just in case hostilities broke out over enforcement of the acts against Boston.

18 Jul 1774: A convention of people of Fairfax County, VA, led by George Washington, met to discuss the relations with Great Britain. It issued their sentiments in the Fairfax County Resolves, which concluded in part: a) the most important part of the British constitution was representation of the people; b) people of the colonies are not and cannot be represented in Parliament; c) without representation, Parliament has no power to levy taxes in the colonies; d) the recent acts of Parliament are proof of tyranny against the colonies; and e) a congress should be assembled to discuss a union of the colonies to defend their rights and liberties.

6 Aug 1774: General Gage received the Regulating and Quartering Acts at Boston and immediately started to enforce them.

16-26 Aug 1774: The court established to enforce the Regulating Act was scheduled to convene in Great Barrington, but on 16 Aug 1774 a large number of people surrounded the court and prevented it from conducting any business. Similar disruptions occurred at Worcester and Springfield on 26 Aug, and later in Plymouth, where court officers were intimidated into resigning their seats. In Boston, jurors refused to serve on the grounds that the court itself was illegal. Town meetings met as usual and were better attended than before, despite General Gage's threat to arrest any attendees.

1 Sep 1774: Colonists had been withdrawing gunpowder from the central storage point at Quarry Hill, according to the proportion they had contributed. On 1 Sep 1774, a British detachment from Boston seized all the powder that still remained, about 125 barrels, and transferred it to the garrison at Castle William. This caused many of the local militia to begin a march on Boston, but they were intercepted and turned back by riders from Boston, informing them that this was not the proper time for engaging the British.

2 Sep 1774: General Gage decided to enlist the aid of the Indians against the colonists, contrary to all previous policy of the British. During the French and Indian War, the British paid the Indians to remain neutral, not as actual fighting forces. He sent orders to begin negotiations with the Cherokee, Choctaws, and Mohawks for their services. Carleton, governor of Canada, tried to dissuade Gage from this policy, but was unsuccessful.

5 Sep-26 Oct 1774: The First Continental Congress met at Carpenter's Hall in Philadelphia. Twelve colonies (all except Georgia) sent delegates to debate the political situation between England and the colonies.

6 Sep 1774: A convention of the towns in Suffolk County, Massachusetts convened to debate resolutions on the five acts of Parliament. They issued a resolution: a) they owed no allegiance to the king on the grounds that he had violated their rights; b) the Regulating Act was declared null and void; c) they urged all the court officers appointed by the king to resign within 11 days; d) they ordered tax collectors to refuse to remit revenue to the colony's treasury; e) they advised each town to organize a militia; and f) they warned the governor that they would take royal officers as hostages if the governor attempted to arrest anyone on political charges. It put the people of Suffolk County in actual rebellion against the crown. This document, known as the Suffolk County Resolution, was sent to the Continental Congress on 9 Sep 1774.

Oct 1774: The rural towns of Massachusetts formed all males between ages of 16 and 70 into their militia, drilled them at least weekly, and segregated one-third of them into "minute-men," to be ready for action at immediate notice.

Oct-Nov 1774: The Indians in the western part of Virginia and along the Ohio River had made several raids on the western settlers, starting in Feb 1774. There had been a few reprisal killings by white people in the summer. Lord Dunmore, royal governor of Virginia, called out a large group of backwoodsmen from the western part of Virginia to advance along the Ohio River to suppress the Indians. They defeated the Shawnees, most warlike of the Indians, in a battle at Point Pleasant on 10 Oct 1774. They advanced further to Pickaway and Camp Charlotte, where they negotiated a peace settlement with the Indians on 24 Oct. By conquering the Ohio Valley, the backwoodsmen nullified the Quebec Act by gaining control of the Ohio Valley before the British could organize it. Among the fighters were: Daniel Morgan, Evan Shelby, James Robertson, Valentine Sevier, Andrew Lewis, Charles Lewis, William Fleming, Isaac Shelby, William Campbell, George Matthews, and Andrew Moore. This action became known as Lord Dunmore's War.

5 Oct 1774: The people organized their own government in Massachusetts, convening a convention at Salem, and created a committee of safety charged with ensuring that the colonists had adequate supplies for defense if required. It was adjourned in Dec 1774.

10 Oct 1774: William Howe was appointed to replace General Gage as commander of the British army at Boston. He arrived in Boston in May 1775.

11 Oct 1774: The First Continental Congress passed an endorsement of the Suffolk County Resolution.

14 Oct 1774: The First Continental Congress passed a Declaration of Rights. First, it summarized individual rights: a) to life, liberty, and property; b) to no forfeiture of rights as English subjects; c) to trial before their peers; d) to the privileges of English statutes that existed at the time of colonization and the colonial charters; and e) to assemble peacefully and petition for redress of grievances. Secondly, it declared that: a) maintaining standing armies in the colonies is against the constitution; and b) the colonists have an exclusive power to legislate for themselves. Thirdly, it called for repeal of eleven acts of Parliament that contradicted these rights. The Declaration was addressed not only to the king and Parliament, but also to the people of Great Britain and Canada.

20 Oct 1774: The First Continental Congress passed a resolution that recommended: a) a boycott of British imports; and b) a prohibition of exports to England, Ireland, or the West Indies.

Early 1775: The closure of the port of Boston caused great hardship in Boston, high unemployment, and shortages of food and supplies. But there was no violence.

1 Feb 1775: Another congress in Massachusetts convened in Cambridge, and established a scheme to organize the militia and staff it with officers. Part of the militia were designated "Minutemen," who were to be prepared for immediate callout if Gage attempted to enforce the Regulating Act. Throughout Massachusetts, people began drilling on the village greens; many men of this district were veterans of the French and Indian War.

6 Feb-21 Mar 1775: At the opening of Parliament on 30 Nov 1774, King George III had declared the colonies in open revolt, and Parliament passed a resolution concurring with his opinion. On 6 Feb 1775, Parliament passed an act closing all the ports in New England; on the 20th it passed an act increasing the size of the army at Boston; on 6 Mar it passed an act prohibiting fishing along the coast of Newfoundland; and on 21 Mar it extended the fishing prohibitions to all colonies except New York. Benjamin Franklin had been in contact with both Lord North and Lord Richard Howe, advising them on the conditions in the colonies, and what it would take to reconcile the colonies to Great Britain. His consistent theme was: only recognition of the limited power of Parliament, repeal of all the acts complained of, and recognition of the colonist's right to legislate for themselves would do. On 17 Feb 1775 he advised the two lords: "They that can give up essential liberty to obtain a little temporary safety deserve neither liberty nor safety. Massachusetts must suffer all the hazards and mischief's of war, rather than admit the alteration of their charter and laws by Parliament."

20-24 Mar 1775: The assembly at Virginia adopted the Fairfax Resolves of 18 Jul 1774. They then developed a plan for putting it into operation, including establishing militias in every county and promoting manufactures of military items.

15 Apr 1775: Lord Dartmouth issued an order to General Gage: a) take possession of all forts in the colonies; b) arrest anyone who could be charged with treason; c) secure all the military stores in the colonies; and d) suppress the rebellion by force if necessary. Dartmouth's orders were not received until May 1775, well after the battles of Lexington and Concord. The seizure of arms at these two places was done on Gage's own initiative.

18-19 Apr 1775: Battles of Lexington and Concord, MA: General Gage, commander of British forces at Boston, sent a contingent of troops to accomplish two missions: a) arrest Samuel Adams and John

Hancock for treason while they were staying at a friend's house in Lexington; and b) proceed to Concord and seize the arms being stored up by the colonists. The troops left Boston on the evening of 18 Apr, but Joseph Warren, a leading patriot in Boston, suspecting such an action, sent Paul Revere through Charlestown and William Dawes and Samuel Prescott through Roxbury to warn the rural areas. Revere and Dawes were captured at Lincoln, but Prescott jumped over a wall and rode to Concord. The British troops under Major Pitcairn were met by about 50 militiamen at Lexington on 19 Apr, where a skirmish ensued, in which several colonists were killed. The British force moved on to Concord and managed to destroy some of the arms. However, the surrounding areas got word of the engagements, organized themselves, and proceeded to attack the British at Concord, and forced them back across the bridge. The British retreated back toward Charlestown, but were ambushed at every turn by the local militias until they were rescued by a force under Lord Percy. The British endured heavy casualties, and the militia was dispersed only through reinforcements sent by Gage. This was the engagement the Americans had been waiting for: they knew that the British would have to fire the first shot if the colonies were to be united against the crown. The engagement at Lexington has since become known as "the shot heard around the world," since it marked the beginning of the shooting war that would deprive Great Britain of the colonies with the greatest potential. News of the engagement was sent by fast riders throughout the colonies.

20-21 Apr 1775: Men from towns in Massachusetts, Connecticut, and New Hampshire converged on Boston upon hearing of the battles at Lexington and Concord. On the evening of 21 Apr, they had cornered the British garrison at Boston under General Gage.

21-29 Apr 1775: The governor of Virginia sent a force on 21 Apr to secure all the gunpowder being stored at Williamsburg. This aroused the militia in Virginia, and they began to march on 29 Apr from Fredericksburg, but George Washington and Peyton Randolph convinced them to disperse.

10 May 1775: A large number of militia from Massachusetts (under Benedict Arnold), Connecticut (under Ethan Allen), and the Vermont portion of New York (under Seth Warner) had set out in early April to the northeastern section of New York. On 10 May 1775, they captured the British forts at Ticonderoga and Crown Point.

10 May 1775-1 Aug 1775: The Second Continental Congress assembled at Philadelphia, with delegates including Washington, Franklin, John Adams, Samuel Adams, Richard Henry Lee, Patrick Henry, George Clinton, John Jay, and Robert Livingston. With the recent disturbances at Lexington and Concord, the colonists decided to develop appropriate responses to the actions of the British. The situation was very unfavorable to the colonies. First, colonial policies during that era were based on the notion that the colony existed for the economic benefit of the mother country. Since the greatest wealth accrues from manufacturing, the British policy had been to ensure the colonies were dependent on England, and to suppress the widespread growth of manufacturing capabilities in the colonies. The colonies did not have the facilities or the tools necessary to establish a viable industrial base. Secondly, with the British monopoly on trade, the colonies had little credit with other foreign nations.

10 May 1775: The Second Continental Congress authorized the issue of Continental currency. The amount of money in circulation at this time in the 13 colonies was estimated to be equivalent to about SM$12,000,000; about $10,000,000 of it in convertible hard money; about $4,000,000 in actual specie. The Continental currency, to be issued as bills of credit on Congress, was not actually issued until 22 Jun 1775.

17 May 1775: The Second Continental Congress resolved that: a) exports to Nova Scotia, Quebec, St. Johns, Newfoundland, East and West Florida, and Georgia (except St. John's) are to be prohibited; and b) provisions to British fisheries on the coasts are to be prohibited.

25 May 1775: The British force at Boston was reinforced by Admiral Richard Howe, General Henry Clinton, and General John Burgoyne, bringing General Howe's forces to 10,000 men.

27 May 1775: A skirmish occurred between British forces and colonists on the islands around Boston; the colonists took control of the islands, and carried off all the livestock.

31 May 1775: A committee from Mecklenburg County, North Carolina passed a resolution, announcing: a) that the local legislatures of each colony had all the executive and legislative powers; b) that such power was to operate independently of Parliament; c) tenure of offices was now by the colonists themselves; and d) all rents and taxes due to the crown were invalid. This became known as the Mecklenburg Resolve.

2 Jun 1775: The Second Continental Congress agreed to several provisions regarding the British in the colonies: a) no bill of exchange presented by any British officer was to be honored; b) no money was to be supplied to any officer or agent of the British army or navy; c) no provisions of any kind were to be furnished for the British army or navy in Massachusetts; and d) no ships carrying British war supplies were to be fitted or freighted.

9 Jun 1775: Governor Carleton of Canada issued a proclamation declaring the colonies bordering Canada to be in open rebellion. He established martial law in Canada and enlisted the French settlers as well as the local Indian tribes to invade New Hampshire, Massachusetts, and New York. The northern colonies had no choice but to organize against Canada.

12 Jun 1775: General Gage imposed martial law on Boston, and outlawed John Hancock and Samuel Adams as traitors, liable for arrest and punishment for treason.

12 Jun 1775: The Virginia House of Burgesses issued a response to an offer by Lord North to repeal the taxes levied by Parliament. Authored by Jefferson, it recounted all the reasons why a simple repeal of taxes would be insufficient: a) eliminating the tea duty did not solve the problem of Parliament claiming arbitrary power; b) Parliament had no right to interfere with the constitutions of the colonies; c) Parliament had no power to appoint local officers; d) the colonists alone were to vote their own taxes; e) Parliament had not redressed its other acts, namely, abolishing trial by jury, changing the government in Quebec, keeping standing armies, and restricting trade by the colonies; and f) that since the colonies were united, they would no longer bother the king with petitions.

15 Jun 1775: The Second Continental Congress appointed George Washington to become the commander of the army at Boston, now called the Continental Army. He was formally commissioned 19 Jun 1775 and left for Boston on 21 Jun 1775. The appointment had been prompted by a letter from Joseph Warren, noting that the militia in Massachusetts was in disarray, and it was necessary for the Congress to take responsibility for the army, and appoint a commander.

17 Jun 1775: Battles of Bunker Hill and Breed's Hill: The Americans under Colonel Prescott, Colonel Stark, and General Warren occupied the two hills northeast of Charlestown with the idea of using them as high ground to siege Boston. But the British under Generals Gage, Pigot, and Howe launched several attacks and defeated the Americans, albeit with heavy losses. The American forces retreated across Charlestown Neck toward Mystic, and the British took both hills, thus negating any threat to Boston. This battle demonstrated that the Americans were a match for the British in pitched battles. The British casualties amounted to about a third of its force (1,054); the American casualties were about one-fourth (449).

17 Jun 1775: The Second Continental Congress selected four major-generals to serve under Washington: a) Artemas Ward; b) Charles Lee, a former English officer and adventurer who cared nothing for the cause of the colonists; c) Philip Schuyler of New York; and d) Horatio Gates, a retired English officer from Virginia.

22 Jun 1775: The Second Continental Congress issued bills of credit for SM$2,000,000 upon the credit of the twelve colonies (i.e., all except Georgia). This was the beginning of the Continental paper currency. The Continental currency was in addition to a fair amount of paper currency already issued by the colonies.

22 Jun 1775: The Second Continental Congress appointed eight brigadier generals: a) Seth Pomeroy, b) Richard Montgomery; c) David Wooster; d) William Heath; e) Joseph Spencer; f) John Thomas; g) John Sullivan; and h) Nathanael Greene.

3 Jul 1775: George Washington arrived in Cambridge, MA and took command of the Continental Army. At this time it consisted of 11,500 militiamen from Massachusetts, 2,300 from Connecticut, 1,200 from New Hampshire, and 1,000 from Rhode Island. It was augmented with 3,000 regulars from Pennsylvania, Maryland, and Virginia during the next month. The British forces consisted of 6,500 men, mostly deployed on Bunker Hill, Breed's Hill, and Roxbury Neck.

6 Jul 1775: The legislature of Georgia passed a resolution prohibiting the sale of slaves or any employment of slaves.

8 Jul 1775: The Second Continental Congress released the "Olive Branch" petition to King George III, claiming their loyalty to the British Empire, and offering reconciliation if some of the abuses were corrected. The petition specifically called for a repeal of the new administrative system whereby government officials were both appointed by and paid by the crown, and a promise that it would never be attempted again. But it admitted that the colonists were obligated to obey all the acts of Parliament prior to 1763. The petition was written by John Dickinson, and Richard Penn was sent to London to present it to the king.

19 Jul 1775: The assembly of Massachusetts formed a new government by simply declaring the office of governor vacant, and appointed the local council to replace him.

21 Jul 1775: A new government was set up in Massachusetts, with James Bowdoin as President, and John Adams as chief justice.

25 Jul 1775: Congress emitted $1,000,000 in bills of credit (Continental currency). It was to be redeemable in gold or silver in three years.

Aug 1775: Rhode Island became the first state to make the Continental currency full legal tender. Counterfeiting the Continentals was regarded the same as counterfeiting Rhode Island's own currency. All the other states eventually followed suit.

21 Aug 1775: The king refused to accept the "Olive Branch" petition on the grounds that doing so would be an implicit recognition of an unauthorized legislative assembly who had also aided an armed revolt against him.

23 Aug 1775: King George III issued a proclamation in which he declared that his subjects in the colonies had engaged in treason by rebelling against his government, and promised to suppress the rebellion by force. At this point, there was no turning back from war for either the king or the colonists. It arrived in America on 1 Nov 1775.

26 Aug 1775: The Americans invaded Canada, concerned that Guy Carleton, governor of Canada, would try to recover Ticonderoga. The American force consisted of three units: a) under General Montgomery, starting from Ticonderoga, b) under Colonel Benedict Arnold, to advance from Cambridge to Montreal via Maine on 19 Sep; c) under General Schuyler, to start from Albany. Schuyler gave up his part of the campaign due to illness on 7 Sep 1775.

13 Sep 1775: The Second Continental Congress convened again, but is now referred to formally as the Continental Congress.

Mid-Sep 1775: Washington wrote to Congress about the desperate condition of the army: no supplies, gunpowder, fuel, tents, or pay, and that most of the enlistments were to expire in December. Congress responded by sending a committee at the end of September to study the situation.

16 Oct 1775: British Captain Mowatt sailed into Falmouth, MA (now Portland, ME) with four ships and burned nearly the entire town by shelling it. About a thousand people, many of them women and children, were turned out into the wilderness.

26 Oct 1775: King George III opened Parliament with a speech denouncing the activities of the colonists in America, and announced his determination to suppress the rebellion by force. The king's speech arrived in America on 8 Jan 1776.

26-28 Oct 1775: Battle of Hampton Roads, VA: A British force under Lord Dunmore attempted to enter and burn the village of Hampton Roads, but was defeated by a combination of regular army and militia commanded by George Nicholas.

Nov 1775: American General Knox secured 43 cannons at Ticonderoga, and carried them on sleds to Boston, arriving there in Feb 1776.

1 Nov 1775: Lord George Sackville Germain became the secretary for American affairs in the British government. He would be in charge of conducting the war against the colonies, although he was not competent for the office.

3 Nov 1775: American General Montgomery forced the surrender of St. John's after a 50-day siege.

12 Nov 1775: Surrender of Montreal, Canada: American General Montgomery entered Montreal without a fight. He afterward proceeded to Quebec to aid Colonel Arnold.

16 Nov 1775: The British government sent requisitions to the German principalities of Hesse-Casel and Brunswick for men to fight against the colonies as mercenaries. It was the first time the British had proposed the use of foreign troops against their own people, and was considered dishonorable by many of the royal courts in Europe.

19 Nov 1775: Colonel Arnold arrived at Quebec after a 60 day march through snowstorms and flooded creeks, during which many men froze. But he did not have enough men left to lay siege to Quebec, and the British, commanded by Cramahe', refused to surrender. Arnold retreated to Point aux Trembles to wait for Montgomery.

29 Nov 1775: The Continental Congress issued $3,000,000 in bills of credit (Continental currency).

1 Dec 1775: Parliament passed the American Act containing the following provisions: a) repeal of the charter of Massachusetts; b) seizure of the port of Boston; c) prohibition of commerce with American colonies as long as the rebellion continued; and d) authorized capture of American ships, confiscation of cargoes, and impressments of American crews to fight against the colonists.

9 Dec 1775: Battle at Great Bridge, VA: Lord Dunmore, royal governor of Virginia built a fort at Great Bridge, Virginia, hoping to intercept an American force supposed to be coming up from North Carolina to take Norfolk. On 9 Dec 1775, a group of Americans under Colonel Woodford and Lieutenant John Marshall repelled an attack from the fort, defeated the British, and caused them to retreat onto a British ship that had just sailed into Norfolk. The Americans then took Norfolk.

31 Dec 1775: Battle of Quebec: Americans under General Montgomery, Colonel Arnold, and Colonel Morgan laid siege to Quebec in a blinding snowstorm; the British in Quebec were commanded by General Guy Carleton. Montgomery was killed, Arnold was wounded, and Morgan's force was captured. The Americans occupied the areas around Quebec.

1 Jan 1776: Battle of Norfolk, VA: The British under Lord Dunmore burned Norfolk, VA through a naval bombardment, after losing it to the Americans the month before.

5 Jan 1776: The assembly in New Hampshire formed a new government, nearly identical with the colonial charter.

8 Jan 1776: Thomas Paine's "Common Sense" was published, which laid out a rationale for independence, concluding that reconciliation with Great Britain was impossible now that the British had responded with armies to the colonists' rightful petitions. It was widely read in all of the colonies and helped to coalesce them into common cause against the crown. Paine had been solicited to write it in Nov 1775 by Benjamin Franklin.

11 Jan 1776: Congress passed a resolution in which all persons refusing to accept the Continental currency as legal tender "shall be deemed, published, and treated as an enemy of his country and precluded from all trade or intercourse with the inhabitants of these Colonies."

20-22 Jan 1776: Generals Schuyler and Herkimer with militia succeeded in surrounding Sir John Johnson and his Indian and Highlander allies at Johnstown, NY, and forced them to disarm.

5 Feb 1776: Sir James Wright, royal governor of Georgia, fled by sea, writing to the king that Georgia was under the control of the Carolina rebels. The people of Georgia set up their own government, with a constitution established 15 Apr 1776.

17 Feb 1776: The Continental Congress authorized $4,000,000 in bills of credit (Continental currency).

27 Feb 1776: Battle of Moore's Creek, NC: A large group of Scottish loyalists from North Carolina under Donald Macdonald fought against about 1,000 militia under Colonel Richard Caswell. The Americans defeated Macdonald and captured him along with 900 other prisoners and 15,000 pounds in gold. British General Henry Clinton was at this time on his way from Boston. By the time he arrived at Cape Fear River by sea, he found 10,000 militiamen ready to oppose him. He decided to remain on the ships and wait for a fleet commanded by Sir Peter Parker to join him from Ireland. The next objective of the British forces was to attack South Carolina.

1 Mar 1776: The Continental Congress issued $4,000,000 in bills of credit (paper currency), having been authorized 17 Feb 1776. It was about this time that depreciation of the Continental currency began, since the amount issued all total thus far had become a significant fraction of the hard money in circulation at the start of the war.

4-17 Mar 1776: Battle of Boston: Americans under Washington laid siege to Boston from Dorchester Heights, aided by a large number of cannons that had been removed from Ticonderoga. With the British forces surrounded, and the memory of the large losses incurred at Bunker Hill, Gen. Howe decided to evacuate, but made it known he would burn the town if his forces were fired upon. Washington allowed the British to evacuate on 17 Mar 1776, taking with them about 900 loyalist citizens. The Americans secured 200 cannon, a large quantity of powder, and other military stores that the British left behind.

23 Mar 1776: Congress responded to the impressment edict of 1 Dec 1775 by: a) issuing letters of marque authorizing privateers to attack and seize ships and cargo belonging to any British subject except those living in Ireland or the West Indies; and b) recommending that all the colonies take steps to disarm the loyalists.

26 Mar 1776: An independent American government was established by a constitution in South Carolina; it instructed its delegates in Congress to assist the other colonies in any action they deem necessary regarding relations with Great Britain.

6 Apr 1776: Congress passed a resolution opening all ports in the colonies to ships of all nations, in direct contradiction to the traditional Navigation Acts.

12 Apr 1776: The legislature of North Carolina instructed its delegates in Congress to advocate for independence from Great Britain.

May 1776: Widespread town hall meetings were held in Massachusetts, and all of them voted to encourage Congress to declare independence from Great Britain.

1 May 1776: The Massachusetts legislature abolished the royal style, and began to claim authority by "the government and people." This was an implicit declaration of independence.

1 May 1776: Archibald Bulloch, president of the newly-formed government of Georgia, was ordered by the council of safety to cooperate with all the resolutions of Congress.

4 May 1776: The assembly of Rhode Island rejected the notion of any lingering allegiance to King George III, eliminated the references to the king in its official documents, and instructed its delegates

to go along with whatever resolutions Congress might adopt with regard to Great Britain. Rhode Island was already republican, so this amounted to forming a new government.

6 May 1776: An American army had been sent to Canada in April, but had been decimated by smallpox. The units had been ordered to Canada by Congress, thus reducing Washington's forces at New York. On 1 May 1776, General John Thomas took command, but he immediately recognized that he could not take Canada: a) he was outnumbered 3 to 1; b) his army had no supplies and no money; c) the Americans were rejected by the Canadian people; and d) the army was suffering from widespread sickness. On 6 May 1776, while the Americans were attempting to retreat, they were attacked by the British at St. John's and St. Louis; many of the Americans were captured and treated in British hospitals. The rest of the Americans retreated to Deschambault, leaving most of their supplies behind.

~7 May 1776: The king of France authorized a loan to the American colonies, to be sent secretly through a commercial firm, of 1,000,000 *livres* (SM$194,000).

15 May 1776: A convention in Virginia voted: a) to instruct the delegation to the Continental Congress to advocate for independence from Great Britain; and b) to form a new government for Virginia. The resolution was sent to the other colonies in a circular letter. This resolution was partially motivated by the burning of Norfolk.

15 May 1776: Congress passed a resolution recommending all the colonies form independent governments on the ground that no allegiance to the crown could be justified because the king had failed to protect the colonists.

~25 May 1776: The king of Spain authorized a loan of 1,000,000 *livres* (SM$194,000) to the Americans, which was secretly funneled through France.

27 May 1776: The Continental Congress issued $5,000,000 in bills of credit (Continental currency), having been authorized 9 May 1776.

4 Jun 1776: The state of Virginia appointed a commission to investigate why the Continental currency was beginning to depreciate.

5-14 Jun 1776: The American army in Canada had spent the past few weeks retreating, and was now at Sorel. Its commander, General Thomas, had died of smallpox on 2 Jun, and was replaced by General John Sullivan on 5 Jun when he arrived at Sorel with his force. Sullivan decided to halt the retreat, and ordered part of his force to advance to Three Rivers, where they were defeated by the British under Carleton and Burgoyne. The Americans then continued the retreat, including General Arnold's force from Montreal. The Americans finally arrived at Crown Point, NY in early July. This was the last attempt to bring Canada into the war.

11 Jun 1776: A committee was set up by the Continental Congress to devise a plan to unite the colonies in the expected contest against Great Britain.

11 Jun 1776: The local assembly at New York passed a resolution by which the delegates that were about to be elected to Congress were to have the powers of establishing a new constitution and deciding on the issue of independence. This was a political maneuver by John Jay to ensure that the issue of independence was to be decided by those who were authorized to do so.

12 Jun 1776: The legislature of Virginia adopted a resolution known as the "Declaration of the Rights of Man," written mostly by George Mason, and modified by James Madison. It proposed that all men are free by nature and have the inherent general right to: a) enjoyment of life and liberty; b) acquire and possess property; and c) pursue happiness and safety. Secondly, governments are to be regulated: a) all governmental power is derived from the people; b) governments exist for the common benefit and security of the people, and are answerable to them; c) people have a legitimate right to abolish or modify any government inadequate or deficient in its duties; d) that offices should not be hereditary; e) that the military power is subordinate to the civil power; and f) that governments should have its powers divided into executive, legislative, and judicial branches. It also listed specific rights of individuals: a) no excessive bail; b) no general warrants; c) punishment only by conviction under

law; d) trial by jury; e) freedom of the press; f) to possess arms, as the militia is the natural defense of a free state; and g) freedom of religion.

14 Jun 1776: The Connecticut legislature endorsed independence. It ended the use of the king's name, and since it was already republican, was a change of government. It was confirmed on 10 Oct 1776 and made permanent.

14 Jun 1776: The Delaware legislature endorsed independence.

15 Jun 1776: The legislature of New Hampshire endorsed independence.

21-22 Jun 1776: The New Jersey legislature established a new government on 21 Jun, after the royal governor had been arrested on the 15th, and on 22 Jun 1776, endorsed independence.

24 Jun 1776: The Pennsylvania legislature endorsed independence, having declared on 19 Jun that the old royal government was incompetent, and that a new one was necessary.

24 Jun 1776: Congress passed a resolution proclaiming anyone who lived in the colonies and continued to be loyal to King George III was a traitor.

28 Jun 1776: The Maryland legislature endorsed independence out of sympathy for the other colonies, and in a spirit of unity; Maryland had not experienced any harm by the British. Maryland thus became the twelfth colony to vote for independence. New York was now the only holdout, since there were many loyalists there.

28 Jun 1776: Lord Howe landed the British troops at New York without opposition from General Washington. Washington only had 8,000 men under his command, which was not enough to contest the landing.

28 Jun 1776: Battle of Sullivan's Island (Fort Moultrie), SC: The British force under General H. Clinton that had intended to land at Moore's Creek was joined by a fleet commanded by Sir Peter Parker, who had sailed from Ireland, and had brought with him Lord Cornwallis. They met in May 1776. Their plan was to take Charleston, since they believed there were a large number of loyalists there. In fact, most of the people there wanted independence. Meanwhile, American Colonel Moultrie had constructed a fort on Sullivan's Island, although the method of construction was denigrated by General C. Lee. On 28 Jun 1776, the British landed the infantry, but were prevented from attacking the fort by the high water across the estuary, even at low tide. The battle then became a ship-to-shore bombardment; the British aimed poorly and generally missed the fort, but the Americans successfully damaged most of the British fleet. The British then sailed for New York, and South Carolina was not visited by the British for two more years.

29 Jun 1776: Virginia established a new constitution, with a bill of rights, and a declaration of independence.

1 Jul 1776: Congress received a letter from General Washington outlining the situation of his forces in New York: he had a total of 7,754 men, 2,200 of which either had defective firelocks or none at all; about 4,000 had no bayonets; of the 6,000 militia ordered by Congress, only 1,000 had shown up. Meanwhile, the British were expected to land about 30,000 troops in New York.

1-15 Jul 1776: Indians invaded the rural areas and massacred many settlers in western South Carolina. The settlers retreated to forts or to Charleston.

2 Jul 1776: New Jersey modified its charter and established a new government.

2 Jul 1776: A declaration of independence was unanimously approved in Congress by twelve colonies. It read in part, "That these colonies are, and of right ought to be, free and independent states; that they are absolved from all allegiance to the British crown, and that all political connection between them and the state of Great Britain is, and ought to be, dissolved." The delegates from New York did not vote because they were not authorized to vote for independence. A committee was appointed to determine how it would be announced.

3 Jul 1776: The legislature of Maryland established a new government.

4 Jul 1776: A formal Declaration of Independence, as written by Jefferson with some alterations by Franklin and Adams, was reviewed and approved by members of the Continental Congress from twelve of the colonies, and signed by John Hancock and a few other members (according to Jefferson). From this day forward, the colonies were each independent of Great Britain, but united together in a common cause to exercise the necessary sovereign powers to conduct the war against Great Britain. Several copies were made, and these were signed by the members of Congress over the next few weeks. The delegates from New York were not authorized to sign it until 9 Jul.

12 Jul 1776: A committee in the Continental Congress issued a report proposing the terms of a confederation. It is supposed to have been written by John Dickinson, but the authorship is uncertain since no formal notes were ever published. The Continental Congress debated these throughout 1776 and most of 1777.

20 Jul 1776: Battle of Island Flats, NC (now TN): Settlers in western North Carolina, now part of Tennessee, defeated a large group of Cherokee Indians enlisted by the British. This was followed by a series of skirmishes at Fort Watauga and other places along the Tennessee River, until the Cherokees agreed to a peace.

Aug-Sep 1776: South Carolina militia under Williamson invaded western South Carolina and defeated the Cherokee Indians on the Keowee, Seneca, Tugaloo, Whitewater, Toxaway, and Estatoe Rivers. He was joined in September by North Carolina fighters under Rutherford, and destroyed 36 Indian settlements on the western side of the Alleghany Mountains. The Cherokees made peace, and this territory came firmly under control of the Americans.

13 Aug 1776: The Continental Congress issued $5,000,000 in bills of credit (Continental currency), having been authorized 22 Jul 1776.

27-29 Aug 1776: Battle of Long Island, NY: The British force numbering 25,000 defeated the Americans numbering about 18,000 at Long Island, New York. The British were commanded by Generals Howe, Clinton, Grant, Percy, and Lord Cornwallis, with their Hessian allies commanded by von Heister. The Americans were commanded by Putnam, W. Alexander (a.k.a. Lord Stirling), and Sullivan. The Americans retreated north across the western edge of Long Island to Brooklyn Heights on the 27th. Sullivan was captured by the British. On the 29th, Washington arrived from his headquarters and engineered a retreat across the East River to Manhattan. The Americans were aided by a dense fog that covered their movements across the East River.

The British had the advantages of numerical superiority and of secrecy because many people in the area were loyalists. This was the best opportunity the British ever had to inflict a decisive defeat on the Americans.

15-16 Sep 1776: Battle of Manhattan, NY: The British had no trouble taking Manhattan after the victory at Long Island. Two brigades under General Washington came to assist General Putnam, but exhibited poor discipline, and retreated almost as soon as they were fired upon. Fortunately, General Howe was delayed for two hours because he accepted an invitation to tea by Mrs. Lindley Murray; this allowed Putnam to retreat to Harlem Heights. The British attempted to dislodge the Americans at Harlem, but were repulsed; meanwhile, the British controlled Manhattan.

21 Sep 1776: Delaware formed a new government by completing a new constitution, including a bill of rights. It included a prohibition on the importation and sale of slaves.

24 Sep 1776: Five hundred American prisoners of war taken in the invasion of Canada arrived at Elizabeth Point, NJ, having been paroled by Governor Carleton of Canada. Among those released was Daniel Morgan.

28 Sep 1776: Pennsylvania established a new constitution, but it disenfranchised the Quakers, and so its ratification was delayed until Feb 1777.

11-13 Oct 1776: Battle of Valcour Island (Lake Champlain), NY: Sir Guy Carleton had spent the summer constructing a fleet on Lake Champlain by which he hoped to recapture Ticonderoga. The basis of his fleet had sailed from England to the St. Lawrence, then carried overland in pieces and reconstructed on the lake. General Benedict Arnold had assembled a small fleet from scratch, and sailed it to Valcour Island. The two fleets engaged in a naval battle 11-13 Oct, in which the British totally destroyed the American fleet, but sustained considerable damage itself. Arnold and his men escaped on 13 Oct and marched to safety at Fort Ticonderoga; Carleton decided not to attack it, but instead retreated back to Canada on 3 Nov, content with controlling Lake Champlain. Carleton's retreat did not make sense from a military standpoint, and he was later criticized for it by the other British generals. General Gates was in command at Ticonderoga, and took credit for the stalling of Carleton.

12-18 Oct 1776: General Washington evaded the British under General Howe, and successfully retreated from Harlem Heights to White Plains. He was joined by Morgan (having been released by Carleton), Alexander, Sullivan (who had been released by the British) and C. Lee, who had returned from South Carolina. The Americans had thus evacuated all of Manhattan except Fort Washington.

17 Oct 1776: Washington ordered General C. Lee to bring the army from New Castle over to New Jersey to join up with the rest of the Americans. Lee pretended not to understand, or made excuses why he couldn't cross over in an attempt to undermine Washington. Lee claimed to engage in "brave, virtuous treason" in order to save the state. His goal was to show that Washington was incompetent, and thus get himself promoted to commander. It was not until 2 Dec 1776 that Lee crossed into New Jersey.

28 Oct 1776: Battle of White Plains, NY: The British advanced to Chatterton Hill, but were fought to a draw by the Americans under Macdougall. Washington, then at White Plains, withdrew his forces to New Castle and placed them under General C. Lee, who occupied a very strong position. Washington went to West Point to survey that area. Howe then decided to move back south along the Hudson in order to attack Fort Washington, or invade New Jersey, or march on Philadelphia. The main British objective was to lure the Americans out of their stronghold.

9 Nov 1776: Maryland established a new government by ratifying a constitution written in Aug.

16 Nov 1776: Battle of Fort Washington, NY: The British under General Howe attacked and took Fort Washington, commanded by Colonel Magaw. More than 2,600 Americans were captured, and many were murdered by Hessians after they had surrendered. The battle occurred partly because Congress interfered in the military chain of command: Washington had ordered Greene to evacuate Fort Washington, but Greene had also received an order from Congress that it should not be abandoned except under most dire circumstances. Greene misjudged the British, and opted to reinforce the fort and be attacked.

18 Nov 1776: Congress authorized a lottery to raise money. The idea was to take in hard money in return for paper bills of credit to be redeemed in a few years at 5% interest. But people were not enticed to give ready money now in return for a paper promise.

20 Nov 1776: Evacuation of Fort Lee, NY: American General Greene failed to post lookouts at Fort Lee. The British under General Howe surprised the Americans and Greene evacuated 2,000 men without a fight. The British took the fort and all the supplies left behind. Greene retreated to Hackensack, NJ to join with the main force.

28 Nov 1776: The new government of Pennsylvania was in turmoil as Washington was retreating through New Jersey, as Howe was offering amnesty and pardons to anyone who would abandon the rebellion. Several prominent people in Pennsylvania accepted it: Colonel Reed of the militia, Samuel Tucker, chairman of the committee of safety, Joseph Galloway, and Andrew Allen, who had been a member of the Continental Congress.

28 Nov-12 Dec 1776: The main American army under Washington retreated through New Jersey, being chased by the British under Cornwallis. Lee finally crossed the remainder of his force across the Hudson on 4 Dec, but not to reinforce Washington. Lee's objective was to intimidate the militias into providing their best men, and to intercept the reinforcements sent by Schuyler to Washington, put them under his command, and fight the British on his own to recover New Jersey. On 8 Dec, Wash-

ington retreated across the Delaware River into Pennsylvania, just north of Trenton. Lee and Sullivan's force marched to Vealtown on 12 Dec 1776, and then Lee himself went to Baskingridge to spend the night at White's tavern. Meanwhile there was considerable confusion among the Americans: General Schuyler, coming from New York, joined with Lee's army, and General Gates was elsewhere in New Jersey, trying to locate Washington. British troops under Cornwallis arrived at Trenton on the 8th and just missed the Americans. But Washington had secured every boat for a distance of 70 miles, and the British were unable to cross the river.

The Americans were in a bad position, having lost New York and now holed up in Pennsylvania with a small army whose enlistments were to expire 1 Jan 1777. The rest of the army was scattered across New Jersey.

Dec 1776: Hessians in New Jersey were allowed to steal anything they could, as plunder was the only way to prevent their desertion. They had been told while still in Europe that their deployment would pave the way for private fortune.

7 Dec 1776: The British captured the island of Rhode Island, and used it as a base for several years to conduct raids on the coast of Connecticut and Massachusetts.

9 Dec 1776: Franklin received assurances from the Spanish that American privateers would be sheltered in Spanish ports.

12 Dec 1776: With the British fleet closing in on Philadelphia, Congress adjourned to Baltimore. Putnam was left in command of the small American garrison in Philadelphia.

13 Dec 1776: General C. Lee was captured by the British at Baskingridge and held as a deserter, clearly the best thing that happened for the American side in recent months. But Lee was popular in the states, and his capture served to lower morale. Lee tried to convince the British that he was the American commander.

18 Dec 1776: North Carolina ratified its constitution and established a new government.

20 Dec 1776: Washington's force was joined south of the Delaware in Pennsylvania by Americans under Generals Sullivan (who had succeeded Lee), Gates, and Stark.

25 Dec 1776: A convention met in Providence, RI, consisting of representatives of the New England states, to discuss the problem of finances. They issued a recommendation that prices be fixed, loans regulated, and that the individual states stop issuing their own paper money.

26-29 Dec 1776: Battle of Trenton, NJ: General Washington, knowing that some kind of victory was necessary to keep the army from dissolving, made a daring midnight crossing of the Delaware River at Mackonkey's Ferry, and attacked the Hessians under Colonel Rahl at Trenton, capturing 1,000 Hessians. The Americans were also led by Generals Greene, Mercer, Alexander, Sullivan, Stark, Hand, Glover, Knox, Webb, Scott, and Captains William Washington, James Monroe, and Alexander Hamilton. General Gates was supposed to have attacked from Bristol, and Putnam from Philadelphia, but neither did so. Griffin was supposed to harass the Hessians at Mt. Holly, but retreated instead. Cadwalader could not make the crossing at Dunk's Ferry. General Grant had warned General Donop and Colonel Rahl that Washington was likely to try such a move, but they rejected Grant's suspicion. Washington recrossed the river afterward, but then returned and occupied Trenton on 29 Dec.

27 Dec 1776: Congress issued a grant of nearly dictatorial powers to Washington for six months, authorizing him: a) to raise 16 battalions of infantry, 3 regiments of artillery, 3,000 light cavalry and engineering corps; b) to appoint all officers up to and including full colonel; c) to seize private property as necessary to conduct the war, with compensation to the owners; and d) to arrest anyone who refused to accept the Continental currency, or demonstrated sympathy with the British. However, these offenses were to be tried in civil courts.

28 Dec 1776: The Continental Congress issued $5,000,000 in bills of credit (Continental currency), having been authorized 2 Nov 1776.

28 Dec 1776: Franklin received assurances from the French foreign minister Vergennes that American privateers would be sheltered in French ports.

1 Jan 1777: Their enlistments had run out, but the American militia chose to remain in the field; Washington, Stark, and other officers pledged their own fortunes to pay them. On 1 Jan 1777, Robert Morris went house to house in Philadelphia borrowing money from whomever he could; he raised $50,000 and sent it to General Washington.

1 Jan 1777: The Continental dollar was valued at SM$0.80.

3 Jan 1777: Battle of Princeton, NJ: Americans under Generals Washington and Mercer evaded Cornwallis at Trenton, and advanced to Princeton, where they defeated British forces under Colonel Mawhood. The British retreated toward New Brunswick and Trenton, while the American main force moved to Morristown, as General Putnam came in from Philadelphia to occupy Princeton. Mercer was killed in action.

5 Jan 1777: Americans under General G. Clinton forced the British to evacuate Hackensack, NJ, and took possession of the town. Meanwhile, some Hessians were defeated at Springfield, NJ, by local militia.

7 Jan 1777: Americans under General Maxwell defeated the British at Elizabethtown, NJ, and occupied Newark, NJ.

13 Jan 1777: Franklin and his associates had requested direct military aid from the king of France on 5 Jan 1777, including provision of eight warships. On the 13th, the king replied that he would not be able to provide military supplies directly because of treaty obligations with Great Britain, but did agree to secretly provide financing to the Americans. Louis XVI agreed to loan the Americans 500,000 *livres* (SM$97,000) quarterly, with the first installment to be issued 16 Jan 1777. France also advanced 1,000,000 *livres* (SM$194,000) on a consignment of tobacco. American privateers were allowed to be outfitted in French ports to prey on the British. The French were not yet ready to commit troops, especially since King Louis XVI was somewhat sympathetic to King George III; French society was occupied with popular government and there was considerable agitation against the monarchy in France.

14 Jan 1777: Congress imitated the example set in the 25 Dec 1776 convention at Providence, RI and adopted a resolution asking the other states to: a) abolish state issues of paper money, and b) give Congress sole authority to issue currency.

14 Jan 1777: The depreciation of the Continental currency had advanced so far that Congress issued a resolution asking all the states to pass legislation that would make the Continental legal tender for all debts, and secondly, that any refusal to accept them would nullify the debt. Congress itself declared that anyone who failed to receive them at par was a public enemy, and his goods were liable to forfeit. The Continental at this time had depreciated to about 2:1 in some places. The states were obligated to redeem the Continental in proportion to their respective populations, so most of the states complied with this resolution.

15 Jan 1777: The people of several counties in the territory disputed by New York and New Hampshire declared independence from both states, and set up a new state which they called "New Connecticut" (changed to "Vermont" on 8 Jul 1777). New Hampshire recognized its independence early on. The secession led to a low-level civil war in this area between forces from New York and the settlers in the region, which earned some New York men the enmity of members of Congress from the New England states. The New Connecticut legislature petitioned Congress to be recognized as one of the states in the war against Britain. However, the New York delegation succeeded in pre-empting a vote, and it was not recognized as a state until after the war. The constitution of New Connecticut prohibited slavery.

20 Jan 1777: British now controlled only Brunswick, Amboy, and Paulus Hook (Jersey City) in New Jersey.

25 Jan 1777: General Washington issued a proclamation in which he declared that anyone who had accepted an amnesty offered by the British had two choices: either move to places held by the British for protection, or come forward and take an oath of allegiance to the United States. Many in New Jersey came forward and took the oath, after having had their property destroyed by the British and Hessians.

5 Feb 1777: Georgia ratified a new constitution and established a new government.

19 Feb 1777: Congress promoted five from Brigadier General to Major General: Alexander, Mifflin, St. Clair, Stephen, and Lincoln, passing over Arnold. Washington talked Arnold out of resigning, since he had proven to be one of his best generals. Congress passed over Arnold because two men from Connecticut already held the rank of Major General, and it was thought unfair to promote Arnold.

26 Feb 1777: The Continental Congress issued $5,000,000 in bills of credit (Continental currency).

30 Mar 1777: The American General Charles Lee had been confined in New York since his capture the previous December. Since he was a former Lieutenant Colonel in the British army, he was liable to be executed for treason. However, General Washington sent a note to General W. Howe that he was in possession of five Hessian officers, and offered to trade them for Lee if and when the time arose. Howe did not have authority to make that decision, so some delay was incurred obtaining permission from the king. Meanwhile, Lee, in an attempt to show himself useful to the British and save himself if Washington's offer was refused, wrote out a detailed plan by which the British could win the war, which he provided to Howe on 30 Mar 1777. Lee's plan was to take Philadelphia with the main army, and send another contingent to take Annapolis and Alexandria. By doing so, Howe could then enlist the aid of a large number of loyalists in Pennsylvania and Maryland, paralyze the actions of Congress at Philadelphia, and separate New England from the southern states. Lee's plan had several flaws regarding the value of Philadelphia, but Howe decided to pursue it.

20 Apr 1777: New York, last of the thirteen, established a new constitution and government.

27 Apr 1777: Battle of Ridgefield, CT: A British force under Tryon, former royal governor of North Carolina, destroyed American supplies at Danbury, CT on 26 Apr 1777 and burned most of the town. American militia under General Wooster responded, but Wooster was killed. General Arnold, who was nearby visiting his children, took command of the militia, and defeated the British at Ridgefield, CT, forcing them to retreat by sea. Arnold afterward received a promotion to Major General for this action.

20 May 1777: The Continental Congress issued $5,000,000 in bills of credit (Continental currency).

Summer 1777: The British began execution of their complicated plan to take central New York, and thus cut the American territory in two. The plan was that General Howe was to advance to Albany via the Hudson from New York. He was to be met there by an army from Canada commanded by General Burgoyne, which was to travel from Lake Champlain to Ticonderoga, take it, and then sail down the Hudson to Albany. Burgoyne's command also included Generals Phillips, Fraser, and Riedesel. A third force under Colonel St. Leger was to start on the St. Lawrence, march to Oswego, then come down the Mohawk Valley and take Fort Stanwix. St. Leger was to be aided by Sir John Johnson and his Indian force. During this time, Canada would be secured by Carleton's army in Quebec. This complex plan was made worse because Howe decided to take (American) General Lee's advice and attack Philadelphia first, then advance up to Albany.

Jun 1777: The Continental dollar was valued at SM$0.40.

12-30 Jun 1777: In Jun 1777, General Howe attempted to pass through New Jersey to attack Philadelphia, but was outmaneuvered by Washington, who kept a step ahead of the British, and always occupied strong locations. There was a skirmish between Morgan and Cornwallis at Piscataway on 22 Jun, and the British defeated Alexander at Machoutin on 24 Jun 1777, but there were no large scale battles. Howe was unwilling to take a risk on an open battle, so he took his army back to Staten Island at the end of June. This delay would turn out to be costly for the British in the wilderness up north. Howe spent the next few weeks sailing his men around New York, trying to confuse the Americans as to what his real destination was. Some thought he would go to Philadelphia, some to Boston, some to Charleston, but all on the American side agreed that he should proceed to assist Burgoyne by going up the Hudson. However, Howe's real objective was to take the long way around and attack Philadelphia.

4-7 Jul 1777: Battle of Hubbardton, NY: British under General Phillips seized Mount Defiance, which overlooked Fort Ticonderoga. With the high ground, bombarding Fort Ticonderoga would be an easy victory, but American General St. Clair evacuated the fort on 5 Jul 1777 and retreated toward the Green Mountains. The British under Fraser pursued them, and caught up to the Americans at Hubbardton on 7 Jul; Fraser was defeated by militia under Colonels Warner and Francis. St. Clair was able to continue the retreat to Fort Edward, where he joined with General Schuyler. Schuyler received the blame for the defeat, mostly out of hostility on the part of New England men in Congress. The failure to secure Mount Defiance was actually due to St. Clair, and to Gates, who had commanded Ticonderoga on and off between the fall of 1776 and Jun 1777.

10 Jul 1777: William Barton, Lieutenant Colonel of the Rhode Island militia, made a daring raid and kidnapped General Prescott, commander of the British in Rhode Island, from his headquarters near Newport. Prescott was quickly transported to Providence, and was later exchanged for Gen. C. Lee.

30 Jul 1777: Burgoyne reached Fort Edward, only to find that the Americans under General Schuyler had evacuated over the Hudson to Stillwater. The British occupied Fort Edward.

1 Aug 1777: The Continental Congress issued $1,000,000 in bills of credit (paper currency).

1-4 Aug 1777: General Schuyler was relieved of command of the northern department on 1 Aug 1777. He was replaced on 4 Aug by General Gates. This was a very bad decision on the part of Congress, as Gates' only talent was to take credit for other people's efforts. Schuyler was replaced mostly because he was hated by the New Englanders, and Congress was afraid that an insufficient number of men would re-enlist if he continued in command.

6 Aug 1777: Battle of Oriskany, NY: The British force commanded by Colonel St. Leger arrived at Fort Stanwix early in the month. The commander of the American-held fort, Colonel Peter Gansevoort, rejected St. Leger's demand to surrender. A local militia of Tryon County, commanded by General Nicholas Herkimer, attempted to aid Gansevoort by mounting a rear attack against St. Leger. At the same time, the personnel in the fort were to come out and attack St. Leger in front. Unfortunately, the arranged timing was poorly executed, and a British force, assisted by their Indian allies under John Johnson, trapped Herkimer's militia in a ravine two miles west of Oriskany, NY, about six miles east of Ft. Stanwix. The British and Indians were forced to retreat after a fierce battle, although the Americans were unable to pursue them. The Americans retreated back to Oriskany. Afterward, a sortie from the fort under Colonel Willett defeated Johnson, and the British retreated back over the Mohawk River. This turned out to be a nominal victory for the Americans, but did not affect St. Leger's general plan, as he was still able to lay siege to Fort Stanwix.

15 Aug 1777: The Continental Congress issued $1,000,000 in bills of credit (Continental currency).

16 Aug 1777: Battle of Bennington, NY: Hessians under Lieutenant Colonel Baum (of Burgoyne's army) advanced to Bennington, New York (now Vermont) to seize American stores; he was defeated there by American militia under General Stark, Ethan Allen (civilian), and Colonel Seth Warner. A relieving force under Breymann was defeated the same day by militia under Warner and Stark. Nearly all of Baum's force was killed or captured, but a small remnant escaped back to Ft. Edward.

22 Aug 1777: Retreat of St. Leger from Ft. Stanwix, NY. General Arnold had volunteered on 1 Aug 1777 to lead an expedition to relieve the siege of Ft. Stanwix by the British under St. Leger. He did so through a brilliant deception, after a difficult advance to German Flats, about 20 miles from Ft. Stanwix. Having caught several loyalist spies and sentenced them to death, he chose one of them, a slightly crazy man named Yan Yost Cuyler to spread panic in the British camp. His fidelity to the mission was secured by holding his brother hostage. Cuyler went through the forest, making contact

with St. Leger's scouts, and passed the word that Burgoyne had been defeated, and that a large American force was advancing to Ft. Stanwix. On the evening of 21 Aug, Cuyler came running into the British camp with fake bullet holes in his coat, claiming he had just narrowly escaped the Americans. Because Cuyler was a known loyalist and spy, the British believed him, and this caused a panic. The Indian allies deserted St. Leger, and spent the night getting drunk. The next day, the British main force abandoned the siege of Ft. Stanwix. As they were leaving, the Americans at the fort made another sortie, and pursued the British for a short distance. But St. Leger's former Indian allies pursued him all the way to Oswego.

25 Aug-8 Sep 1777: Howe finally managed to arrive by sea at Elkton, at the head of Chesapeake Bay, to attack Philadelphia on 25 Aug 1777. He advanced to Kennett Square by early September. Meanwhile, Washington had determined Howe's objective, and deployed his forces at Brandywine Creek.

11 Sep 1777: Battle of Brandywine Creek, PA: The British under General Howe, General Agnew, General Knyphausen, and Lord Cornwallis defeated Americans under Washington, Sullivan, Greene, Wayne, Stephen, and Armstrong at Brandywine Creek, southwest of Philadelphia. The British capitalized on their numerical superiority and training; Cornwallis executed a flawless maneuver on the Lancaster Road; Sullivan failed to ford the creek to cut off Howe and Cornwallis, and the Americans suffered from poor intelligence on British actions. Washington's objective was to detain Howe as long as possible so that he would not be able to aid Burgoyne. By delaying tactics and maneuvers, he managed to prevent Howe from occupying Philadelphia for two weeks.

18 Sep 1777: Congress fled from Philadelphia to Lancaster after the loss at Brandywine Creek.

19 Sep 1777: First Battle at Freeman's Farm, NY: British General Burgoyne, after the retreat of St. Leger and the defeat of Baum, did not have any good options. The American militia was now infesting the area making a retreat to Ticonderoga dangerous, and he risked being cut off entirely if he went to Albany. Believing General Howe was still coming up the Hudson, he decided to engage the Americans directly to buy time for the rendezvous with Howe; failing that, a retreat to Canada. On 13 Sep 1777, Burgoyne, Fraser, Phillips, and Riedesel crossed the Hudson River from Bennington to Schuylerville and proceeded to Bemis Heights. They were intercepted at Freeman's farm, just north of Bemis Heights, by Generals Arnold, Morgan, and Lincoln, after General Gates (in command) reluctantly allowed them to leave their fortified position. This battle was a draw, but Gates took credit for a victory. In reality, it could have been a decisive victory for the Americans if Gates had provided reinforcements to Arnold when requested.

26 Sep 1777: The British under Lord Cornwallis (part of Howe's army) occupied Philadelphia unopposed.

4 Oct 1777: Battle of Germantown, PA: Americans under Washington, Greene, Sullivan, Maxwell, Wayne, Conway, McDougal, Stephen, and Smallwood attacked the British at Germantown, Pennsylvania, intending to force the British to surrender their entire army if cornered against the Schuylkill River. The British were commanded by Lord Cornwallis, General Knyphausen, General Grant, Sir Charles Grey, and Colonel Musgrave. The Americans were defeated, mostly through the ineptness or drunkenness of Stephen, who had attacked Wayne in the fog, mistaking his troops for the British. General Greene also arrived too late.

7 Oct 1777: Second Battle at Freeman's Farm, NY: On 21 Sep 1777, American General Lincoln began an assault on Fort Ticonderoga, and sent his main army down toward Bemis Heights to engage Burgoyne's army. By this time, the Americans (mostly militia) numbered about 16,000, three times the size of Burgoyne's army. Since Gen. H. Clinton had not arrived with reinforcements, Burgoyne elected to try to escape, which led to the second battle at Freeman's Farm on 7 Oct 1777. The British army, commanded by Generals Burgoyne, Fraser, Philips, Riedesel, Ackland, Colonel Breymann, and Lord Balcarras, were defeated by the Americans under Generals Arnold, Greene, and Morgan. Arnold was wounded in the action; Breymann and Fraser were both killed. The British retreated to

Saratoga, with Gates in pursuit. The retreating British were surrounded south of Fort Edward, but manage to stave off the Americans temporarily.

17 Oct 1777: General H. Clinton was unable to reinforce Burgoyne, who was now surrounded at Saratoga, so Burgoyne entered into negotiations with General Gates on terms of surrender. The terms were concluded on 17 Oct 1777. They included four provisions: a) British were to exit their camp under full honors and pile their weapons in a field; b) the British were to march to Boston and sail for Europe, never to return to America for the duration of the war; c) officers were to keep their private arms; and d) there would be no searches of private luggage. In all, the British surrendered 5,791 men, six of whom were members of Parliament. The surrender of Burgoyne at Saratoga is now regarded as the turning point of the war in favor of the Americans; but it was not perceived that way at the time.

22 Oct 1777: A force of Hessians under General Donop was defeated at their attempt to take Fort Mercer (Red Bank) on the Delaware River, commanded by American colonel Christopher Greene.

7 Nov 1777: The Continental Congress issued $1,000,000 in bills of credit (Continental currency).

15 Nov 1777: The Continental Congress agreed upon the terms of the Articles of Confederation, and sent a letter on 17 Nov to the state legislatures for review, and asking them to instruct their Congressional delegates to ratify it if they found it acceptable.

16 Nov 1777: British took Fort Mercer (Red Bank) on the Delaware River.

16 Nov 1777: British under both Howe's took Fort Mifflin (Mud Island) on the Delaware River, commanded by Major Simeon Thayer and Major Fleury. The British then controlled the entire river leading into Philadelphia.

22 Nov 1777: Congress issued a recommendation that the states raise $5,000,000, apportioned according to population, to be paid in quarterly installments starting 1 Jan 1778 to pay the expenses for 1778.

3 Dec 1777: The Continental Congress issued $1,000,000 in bills of credit (Continental currency).

17 Dec 1777: Louis XVI of France decided to recognize America as independent states. He ordered negotiations for treaties to begin with the American envoys.

17 Dec 1777: Washington moved his army to winter at Valley Forge, arriving there on the 19th. There was great suffering among the troops, and their movements could be traced by following their bloody footprints in the snow. Most of the needs went unfulfilled owing to an inefficient requisition and supply system, run by incompetents appointed by Congress. There was a general lack of food, and the men had to build huts in the forest for shelter. However, the army became well-trained during this period, owing to training by the German Major General Baron von Steuben, who arrived in camp 23 Feb 1778. He had been encouraged to come to train the American army by the French.

22-23 Dec 1777: Washington was unable to make a move against General Howe because of a shortage of supplies in the army; two of his brigades bordered on mutiny because they had not received rations for three days. On 23 Dec, Washington reported he had 8,200 men fit for duty and 2,898 unfit for duty because of lack of shoes or clothing. Washington also responded to the undermining of his command by Gates, Conway, and Mifflin.

31 Dec 1777: The Continental dollar was valued at about SM$0.25.

Jan 1778: Congress attempted to borrow $10,000,000, but found it had no credit.

Jan 1778: Louis XVI of France promised a loan of 3,000,000 *livres* (SM$582,000), with an equal amount to be secretly loaned by Spain.

3 Jan 1778: Burgoyne's army had marched from Saratoga to Boston in preparation for the evacuation back to England per the terms of his surrender. General Howe proposed that they leave from Newport, but Washington refused to allow any deviation from the surrender. Congress used Howe's request to falsely accuse Howe of attempting to divert the British troops to New York, to be re-employed in the war. Congress heard that Burgoyne had protested an order to list the names of all

his men, and concluded that Burgoyne was accusing the Americans of bad faith. On 3 Jan 1778, Congress directed that the departure of the British was to be delayed until a British delegation ratified the terms of surrender. Burgoyne's troops were marched from Boston to Charlottesville, Virginia in the fall of 1778, where most of them remained until 1780, when they were transferred to Winchester, VA, then to Frederick, MD, and finally to Lancaster, PA. Eventually those who wished to go back to Europe did so, but most of the Germans settled in America after the war. Burgoyne himself returned to England in the spring of 1778, where he took his seat in Parliament and ironically defended the American cause. Overall, the action by Congress regarding the disposition of Burgoyne's army was without excuse; it was Congress who demonstrated bad faith.

8 Jan 1778: Congress issued $1,000,000 in bills of credit (Continental currency).

22 Jan 1778: Congress issued $2,000,000 in bills of credit (Continental currency).

6 Feb 1778: Treaties of alliance and commerce were concluded between the American states and France. For its part, France agreed: a) to recognize the independence of the American states from Great Britain; and b) to provide military support. The Americans agreed: a) not to ratify a peace treaty with Great Britain unless recognition of independence was included; and b) to conclude peace with Great Britain only if France was a party to the treaty. Both nations extended most-favored trading rights to the other. The Americans recognized French rights to fish along the Newfoundland coast. France also promised to use its influence with the Barbary principalities of the Mediterranean. A secret provision invited Spain into the treaty. The treaty was not entirely popular in America, since the people of New England were irritated by an association with a Catholic power. Meanwhile, the British ministry through their spies found out about the treaty less than two days after it was signed, but kept it secret.

16 Feb 1778: Congress issued $2,000,000 in bills of credit (Continental currency).

17 Feb-11 Mar 1778: British Prime Minister Lord North introduced a bill on 17 Feb designed to achieve reconciliation with the Americans. It would: a) repeal the Tea Act; b) repeal the Regulating Act of 20 May 1774 that changed the charter of Massachusetts; c) eliminate Parliament's power to raise revenue in America; and d) appoint commissioners to order a truce, grant pardons, and negotiate a peace settlement. The commissioners would also have the power to suspend any act of Parliament active in America since 1763 and to issue amnesty for all political offenses. It was everything Samuel Adams had demanded four years earlier; but it was now far too late, especially after the defeat of Burgoyne at Saratoga. It was initially poorly received in Parliament, but passed in Commons on 17 Feb, later in the House of Lords, and was signed by King George III on 11 Mar. It became known as the Reconciliation Act.

19 Feb 1778: Captain James Willing and a group of about 100 American regulars captured Natchez on the Mississippi River, evicting the British who had been instigating the Indians to attack the settlements in western Georgia and South Carolina.

26 Feb 1778: Congress authorized a draft to obtain soldiers; but it was imposed at the state level as militia, with terms of enlistment to be 9 months. The states were to provide in total 79 battalions, apportioned according to state population. This system worked well enough to maintain the army, albeit at levels below what General Washington desired. In Rhode Island, enlisted slaves were emancipated, and their masters compensated.

5 Mar 1778: The Continental Congress issued $2,000,000 in bills of credit (Continental currency).

13 Mar 1778: The French envoy to England announced the treaties between America and France that had been concluded in Feb 1778. Parliament declared war against France.

19 Mar 1778: The legislature of South Carolina approved a new constitution, which was to go into effect 29 Nov 1778. It required everyone above the age of 16 to take an oath against the King of England, or be exiled.

Apr 1778: Congress permitted checks to be drawn for SM$6,000,000 (31,500,000 *livres*) on accounts in France; Franklin was informed that he would have to find the money in France to make good on the notes.

4 Apr 1778: Congress issued $1,000,000 in bills of credit (Continental currency).

11 Apr 1778: The Continental Congress issued $5,000,000 in bills of credit (Continental currency).

18 Apr 1778: Congress issued $500,000 in bills of credit (Continental currency).

22 Apr 1778: Congress rejected the Reconciliation Act, issuing a resolution that said in part, that it would "hold no conference or treaty with any commissioners on the part of Great Britain, unless they shall, as a preliminary thereto, either withdraw their fleets and armies, or in positive and express terms acknowledge the independence of the states."

May 1778: The news of the alliance with France became public, and the Continental dollar appreciated from 6:1 to 4:1.

4 May 1778: Congress ratified the treaties with France.

15 May 1778: Congress agreed to give officers who serve to the end of the war half-pay for seven years, and common soldiers to receive $80.

22 May 1778: Congress issued $5,000,000 in bills of credit (Continental currency). The total amount in circulation at this time was about $56,500,000, and had depreciated to 6:1.

24 May 1778: Sir William Howe resigned as commander of the British forces, and was replaced by Sir Henry Clinton.

Jun 1778: The Continental dollar was valued at SM$0.25.

6 Jun 1778-3 Oct 1778: Commissioners from Great Britain attempted to promote the virtues and benefits of the Reconciliation Act passed by Parliament, but were unsuccessful. One of the objectives of the Reconciliation Act was to allow events to develop such that the North ministry could plausibly convince the English people back home of the necessity of continuing the war. On the other hand, there was growing sentiment among the members of Parliament that the states could not be brought under Great Britain by force. Congress would agree to nothing until independence was first acknowledged by the British. General Clinton was under orders, that if the Reconciliation Act were not accepted by the Americans, to adopt the following strategy: a) retain New York and Rhode Island; b) destroy the coastal towns of Virginia by naval bombardment; c) destroy all the ports north of New York to Nova Scotia; d) support the Indians in their marauding and massacres in the west; and e) occupy the western territories to prevent the states from expanding westward.

17 Jun 1778: Congress rejected the Reconciliation Act for a second time.

18 Jun 1778: The British had found that Philadelphia was of little military value, and evacuated it on 18 Jun 1778 along with a large number of loyalists. An American garrison returned the next day, commanded by Arnold.

20 Jun 1778: Congress issued $5,000,000 in bills of credit (Continental currency).

26 Jun-30 Jul 1778: A large group of backwoodsmen from western Virginia (referred to at this time as the county of Kentucky), led by George Rodgers Clark, William Harrod, Leonard Helm, Joseph Bowman, and John Montgomery, began a campaign to secure the Ohio and Mississippi Rivers from the British and their Indian allies. They seized Kaskaskia on 4 Jul, Kahokia later in the month, and obtained the allegiance of the people at Vincennes. They then sent out notices to the Indians that they intended to conquer the entire territory. The British were led by Lieutenant-Governor Hamilton of the Detroit territory, who was able to take Vincennes.

28 Jun 1778: Battle of Monmouth, NJ: The Americans, commanded by Washington, C. Lee, Wayne, von Steuben, Greene, Alexander, Morgan, Maxwell, and Lafayette fought to a draw against the British force commanded by H. Clinton, Knyphausen, and Cornwallis. It was in this battle that C. Lee disobeyed Washington's order to attack; instead he ordered a retreat, which put Wayne's and Lafa-

yette's forces in danger. Many of Lee's men got bogged down in the swamp until Washington rallied them personally. Lee was court-martialed for his action, and sentenced to a suspension from service for one year. The battle turned out to be a moral victory for the Americans, as 2,000 Hessians deserted the British in the following weeks. It was in this battle that 700 black men fought on the side of the Americans.

3-4 Jul 1778: Massacre at Wyoming Valley, PA: Several British officers (Sir William Johnson, his son Walter Johnson, Col. John Butler, and his son Walter Butler), had organized the Indian tribes of western and central New York (Iroquois, Mohawk, and the Six Nations except the Oniedas and Tuscaroras) to fight on the British side. They mostly engaged in pillaging the frontier. On this occasion Col. John Butler, Johnson, and a band of Senecas attacked the Wyoming Valley along the Susquehanna in Pennsylvania. The Indians and loyalists massacred nearly everyone in the valley.

9 Jul 1778: Eight states (New Hampshire, Massachusetts, Rhode Island, Connecticut, New York, Pennsylvania, Virginia, and South Carolina) ratified the Articles of Confederation.

Congress was the only instrument of the federation. It was to convene on the first Monday in November and continue for a period not longer than six months. When it adjourned, the government was maintained by an executive committee consisting of one delegate from each state. Congress elected a President, who was only the nominal leader of Congress, and had the same powers as any other delegate. Congress published a monthly journal of its proceedings.

Each state was allowed to send between two and seven delegates, but since it was a confederation of states, each state had a single vote. The delegates were paid by their respective states, not out of a federal treasury. Instead of administrative departments, the various functions were allocated to committees. This proved to be inefficient, and later on some functions were allocated to individuals in the interest of expediency.

Congress was granted the following powers: a) to borrow money; b) to appropriate requisitions of money, men, and equipment from each of the states, but could not raise revenue on its own; c) to resolve issues between the states; d) to enact treaties with foreign powers; e) to establish an army and navy; and f) to issue a currency as an obligation to repay loans. One of the great defects of the Confederation was Congress' inability to raise revenue aside from requesting it from the states. The idea was that Congress would make requisitions from the states based on the proportional value of real estate in each state. The states were then free to raise the requisition by taxing their own citizens. Normally the states levied direct taxes and imposed duties on both imports and exports, unless they contradicted any treaty provision made by Congress. But states often did not comply with the requisitions, and Congress was powerless to do anything about it. Also, states were allowed to coin money, issue bills of credit, and make their notes legal tender.

Concurrence of two-thirds of the states was required for any of the following actions: a) to engage in war; b) to make treaties; c) to coin money; d) to borrow or appropriate money; e) to assign quotas of revenue to the states; and f) to appoint commanders of the army.

Under the Articles, the states were required to grant every freeman the same rights and privileges. Every state was compelled to recognize the records and acts of every other state. The states were obligated to extradite persons found in their state who were wanted on criminal charges in another state. Otherwise, all the other powers were left to the states with the following prohibitions: a) a state could not maintain an army or a navy, except for the militia; b) a state could not enter into treaties with foreign nations; c) a state could not form alliances with any of the other states without the consent of Congress; and d) each state was prohibited from entering into any other wars except against the Indians.

The Articles could be amended only by concurrence of all member states.

20 Jul 1778: Washington placed the main army at White Plains, New York, while the British under H. Clinton occupied New York City. The two armies now occupied about the same positions as in 1776.

21 Jul 1778: North Carolina (9) ratified the Articles of Confederation (by delegates to the Continental Congress).

24 Jul 1778: Georgia (10) ratified the Articles of Confederation (by delegates to the Continental Congress).

29 Jul-15 Aug 1778: Failed attempt to take Newport, RI: A force of American regulars under Greene, Lafayette, and Sullivan, aided by Massachusetts militia under Hancock and a French naval force under d'Estaing, failed to take Newport, Rhode Island. The land assault was not well-coordinated. A British fleet arrived on the 30th, and both fleets went to sea for a naval battle, but the battle was precluded by a particularly bad storm. In late August, the French fleet sailed for Boston to be refit.

30 Jul 1778: Congress issued $5,000,000 in bills of credit (Continental currency).

29 Aug 1778: Battle of Butts Hill, RI: The Americans under Sullivan had taken up a strong position on Butts Hill (also called Honyman's Hill), Rhode Island; an assault by the British under Pigot failed. However, with British reinforcements on the way, and the American militia already gone, the Americans evacuated and the siege was abandoned.

5 Sep 1778: Congress issued $5,000,000 in bills of credit (Continental currency).

5-6 Sep 1778: The British burned the towns of New Bedford and Fair Haven, CT.

10-14 Sep 1778: The British pillaged Martha's Vineyard.

25 Sep 1778: Congress replaced General Robert Howe with General Benjamin Lincoln as commander of the southern department. He arrived in Charleston in December.

26 Sep 1778: The Continental Congress issued $10,000,000 in bills of credit (Continental currency).

3 Oct 1778: The British commissioners departed for Great Britain, frustrated that the Americans had rejected the Reconciliation Act. They published a "farewell" address, in which they outlined the new British policy, which was to destroy as much of the country as possible in an effort to wear down the desire for independence. But many in Parliament disavowed and denounced the proclamation, including Burke, Rockingham, and Coke. At about the same time, the ministry decided that the focus of the war should be changed to the southern states.

Nov 1778: A series of skirmishes and protracted guerilla war was fought in southern Georgia and northern Florida (still held by the British). On several occasions, British under General Augustine Prevost ruined plantations in Georgia and kidnapped slaves, which were later re-sold in Europe.

4 Nov 1778: The Continental Congress issued $10,000,000 in bills of credit (Continental currency).

10 Nov 1778: Massacre at Cherry Valley, NY: Walter Butler and his Indian allies conducted a massacre at the small village of Cherry Valley, New York.

26 Nov 1778: New Jersey (11) ratified the Articles of Confederation (by delegates to the Continental Congress).

Dec 1778: Americans tried to call out the militia of South Carolina, but they did not appear because they were afraid that their slaves would stage a revolt in their absence. Relations between masters and slaves were not as good as they were elsewhere, and the whites constantly had to suppress minor rebellions and capture and return fugitive slaves.

14 Dec 1778: The Continental Congress issued $10,000,000 in bills of credit (Continental currency).

15 Dec 1778: Maryland's legislature directed its delegates to Congress not to ratify the Articles of Confederation unless all the states ceded their land claims west of the Appalachians to Congress. This was a very wise move on the part of Maryland, because it brought the problem of conflicting land claims by the states into the forefront. At this time, New York claimed all the land north of the Ohio River up to the Miami River, based on the colonial charter and the influence of New York over the Indian tribes in those areas. But Virginia claimed all the land to Lake Superior, based on old colonial charters and the conquests made in Lord Dunmore's war of 1774. Massachusetts and Connecticut claimed all the land at their respective latitudes extending to the Pacific Ocean based on its earliest

charters. The Maryland legislature realized early on that these would have to be settled sooner or later, and making the Confederacy dependent on it was a useful expedient to force the issue.

29 Dec 1778: A British force under Colonel Campbell defeated the Americans under Gen. Robert Howe at Savannah; the British took Savannah and all the supplies stored there, but was evacuated by the British a month later.

31 Dec 1778: The Continental dollar was judged to be worth SM$0.16 in the northern states and SM$0.12 in the south. The expenses for 1778 were about $62,166,000 in paper currency and about $84,000 in hard money.

5 Jan 1779: The Continental Congress issued a requisition to the states for SM$15,000,000 for 1779. None of it would ever be paid.

9 Jan 1779: British under General Prevost invaded Georgia from Florida and captured Sudbury. The British proceeded to pillage the countryside.

14 Jan 1779: The Continental Congress issued $50,000,400 in bills of credit (paper currency). The total issue of Continentals to this point amounted to about $130,000,000.

14 Jan 1779: The French had negotiated an agreement by which one of the articles of the 6 Feb 1778 treaty was clarified in spite of the French treaty with Spain; namely, that neither France nor the American states would conclude peace with Great Britain without consent of the other party. Congress ratified it based on a report by Jay and Samuel Adams on 14 Jan 1779.

3 Feb 1779: The Continental Congress issued $5,000,160 in bills of credit (Continental currency), and authorized that SM$20,000,000 be borrowed from loan offices on the credit of the United States.

3 Feb 1779: The British under General Prevost attacked Port Royal, but were defeated by American militia under General Moultrie.

14 Feb 1779: Battle of Kettle Creek, GA: A loyalist militia under Boyd was defeated outside of Kettle Creek, GA by militia under Colonel Pickens.

19 Feb 1779: The Continental Congress issued $5,000,160 in bills of credit (Continental currency).

24 Feb 1779: Colonel Clark and the Virginians trapped British Lieutenant-Governor Hamilton at Vincennes and forced him to surrender. This was followed by the capture of supply boats from Detroit. This ended the war in the northwest, securing to Virginia all the territory as far west as present-day St. Louis, including territory that would eventually become Wisconsin, Michigan, Indiana, and Illinois.

3 Mar 1779: Battle of Briar Creek, GA: American militia under General Ashe was defeated by the British under Colonel Campbell. The British were later able to maintain their hold on Augusta, and re-established the royal government in Georgia.

Apr 1779: The Continental dollar was valued at about SM$0.05.

Apr 1779: Backwoodsmen from North Carolina and Virginia attacked the Cherokees in the southwest, ending the attacks upon settlements.

1 Apr 1779: The Continental Congress issued $5,000,160 in bills of credit (Continental currency).

12 Apr 1779: France and Spain signed a treaty of mutual assistance against Great Britain: a) France was to invade either Ireland or England; b) if Newfoundland were taken from Great Britain, it was to be shared between France and Spain; c) France was to aid Spain in recovering Minorca, Pensacola, Mobile, and Honduras; and d) neither would accept a truce or peace with Great Britain until Gibraltar was recovered for Spain. There were two underlying motives for this alliance. First, each obtained aid against their mutual enemy. The second objective was to retard the westward expansion by the Americans by controlling the Mississippi, on the south by Spain, and in the north by France. France was not obligated under its treaty with America to recognize the American claims to the Ohio Valley. This agreement implicitly altered the treaty between America and France: since America was

not obligated to continue the war against Great Britain over Gibraltar, America was free to enact a separate peace with Great Britain without France.

28 Apr-11 May 1779: British under General Prevost waged a war of total destruction throughout Georgia as the army advanced from Savannah to Charleston SC. He routinely invaded the plantation homes and carried off everything of value, while burning crops and killing livestock. The British also carried off many of the slaves. He also had some Cherokee allies, who scalped many of the victims. There was a famine in the area, and about 1,000 slaves died of starvation. The British did not attack Charleston, since the locals of Charleston aided by militia under Rutledge and Moultrie had fortified the neck, but did establish a garrison at Beaufort, SC.

5 May 1779: The Continental Congress issued $10,000,100 in bills of credit (Continental currency).

5 May 1779: Delaware (12) ratified the Articles of Confederation (by delegates to the Continental Congress).

7 May 1779: The Continental Congress issued $50,000,100 in bills of credit (Continental currency), having been authorized 4 Jan 1779.

10 May 1779: The British under General Matthew pillaged the towns of Portsmouth and Norfolk, VA and burned nearly every house in Suffolk County.

19 May 1779: Congress requisitioned $45,000,000 from the states; none of it would ever be paid.

31 May-2 Jun 1779: The British captured the fort at Stony Point, NY on 31 May and Verplanck's Point surrendered on 2 Jun 1779. These two controlled King's Ferry, and the Americans could now communicate between New York and New Jersey only by way of the mountains.

Jun 1779: The Continental dollar was valued at SM$0.05.

4 Jun 1779: The Continental Congress issued $10,000,100 in bills of credit (Continental currency).

15 Jun 1779: France granted a loan of SM$3,000,000 to Congress, to be repaid with interest after the war.

16 Jun 1779: Spain declared war on England, but was done independently of any consideration for the Americans. Spain did not recognize the independence of the American states, and did not enter into any type of alliance. The Spanish had numerous reasons of their own to attack Great Britain: a) revenge for losses suffered in the Seven Years War; b) to prevent the spread of the Protestant religion; and c) attempt to regain Gibraltar or Minorca. But the Spanish also hated the American states for revolting against Great Britain, afraid that her colonies in the Western hemisphere might try to imitate the Americans.

21 Jun 1779: King George III gathered the prominent men of Parliament in a private meeting, and explained that he intended to continue the war against the Americans. This was his way of controlling the debate in Parliament, where many of the members were inclined to recognize American independence, owing to the cost of the war and the lack of success prosecuting it.

5-11 Jul 1779: British under General Tryon pillaged and burned part of New Haven, CT on 5 Jul, then burned Fairfield and Green Farms on the 7th and 8th, and Norwalk on 11 Jul 1779. The Hessians were allowed to plunder anything they could.

16 Jul 1779: Americans under Wayne attacked Stony Point, NY with two simultaneous bayonet charges under Fleury and Stewart, defeated the British garrison, and re-occupied the fort. But it was not regarded as worth defending, and the Americans destroyed and evacuated it on the 19th.

17 Jul 1779: The Continental Congress issued $15,000,280 in bills of credit (Continental currency).

18 Aug 1779: Americans under Major Henry Lee made a daring raid and captured a British fort at Paulus Hook (now Jersey City, NJ).

29 Aug 1779: Battle of Newtown, NY: An American force under Generals Sullivan and James Clinton had advanced up the Susquehanna and Mohawk Rivers to find and destroy the Indians who had been conducting raids on the frontier, and especially in revenge for the massacres at Cherry Valley and

Wyoming Valley. The Americans caught up to the Indians under both Butlers and Sir John Johnson at Newtown (now Elmira, New York), and defeated them. Afterward, the Americans destroyed 40 villages and fields belonging to the Seneca and Cayuga tribes; many of them later died of exposure and hunger during the very cold winter of 1779-1780. For the next two years, the towns of central New York were preyed upon by the Indians; some counties were nearly decimated by the constant Indian attacks.

3 Sep 1779: Congress calculated that the outstanding issues of Continentals amounted to $159,948,880. It passed a resolution limiting the amount in circulation at any one time to be $200,000,000.

17 Sep 1779: Congress issued $15,000,360 in bills of credit (Continental currency).

21 Sep 1779: The Spanish under Governor Galvez forced the British at Baton Rouge to surrender the fort.

Oct 1779: The British evacuated Newport, RI; they did not have enough forces in the north to keep both Newport and New York. Washington, meanwhile, did not have enough forces to do much except monitor Clinton's army at New York City. The two northern armies settled into a stalemate while the focus of the war now shifted to the southern states.

Oct 1779: Congress appointed Henry Laurens to go to the Netherlands and obtain a loan of SM$10,000,000. Laurens would not be successful.

7 Oct 1779: Congress asked the states once again to pay the SM$15,000,000 requisitioned on 5 Jan 1779. None of it would ever be paid.

9 Oct 1779: Battle of Savannah, GA: An American force under General Lincoln and Count Pulaski, assisted by a French naval force under d'Estaing failed to recapture Savannah from the British. The French fleet returned to the West Indies. Lincoln moved his army to Charleston while the militiamen went home. The British sold all the captured slaves into slavery again in the West Indies. Also, the British and their Indian allies continued to rob and pillage anything they could find in Georgia and South Carolina, including turning people out into the wilderness after burning their homes.

14 Oct 1779: The Continental Congress issued $5,000,180 in bills of credit (Continental currency).

17 Nov 1779: The Continental Congress issued $10,050,540 in bills of credit (Continental currency).

Nov 1779: Congress authorized a draft of SM$10,000,000 on account of Henry Laurens, although he had not secured a loan from the Netherlands. They also authorized a draft for the same amount on account from Spain, although John Jay had been unsuccessful in obtaining a loan there.

29 Nov 1779: The Continental Congress issued $10,000,140 in bills of credit (Continental currency). The total authorized came to $241,552,280, and the Continental was worth about SM$0.03.

Dec 1779: Congress was unable to obtain any money. There was so much depreciated paper currency in circulation that no one would loan hard money in return for a promise to repay in paper. The large issues of paper Continentals had ruined both commerce and the nation's credit. Congress had tried many methods to sustain the value of the paper, including the legal tender acts and price controls, but in the end the people simply lost confidence in the promises of Congress.

26 Dec 1779: A large British force under General Clinton and Lord Cornwallis left New York by sea to capitalize on the recent successes in the south. The British remaining at New York were commanded by Knyphausen. Washington accordingly sent some of his forces south to reinforce General Lincoln, and was therefore still too weak to attack New York. But the British fleet encountered several storms, some of which carried the ships to England. The British finally arrived in Georgia at the end of January 1780.

Jan 1780: The Continental dollar was valued at between SM$0.02 and 0.03 at this time.

Jan 1780 ff: From this point on, there was a large influx of hard money into the states. There were three main sources of the coin: a) English procurement of supplies for men and ships; b) French payments for its men and ships (totaling about SM$3,000,000); and c) loans from other foreign nations.

9 Feb 1780: Congress passed a resolution authorizing 35,211 men for the army, to be obtained by requisitions from the states. It also directed the states to forward money to pay and supply the army at SM$1,250,000 in hard money every month, or in paper currency at 40:1. All old paper currency brought in was to be destroyed and new currency was to be issued at a ratio of 1 new for every 20 old. Congress was now deferring everything to the states, having insufficient means to do for itself.

26 Feb-12 May 1780: British forces under General Clinton began the siege of Charleston, SC, on 26 Feb 1780. General Lincoln should have evacuated it as soon as the superior British force arrived, but decided to fight it out. By early May the British had surrounded Charleston, and were able to sail past Fort Moultrie without resistance.

29 Feb 1780: Pennsylvania passed a law that children of slaves were to be free; this was a means to gradually abolish slavery.

8 Mar-25 Apr 1780: Russia issued a declaration of neutrality on the seas on 8 Mar 1780, in which neutral ships were to enjoy free navigation to and from all ports; the only contraband were arms and ammunition. This was directed at England and Spain, whose navies had been attacking ships of all powers in the Atlantic, especially those of the Netherlands. Russian policy then dictated that all of its merchant ships would be escorted by warships. Spain agreed with this approach on 18 Apr, and France joined on 25 Apr. This agreement became known as the Armed Neutrality Treaty. To the British, this indicated that the other nations intended to reduce British supremacy on the seas, and Parliament resolved to attack ships from any nations that supported it.

18 Mar 1780: The Continental Congress issued a report acknowledging that the Continental currency and bills of credit had depreciated to 1/40th (0.025) of their face value, and urged the states to pay the $15,000,000 requisitioned on 5 Jan 1779, which had been repeated on 7 Oct 1779.

10 Apr 1780: The army had not been paid for about 5 months. Congress issued a resolution assuring the army that it would be paid in full, but in fact did not have the resources to do so. The men did not believe the promise anyway.

14 Apr 1780: British under Colonel Tarleton defeated American cavalry at Cooper River, SC, which cut off Charleston from the north.

19 Apr 1780: The legislature of New York authorized Congress to determine the western boundaries of New York, which would supersede the original grants from Charles II. This is the first in a series of territorial questions that the states allowed to be settled by Congress, which greatly aided the union.

12 May 1780: Surrender of Charleston, SC: General Lincoln, American commander at Charleston, surrendered it to the British. The British had surrounded the city and controlled the outlying districts, and fighting a battle here was useless to the Americans. All of the American regulars became prisoners of war, but members of the militia were allowed to leave and return home on good behavior. The British confiscated everything of value in the city.

22 May 1780: British General H. Clinton issued a proclamation requiring every person in South Carolina to declare for or against the British; those who did not take an oath of allegiance were to be treated as traitors. Many people were inclined to accept neutrality, but would not go over to the British. This order had the effect of starting many small skirmishes and gang warfare on both sides. Clinton then sailed back to New York, having transferred to Lord Cornwallis command of British forces in the south. Cornwallis was able to raise some loyalist militia. Meanwhile, he persecuted many who refused to take an oath of loyalty to the king.

29 May 1780: Battle of Waxhaws, SC: British under General Tarleton defeated Americans under Colonel Buford at Waxhaws, SC. Some of the Americans escaped, but about 250 were massacred after they surrendered. There was now no regular American force left in South Carolina.

Jun 1780: The Continental dollar was valued at between SM$0.01 and 0.02 at this time.

Jun 1780: Maryland issued 30,000 pounds (SM$79,800) in paper currency (bills of credit), and required it to be regarded as legal tender.

Jun-Oct 1780: The Americans waged a guerrilla war in South Carolina, led by James Williams, Thomas Sumter, Andrew Pickens, and Francis Marion. They commanded very small forces, but were skilled backwoodsmen, maintained excellent secrecy of their operations, and were successful at making raids on the British patrols whenever they could.

Jun 1780-Jun 1782: The British under Tarleton waged a reign of terror in the Carolinas, believing that ruining the south would bring the Americans back into the empire. There were random killings, burning of homes and farms, turning women and children out, etc. The actions were far worse in the rural areas, where local British agents could do as they pleased without supervision by Cornwallis. Many of the prisoners taken at Charleston were put on prison ships and either died from disease or were impressed into the British navy. This continued for two years.

1 Jun 1780: Washington's army consisted of 3,760 men who were fit for duty, but Congress was unable to raise enough money to pay them or provide adequate rations.

6-7 Jun 1780: Battle of Elizabethtown, NJ: Three divisions of British troops under Knyphausen, Robertson, Tryon, Stachenberg, and Matthews advanced from New York City to attack the Americans at Morristown. They were defeated by regulars under General Maxwell and militia under Colonel Dayton at Elizabethtown and along the road to Connecticut Farms. Regulars under Washington repelled the British attack on Springfield. There were members of Congress with Washington's army, and he explained to them the difficulty of maintaining the war by relying on militia.

13 Jun 1780: Congress appointed General Gates as commander over the forces in the south, over the objections of Washington, who wanted Greene instead. Gates had been in retirement on his plantation in Virginia; he arrived 19 Jul 1780 at Hillsborough, NC to take command.

19 Jun 1780: General Clinton had arrived back in New York on 17 Jun. Although his force outnumbered Washington's army by four to one, he declined to attack, contenting himself with a few minor skirmishes at Elizabeth Point and Springfield, after which the British burned Springfield. Clinton thought it an inopportune time to attack the Americans, and situated his army on Staten Island.

8 Jul 1780: Denmark joined the Armed Neutrality Alliance.

10 Jul 1780: The first contingent of a French army arrived in Newport, RI, in a fleet commanded by Admiral Ternay, with 6,000 men under Count Rochambeau, Duke de Lauzon-Biron, and Marquis de Chastellux. The French put themselves under Washington's command, and American officers of rank equal to the French took precedence. French ground forces were well-trained and well-commanded, and were exactly what the American cause needed at this point in the war. A second contingent was scheduled to arrive later, but was blockaded by the British navy in Brest, France.

11 Jul 1780: Congress fixed the redemption schedule of Continental currency and bills of credit at 40 to 1. Its reckoned value was about 65 to 1 at this time.

12 Jul 1780: American militia under General Sumter defeated a British force under Captain Huck at Cross Roads, SC.

21 Jul 1780: Sweden joined the Armed Neutrality Alliance.

30 Jul 1780: Americans under Sumter failed to take Rocky Mount, NC.

6 Aug 1780: Americans under Sumter attacked and defeated the British at Hanging Rock, NC.

15 Aug 1780: Americans under General Sumter attacked a British supply convoy along a road leading to Charleston, SC, capturing all the provisions and 100 prisoners.

16 Aug 1780: Battle of Camden, SC: The British under Lord Cornwallis, Lord Rawdon, General Tarleton, and Colonel Webster, defeated the Americans under Generals Gates, Kalb, Stevens, Caswell, Gist, Gregory, and Colonel Porterfield at Camden, SC. The Americans, mostly raw militia, were routed, and lost nearly all of their supplies. It was the culmination of several errors by Gates, including: a) taking a shorter but more dangerous road from Hillsborough (in which the men suffered from hunger on the march), b) incorrect application of intelligence on the British activities, c) needless de-

lays in attacking the British when opportunities arose; and d) sending his most experienced troops under Sumter to fight a skirmish between Camden and Charleston. Porterfield and Kalb were both killed in action; Gates fled back to Hillsborough. This was the worst defeat of the war for the Americans. With the American army virtually destroyed in the south, this victory made an attack on North Carolina attractive to the British.

18 Aug 1780: British under General Tarleton defeated Americans under General Sumter at Fishing Creek, SC, and freed all the British prisoners Sumter had taken on the 15th.

18-20 Aug 1780: American raiders under Colonel Williams defeated British and loyalists at Musgrove's Mills, SC on 18 Aug. Another group of raiders under Marion defeated a British contingent at Nelson's Ferry on 20 Aug. But these relatively minor battles only showed that there was some resistance left in South Carolina; after the defeat of Gates at Camden, the British controlled the entire state.

3 Sep 1780: An English ship captured an American ship off Newfoundland. Upon searching it, the English discovered Henry Laurens, who had been President of Congress from 1 Nov 1777 to 9 Dec 1778. Laurens' papers showed that he had been involved in negotiations between the United States and Holland. This caused a major diplomatic incident between England and Holland; England demanded a declaration from Holland that the negotiations were not aimed at assisting the Americans, which Holland refused to give. The respective ambassadors were recalled.

22-25 Sep 1780: Discovery of General Arnold's treason: Arnold had been unfairly charged with abuse of authority as commander in Philadelphia, and had gotten into many arguments with Congress. He was acquitted of the serious charges brought in Jan 1779 by Congress, but others were referred to a court martial on 3 Apr 1779. The Council of Pennsylvania delayed the court martial by asking for more time to gather evidence against Arnold. The court martial finally began on 19 Dec 1779 and delivered its verdict on 26 Jan 1780, convicting him of two minor charges for which Washington was required to reprimand him. Arnold had also married into a family of loyalists in Philadelphia, and was accused of associating with the enemy. He gave lavish parties, which irritated the people of Philadelphia, and incurred enormous debts. Arnold was probably being paid by General H. Clinton, and providing the British with intelligence since early 1779. Whether he was influenced by the loyalists, or whether he actually came to believe that the American cause was lost is unknown, but he did want revenge against Congress. He accordingly decided to go over to the British in a big way: by securing a command of an important location, and handing it with all the men over to the British. In Jul 1780, he obtained the command of West Point, NY from his friend Washington. Meanwhile he secretly conspired with Major Andre, assistant to Clinton, to give the fort to the British at a time when Washington was expected to be nearby. The idea was that Clinton would have a large enough force close at hand to defeat and capture Washington if he attempted to regain West Point. The plot was discovered when Major Andre was captured on his way back to New York by three patriots named John Paulding, David Williams, and Isaac van Wart who kept watch on the road. They discovered papers in his stockings, realized he was a spy and handed him over to the American garrison at North Castle. Andre was allowed to inform Arnold of his capture. Arnold fled West Point on the 25th when he received Andre's letter. Fortunately, Hamilton was in Arnold's house at the time of Arnold's escape, and Lafayette, Washington, and Knox were nearby, returning from a visit to Hartford to meet Rochambeau for the first time. The actual transfer to the British was never accomplished. Andre was hanged as a spy; Arnold became a Brigadier General in the British army.

28 Sep 1780: American militia under Marion defeated British and loyalist militia at Black Mingo, SC.

Oct 1780: Connecticut ceded all its claims to western lands to Congress, except it reserved some land on the southern shore of Lake Erie. This was eventually worked out in 1786.

Oct 1780: Connecticut issued regulations distinguishing between contracts payable in specie vs. those payable in paper currency, and established equitable rules for depreciation of the paper currency. Disputes were to be handled by the courts of equity. These provisions maintained equity between debtors and creditors, and prevented the problems experienced in other states regarding the enforcement of contracts. Connecticut also returned to a coin system in 1780, which avoided the rampant inflation experienced elsewhere.

5 Oct 1780: Congress adopted "armed neutrality" as a maritime code. It was later referenced in treaties with Prussia, the Netherlands, and Sweden.

5 Oct 1780: With the defeats in the south because of Gates' incompetence, Congress finally got out of the way and deferred to Washington regarding Gates' successor; Washington chose Greene on 14 Oct, whom he had wanted all along. Greene took command at Charlotte, NC on 2 Dec 1780.

7 Oct 1780: Battle of King's Mountain, SC: A British force under Major Patrick Ferguson was attacked and defeated at King's Mountain, SC by a collection of militia groups from North Carolina, South Carolina, Virginia, Tennessee, and Kentucky, commanded by William Campbell, James Williams, Benjamin Cleveland, Charles MacDowell, Isaac Shelby, and John Sevier. Ferguson's entire force was either killed or captured. Ferguson and Williams were killed in battle. Ferguson's main mission had been to travel through the back country and assemble an army of loyalists, which were to join Cornwallis' main army at Charlotte, NC. The militiamen all went back home after the battle, which gave Cornwallis enough time to concentrate his army at Winnsboro, SC. Meanwhile, this victory inspired the patriots of North Carolina to organize, while suppressing the desire of the loyalists.

10 Oct 1780: Congress agreed to a method of establishing new states out of the Northwest Territories (Ohio Valley) if those lands were to be ceded by the states currently claiming them. The provisions of this resolution were: a) territory was to be divided into several republican states to be admitted into the Confederacy; b) new states shall have the same rights of freedom, independence, and sovereignty; c) each state shall be not less than 100 miles or more than 150 miles square; and d) each state shall be reimbursed for any expenses incurred fighting the British.

21 Oct 1780: In order to stabilize the command structure of the army, Congress passed a resolution promising officers half-pay for life. However, Congress did not actually have the money to pay them. There was great concern that many of the officers would leave.

25 Oct 1780: A new constitution for Massachusetts went into effect, which included a prohibition on slavery.

Nov 1780: As the British under Cornwallis retreated from Charlotte, NC to Winnsborough, SC; General Gates' army moved in from Hillsborough and occupied Charlotte. Gates was joined by reinforcements under General Morgan.

4 Nov 1780: Congress requisitioned SM$6,000,000 in silver from the states. None of it would ever be paid.

9 Nov 1780: Americans under Gen. Sumter defeated a British force under Major Wemyss at Fishdam, SC.

20 Nov 1780: Battle of Blackstock Hill, SC: American militia under Sumter defeated the British under General Tarleton at Blackstock Hill, SC.

10 Dec 1780: Holland joined the Armed Neutrality Alliance. This was the last stage in a European alliance against Great Britain, which had the effect of diverting resources away from the war against the Americans.

14 Dec 1780: England declared war on Holland in revenge for Holland's joining the Armed Neutrality Alliance and the incident involving Henry Laurens gave the British the immediate excuse they were looking for. War against Holland was a matter of convenience, since Holland was wealthy, but weak militarily. Although Holland had been Great Britain's ally for a century, the British simply took advantage of the fact that Holland's carrying trade was easy prey.

30 Dec 1780: American militia under Colonels W. Washington and McCall attacked and defeated loyalists at Fair Forest, GA.

31 Dec 1780: The Continental dollar was valued at about SM$0.01.

1-7 Jan 1781: About 1,300 troops stationed at Morristown, NJ under General Wayne began a mutiny, and marched to Princeton to protest the poor provisions, lack of clothing, and lack of pay. They demanded to be discharged on the grounds they had served their three years under their contracts. President Reed of Pennsylvania went to their camp on 7 Jan 1781, and made a proposition that was immediately accepted: a) those that had served for three years were to be discharged; b) the men would be provided with proper clothing; and c) the men were issued certificates for back pay. This ended the mutiny.

2 Jan 1781: Virginia ceded its claims to western lands to Congress on the condition that Virginia could keep what is now Kentucky. This requirement was later dropped in 1786.

5-6 Jan 1781: British under General Benedict Arnold (now fighting for the British) burned Richmond, VA.

17 Jan 1781: Battle of The Cowpens, SC: American regulars under General Morgan and militia under Colonels Pickens, Washington, and Howard defeated the British under General Tarleton at The Cowpens, SC (about 16 miles from Spartanburg, and about 5 miles from the state line with North Carolina). Nearly the entire British force was killed or captured.

20 Jan 1781: Some soldiers staged a mutiny at Pompton, NJ, and intended to march on Philadelphia. But Washington sent a force down to suppress the men, which was ended without violence, although two of the mutiny leaders were executed.

30 Jan 1781: Maryland authorized its delegates to the Continental Congress to ratify the Articles of Confederation because the other states except Massachusetts (whose claim was weak) had fulfilled the demand of ceding land in the west to Congress.

3 Feb 1781: Congress passed a resolution urging the states to grant Congress a power to impose a 5% duty on all imports from foreign countries except: a) arms and ammunition; b) clothing; c) items imported by the United States or any of them; d) wool and cotton cards; and e) salt. The revenue was to be used to discharge the debts contracted in the prosecution of the war. No immediate action was taken by the states.

3 Feb 1781: A British fleet took the Dutch island of St. Eustatius in the West Indies without firing a shot, as the Dutch were not aware of a state of war. The British confiscated everything on the island, including the private property of British citizens. But the British continued to fly the Dutch flag as a ruse, and in the next few months, 50 American ships were seized and confiscated. The unjustified British war against Holland caused all the other powers in Europe to oppose Britain.

1 Mar 1781: Maryland (13) became the final state to ratify the Articles of Confederation.

2 Mar 1781: Congress convened under the powers of the Articles of Confederation.

15 Mar 1781: Battle of Guilford, NC: British under Lord Cornwallis defeated a combined force of regulars and militia under General Greene and Colonels Campbell, Lee, Lawson, Butler, Eaton, and Washington. General Morgan had resigned on 9 Feb due to rheumatism and fever. But the British had gone too far from their supply lines and could not remain in north-central North Carolina; Cornwallis accordingly retreated a few days later to Wilmington, NC in order to be resupplied by sea. Cornwallis soon realized that North Carolina was lost, and decided to advance into Virginia.

Apr 1781: Henry Laurens arrived at Versailles to ask for a loan of 25,000,000 *livres*; he was supported by letters previously sent by Rochambeau, Lafayette, and Franklin. The king of France agreed to a gift of 6,000,000 *livres* (SM$1,164,000), a loan of 14,000,000 *livres* (SM$2,716,000) from France, and also agreed to guarantee a future loan of 10,000,000 *livres* (SM$1,940,000) from Holland.

23 Apr 1781: Surrender of Fort Watson, SC: An American force under H. Lee and Marion cut down trees in a pine forest, and then dragged the timber to a spot in front of Fort Watson, SC; the British in the fort surrendered since they had no cannon to fight with. This was an important event, as Fort Watson lay on the communications line between Camden and Charleston, SC.

25 Apr 1781: Battle of Hobkirk's Hill, SC: The British under Lord Rawdon defeated the Americans under General Greene at Hobkirk's Hill, SC, just north of Camden. Greene retreated to Clermont. However, with the loss of Fort Watson, Rawdon realized Camden was too isolated to hold.

1 May 1781: Gen. Washington assessed the situation: a) the army only had small provisions, which were scattered throughout the states; b) the arsenals were poorly provided, and the workmen were about to leave; c) there was no money to pay for equipment or transportation; d) the states had supplied less than one-eighth of their requisition in men; and e) there was no hope of an offensive campaign without aid from France, especially a navy that could counteract Britain's command of the sea lanes.

7 May 1781: Prussia joined the Armed Neutrality Alliance.

9 May 1781: The Spanish army conquered Pensacola, Florida, stripping the British of their last stronghold in Florida.

10-15 May 1781: With supply lines cut off, the British realized they could not hold Camden, SC, so they burned it and evacuated it on 10 May. The British garrison on Orangeburg surrendered 11 May; Fort Motte surrendered 12 May; the British gave up Nelson's ferry on 14 May, and surrendered Fort Granby on 15 May.

14 May 1781: Robert Morris was appointed superintendent of finance. It was the genius of Morris that allowed the Americans to continue the war after the collapse of the Continental currency.

22 May 1781: Americans under Greene failed to take Ninety-Six, SC.

31 May 1781: The Continental currency was abolished as circulating money. It was exchanged at between 200:1 and 500:1 relative to silver (Continental dollar equal to between SM$0.002 and 0.005).

5 Jun 1781: Surrender of Augusta, GA: British surrendered Augusta to Americans under H. Lee.

29 Jun 1781: The British abandoned Ninety-Six, SC; this was the last inland post occupied by the British. It was made necessary by the loss of all the other inland posts, since the British were too far from the sea to keep a force at Ninety-Six.

6 Jul 1781: Battle of Green Springs, VA: British under Cornwallis and Tarleton defeated an American force under Lafayette, Wayne, and von Steuben at Green Spring, VA. It was the culmination of a series of marches and counter-moves by both armies. The British ruined many plantations in the area, plundering as they pleased, and carried off slaves to be re-sold in the West Indies. Lafayette did not have sufficient resources to attack Cornwallis directly, and Cornwallis was unable to attack any significant points in the interior of the state. Afterward, Cornwallis moved his army to Yorktown, and Lafayette moved his to Malvern Hill.

13 Jul 1781: Robert Morris appealed to John Jay, ambassador at Madrid, to try to get a loan from Spain in order to fund a national bank. But Jay was unable to obtain a loan, given the poor credit standing of the United States.

14 Aug 1781: Washington, still at White Plains, had been considering whether to attack the British at New York or assist Greene in the south. He received news on 14 Aug that Cornwallis, confident that the British would continue to have unfettered control of the seacoast, had deployed his army on the peninsula at Yorktown, VA. At the same time, he received news from French Admiral de Grasse that the French fleet had left the West Indies and was available for action in the north, but only until Oct 1781. Washington then decided to capitalize on the availability of the French fleet to block Cornwallis' escape by sea while trapping him with a large enough force to prevent him from fighting his way off the peninsula. To do so meant he would have to march most of his army from New York to Virginia.

19 Aug-21 Sep 1781: Washington left General Alexander and General Heath with small garrisons at Saratoga and West Point, respectively, while his main army, now combined with Rochambeau's French army from Rhode Island, marched from New York to Virginia. They crossed the Hudson River on 23 and 24 Aug. Gen. Clinton was expecting to be attacked at New York, so Washington arranged his movements to be consistent with Clinton's expectation. Although the Hessian Colonel Wurmb

continued to warn Clinton that Washington was moving south, Clinton did not accept that possibility until 2 Sep. Washington's force consisted of 2,000 American regulars, and Rochambeau's army consisted of 4,000 French troops. Meanwhile, the French fleet under de Grasse arrived outside of Yorktown on 31 Aug.

5-7 Sep 1781: A British fleet under Sir Samuel Hood and Admiral Graves (19 ships, about 2,500 men) and a French fleet under de Grasse (28 ships, about 4,000 men) fought a naval battle at the entrance to Chesapeake Bay. The engagement itself was indecisive. After a few days of maneuvering, the British fleet sailed to New York, and the French sailed to the York River between Yorktown and Gloucester and landed 3,000 troops under Marquis de Saint-Simon. Lafayette and de Saint-Simon occupied Williamsburg, VA on 7 Sep, cutting off Cornwallis' ability to retreat into North Carolina. Cornwallis delayed attacking Lafayette, who was still camped at Malvern Hill.

6 Sep 1781: General H. Clinton had received intelligence on the American movements that revealed Washington's plan. He decided to launch a counterstrike in the north to bait the Americans to return north. On 6 Sep 1781, British under General Arnold attacked and captured Fort Griswold, CT, and then massacred nearly the entire American garrison. New London, CT was then burned to the ground.

8 Sep 1781: Battle of Eutaw Springs, SC: The British under Colonel Stewart (who had succeeded Lord Rawdon) defeated Americans under Greene, Sumter, Marion, Pickens, Campbell, Williams, and H. Lee at Eutaw Springs, South Carolina. Although the British retained control of the battlefield, they were compelled to retreat to Charleston Neck, South Carolina. It turned out to be a strategic victory for the Americans.

18-26 Sep 1781: Washington and Rochambeau arrived with the army from the north at Williamsburg, VA. Their forces combined with Lafayette and de Saint-Simon amounted to 16,000 men, and had Cornwallis trapped at Yorktown.

6-19 Oct 1781: Battle of Yorktown, VA. Lord Cornwallis with 7,000 men was positioned at Yorktown, and was attacked by the Americans under Washington, von Steuben, Lincoln, and Colonel Hamilton, along with the French army under de Viomenil, Rochambeau, and Lafayette. The American force consisted of about 3,500 militia and 5,500 regular army; the French army consisted of about 7,000 men. Meanwhile, the French fleet of 36 ships under de Grasse blockaded the harbor to preclude Cornwallis from escaping by sea. Cornwallis surrendered on 19 Oct 1781. This victory by the Americans ended the war for practical purposes. The British regulars became prisoners of war, and the Americans allowed Cornwallis to send American loyalists in his army on a ship to New York, without having to give any details about them. Afterward, Washington took his army back to New York, Wayne aided Greene in the south, and the French fleet sailed to the West Indies.

23 Oct 1781: General H. Clinton arrived by sea at the mouth of the Chesapeake from New York with 35 ships and 7,000 men, but he discovered he was too late. The war was over, except for a few minor skirmishes.

30 Oct 1781: Congress issued its first requisition under the Confederation from the states for an amount of SM$8,000,000. By the end of 1783, only SM$1,486,511 will be paid [2]; by the end of 1785, a total of SM$1,600,000 would be paid.

Winter 1781-Spring 1782: American forces under General Wayne defeated the remaining British forces in Georgia and forced them to evacuate the state, except for the city of Savannah.

Nov 1781: Virginia passed a law abolishing its paper currency: a) it proclaimed that Virginia's paper currency was no longer legal tender for debts, but was accepted for taxes; b) it stated that paper currency became redeemable at loan offices at a ratio of 1,000 to 1; and c) it returned to coinage system. By this means, Virginia succeeded in taking the paper out of circulation, and relied on coinage afterward. Virginia had issued the most paper currency of any state during the Revolution.

25 Nov 1781: The news of Cornwallis' surrender reached London. It was now only a matter of time before Lord North's government would fall. Several English statesmen, including the Duke of Richmond, Charles Fox, and William Pitt Jr. were happy about the defeat, having always believed that Britain's policy was unjustified. King George III was not ready to give up yet; he replaced Clinton with Sir Guy Carleton, and instructed him to do what he could to retain Georgia, Charleston, SC, and New York City.

31 Dec 1781: Congress established the Bank of North America, chartered with SM$400,000 in capital.

1 Jan 1782: The expected expenses of the nation for 1782 totaled SM$9,000,000 but only SM$422,000 would be collected from the states; Georgia, North Carolina, South Carolina, and Delaware made no contributions at all. From Jan May 1782, only SM$20,000 was collected.

7 Jan 1782: The Bank of North America began operations in Philadelphia with SM$70,000 in hard money from individuals, and SM$254,000 from Congress, using money left over from a foreign loan. The bank played no part in the prosecution of the war since hostilities had ceased, but it did facilitate commerce.

Feb 1782: South Carolina repealed its legal tender law on its paper currency.

27 Feb 1782: The British House of Commons passed a resolution declaring that the war in America was over, and informed King George III that Parliament would regard anyone who advised him to continue the war as an enemy of Great Britain.

12 Apr 1782: A British fleet under Admiral Rodney defeated the French fleet under de Grasse near Sainte-Marie-Galante, an island in the French West Indies. The French naval influence in the western hemisphere was eliminated, and Britain maintained control of the ocean in the Caribbean. The British, now confident of having regained control of the seas, became more comfortable about settling a peace treaty with the Americans.

19 Apr 1782: The Netherlands recognized the independence of the United States.

5 May 1782: Sir Guy Carleton succeeded General Henry Clinton as commander of British forces in America.

22 May 1782: Congress' inability to pay the Army had reached a critical stage. The officers who were promised half-pay for life in 1780 still had not received anything. Many of the officers openly doubted that they would ever be paid, especially since the promise had been made before the Articles had been ratified by all the states, and there would likely be a challenge made to the payments. This was further aggravated by the fact that the general public opposed the payment provision.

Colonel Louis Nicola of Pennsylvania reasoned that these financial difficulties could be solved if the nation had a strong leader to inspire the people and put pressure on Congress to do its duty. Nicola was seeking a means to resolve the morale issues. He wrote a long letter dated 22 May 1782 to Washington in which he reviewed the difficulties of the soldiers, their hardships, lack of pay, etc., and laying out the case for monarchy, ostensibly on behalf of some officers (although to what extent is unknown), and implying support for Washington if he would assume a crown. His letter reads in part, "This war must have shown to all, but to military men in particular the weakness of republics.... Some people have so connected the ideas of tyranny and monarchy as to find it very difficult to separate them, it may be therefore requisite to give the head of such a constitution as I propose, some title more moderate, but if all other things are once adjusted I believe strong arguments might be produced for admitting the title of king, which I conceive would be attended with some material advantage."

Washington replied with a scathing rebuke. It is worth quoting in full, dated also 22 May 1782, from Newburgh [3]: "Sir: With a mixture of great surprise and astonishment I have read with attention the sentiments you have submitted to my perusal. Be assured Sir, no occurrence in the course of the war, has given me more painful sensations than your information of there being such ideas existing in the Army as you have expressed, and I must view with abhorrence, and reprehend with severity. For the present, the communication of them will rest in my own bosom, unless some further agitation of the matter, shall make a disclosure necessary.

"I am much at a loss to conceive what part of my conduct could have given encouragement to an address which to me seems big with the greatest mischiefs that can befall my country. If I am not deceived in the knowledge of myself, you could not have found a person to whom your schemes are more disagreeable; at the same time in justice to my own feelings I must add, that no man possesses a more sincere wish to see ample justice done to the Army than I do, and as far as my powers and influence, in a constitutional way extend, they shall be employed to the utmost of my abilities to affect it, should there be any occasion. Let me conjure you then, if you have any regard for your country, concern for yourself or posterity, or respect for me, to banish these thoughts from your mind, and never communicate, as from yourself, or any one else, a sentiment of the like nature. With esteem I am."

Nicola wrote again three more times on 23, 24, and 28 May, apologizing for his original letter.

11 Jul 1782: Americans under General Wayne forced the British to surrender Savannah, GA. The regular British army marched to Charleston, SC while the loyalists fled to Florida.

16 Jul 1782: A contract was drawn up between the French government and America, negotiated by Benjamin Franklin, summarizing the loans that had been made or guaranteed by France to America, with a repayment schedule. From the initial treaty in 1778, the king of France had loaned Congress a total of 18,000,000 *livres* (SM$3,492,000) at 5 percent interest between 28 Feb 1778 and 5 Jul 1782: a) in 1778: 750,000 each on 28 Feb, 19 May, 3 Aug, and 1 Nov; b) in 1779: 250,000 each on 10 Jun, 16 Sep, 4 Oct, and 21 Dec; c) in 1780: 750,000 each on 29 Feb, 23 May, 21 Jun, and 5 Oct plus 1,000,000 on 27 Nov; d) in 1781: 750,000 each on 15 Feb, 15 May, 15 Aug, and 15 Nov with an additional loan of 1,000,000 on 1 Aug; e) in 1782: 1,500,000 each on 10 Apr and 1 Jul, plus another 3,000,000 on 5 Jul. The king of France had also guaranteed the 5,000,000 *florin* (10,000,000 *livre*) loan made by the Netherlands on 5 Nov 1781. It was ratified by Congress on 22 Jan 1783. The king of France also waived all interest due until the conclusion of the peace treaty with Great Britain [4].

31 Jul 1782: Robert Morris provided to Congress his estimate of expenses for 1783 totaling SM$9,000,000. He did not have any idea how to raise this much; he recommended borrowing SM$4,000,000 and requisitioning SM$5,000,000 from the states.

4 Sep 1782: Congress requisitioned SM$1,200,000 from the states, but did not require it be paid directly to Congress. The states were to use the revenue to pay down interest in their own states [5].

3 Oct 1782: Congress agreed on the terms it would demand in the peace with Great Britain: a) states would retain territory claimed; b) states would have full access to fisheries; c) states would have free navigation of the Mississippi River; and d) states would pay no compensation to loyalists who had fled with the British.

8 Oct 1782: John Adams negotiated a treaty of "amity and commerce" with the Netherlands; it was ratified in Congress on 23 Jan 1783.

16 Oct 1782: Congress requisitioned another SM$2,000,000 from the states. None of this would ever be paid [6].

30 Nov 1782: Preliminary articles of peace were signed in Paris between Britain and America. The British were anxious for a settlement of some kind, since a continuation of the war only aided the French and the Spanish against Britain. The existing treaty between France and America, however, stipulated that America and France could establish peace with Britain only by joint agreement (no separate peace). The terms of the preliminary articles included: a) Britain would recognize the independence of the American states; b) there was agreement on fishing rights off Newfoundland; c) Britain would indemnify American loyalists for their losses during the war (estimated at 10,000,000 pounds sterling); d) Congress would recommend to the states to enact compensation to loyalists for losses incurred to their professions or businesses during the war; and e) no persecutions of loyalists and all

current prosecutions to be terminated. Negotiations between France, Britain, and Spain began soon afterward, which resulted in the agreement of 20 Jan 1783.

30 Nov 1782: Rhode Island notified Congress that it had passed a resolution 1 Nov 1782 rejecting the system of import duties proposed by Congress on 3 Feb 1781. The state legislature cited three reasons for opposing it: a) an import duty as proposed would impose financial hardships on the commercial states; b) concern that the revenue officers would be persons unknown to and not answerable to officials of Rhode Island; and c) Congress would not be adequately accountable for how the revenue would be spent; i.e., Congress, having a funding source separate from the states, would be able to act independently of the states. Because the Articles of Confederation required unanimity for amendments, this refusal by Rhode Island doomed this attempt to give Congress power to raise money independently.

7 Dec 1782: Virginia withdrew its earlier consent to amend the Articles of Confederation in order to give Congress a power to impose import duties. The withdrawal resolution was led by Richard Henry Lee and others who were concerned that such an import duty would weaken the sovereignty of the individual states, and could be indirectly injurious to individuals. This action was indicative of the debate between those who favored a loose coalition of states and those who favored some sort of central union.

24 Dec 1782: French forces left Boston for the West Indies, except for one regiment that was to follow soon after. The French were greatly respected and admired in America for the invaluable aid they had provided during the Revolution.

28 Dec 1782: The state legislature in Virginia passed a resolution informing Congress that Virginia would pay only a fraction of the requisitions imposed on it for 1782.

30 Dec 1782: The special court established by Congress to resolve the Wyoming County dispute between Pennsylvania and Connecticut announced its verdict. It ruled that Wyoming County (along the Susquehanna River north of present-day Scranton, PA), although settled by people from Connecticut and claimed by Connecticut, should be transferred under the sovereignty of Pennsylvania. This was a sensible decision, since the territory in question was not contiguous with any other portion of Connecticut. The decision was accepted by both sides.

6 Jan-13 Jan 1783: Major General Macdougall, Colonel Brooks, and Colonel Ogden delivered an address to Congress, outlining the situation regarding the army in the field: a) the fact that the army had not been paid; b) were owed compensation for out-of-pocket expenses; c) that many in the army were getting restless; and d) there was growing dissatisfaction about how Congress was treating them. Although the army had heard complaints from the people about the amount of taxes they were paying to their states, the army had not seen any of it from Congress. One of the recommendations in this address was to exchange the half-pay for life provision to full pay for a fixed number of years, or a lump sum.

Robert Morris reported to Congress that there was no money in the treasury, and that he had in fact overdrawn 3,000,000 *livres* (SM$582,000) on his foreign accounts. He advised Congress that no payment to the army could be made. He proposed that he be authorized to draw advances on expected loans from Holland and France, which Congress did in a secret resolution of 10 Jan 1783.

Macdougall and the other two officers met with the finance committee on 13 Jan 1783, and impressed on the members that some payment was necessary, especially since it was well-known in the army that legislatures never adjourned without being paid, and that all the civil servants were being paid; it was manifestly unfair that only the military was forgotten. But Congress simply did not have the means to meet the need; it could only rely on delaying tactics.

14 Jan 1783: Congress began debate on the terms of the treaty with Great Britain. There were widespread objections to the provision calling for return of loyalist refugees and repayment of debts owed to loyalists. The people were strongly divided on the issue of how to deal with loyalists. One faction believed all loyalists should be banished from the thirteen states. Another faction was opposed to

banishment but still wary of allowing any loyalists to gain influence in the governments. The provision regarding refugees was rightly regarded as an attempt by the British to tell Americans how to treat their own citizens. The resentment on the part of the patriots was fueled in part by atrocities committed by the Indians during the war as allies of the loyalists. This was especially true in New York and South Carolina. There was some fear that wealthy loyalists would gain control of the government and set up an aristocracy. Many people were resentful toward Congress for even considering a provision that would allow loyalists who had fled to return, or allow them to collect debts they were owed.

20 Jan 1783: Britain, France, Spain, and the U. S. signed the preliminary articles of the Treaty of Paris, which, if ratified, would end the Revolutionary War. The terms regarding America were unchanged from 30 Nov 1782, and the terms between the European powers included: a) Great Britain retained Gibraltar (a concession by Spain); b) Netherlands agreed to an end to hostilities; c) France recovered St. Pierre and Miquelon in the West Indies; d) France received a share in Newfoundland fishing rights; e) Spain retained the island of Minorca; and f) Spain retained both Floridas. It was signed by John Adams and Benjamin Franklin on behalf of America.

Spain had recently incurred a large loss of blood and treasure suppressing the revolt in South America. The wisest in the Spanish government realized the long-term difficulty of maintaining its colonies in the Western Hemisphere, given what had just happened to Britain. The prospect of a unification of the thirteen states alarmed the Spanish, since such a nation could control all the territory from the Atlantic to the Mississippi River, which was the main port of entry for Spanish commerce with the interior. Although Spain retained the Floridas, its long-term prospects for holding it would be reduced by any unification of the states.

24 Jan 1783: Robert Morris sent his letter of resignation, effective the end of May 1783, on the grounds that he would not be a part of injustice toward the nation's creditors, especially the army. By doing so, he attempted to coerce Congress into implementing some means to obtain the required revenues. He correctly pointed out that many members of Congress were reluctant to do what was necessary out of fear of reaction within their states. Congress could do nothing about the money issue. It was clear that if the nation's financial destitution became public, it could serve as a great encouragement to Great Britain to resume the war, may provoke revolts in the army, and could ruin what little foreign credit was available. The members of Congress initially resolved to keep Morris' letter of resignation secret. But Morris obtained permission at the end of February to release his letter, and it was published throughout the country in newspapers. However, he continued in office until Nov 1784.

5 Feb 1783: Congress passed a resolution in which officers received one month's pay in notes; private soldiers received one month's pay which was delivered in weekly installments of 50 cents each. The total for this one month's pay was SM$256,232.86.

7 Feb-21 Feb 1783: Hamilton wrote to Washington, and Gouverneur Morris wrote to General Knox implying that the army might prove useful for forcing Congress to establish a necessary revenue source. Morris' letter to Knox has been lost, but was intended as a means to address Washington through Knox. Knox replied to Morris on 21 Feb 1783 with Washington's advice, which was that the army was not qualified to participate in political contests, and that the best course of action was for Congress to call a convention to establish a new constitution to address the deficiencies of the Confederation.

12 Feb 1783: Congress passed a resolution, based on a proposal from Madison and Hamilton, in which Congress should have the power to impose a poll tax and land tax. It was affirmed by all seven of the states present, but could not go into effect until all 13 agreed to amend the Articles of Confederation.

21 Feb 1783: Robert Morris had communicated in Dec 1782 to Benjamin Franklin, ambassador to France, the need for a loan from France for 20,000,000 *livres*. But King Louis XVI agreed only to 6,000,000 for 1783, documented in a contract dated 21 Feb 1783. Franklin received the first 600,000

(SM$116,400) immediately. The terms for repayment were ratified by Congress on 31 Oct 1783. But Vergennes, the French minister of foreign affairs, informed Chevalier de la Luzerne, the French minister in America, that Louis XVI was unwilling to make any further loans to America because of American inability to establish creditworthiness. Luzerne passed this onto his contacts in America.

Mar 1783: South Carolina published a table of depreciation such that debts denominated in the paper currency could be settled per their real value at the time of the contract.

Mar 1783: Greene had received G. Morris' suggestions that the army might be useful in prodding the states to provide revenue for Congress. Greene wrote a letter to Governor Guerard of South Carolina, implying the army may have to take action, stating in part, "the eyes of the army are turned upon the states, whose measures will determine their conduct." The reading of the letter in the legislature was interrupted by shouts of "No dictation by a Cromwell." To spite Greene, and to demonstrate that it would not be intimidated, the legislature revoked its previous concurrence with the 3 Feb 1781 resolution by Congress asking for power to impose a 5% import duty.

4 Mar 1783: Washington replied to Virginia Governor Harrison's letter of 31 Jan 1783. Harrison had asked Washington what his expectations for peace were. Washington's reply was that he did not have good sense of it, but addressed the issues of payment to the army and the inability of Congress to properly manage its affairs: a) asking Harrison what could have possessed Virginia to rescind its concurrence to the proposed import duties; b) rejecting Rhode Island's claim that Congress could not be trusted with revenues from it; and c) stressing that the powers of Congress must be expanded, otherwise the benefits of the Revolution will be lost as the states sink into anarchy.

Washington also wrote to Hamilton the same day expressing similar sentiments, warning him that a political dissolution of the army for lack of pay would probably lead to "civil commotions." He impressed upon Hamilton the just demands of the army for payment; that the army should stay out of the political debate; and that the limitations of the Confederation be placed before the States for their consideration [7].

11-15 Mar 1783: The army was encamped at Newburgh, NY, for the winter. General Gates had been conspiring for some time with Major John Armstrong and assistant adjutant-general Colonel Barber to hold a meeting of officers regarding payment. Their idea was to exploit the doubts among the army officers about getting their rightful pay. They also were attempting to capitalize on the fact that many of Congress' creditors were looking to the army to help resolve the issue of non-payment of debts by Congress. A circular, instigated by Gates, but authored anonymously by Armstrong, was circulated secretly among the officer corps by Barber, implying that Washington had not done enough to force Congress to meet its obligations. Washington obtained a copy of it early 11 Mar. He issued a general order prohibiting the gathering, but offered to meet with the interested parties on 15 Mar and listen to their complaints.

The meeting with Washington convened at Newburgh on the 15th. Washington read the anonymous tract to the entire assembly and issued his analysis of it. In doing so, he pointed out that he had been in the field for nearly all of the war; he was fully aware of their needs; but provoking Congress would not help matters. He expressed his confidence that Congress would make good on their promises if the army demonstrated due patience and allowed Congress to work out the political problems. He warned them not to do anything that would diminish the high esteem they currently enjoyed in the public mind by staging a revolt or taking sides in a political debate; the goal was to continue to show patriotism and virtue. This became known as the "Newburgh Address." The officers came over to Washington's point of view, and issued a resolution asking only that Washington appeal to Congress for relief, but making no other demands. General Gates then asked for a vote to "reject with disdain" the anonymous circular which he himself had helped perpetrate; the officers condemned it unanimously.

17 Mar 1783: The Trespass Act was passed in New York, the main purpose of which was to persecute loyalists living in New York. The law permitted anyone who had left their home in New York at any

time during the war because of the presence of the British military to sue the present occupants as having trespassed on the property. The loyalist defendants were not allowed to claim that the change in possession was due to military causes. This law gave rise to a large number of lawsuits against loyalists, as nearly every house in New York had changed hands at least once during the war. Plaintiffs were demanding exorbitant damages, which continued until several adverse rulings nullified it in 1784. The Trespass Act violated the traditional law of nations (in which property taken in war was retained by the taker so long as he remained in possession of it), and it also violated the peace treaty with Great Britain.

18 Mar 1783: General Washington wrote an appeal to the President of Congress and its members on behalf of the "Patriot Army." In it he recounted the Newburgh circular, his address on it, and the favorable response he received from the officers; he reiterated the army's long sufferings; he noted the obligation of Congress to treat the army justly; he reminded them of previous assurances given by Congress; and finally he urged Congress not to leave the army in want and destitution, as it would always be remembered as a sign of Congress' ingratitude for services rendered by the army [8]. He also recommended that men who had been promised half pay for life would be better served by full pay for a fixed number of years.

22 Mar 1783: Congress agreed to a resolution per General Washington's suggestion on payment to the army. It modified the pay provision for soldiers from half-pay for life to full pay for five years at once, known as the commutation. The lump sum was to be paid by issuing certificates bearing 6% interest. This was a good bargain for the government, as it would reduce the total outlay, since most soldiers would likely live more than ten years. It would also benefit the soldiers, who, having left their farms and occupations, would find a lump sum handy in getting back on their feet. But the public was opposed to it, angry that such a large amount was to be paid at once, since their wages were small in comparison. The public had forgotten the sacrifices made by the army, and became occupied with their own problems.

23 Mar 1783: Congress received news that the preliminary articles of peace had been signed on 20 Jan 1783.

31 Mar 1783: General Washington wrote to Hamilton that there was a great need for a union, noting that the history of the war had proven that individual state actions could not be relied upon, that: a) the states were too preoccupied with their prejudices and jealousies; b) unless united, the 13 states would be manipulated individually by the European powers; and c) the limitations upon Congress had prolonged the war and overall expenses, which in turn had caused morale problems in the army. He concluded with a recommendation that the Confederation be reformed.

Apr 1783: North Carolina issued 100,000 pounds (SM$250,000) in bills of credit (paper currency).

3 Apr 1783: Benjamin Franklin concluded a treaty with Sweden. The king of Sweden had sent a message to Franklin in May 1782, expressing his desire for a treaty with America; he was the first European power to do so without being solicited by the Americans. The provisions of this treaty included: a) reciprocal most-favored nation status; b) free trade in goods, except for a small number of products that were prohibited; and c) unrestricted passage of persons. It contained an additional provision that if both the U. S. and Sweden were neutral in a state of maritime war, both nations would render mutual assistance and protection to each other's ships. It was ratified by Congress on 29 Jul 1783.

4 Apr 1783: General Washington wrote to Theodorick Bland, a member of the finance committee in Congress, advising him that: a) the army should not be disbanded before each member of the army was advised of the full amount due him; b) all the accounts should be settled with the army as a whole instead of along state lines; and c) informing him that there was a universal expectation in the army of one month's pay in hand, and an absolute assurance of two more months pay to follow soon thereafter.

8 Apr 1783: The Grand Committee of Congress issued its report on the financial condition of the nation: a) foreign debt amounted to SM$7,885,085; b) domestic debt amounted to SM$28,615,290; and c) interest due was SM$2,362,320. The SM$28,000,000 cited here did not include any funds for the commutation of 22 Mar 1783.

14 Apr 1783: Robert Morris advised Congress that the amount requested by General Washington of three months pay for the army was greater than all the revenues received from the states going back to 1781. Congress could only issue paper, and it would be redeemable only if Congress could get a loan.

15 Apr 1783: Congress ratified the peace treaty with Great Britain. The treaty contained nine acknowledged articles plus a "separate" (secret) one. The articles were: 1) the king of Great Britain recognized the independence of the thirteen states; 2) defined the northern and southern borders between Canada and the territories held by Spain in the west and south; 3) Americans were to have fishing rights off Newfoundland and Nova Scotia, except for drying of fish; 4) both sides agreed not to impede creditors in seeking payment for debts; 5) Congress would recommend to the states that British subjects be compensated for property confiscated during the war; 6) no confiscations or persecutions on either side for actions committed during the war; 7) permanent peace, and return of prisoners on both sides; 8) free navigation of the Mississippi River for both British and Americans; and 9) territories conquered before ratifications are exchanged to be returned without compensation. The secret provision stated that if Great Britain were to recover or come into possession of West Florida, the northern boundary between West Florida and the United States shall be a line from the junction of the Yassous (Yazoo) and Mississippi Rivers east to where the Yassous joins the Apalachicola River (from present-day Vicksburg, MS to Columbus, GA) [9]. The secret provision would turn out to be the source of an important diplomatic issue between America and Spain.

18 Apr 1783: Congress passed a resolution to recommend to the states that Congress be given a power to levy duties for a period of 25 years on certain imported items in order to raise revenues to pay the debts of the war. The items on which duties were to be paid amounted to between 1.1% to 26.6% on rum and other liquors, wines, tea, pepper, sugar, molasses, cocoa, and coffee; in addition to a 5% duty on all other items. It was estimated at this time that the import duties would bring about SM$1,000,000 annually to Congress. The resolution also recommended that a standing annual requisition of SM$1,500,000 be apportioned to the various states according to population (New Hampshire: SM$52,708; Massachusetts: SM$224,427; Delaware: SM$22,443; Maryland: SM$141,517; Rhode Island: SM$32,318; Virginia: SM$256,487; Connecticut: SM$132,091; North Carolina: SM$109,006; New York: SM$128,243; South Carolina: SM$96,183; New Jersey: SM$83,358; Georgia: SM$16,030; and Pennsylvania: SM$205,189). It was sent to the states on 26 Apr 1783 with an address by James Madison, Alexander Hamilton, and Oliver Ellsworth in which they outlined the need for revenue, as the current debt amounted to SM$42,000,325 (including SM$5,000,000 for the commutation) with an annual interest due of SM$2,415,956. Congress remained helpless in the meantime, since all thirteen states would have to ratify this amendment to the Articles before the revenue could be collected.

There had been considerable debate within Congress on how to count slaves for revenue purposes. The southern states, with large slave populations, made the argument that slaves were an economic burden, and should be counted as only half a person for revenue purposes. Madison and Rutledge proposed a compromise of counting slaves as three-fifths of a freeman for revenue purposes, which was acceptable to all. This provision had no effect on representation in Congress, since each state was represented equally.

19 Apr 1783: The Americans ended formal hostilities against the British. This date was chosen to coincide with the anniversary of the battles at Lexington and Concord in 1775; there had been no action in the war since the American victory in Georgia in 1782.

28 Apr 1783: Congress appointed a committee, led by Ellsworth, to study and make a recommendation on a resolution by New York's assembly of Jul 1782 to hold a general convention on revising the Articles of Confederation. The other members were Carroll, Duane, Gorham, Hamilton, Izard, McHenry, Peters, and Wilson.

6 May 1783: This date marks the culmination of a debate that had raged in British Parliament regarding commercial relations with America. Some members desired entirely free trade with America, but others wanted even greater restrictions to be imposed than had been enacted during the war. Adams and Franklin attempted to negotiate a treaty containing reciprocal terms, but Parliament refused to agree. Finally Parliament decided to repeal some restrictions imposed during the war, but otherwise transferred the power of regulating commerce with America to the king in council. The members of Parliament correctly regarded America as lacking a government competent to negotiate or to abide by any commercial treaty, knowing that Congress lacked the power to do so under the Articles of Confederation. Secondly, it was impractical for the British to attempt to negotiate commercial treaties with thirteen different states, so the British simply took the initiative and decided to allow the king to impose conditions unilaterally.

2 Jun 1783: The Continental Army received papers giving immediate furloughs, and which contained on the back a full discharge effective the day of a formal peace treaty with Great Britain. Congress was unable to meet its obligations for the three month's pay that General Washington asked for in Apr 1783. The soldiers received only paper notes, the same as all the other notes issued by Congress, payable in 6 months and bearing 6% interest; their cash value was estimated at 1:10. The soldiers of the Continental Army, who had defeated the British Empire and freed the states from the tyranny of colonialism, dispersed peacefully and went home with no money.

5 Jun 1783: Congress received the cession by Virginia of its claims to the Ohio Valley. The resolution directed that the lands be divided into districts of 2 degrees of latitude by 3 degrees of longitude and townships of 6 miles square. Other provisions included: a) when any district attained a population of 20,000 inhabitants, it was to be admitted to the Confederacy; b) soldiers who had served for 3 years were to receive lands plus 30 acres for every dollar owed them by Congress; and c) one-tenth of the land was to be reserved for forts, schools, and the navy.

8 Jun 1783: General Washington issued a circular letter to the governors of the 13 states, urging them to support a permanent central government that could adequately pay its debts, conduct foreign affairs, enforce its laws, organize the militia throughout the country, and do what was necessary to preserve peace and unity. He recommended a federal constitution to be endorsed by the general public, and urged the people to set aside their local prejudices and regard themselves as citizens of one nation. It was published in many newspapers throughout Jul 1783.

11 Jun 1783: The legislature of Virginia passed a resolution that rejected giving Congress a power to levy an import duty, citing many of the same reasons as had Rhode Island: a) the revenue collectors would not be accountable to the state of Virginia; b) perceived risk of delegating revenue power to Congress; and c) money from Virginia citizens would be transferred directly to Congress (bypassing the state government of Virginia). But, Virginia also agreed to establish its own customs-house, from which Virginia would grant its revenue to Congress for 25 years.

~15 Jun 1783: Delaware's legislature passed a resolution granting Congress the power to impose the import duty (proposed 18 Apr 1783).

~15 Jun 1783: New Jersey's legislature passed a resolution granting power to Congress to levy an import duty, and provided that 90,000 pounds (SM$239,400) be raised in taxes to be forwarded to Congress to pay down the war expenses.

19-30 Jun 1783: About 300 soldiers stationed in Philadelphia and Lancaster became angry about not being paid. They formed together, and marched on Philadelphia, got drunk, surrounded Congress, and demanded their pay. They threatened to kidnap members of Congress, and to break into the bank where federal deposits were held. Congress called for aid from the Pennsylvania militia, but the government of Pennsylvania refused on the grounds that the soldiers had not committed any open violence. Congress then fled to Princeton after being forced to walk a gauntlet of the soldiers. The soldiers heard false rumors that General Washington was on his way to deal with the situation and dispersed back to their barracks.

2 Jul 1783: King George III issued an order in council defining the terms of trade between Great Britain and America. It was a return to the Navigation Acts: a) trade between America and the British West Indies to be conducted only in ships built, manned, and navigated by British subjects; b) American ships landing in British ports were permitted to bring in only items produced in states of which the ship's owners were citizens. The first of these had a severe impact on the shipbuilding industry in America, especially in the New England states, and the second one provoked a desire for retaliation. Prior to the war, about a third of colonial-British commerce was conducted in American-built ships; now, very few ships would be built even though they were much cheaper to build in America. Britain imposed these provisions as a means to weaken American commerce as part of its general mercantile policy. The great overriding fear in Britain was that the American traders would supplant Britain in the carrying trade in Western Europe. Afterward, John Jay used this action by Britain to argue that Congress should be given powers to negotiate consistent commercial treaties. But the states at this time were wary of granting any additional power to Congress to formulate a uniform trade policy.

29 Jul 1783: Congress ratified the commercial treaty with Sweden of 3 Apr 1783.

7 Aug 1783: King George III decided that he would receive ambassadors only from the thirteen American states separately, not from the United States as a whole.

13 Aug 1783: The legislature of South Carolina, reflecting on General Washington's circular letter of Jun 1783, passed a resolution authorizing the import duty, but inserted the caveat that the duty could only be collected by officers of the South Carolina government, which would then be forwarded to Congress in fulfillment of the requisitions due from South Carolina.

Sep-Dec 1783: Many loyalists left New York for the Bahamas, Nova Scotia, or the West Indies in anticipation of persecution or riots in December, when the British army was scheduled to evacuate New York. The ones who emigrated to Nova Scotia later became competitors for fishing rights in Newfoundland. After these loyalists left, many patriots returned to New York from New Jersey, and were instrumental in getting many anti-loyalist laws passed. This effort was led by Governor George Clinton.

2 Sep 1783: The Committee of Apr 1783, who had been tasked to consider a suggestion made by New York's delegation that a convention be called to address the deficiencies of the Confederation, issued a report recommending that any convention be postponed until the revenue issue could be resolved. This marked the end of the convention movement for the time being.

3 Sep 1783: British negotiators signed the Treaty of Paris, ending the Revolutionary War. The terms of the treaty included the following provisions: a) loyalists were to be compensated for loss of property suffered during the war; b) British creditors holding private debt were to be paid in full; c) there would be no persecution of loyalists; d) opportunity would be provided for loyalists to recover estates lost during the war; e) private debts owed to loyalists would be paid in sterling; and f) Britain would give up forts in the western New York and the Ohio Valley. But Congress had no power to force any of the states to observe any of these provisions.

At the return of peace, trade between the states and England resumed, as there was still considerable demand for English products. However, since the Continental currency had collapsed, the Americans had to pay for imports in hard money. The war had left many areas ruined. In the south, the farms had not recovered enough to resume trading in indigo, rice or tobacco. The same problem prevailed in the middle states, and they were unable to pay as they normally would, by exporting wheat and furs. The New England states fell on hard times because shipping had become unprofitable owing to the Navigation Acts. Many in the states were living off the land, and resorted to barter to obtain what they needed. Many demagogues claimed that the remedy was cheap paper money, and some states began to issue worthless paper in order to give the illusion of prosperity.

Although not perceived as such at the time, the treaty ending the war began the most crucial period in the history of America. The American states were surrounded on the south and west by Spanish lands, and on the north by Canada, which was still a British colony. The big risk was that the states now had no common enemy, and without some sort of unifying force, would degenerate into thirteen petty republics bickering among themselves. They were also vulnerable to encroachment by the larger and more organized European powers.

16 Oct 1783: The legislature of Massachusetts approved giving Congress the power to levy an import duty.

3 Nov 1783: The Continental Army was formally disbanded, even though the British still occupied New York City. The main problem was that Congress could no longer afford to maintain the army; in fact, it owed considerable back pay to the soldiers. Many soldiers begin to think they would never get paid, and there was widespread dissension and distrust of Congress. Many members of the army from Pennsylvania, Maryland, Delaware, and Virginia had been previously furloughed on 26 May, 11 Jun, 9 Aug, and 26 Sep 1783.

25 Nov 1783: The British army under Sir Guy Carleton left New York City, but Britain retained all its garrisons in the northwest, even though they were obligated by the peace treaty to evacuate them. The British realized correctly that Congress was unable to force Britain to comply with this article. In fact, they left New York only because it had become too expensive to maintain the army there. At the close of the war, Great Britain's national debt was about £270,000,000 sterling, having doubled in the course of the war.

Dec 1783: The New Jersey legislature issued 31,000 pounds (SM$82,460) in paper currency.

Dec 1783: The financial situation had become so bad that the U. S. government finance directors resorted to underhanded schemes to raise money. One of the means was to create bank drafts on foreign accounts, knowing full well that there was no credit available, and sell these in America for cash. The drafts were then sent to the American envoys in those foreign countries, and they were required to find the money to make good on the notes or else they would go back to America as defaults. Robert Morris wrote checks for 1,000,000 florins (SM$383,000), but only had 400,000 (SM$153,200) on account; of the checks outstanding about 200,000 florins (SM$76,600) had already been cashed. He was able to put off the creditors with excuses, but sent an urgent note to John Adams, the ambassador to Holland, to ask him to obtain a loan to cover the checks.

4 Dec 1783: General Washington gave a farewell address to his officers in New York City.

9 Dec 1783: Virginia's legislature passed a resolution authorizing Congress to develop a response to the British Navigation Acts. Governor Harrison of Virginia also sent a circular letter to all the other states requesting they issue a similar grant of power.

21 Dec 1783: Virginia's legislature confirmed its cession of western lands in the Ohio Valley to Congress.

22 Dec 1783: Congress agreed to a set of principles regarding foreign commerce given as instructions to the ambassadors in France, so long as they were reciprocal with the other treaty members: a) no navigation laws; b) equal status of ports; c) each nation shall be able to carry its own products on its own ships and to take other nations' products out; d) prefer free trade, but if duties are to be paid, they shall be only in accordance with most-favored nation status; e) no privateering in wartime; f) minimal interference in land industries; g) fishermen not to be interfered with; h) limitations on definition of contraband; i) free commerce between neutrals and belligerents in non-contraband; j) to be negotiated for a period not exceeding 10 years; and k) to require ratification by Congress (treaties to be represented as with the U. S. as a nation).

23 Dec 1783: George Washington resigned his command of the Continental Army to Congress at Annapolis, and retired to his home at Mount Vernon, Virginia. He had presented an account of his personal expenses incurred during the war at Philadelphia a few days earlier; it amounted to SM$65,315.

29 Dec 1783: The legislature of Virginia reversed its 11 Jun 1783 resolution upon consideration of the arguments made by General Washington in his Jun 1783 circular.

31 Dec 1783: The population of the 13 states at the end of 1783 has been estimated at about 3.5 million. It is not certain how accurate this number is, since the first census was not conducted until 1790. Of the 3.5 million, about one-third were in the New England states (Massachusetts, Connecticut, New Hampshire, Rhode Island, and Connecticut), about one third in the middle states (New York, New Jersey, Pennsylvania, and Delaware), and the remaining third in Maryland, Virginia, North and South Carolina, and Georgia. Virginia, Pennsylvania, and Massachusetts had the highest populations, and Rhode Island and Georgia the lowest. New York State was still mostly Indian country. Throughout the states, the population was centered east of the Appalachian Mountains. Of the 3.5 million, about 600,000 were slaves. By the end of the war, only Massachusetts had outlawed slavery altogether, but Pennsylvania was in the process of freeing slaves in that state. All the other states tolerated slavery, but all had passed laws prohibiting further importation of slaves.

1 Jan 1784: The financial situation of the United States at this time can be summarized as follows. Most of these figures are derived from best estimates and there is considerable conjecture in them owing to the depreciation of the paper currency. Jefferson calculated the cost of the war from Apr 1775 to Apr 1783 as about SM$140,000,000. He estimated that Congress had emitted paper Continentals during this time having a face value of about $200,000,000; but whose actual value was about SM$36,000,000. The several states had likewise printed a great deal of paper currency, and Jefferson reckoned its true value also at SM$36,000,000. As of Apr 1783, the national debt of the American states amounted to SM$36,500,000. As of 1 Jan 1784, the national debt had grown to SM$68,000,000 (this last figure obtained by subtracting the true value of the Continentals and state currency from the cost of the war). Of the SM$68,000,000 total debt, about SM$8,000,000 was still outstanding from loans given by foreign nations, and the rest was owed either to private citizens or the states.

The status of requisitions at this time was as follows. The states were credited with having paid the SM$1,200,000 requisitioned on 4 Sep 1782 as it was for local interest payments. Of the requisition of 16 Oct 1782 for SM$2,000,000, none had been paid. Of the original requisition of 30 Oct 1781 for SM$8,000,000, a total of SM$1,486,511 had been paid. It is interesting to note that the states were very uneven in their payments. The amount of the SM$8,000,000 paid per its apportionment of each state was as follows [10]: a) New Hampshire paid $3,000 of $373,598; b) Massachusetts paid $247,677 of $1,307,596; c) Rhode Island paid $67,848 of $216,684; d) Connecticut paid $131,578 of $747,196; e) New York paid $39,064 of $373,598; f) Pennsylvania paid $346,633 of $1,120,794; g) Delaware paid nothing of $112,085; h) Maryland paid $89,302 of $933,996; i) Virginia paid $115,104 of $1,307,594; j) North Carolina paid nothing of $622,677; k) South Carolina paid $344,302 of $373,598; and l) Georgia paid nothing of $24,905.

The French had been exceedingly generous with the terms of loans made to Congress, having volunteered to forgo repayment during the war and for a short period thereafter. Beginning in 1784, France allowed interest-only payments on the loans.

24 Jan 1784-29 Feb 1784: John Adams had received the note from Morris from Dec 1783 while in London, and finally arrived in Amsterdam after a 3-week ordeal on 24 Jan 1784 to try and find a loan to cover the outstanding checks. There he met with Dutch bankers, but they refused to extend credit as they did not believe America would be able to repay it. Neither the government of Holland nor the main bankers would consider lending the U. S. money; American credit was dead. By the end of Feb 1784, Adams was able to get a loan of 1,000,000 guilders (SM$388,000) at "ruinous interest"

from brokers and moneylenders. John Jay, ambassador to Spain, experienced the same financial demands as Adams had faced in Holland.

1 Mar 1784: Virginia ceded to Congress all of its land claims lying northwest of the Ohio River, removing its earlier demand to keep Kentucky. The purpose of doing so was to facilitate the settlement of the new lands, open communications, and develop them into new states per the 1780 act of Congress.

Mar-Jul 1784: The winter of 1783-1784 had been cold and snowy in northeastern Pennsylvania. There was a sudden thaw and the Susquehanna River flooded the Wyoming Valley, the same territory that had been contested between Connecticut and Pennsylvania in 1782. Many of the houses were washed away, and most of the cattle drowned. A large buildup of ice had swept down the river, and the portion of it that reached Wilkes-Barre would not melt until mid-summer. The people of the Wyoming Valley, most of whom had come to the area as citizens of Connecticut, suffered greatly during the floods from cold and hunger. However, the legislature of Pennsylvania initially refused to help them. The state did eventually send a militia to the area, commanded by Justice Patterson, but instead of helping them, he proceeded to insult and harass the people, and his men stole whatever was available. His objective was to rid the area of the Connecticut settlers. His men blocked roads with trees and pieces of fencing, and prohibited the settlers from hunting, fishing, or drawing water from wells. Naturally, the settlers resisted this treatment. Patterson wrote to President Dickinson that the residents of the Wyoming Valley were participating in sedition against the state, and that he would correct the situation with a show of force. Patterson and his men then attacked the settlements in the valley, burning down houses and forcing about 500 people into the wilderness, many of whom were children and the elderly. Residents were told to go back to Connecticut, and were forced to take an abandoned road out of the valley. The legislature realized that Patterson had gone too far, so he was recalled. However, Patterson did not withdraw as ordered, but retreated to the hills and maintained a guerilla war against the valley residents. Settlers from around the area gathered together an army and attacked and laid siege to Patterson's hideout. The legislature then ordered a regiment from Philadelphia under Colonel John Armstrong (author of the Newburgh circular) to settle the problem. When Armstrong arrived in the valley, he negotiated a truce with the Connecticut settlers, convinced them to disarm, and promised that he would also force Patterson's group to disarm. However, Armstrong arrested 76 of the Connecticut men and marched them to prisons in Easton and Northumberland. Armstrong then left for Philadelphia.

This episode caused quite a commotion in the New England states, and there was a real possibility of war between Pennsylvania and Connecticut over it. Pennsylvania had a provision in its constitution calling for a Council of Censors to meet every seven years and issue an opinion on the conduct of the government. Fortunately, such a meeting was scheduled just after this Wyoming incident. The Council summarily condemned the actions of Patterson and Armstrong, found that they were in violation of the Constitution, and ordered them to produce documents, which they refused. The people had supported the legislature against the settlers, but reacted against Armstrong and Patterson for rejecting the order of the Council of Censors. The public then turned against Armstrong, Patterson, and the legislature. Although the action of the Council stirred up a lot of controversy between itself and the legislature, eventually the public came to see the evil that had been done. In the end, the Pennsylvania legislature ordered a full restitution to the settlers of the Wyoming Valley, thus avoiding a war with Connecticut.

26 Mar 1784: South Carolina passed a law allowing debts to be paid in four annual installments starting in Jan 1786, owing to the shortage of stable money.

26 Mar 1784: Congress adopted a resolution stating that the several states would be considered one nation with regard to treaties and all issues arising under them.

5 Apr 1784: Thomas Jefferson, as head of a finance committee in Congress, delivered a report on the finances of the Confederacy. The expenses for 1784 were estimated as: a) SM$457,525 for public services; b) SM$442,648 for interest on foreign debt; c) SM$3,580,030 for interest on domestic debt;

and d) SM$1,000,000 debts contracted but still unpaid from 1782 and 1783, which totaled to about SM$5,480,203. This figure was not practical as a revenue target. Jefferson proposed that the states be given credit for the SM$1,200,000 that had been requisitioned on 4 Sep 1782 (included in the SM$3,580,030 number), since it had given the states leeway to use it to pay interest due on certificates issued by the states and other liquidated debts. He then recommended that a new requisition be ordered that would get the states up to three-fourths of the original SM$8,000,000 that had been requisitioned on 30 Oct 1781. He calculated the apportionment, deducting for some receipts that had been made, and requested a requisition for 1784 of SM$4,577,591. This would be enough to meet the current needs. It was voted down by Congress, probably realizing the demands on the states were too great [11].

19 Apr-23 Apr 1784: Congress debated the rules for admission of new states. It generally retained the principles laid out in Oct 1780, except the prohibition on slavery after 1800 was deleted. On 19 Apr, Richard Spaight and Jacob Read, of North and South Carolina respectively, proposed that the prohibition of slavery be deleted. Only ten states were present, thus the vote of seven states was required to keep the prohibition. Massachusetts, Connecticut, New Hampshire, Rhode Island, New York, and Pennsylvania voted to keep the prohibition. New Jersey refused to vote since only one of its delegates was present. North Carolina was divided. Virginia, South Carolina, and Maryland voted against keeping the prohibition. But Virginia's vote was due to the fact that James Monroe had been absent due to illness. Had he been present, Virginia's delegation would have been divided, and slavery prohibition would have been retained by a 6-2 vote. The modified measure was adopted 23 Apr 1784 as the Ordinance of 1784. The territorial provisions included: a) townships of 6 miles square; b) allocations to states for distribution by lot, to be sold publicly in the states; c) simple registration of land titles; d) allowed slavery in the northwest territories until 1 Jan 1801; e) Virginia received the area between the Little Miami and Scioto Rivers as compensation for conquering this territory during the war; f) territories required to have a republican form of government; g) land was to be first purchased from the Indians; h) the settlers were to form temporary governments until the population reached 20,000, at which time the territory would set up a permanent government and be admitted with a non-voting seat in Congress; and i) when the population of the territory became equal to the population of the least populated of the thirteen original states, the territory would be admitted into the Confederation upon a concurring vote of nine of the original thirteen. The provisions also imposed these conditions upon admission to the Confederacy: a) to become permanent members of the Confederacy; b) equal in status with the original thirteen states; and c) were obligated to pay requisitions ordered by Congress.

27 Apr 1784: Jefferson revised his report on the finances. Jefferson decided to credit the states for the requisitions received from the original SM$8,000,000 and to set as a goal for 1784 a new requisition that would fulfill the first half of the initial SM$8,000,000. Since SM$1,436,511 had been received of the SM$8,000,000 requisitioned on 30 Oct 1781, he re-apportioned SM$2,670,988 as a new requisition for 1784, and it allocated to all the states on the basis of their respective populations. If that could be collected, it would meet the immediate minimal needs of the government, and might serve to improve creditworthiness [12].

30 Apr 1784: Great Britain's Navigation Acts (2 Jul 1783) had greatly impaired America's ability to conduct commerce in the West Indies. The American people began to demand retaliation against the British policy. However, Congress had no means to force reciprocal restrictions on Great Britain, or to threaten them in order to prod Great Britain into opening up trade. To meet this need, Congress passed a resolution recommending to the states that Congress be given power, for a period of 15 years, to "prohibit any goods, wares, or merchandise, from being imported into, or exported from, any of the states, in vessels belonging to, or navigated by, the subjects of any power with whom these states shall not have formed treaties of commerce."

May 1784: Virginia passed a resolution granting powers to Congress to respond to the Navigation Acts. This action was promoted by Madison and Jones, and was even supported by Patrick Henry, who had lately come around to the view that Congress needed some means to enforce its demands. The idea was to pass a resolution in Virginia in hope that the other states would emulate it. The provisions of the Virginia resolution included: a) granting Congress power for 15 years to prohibit imports or exports out of Virginia by foreign nations that did not have a commercial treaty with the United States; b) Virginia's fulfilling its requisitions from Congress, counting slaves as three-fifths for revenue purposes; and c) recommending that accounts between Congress and the states be settled, and the balance due Congress should be paid.

7 May 1784: John Adams, Benjamin Franklin, and Thomas Jefferson were commissioned to negotiate treaties in accordance with the principles adopted in Dec 1783; the commission was valid for two years, and the maximum length of treaties negotiated under it was to be 15 years.

12 May 1784: A formal exchange of the ratifications of the peace treaty between Great Britain and America was held at Paris.

25 May 1784: Congress considered establishing a permanent location to meet.

26-27 May 1784: Congress approved a resolution to establish a standing army of 780 men, eighty of whom were to be under the direct command of Congress. Twenty-five of the eighty were to guard the stores at Fort Pitt [Pittsburgh, PA], and fifty-five of the eighty were to be stationed at West Point. The other 700 were requisitioned from New York, Connecticut, New Jersey, and Pennsylvania, and were to be used to garrison the frontier outposts for one year.

2 Jun 1784: North Carolina passed a resolution granting Congress the power to impose import duties, but it contained a large number of caveats.

26 Jun 1784: Congress convened at Philadelphia, having adjourned on 3 Jun, but delegates from nine states did not show up until 8 Jul. It could not do much business, because nine states were required for any important action; one state could stop all activity.

11 Aug 1784: The three New England states left Congress in a dispute with the others, which left Congress without a quorum.

17 Aug 1784: Robert Morris informed French officials that the United States would not be able to pay interest on a 10,000,000 *livre* (SM$1,940,000) loan that had been obtained from Holland (5 Nov 1781), for which France was the guarantor. He also informed them that no interest could be paid on the direct loans from France. These defaults ruined American credit abroad.

19 Aug 1784: The remaining delegates to Congress left, since no business could be done. The members of Congress had grown tired of sitting at Annapolis with no power to do anything. The U. S. was left without a government until Oct 1784, when Congress reconvened in Trenton.

1 Nov 1784: Robert Morris resigned as superintendent of finances. He was replaced by a committee of finance, but they were unable to continue the work of Morris. Ultimately, the states entered into financial desperation. Meanwhile, Congress convened at Trenton, but only five states sent delegates.

26 Nov 1784: There was still no quorum in Congress. The members were arriving so slowly that many prominent persons, including Richard Henry Lee of Virginia, J. F. Mercer, and French officials started to believe that the Confederacy was unraveling.

30 Nov 1784: Congress finally reached a quorum.

15 Dec 1784: Congress received a letter from the agent for the Spanish government dated 19 Nov 1784, which contained a letter from the Spanish foreign minister Joseph de Galvez dated 26 Jun 1784. The letter from the Spanish government announced that Spain would not permit any American ships to navigate the Mississippi River. The Spanish court had found out about the secret provision of the peace treaty with Great Britain about six months after the fact. They viewed the secret provision rightly as a conspiracy by which Great Britain and America would cede territory to each other notwithstanding that Spain had some legitimate claim to it, since Spain possessed Florida, controlled the mouth of the river at New Orleans, and had garrisons along the river as far as Natchez. The territory in question is a rectangle with the Mississippi River on the West, the Apalachicola River on the East,

the 31st parallel of latitude on the South (present border of Florida and Georgia), and a line from present-day Vicksburg, MS to Columbus, GA on the North.

This news caused the Americans to divide into three opposing factions. There were some who wanted to take the entire Mississippi by force, although such an undertaking was probably unaffordable. The New England states, desperate for resumption of any kind of trade and revenue, wanted to give up navigation of the Mississippi in order to conclude a commercial treaty with Spain. Friendly relations with Spain would also be of some aid against the pirates in the western Mediterranean, where the Spanish had a strong presence and would serve to expand trade in general with the Spanish possessions. The southern states saw the problem most clearly: it was essential for their future to maintain a claim to navigation of the Mississippi. Although a war to conquer it was out of the question now, the immediate goal was to obtain whatever treaty could be had with Spain, but maintain some rights to the Mississippi. Navigation up the river was necessary in order to maintain contact with the newly settled territories in the west and prevent them from becoming aligned with either Great Britain or Spain. It was important to prevent such a trend, as the thirteen American states would then be completely surrounded by hostile powers: Great Britain on the north and northwest, and Spain on the south and southwest.

Jan-May 1785: Protectionist sentiment grew in Massachusetts against the Navigation Acts. It was widely recognized by this time that peace did not bring prosperity, since the inability of Congress to regulate trade meant that foreign nations were able to impose their mercantile policies on American merchants.

~11 Jan 1785: The New York legislature levied a double duty on all goods arriving into New York on British ships, as a retaliatory measure against the British Navigation Acts.

Feb 1785: The Georgia legislature passed a law redeeming its bills of credit at a ratio of 1,000 to 1, in specie certificates.

Feb 1785: The Delaware legislature passed a law in which all of its outstanding paper currency (bills of credit) was recalled, to be redeemed at a ratio 75 to 1.

Mar 1785: The British foreign minister, the duke of Dorset, informed Franklin, Adams, and Jefferson that Great Britain would not enter into trade negotiations with them because of the ambiguity surrounding the powers held by the three Americans. The British were uncertain (or claimed to be uncertain) as to whether they were authorized to negotiate for all thirteen states, or for each of them individually. The British correctly noticed that treaty negotiations may be a waste of time since the states were passing their own laws which could nullify or conflict with the resulting treaty. Secondly, the British had no particular incentive to negotiate a treaty with the Americans, as all the commercial advantages accrued to Britain: a) Americans desired British goods; b) Britain was able to maintain its Navigation Acts benefitting British traders; and c) the thirteen states were weak and bogged down in their own rivalries. The British did not expect the American states to ever establish a strong union.

8 Mar 1785: Henry Knox was appointed Secretary of War. The standing army under his control numbered 600 men.

19 Mar 1785: The New York state legislature appointed delegates to Congress who were opposed to any type of union. They were in agreement with Richard Henry Lee of Virginia, now the president of Congress. Between them, they were able to prevent any move toward modification of the Articles of Confederation.

28 Mar 1785: Several prominent leaders from Virginia and Maryland (George Mason, Alexander Henderson, Daniel of St. Thomas Jenifer, Thomas Stone, and Samuel Chase) met at Alexandria to discuss a system of commercial regulations on the Chesapeake and Potomac River. Their goal was to submit proposals for legislation to both Virginia and Maryland. Some sort of accommodation had been urged on these members by George Washington. They issued a request to their respective

states, and also asked Pennsylvania for permission to use the branches of the Ohio River for a canal between the Chesapeake and Delaware River.

Apr 1785: By this time, Britain's Navigation Act had ruined the economies of the New England states. Because only English ships could import or export out of England, carrying trade by the New England states came to a virtual standstill, with ships lying in harbors. Secondly, a duty in England of 18 pounds sterling per ton on whale oil ruined the whaling trade. Fish could be carried to the British West Indies only by British ships, which ruined the fishing trade. Last, there was a great demand for English manufactures after the war, so the people foolishly went into debt to obtain them, thus draining the New England states of money when its own ability to generate revenue was impaired. At the same time, the British came to dominate trade in the southern states. Since the southern states did not have large contingents of merchants or a fleet, the British naturally filled that void by underselling Dutch and French merchants, and obtained a de facto monopoly on trading in the south. Many people in the south were going into debt to pay for British imports, and the British were taking Americans to court to obtain judgments for repayment. In Virginia, farmers were being forced to sell their commodities at low prices and buy imports at high prices because British merchants dominated the trading there. The British had all the advantages in Virginia, and exploited them as best they could. In fact, even the carrying trade on the rivers was dominated by the British.

15 Apr-3 May 1785: Merchants and artisans in Boston held a series of meetings to discuss what could be done about the decline in the economy caused by the Navigation Acts. They agreed among themselves not to buy British goods from local British-owned companies or their agents in an attempt to reduce the large amount of British imports. They also sent letters to Congress and the state legislature explaining the general problems and organized a Committee of Correspondence to write to merchants in the seaports of the other states to urge them to join in the boycott of British goods.

19 Apr 1785: Massachusetts ceded all its claims to western land to Congress.

10 May 1785: The legislature of Pennsylvania authorized paper money, starting with 7,000 pounds (SM$18,620). Ultimately it issued 150,000 pounds (SM$399,000) in bills of credit, and another 50,000 pounds (SM$133,000) in bills of credit on loans. These were treated the same as silver and gold with respect to taxes owed the state, but were not made legal tender. Generally they were used as loans to farmers on their lands and were used to pay off public creditors.

23 May 1785: Congress passed a resolution urging North Carolina to cede its territory west of the Appalachian Mountains. The people of that district had already formed a new state called Franklin. They had been abandoned by the legislature of North Carolina, and their calls for help to Congress had been ignored. By this time, the people of western North Carolina had drafted a constitution and their legislature was already in session.

1 Jun 1785: John Adams, ambassador to Great Britain, met King George III for the first time. The king told Adams that although he had held out to the very end in opposing American independence, he was amenable to friendly relations with America.

23 Jun 1785: The New Hampshire legislature authorized a grant of power to Congress to levy import duties for a period of 15 years, but was inoperative until the other states passed similar resolutions.

1 Jul 1785: Governor Bowdoin of Massachusetts had recommended on 31 May that the state legislature appoint delegates to meet with delegates from other states to discuss the amount of power that should be given to Congress to regulate foreign trade. On 1 Jul, the legislature passed a resolution doing so, and a circular letter was sent to the president of Congress, which was then forwarded to each of the respective state governors, urging them to consider how the Confederation's defects could be corrected. But the Massachusetts delegates to Congress refused to bring the resolution before Congress, as they were afraid that such a meeting would lead to a general revision of the Confederation, and in turn would cause the establishment of an aristocracy.

6 Jul 1785: Congress adopted the Morris coinage system, as modified by Jefferson, in which the standard was to be a silver coin similar to the Spanish milled dollar, but divided into 100 cents (the decimal system). The weight of the coin was not fixed until 1786.

~7 Jul 1785: The Massachusetts legislature passed a law regulating commerce in the state: a) prohibited exports from being carried by British ships; b) levied a tonnage duty on all foreign ships; and c) imposed a quadruple duty on foreign manufactures as a means to protect domestic producers.

13-14 Jul 1785: A committee in Congress led by James Monroe produced a motion to amend the Articles of Confederation to grant Congress the power to regulate foreign commerce, levy import duties, send and receive ambassadors, enter treaties and alliances, and establish courts for trial of piracy, if eleven states were agreeable. Monroe's committee had concluded that granting such a power was desirable: a) a tax on foreign goods would aid domestic manufacturers; b) Congress would be able to deal reciprocally with foreign powers, such that America would not always be at a disadvantage; c) it would allow uniform commercial rules among the states; and d) it would prepare the way for the establishment of a navy to protect commerce. Richard Henry Lee of Virginia led the opposition to it, noting that granting powers to Congress would: a) endanger liberty; b) may tempt Congress to expands its powers even further; and c) increase the risk of undue foreign influence upon Congress if powers affecting foreign nations were concentrated in Congress. He also argued that the interests of the northern and southern states were different. Lee feared that the northern states would use their numerical advantage to vote themselves benefits in the carrying trade that would serve to impoverish the southern states (since it had no shipping industry). Congress took no action on it, preferring to leave propositions for amending the Articles to the several state legislatures.

~15 Jul 1785: The legislatures of New Hampshire and Rhode Island passed trade regulations nearly identical to that of Massachusetts (7 Jul 1785).

24 Aug 1785: British Prime Minister William Pitt had a conversation with John Adams, the U. S. ambassador. They discussed some general issues of disagreement between the two nations: a) black people having been carried away by the British military; b) seizing of American ships; c) the terms of the Navigation Act; and d) the amount owed to British creditors. On this last point, contracts were traditionally considered cancelled during war, but the British position was that interest on debts continued to accumulate during the war. They also discussed some areas of mutual non-compliance with the peace treaty: a) Britain's refusal to give up garrisons in the Northwest Territories; b) America's continued engagement in the slave trade; and c) America's slow payment of debts owed to British creditors. Adams rejected Pitt's proposition for a treaty favorable to England at the expense of the French. Adams proposed a free-trade framework, but Pitt rejected it. Pitt afterward adopted a policy of strict enforcement of the Navigation Acts. Adams afterward recommended to Congress that it impose a retaliatory Navigation Act on the British, but Congress could never get enough states to agree to it.

25 Aug 1785: Congress passed a resolution instructing Foreign Secretary John Jay to continue to insist on navigation rights on the Mississippi in his negotiations with Spain.

20 Sep 1785: The Pennsylvania legislature enacted a law imposing import duties on seventy items, especially those of iron manufacture, and also placed a tonnage duty upon ships from any nations that did not have a commercial treaty with Congress. This law was the culmination of six months debate in Pennsylvania.

27 Sep 1785: Congress requisitioned SM$3,000,000 from the states. None of it would ever be paid.

Oct 1785: South Carolina's legislature passed what became known as "the barren land law:" debts could be paid in land, and the creditor was obliged to accept the land at 75% of its appraised value. Naturally, debtors gave their worst land to pay their debts. The law also authorized an issue of 700,000 pounds (SM$2,800,000) in bills of credit to be loaned at 7% interest.

20 Oct 1785: New Jersey's legislature voted to refuse to send requisitions to Congress until all the states had agreed to the import duty proposed in Apr 1783. New Jersey favored a power in the hands of Congress because residents of New Jersey were paying high prices on foreign goods transferred from

New York, due to the import duties imposed at the port of New York. New Jersey was serving notice that it was abandoning the Confederation by refusing to support it financially.

Nov 1785: North Carolina's legislature issued 100,000 pounds (SM$250,000) in bills of credit, and made it legal tender for all debts. The state ordered large purchases of tobacco, and paid for it in paper at twice the face value the tobacco would have sold for in hard money, in order to get the paper currency into circulation. It soon depreciated 30%, and North Carolina continued on a path to ruin with nearly worthless paper currency.

Nov 1785: The Maryland legislature agreed to the proposal for joint jurisdiction of the Chesapeake and Potomac per the recommendation from the meeting at Alexandria (28 Mar 1785); it also invited Delaware and Pennsylvania to consider a canal between the Delaware and Chesapeake.

23 Nov 1785: Congress convened late, with only seven states present. It elected a president, but could do no other business until mid-Dec 1785.

30 Nov 1785: Virginia's legislature passed a resolution granting Congress power over trade regulations, but only for a period of 13 years. This was a compromise between those who feared Congress would overstep its bounds and those who thought a general power in Congress' hands was necessary. The opponents finally agreed to allow temporary measures in order to test how well they worked.

5 Dec 1785: The Virginia legislature passed a law confirming the agreement with Maryland, known as the Compact of 1785. The confirmation sent from the Maryland legislature to the Virginia legislature had also recommended that a set of commissioners meet to discuss commercial issues for all the states in general. Madison saw an opportunity to make such a meeting into a forum for airing political and commercial problems alike. He worked with John Tyler of Virginia in crafting an invitation to all the states.

31 Dec 1785: Of the original SM$8,000,000 requisition of 30 Oct 1781, about SM$1,600,000 had been paid by the states.

16 Jan 1786: The Virginia legislature proposed a law separating church and state, declaring that freedom of religion is a natural right of mankind. It adopted the original text recommended by Jefferson in 1779: "No man shall be compelled to frequent or support a religious worship, place, or ministry whatsoever, nor shall suffer on account of his religious opinions or belief; opinion on matters of religion shall in no wise diminish, enlarge, or affect civil capacities. The rights hereby asserted are of the natural rights of mankind." Religious freedom was adopted in Maryland soon after.

21 Jan 1786: John Tyler and James Madison had written a proposal in the Virginia legislature, capitalizing on Maryland's recommendation for a general commercial meeting, to recommend to all the states that delegates be sent to discuss giving Congress powers over regulation of trade. The strategy was that the meeting would issue a report with recommendations that would go into effect only after all the states had agreed. Annapolis was chosen as the meeting site, as it was considered suitably far away from Congress, and to commence in Sep 1786. On 21 Jan 1786, the invitations were sent to the other states by Patrick Henry, governor of Virginia.

Feb 1786: A representative of Tripoli entered into negotiations with John Adams regarding the piracy against American vessels in the Mediterranean. It was common throughout this period for pirates to attack American ships, carry off the cargo, and either murder the crew or sell them into slavery in Algiers or Tripoli. It was safe work, since the pirates knew that America could do nothing about it. They also engineered kidnappings for ransom of prominent people. These pirates were usually private individuals who acted by endorsement from and under the protection of the local Barbary state monarchs; in return, the pirates paid a tribute from the haul. These "monarchs" were little more than professional gangsters who had risen to the top because they possessed the best combination of subterfuge and ruthlessness. The representative from Tripoli made Adams an offer: the pirates of Tripoli would stop attacking American vessels if a tribute of SM$1,000,000 was to be made to the king of Tripoli. This was an attractive offer in the sense that it would be cheaper than warfare to defeat the pirates; on the other hand, it would be an admission of weakness. It didn't matter though, because

Congress did not have the means to pay. It could not finance a navy; it could not finance a just war even if it had a navy; and it could not finance a payoff to avoid a war. All Congress could do was accept the losses, demonstrating to everyone that the central government, such as it was, could not do the most important thing a legitimate government does, which is to protect its citizens from other governments. The pirate attacks continued into the early 1800s.

15 Feb 1786: Congress issued a report by a committee consisting of Pinckney, King, Kean, Monroe, and Pettit, declaring that the Articles of Confederation were inadequate. It laid out the following conclusions: a) the requisition system of raising revenues had been a failure for its entire eight year duration; b) the requisition system could not be relied upon in the future either; c) it would be impossible to maintain any faith in the Congress unless the states authorized Congress to receive an independent revenue per the 18 Apr 1783 request; and d) Congress had a duty to announce the conditions that had caused problems to reach the crisis stage. It furthermore recommended that an appeal to the people be made to determine if the people would allow Congress to have the import duty authority, or if they would allow the nation to crumble for lack of revenue. The committee made it clear that Congress had three options: a) it could step aside and wait for the states to call a general convention; b) it could propose amendments to the Articles and seek consent to them; or c) it could work together within Congress to make the existing Articles function better. Congress agreed to debate the issue of calling for a convention, which it did for the next six months.

The minimum anticipated expenses for 1787 associated with payment of interest on foreign loans and other foreign obligations was SM$1,566,523, including: a) interest on loans from France; b) interest on a loan from Spain (to Mar 1787) (SM$48,596); and c) interest on a loan from Holland (to Jun 1787) (SM$265,600). The total receipts since 1781 amounted to SM$2,457,987: a) from requisitions made between 1 Nov 1781 and 1 Nov 1784, SM$2,025,089; b) from requisitions made between 1 Nov 1784 and 1 Jan 1786, SM$432,898 [13].

20 Feb 1786: The legislature of New Jersey voted to refuse to pay any requisitions at all. The rationale was that there was no point in supporting a weak Congress that was unable to aid New Jersey against the economic warfare being waged by the state of New York. People in New Jersey felt ill-used, and were not going to cave in any longer until their complaints had been addressed.

28 Feb 1786: Carmarthen, the British secretary of state, notified John Adams that Britain would continue to hold the outposts in the west until the states paid off British creditors. Congress had been trying to get these claims resolved through the state courts, but it had no power to force the states to pay them. This showed the inability of Congress to maintain one of its obligations under the peace treaty that ended the Revolution.

Mar 1786: A public debate over a new issue of paper currency occurred in New York State, conducted by commentary and letters published in the newspapers. The advocates for paper money included most shopkeepers, merchants, manufacturers, and debtors; those opposed included speculators, importers, stockholders, and creditors. One of the most important pamphlets against it was Thomas Paine's "The Affairs of the Bank, and Paper Money" in which Paine pointed out that no law can really equate paper with gold, and that the "value" of paper currency could be arbitrarily changed from year to year by the government. But a paper money bill passed, in which 200,000 pounds (SM$500,000) was to be issued starting in Jul 1786. However, it was made legal tender only for the proceeds from lawsuits, and was loaned only to those with excellent credit.

3 Mar 1786: Congress reviewed the actions of the states with regard to the recommendation issued by Congress on 30 Apr 1784, in which Congress requested authority to regulate foreign commerce in response to the Navigation Acts of Great Britain. Massachusetts, New York, New Jersey, and Virginia had passed laws granting Congress the power. Rhode Island, North Carolina, and New Hampshire had passed resolutions favoring it, but they were contingent on all the other states doing the same. Pennsylvania, Maryland, and Connecticut had complied also, but had fixed the dates of operation. Delaware, South Carolina, and Georgia had taken no action. Congress issued another recom-

mendation urging Rhode Island, North Carolina, New Hampshire, Pennsylvania, Maryland, and Connecticut to revise their acts to bring them into conformance with the original 30 Apr 1784 request, and urging Georgia, Delaware, and South Carolina to consider it.

11 Mar 1786: The South Carolina legislature passed a resolution authorizing Congress to regulate foreign trade for a period of 15 years from this date.

~20 Mar 1786: Congress recognized that the example set by New Jersey's failure to pay any requisitions would be fatal, since there was no way to prevent the other states from following suit. It sent a committee to meet with the New Jersey legislature, in which Charles Pinckney of South Carolina entreated the legislature to reconsider its law of 20 Feb 1786. His arguments were: a) each state had entered voluntarily into the Confederation and was bound by honor to meet its commitments; b) New Jersey had agreed to the requisition system; c) New Jersey had the remedies to deal with New York by imposing its own fees and duties; and d) if New Jersey failed to pay, it would weaken the Confederacy and make things worse for New Jersey as well as every other state. His last point was especially evident from the hostility of Britain's Navigation Acts and the holding of garrisons in the northwest. New Jersey agreed to send delegates to the convention at Annapolis, hoping that some consensus could be reached on the revenue and import duty issues. It also repealed its 20 Feb 1786 law refusing to pay requisitions, but it did not promise to pay them either.

May 1786: The New Jersey legislature issued 130,000 pounds (SM$345,800) in paper currency, and was made legal tender for business transactions. If refused, the law allowed the debt to be suspended for 12 years. But it was refused by merchants in both New York and Pennsylvania, and it soon became worthless.

May 1786: The legislature in Pennsylvania passed a resolution rejecting the requisition system unless Congress adopted some additional revenue source.

May 1786: The Rhode Island legislature issued about 100,000 pounds (SM$333,300) in paper money to be loaned to farmers at 4% for seven years in which they could pledge their farms as collateral. This was a popular idea with the farmers, since they were desperate to pay off their debts. The paper currency was sold at a 50% discount, and the farmers had to agree to take a 14-year mortgage on their farms for twice the assessed value before they could obtain the money. This was thought to be an adequate insurance against the risk of inflation. But the merchants knew full well that the paper currency would depreciate in value, and accepted it only at a discount. Sometimes the merchants refused to accept the paper at all. The legislature reacted by passing a Forcing Act with the following provisions: a) the paper currency was made legal tender; b) the penalty for refusing to accept it was a 100 pound (SM$333) fine and loss of the right to vote; c) offenses to be tried within three days of the complaint; d) cases for offenses to be tried by a panel of three judges; e) decisions of the trial judges were final, with no appeal; f) those who did not abide by the judges' decision were to be jailed; g) anyone who turned in a person who refused the currency received half of the SM$333 fine as a bounty; and h) if a merchant rejected the currency, the debtor could have the debt discharged. The judicial edicts started with the phrase "Know Ye," and Rhode Island became the subject of ridicule as the home of "Know Ye Men."

4 May 1786: At this point, all the states except New York had passed some kind of resolution authorizing the import duty power of Congress. But the prevailing opinion in New York ran counter to any grant being provided. First, the provisions of the state constitution and the Confederacy had to be upheld. Secondly, giving Congress independent powers to levy duties would weaken the state and constitute a transfer of power to Congress. Third, it would ruin the liberty of the states and eventually abolish them if Congress, having an independent revenue source, would appropriate all the powers of government to itself, and become despotic. Fourth, the only protection for liberty was in small republics. On 4 May 1786, New York imposed a 5% duty on all imports, but this revenue was to be collected by state agents and was provided to New York.

17 May 1786: Congress ratified a commercial treaty with Prussia that had been negotiated in May 1785. Frederick the Great was one of the few monarchs of Europe that saw fit to come to terms with America as a sovereign nation. The terms of this treaty, to be in effect for ten years, included: a) free trade between Prussia and the American states; b) permitting ships to carry arms and munitions as neutrals; b) merchant ships to be allowed safe passage even in war; c) prohibition of privateering on both sides; d) freedom of religion for citizens living in the opposite country; and e) merchants and workmen may continue employment even in case of war between the two parties.

31 May 1786: Foreign Secretary John Jay wrote a letter to Congress informing them that he required direction on how to negotiate with Spain. Jay preferred to be released from the condition imposed by Congress on 25 Aug 1785, in which he was instructed to demand navigation rights on the Mississippi. This was the one impediment to a commercial treaty with Spain. The Spanish had consistently refused to permit navigation by American ships up the Mississippi River, which was controlled by Spain from New Orleans to Natchez. Jay then began work with a committee in Congress to establish a policy.

6 Jun 1786: Thomas Amis, a resident of Kentucky, had outfitted a boat and had sailed down the Mississippi River, intending to sell his goods in the Spanish towns along the river. However, he was intercepted on 6 Jul 1786 at Natchez by the Spanish, who confiscated his boat and goods. The Spanish were enforcing their prohibition upon American navigation on the Mississippi. Amis was released, and went back to Kentucky overland, telling his story to many people on the way.

Jul 1786: By the summer of 1786 nearly all business stopped in Newport and Providence, RI leading to fights and riots over the financial policies. The farmers were angry at the merchants for refusing to accept the paper currency, so they decided to boycott the city and starve the urban residents into submission. In the meantime, the farmers had no choice but to offload their products in Boston or New York, but had difficulty selling there because the residents of those cities did not want to aid the cause of paper money. The farmers of Rhode Island ended up destroying their products, resulting in food shortages and high prices in most Rhode Island towns. By Aug 1786, the Rhode Island paper currency had depreciated to 4:1.

4 Jul 1786: Vermont formally separated from New York, and established a new government with a constitution that included a bill of rights.

21 Jul-30 Aug 1786: Congress debated the merits of proposing amendments to the Articles. These were referred to a committee led by Pinckney. His committee issued a recommendation that seven new provisions be added to the Articles of Confederation. First, Congress was to have the power to regulate foreign and domestic trade without infringing on state constitutions, and that revenue collected under this provision would be paid to the states. Secondly, Congress would continue the requisition system, but have a power to force the states to pass laws requiring the states to pay them; states would be charged 12% on arrears on the portion of the requisition devoted to the army, 10% otherwise. Third, if a state was delinquent on its requisitions for ten months, and a majority of the states were in compliance, Congress shall have a power to assess the amount due to counties and townships in the offending state, and these would be collected by the agents that collected the last tax. If they did not act, Congress could then appoint federal collectors. Fourth, Congress would allow interest to be paid if states provided requisitions early, and charge interest for late payments. Fifth, a new revenue system could be established with the concurrence of eleven states, and the number required for approval would be raised commensurate with additional states being admitted to the Confederation. Sixth, Congress would receive three new general powers: a) to define and punish treason; b) to define and punish piracy and felonies at sea; and c) to establish a federal court which would serve as a court of appeals from states concerning treaties, the law of nations, commerce, federal revenue, and others where the United States was a party. Seventh, Congress would have a power to force attendance by delegates from the states. No action was taken on these proposals; in all likelihood they would not have been ratified.

Aug 1786: The Georgia legislature authorized an issue of 50,000 pounds (SM$200,000) in bills of credit, to be made legal tender in the state, to be secured by a mortgage on a large tract of fertile state-owned land. There subsequently was a vigorous debate on the merits of paper money before it was actually issued.

1 Aug 1786: The paper currency issued by Pennsylvania in 1785 had depreciated by 12%.

2 Aug 1786: The Georgia legislature passed a resolution authorizing Congress to regulate foreign trade.

3-24 Aug 1786: John Jay concluded his work with the committee in Congress, and laid out his case regarding a treaty with Spain. It was clear that a commercial treaty would be of great benefit to the thirteen states, but the Spanish were inflexible on the issue of American navigation on the Mississippi. Jay proposed that the Mississippi problem be postponed for 25 years, and recommended a treaty with Spain be negotiated as soon as possible. Congress debated the policy for three weeks. The states continued to be divided on how to proceed. The New England states wanted a treaty with Spain, and did not care about navigation on a faraway river. They were joined by Pennsylvania and New Jersey. The southern states were prepared to deal with it directly, and advocated that Jay be instructed to cease all negotiations with Spain. The position taken by New York was unknown, but would likely lean toward what was in the immediate best interest of New York, meaning a treaty with Spain without rights on the Mississippi. The New England states failed to see the long-term importance of the Mississippi: it would open up the entire west as a market for the manufactured goods from New England.

8 Aug 1786: Congress established a coinage standard, per the decimal system organized in Jul 1785. A dollar was defined as 375.64 grains of pure silver, or 24.6268 grains of pure gold. The fineness of the coinage was to be 11/12 (0.91666 fine). The ratio of gold to silver was thus 15.253 to one. Congress authorized $5 and $10 coins of gold; dollars, half-dollars, dimes, and double-dimes of silver; and copper pennies and half-pennies. However, only the copper coins were actually minted.

11 Aug 1786: Congress passed a resolution asking George Clinton, governor of New York State, to call a special session of the legislature to reconsider the import law passed on 4 May 1786, which required that only New York collectors receive the duties. This was a very important matter to the Confederacy, as New York was the only state that had not as yet granted Congress a power to levy an import duty.

15-20 Aug 1786: The anger at lawsuits for debt and seizures of property in Vermont reached a breaking point. Petitions had been sent up from several of the townships to the state legislature, complaining of high taxes, too many lawyers, and high court costs. There were street riots in Rutland and Wind sor during mid-Aug 1786.

16 Aug 1786: Governor Clinton of New York notified Congress that he would not call the legislature into special session, since he was authorized to call a special session only for "extraordinary occasions." He regarded the issue of the import duty as simply not important enough. Clinton's objective since the end of the war had been to promote New York at the expense of both the Confederacy and the other states by any means available.

22-25 Aug 1786: The people of Massachusetts, desperate for money and unable to obtain any satisfaction from the state legislature, began to call conventions of their own in the various prominent towns to discuss what should be done. One of the most influential was the one convened at Hatfield (Hampshire County, MA) on 22 Aug 1786, although others sat around the same time in the counties of Worcester, Middlesex, Bristol, Lenox, and Berkshire. Mainly these were attended by people who were deep in debt, and had seen their farms seized for payment; or who had prosperous farms but were unable to sell their produce because of the lack of circulating medium and had to resort to barter for necessities. It was true that hard money was in short supply, but many people added to the problem by spending what little there was on luxuries imported from Great Britain, for which the British demanded hard money. The convention at Hatfield formulated a petition of 25 articles summarizing their complaints: a) the state Senate was derelict in its duty, and ought to be abolished; b) the Court of Common Pleas should be abolished; c) there were too many lawyers in the state prospering from the numerous debt-related lawsuits; d) import duties and excise taxes devoted to paying Massachusetts' portion of the requisitions by Congress and payments to the army was denounced; e) the method of apportioning taxes declared to be unfair; and f) an urgent need for paper money. It also denounced any use of mobs to influence the legislature, but it was too late; the people were agitated enough to take direct action. The Court of Common Pleas was an object of hatred, because distress sales and seizures for non-payment of debt were adjudicated there. The resolutions adopted at Hatfield were imitated in other conventions, and large groups of men decided to take action by forming mobs and disrupting court proceedings in the various counties in Massachusetts.

29 Aug 1786: The Court of Common Pleas at Northampton, MA was disrupted by a mob of 1,500 armed men, who had occupied the court before the judges arrived. This encouraged other groups to do the same in other towns.

5 Sep 1786: The Court of Common Pleas at Worcester, MA was disrupted by an armed mob. The local militia sided with the mob, and the court was adjourned.

11-14 Sep 1786: The convention at Annapolis opened to discuss a system of uniform trade regulations. Unfortunately, only delegates from Virginia, New York, New Jersey, Delaware, and Pennsylvania were present. Although most of the other states had committed to sending representatives, they had not followed through, and it was not possible to take any meaningful action. But Alexander Hamilton took the opportunity to send a message to all the state legislatures urging them to appoint delegates to meet in May 1787 at Philadelphia to consider matters of general importance to the states, to report to Congress of their recommendations, and hopefully have them endorsed by the legislatures of the states in order for them to go into effect. Hamilton's actions were prompted partly by his desire to advance a union of the states, and partly by the fact that the delegates from New Jersey had already been instructed to discuss not only commercial problems but other items that would promote the common interests of the states.

12 Sep 1786: The Courts of Common Pleas at Concord and Great Barrington, MA were disrupted by armed mobs. At Great Barrington, the mob broke into the jail and set the prisoners free, and intimidated three of the four judges to sign papers stating they would not exercise their duties until the complaints of the people had been addressed by the legislature.

Mid-Sep 1786: The problem with the paper money in Rhode Island came to a head when John Trevett tried to pay the butcher John Weeden in the paper money, which Weeden refused except at a large discount. Trevett turned Weeden in per the Forcing Act of May 1786, and the case went to court in mid-Sep 1786. The court found the Forcing Act to be unconstitutional. In order to maintain the viability of the paper currency, the Rhode Island legislature removed four of the five judges who had decided the case, and proposed a new law called the Test Oath in which an oath to accept the currency at par was required before: a) anyone could vote; b) anyone could hold office; c) lawyers could practice; or d) ships captains could leave port.

19-21 Sep 1786: The Supreme Court of Massachusetts was scheduled to open at Springfield. In light of the disruptions of the past few weeks, Governor Bowdoin ordered General Shepard and his militia to occupy the courthouse beforehand in order to ensure that it could do business. But the militia was met by a group of rebels, who called themselves The Regulators, led by Daniel Shays, who had served as a captain during the war. There was a tense standoff between the Regulators and the militia, and the court adjourned 21 Sep 1786 when it could not do business owing to a lack of jurors.

20-21 Sep 1786: A group of about 400 armed men assembled in Kingston, NH, where the General Court was in session. They marched to Exeter, where the House and Senate were in session. There they demanded an answer to an earlier petition, which had demanded paper money, equal distribution of property, and release from debts. The Senate refused to be intimidated by the show of force, and rejected their demands. The mob kept a vigil outside the Assembly until late that night, when they retreated after hearing what they believed to be a militia coming to assist the government. On 21 Sep, a group of men from the town formed a militia, led by the president of New Hampshire, and pursued the rebels to a tavern nearby. The rebels retreated to Kings Fall bridge and made a stand. They were defeated by the militia, and about forty were taken prisoner. The prompt action by the government prevented a long popular revolt in New Hampshire.

26-27 Sep 1786: Shays heard a rumor that the Massachusetts Supreme Court was not going to convene at Great Barrington as scheduled. But he believed this to be a ruse, and marched his "Regulators" there and occupied the town. But when they got there, they found the court was in fact to sit at Boston. Disappointed, the rebels started a riot, searched some houses, and ran a few government officials out of town. The Court convened without incident at Boston on the 27th.

Early Oct 1786: Three conventions were held in Worcester, Boston, and Middlesex, MA by people angry about the state of the economy and the lawsuits over debt. Each of them filed petitions with the state legislature. The main complaints were about the various courts (General Sessions of the Peace, Common Pleas, Probate, and General), the lack of money, and the manner in which revenues from the import duties and excise taxes were appropriated.

10 Oct 1786: Hamilton's recommendation of a convention in Philadelphia was defeated by arguments made by Rufus King and Nathan Dale before the Massachusetts House of Representatives. Their argument was that: a) legally, only Congress could recommend a conference to consider modifying the Articles; and b) any recommendation for alteration had to be confirmed by the state legislatures, but they could not do so if the recommendation were done by a convention. Massachusetts thus declined to appoint delegates to the proposed convention in Philadelphia.

Mid-Oct 1786: The debate in Georgia over paper money came to an end. Workers and farmers were opposed to paper money, knowing that it always depreciated. In a meeting in Sep 1785 in Savannah, they had issued a resolution noting that paper money had previously been discharged at 1,000 to one, and any new issue was likely to meet the same fate. Their view was that the new paper could not be accepted at par, but only for what could be obtained for it in coin. But the merchants wanted it, and used their political power to force a law through the legislature in mid-October requiring that the new paper be accepted at par. The law required farmers and merchants to certify under an affidavit that they accepted the paper currency at par; if the farmer refused, merchants would boycott his products, and he would be left with unsellable commodities.

16 Oct 1786: Congress passed a resolution establishing a mint.

16 Oct 1786: The Virginia legislature passed a resolution to send delegates to the proposed convention in Philadelphia, based on the recommendation from the meeting at Annapolis and the report made in Congress on 15 Feb 1786. Governor Edmund Randolph of Virginia then sent out a circular letter to the other states asking them to do likewise.

23 Oct 1786: Congress was still trying to obtain sufficient authorization from the states to regulate foreign commerce. At this point, Massachusetts, New York, New Jersey, Virginia, Georgia, Rhode Island, and Delaware had passed resolutions conforming to the required powers. But the measures passed by North Carolina and New Hampshire were too broad and not in compliance with the request; Connecticut, Pennsylvania, Maryland, and South Carolina had passed resolutions but the power to be conveyed was to start and end on different dates, making them also out of compliance. Massachusetts, Virginia, New York, and New Jersey had made their grants contingent on all the others being in operation. Congress again issued a recommendation to the non-complying states to revise their legislation.

Early Nov 1786: Most people of Rhode Island were not willing to endorse the severe restrictions per the proposed Test Oath act that would prop up the paper currency, and it failed in a general referendum. By Nov 1786, the paper currency that had been issued in May had depreciated to 6:1.

Mid-Nov 1786: The legislature of Vermont had passed a paper money decision over to the General Court at Rutland for their advice. During the session, a group of armed men calling themselves the "Regulators" came into town and tried to influence the court with a show of force. The sheriff called out the local militia, and after a few days standoff, the men dispersed.

18 Nov 1786: The state legislature in Massachusetts adjourned, having addressed (so they thought) the concerns expressed by the petitions presented by the three conventions in Middlesex, Boston, and Worcester in October. But the remedies suggested by the legislature proved to be the spark that set off Shays' Rebellion.

21 Nov 1786: The Court of General Sessions was prevented from sitting at Worcester, Massachusetts due to the court being occupied by a band of armed men.

23 Nov 1786: A convention assembled at Worcester read the resolutions adopted by the legislature of Massachusetts in response to the petitions of Oct 1786. These were condemned as the work of people out of touch with the common people. The members of the legislature were accused of being men of affluence, of never having experienced being sued for non-payment of debts or having their property seized for inability to pay the high property taxes (all of which was true). The convention likewise condemned the interference with the courts, but to no avail.

23 Nov 1786: The New Jersey legislature voted to send delegates to the convention at Philadelphia.

25 Nov 1786: A large group of rebels from Bristol, Worcester, Hampshire, and Middlesex met at Middlesex, despite a previous pledge to prominent people of Middlesex that they would not assemble.

29-30 Nov 1786: Governor Bowdoin of Massachusetts had issued orders a few weeks earlier against the rebel leaders, and called out a posse to capture them. On the 29th, they captured two of the rebels, Parker and Page, but Shattuck had escaped. The posse went to Shattuck's house in Groton, where Shattuck was found hiding in the nearby woods; after a brief fight, they wounded and captured Shattuck.

~2 Dec 1786: A large band of rebels under Shays assembled at Worcester, despite freezing cold and deep snow. He imposed on residents of the town to house his men, which provoked many people in the state against him when the news got out.

4 Dec 1786: The militia was called out in Boston to defend the city against an attack by Shays' Regulators, to be commanded by General Lincoln.

4 Dec 1786: Virginia selected Washington, Madison, Mason, and Randolph to be delegates to the Philadelphia convention. Virginia played a very important part in getting the convention to meet, for choosing Washington as a delegate underscored the gravity of the situation and made it very difficult for the other states to refuse.

9 Dec 1786: Shays decided to retreat from Worcester rather than attack Boston; it was very confused and haphazard, as his men were not well-trained. A few died of exposure, and nearly all suffered some frostbite.

Mid-Dec 1786: Governor Bowdoin decided to raise a militia to deal with Shays, but was careful to select militiamen who did not reside in the same areas as Shays' men. This was done to prevent a situation in which friends and neighbors would fight each other in the fields. A force of 4,400 was called up: 500 from Essex, 700 from Suffolk, 800 from Middlesex, 1,200 from Hampshire, and 1,200 from Worcester. The contingents from Suffolk and Essex were to be stationed in Boston; those from Hampshire to be stationed in Springfield, and the men from Worcester to be stationed at the eastern part of the county. They were enlisted for 30 days starting from 18 Jan 1787. General Lincoln was in overall command, assisted by Generals Tupper, Shepard, and Patterson. But it was soon discovered that there was no money in the treasury to pay them, and the legislature was out of session. Even if it were called in, any tax levied would be too late to make timely payment to the soldiers. A group of wealthy businessmen volunteered to fund the militia.

30 Dec 1786: The Pennsylvania legislature voted to send delegates to the convention at Philadelphia, based on the suggestion made by the legislature of Virginia (16 Oct 1786).

31 Dec 1786: Congress had received only SM$500,000 of the money requisitioned from the states over the past two years. Congress was delinquent on its interest payments. The response from the states was not uniform: New York, Pennsylvania, Maryland, and Virginia were paid up; Massachusetts, Rhode Island, New Hampshire, and Connecticut had paid some, but were in arrears; North Carolina, South Carolina, and Georgia had not made much payment at all since the end of the war.

Jan 1787: By this time, Congress as an institution was considered practically useless. It was disrespected even by its own members; it did not even have a consistent meeting location. It had been chased out of Philadelphia by some rowdy soldiers. It had been formed in wartime to meet an immediate need, which was now passed. The states held nearly all the relevant powers that were needed in peacetime. Although the states were united in a confederation, and had benefitted by being allied in a single object of obtaining freedom from the British, the people of the respective states were too provincial in their views and their politicians were too occupied with maintaining their power. Congress had made treaties, but the states violated the provisions; Congress had borrowed money, but the states refused revenue to repay the loans; Congress had proposed good resolutions, but they were negated by the action of a single state; Congress could establish an army, but the states could refuse to supply it. In short, Congress was powerless to act in a national spirit when it was called for.

6 Jan 1787: North Carolina agreed to send delegates to the convention at Philadelphia.

24-30 Jan 1787: Shays had marched his men to Springfield, planning to capture the supplies at the arsenal there by defeating Shepard before Lincoln could arrive from Worcester. His men were split into three groups commanded by Luke Day, Eli Parsons, and Shays himself. Shepard had already arranged his troops on the heights surrounding the town. On the 24th, Shays ordered Day to attack on the 25th, but Day, determined to gain all the glory for himself, sent a message back to Shays informing him that he would not attack until the 26th. But Day's message to Shays was intercepted and sent to Lincoln. Shays attacked Shepard on the 26th, but his inexperienced men panicked after a few casualties, and most of his men retreated to Ludlow. On the 26th, they met with Parsons at Chicopee, and found that 200 had deserted. Parsons escaped over the border to New Hampshire and then to New York. Shays remained in Springfield with a small force. On the 27th, Lincoln arrived in Springfield, and had a skirmish with Shays; Shays' army retreated to and pillaged S. Hadley, then continued to Amherst. The retreat was so disorderly that Shays' men killed some of their own when they mistook their rear guard for Lincoln's men. Lincoln pursued Shays as far as Amherst on the 28th, but Shays had by that time moved to Pelham and took up a strong position in the hills. Meanwhile, Day had captured a few of Shepard's men, so Gen. Tupper was dispatched to rescue them. They located the captured men at Middlefield, rescued them, and captured a small band of rebels under Luddington.

27-30 Jan 1787: A group of rebels under Hubbard had assembled at W. Stockbridge; their plan was to aid Shays by diverting the army to several places at once. However, Hubbard was defeated by General Patterson and was captured. The ones who escaped retreated, but were pursued and defeated by Patterson at Adams and Williamstown. The rebels then began to move on Washington (MA).

1-5 Feb 1787: Lincoln traded messages with Shays about a meeting to discuss a truce and pardon. They agreed to meet on 3 Feb, but Shays used it as a ruse to escape. He assembled his force, and marched to Petersham on the 2nd. Lincoln pursued him on the 3rd, and arrived in Petersham on the 4th. His army was strung out for 5 miles along the road owing to the cold and wind. Even so, Shays' men had gotten comfortable in Petersham, and were taken by surprise. They had not expected to be pursued promptly, and when they were warned of Lincoln's arrival, they dispersed without a fight, although some of them regathered at Northfield. Daniel Shays was captured. With Shays' men now scattered, Lincoln was confident that the revolt was over; he marched to Pittsfield via Amherst, Hadley, Chesterfield, Partridgefield, and Worthington, and ordered Shepard to meet him there.

3 Feb 1787: The Delaware legislature agreed to send delegates to the Philadelphia convention, based on the suggestion from the legislature of Virginia.

10-25 Feb 1787: Eli Parsons, having escaped capture in Massachusetts, traveled from town to town in Vermont and New York, trying to get up a force to fight Lincoln. He was successful, especially since the people of Vermont were favorably disposed to the motives of Shays.

10 Feb 1787: The Georgia legislature voted to send delegates to the convention in Philadelphia.

15 Feb 1787: The legislature of New York gave its final refusal to give Congress a power to raise revenues via an import duty. This proved to be fatal to the Confederation, as Congress was forced to accept that there was no hope of a stable revenue stream, even though the other twelve states had approved it. It led to the reconsideration by Congress of a convention at Philadelphia to modify the Articles.

21 Feb 1787: The state legislature in Massachusetts approved sending delegates to a general convention in Philadelphia; it was the seventh to do so and thus met the requirement for a quorum.

21 Feb 1787: Congress reconsidered Hamilton's recommendation made at Annapolis in Sep 1786 for a convention at Philadelphia. Congress was under great political pressure to deal with the problems among the states, especially in view of Shay's rebellion, the talk of secession by some states, and its own inability to accomplish anything. At this point, Massachusetts and New York were on record as being opposed to the Annapolis recommendation on the ground that a convention was illegitimate unless called by Congress. On 21 Feb 1787 Congress passed a carefully crafted resolution that would preserve the endorsements already received per the recommendation out of Annapolis, but would allay the concerns of Massachusetts and New York. Unknown to Congress, Massachusetts had that same day passed a resolution approving attendance at the convention. The appointed day was 14 May 1787. Many of the states had already chosen their delegates. Virginia had chosen Washington to be one of its delegates, and by doing so eased the opposition to the convention.

The resolution reads [14]: "Whereas there is provision, in the Articles of Confederation and Perpetual Union, for making alterations therein, by the assent of a Congress of the United States, and of the legislatures of the several states; and whereas experience hath evinced that there are defects in the present Confederation; as a means to remedy which, several of the states, and particularly the state of New York, by express instructions to their delegates in Congress, have suggested a convention for the purposes expressed in the following resolution; and such convention appearing to be the most probable means of establishing in these states a firm national government, -- Resolved, That in the opinion of Congress, it is expedient that, on the second Monday in May next, a convention of delegates, who shall have been appointed by the several states, be held in Philadelphia, for the sole and express purpose of revising the Articles of Confederation, and reporting to Congress and the several legislatures such alterations and provisions therein as shall, when agreed to in Congress, and confirmed by the states, render the federal Constitution adequate to the exigencies of government and the preservation of the Union."

26 Feb-1 Mar 1787: A rebel force from New York, assembled by Parsons, and commanded by Hamlin, invaded Stockbridge, plundered it, and took some prominent men as hostages. The militia at Sheffield and Great Barrington were called out, and they marched around trying to find Hamlin. They stumbled across him by accident at Springfield. They defeated Hamlin and captured him, and this ended Shays' Rebellion. Hamlin had missed a golden opportunity; if he had attacked a few days earlier, he would have been unopposed, since the militia's enlistments had run out on the 21st, and for a few days, Lincoln only had 30 men in the field.

28 Feb 1787: The New York legislature agreed to send delegates to the convention at Philadelphia, but did not mention either the resolution of Congress or the recommendation made from the meeting at Annapolis.

8 Mar 1787: The South Carolina legislature voted to send delegates to the convention in Philadelphia.

10 Mar 1787: The legislature of Massachusetts, hard pressed by inability to pay its debts, and faced with riots and rebellions, recognized that a stronger union was necessary in order to solve the financial

problems of the states. It voted to endorse Congress' recommendation of 21 Feb 1787 and send delegates to Philadelphia.

Apr 1787: James Madison wrote an essay called "Vices of the Political System of the United States" [15]. He provided a brief summary of the problems encountered under the Articles of Confederation: a) states were unwilling to supply the requisitions ordered by Congress; b) violations of the Articles by some states, especially with regard to treaties with the Indians and treaties among themselves; c) violations by the states of treaties made with Great Britain, France, and Holland; d) economic feuds between the states; e) inability of the states to form a united front with regard to commercial relations with foreign nations; f) inability to deal with rebellions in the states; g) inability of Congress to enforce its decisions on the states; h) the fact that the Articles were not adopted in the same way in all states (in some it was referenced in their constitutions, in others by a simple statute); i) expansion of laws in the states and constant alteration of them; and j) unjust laws passed in some states.

12 May 1787: The Connecticut legislature voted to send delegates to the convention in Philadelphia.

25 May-17 Sep 1787: A quorum of seven states was required to begin the convention at Philadelphia. The original opening day was supposed to have been 14 May 1787, but many were delayed in getting to Philadelphia. On 25 May 1787, delegates from nine states (Massachusetts, New York, New Jersey, Pennsylvania, Delaware, Virginia, North Carolina, South Carolina, and Georgia) assembled at Independence Hall in Philadelphia to debate modifications to the Articles of Confederation. George Washington was chosen to be the president of the Convention. Delegates from Connecticut and Maryland arrived on 29 May, and those from New Hampshire arrived on 23 Jul. Rhode Island never did participate. It became apparent early on that modification of the Articles was impractical, and the delegates set about framing a new Constitution. After several months of negotiations, all done in secret, the delegates issued a proposed Constitution on 17 Sep 1787, and submitted it to the states for ratification. James Madison took extensive notes of the proceedings, but they were kept secret until 1830, when he began editing them for publication, a task he never completed.

26 May 1787: The Maryland legislature voted to send delegates to the convention in Philadelphia.

Jun 1787: The paper currency issued by Rhode Island in May 1786 had depreciated to 8:1. The farmers of Rhode Island began to resort to barter, and land rents were paid in corn.

27 Jun 1787: New Hampshire's legislature voted to send delegates to the convention in Philadelphia.

13 Jul 1787: Congress passed the Northwest Ordinance. This law consolidated the lands in the northwest into the Territory of Ohio, with a prohibition on the institution of slavery in that territory and any states that would ultimately be formed from it. The conditions set out included the following: a) intestate property was to be divided equally among all children, or in case of no children, progressing to next of kin; b) offices of governor and judges were established; c) the militia was placed under control of the governor; d) counties or townships obtained representation in the assembly when the adult male population exceeded 5,000; e) the territory was eventually to be divided into three to five states; f) religious freedom was guaranteed; g) people were guaranteed rights of habeas corpus, trial by jury, compensation for property taken for public use; h) people with 50 acres of property would be eligible to vote; i) slavery was prohibited; and j) the 23 Apr 1784 Ordinance was repealed. Under the Articles, Congress did not actually have authority to pass this Ordinance, but had done it out of necessity.

18 Jul 1787: Congress ratified a treaty with the "Emperor" of Morocco to end the piracy upon American ships in the Mediterranean, which had been negotiated on 28 Jun 1786. An additional article covering the status of ships in a war zone was added on 15 Jul 1786. It contained the following provisions: a) both parties to remain neutral if the other is in a state of war; b) immunity of ships in war; c) no piracy by either party; d) each to open ports for resupply of ships; e) mutual defense at sea; f) no searches of ships in ports; g) most favored nation trading status; and h) in case of war between parties, prisoners to be exchanged instead of being sold into slavery.

17 Sep 1787: The constitutional convention at Philadelphia closed, and sent the proposed Constitution to Congress, to be transmitted to the states for ratification.

27 Oct 1787-28 May 1788: *The Federalist Papers*, authored by John Jay, Alexander Hamilton, and James Madison, were published as a series of essays under the pen name Publius in various newspapers throughout the state of New York. Their purpose was to convince the people of New York and their delegates of the necessity of a federal union per the proposed Constitution.

By the time the last essay was published, eight states had already ratified the Constitution: 1) Delaware, 6 Dec 1787; 2) Pennsylvania, 12 Dec 1787; 3) New Jersey, 18 Dec 1787; 4) Georgia, 2 Jan 1788; 5) Connecticut, 9 Jan 1788; 6) Massachusetts, 6 Feb 1788; 7) Maryland, 28 Apr 1788; and 8) South Carolina, 23 May 1788.

21 Jun 1788: New Hampshire ratified the Constitution, which was the critical ninth state to ratify, and caused the Constitution to go into effect for those nine states.

25 Jun 1788: Virginia ratified the Constitution.

16 Jul 1788: The state of New York, to which *The Federalist Papers* was directed, ratified the Constitution.

16 Sep 1788: Congress ceased operations under the authority of the Articles of Confederation. Its last act was to defer negotiations with Spain until the new government under the Constitution convened.

24, 25 Nov 1788: South Carolina held elections for members of Congress.

26 Nov 1788: Pennsylvania held elections for members of Congress.

15 Dec 1788: Voting for the office of President began in the States (cf. 10 Jan 1789). Also, New Hampshire held elections for members of Congress.

18 Dec 1788: Massachusetts held elections for members of Congress.

22 Dec 1788: Connecticut held elections for members of Congress.

4 Mar 1789: The federal government of the United States of America went into operation with the swearing-in of Congress.

30 Apr 1789: George Washington was sworn in as the first President of the United States.

21 Nov 1789: North Carolina ratified the Constitution and joined the union (12th state).

29 May 1790: Rhode Island ratified the Constitution and joined the union (13th state).

References

[1] *The Secret Journal of the Acts and Proceedings of Congress*, Boston: Thomas B. Wait, 1821, Vol. 3, pp. 417-436

[2] Gaillard Hunt, ed., *Journals of the Continental Congress*, Washington DC: U. S. Government Printing Office, 1928, Vol. 26, pp. 185-198

[3] John C. Fitzpatrick, ed., *The Writings of George Washington*, Vol. 24, pp. 272, 273. Washington DC: The U. S. Government Printing Office, Jan. 1938

[4] The Secret Journal of the Acts and Proceedings of Congress, Boston: Thomas B. Wait, 1821, Vol. 3, pp. 281-289

[5] Gaillard Hunt, ed., *Journals of the Continental Congress*, Washington DC: U. S. Government Printing Office, 1928, Vol. 26, pp. 185-198

[6] ibid., pp. 185-198

[7] John C. Fitzpatrick, ed., *The Writings of George Washington*, Vol. 26, pp. 183-188. Washington DC: The U. S. Government Printing Office, Jul. 1938

[8] ibid., pp. 229-232

[9] *The Secret Journal of the Acts and Proceedings of Congress*, Boston: Thomas B. Wait, 1821, Vol. 3, pp. 327-338

[10] Gaillard Hunt, ed., *Journals of the Continental Congress*, Washington DC: U. S. Government Printing Office, 1928, Vol. 26, pp. 297-310
[11] ibid., pp. 185-198
[12] ibid., pp. 297-310
[13] ibid., Vol. 30, pp. 70-76
[14] Jonathan Elliot, *The Debates in the Several State Conventions on the Adoption of the Federal Constitution*, Vol. 1, pp. 119, 120. Philadelphia: J. B. Lippincott & Co., 1881
[15] James Madison, *Writings*, New York: Literary Classics of the United States, 1999, pp. 69-80

Bibliography

1. David Hume, *A History of England*, New York: Harper & Brothers, 1869
2. James Madison, *Notes of Debates in the Federal Convention of 1787*, Athens, OH: Ohio University Press, 1965 (a reprint of C. C. Tansill, "Madison's Notes", contained in *Documents Illustrative of the Formation of the Union of the American States*, House Document No. 398, Washington: U. S. Government Printing Office, 1927)
3. Jonathan Elliot, *The Debates in the Several State Conventions on the Adoption of the Federal Constitution*, Philadelphia: J. B. Lippincott & Co., 1881
4. Sir A. W. Ward, Sir G. W. Prothero, Sir Stanley Leathes, ed., *The Cambridge Modern History, Vol. VII: The United States*, New York: The Macmillan Co., 1934
5. A. Barton Hepburn, *A History of Currency in the United States*, New York: The Macmillan Co., 1924
6. William G. Sumner, *A History of American Currency*, New York: Henry Holt & Co., 1878
7. George Bancroft, *History of the United States of America*, New York: D. Appleton & Co., 1888
8. James Schouler, *History of the United States of America under the Constitution*, New York: Dodd, Mead, and Co., Revised Edition, 1908
9. John B. McMaster, *A History of the People of the United States from the Revolution to the Civil War*, New York: D. Appleton & Co., 1900
10. John Fiske, *John Fiske's Historical Writings*, New York: Houghton, Mifflin and Company, 1901

The Defects of the Articles of Confederation

Note: This essay describes the main defects of the Articles of Confederation under which the American states organized themselves during the Revolutionary War until the adoption of the Constitution in 1788. It was previously published as a series of 16 essays between 30 Jun 2011 and 21 Nov 2011.

1 Historical Background

It must be recalled that the Revolution of the American colonies against the British was not the result of some grand conspiracy. The main source of irritation between the colonies and the mother country was a series of Acts of Parliament that constituted undue interference in the colonies' traditional rights of self-government. Among the offenses were alteration of the colonial charters, in which land grants were withdrawn and sold again; the imposition of taxes without consulting the colonies; the gradual usurpation of the rights of the colonists to elect their own government; and the intensification of economic burdens designed to benefit England at the expense of the colonies. All of these were more or less the consequence of King George III's desire to rule both England and the colonies as a personal autocracy. But even in the early 1770's, many people in the colonies preferred to remain Englishmen, hoping that they could somehow reach a compromise with Great Britain. Only when the British crown sought to make Massachusetts an example by imposing severe constraints on her in 1775 did the colonies awake to the fact that Parliament would not retract any of their excesses.

The colonies were not closely aligned politically during the immediate pre-war period. There had never been any desire on the part of any of the colonies to form associations or leagues; all were content to operate as independently of each other as possible as direct subordinates to the crown. But when the British Parliament began to impose repressive measures, some of the colonists saw a need to act together to seek remedies. They appointed a Congress of delegates from the several colonies to meet in May 1774; its purpose was to defend the rights of the colonies. It was not entirely clear how to get Parliament's attention; and Congress as such had no real authority to do much anyway. The main result of this first Congress was a debate on the legitimate powers held by Parliament, in view of the colonial charters and the traditional rights as Englishmen. A break with England was not seriously considered yet. It published a petition calling on Parliament to repeal all the offensive laws passed since 1763. Suffice to say, it was summarily ignored by Parliament.

By the fall of 1774, the abuses by Parliament against Massachusetts led to the people beginning to reject the powers of the crown outright; this tension promoted by some in America who saw that the Americans were ripe for independence, and by the British, who desired to bring each of the colonies under direct rule by the king. Eventually the British attempted to end the dispute by arresting leaders of the independence movement; this led to the battles at Lexington and Concord in April 1775. There was now no going back; the issue of Parliament's powers, and if they were to have any over the colonies, would be decided by force.

The Second Continental Congress convened in May 1775. Its charter was to do what was necessary and proper to convince Parliament to undo its abuses. But with the battle of Bunker and Breed's Hill in June, the assembly of a large number of militiamen around Boston to threaten the British army there, the establishment of new governments in Massachusetts and New Hampshire, and the expansion of fighting throughout the northeast, Congress became a de facto revolutionary government. Having gained the confidence of the people, it simply assumed command of the shooting war, appointing Washington as commander, issuing currency on its own credit, and generally organizing the war effort. The Americans launched an invasion of Canada in August 1775, and the British responded militarily in earnest in October of 1775. A formal break with Great Britain was now inevitable, and was announced by the Declaration of Independence on 4 Jul 1776.

Congress assumed the powers of a government without any particular authorization outside of the military emergency. Because the delegates could not agree on the relative weighting by population or wealth, or any other method of apportioning votes, it adopted by default a purely federal system in which each former colony, referring to themselves now as states, had one vote. Congress appointed a committee on 10 Jun 1776 to devise a permanent government for the thirteen states; it reported out a draft of the Articles of Confederation on 12 Jul 1776. The Articles were debated from 12 Jul 1776 to 20 Aug 1776 and again from 8 Apr 1777 until their form was agreed to on 15 Nov 1777, which is to say, it was suitable to send to the states for ratification. On 9 Jul 1778, delegates from eight states ratified the Articles (Connecticut, New Hampshire, Rhode Island, Massachusetts, New York, Pennsylvania, Virginia, and South Carolina). North Carolina followed suit on 21 Jul 1778, Georgia on 24 Jul 1778; New Jersey on 26 Nov 1778, Delaware on 5 May 1779, and Maryland on 1 Mar 1781. The Articles required that all thirteen states ratify it before it could go into effect; hence Congress did not convene under the powers granted by the Articles until 2 Mar 1781.

The main features of the Articles, which will be examined more closely in the next sections, were:

a. Congress was the only instrument of the federation. It was to convene on the first Monday in November and continue for a period not longer than six months. When it adjourned, the government was maintained by an executive committee consisting of one delegate from each state. Congress elected a President, who was only the nominal leader of Congress, and had the same powers as any other delegate. Congress published a monthly journal of its proceedings.

b. Each state was allowed to send between two and seven delegates, but since it was a confederation of states, each state had a single vote. The delegates were paid by their respective states, not out of a federal treasury. Instead of administrative departments, the various functions were allocated to committees. This proved to be inefficient, and later on some functions were allocated to individuals in the interest of expediency.

c. Congress was granted the following powers: a) to borrow money; b) to appropriate requisitions of money, men, and equipment from each of the states, but could not raise revenue on its own; c) to resolve issues between the states; d) to enact treaties with foreign powers; e) to establish an army and navy; and f) to issue a currency as an obligation to repay loans. Congress had the power to establish requisitions from the states based on the proportional value of real estate in each state. The states were then free to raise the requisition by taxing their own citizens.

d. Concurrence of two-thirds of the states was required for any of the following actions: a) to engage in war; b) to make treaties; c) to coin money; d) to borrow or appropriate money; e) to assign quotas of revenue to the states; and f) to appoint commanders of the army.

e. The states were required to grant every freeman the same rights and privileges. Every state was compelled to recognize the records and acts of every other state, and obligated to extradite persons found in their state who were wanted on criminal charges in another state. Otherwise, all the other powers were left to the states with the following prohibitions: a) a state could not maintain an army or a navy, except for the militia; b) a state could not enter into treaties with foreign nations; c) a state could not form alliances with any of the other states without the consent of Congress; and d) each state was prohibited from entering into any other wars except against the Indians.

f. The Articles could be amended only by concurrence of all member states.

The remaining sections discuss how these provisions worked in practice at the return of peace: the military establishment, to make treaties, allocate powers, regulate commerce and coinage, preserve the republican form of government, obtain necessary revenue, and methods of ratifying and amending.

2 The Power to Raise an Army and Navy

No matter how a government is constituted, its first duty is to protect the people from other governments and other factions which intend to invade its territory, attack the people, or infringe upon their legitimate interests. Any government unwilling or unable to perform this task will soon lose all legitimacy; first, it will excite the ambition of other governments of factions; secondly, it will earn the contempt of the domestic population. No sensible people can prosper or seek happiness if subject to coercion or invasion by armies in the service of other governments or by armed factions; the uncertainty and fear among the people is certain to restrain the promotion of progress. What population will support a government that allows invasions and attacks upon them without a commensurate response? They may as well avoid the expense of the government and take measures into their own hands. To remain viable then, every government must enjoy the confidence of the people that it can and will deter or respond to outside threats. Once that confidence is lost, such a government is ripe for replacement either by a domestic revolt of conquest.

It is instructive first to review the difficulties encountered before the Articles formally went into effect on 2 Mar 1781. By the time Congress issued the Declaration of Independence on 4 Jul 1776, the states were already involved in a shooting war. The war had been fought entirely by militia at Lexington and Concord (18, 19 Apr 1775) and Bunker Hill and Breed's Hill (17 Jun 1775). When George Washington took over as commander of the Continental army at Cambridge on 3 Jul 1775, it consisted of 3,000 regular troops authorized by Congress and 16,000 militiamen from the northern states. The militia continued to be the dominant force throughout the battles of Hampton Roads, VA (26-28 Oct 1775); Montreal (12 Nov 1775); Great Bridge, VA (9 Dec 1775); Quebec (31 Dec 1775); Moore's Creek, NC (27 Feb 1776); Boston (4-17 Mar 1776); and the remaining defeats in Canada up to June of 1776. Washington recognized early on the great risk associated with fighting a protracted war using militiamen with short terms of service. In his letter to Congress 2 Sep 1776, he wrote in part, concerning the lack of discipline among the militia, and their enlistments [1]:

> All these circumstances fully confirm the opinion I ever entertained, and which I more than once in my letters took the liberty of mentioning to Congress, that no dependence could be in a militia or other troops than those enlisted end embodied for a longer period than our regulations heretofore have prescribed. I am persuaded and as fully convinced, as I am of any one fact that has happened, that our liberties must of necessity be greatly hazarded, if not entirely lost, if their defense is left to any but a permanent standing army, I mean one to exist during the war.

By his last qualification, "during the war", he is no doubt referring to the suspicion held by many in the states at that time, that a standing army leads invariably to domestic tyranny engineered by whoever controlled the army. He did not have enough troops of sufficiently durable enlistments to defend New York; losing at Long Island (27-29 Aug 1776); Manhattan (15, 16 Sep 1776); White Plains (28 Oct 1776); Ft. Washington (16 Nov 1776); the evacuation of Ft. Lee (20 Nov 1776); and the retreat through New Jersey (28 Nov - 12 Dec 1776).

On 16 Sep 1776, Congress responded to his letter of 2 Sep, authorizing 88 battalions to be raised by the states according to quota and pay schedule established by Congress. They were to be paid and outfitted by the states, and each state was to appoint all officers of rank colonel and below. Although these troops were authorized as part of a regular army, their existence was still too dependent on the states. First, promotion below colonel could not be done based on merit in the field; it could be done by whatever system the states adopted back home. Secondly, the pay set by Congress was too low; men found they could do better by waiting for an appointment to a state militia.

The Continental army, or what was left of it, was in an exceedingly precarious situation at the close of 1776. It still consisted mostly of militia, and those enlistments were about to run out. Having been faced with continuous defeats the past six months, this army, barring some miracle, was at risk of simply melting away at the first of the year. Washington revisited this same topic again in a letter of 16 Dec 1776 [2] to the President of Congress, writing in part:

> Sir: In a late letter which I had the honor of addressing you, I took the liberty to recommend that more battalions should be raised for the new army, than what had been voted. Having fully considered the matter I am more and more convinced not only of the propriety, but of the necessity of the measure. That the enemy will leave nothing unessayed in

> the course of the next campaign, to reduce these states to the rule of a most lawless and insufferable tyranny must be obvious to everyone, and that the militia is not to be depended on, or aid expected from them, but in cases of the most pressing emergency, is not to be doubted. The first of these propositions is unquestionable, and fatal experience has given her sanction to the truth of the latter; indeed their lethargy of late and backwardness to turn out at this alarming crisis, seem to justify an apprehension, than nothing can bring them from their homes. ... In a word, the next will be a trying campaign and as all that is dear and valuable may depend on the issue of it, I think no measure would advise that nothing should be omitted to ensure that shall seem necessary to our success. Let us have a respectable army, and such as will be competent to every exigency. I will also add that the critical situation of our affairs and the dissolution of our present force, (now at hand) require that every nerve and exertion be employed for recruiting the new battalions.

It was Washington's brilliant attack on Trenton, NJ (26-29 Dec 1776) by crossing the Delaware River in the dead of winter, followed by victories at Princeton, NJ (3 Jan 1777) and Elizabethtown, NJ (7 Jan 1777) that induced many to remain in the army.

Afterwards, as Congress' authorization of 16 Sep 1776 took effect, there was greater balance in the makeup of the army. It should be noted however, that the militia played an important role in two areas: a) the defeat of several Hessian and British detachments at Hubbardtown, NY (4-7 Jul 1777), Oriskany, NY (6 Aug 1777), and Bennington, NY (16 Aug 1777); all of these contributed to Burgoyne's surrender after the second battle of Freeman's Farm (7 Oct 1777). Also, the militia was instrumental in keeping the war in the south alive after General Horatio Gates was defeated by Lord Cornwallis at Camden, SC (16 Aug 1780). It was not until March of 1781, after Nathaniel Greene replaced Gates, when the regular American army resumed fighting the British in the south; Greene and Lafayette were able to deprive Cornwallis of his interior lines and forced him to retreat to Yorktown, VA. The French fleet blocked Cornwallis' attempt to evacuate by sea, Washington led a forced march from New York, and Cornwallis was defeated at Yorktown 19 Oct 1781.

The portions of the Articles of Confederation attendant to our subject are found in Article VI, paragraphs 4 and 5; and Articles VII and VIII, as follows:

> [**Article VI**, paragraphs 4 and 5] No vessels of war shall be kept up in time of peace by any State, except such number only as shall be deemed necessary by the United States, in Congress assembled, for the defense of such State or its trade; nor shall any body of forces be kept up by any State, in time of peace, except such number only as, in the judgment of the United States, Congress assembled, shall be deemed requisite to garrison the forts necessary for the defense of such State; but every State shall always keep up a well regulated and disciplined militia, sufficiently armed and accoutered, and shall provide and constantly have ready for use, in public stores, a due number of field-pieces and tents, and a proper quantity of arms, ammunition and camp equipage.
>
> No State shall engage in any war without the consent of the United States, in Congress assembled, unless such State be actually invaded by enemies, or shall have received certain advice of a resolution being formed by some nation of Indians to invade such State, and the danger is so imminent as not to admit of a delay, till the United States, in Congress assembled, can be consulted; nor shall any State grant commissions to any ships or vessels of war, nor letters of marque or reprisal, except it be after a declaration of war by the United States, in Congress assembled, and then only against the kingdom or state and the subjects thereof against which war has been so declared, and under such regulations as shall be established by the United States, in Congress assembled, unless such State be invested by pirates, in which case vessels of war be fitted out for that occasion, and kept so long as the danger shall continue, or until the United States, in Congress assembled, shall determine otherwise.

> **Article VII.** When land forces are raised by any State for the common defense, all officers of or under the rank of colonel, shall be appointed by the legislature of each State respectively by whom such forces shall be raised, or in such manner as such State shall direct, all vacancies shall be filled up by the State which first made the appointment.
>
> **Article VIII.** All charges of war, and all other expenses that shall be incurred for the common defense or general welfare, and allowed by the United States, in Congress assembled, shall be defrayed out of a common treasury, which shall be supplied by the several States, in proportion to the value of all land within each State, granted to, or surveyed for, any person, as such land and the buildings and improvements thereon shall be estimated according to such mode as the United States in Congress assembled, shall from time to time direct and appoint. The taxes for paying that proportion shall be laid and levied by the authority and direction of the legislatures of the several States, within the time agreed upon by the United States, in Congress assembled.

It is easily seen from these provisions that the main sources of complaint by Washington continued. Although Congress had the authority to establish a regular army, it was to be largely commanded, except at the flag-rank, by men chosen by the state legislatures. The states were properly restrained from declaring war on their own. But the most serious defect that affected the military was Article VIII, in which the army was to be paid by Congress, but the money was to come from requisitions upon the states. Congress appropriated requisitions, but the states simply refused to pay, or paid only a fraction of their requisition. Congress issued its first requisition under the Confederation on 30 Oct 1781 for $8,000,000 in Spanish milled dollars (1 SM$ = 386.7 grains of silver). By the end of 1785, only $1,600,000 would be paid. Congress made other requisitions, none of which were ever paid. The net result was that Congress was unable to pay the army; this led to several revolts throughout 1783. Congress was forced to adopt a half-pay-for-life provision as a way to keep men in the field; it was later changed to a "commutation" of five years pay immediately. The truth was that Congress could not pay either one; it simply issued notes that matured some years later at 6% interest, or provided land in the western territories. The situation became so bad in 1786 that Congress was unable to raise a force to put down Shays' rebellion in Massachusetts (19 Sep 1786 - 1 Mar 1787), which was a popular tax revolt against the foreclosure of farms.

The U. S. Constitution remedies these defects by giving power to the federal government to lay taxes necessary to raise an army and navy, and to make rules for their discipline. It retained the militia system for two reasons: a) to aid the regular army if called upon; and b) as a means for an armed population to repel any attempt at domestic tyranny. The provisions of interest are contained in Article 1, Section 8, reading in part:

> **[Article 1, Section 8.]** The Congress shall have Power To lay and collect Taxes, Duties, Imposts and Excises, to pay the Debts and provide for the common Defense and general Welfare of the United States; but all Duties, Imposts and Excises shall be uniform throughout the United States;
>
> To raise and support Armies, but no Appropriation of Money to that Use shall be for a longer Term than two Years;
>
> To provide and maintain a Navy;
>
> To make Rules for the Government and Regulation of the land and naval Forces;
>
> To provide for calling forth the Militia to execute the Laws of the Union, suppress Insurrections and repel Invasions;
>
> To provide for organizing, arming, and disciplining the Militia, and for governing such Part of them as may be employed in the Service of the United States, reserving to the States respectively, the Appointment of the Officers, and the Authority of training the Militia according to the discipline prescribed by Congress;

Congress under the Constitution now has the ability to organize and equip a regular army and navy, establish rules for their deployment, and levy taxes directly for their support without depending on the states. The only limitation, deferring to the continuing (and legitimate) suspicions against standing armies, was that appropriations for the military had to be renewed at least every two years. Alexander Hamilton explained the underlying reasoning behind these provisions, as compared to the corresponding ones in the Articles in the *Federalist Papers* #23:

> The principal purposes to be answered by union are these -- the common defense of the members; the preservation of the public peace as well against internal convulsions as external attacks; the regulation of commerce with other nations and between the States; the superintendence of our intercourse, political and commercial, with foreign countries.
>
> The authorities essential to the common defense are these: to raise armies; to build and equip fleets; to prescribe rules for the government of both; to direct their operations; to provide for their support. These powers ought to exist without limitation, because it is impossible to foresee or define the extent and variety of national exigencies, or the correspondent extent and variety of the means which may be necessary to satisfy them. The circumstances that endanger the safety of nations are infinite, and for this reason no constitutional shackles can wisely be imposed on the power to which the care of it is committed. This power ought to be coextensive with all the possible combinations of such circumstances; and ought to be under the direction of the same councils which are appointed to preside over the common defense.
>
> This is one of those truths which, to a correct and unprejudiced mind, carries its own evidence along with it; and may be obscured, but cannot be made plainer by argument or reasoning. It rests upon axioms as simple as they are universal; the means ought to be proportioned to the end; the persons, from whose agency the attainment of any end is expected, ought to possess the means by which it is to be attained.
>
> Whether there ought to be a federal government intrusted with the care of the common defense, is a question in the first instance, open for discussion; but the moment it is decided in the affirmative, it will follow, that that government ought to be clothed with all the powers requisite to complete execution of its trust. And unless it can be shown that the circumstances which may affect the public safety are reducible within certain determinate limits; unless the contrary of this position can be fairly and rationally disputed, it must be admitted, as a necessary consequence, that there can be no limitation of that authority which is to provide for the defense and protection of the community, in any matter essential to its efficacy -- that is, in any matter essential to the formation, direction, or support of the national forces.
>
> Defective as the present Confederation has been proved to be, this principle appears to have been fully recognized by the framers of it; though they have not made proper or adequate provision for its exercise. Congress have an unlimited discretion to make requisitions of men and money; to govern the army and navy; to direct their operations. As their requisitions are made constitutionally binding upon the States, who are in fact under the most solemn obligations to furnish the supplies required of them, the intention evidently was that the United States should command whatever resources were by them judged requisite to the "common defense and general welfare." It was presumed that a sense of their true interests, and a regard to the dictates of good faith, would be found sufficient pledges for the punctual performance of the duty of the members to the federal head.
>
> The experiment has, however, demonstrated that this expectation was ill-founded and illusory; and the observations, made under the last head, will, I imagine, have sufficed to convince the impartial and discerning, that there is an absolute necessity for an entire change in the first principles of the system; that if we are in earnest about giving the Union energy and duration, we must abandon the vain project of legislating upon the States in their collective capacities; we must extend the laws of the federal government to

> the individual citizens of America; we must discard the fallacious scheme of quotas and requisitions, as equally impracticable and unjust. The result from all this is that the Union ought to be invested with full power to levy troops; to build and equip fleets; and to raise the revenues which will be required for the formation and support of an army and navy, in the customary and ordinary modes practiced in other governments.

The militia, which is the entire armed population, is intended partly to aid the regular army when called and partly to restrain the forces of ambition within the federal government. I mention this only because there are those who maintain a fiction that the National Guard is now the militia mentioned in the Constitution. But the concept that a perpetually armed population is necessary to deter domestic tyranny is confirmed by Madison's comments in the *Federalist Papers* #46:

> The only refuge left for those who prophesy the downfall of the State governments is the visionary supposition that the federal government may previously accumulate a military force for the projects of ambition. The reasonings contained in these papers must have been employed to little purpose indeed, if it could be necessary now to disprove the reality of this danger. That the people and the States should, for a sufficient period of time, elect an uninterrupted succession of men ready to betray both; that the traitors should, throughout this period, uniformly and systematically pursue some fixed plan for the extension of the military establishment; that the governments and the people of the States should silently and patiently behold the gathering storm, and continue to supply the materials, until it should be prepared to burst on their own heads, must appear to every one more like the incoherent dreams of a delirious jealousy, or the misjudged exaggerations of a counterfeit zeal, than like the sober apprehensions of genuine patriotism. Extravagant as the supposition is, let it however be made. Let a regular army, fully equal to the resources of the country, be formed; and let it be entirely at the devotion of the federal government; still it would not be going too far to say, that the State governments, with the people on their side, would be able to repel the danger. The highest number to which, according to the best computation, a standing army can be carried in any country, does not exceed one hundredth part of the whole number of souls; or one twenty-fifth part of the number able to bear arms. This proportion would not yield, in the United States, an army of more than twenty-five or thirty thousand men. To these would be opposed a militia amounting to near half a million of citizens with arms in their hands, officered by men chosen from among themselves, fighting for their common liberties, and united and conducted by governments possessing their affections and confidence. It may well be doubted, whether a militia thus circumstanced could ever be conquered by such a proportion of regular troops. Those who are best acquainted with the last successful resistance of this country against the British arms, will be most inclined to deny the possibility of it. Besides the advantage of being armed, which the Americans possess over the people of almost every other nation, the existence of subordinate governments, to which the people are attached, and by which the militia officers are appointed, forms a barrier against the enterprises of ambition, more insurmountable than any which a simple government of any form can admit of. Notwithstanding the military establishments in the several kingdoms of Europe, which are carried as far as the public resources will bear, the governments are afraid to trust the people with arms. And it is not certain, that with this aid alone they would not be able to shake off their yokes. But were the people to possess the additional advantages of local governments chosen by themselves, who could collect the national will and direct the national force, and of officers appointed out of the militia, by these governments, and attached both to them and to the militia, it may be affirmed with the greatest assurance, that the throne of every tyranny in Europe would be speedily overturned in spite of the legions which surround it. Let us not insult the free and gallant citizens of America with the suspicion, that they would be less able to defend the rights of

> which they would be in actual possession, than the debased subjects of arbitrary power would be to rescue theirs from the hands of their oppressors. Let us rather no longer insult them with the supposition that they can ever reduce themselves to the necessity of making the experiment, by a blind and tame submission to the long train of insidious measures which must precede and produce it.

Thus the Constitution remedied the defects of the Articles of Confederation with respect to the maintenance of regular military institutions. The federal government has always been able to suitably field necessary armies, navies, and other forces as necessary. All Americans should be grateful that the U. S. military has been exceptional throughout its history in maintaining fidelity to the Constitution - very different from the experiences of most nations. That said however, no free people will ever allow themselves to be disarmed, no matter how well the military behaves.

3 The Power to Make Treaties

A treaty is nothing more than an agreement between nations. But unlike the numerous pacts, communiqués, diplomatic memorandums and the like that occur commonly in foreign relations, a treaty normally imposes solemn obligations on both sides. Therefore, they are not to be entered into lightly, because they represent promises made by a nation in return for promises to be kept by the other party. A treaty must be established by knowledgeable persons, since violations of a treaty could be a just cause for war, loss of national prestige, loss of confidence by other nations, or many types of economic retaliation. It is of utmost importance then, that a treaty be entered into for sound reasons, that is, for reasons that promote the national interest; but once entered into, be adhered to in good faith. All of this explains why treaties must be negotiated by experienced people, capable of understanding a nation's long-term interests and the threats to them. Otherwise, a detrimental treaty may result, in which case there is no choice but to ask for renegotiation, adhere to it as best as can be done, or take the risk of violating it.

We can observe from history in general some requirements for a successful treaty: a) each party enters into obligations in return for obligations to be observed by the other; b) the provisions are consistent with the long-term goals and interests of the entire nation, not just a portion thereof or one faction; c) it should be made either for a term of years, or to be operable so long as a certain set of conditions prevails; d) should take the long-term view, unless made for a term of years; not focusing only on immediate problems that may be solved with the passage of time, or risking long-term interests for short-term gain; and e) contain a means of termination should both parties find it advisable, or as a means to address violations.

Likewise, conditions conducive to successful negotiations include: a) that both parties have confidence of good faith by the other; in many cases this is known not to be true, in which case, no treaty should be signed without numerous caveats and conditions; b) ability to maintain secrecy if necessary and prudent; and c) that both side believe they will achieve a net gain for their interests.

Congress had full powers to enact treaties under the Articles of Confederation, and the States were likewise constrained, by the first three paragraphs of Article VI and by the first and next-to-last paragraphs of Article IX, as follows:

> **Article VI.** No State, without the consent of the United States, in Congress assembled, shall send any embassy to, or receive any embassy from, or enter into any conference, agreement, alliance or treaty with any king, prince or state; nor shall any person holding any office of profit or trust under the United States, or any of them, accept of any present, emolument, office, or title of any kind whatever, from any king, prince or foreign state; nor shall the United States, in Congress assembled, or any of them, grant any title of nobility.
>
> No two or more States shall enter into any treaty, confederation, or alliance whatever between them, without the consent of the United States, in Congress assembled, specify-

ing accurately the purposes for which the same is to be entered into, and how long it shall continue.

No State shall lay any impost or duties, which may interfere with any stipulations in treaties entered into by the United States, in Congress assembled, with any king, prince, or state, in pursuance of any treaties already proposed by Congress to the courts of France and Spain.

Article IX. The United States, in Congress assembled, shall have the sole and exclusive right and power of determining on peace and war, except in the cases mentioned in the sixth Article; of sending and receiving ambassadors; entering into treaties and alliances, provided that no treaty of commerce shall be made whereby the legislative power of the respective States shall be restrained from imposing such imposts and duties on foreigners, as their own people are subjected to, or from prohibiting the exportation or importation of any species of goods or commodities whatsoever; of establishing rules for deciding, in all cases, what captures on land or water shall be legal, and in what manner prizes taken by land or naval forces in the service of the United States shall be divided or appropriated; of granting letters of marque and reprisal in times of peace; appointing courts for the trial of piracies and felonies committed on the high seas; and establishing courts for receiving and determining finally appeals in all cases of capture; provided that no member of Congress shall be appointed a judge of any of said courts.

The United States, in Congress assembled, shall never engage in war, nor grant letters of marque and reprisal in time of peace, nor enter into any treaties or alliances, nor coin money, nor regulate the value thereof, nor ascertain the sums and expenses necessary for the defense and welfare of the United States, or any of them, nor emit bills, nor borrow money on the credit of the United States, nor appropriate money nor agree upon the number of vessels of war to be built or purchased, or the number of land or sea forces to be raised, nor appoint a commander-in-chief of the army or navy, unless nine States assent to the same, nor shall a question on any other point, except for adjourning from day to day, be determined, unless by the votes of a majority of the United States, in Congress assembled.

Congress' power of commercial treaties was limited by two exemptions which the states reserved to themselves: a) no commercial treaty negotiated by Congress could prevent the states from imposing duties on foreigners so long as they were equivalent to those imposed on Americans; and b) the states had powers to determine prohibitions on imports and exports. However, the states were prohibited from interfering with treaties under negotiation with France and Spain. The ratification of treaties required the concurrence of nine states (i.e., two-thirds of thirteen), same as most other major topics of government.

After the return of peace in 1781, there arose three major problems with the treaty provisions of the Articles. The first was the inability of Congress to conclude any type of commercial treaty with uniform regulations. A major factor was Great Britain's return to the Navigation Acts on 2 Jul 1783, when King George III issued an order in council regarding trade with the Americans. Britain's main fear was that the Americans would replace the British in the carrying trade in the western Mediterranean; in order to prevent it, Britain sought to weaken American commerce in general. Therefore, Britain imposed regulations designed to weaken the New England states: a) trade between America and the British West Indies could only be conducted in ships built, manned and navigated by British subjects; and b) American ships landing in British ports were permitted to bring in only items produced in states of which the ships' owners were citizens. The first of these nearly ruined the shipbuilding trade in the New England states, and greatly reduced the demand for its fisheries. The second greatly reduced the ability of the southern states to export their products, as none of them had a shipping industry. In fact, the weakness of the southern states with regard to shipping resulted in the British controlling nearly all trade in the southern states, even along the inland waterways. As a result, the states ended up attempting to raise revenues by imposing duties on imports from Europe. This led to a feud between New Jersey and New York, since nearly everything imported into New Jersey had to pass through the port of New York. Meanwhile, although there were demands for Congress to respond to the Navigation Acts, Congress could not get nine states to agree to give Congress suitable power to regulate commerce.

The second major problem was the issue of navigation rights on the Mississippi River. With British trade restricted, the New England states were very interested in obtaining a trade agreement with Spain. But, Spain was adamant in its rejection of American demands that any trade treaty allow American navigation on the river. The southern states wisely recognized that this was an essential point, and important for the future of the nation, since Spanish control of the Mississippi might tempt the western territories to align with Spain, thus causing all of the states to be surrounded by hostile powers. This dispute led to a north-south split among the states, which was not resolved until after the adoption of the Constitution.

The third major problem was that Great Britain refused to enter into any negotiations at all, on the grounds that since the thirteen states each retained powers over trade, there was little point in attempting to negotiate with Congress. It made little sense, from the British view, to conclude a treaty with Congress that could be violated by the states individually. Britain accordingly sought to deal with each state individually, albeit indirectly, by altering regulations that affected one or a few states; i.e., playing the states against one another and weakening all of them. This tempted some of the states to think about entering into commercial leagues among a few states, which were clearly prohibited by the Articles; but the general crisis of the Articles led to the adoption of the Constitution before any of these could materialize. It should be noted, however, that Congress did successfully ratify treaties with Holland (23 Jan 1783), Sweden (29 Jul 1783), and Prussia (17 May 1786).

The U. S. Constitution remedied these problems under several provisions. Two of these are found in Article I, Section 10, which imposes restrictions on State powers:

> No State shall enter into any treaty, alliance, or confederation...
>
> No State shall, without the consent of Congress, enter into any agreement or compact with another State, or with a foreign power...

The provisions under Article 1 make it clear that the federal government has a monopoly on the power to make treaties, and in fact, these two provisions were simply carried over from Article VI of the Articles of Confederation. The immediate consequence was to terminate any activities by the respective states to engage in independent agreements with foreign nations to the detriment of other states. In the long run, these provisions ensure that treaties are made by and with the United States as a uniform whole, preventing foreign nations from pitting one state or group of states against another, thus weakening all. It ensures that treaties are of a purely national character; a provision of this sort is necessary especially in compound-republic American system. It corrects one of the more notorious problems with the Articles of Confederation, as Hamilton notes in the *Federalist Papers* #22:

> The treaties of the United States, under the present Constitution [i.e., the Articles of Confederation], are liable to the infractions of thirteen different legislatures, and as many courts of final jurisdiction, acting under the authority of those legislatures. The faith, the reputation, the peace of the whole Union, are thus continually at the mercy of the prejudices, the passions, and the interests of every member of which it is composed. Is it possible that foreign nations can either respect or confide in such a government? Is it possible that the people of America will longer consent to trust their honor, their happiness, their safety, on so precarious a foundation?

Another is in Article II, Section 2, which grants certain powers to the Executive:

> He shall have power, by and with the advice and consent of the Senate, to make treaties, provided two thirds of the Senators present concur...

The provisions of Article II are designed to enhance the dignity of the power of making treaties but tempering it with a review and confirmation by the Senate. The President is the only officer in the American system that is elected, albeit indirectly, by the whole voting population; hence he has the dignity of representing the entire people. It served as a signal to foreigners that the President and his delegates, in his treaty-making capacity, were empowered to negotiate on behalf of the entire nation. But, it would be unwise to place the entire power in the hands of one person, so this same provision requires that two-thirds of the Senators present confirm, or ratify, and treaty presented to them. The Senate was chosen for this task instead of the House because the Senators, being elected to terms of six rather than two years, are more likely to have the maturity and experience from continuity in office to the implications of proposed treaties, especially prior to the 17th Amendment, when members of the Senate were appointed by state legislatures instead of being popularly elected. Note that the number of votes necessary to ratify a treaty is not fixed in the Constitution: it requires only that two-thirds of the Senators present ratify it, as opposed to the provision in the Articles, which required two-thirds of all the states. No doubt this was intended as a compromise between the high threshold of two-thirds of the states, which became a problem under the Articles, and the necessary reduction of risk to the interests of the states. In summary, it was unlikely in the founders' view that both the President and the Senate could make a serious mistake compromising the nation's health.

The next important power regarding treaties occurs in Article III, section 2, describing the powers of the Supreme Court:

> The judicial power shall extend to all cases, in law and equity, arising under this Constitution, the laws of the United States, and treaties made, or which shall be made...

Last, Article VI states the legal status of treaties made under the Constitution as compared to domestic laws:

> This Constitution, and the laws of the United States which shall be made in pursuance thereof; and all treaties made, or which shall be made, under the authority of the United States, shall be the supreme law of the land ...

The provisions of Articles III and VI provide confidence to foreign nations that the U. S. takes foreign relations seriously, since treaties are to have the force of law equally with the Constitution itself. But the Supreme Court still has a review authority, since clearly, in the American system, no treaty obtained by fraud, or one that contradicts the Constitution or one which reduces the liberties of the people can be valid, even if it was ratified. A treaty with any of these defects is voided the same as any law passed by Congress in violation of the constitution.

4 Division of Government Powers

James Madison mentions in the *Federalist Papers* #38 that putting all government powers in the hands of a few is inherently risky. He is referring to the fact that Congress was the only institution under the Articles of Confederation, a purely federal union organized under emergency conditions at the beginning of the Revolutionary War. He writes:

> Is it improper and unsafe to intermix the different powers of government in the same body of men? Congress, a single body of men, are the sole depositary of all the federal powers.

The issues that arose specifically from this feature are due partly to the nature of deliberative legislative bodies, and partly to the concentration of such a wide variety of powers in a few hands. (The lack of adequate powers will be the subject of later sections.) When an issue of importance came up, there was no mechanism within the Congress to address it, other than to debate or send to a committee for consideration, whereupon some resolution would be passed or defeated. It ended up being tasked with every type of problem, but was not ideally suited for those that required immediate attention or a definite determination. It had a nominal judicial function to render certain types of findings in disputes between the states, but no regular judicial function. It was also charged with managing the war effort and foreign relations, which sometimes require quick action.

But the larger risk was that all of these powers were lodged in one place. It was common knowledge among the leaders in the founding generation, from their knowledge of history and the observations of the great political theorists, that the best structure for both efficiency and protection of liberties was an inherent division of power within the government. Certain structures are inherently more efficient for certain objectives; but efficiency in government, carried too far, leads to a grasping for more powers to do more things efficiently; which in turn leads to a reduction in liberty as the government wields greater power. The best solution was to divide the government into branches with narrowly-defined powers, and let the mutual ambitions of each cancel each other out. While each branch has its legitimate sphere of power, the jealousy of the other branches keeps it within its proper limits.

One of the political theorists familiar to the founding generation was Charles de Montesquieu, who laid out his observations on divided government in his book *The Spirit of Laws* (1748). In Book IX, he points out the one nation on earth in which political liberty was the main objective of its constitution, that is to say, England. He proceeds to dissect the characteristics of the English system and how it promoted liberty in a general sense, writing in part:

> "6. Of the Constitution of England. In every government there are three sorts of power: the legislative; the executive in respect to things dependent on the law of nations; and the executive in regard to things that depend on the civil law.
>
> By virtue of the first, the prince or magistrate enacts temporary or perpetual laws, and amends or abrogates those that have already been enacted. By the second, he makes peace or war, sends or receives embassies, establishes the public security, and provides against invasions. By the third, he punishes criminals, or determines the disputes that arise between individuals. The latter we shall call the judiciary power, and the other simply the executive power of the state.
>
> The political liberty of the subject is a tranquility of mind arising from the opinion each person has of his safety. In order to have this liberty, it is requisite the government be constituted as one man need not be afraid of another.
>
> When the legislative and executive powers are united in the same person, or in the same body of magistrates, there can be no liberty; because apprehensions may arise, lest the same monarch or senate should enact tyrannical laws, to execute them in a tyrannical manner.
>
> Again, there is no liberty, if the judiciary power be not separated from the legislative and executive. Were it joined with the legislative, the life and liberty of the subject would be exposed to arbitrary control; for the judge would then be the legislator. Were it joined to the executive power, the judge might behave with violence and oppression.
>
> There would be an end to everything, were the same man or the same body, whether of the nobles or of the people, to exercise those three powers, that of enacting laws, that of executing the public resolutions, and of trying the causes of individuals.
>
> As in a country of liberty, every man who is supposed a free agent ought to be his own governor; the legislative power should reside in the whole people. But since this is impossible in large states, and in small ones is subject to many inconveniences, it is fit the people should transact by their representatives what they cannot transact by themselves."

The desirability of a system of functional branches was so evident to the delegates to the federal convention, that the first set of resolutions on a new plan, offered by Edmund Randolph on 29 May 1787, called for separate legislative, executive, and judicial departments. On the same day (the fourth of the convention), Charles Pinckney put forward a draft of a constitution; it also called for the same three separate branches. The next day, Nathaniel Gorham proposed, and his motion was carried, to postpone the discussion of Randolph's first proposition about the general enlargement of the Articles of Confederation, and consider directly a general revision of the government, in these words [3]:

> 1. That a union of the states merely federal will not accomplish the objects proposed by the Articles of Confederation – namely, common defense, security of liberty, and general welfare.
> 2. That no treaty of treaties among the whole or part of the states, as individual sovereignties, would be sufficient.
> 3. That a national government ought to be established, consisting of a supreme legislative, executive, and judiciary.

The story of the Convention is how the delegates conducted the debate about the exact character of the government; whether it should be entirely national or entirely federal, or a mix; how the members thereof should be chosen, and what the duration of their offices would be; but from this point forward, there was little debate about the necessity and utility of a government with the three familiar branches, instead of Congress alone.

5 Regulation of Foreign Commerce

Every successful nation that intends to remain independent requires the ability to regulate commercial activities with foreign nations. Historically, national governments have used the management of foreign trade for several purposes, including: a) generation of domestic revenue through imposition of duties and tariffs; b) restrictions or prohibitions on the exportation of certain items which would give competing nations an equal or superior military advantage (such as the U. S. Munitions List); c) regulation on the quality of articles that can be imported (such as consumer safety); d) as a means of promoting trade and closer relations with certain "favored nations"; e) outright prohibition on the importation of articles deemed dangerous (such as "illegal drugs"); f) restrictions on imports to protect domestic industry or stimulate domestic investment and production; g) management of boycotts of certain enemy nations; and h) indirect means to influence domestic policies in a foreign nation (such as restrictions on goods imported from nations that allow child labor). Nearly all of these have been tried in different times and to different degrees by every nation. While the first four are eminently practical and wise, the last two are useful only for making symbolic political statements. The remaining two are generally well-meaning but ineffective, and may sometimes be dangerous. Regardless of their wisdom or lack thereof, the main point is that every nation has a legitimate power to pass laws regulating foreign commerce as a means to advance or protect its interests. The consequences of an inability to do so can be illustrated by a review of the events in this area while the Articles of Confederation were in effect.

The states were prohibited by Article VI of the Articles of Confederation from contradicting any provision in any subsequent treaty then in negotiations with France and Spain. Also, they retained powers over the most important aspects of commercial treaties.

> **Article VI.** No State, without the consent of the United States, in Congress assembled, shall send any embassy to, or receive any embassy from, or enter into any conference, agreement, alliance or treaty with any king, prince or state; nor shall any person holding any office of profit or trust under the United States, or any of them, accept of any present, emolument, office, or title of any kind whatever, from any king, prince or foreign state; nor shall the United States, in Congress assembled, or any of them, grant any title of nobility.
>
> No two or more States shall enter into any treaty, confederation, or alliance whatever between them, without the consent of the United States, in Congress assembled, specifying accurately the purposes for which the same is to be entered into, and how long it shall continue.
>
> No State shall lay any impost or duties, which may interfere with any stipulations in treaties entered into by the United States, in Congress assembled, with any king, prince, or state, in pursuance of any treaties already proposed by Congress to the courts of France and Spain.

> **Article IX.** The United States, in Congress assembled, shall have the sole and exclusive right and power of determining on peace and war, except in the cases mentioned in the sixth Article; of sending and receiving ambassadors; entering into treaties and alliances, provided that no treaty of commerce shall be made whereby the legislative power of the respective States shall be restrained from imposing such imposts and duties on foreigners, as their own people are subjected to, or from prohibiting the exportation or importation of any species of goods or commodities whatsoever; of establishing rules for deciding, in all cases, what captures on land or water shall be legal, and in what manner prizes taken by land or naval forces in the service of the United States shall be divided or appropriated; of granting letters of marque and reprisal in times of peace; appointing courts for the trial of piracies and felonies committed on the high seas; and establishing courts for receiving and determining finally appeals in all cases of capture; provided that no member of Congress shall be appointed a judge of any of said courts.

By the ninth Article, the states had the power to regulate commerce by imposts and duties, so long as foreigners were treated equally with Americans, and also retained the power to prohibit exports or imports as they saw fit. During the war, the ability to make meaningful trade regulations in the states was limited. After the war, the states naturally proceeded to enact laws that they believed best advanced their interests. One of the main issues, as detailed in section 3, was how to respond to Great Britain's Navigation Acts. Recall that these were designed to limit America's ability to conduct trade with British territories; in fact was designed to prevent the Americans from gaining a significant share of the carrying trade in the western Mediterranean. Britain was able to capitalize on the weakness of each state, and the inability of Congress to form a united front in its alleged capacity to negotiate treaties for all thirteen states.

On 26 Apr 1784, Congress passed a resolution stipulating that all treaties were to be represented as an agreement with all thirteen states. But since the Articles of Confederation allowed the states to determine import and export rules as well as the setting of duties, which constituted important provisions in commercial treaties, Congress in effect was not able to force the states to abide by any treaties that were negotiated by the ambassadors. There was therefore little incentive for foreign nations to enter into treaties with the United States. Great Britain chose to adopt a policy of negotiating with each of the states separately; but any state that did so would be in violation of the Articles prohibiting separate treaties by states.

By the end of 1783, Britain's Navigation Acts had ruined much of the commercial activity in the states. The Virginia State legislature had passed a resolution in which they urged all the other states to grant Congress a power to respond to them. On 30 Apr 1784, Congress passed a resolution recommending to the states that it be given power for 15 years to develop and enforce regulations in response to the Navigation Acts. But the states never did agree to grant Congress this power, as there was considerable suspicion among the states that Congress would be unable or unwilling to develop rules that were equally fair to all the states. By Mar 1786, several states had granted some powers to Congress to either regulate trade or impose a revenue duty, but they were inconsistent and could not be used to justify a modification to the Articles. All Congress could do was to issue another request for consideration of the initial resolution.

Meanwhile, a general authority lacking in Congress, the states did as they believed best for themselves. In Jan 1785, New York imposed a two-fold duty on goods arriving in British ships, as retaliation for the Navigation Acts. These were passed onto the residents of New Jersey, since they imported their goods from New York. The residents of New Jersey were thus forced to pay a duty to New York, without any corresponding advantage to their treasury. By the spring of 1785, merchants in Massachusetts organized a boycott of all British-owned businesses in the state. In Jul 1785, Massachusetts prohibited exports carried on British ships, levied a tonnage duty, and imposed high duties on certain foreign goods in order to protect domestic manufacturers. New Hampshire and Rhode Island passed nearly identical laws a week or two later. Connecticut then opened its ports to British ships, and imposed a tax on imports from Massachusetts. In Sep 1785, Pennsylvania passed a law imposing duties on 70 items, especially iron manufactures, and imposed a tonnage duty on the ships of any nation that did not have a commercial treaty with Congress. Pennsylvania also passed laws against trade with Delaware and New Jersey. As states levied duties on imports, the trade was simply carried to ports in other states, negating the alleged benefits of a revenue duty. New York imposed heavy duties on imports from Connecticut and New Jersey, including a requirement that every shipment, no matter how small, be obliged to clear customs upon entering any port in New York. Connecticut responded with a boycott on commerce with New York. New Jersey retaliated by imposing a large tax on a lighthouse owned by New York, but sitting on an island off the coast of New Jersey. Most of the states violated the most-favored-nation provisions of the treaties with Holland and France. In other words, America was in the midst of a trade war among the states, and in violation of agreements with other nations. Fortunately, the Convention of 1787 occurred before any shooting wars between the states, and the Constitution that resulted resolved the commercial trade issues.

The lack of requisite powers over trade in the Articles of Confederation was so obvious to the delegates at the Convention, that there was little argument over giving them generally to the federal government. Ultimately, the U. S. Constitution as devised at the Convention addressed all these difficulties by four methods. First, in regard to treaties in general, the Executive was given power to negotiate them, but they require ratification by the Senate, as detailed in section 3 (Article 1, Section 10; Article 2). Second, Congress was given general legislative power over foreign trade not covered by treaty (Article 1, Section 8). Third, Congress was given legislative power to regulate trade between the states and the Indian tribes (Article 1, Section 8) with the caveats per Article 1, Section 9. Fourth, the states are prohibited from imposing import and export levies except for the costs of inspection, and any excess revenue is to be devoted to the United States (Article 1, Section 10). The relevant texts are:

Article 1, Section 8, First and Third Clauses:

> The Congress shall have Power To lay and collect Taxes, Duties, Imposts and Excises, to pay the Debts and provide for the common Defense and general Welfare of the United States; but all Duties, Imposts and Excises shall be uniform throughout the United States;
>
> To regulate Commerce with foreign Nations, and among the several States, and with the Indian Tribes;

Article 1, Section 9, Fifth and Sixth Clauses:

> No Tax or Duty shall be laid on Articles exported from any State.
>
> No Preference shall be given by any Regulation of Commerce or Revenue to the Ports of one State over those of another: nor shall Vessels bound to, or from, one State, be obliged to enter, clear, or pay Duties in another.

Article 1, Section 10:

> No State shall enter into any Treaty, Alliance, or Confederation; grant Letters of Marque and Reprisal; coin Money; emit Bills of Credit; make any Thing but gold and silver Coin a Tender in Payment of Debts; pass any Bill of Attainder, ex post facto Law, or Law impairing the Obligation of Contracts, or grant any Title of Nobility.
>
> No State shall, without the Consent of the Congress, lay any Imposts or Duties on Imports or Exports, except what may be absolutely necessary for executing its inspection Laws: and the net Produce of all Duties and Imposts, laid by any State on Imports or Exports, shall be for the Use of the Treasury of the United States; and all such Laws shall be subject to the Revision and Control of the Congress.
>
> No State shall, without the Consent of Congress, lay any duty of Tonnage, keep Troops, or Ships of War in time of Peace, enter into any Agreement or Compact with another State, or with a foreign Power, or engage in War, unless actually invaded, or in such imminent Danger as will not admit of delay.

6 Disputes Between States

Before reviewing how the Articles of Confederation operated with respect to territorial issues, it is first necessary to recall that the states retained land claims under the ancient colonial English charters. The charters of Massachusetts and Connecticut extended ostensibly all the way to the western end of the continent. The colony of New York had been established during the reign of Charles II; as a result, Massachusetts and Connecticut exempted that area, but continued to claim all the lands to the west at their respective latitudes. Massachusetts also held the territory of what is now the state of Maine. During the period from its establishment to the Revolution, the colony of New York gradually gained influence over the Iroquois Indians and the other tribes that had accepted the nominal sovereignty of the Iroquois. Consequently, New York claimed all the land occupied by these tribes, which extended westward nearly to what is now Michigan. After the Spanish gained control of the southwest it was recognized that these claims now extended only to the Mississippi River.

The original charters of Virginia, North Carolina, and Georgia also extended to the western sea, although by the time of the Revolution was valid only to the Mississippi River given the Spanish occupation of the southwest. South Carolina likewise had some claims to territory in the west, but was not clearly specified.

The claims of Virginia were further enhanced by the fact that two earlier expeditions had led to the conquest of some western territory. In 1774, after Parliament had passed the Quebec Act, Lord Dunmore, governor of Virginia, called out a large number of settlers in western part of the colony to suppress an Indian uprising against some of the settlers along the Ohio River. In November of that year, this force defeated the Shawnees at Point Pleasant and established peace with the Shawnees and their allies. Virginia then exerted indirect control over the Ohio Valley even before the Revolution; this action, known in history as Lord Dunmore's War, effectively nullified the British Quebec Act since the colonial settlers controlled it before the British could organize it directly under a government set up by Parliament. A second action during the Revolution furthered Virginia's claims. An expedition led by George Rodgers Clarke began a campaign in Jun 1778 to defeat the British and their Indian allies along the Mississippi and Ohio Rivers. By the end of July, they had taken Cahokia and Kaskaskia. By Feb 1779, Clarke had taken Vincennes; this gave Virginia physical control of all the territory along the Ohio River as far as present-day Detroit and westward to present day St. Louis.

The powers given to Congress under the Articles of Confederation to determine territorial questions between the states was contained in the second and third paragraphs of Article IX:

> The United States, in Congress assembled, shall also be the last resort on appeal, in all disputes and differences now subsisting, or that hereafter may arise between two or more States concerning boundary, jurisdiction, or any other cause whatever; which authority shall always be exercised in the manner following: Whenever the legislative or executive authority, or lawful agent of any State in controversy with another, shall present a petition to Congress, stating the matter in question, and praying for a hearing, notice thereof shall be given by order of Congress to the legislative or executive authority of the other State in controversy, and a day assigned for the appearance of the parties by their lawful agents, who shall then be directed to appoint, by joint consent, commissioners or judges to constitute a court for hearing and determining the matter in question; but if they can not agree, Congress shall name three persons out of each of the United States, and from the list of such persons each party shall alternately strike out one, the petitioners beginning, until the number shall be reduced to thirteen; and from that number not less than seven, nor more than nine names, as Congress shall direct, shall, in the presence of Congress, be drawn out by lot, and the persons whose names shall be so drawn, or any five of them, shall be commissioners or judges, to hear and finally determine the controversy, so always as a major part of the judges who shall hear the cause shall agree in the determination; and if either party shall neglect to attend at the day appointed, without

> showing reasons which Congress judge sufficient, or being present, shall refuse to strike, the Congress shall proceed to nominate three persons out of each State, and the secretary of Congress shall strike in behalf of such party absent or refusing; and the judgment and sentence of the court, to be appointed in the manner before prescribed, shall be final and conclusive; and if any of the parties shall refuse to submit to the authority of such court, or to appear or defend their claim or cause, the court shall, nevertheless proceed to pronounce sentence or judgment, which shall in like manner be final and decisive; the judgment or sentence and other proceedings being in either case transmitted to Congress, and lodged among the acts of Congress for the security of the parties concerned; provided, that every commissioner, before he sits in judgment, shall take an oath, to be administered by one of the judges of the supreme or superior court of the State where the cause shall be tried, "well and truly to hear and determine the matter in question, according to the best of his judgment without favor, affection, or hope of reward." Provided, also, that no State shall be deprived of territory for the benefit of the United States.
>
> All controversies concerning the private right of soil claimed under different grants of two or more States, whose jurisdictions, as they may respect such lands, and the States which passed such grants, are adjusted, the said grants or either of them being at the same time claimed to have originated antecedent to such settlement of jurisdiction, shall, on the petition of either party to the Congress of the United States, be finally determined, as near as may be, in the same manner as is before prescribed for deciding disputes respecting territorial jurisdiction between the different States.

As seen by this provision, the method of resolution was to be a determination by a special court appointed under the supervision of Congress. These judges, or commissioners, would then be tasked with formulating a decision on any territorial disputes between states. This presented three problems. First, it was not particularly efficient, as each case was to be handled in isolation from every other. It was probably not a feasible system for resolving large-scale competing territorial claims. Secondly, there was no provision for conflicts within a state in which one part wished to separate from the other. Third, there was no provision by which additional states could be added to the Confederation out of any western lands.

The legislature and delegates to Congress from the state of Maryland performed a very useful service to the eventual union by helping to resolve the first of these defects. The Articles were agreed to and recommended to the states on 15 Nov 1777, and were ratified by eight states on 9 Jul 1778. But, unlike our Constitution, which could be activated through ratification by any nine of the thirteen states, the Articles required all the states to ratify it before it could go into effect. The legislature in Maryland, recognizing the difficulties that would ensue over the colonial charters, passed a resolution on 15 Dec 1778 stating their refusal to consider ratification of the Articles until all the states had conveyed their land claims to Congress. Maryland thus wisely made the activation of the Confederation dependent upon cession of all the competing claims to the western lands.

The states responded to Maryland's challenge in a most commendable way. On 19 Apr 1779, New York conceded that Congress should have power to determine its western boundary. In Oct 1780, Connecticut ceded its western claims except for a small slice of territory just east of what is now Cleveland. Virginia, who had not only strong claims to western lands, but was actually in control of a great deal of it, magnanimously ceded its claims to Congress on 2 Jan 1781. Since the claim of Massachusetts was weak, and the territories claimed by North Carolina and Georgia were mostly still wilderness, Maryland authorized its delegation to ratify the Articles on 30 Jan 1781. Maryland, the final state to ratify, did so on 1 Mar 1781, and Congress officially assumed authority under the Articles on 2 Mar 1781.

The provision contained in the Articles was used once, in the long-standing feud between Pennsylvania and Connecticut regarding the Wyoming Valley, situated in Pennsylvania just north of what is now Scranton. Although contained entirely within Pennsylvania, the area had been settled by settlers from

Connecticut, and was claimed by that state. A special court convened under the Articles settled this dispute in a ruling on 30 Dec 1782, which was accepted by both sides.

But the power conveyed under the Articles proved insufficient to deal with disputes within the states. The Maine district of Massachusetts desired to break away and form an independent state. There had been a long-running feud between New Hampshire and New York regarding the territory now known as Vermont. This district, although belonging in strictness to New York, desired independence before the Revolution. It declared itself independent on 15 Jan 1777, calling itself "New Connecticut", and petitioned for entry into Congress as a fourteenth state. The name was changed on 8 Jul 1777 to "Vermont". The delegation from New York successfully prevented this request from coming before Congress, and it remained unresolved until Vermont formally seceded from New York on 4 Jul 1786.

The case of North Carolina is unique. In Jun 1784, North Carolina ceded its western claims to Congress on the condition that Congress would have two years to decide how to allocate it. But the settlers in that area, beset by problems with Indians, were refused help from both Congress and North Carolina, and accordingly set up their own state, named Franklin in 1786. This led to a low-level civil war in this region, now the state of Tennessee, until 1788, when it was rejoined to North Carolina. The important point here is that Congress was too weak to resolve the conflict either way.

Last, we must take notice of the Northwest Ordinance of 13 Jul 1787, passed by Congress to determine the conditions of settlement and eventual statehood for all the lands in the west that had been ceded to Congress. It was an admirable law, providing an excellent method of settlement, governance as a territory, a prohibition of slavery, and guarantees of certain civil rights. It superseded an earlier one of 28 Jun 1786, which contained the great defect of permitting slavery in the west. While the Northwest Ordinance proved to be an excellent expedient, it was done without outside any specific authority in the Articles. As a result, Congress simply treated this vast territory as a traditional English folk land, in which it is divided and administered ad-hoc as the population increases. Congress passed it of necessity, as the population was growing. But the fact that it had no authority to exercise any sovereign authority of this nature only proved the general deficiency of the Articles, for the powers granted would have to be violated as circumstances arose; that could only lead to quarrels and instability among the states.

The requisite power over territory, lacking in the Articles, was granted to Congress under the federal Constitution in Article IV, Section 3:

> **Article IV, Section 3.** New States may be admitted by the Congress into this Union; but no new State shall be formed or erected within the Jurisdiction of any other State; nor any State be formed by the Junction of two or more States, or parts of States, without the Consent of the Legislatures of the States concerned as well as of the Congress.
>
> The Congress shall have Power to dispose of and make all needful Rules and Regulations respecting the Territory or other Property belonging to the United States; and nothing in this Constitution shall be so construed as to Prejudice any Claims of the United States, or of any particular State.

7 Division of Legislative Power Among the States

A republican political system is one in which a large fraction of the general population exerts power indirectly through representatives of their choice. The great attraction of a republic is that those representatives will, over the long run, reflect the views of a majority of the people, but at the same time, will tend to attenuate excessive demands by the public in times of difficulty or uncertainty. A republic is therefore somewhere in the center of the styles of political organization. At one end are the forms in which power is concentrated in a few people. Among these are: a) a dictatorship or absolute monarchy, in which one person has nearly all the power; b) a monarchy and hereditary nobility composed of a small but stable number of people; and c) ruling oligarchies, in which power is assumed by a small number of people who are not members of a permanent class. At the other extreme is pure democracy, in which every eligible person has a direct voice in public affairs.

There are two main classes of systems that can be correctly called republics. In the first type, a purely federative style, the members of the federation are actually subordinate political divisions. Each political subdivision chooses delegates to represent it at an upper political level. In the second type, the general public chooses delegates to the top political level in their capacity as individuals. A mixture of these prevailed under the Articles of Confederation: the eligible voting public, in their capacity as individuals, chose delegates to their state legislatures; those state legislators in turn chose delegates to Congress. In Congress, each state had an equal vote. At the state level then, it was of the second type of republic, but at the national level, was purely federative. The provision in the Articles of Confederation is found in the first portion of Article V:

> **Article V.** For the more convenient management of the general interests of the United States, delegates shall be annually appointed in such manner as the legislature of each State shall direct, to meet in Congress on the first Monday in November, in every year, with a power reserved to each State to recall its delegates, or any of them, at any time within the year, and to send others in their stead for the remainder of the year.
>
> No State shall be represented in Congress by less than two, nor by more than seven members; and no person shall be capable of being a delegate for more than three years in any term of six years; nor shall any person, being a delegate, be capable of holding any office under the United States, for which he, or another for his benefit, receives any salary, fees or emolument of any kind.
>
> Each State shall maintain its own delegates in a meeting of the States, and while they act as members of the committee of the States.
>
> In determining questions in the United States, in Congress assembled, each State shall have one vote.

It is clear that such a system is republican in the sense that the public chose representatives at the state level who in turn represented the state in Congress. The people thus had an indirect choice in who represented them in Congress. This is a satisfactory system, because ultimately the people are able to determine the makeup of Congress, although the process is one step removed from direct election. But, if we recall the basic premise of a republic, that the views of a majority of the people will usually prevail, it is equally clear that a purely federative system such s the Articles can maintain this premise only if each state has approximately the same population. Such was not the case with the original thirteen states. As Hamilton pointed out in the *Federalist Papers* #22, seven states (Delaware, Georgia, Maryland, New Hampshire, New Jersey, Rhode Island, and South Carolina) could constitute a majority of votes in Congress, yet their combined population was not more than a third of the entire population. On the face of it, there was no remedy for this problem other than the hope that these states would have such diverse interests that they would not combine together, thus requiring that some other combination of states vote one way or the other, and that by this means, opinions shared by of a majority of the population could be expressed. It is true that these seven states rarely agreed, so little harm was done, but it was accidental, not by virtue of the system.

The Articles did contain one other provision that tended to mitigate this problem somewhat, at least at first glance. It is found in the second-to-last paragraph of Article IX:

> The United States, in Congress assembled, shall never engage in war, nor grant letters of marque and reprisal in time of peace, nor enter into any treaties or alliances, nor coin money, nor regulate the value thereof, nor ascertain the sums and expenses necessary for the defense and welfare of the United States, or any of them, nor emit bills, nor borrow money on the credit of the United States, nor appropriate money nor agree upon the number of vessels of war to be built or purchased, or the number of land or sea forces to be raised, nor appoint a commander-in-chief of the army or navy, unless nine States assent to the same, nor shall a question on any other point, except for adjourning from day to

> day, be determined, unless by the votes of a majority of the United States, in Congress assembled.

As seen here, concurrence of nine of the thirteen states was required to enact legislation on the important issues, such as treaties, coining money and issuing currency, and military expenditures. In this way, the defect mentioned earlier was avoided: any nine states, including the seven whose population totaled only one-third, would likely constitute a majority of the people. Secondly, history shows that requiring a supermajority on important issues having a great impact on the whole is an excellent idea. But the wide diversity of state populations, the provincial outlook of many states, and the nine-of-thirteen rule sometimes led to a pernicious defect in the operation of the Articles when taken together. For, if nine states were required to pass significant legislation, a combination of five states, whose combined population may total only 20% of the entire American population, could prevent necessary legislation from being passed – rule by the minority, contrary to the basic goal of a republic. It was similar to, but not quite as bad as the Polish system, which required unanimity on every issue.

Two examples illustrate the problem. In 1784, Congress was deprived of a quorum to do business from 11 Aug to 30 Nov because three New England states decided not to attend. An even worse example was a vote taken on 23 Apr 1784 regarding the administration of western lands. The issue was whether slavery would be allowed in those territories. Because not all the states were present this vote required 7 of 10 states to retain a previous resolution that prohibited slavery. New Jersey's lone delegate refused to vote, and the delegation from North Carolina was divided. So, the previous resolution was repealed by the votes of three states: Virginia, South Carolina, and Maryland; thus three states, with a combined population very much in the minority compared to the whole, was able to re-institute slavery in all the western territories. Fortunately, this act of 1784 was superseded by the Northwest Ordinance of 13 Jul 1787.

The U. S. Constitution as proposed in 1787 preserved the excellent feature of a two-thirds requirement to confirm treaties in the Senate, which represented the states in their sovereign capacity. But to avoid the main representative defect discussed here, most other legislation was to be decided by a simple majority in both branches of Congress: the House, which represents the people through their directly-elected representatives, and the Senate representing the states. In this way, the sentiments of a majority of the people, through representation in the House, are always guaranteed a voice in every vote. These provisions lay out a workable framework by cannot address the case wherein the interests of the members of Congress diverge from the interests of the people; there is no cure for that except elections.

8 Mutual Guarantee between States and Federal Government

One of the problems of the Articles of Confederation is that it contained no implicit or explicit guarantee that the states would remain qualified to be in the Confederacy. It was conceivable that a state could end up with a form of state government unsuitable for participation in a federal system. While Article VI addressed instances where Congress could respond if a state was invaded by Indians or other nations, and Article IX addressed how disputes between states were to be handled, neither of them addressed the problem of an internal rebellion that affected the state constitution. In short, every state was left at risk to handle any internal violence, and could expect no assistance from other states or from Congress.

Hamilton addressed this problem, namely the inability of Congress under the Articles to take action to preserve a state government, in the *Federalist Papers* #21:

> The want of a mutual guaranty of the State governments is another capital imperfection in the federal plan. There is nothing of this kind declared in the articles that compose it; and to imply a tacit guaranty from considerations of utility, would be a still more flagrant departure from the clause which has been mentioned, than to imply a tacit power of coercion from the like considerations. The want of a guaranty, though it might in its consequences endanger the Union, does not so immediately attack its existence as the want of a constitutional sanction to its laws.

> Without a guaranty the assistance to be derived from the Union in repelling those domestic dangers which may sometimes threaten the existence of the State constitutions, must be renounced. Usurpation may rear its crest in each State, and trample upon the liberties of the people, while the national government could legally do nothing more than behold its encroachments with indignation and regret. A successful faction may erect a tyranny on the ruins of order and law, while no succor could constitutionally be afforded by the Union to the friends and supporters of the government. The tempestuous situation from which Massachusetts has scarcely emerged, evinces that dangers of this kind are not merely speculative. Who can determine what might have been the issue of her late convulsions, if the malcontents had been headed by a Caesar or by a Cromwell? Who can predict what effect a despotism, established in Massachusetts, would have upon the liberties of New Hampshire or Rhode Island, of Connecticut or New York?

Hamilton is alluding here to Shays' rebellion, a tax revolt in Massachusetts that had just concluded in Feb 1787. It was not necessary for Hamilton to mention those names and battles directly, as they were fresh in the mind of the readers of the *Federalist Papers* essays. But if we are to understand Hamilton's argument, it is helpful for us to review Shay's Rebellion, and how it influenced the movement toward a replacement of the Articles with the U. S. Constitution. As mentioned in section 3, an economic depression occurred after the war owing to Britain's enforcement of its Navigation Acts coupled with Congress' inability to respond accordingly. Meanwhile, the states passed their own laws, some of which negatively affected neighboring states. But the shortage of ready money and the seizure of farms in lieu of unpaid taxes continued in Massachusetts, which led to the following events.

The people of Massachusetts, desperate for money and unable to obtain any satisfaction from the state legislature, began to call conventions in prominent towns to discuss what should be done about economic conditions. One of the most influential of these was convened at Hatfield (Hampshire County, MA) on 22 Aug 1786; and others occurred about same time in Worcester, Middlesex, Bristol, Lenox, and Berkshire. Mainly these were attended by people who had seen their farms seized for payment of taxes or debt; or who had prosperous farms but were unable to sell their produce because of the lack of circulating medium. Hard money was in short supply, due partly to Britain's policies but also to the foolishness of the people, who continued to buy luxuries they could not afford. The convention at Hatfield formulated a petition of 25 articles summarizing their complaints: a) the state Senate was derelict in its duty, and ought to be abolished; b) the Court of Common Pleas should be abolished; c) there were too many lawyers in the state prospering from the numerous debt-related lawsuits; d) import duties and excise taxes devoted to paying Massachusetts' portion of the requisitions by Congress and payments to the army was denounced; e) the method of apportioning taxes declared to be unfair; and f) an urgent need for paper money. The Court of Common Pleas was an object of hatred, because distress sales and seizures for non-payment of debt were adjudicated there. The resolutions adopted at Hatfield were imitated in other conventions, and large groups of men decided to take action by forming mobs and disrupting court proceedings in the various counties in Massachusetts.

The Court of Common Pleas at Northampton, MA was disrupted on 29 Aug 1786 by a mob of 1,500 armed men, who had occupied the court before the judges arrived. This encouraged other groups to do the same in other towns. On 5 Sep, the Court of Common Pleas at Worcester, MA was also disrupted by an armed mob. The local militia sided with the mob, and the court was adjourned. Likewise, the Courts of Common Pleas at Concord and Great Barrington, MA were disrupted by armed mobs on 12 Sep 1786. At Great Barrington, the mob broke into the jail and set the prisoners free, and intimidated three of the four judges to sign papers stating they would not exercise their duties until the complaints of the people had been addressed by the legislature. The Supreme Court of Massachusetts was scheduled to open on 19 Sep 1786 at Springfield. In light of the disruptions of the past few weeks, Governor Bowdoin ordered General Shepard and his militia to occupy the courthouse beforehand in order to ensure that it could do business. But the militia was met by a group of rebels, who called themselves The Regulators, led by Daniel Shays, who had served as a captain during the war. There was a tense standoff between the Regulators and the militia, and the court adjourned 21 Sep 1786 when it could not do business owing to a lack of jurors.

At the end of September, Shays heard a rumor that the Massachusetts Supreme Court was not going to convene at Great Barrington as scheduled. But he believed this to be a ruse, and marched his "Regulators" there and occupied the town. But when they got there, they found the court was in fact to sit at Boston. Disappointed, the rebels started a riot, searched some houses, and ran a few government officials out of town. The Court convened without incident at Boston on 27 Sep 1786.

Three more conventions were held in Worcester, Boston, and Middlesex, MA in early Oct 1786 by people angry about the state of the economy and the lawsuits over debt. Each of them filed petitions with the state legislature. The main complaints were about the various courts (General Sessions of the Peace, Common Pleas, Probate, and General), the lack of money, and the manner in which revenues from the import duties and excise taxes were appropriated. The state legislature in Massachusetts passed legislation on 18 Nov 1786 which they believed addressed the concerns expressed by the petitions presented by the three conventions in Middlesex, Boston, and Worcester in October. But the remedies suggested by the legislature proved to be the spark that set off Shays' Rebellion.

The Court of General Sessions was prevented from sitting at Worcester, MA on 21 Nov 1786 due to the court being occupied by a band of armed men. On 23 Nov 1786, a convention assembled at Worcester read the resolutions adopted by the legislature of Massachusetts in response to the petitions of Oct 1786. These were condemned as the work of people out of touch with the common people. The members of the legislature were accused of being men of affluence, of never having experienced being sued for non-payment of debts or having their property seized for inability to pay the high property taxes (all of which was true). The convention likewise condemned the interference with the courts, but to no avail. In the next few weeks, a large group of rebels from Bristol, Worcester, Hampshire, and Middlesex met at Middlesex, despite a previous pledge to prominent people of Middlesex that they would not assemble.

On 2 Dec 1786, a large band of rebels under Shays assembled at Worcester, despite freezing cold and deep snow. He imposed on residents of the town to house his men, which provoked many people in the state against him when the news got out. The militia was called out on 4 Dec 1786 in Boston to defend the city against an attack by Shays' Regulators, to be commanded by General Lincoln. Shays decided to retreat from Worcester rather than attack Boston. By mid-December, Governor Bowdoin decided to raise a militia to deal with Shays, but was careful to select militiamen who did not reside in the same areas as Shays' men. This was done to prevent a situation in which friends and neighbors would fight each other in the fields. A force of 4,400 was called up: 500 from Essex, 700 from Suffolk, 800 from Middlesex, 1,200 from Hampshire, and 1,200 from Worcester. The contingents from Suffolk and Essex were to be stationed in Boston; those from Hampshire to be stationed in Springfield, and the men from Worcester to be stationed at the eastern part of the county. They were enlisted for 30 days starting from 18 Jan 1787. General Lincoln was in overall command, assisted by Generals Tupper, Shepard, and Patterson. But it was soon discovered that there was no money in the treasury to pay them, and the legislature was out of session. Even if it were called in, any tax levied would be too late to make timely payment to the soldiers. A group of wealthy Boston businessmen volunteered to fund the militia.

Shays marched his men to Springfield at the end of January 1787, planning to capture the supplies at the arsenal there by defeating Shepard before Lincoln could arrive from Worcester. His men were split into three groups commanded by Luke Day, Eli Parsons, and Shays himself. Shepard had already arranged his troops on the heights surrounding the town. On the 24th, Shays ordered Day to attack on the 25th, but Day, determined to gain all the glory for himself, sent a message back to Shays informing him that he would not attack until the 26th. But Day's message to Shays was intercepted and sent to Lincoln. Shays attacked Shepard on the 26th, but his inexperienced men panicked after a few casualties, and most of his men retreated to Ludlow. On the 26th, Shays' men met with Parsons at Chicopee, and found that 200 had deserted. Parsons escaped over the border to New Hampshire and then to New York while Shays remained in Springfield with a small force. On the 27th, Lincoln arrived in Springfield, defeated Shays in a skirmish, and Shays' army retreated to and pillaged S. Hadley, then continued to Amherst. Lincoln pursued Shays as far as Amherst on the 28th, but Shays had by that time moved to Pelham and took up a strong position in the hills.

Meanwhile, a group of rebels under Hubbard had assembled at W. Stockbridge; their plan was to aid Shays by diverting the army to several places at once. However, Hubbard was defeated by General Patterson and was captured. Hubbard's men retreated, but were pursued and defeated by Patterson at Adams and Williamstown. Lincoln pursued Shays' army for several days in early February, and Shays was captured on 5 Feb 1787. With Shays' men now scattered, Lincoln was confident that the revolt was over; he marched to Pittsfield via Amherst, Hadley, Chesterfield, Partridgefield, and Worthington, and ordered Shepard to meet him there. But Shays' ally, Eli Parsons, having escaped capture in Massachusetts, traveled from town to town in Vermont and New York, successfully raising another army to oppose Lincoln. On 26 Feb 1787 Parson's rebel force from New York, commanded by Hamlin, invaded Stockbridge, plundered it, and took some prominent men as hostages. The militia at Sheffield and Great Barrington were called out, and they marched around trying to find Hamlin. They stumbled across him by accident at Springfield. They defeated Hamlin and captured him, and this ended Shays' Rebellion. Hamlin had missed a golden opportunity; if he had attacked a few days earlier, he would have been unopposed, since the militia's enlistments had run out on the 21st, and for a few days, Lincoln only had 30 men in the field.

It is easy to see that a victory by Shays would have produced a very serious situation: at minimum, a state would have been held hostage to the demands of the leaders of an armed revolt. Suppose Shays had decided to set up a monarchy or a dictatorship? Clearly Massachusetts would no longer be eligible for membership in the Confederation, and the entire system could have collapsed over that issue. It is important to recall that all during this period, Congress was aware of these events, but took no action. It was unwilling or unable to act in the interest of preserving the confederation upon which its existence was founded. Shay's revolt was in fact one of the two primary factors that led to the states' assent to the Constitutional Convention in 1787 (the other was inability to raise revenue).

There was also a currency revolt in Rhode Island in 1786 which caused considerable political distress, symptomatic of the instability that could occur in the states due to poor policies. The details will be covered in section 10; for our purposes here, it is important to note that the government of Rhode Island actually passed a requirement that the people pledge an oath to accept the state paper currency at par or else they would lose the right to vote (among other penalties). This was a most un-republican development; one which Congress under the Articles could not address.

The general problem of ensuring state stability was resolved by the adoption of a provision in the U. S. Constitution granting power to the federal government to suppress revolts directly. It is in effect a guarantee by all the states that none of them could be overthrown by a domestic insurrection. It is found in the fourth section of Article IV:

> **Article IV, Section 4.** The United States shall guarantee to every State in this Union a Republican Form of Government, and shall protect each of them against Invasion; and on Application of the Legislature, or of the Executive (when the Legislature cannot be convened) against domestic Violence.

This provision does not prevent the people of a state from changing their constitution by peaceful means, but only gives power to the federal government to act when violent means are attempted. However, in order to maintain the consistency of the union, every state is also required to maintain a republican form of government. Section 4 above discussed the general requirement for republican governments.

9 Necessary Revenues

Every viable government must possess the means to fulfill its duties and to keep its promises. A national or federal government, whether it is a republic, aristocracy, or some other, naturally has the duty to manage the nation's defenses, engage in diplomacy, manage trade relations, and maintain a judicial system; all these must be paid for in some way or another. In the American system, the states likewise exercise many powers for which considerable revenue is required, and so on down to the local level. Our early history instructs us on one thing in particular with regard to finances: a government must have the financial means to execute its respective powers and duties. It cannot, in the long run, depend on another level of government for money; it will become captive to the interests and prejudices of the politicians and bureaucrats within the other government entity. A prime example of this principle is contained in the most serious defect of the Articles of Confederation: Congress, as the only federal power, was dependent entirely on the states for revenue. This disconnect caused a radical divergence between need and ability: Congress' needs were great, even after the war, but the states, attending to their own problems, soon found ready excuses not to meet their financial obligations to Congress. By the mid-1780's, Congress had neither credit nor credibility, and the thinkers of that time realized that Congress' lack of a revenue stream caused many other problems. If the states were to stay together, a more consistent federal government would be required, and that government must have its own independent revenue source.

At the beginning of the Revolutionary War, Congress assumed emergency powers to manage the war effort. Although the Articles of Confederation were proposed and debated from 1776 to 1778, they did not actually go into operation until the spring of 1781. Congress attempted to fund the war effort prior to the implementation of the Articles by three means: borrowing, issuing its own currency, and asking requisitions from the states. The first two will form the subject of section 10, but the last will be considered here since it emulates so closely the provision in Article VIII of the Confederation:

> **Article VIII.** All charges of war, and all other expenses that shall be incurred for the common defense or general welfare, and allowed by the United States, in Congress assembled, shall be defrayed out of a common treasury, which shall be supplied by the several States, in proportion to the value of all land within each State, granted to, or surveyed for, any person, as such land and the buildings and improvements thereon shall be estimated according to such mode as the United States in Congress assembled, shall from time to time direct and appoint. The taxes for paying that proportion shall be laid and levied by the authority and direction of the legislatures of the several States, within the time agreed upon by the United States, in Congress assembled.

Under this system, Congress allocated to each state a requisition, based on an estimate of the total value of land and buildings. The state was obligated to raise this sum by internal taxation, which was then to be forwarded to Congress. The system never worked as envisioned, and the proof of it lies in these facts. In the following, all amounts have been converted to Spanish milled dollars, a coin in common use at the time, which was reckoned at 386.7 grains of pure silver.

First, consider requisitions issued by Congress prior to the ratification of the Articles of Confederation:

> 22 Nov 1777: Congress issued a recommendation that the states raise SM$5,000,000, apportioned according to population, to be paid in quarterly installments starting 1 Jan 1778 to pay the expenses for 1778.
>
> 5 Jan 1779: Congress issued a requisition to the states for SM$15,000,000 for 1779. Congress passed additional resolutions urging the states to pay it on 7 Oct 1779 and 18 Mar 1780.
>
> 19 May 1779: Congress requisitioned SM$45,000,000 from the states.

None of the above requisitions were ever paid. In fairness to the states, Congress was not acting under any constitutional authority, only as an emergency institution.

But the requisition system under the Articles, in which the states were obligated by the compact, did not fare much better:

> 30 Oct 1781: Congress issued its first requisition to the states under the Articles of Confederation for SM$8,000,000.

4 Sep 1782: Congress requisitioned SM$1,200,000 from the states, but did not require it be paid directly to Congress. The states were to use the revenue to pay down interest in their own states.

16 Oct 1782: Congress requisitioned another SM$2,000,000 from the states.

18 Apr 1783: A standing annual requisition of SM$1,500,000 was requested as part of resolution to give Congress the power to levy import duties.

27 Apr 1784: Of the SM$8,000,000 requisitioned on 30 Oct 1781, SM$1,436,511 had been received from the states. The states were credited with having paid the SM$1,200,000 requisitioned on 4 Sep 1782 as it was for local interest payments. Of the requisition of 16 Oct 1782 for SM$2,000,000, none had been paid. The request for the standing requisition of 18 Apr 1783 had been ignored. Congress decided to lower its expectations down to half of the original requisition of SM$8,000,000, subtracted the amount paid, and accordingly requisitioned SM$2,670,988 for 1784. This amount would meet the immediate minimal needs of the government.

27 Sep 1785: Congress requisitioned SM$3,000,000 from the states.

31 Dec 1785: Of the original SM$8,000,000 requisition of 30 Oct 1781, about SM$1,600,000 had been paid by the states.

15 Feb 1786: The total receipts since 1781 amounted to SM$2,457,987: a) from requisitions made between 1 Nov 1781 and 1 Nov 1784, SM$2,025,089; b) from requisitions made between 1 Nov 1784 and 1 Jan 1786, SM$432,898.

31 Dec 1786: Congress had received only SM$500,000 of the money requisitioned from the states over the past two years.

In summary, ignoring the standing requisition of 18 Apr 1783 and the requisition of 4 Sep 1782, Congress had requisitioned SM$13,000,000 from the states, but had received about SM$2,525,000, which is a little less than 20%. This was clearly not a workable system; Congress could not meet its basic obligations (including paying the men in the army). Congress survived on borrowed money, usually at very high interest rates, because its credit and means were so bad.

During the debate leading up to the 15 Feb 1786 requisition, Congress issued a report by a committee consisting of Pinckney, King, Kean, Monroe, and Pettit, declaring that the Articles of Confederation were inadequate. It laid out several conclusions, two of which were: a) the requisition system of raising revenues had been a failure for its entire eight year duration; and b) the requisition system could not be relied upon in the future.

There were some proposals to alter the Articles to give Congress an independent revenue source by granting it a power to levy duties on imports. Twelve of the states agreed to it, but New York refused on the grounds that a general import duty levied by Congress would serve to weaken New York's position as a trade center. The persistent financial crisis and New York's intransigence, coupled with Shays' Rebellion, led to the calling of the Constitutional Convention in 1787.

James Madison wrote an undated paper near the end of his life in which he recounted this period as Congress and the nation as a whole suffered under this defect [4]:

> But the radical infirmity of the "Articles of Confederation" was the dependence of Congress on the voluntary and simultaneous compliance with its requisitions by so many independent communities, each consulting more or less its particular interests and convenience, and distrusting the compliance of the others.

This problem was resolved by the adoption of the U. S. Constitution, in which Congress was given power to raise revenue independent of state influence:

> **[Article 1] Section 8.** Congress shall have the power to lay and collect taxes, duties, imposts, and excises to pay the debts and provide for the common defense and general wel-

> fare of the United States; but all duties, imposts, and excises shall be uniform throughout the United States.

10 Coinage and Currency

In order to fully appreciate the situation regarding coinage and debt under the Articles of Confederation, and how it was addressed by the Constitution, it is necessary to review some basic facts. First, Congress became the symbol of the Revolution as the only institution recognized by all the states. Secondly, it came into being under emergency circumstances in order to coordinate the war effort. Recognizing a need for a formal arrangement governing relations among the states, the men of Congress first proposed the Articles of Confederation shortly after the Declaration of Independence, but they were not established in final form until November of 1778, when they were submitted to the state legislatures for consideration. They did not go into effect until all thirteen states had sanctioned them which occurred in March of 1781. The provisions concerning money and credit are as follows:

> **[Paragraph 4 of Article IX]** The United States, in Congress assembled, shall also have the sole and exclusive right and power of regulating the alloy and value of coin struck by their own authority, or by that of the respective States; fixing the standard of weights and measures throughout the United States; regulating the trade and managing all affairs with the Indians not members of any of the States; provided that the legislative right of State, within its own limits, be not infringed or violated; establishing and regulating post-offices from one State to another throughout all the United States, and exacting such postage on the papers passing through the same as may be requisite to defray the expenses of the said office; appointing all officers of the land forces in the service of the United States, excepting regimental officers; appointing all the officers of the naval forces, and commissioning all officers whatever in the service of the United States; making rules for the government and regulation of said land and naval forces, and directing their operations.

> **[Paragraph 7 of Article IX]** The United States, in Congress assembled, shall never engage in war, nor grant letters of marque and reprisal in time of peace, nor enter into any treaties or alliances, nor coin money, nor regulate the value thereof, nor ascertain the sums and expenses necessary for the defense and welfare of the United States, or any of them, nor emit bills, nor borrow money on the credit of the United States, nor appropriate money nor agree upon the number of vessels of war to be built or purchased, or the number of land or sea forces to be raised, nor appoint a commander-in-chief of the army or navy, unless nine States assent to the same, nor shall a question on any other point, except for adjourning from day to day, be determined, unless by the votes of a majority of the United States, in Congress assembled.

> **Article XII.** All bills of credit emitted, moneys borrowed, and debts contracted by or under the authority of Congress, before the assembling of the United States, in pursuance of the present Confederation, shall be deemed and considered as a charge against the United States, for payment and satisfaction whereof the said United States and the public faith are hereby solemnly pledged.

Under Art. IX, paragraph 4, Congress had the power to regulate the nature of coin, but the states were allowed to coin their own money under that regulation. The states also had the power (already existing) to issue their own paper currency. Under paragraph 7 of Art, IX, Congress had the power to issue "bills of credit", which are notes issued on the credit of the United States; they functioned in the same manner as a paper currency. Last, Article XII states that Congress shall be liable for full payment of all debts and bills of credit issued before the Articles are ratified. That means we must first review the progression of the "Continental money", which was mostly issued as bills of credit, but occasionally as paper currency. These were issued directly by Congress as shown in Figure 1, denominated in dollars, ostensibly to be regarded at the same value as the Spanish milled dollar (SM$) then in common use (reckoned as

386.7 grains of silver). The reckoned value of the Continental bills of credit and currency depreciated rapidly, and those estimates compared to the Spanish Milled dollar are shown in the fourth column of each section.

Date	Amount Authorized	Total Authorized	Value WRT Spanish Milled Dollar (SM$)	Date	Amount Authorized	Total Authorized	Value WRT Spanish Milled Dollar (SM$)
22 Jun 1775	2,000,000	2,000,000	1.00	22 May 1778	5,000,000	56,500,000	0.25
25 Jul 1775	1,000,000	3,000,000	1.00	20 Jun 1778	5,000,000	61,500,000	0.25
29 Nov 1775	3,000,000	6,000,000	0.80	30 Jul 1778	5,000,000	66,500,000	0.20
17 Feb 1776	4,000,000	10,000,000	0.67	5 Sep 1778	5,000,000	71,500,000	0.20
27 May 1776	5,000,000	15,000,000	0.50	26 Sep 1778	10,000,000	81,500,000	0.20
13 Aug 1776	5,000,000	20,000,000	0.40	4 Nov 1778	10,000,000	91,500,000	0.17
28 Dec 1776	5,000,000	25,000,000	0.40	14 Dec 1778	10,000,000	101,500,000	0.14
26 Feb 1777	5,000,000	30,000,000	0.40	3 Feb 1779	5,000,160	106,500,160	0.13
20 May 1777	5,000,000	35,000,000	0.33	19 Feb 1779	5,000,160	111,500,320	0.10
15 Aug 1777	1,000,000	36,000,000	0.33	1 Apr 1779	5,000,160	116,500,480	0.10
7 Nov 1777	1,000,000	37,000,000	0.33	5 May 1779	10,000,100	126,500,580	0.06
3 Dec 1777	1,000,000	38,000,000	0.33	7 May 1779	50,000,100	176,500,680	0.04
8 Jan 1778	1,000,000	39,000,000	0.33	4 Jun 1779	10,000,100	186,500,780	0.05
22 Jan 1778	2,000,000	41,000,000	0.25	17 Jul 1779	15,000,280	201,501,060	0.05
16 Feb 1778	2,000,000	43,000,000	0.25	17 Sep 1779	15,000,360	216,501,420	0.05
5 Mar 1778	2,000,000	45,000,000	0.20	14 Oct 1779	5,000,180	221,501,600	0.04
4 Apr 1778	1,000,000	46,000,000	0.20	17 Nov 1779	10,050,540	231,552,140	0.03
11 Apr 1778	5,000,000	51,000,000	0.17	29 Nov 1779	10,000,140	241,552,280	0.03
18 Apr 1778	500,000	51,500,000					

1. Source: Joseph Nourse, Register of the Treasury, in a letter 30 Jan 1828 to the House of Representatives, cited by Schuckers, "Finances and Paper Money of the Revolutionary War", NY: Sanford J. Durst, 1978, p. 125

2. Of the $50,000,100 authorized 7 May 1779, $25,552,780 was to replace old bills (cf. Schuckers, p. 126). It is not clear if the amount authorized was $50,000,100 or $50,000, 400.

Figure 1: "Continental" Bills of Credit and Paper Currency Authorized by Congress 1775-1779

By the end of 1779, the "Continental" was worth about 2 cents in hard money; by Jun 1780, it was valued at about one cent. It then became the object of ridicule and simply went out of circulation. Finally, on 11 Jul 1780, Congress published a redemption schedule for all the Continental bills and currency: they would be redeemed at 40 to 1 (SM$ 0.025), although their reckoned value by that time was about 65 to 1 (i.e., worth about SM$ 0.015). Thus the $232,000,000 or so Continentals that were still in circulation ultimately was reduced to SM$5,8000,000 in actual redemption value. Because Congress could not raise any revenue on its own, as mentioned in section 9, this was simply added to the national debt. Keep in mind that all this occurred prior to the formal operation of the Articles of Confederation (2 Mar 1781). What happened to all the people that accepted the Continental at face value? They were robbed.

Why did the Continental depreciate so quickly? For the same two reasons any fiat currency depreciates: a) in the short run, the issuer knows it has no value that he is responsible for, so he issues as much as he can without startling the public or the business community; and b) in the long run, the public loses confidence in it once they realize it has no true value. These explain why every fiat currency requires a "legal tender" law in order to force the public and the business community to pretend that it actually does have value. That continues until the issuer decides to get out of the business (having made his money on interest payments) and simply abolishes the fiat currency, thus robbing those who accepted it. Going back to the case of the Continental, Congress issued it under emergency conditions, that is, to fight the war against Britain. Perhaps it was necessary and justifiable to do so, given the enormous benefits to be derived from independence; but it corrupted the economy.

The states had also issued a great deal of paper money during the war, and their currency had also depreciated somewhat. Although the Articles permitted Congress to issue bills of credit, it no longer did so, having learned its lesson from the history of the Continental currency. But the evil of paper money was not solved thereby, since some of the states continued to issue paper money after the war, which also depreciated. Georgia redeemed its paper money at 1,000 to 1 in Feb 1785; Delaware redeemed its paper in the same month at 75 to 1. Pennsylvania issued paper money in May 1785; by Aug 1786, it had already depreciated 12%. South Carolina issue paper currency in Oct 1785; followed by North Carolina in Nov 1785, New York in Mar 1786; New Jersey and Rhode Island in May 1786; and Georgia in Aug 1786. By Aug 1786, New Jersey's currency had become worthless, and Rhode Island's paper had depreciated to 4:1. The other paper issued by the states suffered similar fates, especially in North and South Carolina. It was the debate over paper currency that started Shays' rebellion in Massachusetts (a case where the people wanted it).

Simply issuing paper at the state level was not the only problem; it was coupled with constant alterations in its official value, which affected contracts between parties in different states. Certainly there is no incentive to extend credit if the currency can be manipulated, or as in South Carolina and Virginia, terms of contracts were altered to allow payments in land or tobacco, or as again in South Carolina, contracts were altered to require different payment schedules.

Such was the situation at the Constitutional Convention in 1787. Providing Congress a power to borrow money and establish coinage was agreed to easily. Likewise, the states were prohibited from coining money or issuing bills of credit; furthermore, only gold and silver could be made legal tender in the states. The corrective provisions in the U. S. Constitution read:

> **[Article I, Section 8]** The Congress shall have Power To lay and collect Taxes, Duties, Imposts and Excises, to pay the Debts and provide for the common Defense and general Welfare of the United States; but all Duties, Imposts and Excises shall be uniform throughout the United States;
>
> To borrow money on the credit of the United States;
>
> **[Article I, Section 10]** No State shall enter into any Treaty, Alliance, or Confederation; grant Letters of Marque and Reprisal; coin Money; emit Bills of Credit; make any Thing but gold and silver Coin a Tender in Payment of Debts; pass any Bill of Attainder, ex post facto Law, or Law impairing the Obligation of Contracts, or grant any Title of Nobility.

It is of great interest while on this subject to examine the debate in the Constitutional Convention about whether the federal government shall have a power to emit bills of credit. A draft had been presented on 6 Aug 1787, containing a provision [Art. VII, Section 1] stating "The legislature of the United States shall have the power ... to borrow money, and emit bills, on the credit of the United States." This clause was debated on 16 Aug 1787, as follows per Elliot [5]:

> Mr. Gouverneur Morris moved to strike out "and emit bills on the credit of the United States." If the United States had credit, such bills would be unnecessary; if they had not, unjust and useless.
>
> Mr. Butler seconds the motion.
>
> Mr. Madison. Will it not be sufficient to prohibit the making them a tender? This will remove the temptation to emit them with unjust views; and promissory notes, in that shape, may in some emergencies be best.
>
> Mr. Gouverneur Morris. Striking out the words will leave room still for notes of a responsible minister, which will do all the good without the mischief. The moneyed interest will oppose the plan of government, if paper emissions be not prohibited.
>
> Mr. Gorham was for striking out without inserting any prohibition. If the words stand, they may suggest and lead to the measure.
>
> Mr. Mason had doubts on the subject. Congress, he thought, would not have the power, unless it were expressed. Though he had a mortal hatred to paper money, yet, as he could not foresee all emergencies, he was unwilling to tie the hands of the legislature. He observed that the late war could not have been carried on, had such a prohibition existed.

Mr. Gorham. The power, as far as it will be necessary or safe, is involved in that of borrowing.

Mr. Mercer was a friend to paper money, though, in the present state and temper of America, he should neither propose or approve of such a measure. He was consequently opposed to a prohibition of it altogether. It will stamp suspicion on the government, to deny it a discretion on this point. It was impolitic, also, to excite the opposition of all those who were friends to paper money. The people of property would be sure to be on the side of the plan, and it was impolitic to purchase their further attachment with the loss of the opposite class of citizens.

Mr. Ellsworth thought this a favorable moment to shut and bar the door against paper money. The mischief's of the various experiments which had been made were now fresh in the public mind, and had excited the disgust of all the respectable part of America. By withholding the power from the new government, more friends of influence would be gained to it than by almost anything else. Give the government credit, and other resources will offer. The power may do harm, never good.

Mr. Randolph, notwithstanding his antipathy to paper money, could not agree to strike out the words, as he could not foresee all the occasions that might arise.

Mr. Wilson. It will have a most salutary influence on the credit of the United States, to remove the possibility of paper money. This expedient can never succeed whilst its mischief's are remembered; and, as long as it can be resorted to, it will be a bar to other resources.

Mr. Butler remarked, that paper was a legal tender in no country in Europe. He was urgent for disarming the government of such a power.

Mr. Mason was still averse to tying the hands of the legislature altogether. If there was no example in Europe, as just remarked, it might be observed, on the other side, that there was none in which the government was restrained on this head.

Mr. Read thought the words, if not struck out, would be as alarming as the mark of the beast in Revelation.

Mr. Langdon had rather reject the whole plan, than retain the three words, "and emit bills."

On the motion for striking out, --

New Hampshire, Massachusetts, Connecticut, Pennsylvania, Delaware, Virginia, North Carolina, South Carolina, Georgia, aye, 9; New Jersey, Maryland, no, 2.

The clause for borrowing money was agreed to, *nem. con.*

Adjourned.

Elliot added a footnote regarding Virginia's positive vote to strike out "and emit bills." It reads:

This vote in the affirmative by Virginia was occasioned by the acquiescence of Mr. Madison, who became satisfied that striking out the words would not disable the government from the use of public notes, as far as they could be safe and proper; and would only cut off the pretext for a paper currency, and particularly for making the bills a tender, either for public or private debts.

Madison defended this view more directly in the *Federalist Papers* #44:

The right of coining money, which is here taken from the States, was left in their hands by the Confederation, as a concurrent right with that of Congress, under an exception in favor of the exclusive right of Congress to regulate the alloy and value. In this instance, also, the new provision is an improvement on the old. Whilst the alloy and value depended on the general authority, a right of coinage in the particular States could have no other effect than to multiply expensive mints and diversify the forms and weights of the circulating pieces. The latter inconveniency defeats one purpose for which the power was originally submitted to the federal head; and as far as the former might prevent an inconvenient remittance of gold and silver to the central mint for recoinage, the end can be as well attained by local mints established under the general authority.

The extension of the prohibition to bills of credit must give pleasure to every citizen, in proportion to his love of justice and his knowledge of the true springs of public prosperity. The loss which America has sustained since the peace, from the pestilent effects of paper money on the necessary confidence between man and man, on the necessary confidence in the public councils, on the industry and morals of the people, and on the character of republican government, constitutes an enormous debt against the States chargeable with this unadvised measure, which must long remain unsatisfied; or rather an accumulation of guilt, which can be expiated no otherwise than by a voluntary sacrifice on the altar of justice, of the power which has been the instrument of it. In addition to these persuasive considerations, it may be observed, that the same reasons which show the necessity of denying to the States the power of regulating coin, prove with equal force that they ought not to be at liberty to substitute a paper medium in the place of coin. Had every State a right to regulate the value of its coin, there might be as many different currencies as States, and thus the intercourse among them would be impeded; retrospective alterations in its value might be made, and thus the citizens of other States be injured, and animosities be kindled among the States themselves. The subjects of foreign powers might suffer from the same cause, and hence the Union be discredited and embroiled by the indiscretion of a single member. No one of these mischief's is less incident to a power in the States to emit paper money, than to coin gold or silver. The power to make anything but gold and silver a tender in payment of debts, is withdrawn from the States, on the same principle with that of issuing a paper currency.

11 Slavery

Recorded human civilization is probably about 10,000 years old. It is fascinating to consider that chattel slavery has existed for 98.5% of that entire period, having ended only about 150 years ago. While it is nothing new in the history of mankind, it is more revolting to the modern mind. In America we continue to be preoccupied with it since American slavery was uniquely racial in its implementation. That, combined with the fact that there are Americans still living who knew, as children, people who had been slaves, causes slavery to remain fresh in our debates. But those among us who impute universal racism to white people would do well to remember that far more white people than black have been slaves throughout history. The enslavement of blacks began in Africa, just as the enslavement of whites originated in Greece and Rome. Does racism exist in America? Of course; it always has and it always will so long as people of one racial group desire to feel superior to some other. There are and always will be a few who join the Ku Klux Klan or sympathize with them and their equivalents; there are likewise on the other side always a few who embrace Black Liberation theology and its various mutations. I digress -- our subject is the issue of slavery at the forming of the United States.

Slavery was practiced throughout the 13 colonies from the mid-1600's onward, especially in the south. It became apparent soon after the colonies were established that black people were better suited to the hard labor required in an agricultural economy in the sub-tropical conditions of the south. Or at least the white people discovered that claim as a convenient excuse. In any case, many of that era believed that slavery was an efficient economic system. Secondly, slavery was important to the British crown as a source of revenue, and was not only encouraged in the colonies, it was sometimes vigorously promoted since there was a great deal of money to be made buying/capturing slaves and selling them in the colonies once Britain obtained a lock on the slave trade in the early 1700's.

The institution of slavery was not uniformly embraced in all the colonies. In the north, the religious ethic rejected slavery on moral grounds, and it did not take hold there as it did in the southern colonies, where the (false) economic argument was firmly planted. There were many attempts prior to the Revolutionary War to limit slavery in the colonies. A few examples are as follows.

In Virginia, the state Assembly imposed a series of import duties from 1732 on the importation of slaves that nearly amounted to a prohibition (up to 40% of the slaves' value). In 1772 the Virginia Assembly wrote to King George III, asking him, unsuccessfully, to abolish the slave trade [6]:

> We implore your Majesty's paternal assistance in averting a calamity of a most alarming nature. The importation of slaves into the colonies from the coast of Africa hath long been considered a as a trade of great inhumanity, and under its present encouragement we have too much reason to fear will endanger the very existence of your Majesty's American dominions. We are sensible that some of your Majesty's subjects may reap emoluments from this sort of traffic, but when we consider that it greatly retards the settlement of the colonies with more useful inhabitants and may in time have the most destructive influence, we presume to hope that the interest of the few will be disregarded when placed in competition with the security and happiness of such numbers of your Majesty's dutiful and loyal subjects. We therefore beseech your Majesty to remove all those restraints on your majesty's governors in this colony which inhibit their assenting to such laws as might check so pernicious a consequence.

The Rhode Island legislature passed a law in 1774 whereby all slaves brought into state by citizens of other states were to be free, except those passing through with their master; also, Rhode Island citizens bringing in slaves had to remove or free them in one year [7]. In Connecticut, the Assembly passed a law in 1774 stating [8] "No Indian, mulatto, or negro slave shall at any time hereafter be brought or imported into this state, by sea or land, from any place or places whatsoever, to be disposed of, left, or sold within the State." New Jersey had attempted in 1744 and 1761 to essential prohibit importation by imposing large import duty [9], but it was rejected by the Provincial Council as injurious to crown revenue. In Pennsylvania, the influence of the Quakers led to the voluntary freeing of many slaves from 1725 onward [10]. Massachusetts attempted in 1774 to prohibit the importation of slaves outright [11], but this motion was rejected by Gov. Hutchinson as it would reduce revenue to the crown.

The Articles of Confederation was silent on the entire issue of slavery; each state enacted legislation as it saw fit. In 1775, slavery existed in all 13 states but there was a great deal of activity in the states toward reducing slavery from the start of the Revolution through the period of the Articles. In 1776 Delaware prohibited further importation through a provision in its new Constitution, which read: "No person hereafter imported into this state from Africa ought to be held in slavery under any pretense whatever, and no Negro, Indian or mulatto slave ought to be brought into this state for sale from any part of the world." Unfortunately, free blacks were occasionally kidnapped & sold. In 1776, Rhode Island passed legislation that made all children of slaves born in 1776 and after free; and promoted the gradual liberation of existing slaves by regulation [12]. In 1778, Virginia prohibited further importation of slaves, although probably more out of fear of a large population of slaves starting an uprising than out of widespread disapprobation of the institution itself [13]. Pennsylvania passed a law in 1780 that prohibited further importation, and made all persons born after 1 Mar 1780 servants only until age 28, after which they were then free [14]. It was not abolished outright until 1847.

Massachusetts adopted a new Constitution in 1780, the first article of which read: "All men are born free and equal, and have natural, essential, and unalienable rights; among which may be reckoned the right of enjoying, and defending their lives and liberties; that of acquiring, possessing, and protecting property; in fine, that of seeking and obtaining their safety and happiness." It was not intended by these words to abolish slavery, but a series of court rulings on the Constitution in 1781 and afterward serve to gradually reduce slavery; the people considered it abolished for practical purposes [15]. In 1788, importation of slaves was prohibited directly [16].

Maryland prohibited further importation in 1783 (but slavery was not abolished until 1864). New Hampshire passed a law in 1783 that was similar to the 1780 Pennsylvania law; in 1784, Connecticut did the same [17]. New York followed suit in 1785, except the children of slaves gained full voting rights. Starting in 1782, New Jersey freed all the slaves that had been owned by Tories [18]. In 1786 the legislature passed provisions for voluntary gradual freeing of slaves of a certain age [19]; in that same year prohibited further importation; and in 1788 also prohibited exportation [20]. Gradual mandatory emancipation did not begin until 1804, and slavery was not abolished entirely in New Jersey until 1846.

In 1786 the state of North Carolina imposed a 5 pound sterling duty on importation to discourage the trade. Only in Georgia and South Carolina was the slave trade entirely unrestricted.

The weakness of the Articles of Confederation in this regard was that there was no limitation on the importation of slaves as a general rule. It was gradually being phased out in the north, while importation continued unabated in the south. As the debates at the Constitutional Convention got underway, it was soon apparent that many in the north would have preferred to abolish slavery entirely, but the Georgia and South Carolina delegations made it clear that they would never join the union if there was any attempt to remove slavery as an institution – it was, they believed, too important for the function of their economy [21, 22]. This condition determined the debate, as Georgia and South Carolina were essential for the preservation of the union. It was necessary to keep those two states in the union, since they would serve to deter a serious military threat from Spain in the south. Secondly, if they did not join the union, it is likely they would have attempted to rejoin Great Britain in order to gain an ally in any controversy with Spain over navigation rights on the Mississippi. These two southern states were however, willing to accept the prohibition on the importation of slaves after 1808. The provision in the U. S. Constitution reads:

> **Article 1, Section 9.** The Migration or Importation of such Persons as any of the States now existing shall think proper to admit, shall not be prohibited by the Congress prior to the Year one thousand eight hundred and eight, but a tax or duty may be imposed on such Importation, not exceeding ten dollars for each Person.

The provision did not affect existing slaves, but it was an improvement over the Articles since it universally limited importation after 1808. In effect, it imposed on all the states, even those where slavery was most entrenched, the same trend that had occurred in the northern states throughout the previous decade.

12 Amendments

Change is the one unchanging constant of human history. By way of application, it must be admitted that any rules for governance among people must contain a provision by which those rules may be altered in an orderly fashion in order to accommodate changing conditions. The Articles of Confederation contained such a provision as follows:

> **Article XIII.** Every State shall abide by the determinations of the United States, in Congress assembled, on all questions which by this Confederation are submitted to them. And the Articles of this Confederation shall be inviolably observed by every State, and the Union shall be perpetual; nor shall any alteration at any time hereafter be made in any of them, unless such alteration be agreed to in a Congress of the United States, and be afterwards confirmed by the legislatures of every State.

The concurrence of every state legislature was required to make any change in the Articles. Section 9 discussed the main problem with the revenue provisions of the Articles, namely that Congress was entirely dependent on the states through the requisition system. But the Articles could not be amended, because one state (New York) refused to permit Congress a power to establish an independent revenue source to meet the needs at the national level. The conflict over Congress' revenue started on 3 Feb 1781, when Congress, realizing that the requisition system was not working, recommended that the Articles be amended to allow Congress to impose an import duty. With such a power, Congress could raise revenue necessary to perform its minimum duties, such as paying the army. Rhode Island was the first to reject the concept on 1 Nov 1782, arguing among other things, that the revenue collectors would not be answerable to Rhode Island. Virginia was initially in favor of the import duty, but revoked its agreement on 11 Jun 1783. But in that same month, Delaware and New Jersey agreed to it; South Carolina followed suit on 13 Aug 1783 but with difficult caveats; Massachusetts concurred on 16 Oct 1783; Virginia reversing itself once again in favor on 29 Dec 1783; North Carolina agreed on 2 Jun 1784; and New Hampshire agreed on 23 Jun 1785. All the other states except New York did likewise by May 1786.

But the government of the state of New York, interested only in its own revenues, refused to allow Congress to impose any import duties. On 16 Aug 1786, Governor Clinton of New York notified Congress that he would not call the state legislature into session to consider the proposal; although Congress was desperate for money, he did not consider the situation important enough. On 15 Feb 1787, New York gave its final refusal to consider the matter. This proved fatal to the Confederation, as Congress realized it now had no hope of a stable revenue stream. It caused Congress endorse the idea of a convention of the states to modify the Articles, which became the convention that wrote the Constitution.

The Constitution permits amendments in a manner superior to the Articles of Confederation:

> **Article V.** The Congress, whenever two thirds of both Houses shall deem it necessary, shall propose Amendments to this Constitution, or, on the Application of the Legislatures of two thirds of the several States, shall call a Convention for proposing Amendments, which, in either Case, shall be valid to all Intents and Purposes, as part of this Constitution, when ratified by the Legislatures of three fourths of the several States, or by Conventions in three fourths thereof, as the one or the other Mode of Ratification may be proposed by the Congress; Provided that no Amendment which may be made prior to the Year One thousand eight hundred and eight shall in any Manner affect the first and fourth Clauses in the Ninth Section of the first Article; and that no State, without its Consent, shall be deprived of its equal Suffrage in the Senate.

Under this provision, amendments to the Constitution may be initiated in two ways: a) if two-thirds of both Houses of Congress pass an amendment; or b) if two-thirds of the states call for a convention for the purpose of proposing amendments. In each case, concurrence of three-fourths of the states, either by their legislatures or by ratifying conventions, is required before such proposed amendments take effect.

James Madison defended this provision in the *Federalist Papers #43*:

> That useful alterations will be suggested by experience, could not but be foreseen. It was requisite, therefore, that a mode for introducing them should be provided. The mode preferred by the convention seems to be stamped with every mark of propriety. It guards equally against that extreme facility, which would render the Constitution too mutable; and that extreme difficulty, which might perpetuate its discovered faults. It, moreover, equally enables the general and the State governments to originate the amendment of errors, as they may be pointed out by the experience on one side, or on the other.

Alexander Hamilton answered critics of the provision, and gave his opinion on the nature of amendments were they to occur, in the *Federalist Papers #85*:

> In opposition to the probability of subsequent amendments, it has been urged that the persons delegated to the administration of the national government will always be disinclined to yield up any portion of the authority of which they were once possessed. For my own part I acknowledge a thorough conviction that any amendments which may, upon mature consideration, be thought useful, will be applicable to the organization of the government, not to the mass of its powers; and on this account alone, I think there is no weight in the observation just stated. I also think there is little weight in it on another account. The intrinsic difficulty of governing thirteen States at any rate, independent of calculations upon an ordinary degree of public spirit and integrity, will, in my opinion constantly impose on the national rulers the necessity of a spirit of accommodation to the reasonable expectations of their constituents. But there is yet a further consideration,

> which proves beyond the possibility of a doubt, that the observation is futile. It is this that the national rulers, whenever nine States concur, will have no option upon the subject. By the fifth article of the plan, the Congress will be obliged "on the application of the legislatures of two thirds of the States [which at present amount to nine], to call a convention for proposing amendments, which shall be valid, to all intents and purposes, as part of the Constitution, when ratified by the legislatures of three fourths of the States, or by conventions in three fourths thereof." The words of this article are peremptory. The Congress "shall call a convention." Nothing in this particular is left to the discretion of that body. And of consequence, all the declamation about the disinclination to a change vanishes in air. Nor however difficult it may be supposed to unite two thirds or three fourths of the State legislatures, in amendments which may affect local interests, can there be any room to apprehend any such difficulty in a union on points which are merely relative to the general liberty or security of the people. We may safely rely on the disposition of the State legislatures to erect barriers against the encroachments of the national authority.

Hamilton was almost right when he wrote that subsequent amendments would mostly change the organization of the government, not its powers. In fact, the first ten Amendments confirmed the existing rights of the people and the states relative to the federal government, thus expressly limiting the federal government's power if there was any room for doubt among rational people. There are only two cases where the federal government expanded its powers by amending the Constitution. The first was the patently moronic Prohibition (Amendment 18, subsequently repealed by Amendment 21), which led to the rise to a permanent criminal class (Irish and Italian mafias) with the means and willingness to corrupt the government. Although alcohol prohibition was repealed, it was replaced with other equally detrimental prohibitions that have kept the criminal elite employed for decades. The second case of an expansion of power is Amendment 16, which gave Congress a power to tax incomes.

In general, this method of amendment has the virtue of making amendments fairly difficult, thus enhancing the stability of the Constitution. At the same time it permits necessary amendments, but only if a great majority of the people, acting through their state legislators or conventions, agree to it. It has proven over time to be a most beneficial system, since very few of the numerous and ridiculous proposed amendments ever come to the states for consideration -- they die in Congress as they deserve.

13 Method of Ratification

It was only a week after the Declaration of Independence that a committee in the Continental Congress reported out an initial plan for organizing a confederation of the states to be united in the effort against Great Britain. Although reported out of this committee on 12 Jul 1776, it could have no practical effect until the members of Congress agreed to all of its terms and proposed it to the states. This was a sensible approach, given that the Articles represented a purely federal system, that is, a compact between states in their sovereign capacity. Congress debated these for nearly 18 months; on 15 Nov 1777, having reached agreement on the terms thereof, a letter dated 17 Nov 1777 was sent to every state, asking those states to ratify the Articles. The legislatures of eight states passed legislation in the next 6 months by which their delegates to Congress were authorized to approve the Articles. The delegates from those states (New Hampshire, Massachusetts, Rhode Island, Connecticut, New York, Pennsylvania, Virginia, and South Carolina) formally ratified the Articles on 9 Jul 1778. The provision is contained in Article XIII:

> **Article XIII.** Every State shall abide by the determinations of the United States, in Congress assembled, on all questions which by this Confederation are submitted to them. And the Articles of this Confederation shall be inviolably observed by every State, and the Union shall be perpetual; nor shall any alteration at any time hereafter be made in any

of them, unless such alteration be agreed to in a Congress of the United States, and be afterwards confirmed by the legislatures of every State.

And whereas it hath pleased the great Governor of the world to incline the hearts of the legislatures we respectively represent in Congress to approve of, and to authorize us to ratify the said Articles of Confederation and perpetual Union, Know ye, that we, the undersigned delegates, by virtue of the power and authority to us given for that purpose, do, by these presents, in the name and in behalf of our respective constituents, fully and entirely ratify and confirm each and every of the said Articles of Confederation and perpetual Union, and all and singular the matters and things therein contained. And we do further solemnly plight and engage the faith of our respective constituents, that they shall abide by the determinations of the United States, in Congress assembled, on all questions which by the said Confederation are submitted to them; and that the Articles thereof shall be inviolably observed by the States we respectively represent, and that the Union shall be perpetual. Done at Philadelphia, in the State of Pennsylvania, the ninth day of July, in the year of our Lord 1778, and in the third year of the Independence of America.

But the Articles did not contain a provision by which it would go into effect for those states that ratified it; the intent was that all 13 states were to be united in the war effort. Therefore, the Articles did not formally go into effect until 2 Mar 1781, the day after Maryland's legislature ratified the Articles. This unanimous requirement for both ratification and amendment proved to be a serious defect, as already cited in sections 9 and 12.

The framers of the Constitution were only too familiar with this difficulty, and made provision in the new Constitution by which it would go into effect if a certain number (two-thirds) of the then-existing states were to agree to it:

Article 7. The ratification of the conventions of nine States shall be sufficient for the establishment of this Constitution between the States so ratifying the same.

This may seem contrary to the Preamble in the Constitution, which states:

We the people of the United States, in order to form a more perfect union, establish justice, insure domestic tranquility, provide for the common defense, promote the general welfare, and secure the blessings of liberty to ourselves and our posterity, do ordain and establish this Constitution for the United States of America.

How can it be said that the people established it, if in fact it required ratification by the states? The answer lies in the fact that each state that ratified it did so at a ratifying convention called for that purpose in each state, and each delegate sent to it was tasked with representing the people of the state. The U. S. Constitution is the founding document of a compound democratic republic established by republican means, that is, when the people are represented by those they trust, and accept the results of a vote of the specified majority. In this way, although the representatives cast their votes directly, those votes matter only because the full weight of the people's confidence is behind them.

James Madison, writing in the *Federalist Papers* #40, discussed the objections of some who were opposed to the Constitution on the grounds that agreement of all thirteen states should be required before it should go into effect. Madison simply noted that the critics had avoided the fact that unanimity on ratification would be a form of minority rule:

It is worthy of remark that this objection, though the most plausible, has been the least urged in the publications which have swarmed against the convention. The forbearance can only have proceeded from an irresistible conviction of the absurdity of subjecting the fate of twelve States to the perverseness or corruption of a thirteenth; from the example of inflexible opposition given by a *majority* of one sixtieth of the people of America to a measure approved and called for by the voice of twelve States, comprising fifty-nine sixtieths of the people -- an example still fresh in the memory and indignation of every citizen who has felt for the wounded honor and prosperity of his country. As this objection, therefore, has been in a manner waived by those who have criticized the powers of the convention, I dismiss it without further observation.

The "example of inflexible opposition" referred to here was the refusal by the state of New York to allow Congress (under the Articles) to impose an import duty in order to obtain a direct revenue source.

Madison addressed the method of ratification as called out in Article 7 directly in the *Federalist Papers* #43:

> This article speaks for itself. The express authority of the people alone could give due validity to the Constitution. To have required the unanimous ratification of the thirteen States would have subjected the essential interests of the whole to the caprice or corruption of a single member. It would have marked a want of foresight in the convention which our own experience would have rendered inexcusable.

The provision in the Constitution was an improvement over the Articles in two ways: a) nine states could activate it without being held hostage to a minority of states; and b) it was ratified by conventions that represented the people, not just the state governments.

14 Executive and Judicial Function

The Articles of Confederation were initially proposed in the wartime emergency of 1775-1776 and were ratified by all the states by 1781; but the structure of the Confederation was not conducive to long-term stability. Congress was granted certain powers under the Articles: a) to determine the amount of requisitions each state was to pay; b) to declare war and make peace; c) to send and receive ambassadors to foreign nations; d) to negotiate and ratify treaties; e) to determine rules for disposition of captures at sea; f) to grant letters of marque (authorizing private piracy on behalf of the U. S.); g) to convene courts for trials of crimes committed at sea; h) to be the appeal of last resort in disputes between the states; i) to regulate coinage issued by Congress or by the states; j) to establish uniform weights and measures throughout the United States; k) to regulate trade with the Indian tribes; l) to create post offices; m) to exercise overall command and control of the military forces; n) to appoint some officers in the army and all in the navy; and o) to commission all officers in the service of the United States.

One major difficulty was that Congress did not have the ability to regularly enforce any of its laws nor the means to punish violations of them. This essay has presented considerable evidence to that effect, especially concerning Congress' inability to maintain an army, raise revenue, ensure adherence to treaties, manage territories, respond to foreign policies, or regulate commerce. A stable government must, as a minimum, have an executive function to enforce its laws and a judicial system to punish violations of valid laws and to interpret the law itself.

Alexander Hamilton addressed both of these problems in the *Federalist Papers*. First, in the *Federalist Papers* # 21, he cites Congress' inability to enforce any of its laws:

> The next most palpable defect of the subsisting Confederation, is the total want of a SANCTION to its laws. The United States, as now composed, have no powers to exact obedience, or punish disobedience to their resolutions, either by pecuniary mulcts, by a suspension or divestiture of privileges, or by any other constitutional mode. There is no express delegation of authority to them to use force against delinquent members; and if such a right should be ascribed to the federal head, as resulting from the nature of the social compact between the States, it must be by inference and construction, in the face of that part of the second article, by which it is declared, "that each State shall retain every power, jurisdiction, and right, not *expressly* delegated to the United States in Congress assembled." There is, doubtless, a striking absurdity in supposing that a right of this kind does not exist, but we are reduced to the dilemma either of embracing that supposition, preposterous as it may seem, or of contravening or explaining away a provision, which has been of late a repeated theme of the eulogies of those who oppose the new Constitu-

> tion; and the want of which, in that plan, has been the subject of much plausible animadversion, and severe criticism. If we are unwilling to impair the force of this applauded provision, we shall be obliged to conclude, that the United States afford the extraordinary spectacle of a government destitute even of the shadow of constitutional power to enforce the execution of its own laws. It will appear, from the specimens which have been cited, that the American Confederacy, in this particular, stands discriminated from every other institution of a similar kind, and exhibits a new and unexampled phenomenon in the political world.

Hamilton then discusses in the *Federalist Papers* #22, the lack of a judicial system:

> A circumstance which crowns the defects of the Confederation remains yet to be mentioned, -- the want of a judiciary power. Laws are a dead letter without courts to expound and define their true meaning and operation. The treaties of the United States, to have any force at all, must be considered as part of the law of the land. Their true import, as far as respects individuals, must, like all other laws, be ascertained by judicial determinations. To produce uniformity in these determinations, they ought to be submitted, in the last resort, to one SUPREME TRIBUNAL. And this tribunal ought to be instituted under the same authority which forms the treaties themselves. These ingredients are both indispensable. If there is in each State a court of final jurisdiction, there may be as many different final determinations on the same point as there are courts. There are endless diversities in the opinions of men. We often see not only different courts but the judges of the same court differing from each other. To avoid the confusion which would unavoidably result from the contradictory decisions of a number of independent judicatories, all nations have found it necessary to establish one court paramount to the rest, possessing a general superintendence, and authorized to settle and declare in the last resort a uniform rule of civil justice.

In reviewing the chronicle of the Constitutional Convention, it is interesting to note that there was no serious debate about whether an executive or judicial branch should exist. The need for them was pretty much accepted by all the attendees; the main debates were about the exact form, how they would be constituted, and what specific powers they would have. There were some who thought an executive council would carry out the executive function better than a single officer; some preferred a system by which the judicial system would be combined with the legislative; some thought all proposed laws by the legislative should be reviewed and modified by the executive and judicial branches. In the end, the framers developed a Constitution that created three main branches of the federal government, each with defined powers and the means to defend itself from encroachment by the other two. The framers employed methods to ensure that the executive (President) and judicial branches were separate from each other and independent of the legislative. There are some areas of overlap between the executive and the legislative (power of making treaties), and considerable influence of both of these upon the judicial branch (nomination of judges by the President and confirmation by the Senate).

The powers granted to the President are: a) to be Commander-in-Chief of the military; b) to be the point of contact for all foreign dignitaries as the nominal head of state; c) to negotiate treaties (but not to ratify them); d) to nominate ambassadors, judges, and certain other offices subject to Senate confirmation; e) to serve as chief administrator over the government departments that enforce the laws made by Congress; and f) to make lower-level appointments in his executive branches charged with those enforcement tasks.

The general power granted to the federal judicial system is to hear all cases in law and equity arising from treaties, federal laws, and the Constitution itself. The powers are divided as follows: a) creation of a Supreme Court which is to have original jurisdiction in cases affecting ambassadors, public officials, and when a state is a party; and b) creation of lower federal courts to hear cases for which the Supreme Court does not have original jurisdiction. In all cases, the Supreme Court has an appellate jurisdiction to hear appeals from lower federal courts.

15 Miscellaneous Necessary Powers

The first fourteen sections covered in detail some of the most serious problems encountered under the Articles of Confederation. Most of them arose because Congress did not have sufficient power under that agreement to perform necessary duties. It is important to remember that the U. S. Constitution, as a successor to the Articles, represented in some ways, a transfer of power from the several states to a new federal government. There was not much question that a change was necessary -- the nation was beginning to fall apart owing partly to the weakness of Congress and partly to the jealousies of the states.

A formal transfer of power is not to be taken lightly. The people of that era knew full well that if the states agreed to give up powers to the federal government, those powers would never return to the states. It is a testament to the wisdom of those who wrote the Constitution as well as those that urged its ratification on the state level, that the founding generation got the division of power between states and the federal government about right. The system worked well from 1788 to about the time of World War I, when the federal government began in earnest to assert undue powers. That is of course a very big subject for a later time. For now, the following is a summary of the powers that were not granted to Congress under the Articles of Confederation, but were granted to some portion of the federal government in the U. S. Constitution.

1. The creation of an Executive Department per Article 2, to: a) enforce the laws, b) control foreign policy, c) to be Commander-in-Chief of the military, d) make treaties, subject to ratification by the Senate; e) nominate federal officials, including Supreme Court justices, f) is charged with ensuring that the laws are executed faithfully; and g) has power to commission all officers of the U. S. These were discussed in sections 3, 4, 5, and 14.

2. The creation of a judicial system per Article 3, to: a) hear all cases, in law and equity, arising under the Constitution, the laws of the United States, and treaties; b) those affecting ambassadors, other public ministers and consuls; c) of admiralty and maritime jurisdiction; d) those in which the United States is a party; e) between two or more states; and f) certain types of cases involving citizens and states. The Supreme Court also has appellate power in both law and fact except as Congress may determine. This was discussed in 14.

3. The power to obtain direct revenue for the federal government through the "power to lay and collect taxes, duties, imposts and excises, to pay the debts and provide for the common defense and general welfare of the United States; but all duties, imposts and excises shall be uniform throughout the United States." This was discussed in section 9.

4. The power to call out the militia to: a) execute the laws; and b) respond to invasions and revolts. Congress also is granted the power to organize, arm, and determine the actions of the militia when called out to service under the United States. These were discussed in sections 2 and 8.

5. The power to determine regulations for the regular armed forces, transferring the power to provide for the regular army from levies on the states to a central federal power. This was discussed in section 2.

6. The power to guarantee a republican government in every state in order to ensure that the states would be immune from political revolutions. This was discussed in section 8.

7. The power to: a) administrate territories; and b) admit new states. These were necessary in order to regularize the large western area that was rapidly being populated until such time as they qualified for statehood. This was discussed in section 6.

8. The power to regulate: a) foreign commerce; and b) commerce between the states. These powers were necessary to respond to the acts of foreign nations affecting the economy of the U. S and also to control the predatory activities of some states upon the others. These were discussed in sections 3 and 5.

9. The exclusive power to: a) coin money; b) regulate its value; c) regulate the value of foreign money; and d) define and punish counterfeiting of the coin and securities of the U. S. These powers

were necessary to end the abuses of paper currency issued by the states and confusion caused by the different values of state issues. This was discussed in section 10.

10. The power to impose taxes and duties in order to affect the slave trade (section 11).
11. The power to punish offenses against the law of nations.
12. The power to establish uniform rules on bankruptcy.
13. The power to create post-roads.
14. The power to grant patents and copyrights.
15. The power to establish a new class of federal property, such as docks, arsenals, forts, etc.

The next section will review the powers that were originally granted to Congress under the Articles of Confederation, but were modified or clarified in the Constitution.

16 Powers of States

The previous section surveyed the alteration of power at the federal level from the Articles of Confederation gave way to the Constitution. But there were also significant alterations to the powers held by the states. These alterations fall into three categories: a) those powers held by the states under the Articles, but were prohibited in the Constitution; b) those that were retained in the Constitution, but in a modified form; and c) those that were not addressed in the Articles and prohibited by the Constitution. This study closes with a list of powers that were prohibited to the states in the Articles and carried over into the Constitution.

The powers falling under the first category may be summarized as follows:

a. The states were allowed to coin money under the Articles, but are prohibited from doing so under the Constitution. This was to correct the paper-money problem so rampant in the states after the war, as detailed in section 10.

b. The states were allowed to issue bills of credit on their account under the Articles, but are prohibited from doing so under the Constitution. It is worth observing that the federal government likewise falls under the same prohibition. This had been an enormous problem during the war, more so on the part of Congress, as it had issued the Continental bills of credit, which became worthless in a few years. This is also discussed in section 10.

c. Under the Articles, the states could independently issue letters of marque (privateering) with the approval of Congress (which required a declaration of war); under the Constitution, only the federal government can issue them.

The power falling under the second category is the power to levy import duties. Under the Articles, the states retained the power to levy their own import and export duties, unless they conflicted with provisions of treaties that were in negotiation with France and Spain at the time. This power caused several problems after the war. First, the states proceeded to respond to Britain's navigation Acts by imposing tonnage duties and other duties; this was partly a consequence of Congress' inability to negotiate commercial treaties, as detailed in part 5 of this series. The second problem was that the states began to prey on each other in order to gain commercial advantages. The Constitution prohibits the states from these levies, except for any necessary to cover inspection costs. Any revenue collected that is in excess of the inspection costs are to be transferred to the federal treasury.

The powers falling under the third category (not addressed in the Articles, prohibited to the states under the Constitution) include: a) prohibited from passing bills of attainder; b) prohibited from passing ex-post facto laws; c) prohibited from passing laws that inhibit the execution of contracts; d) prohibited from passing a legal tender law, except for gold and silver; and d) prohibited from laying a tonnage duty.

Last, there are powers which were prohibited to the states under the Articles, and were likewise carried over to the Constitution. These prohibitions include: a) creation of titles of nobility; b) establishing treaties with foreign nations; c) forming alliances with foreign nations; d) forming alliances or confederations among any number of states; e) keeping a military navy in peacetime; f) maintaining an army in peacetime except as allowed by Congress; and g) engaging in war without concurrence of Congress, except for emergency situations.

References

[1] John C. Fitzpatrick, editor, *The Writings of George Washington from the Original Manuscript Sources 1745-1799*, Washington: U. S. Government Printing Office, Vol. 6, p. 5.

[2] ibid., Vol. 6, pp. 379, 380

[3] Jonathan Elliot, *Debates on the Adoption of the Federal Constitution, in the Convention Held at Philadelphia in 1787, With a Diary of the Debates in the Congress of the Confederation, as Reported by James Madison,* Philadelphia; J. B. Lippincott & Co., 1881, Vol. 5, pp. 126-134

[4] Jonathan Elliot, *Debates on the Adoption of the Federal Constitution in the Convention Held at Philadelphia in 1787, With a Diary of the Debates of the Congress of the Confederation; As Reported by James Madison*, Philadelphia: J. B. Lippincott & Co., 1881, Vol. 5, p. 112

[5] Jonathan Elliot, *Debates on the Adoption of the Federal Constitution in the Convention Held at Philadelphia in 1787, With a Diary of the Debates of the Congress of the Confederation; As Reported by James Madison*, Philadelphia: J. B. Lippincott & Co., 1881, Vol. 5, pp. 434, 435

[6] James Curtis Ballagh, *A History of Slavery in Virginia*, Baltimore: Johns Hopkins University Press, 1902, p. 22

[7] William D. Johnston, *Slavery in Rhode Island 1755 – 1776*, Providence: Rhode Island Historical Society, 1894, pp. 130, 131

[8] Bernard C. Steiner, "History of Slavery in Connecticut", Johns Hopkins University Studies in Historical and Political Science, Eleventh Series, Baltimore: The Johns Hopkins Press, September-October 1893, p. 16

[9] Henry Scofield Cooley, "A Study of Slavery in New Jersey", Johns Hopkins University Studies in Historical and Political Science, Fourteenth Series, Baltimore: The Johns Hopkins Press, September-October 1896, p. 15,16

[10] Edward Raymond Turner, *The Negro in Pennsylvania: Slavery – Servitude – Freedom 1639 - 1861*, Washington DC: The American Historical Association, 1911, pp. 56 - 61

[11] George H. Moore, *Notes on the History of Slavery in Massachusetts*, New York: D. Appleton & Co. 1866, p. 142

[12] op. cit., Johnston, p. 133

[13] op. cit., Ballagh, p. 23

[14] op. cit., Turner, pp. 77 – 79

[15] op. cit., Moore, pp. 202 - 217

[16] op. cit., Moore, pp. 141, 142

[17] op. cit., Steiner, p. 30

[18] op. cit., Cooley, p. 46

[19] op. cit., Cooley, p. 47

[20] op. cit., Cooley, p. 18, 19

[21] See the text of the debates in the Constitutional Convention on 8 and 22 Aug 1787. The primary source is Jonathan Elliot, *The Debates in the Several State Conventions on the Adoption of the Federal Constitution as Recommended by the General Convention at Philadelphia in 1787; With a Diary of the Debates of the Congress of the Confederation As Reported by James Madison*, Philadelphia: J. B. Lippincott & Co., 1881, Vol. 5, pp . 391-394 and 457-461

[22] Edward D. Duvall, "Regarding the Three-Fifths Rule", 20 Jun 2011, pp. 51-59; it is also shown later in this volume.

Washington's Circular Letter (8 Jun 1783)
(5 Jun 2011)

The year 1783 was not an easy one for the thirteen newly-independent former British colonies. Although formal hostilities had ended, the British continued to interfere with commerce. Congress under the Confederation was proving to be a weak and useless institution, unable to meet its financial obligations, and unable to force the states to meet their obligations to Congress. The financial situation was so bad, in fact, that there were a few conspiracies in which some attempted to enlist the aid of the army to force the states to make good on the requisitions imposed by Congress. General George Washington had himself defused such a conspiracy in Mar 1783, in which some of his senior officers had attempted to instill a revolt in the ranks because Congress had not been able to pay the men. Congress continued to seek authority to establish a steady and reliable revenue stream, but the states were opposed to it.

It was at this time that George Washington, as commander of the army, but intending to resign his commission, took the initiative to outline to each of the 13 state leaders his view on necessary reforms. He wrote a circular letter to each of the governors or presidents of the thirteen states, explaining the current situation as he saw it and what would be necessary to ensure that the Revolution had not been in vain. His letter was made public, and was widely published throughout the states in the summer of 1783. It was an early recognition that some move toward a more firm union of the states to replace the ineffective Articles of Confederation was necessary. Washington wrote in part [1]:

> The citizens of America, placed in the most enviable conditions, as the sole lords and proprietors of a vast tract of continent, comprehending all the various soils and climates of the world, and abounding with all the necessaries and conveniences of life, are now by the late satisfactory pacification, acknowledged to be possessed of absolute freedom and independency; they are, from this period, to be considered as the actors on a most conspicuous theater, which seems to be peculiarly designated by providence for the display of human greatness and felicity; here, they are not only surrounded with every thing which can contribute to the completion of private blessings, by giving a fairer opportunity for political happiness, than any other nation has ever been favored with. Nothing can illustrate these observations more forcibly, than a recollection of the happy conjuncture of times and circumstances, under which our republic assumed its rank among the nations; the foundation of our empire was not laid in the gloomy age of ignorance and superstition, but at an epoch when the rights of mankind were better understood and more clearly defined, than at any former period, the researches of the human mind, after social happiness, have been carried to a great extent, the treasures of knowledge, acquired by the labors of the philosophers, sages, and legislatures, through a long succession of years, are laid open for our use, and their collected wisdom may be happily applied in the establishment of our forms of government; the free cultivation of letters, the unbounded extension of commerce, the progressive refinement of manners, the growing liberality of sentiment, and above all, the pure and benign light of revelation, have had a meliorating influence on mankind and increased the blessings of society. At this auspicious period, the United States came into existence as a nation, and if their citizens should not be completely free and happy, the fault will entirely be our own.
>
> Such is our situation, and such are our prospects: but notwithstanding the cup of blessing is thus reached out to us, notwithstanding happiness is ours, if we have a disposition to seize the occasion and make it our own; yet, it appears to me there is an option still left to the United States of America, that it is in our choice, and depends on their conduct, whether they will be respectable and prosperous, or contemptible and miserable as a nation; this is the time of their political probation, this is the moment when the eyes of the whole world are turned upon them, this is the moment to establish or ruin their national character forever, this is the favorable moment to give such a tone to our federal

> government, as will enable it to answer the ends of its institution, or this may be the ill-fated moment for relaxing the powers of the union, annihilating the cement of the Confederation, and exposing us to become the sport of European politics, which may play one state against another to prevent their growing importance, and to serve their own interested purposes. For, according to the system of policy the states shall adopt at this moment, they will stand or fall, and by their confirmation or lapse, it is yet to be decided, whether the Revolution must ultimately be considered as a blessing or a curse: a blessing or a curse, not to the present age alone, for with our fate will the destiny of unborn millions be involved.
>
> With this conviction of the importance of the present crisis, silence in me would be a crime; I will therefore speak to your Excellency, the language of freedom and sincerity, without disguise; I am aware, however, that those who differ from me in political sentiment, may perhaps remark, I am stepping out of the proper line of my duty, and they may possible ascribe to arrogance or ostentation, what I know is alone the result of the purest intention, but the rectitude of my own heart, which disdains such unworthy motives, the part I have hitherto acted in life, the determination I have formed, of not taking any share in public business hereafter, the ardent desire I fell, and shall continue to manifest, of quietly enjoying in private life, after all the toils of war, the benefits of a wise and liberal government, will, I flatter myself, sooner or later convince my countrymen, that I could have no sinister views in delivering with so little reserve, the opinions contained in this address.
>
> There are four things, which I humbly conceive, are essential to the well being, I may even venture to say, to the existence of the United States as an independent power:
>
> First. An indissoluble union of the states under one federal head.
>
> Secondly. A sacred regard to justice.
>
> Thirdly. The adoption of a proper peace establishment.
>
> Fourthly. The prevalence of that pacific and friendly disposition, among the people of the United States, which will induce them to forget their local prejudices and policies, to make those mutual concessions which are requisite to the general prosperity, and in some instances, to sacrifice their individual advantages to the interests of the community.
>
> These are the pillars on which the glorious fabric of our independency and national character must be supported; liberty is the basis, and who ever would dare to sap the foundation, or overturn the structure, under whatever specious pretexts he may attempt it, will merit the bitterest execration, and the severest punishment which can be inflicted by his injured country.

He then went on at some length to explain each of the first three main points: a) that the federal government requires certain essential enforceable powers; b) that creditors must be paid faithfully, and a certain means of revenue put in place, and secondly, the soldiers of the army must be fairly compensated; and c) that the militia is the backbone of the nation's defenses.

References

[1] John C. Fitzpatrick, editor, *The Writings of George Washington from the Original Manuscript Sources 1745-1799*, Washington: The United States Government Printing Office, (1938); Vol. 26, pp. 483-487

Benjamin Franklin Asks for Prayer (28 Jun 1787)
(2 May 2011)

Benjamin Franklin is widely regarded as an atheist, or at most a deist, when the topic of the religion embraced by the founding fathers comes up. Only God knows the true beliefs of any person. Deism, for those not familiar with it, is the concept that God exists and created the universe, but takes no interest in the affairs of mankind; that God is completely impersonal and uninterested in the fate of His creation.

I will relate a short debate in the Continental Congress in which Franklin discusses his beliefs, not because I have any interest in advancing any theory about Franklin, but because it runs so contrary to what is commonly taught about him. The members of the Convention had spent many days arguing about how the states would be represented in Congress; in fine, how the small states could guard themselves against the expected predations of the larger states, and how all the states could guard themselves against the national government. They were not making much headway. By late Jun 1787, they had agreed to two branches of a national legislature, but could not come to terms with how they should be constituted or how representation therein was to be allocated. On 28 Jun 1787, Dr. Franklin gave a short speech in Convention that sparked a debate on the usefulness of daily prayer. No such thing can be tolerated today in our public offices. But here is the incorrigible Benjamin Franklin [1].

> Dr. FRANKLIN. Mr. President, the small progress we have made after four or five weeks' close attendance and continual reasonings with each other -- our different sentiments on almost every question, several of the last producing as many noes as ayes -- is, methinks, a melancholy proof of the imperfection of the human understanding. We indeed seem to feel our own want of political wisdom, since we have been running about in search of it. We have gone back to ancient history for models of government, and examined the different forms of those republics which, having formed with the seeds of their own dissolution, now no longer exist. And we have viewed modern states all round Europe, but find none of their constitutions suitable to our circumstances.
>
> In this situation of this assembly, groping, as it were, in the dark, to find political truth, and scarce able to distinguish it when presented to us, how has it happened, sir, that we have no hitherto once thought of humbly applying to the father of lights to illuminate our understandings? In the beginning of the contest with Great Britain, when we were sensible of danger, we had daily prayer in this room for the divine protection. Our prayers, sir, were heard, and they were graciously answered. All of us who were engaged in the struggle must have observed frequent instances of a superintending providence in our favor. To that kind Providence we owe this happy opportunity of consulting in peace on the means of establishing our future national felicity. And have we now forgotten the powerful Friend? Or do we imagine that we no longer need his assistance? I have lived, sir, a long time, and, the longer I live, the more convincing proofs I see of this truth -- that God governs in the affairs of men. And if a sparrow cannot fall to the ground without his notice, is it probable than an empire can rise without his aid? We have been assured, sir, in the sacred writings, that "except the Lord build the house, they labor in vain that build it." I firmly believe this; and I also believe that without his concurring aid we shall succeed, in this political building, no better than the builders of Babel. We shall be divided by our little partial local interests; our projects will be confounded; and we ourselves shall become a reproach and by-word to future ages. And, what is worse, mankind may hereafter, from this unfortunate instance, despair of establishing governments by human wisdom, and leave it to war, conquest, and chance.
>
> I therefore beg leave to move that, henceforth, prayers imploring the assistance of Heaven, and its blessings on our deliberations, be held in this assembly every morning

> before we proceed to business, and that one or two or more of the clergy of this city be requested to officiate in that service.

There followed a short debate, in which the proposition was not brought to a vote, and as far as I know, never adopted. Now, (only God knows) maybe old Ben was as cynical as they come, hoping the religious types would be pacified by prayers every morning that would serve to soften them up and make them more willing to give up their rights to the sensible atheists. Maybe (only God knows), he was a true Christian, that is, personal belief in the saving work of Jesus Christ, the God-man. Maybe he was somewhere in between. But let's admit, given what we have been told these many years about Franklin's alleged dim view of Christianity, he made a speech that would get him kicked out of most schools, legislatures, and courthouses today.

References

[1] Jonathan Elliot, *Debates on the Adoption of the Federal Constitution in the Convention held at Philadelphia in 1787; With a Diary of the Debates of the Congress of the Confederation; As Reported by James Madison*, Philadelphia: J. B. Lippincott & Co., 1881, Vol. 5, pp. 253, 254.

Regarding the "Three-Fifths Rule"

Note: This essay was first published 20 Jun 2011. It is important to review the true history of how the "three-fifths rule" came about, since a great many race-baiting political operatives make a good living distorting it. The facts are shown in the following record of the debates on the Articles of Confederation and the Constitution: the "three-fifths rule" came about as a compromise on taxation and representation that had been agreed-to in 1783 (cf. 28 Mar 1783 and 11 Jun 1787 below).

1 Introduction
2 The Debate on the Articles of Confederation (1776)
3 The Articles of Confederation (1778)
4 The Proposed Amendment to the Articles of Confederation (1783)
5 The Constitutional Convention (1787)
6 Summary
References

1 Introduction

Every now and then we Americans find ourselves being subjected to "debates" among the prominent political persons and members of the media as to the lingering consequences of the "three-fifths" rule. It is common for those participants to make allegations about the three-fifths rule that fit their ideology or advance their demands. Rather than intrude on their high-level sloganeering, I shall in what follows simply lay out the true history of the matter, such that you, the honest observer, will be armed with the facts. Then you will be able to judge the merits of any arguments presented in those "debates".

Now I must first give a warning on this subject. The provision in question is contained in the third paragraph of Article 1, Section 2 of the U. S. Constitution. However, this provision was superseded by the 14th Amendment, which was ratified by the required number of states on 9 Jul 1868. So, anyone claiming to have been directly harmed by this "three-fifths" provision would have to have been born prior to that date. I am unaware of any people now living who could make a valid claim. Therefore, it is important to keep in mind that, although it is of great historical interest, this entire subject has now been resolved for practical purposes by Constitutional amendment.

We begin with the statement of the provision itself, extracted from the U. S. Constitution as noted above, as ratified by the last of the thirteen original states on 29 May 1790. Actually, the Constitution went into effect before that, since only nine were required to activate it; that occurred on 21 Jun 1788 with the ratification by New Hampshire. The provision in question reads:

> *Representatives and direct Taxes shall be apportioned among the several States which may be included within this Union, according to their respective Numbers, which shall be determined by adding to the whole Number of free Persons, including those bound to Service for a Term of Years, and excluding Indians not taxed, three fifths of all other Persons.*

This provision concerns the allocation of the number of seats in the House of Representatives, and the method by which "direct taxes" may be imposed by Congress. In this context, "direct taxes" referred to property taxes, head taxes, poll taxes or others which are based directly on population. The number of seats in the House allocated to each state is based on the states' population. In that way, it may be said that the House represents the people, since one seat is given to a certain number of people, regardless of how those are distributed among the states. It is the system by which a highly populated state like California or New York has greater representation in the House than Montana or Wyoming, which are states with comparable or greater land area. Note that four categories of persons are cited in the last part of the provision: a) free persons; b) those bound to a service for a term of years; c) Indians not taxed; and d) three fifths of all other persons. "Those bound to a term of service" refers to "indentured servitude", which was common in the colonial period and early years of the Republic. It refers to people who agreed to work without pay for another person, usually in repayment of the cost of the voyage from Europe. They were "indentured" until the debt was repaid, and then became free. "Indians not taxed" referred to Indians who were living on reservations, with sovereignty under treaties with the U. S. Last, "three fifths of all other persons" is a reference to slaves. The allegation, often made by the illustrious "debaters", is that this provision proves the pervasive hatred and prejudice of the white founders, since they relegated slaves to only three-fifths of a person for determining representation in the House of Representatives. Furthermore, such ratio is alleged to be due to black people being presumed by the founders as less than fully human. As I said, I will provide the facts below, and you may judge for yourselves.

It is important to keep in mind the status of slavery at this time (1788). Of the thirteen original states, only one (Massachusetts) had outlawed slavery altogether. Pennsylvania had passed a law a few years earlier that granted freedom to all persons born to slave parents after a certain date; it would have the effect of gradually eliminating slavery. All the other states permitted slavery, although not all permitted the importation of slaves. It must be said, though, that although slavery existed in twelve of the thirteen states, it was widespread only in four: Georgia, South Carolina, North Carolina, and Virginia.

2 The Debate on the Articles of Confederation (1776)

The earliest widely-available record we have on this subject, that is, the relative ratio of counting free vs. slave persons, is contained in Thomas Jefferson's notes on the debate of the Articles of Confederation in July 1776. Recall that at this time, there was no formal national or federal government of any kind; Congress had appointed itself to regulate the conduct of the war. But a formal union was desirable for many obvious reasons, and one point that must always be considered is to fund such a government. It was agreed in principle that Congress should have the power to requisition funds from each of the states to contribute to the war effort. The question was: upon what basis should Congress requisition various amounts from each state? In other words, should Congress request appropriations on the basis of land, number of people, value of houses, or some other metric? One proposal put forward, and which touches upon our subject, was to base it on the number and type of inhabitants. We pick up now from Jefferson's notes on that debate, reproduced in full without omission or interruption [1].

JEFFERSON'S NOTES OF DEBATE ON CONFEDERATION

> On Friday, July 12, [1776] the committee appointed to draw the Articles of Confederation reported them, and on the 22nd the house resolved themselves into a committee to take them into consideration. On the 30th and 31st of that month, and 1st of the ensuing, those articles were debated which determined the proportion, or quota, of money which each state should furnish to the common treasury, and the manner of voting in Congress. The first of these articles was expressed, in original draft, in these words: --
>
> "Art. XI. All charges of war, and all other expenses that shall be incurred for the common defense, or general welfare, and allowed by the United States assembled, shall be defrayed out of a common treasury, which shall be supplied by the several colonies in proportion to the number of inhabitants of every age, sex, and quality, except Indians not paying taxes, in each colony -- a true account of which, distinguishing the white inhabitants, shall be triennially taken, and transmitted to the Assembly of the United States."
>
> Mr. Chase moved that the quotes should be fixed, not by the number of inhabitants of every condition, but by that of the "white inhabitants". He admitted that taxation should always be in proportion to property; that this was, in theory, the true rule; but that, from a variety of difficulties, it was a rule which could never be adopted in practice. The value of the property in every state could never be estimated justly and equally. Some other measures for the wealth of the state must therefore be devised, some standard referred to, which would be more simple. He considered the number of inhabitants as a tolerably good criterion of property, and that this might always be obtained. He therefore thought it the best mode which we could adopt, with one exception only: he observed that

negroes are property, and, as such, cannot be distinguished from the lands or personalities held in those states where there are few slaves; that the surplus of profit which a northern farmer is able to lay by, he invests in cattle, horses, etc., whereas a southern farmer lays out the same surplus in slaves. There is no more reason, therefore, for taxing the Southern States on the farmer's head, and on his slave's head, than the northern ones on their farmer's heads and the heads of their cattle; that the method proposed would, therefore, tax the Southern States according to their numbers and their wealth conjunctly, while the Northern would be taxed on numbers only; that negroes, in fact, should not be considered as members of the state, more than cattle, and that they have no more interest in it.

Mr. John Adams observed, that the numbers of people are taken, by this article, as an index of the wealth of the state, and not as objects of taxation; that, as to this matter, it was of no consequence by what name you called your people, whether by that of freemen or of slaves; that, in some countries, the laboring poor are called freemen, in others they were called slaves; but that the difference as to the state was imaginary. What matters it whether a landlord, employing ten laborers on his farm, give them annually as much money as will buy them the necessaries of life, or give them those necessaries at short hand? The ten laborers add as much wealth to the state, increase its exports as much, in the one case as in the other. Certainly five hundred freemen produce no more profits, no greater surplus for the payment of taxes, than five hundred slaves. Therefore the state in which the laborers are called freemen, should be taxed no more than that in which those are called slaves. Suppose, by an extraordinary operation of nature or of law, one half the laborers of a state could, in the course of one night, be transformed into slaves; would the state be made poorer, or the less able to pay taxes? That the condition of the laboring poor in most countries -- that of the fishermen, particularly, in the Northern States -- is as abject as that of slaves. It is the number of laborers which produces the surplus for taxation; and numbers, therefore, indiscriminately, are the fair index to wealth; that it is the use of the word "property" here, and its application to some of the people of the state, which produce the fallacy. How does the southern farmer procure slaves? Either by importation, or by purchase from his neighbor. If he imports a slave, he adds one to the number of laborers in his country, and, proportionably, to its profits, and ability to pay taxes. If he buys from his neighbor, it is only a transfer of a laborer from one farm to another, which does not change the annual produce of the state, and therefore should not change its tax; that if a northern farmer works ten laborers on his farm, he can, it is true, invest the surplus of ten men's labor in cattle; but so may the southern farmer, working ten slaves; that a state of one hundred thousand freemen can maintain no more cattle than one of one hundred thousand slaves. Therefore they have no more of that kind of property. That a slave may, indeed, from the custom of speech, be more properly called the wealth of his master, than the free laborer might be called the wealth of his employer; but as to the state, both were equally its wealth, and should therefore equally add to the quota of its tax.

Mr. Harrison proposed, as a compromise, that two slaves should be counted as one freeman. He affirmed that slaves did not do as much work as freemen, and doubted if two effected more than one; that this was proved by the price of labor -- the hire of a laborer in the southern colonies being from £8 to £12, while in the northern it was generally £24.

Mr. Wilson said that, if this amendment should take place, the southern colonies would have all the benefit of slaves, whilst the northern ones would bear all the burden; that slaves increase the profits of a state, which the Southern States mean to take for themselves; that they also increase the burden of defense, which would of course fall so much the heavier on the Northern; that slaves occupy the places of freemen, and eat their food. Dismiss your slaves, and freemen will take their places. It is our duty to lay every discouragement on the importation of slaves; but this amendment would give *jus trium liberorum* to him who would import slaves; that other kinds of property were pretty well equally distributed through all the colonies; -- there were as many cattle, horses, and sheep in the north as the south, and south as the north; but not so to slaves; -- that experience has shown that those colonies have always been able to pay most which have the most inhabitants, whether they be black or white; and the practice of the southern colonies has always been to make every farmer pay poll taxes upon all his laborers, whether they be black or white. He acknowledges, indeed, that freemen work the most; but they consume the most also. They do not produce a greater surplus for taxation. The slave is neither fed nor clothed so expensively as a freeman. Again, white women are exempt from labor generally, but negro women are not. In this, then, the Southern States have an advantage, as the article now stands. It has sometimes been said that slavery is necessary, because the commodities they raise would be too dear for market if cultivated by freemen; but now it is said that the labor of slaves is the dearest.

Mr. Payne urged the original resolution of Congress, to proportion the quotas of the states to the number of souls.

Dr. Witherspoon was of opinion that the value of lands and houses was the best estimate of the wealth of a nation, and that it was practicable to obtain such a valuation. This is the true barometer of wealth. The one now proposed is imperfect in itself, and unequal between the states. It has been objected that negroes eat the food of freemen, and therefore should be taxed: horses also eat the food of freemen; therefore they should also be taxed. It has been said, too, that in carrying slaves into the estimate of the taxes the state is to pay, we do no more than those states themselves do, who always take slaves into the estimate of the taxes the individual is to pay. But the cases are not parallel. In the southern colonies slaves pervade the whole colony; but they do not pervade the whole continent. That, as to the original resolution of Congress, to proportion the quotas according to the souls, it was temporary only, and related to the moneys heretofore emitted; whereas we are now entering into a new compact, and therefore stand on original ground.

August 1. -- The question being put, the amendment proposed was rejected by the votes of New Hampshire, Massachusetts, Rhode Island, Connecticut, New York, New Jersey, and Pennsylvania, against those of Delaware, Maryland, Virginia, North and South Carolina. Georgia was divided.

Note that while these men had differing views on how taxation ought to be levied, there is no evidence that any distinction between freemen and slaves was due to a lesser moral quality of one compared to the other. It was all about the money, and the simplest, most equitable way to establish the quota and to collect it. As Adams observed, it makes no difference what people are called from the standpoint of revenue, one is the same as another, and should be equally taxed. Harrison offered up his compromise of counting slaves as half a freeman only because he estimated that a slave contributed only half as much in profit as a freeman. It was a very sensible observation, having nothing to do with the worth of a person, only the worth, that is, the relative value of their output. Who can doubt it? Why would a slave work as hard as a freeman, when all the benefits went to the master? Wilson was wary of the southern states, where slaves were numerous, taking economic advantage of the northern states, and he points out the hypocrisy of the southerners in pretending that slaves were of great economic necessity, but left the master too poor to pay taxes from the proceeds.

3 The Articles of Confederation (1778)

How did the debate turn out? Did the members of Congress decide that black people in general, and slaves in particular were less than human, and therefore given voting rights in a lesser proportion than whites? Of course not; under the Articles of Confederation, the only institution was Congress: only states were represented, and each state got one vote. It is most comparable to the Senate today, in which each state is represented equally. Representation was not decided by population or proportion between white and black. What about the tax issue? Here is Article 8 of the Articles of Confederation, which states the issue of taxation:

> Art. 8. All charges of war, and all other expenses that shall be incurred for the common defense or general welfare, and allowed by the United States in Congress Assembled, shall be defrayed out of a common treasury, which shall be supplied by the several states, in proportion to the value of all land, within each state, granted to or surveyed for any person, as such land, and the buildings and improvements thereon, shall be estimated, according to such mode as the United States in Congress assembled, shall, from time to time, direct and appoint.
>
> The taxes for paying that proportion shall be laid and levied by the authority and direction of the legislatures of the several states, within the time agreed upon by the United States in Congress assembled.

Referring back to Jefferson's notes, it seems that the opinion by Dr. Witherspoon ultimately was adopted: there is nothing in the Articles by which black and white, free and slave are distinguished. How did this happen? We don't know for sure. Jefferson added a paragraph at the end of his notes simply saying that "These articles, reported July 12, '76, were debated from day to day, and time to time, for two years."

4 The Proposed Amendment to the Articles of Confederation (1783)

The next occasion of debate on our subject occurred in the spring of 1783. The war had been over for all practical purposes since the victory at Yorktown in October of 1781. Unknown to Congress, preliminary articles of peace with Great Britain had been signed in Paris on 20 Jan 1783, but Congress would not learn of it until 23 Mar 1783. Congress was however, mired in debates about how to keep the nation together after the peace. One of the main problems was Congress' inability to borrow money since the collapse of the Continental currency in 1781. Congress had no credit; in fact in the previous year, there was a time when there was no money at all in the treasury. There were essentially two problems. First, the Articles of Confederation did not provide Congress with a revenue stream independent of requisitions from the states; and secondly, the states were not paying their duly assigned requisitions. So, Congress, in early March of 1783, set about debating how to modify the Articles to remedy both of these. On 7 Mar 1783, Congress began debate on a report produced by a Committee on Revenue. It contained eleven sections, of which only the eleventh section relates to our subject (it has two paragraphs). The first ten are recommendations for the imposition of import duties on various items for a period for 25 years, rules for determining which expenses were allowable under the Articles, and the rules by which these changes were to be adopted. Section 11 states [2]:

> 11. "That, as a more convenient and certain rule of ascertaining the proportions to be supplied by the States, respectively, to the common treasury, the following alteration, in the Articles of Confederation and perpetual union between these States, be, and the same is hereby, agreed to by Congress; and the several States are advised to authorize their respective Delegates to subscribe and ratify the same, as part of the said instrument of union, in the words following, to wit:
>
> " 'So much of the eighth of the Articles of Confederation and perpetual union between the thirteen States of America as is contained in the words following, to wit: "All

> charges of war, and all other expenses that shall be incurred for the common defense or general welfare, and allowed by the United States in Congress Assembled, shall be defrayed out of a common treasury, which shall be supplied by the several states, in proportion to the value of all land within each state granted to, or surveyed for, any person, as such land, and the buildings and improvements thereon, shall be estimated according to such mode as the United States in Congress assembled, shall, from time to time, direct and appoint," -- is hereby revoked and made void, and in place thereof it is declared and concluded the same having been agreed to in a Congress of the United States, that all charges of war, and all other expenses that shall be incurred for the common defense or general welfare, and allowed by the United States in Congress assembled, shall be defrayed out of a common treasury, which shall be supplied by the several States in proportion to the number of inhabitants, of every age, sex, and condition, except Indians, not paying taxes in each State; which number shall be triennially taken and transmitted to the United States, in Congress assembled, in such mode as they shall direct and appoint; provided always, that in such numeration no persons shall be included who are bound to servitude for life, according to the laws of the State to which they belong, other than such as may be between the ages of * ---- years.' "

The items relating to the import duties were debated briefly on 11 Mar 1783, but the ones of interest here were not debated again until 27 Mar 1783. In the meantime, Congress learned of and debated the preliminary articles of peace (12-15 Mar 1783), received a note from General Washington on the 17th that there were some members of the business community to whom Congress owed money that were trying to tempt the army to force either the States or Congress to pay them. On the 18th, they modified the rates of import duties. On the 19th they were notified by the Superintendent of Finance that he had received word that Congress could expect no more credit from France or any other European nation. They spent the week from the 20th to the 26th debating various points of the preliminary peace treaty; on a dispute with France about the diplomatic delicacy of signing articles of peace without France's participation; Washington's skill at pre-empting any subversion of the army; and a few items on the import duty issue.

On 27 Mar 1783, Congress resumed debate on the requisition allocation issue in detail. After going over paragraphs 6 through 10 of the 7 Mar 1783 report, they debated the 11th and 12th paragraph (both part of the 11th Section), which is pertinent to our subject. Resuming at the official record, which carried over to 28 Mar 1783, we have, regarding the 11th and 12th paragraphs of the 7 Mar 1783 report, without omission or interruption [3]:

> (Thursday, March 27, 1783)
>
> (Eleventh and twelfth paragraphs) Mr. Bland, in opposition, said that the value of land was the best rule, and that, at any rate, no change should be attempted until its practicability should be tried.
>
> Mr. Madison thought the value of land could never be justly or satisfactorily obtained; that it would ever be a source of contentions among the States; and that, as a repetition of the valuation would be within the course of twenty-five years, it would, unless exchanged for a more simple rule, mar the whole plan.
>
> Mr. Gorham was in favor of the paragraphs. He represented, in strong terms, the inequality and clamors produced by valuations of land in the State of Massachusetts, and the probability of the evils being increased among the States themselves, which were less tied together, and more likely to be jealous of each other.
>
> Mr. Williamson was in favor of the paragraphs.
>
> Mr. Wilson was strenuous in their favor; said he was in Congress when the Articles of Confederation directing a valuation of land were agreed to; that it was the effect of the impossibility of compromising the different ideas of the Eastern and Southern States, as to the value of slaves compared with whites, the alternative in question.

Mr. Clark was in favor of them. He said that he was also in Congress when this article was decided; that the Southern States would have agreed to number in preference to the value of land, if half their slaves only should be included; but that the Eastern States would not concur in that proposition.

It was agreed, on all sides, that, instead of fixing the proportion by ages, as the report proposed, it would be best to fix the proportion in absolute numbers. With this view, and that the blank might be filled up, the clause was recommitted.

(Friday, March 28, 1783)

The Committee last mentioned, reported that two blacks be rated as one freeman.

Mr. Wolcott was for rating them as four to three.

Mr. Carroll as four to one.

Mr. Williamson said he was principled against slavery; and he thought slaves an incumbrance to society, instead of increasing its ability to pay taxes.

Mr. Higginson as four to three.

Mr. Rutledge said, for the sake of the object, he would agree to rate slaves as two to one, but he sincerely thought three to one would be a juster proportion.

Mr. Holten as four to three.

Mr. Osgood said he did not go beyond four to three.

On a question of rating them as three to two, the votes were, New Hampshire, aye; Massachusetts no; Rhode Island, divided; Connecticut, aye; New Jersey, aye; Pennsylvania, aye; Delaware, aye; Maryland, no; Virginia, no, North Carolina, no; South Carolina, no.

The paragraph was then postponed, by general consent, some wishing for further time to deliberate on it; but it appearing to be the general opinion that no compromise would be agreed to.

After some further discussions on the report, in which the necessity of some simple and practicable rule of apportionment came fully into view, Mr. Madison said that, in order to give proof of the sincerity of his professions of liberality, he would propose that slaves should be rated as five to three. Mr. Rutledge seconded the motion. Mr. Wilson said he would sacrifice his opinion on this compromise.

Mr. Lee was against changing the rule, but gave it as his opinion that two slaves were not equal to one freeman.

On the question of five to three, it passed in the affirmative; New Hampshire, aye; Massachusetts, divided; Rhode Island, no; Connecticut, no; New Jersey, aye; Maryland, aye; Virginia, aye; North Carolina, aye; South Carolina, aye.

A motion was then made by Mr. Bland, seconded by Mr. Lee, to strike out the clause so amended, and on the question "shall it stand," it passed in the negative; New Hampshire, aye; Massachusetts, no; Rhode island, no; Connecticut, no; New Jersey, aye; Pennsylvania, aye; Delaware, no; Maryland, aye; Virginia, aye; North Carolina, aye; South Carolina, no; so the clause was struck out.

The arguments used by those who were for rating the slaves high were, that the expense of feeding and clothing them was as far below that incident to freemen as their industry and ingenuity were below those of freemen; and that the warm climate within which the States having slaves lay, compared with the rigorous climate and inferior fertility of the others, ought to have great weight in the case; and that the exports of the former States were greater than of the latter. On the other side, it was said, that slaves were not put to labor as young as the children of laboring families; that, having no interest in their labor, they did as little as possible, and omitted every exertion of thought requisite to facilitate and expedite it; that if the exports of the States having slaves exceeded those of the others, their imports were in proportion, slaves being employed wholly in agriculture, not in manufactures; and that, in fact, the balance of trade formerly was much more against the Southern States than the others.

On the main question, New Hampshire, aye; Massachusetts, no; Rhode Island, no; Connecticut, no; New York (Mr. Floyd, aye); New Jersey, aye; Delaware, no; Maryland, aye; Virginia, aye; North Carolina, aye; South Carolina, no.

We observe here an agreed-to compromise in which slaves were to be counted as three-fifths of a freeman. Note the context of the debate. The Northern states wanted to count slaves as equal, or nearly equal (3 to 4) to a freeman, noting that the expenses associated with providing for a slave was proportional to the lower output of slaves compared to a freeman. At the same time, the output produced by slaves could be exported profitably by the southerners, and therefore they could afford to pay taxes on slaves as equal, or nearly equal to freeman. The southerners argued that the children of freemen went to work at a younger age than slaves, that slaves did as little work as possible, and that the larger exports existed only to pay for the larger imports by the Southern States. In no case did any of these men argue that slaves, or black people in general, were to be rated lower than whites owing to some moral deficiency of black people relative to white. As to Madison's note that some argued on the basis of reduced ingenuity by the slaves, it is obvious that slaves would exhibit less ingenuity since they were deliberately kept uneducated by the masters.

Wilson's comment about the earlier debate being based on the value of slaves relative to whites does not relate to any moral sense; only the to the relative amount slaves contributed to the economy. Again, if slaves produced less per capita than freemen, then it is safe to conclude that it is characteristic of the institution: why would a person in bondage work as hard as a freeman who was able to keep the proceeds of his labor?

Congress resumed its debate on the most important problem, which was how to obtain consistent revenue. The states had mostly been delinquent in the payment of requisitions, which in a sense held Congress hostage, since Congress was not granted any power to raise revenues directly. The sought-for reform was to give Congress the power to impose an import duty to finance the necessary activities of Congress and to pay off the war debts. The culmination of the debate occurred on 18 Apr 1783, in which Congress put forth two recommendations: a) that Congress be allowed to impose an import duty on various products; and b) that Article 8 was to be modified such that requisitions assigned to the states shall be done in proportion to population and not land value. This second recommendation was made as follows [4]:

So much of the 8th of the Articles of Confederation and Perpetual Union, between the thirteen states of America, as is contained in the words following, to wit, "All charges of war, and all other expenses that shall be incurred for the common defense or general welfare, and allowed by the United States in Congress assembled, shall be defrayed out of a common treasury, which shall be supplied by the several states, in proportion to the value of all land within each state, granted to or surveyed for any person, as such land, and the buildings and improvements thereon shall be estimated, according to such mode as the United States in Congress assembled shall from time to time direct and appoint," is hereby revoked and made void; and in place thereof, it is declared and concluded, the same having been agreed to in a Congress of the United States, that all charges of war, and all other expenses, that have been, or shall be, incurred for the common defense and general welfare, and allowed by the United States in Congress assembled, except so far as shall be otherwise provided for, shall be defrayed out of a common treasury, which shall be supplied by the several states in proportion to the whole number of white and other free citizens and inhabitants, of every age, sex, and condition, including those bound to servitude for a term of years, and three fifths of all other persons not comprehended in the

> foregoing description, except Indians not paying taxes, in each state; which number shall be triennially taken an transmitted to the United States in Congress assembled, in such mode as they shall direct and appoint.
>
> On the question to agree to the forgoing act, the yeas and nays required by Mr. Arnold: New Hampshire, aye; Massachusetts, aye, Rhode Island, no; Connecticut, aye; New York, divided; New Jersey, aye; Pennsylvania, aye; Delaware, aye; Maryland, aye; Virginia, aye; North Carolina, aye; South Carolina, aye. So it was resolved in the affirmative.

The Articles of Confederation required that every proposed alteration or amendment be approved unanimously by the thirteen states. This recommendation as cited above was sent out the states, but neither the import duty nor the modification of the provision on determining requisitions was ever agreed to. In fact, the inability of Congress to pay its debts, along with various revolts in the states, and threat of strategic encirclement by Spain and England were the principal causes of the drive for a different type of union, that is, the Constitution of 1787.

At this stage then, Congress had agreed and recommended that requisitions upon the states should be based on population rather than land value, and that slaves were to be counted as three-fifths of a free man for the purpose of assessing the relative ability to pay those requisitions. Nothing else occurred on this topic until the debates in the Constitutional Convention, which is recalled next.

5 The Constitutional Convention (1787)

We come now at last to the debates in Philadelphia that produced the Constitution and the most-hated-and-frequently-debated "three-fifths' rule in its final form. The following narrative contains the progress of the debate on this issue in the Federal Convention of 1787.

The first mention of our topic occurred on 29 May 1787, when Edmund Randolph introduced several resolutions for consideration, the second of which reads [5]:

> 2. Resolved, therefore, that the right of suffrage, in the national legislature, ought to be proportioned to the quotas of contribution, or to the number of free inhabitants, as the one or the other may seem best, in different cases.

On the same day, Charles Pinckney submitted a draft of a Constitution for consideration. Regarding the means of allocating seats in the legislature, Article III states [6]:

> --- and the legislature shall hereafter regulate the number of delegates by the number of inhabitants, according to the provisions hereinafter made, at the rate of one for every ______ thousand.

Pinckney did not spell out the method by which the number of inhabitants was to be counted. He did, however, mention a method of direct taxation in his Article VI [7]:

> The proportion of direct taxation shall be regulated by the whole number of inhabitants of every description; which number shall, within _____ years after the first meeting of the legislature, and within the term of every _____ year, by taken, in the manner to be prescribed by the legislature.

On 30 May 1787, some debate occurred on this subject [8]:

> (Wednesday, May 30)
>
> The following resolution, being the second, proposed by Mr. Randolph, was taken up, viz.:
>
> "That the rights of suffrage in the national legislature ought to be proportioned to the quotas of contribution, or to the number of free inhabitants, as the one or the other rule may seem best in different cases."

Mr. Madison, observing the words "or to the number of free inhabitants" might occasion debates which would divert the committee from the general question whether the principle of representation should be changed, moved that they be struck out.

Mr. King observed, that the quotas of contribution, which would alone remain as the measure of representation, would not answer; because, waiving every other view of the matter, the revenue might hereafter be so collected by the general government that the sums respectively drawn from the states would not appear, and besides would be continually varying.

Mr. Madison admitted the propriety of the observation, and that some better rule ought to be found.

Col. Hamilton moved to alter the resolution so as to read, "that the rights of suffrage in the national legislature ought to be proportioned to the number of free inhabitants." Mr. Spaight seconded the motion.

It was then moved that the resolution be postponed; which was agreed to.

Mr. Randolph and Mr. Madison then moved the following resolution: "That the rights of suffrage in the national legislature ought to be proportioned."

It was moved, and seconded, to amend it by adding, "and not according to the present system;" which was agreed to.

It was then moved and seconded to alter the resolution so as to read, "That the rights of suffrage in the national legislature ought not to be according to the present system."

It was then moved and seconded to postpone the resolution moved by Mr. Randolph and Mr. Madison; which being agreed to, ---

Mr. Madison moved, in order to get over the difficulties, the following resolution: "That the equality of suffrage established by the Articles of Confederation ought not to prevail in the national legislature; and that an equitable ratio of representation ought to be substituted." This was seconded by Mr. Gouverneur Morris, and being generally relished, would have been agreed to; when

Mr. Read moved, that the whole clause relating to the point of representation be postponed; reminding the committee that the deputies from Delaware were restrained by their commission from assenting to any change of the rule of suffrage, and in case such a change should be fixed on, it might become their duty to retire from the Convention.

Mr. Gouverneur Morris observed, that the valuable assistance of those members could not be lost without real concern; and that so early a proof of discord in the Convention as the secession of a state would add much to the regret; that the change proposed was, however, so fundamental an article in a national government, that it could not be dispensed with.

Mr. Madison observed, that, whatever reason might have existed for the equality of suffrage when the union was a federal one among sovereign states, it must cease when a national government should be put into place. In the former case, the acts of Congress depended so much for their efficacy and on the cooperation of the states, that these had a weight, both within and without Congress, nearly in proportion to their extent and importance. In the latter case, as the acts of the general government would take effect without the intervention of the state legislatures, a vote from a small state would have the same efficacy and importance as a vote from a large one, and there was the same reason for different numbers of representatives from different states, as from counties of different extents within particular states. He suggested, as an expedient for at once taking the sense of the members on this point, and saving the Delaware deputies from embarrassment, that the question should be taken in committee, and the clause, on report to the

House, be postponed without a question there. This, however, did not appear to satisfy Mr. Read.

By several it was observed, that no just construction of the act of Delaware could require or justify a secession of her deputies, even if the resolution were to be carried through the House as well as the committee. It was finally agreed, however, that the clause should be postponed; it being understood that, in the event the proposed change of representation would certainly be agreed to, no objection or difficulty being started from any other quarter than from Delaware.

The motion of Mr. Read to postpone being agreed to, the committee then rose; the chairman reported progress; and the House, having resolved to resume the subject in committee tomorrow, adjourned to ten o'clock.

It is important to pause here for clarity. The "rights of suffrage" referred to here does not refer to persons; it refers to how the states would vote in the national legislature. Recall, that in the Articles of Confederation, each state received one vote only. When Madison calls for the elimination of "equality of suffrage", he is recommending that the states have differing numbers of votes, based on some as-yet defined criteria. Two possible criteria had already been proposed: a) Randolph's allocation by the amount contributed to the union by each state; and b) Hamilton's method of allocation by the number of free inhabitants in each state.

The next important facet of this debate came on 31 May 1787, when the members debated the general method by which the members of the first branch of the national legislature (i.e., ultimately the House of Representatives) should be chosen. Some were in favor of election by the people, and some were in favor of some other method. Madison's notes of this debate read [9]:

(Thursday, May 31)

In the committee of the whole on Mr. Randolph's resolution, --- the third resolution, "that the national legislature ought to consist of two branches," was agreed to without debate, or dissent, except that of Pennsylvania, --- given probably from complaisance to Dr. Franklin, who was understood to be partial to a single house of legislation.

The fourth resolution, first clause, "that the members of the first branch of the national legislature ought to be elected by the people of the several states," being taken up, ---

Mr. Sherman opposed the election by the people, insisting that it ought to be by the state legislatures. The people, he said, immediately, should have as little to do as may be about the government. They want information, and are constantly liable to be misled.

Mr. Gerry. The evils we experience flow from the excess of democracy. The people do not want virtue, but are the dupes of pretended patriots. In Massachusetts, it had been fully confirmed by experience, that they are daily misled into the most baneful measures and opinions, by the false reports circulated by designing men, and which no one on the spot can refute. One principal evil arises from the want of any due provision for those employed in the administration of government. It would seem to be a maxim of democracy to starve the public servants. He mentioned the popular clamor in Massachusetts for the reduction of salaries, and the attack made on that of the governor, though secured by the spirit of the constitution itself. He had, he said, been too republican heretofore: he was still, however, republican, but had been taught by experience the danger of the levelling spirit.

Mr. Mason argued strongly for an election of the larger branch by the people. It was to be the grand depositary of the democratic principle of the government. It was, so to speak, to be our House of Commons. It ought to know and sympathize with every part of the community, and ought therefore to be taken, not only from different parts of the whole republic, but also from different districts of the larger members of it; which had in several instances, particularly in Virginia, different interests and views arising from the difference of produce, of habits, etc. etc. He admitted that we have been too democratic, but was afraid we should incautiously run into the opposite extreme. We ought to attend to the rights of every class of the people. He had often wondered at the indifference of the superior classes of society to this dictate of humanity and policy; considering that, however affluent their circumstances, or elevated their situations might be, the course of a few years not only might, but certainly would, distribute their prosperity throughout the lowest classes of society. Every selfish motive, therefore, every family attachment, ought to recommend such a system of policy as would provide no less carefully for the rights and happiness of the lowest, than of the highest, order of citizens.

Mr. Wilson contended strenuously for drawing the most numerous branch of the legislature immediately from the people. He was for raising the federal pyramid to a considerable altitude, and for that reason he wished to give it as broad as basis as possible. No government could long subsist without the confidence of the people. In a republican government, this confidence was peculiarly essential. He also thought it wrong to increase the weight of the state legislatures by making them the electors of the national legislature. All interference between the general and local governments should be obviated as much as possible. On examination, it would be found that the opposition of states to federal measures had proceeded much more from the officers of the states than from the people at large.

Mr. Madison considered the popular election of one branch of the national legislature as essential to every plan of free government. He observed, that, in some of the states, one branch of the legislature was composed of men already removed from the people by an intervening body of electors; that, if the first branch of the general legislature should be elected by the state legislatures, the second branch elected by the first, the executive elected by the second together with the first, and other appointments again made for subordinate purposes by the executive, the people would be lost sight of altogether, and the necessary sympathy between them and their rulers and officers too little felt. He was an advocate for the policy of refining the popular appointments by successive filtrations, but thought it might be pushed too far. He wished the expedient to be resorted to only in the appointment of the second branch of the legislature, and in the executive and judiciary branches of the government. He thought, too, that the great fabric to be raised would be more stable and durable, if it should rest on the solid foundation of the people themselves, than if it should stand merely on the pillars of the legislatures.

Mr. Gerry did not like the election by the people. The maxims taken from the British constitution were often fallacious when applied to our situation, which was extremely different. Experience, he said, had shown that the state legislatures, drawn immediately from the people, did not always possess their confidence. He had no objection, however, to an election by the people, if it were so qualified that men of honor and character might not be unwilling to be joined in the appointments. He seemed to think the people might nominate a certain number, out of which the state legislatures should be bound to choose.

Mr. Butler thought an election by the people an impractical mode.

On the question for an election of the first branch of the national legislature by the people, -- Massachusetts, New York, Pennsylvania, Virginia, North Carolina, Georgia, aye, 6; New Jersey, South Carolina, no, 2; Connecticut, Delaware, divided.

So far, then we have an agreement that the legislative branch will consist of two branches, that the voting rights of the states will not be equal as in the Articles of Confederation, and that the members of the first branch of the legislature will be elected directly by the people.

There was a debate on 7 Jun 1787 regarding suffrage of states, but it related only to the manner of choosing the Senate. Since states are represented equally in the Senate, that debate does not enter into our subject. The rules for the first branch resumed again on 9 Jun 1787 [10]:

(Saturday, June 9)

Mr. Patterson moved, that the committee resume the clause relating to the rule of suffrage in the national legislature.

Mr. Brearly seconds him. He was sorry, he said, that any question on this point was brought into view. It had been much agitated in Congress at the time of forming the Confederation, and was then rightly settled by allowing each sovereign state an equal vote. Otherwise, the smaller states must have been destroyed instead of being saved. The substitution of a ratio, he admitted, carried fairness on the face of it, but, on a deeper examination, was unfair and unjust. Judging of the disparity of the states by the quota of Congress, Virginia would have sixteen votes, and Georgia but one. A like proportion to the others will make the whole number ninety. There will be three large states, and ten small ones. The large states, by which he meant Massachusetts, Pennsylvania, and Virginia, will carry everything before them. It had been admitted, and was known to him facts from within New Jersey, that where large and small counties were united into a district for electing representatives for the district, the large counties always carried their point, and consequently the large states would do so. Virginia with her sixteen votes will be a solid column indeed, a formidable phalanx. While Georgia, with her solitary vote, and the other little states, will be obliged to throw themselves constantly into the scale of some large one, in order to have any weight at all. He had come to the convention with a view of being as useful as he could, in giving energy and stability to the federal government. When the proposition for destroying the equality of votes came forward, he was astonished, he was alarmed. Is it fair, then, it will be asked, that Georgia should have an equal vote with Virginia? He would not say it was. What remedy, then? One only: that a map of the United States be spread out, that all the existing boundaries be erased, and that a new partition of the whole be made into thirteen equal parts.

Mr. Patterson considered the proposition for a proportional representation as striking at the existence of the lesser states. He would premise, however, to an investigation of this question, some remarks on the nature, structure, and powers of the Convention. The Convention, he said, was formed in pursuance of an act of Congress; that this act was recited in several of the commissions, particularly that of Massachusetts, which he required to be read; that the amendment of the Confederacy was the object of all the laws and commissions on the subject; that the Articles of Confederation were therefore the proper basis of all the proceedings of the Convention; that we ought to keep within its limits, or we should be charged by or constituents with usurpation; that the people of America were sharp-sighted, and not to be deceived. But the commissions under which we acted were not the only measure of our power, they denoted also the sentiments of the states on the subject of our deliberation. The idea of a national government, as contradistinguished from a federal one, never entered into the mind of any of them; and to the public mind we must accommodate ourselves. We have no power to go beyond the federal scheme; and if we had, the people are not ripe for any other. We must follow the people; the people will not follow us. The proposition could not be maintained, whether considered in reference to us as a nation, or as a confederacy. A confederacy supposes sovereignty in the members composing it, and sovereignty supposes equality. If we are to be considered as a nation, all state distinctions must be abolished, the whole must be thrown into hotchpot, and when an equal division is made, and then there may be fairly an equality of representation. He held up Virginia, Massachusetts, and Pennsylvania, as the three large states, and the other ten as small ones; repeating the calculations of Mr. Brearly, as to the disparity of votes which would take place, and affirming that the small states would never agree to it. He said there was no more reason that a great individual state, contributing much, should have more votes than a small one, contributing little, than that a rich individual citizen should have more votes than an indigent one. If the ratable property of A was to that of B as forty to one, ought A, for that reason, to have forty times as many votes as B? Such a principle would never be admitted; and, if it were admitted, would put B entirely at the mercy of A. As A has more to be protected than B, so he ought to contribute more for the common protection. The same may be said of a large state, which has more to be protected than a small one. Give the large states an influence in proportion to their magnitude, and what will be the consequence? Their ambition will be proportionally increased, and the small states will have every thing to fear. It was once proposed by Galloway, and some others, that America should be represented in the British Parliament, and then be bound by its laws. America could not have been entitled to more than one third of the representatives which would fall to the share of Great Britain: would American rights and interests have been safe under an authority thus constituted? It has been said that, if a national government is to be formed so as to operate on the people, and not on the states, the representatives ought to be drawn from the people. But why so? May not a legislature, filled by state legislatures, operate on the people who choose the state legislatures? Or may not a practicable coercion be found? He admitted that there was none such in the existing system. He was attached strongly to the plan of the existing Confederacy, in which the people choose their legislative representatives, and the legislatures their federal representatives. No other amendments were wanting than to mark the orbits of the states with due precision, and provide for the use of coercion, which was the great point. He alluded to the hint, thrown out by Mr. Wilson, of the necessity to which the large states might be reduced, of confederating among themselves, by a refusal of the others to concur. Let them unite if they please, but let them remember that they have no authority to compel the others to unite. New Jersey will never confederate on the plan before the committee. She would be swallowed up. He had rather submit to a monarch, to a despot, than to such a fate. He would not only oppose the plan here, but, on his return home, do every thing in his power to defeat it there.

Mr. Wilson hoped, if the Confederacy should be dissolved, that a majority – nay, a minority of the states would unite for their safety. He entered elaborately into the defense of a proportional representation, stating, for his first position, that, as all authority was derived from the people, equal numbers of people ought to have an equal number of representatives, and different numbers of people, different numbers of representatives. This principle had been improperly violated in the Confederation, owing to the urgent circumstances of the times. As to the case of A and B, stated by Mr. Patterson, he observed that, in districts as large as the states, the number of people was the best measure of their comparative wealth. Whether, therefore, wealth or numbers was to form the ratio, it would be the same. Mr. Patterson admitted persons, not property, to be the measure of suffrage. Are not the citizens of Pennsylvania equal to those of New Jersey? Does it require one hundred and fifty of the former to balance fifty of the latter? Representatives of different districts ought clearly to hold the same proportion to each other, as their respective constituents hold to each other. If the small states will not confederate on this plan, Pennsylvania, and he presumed some other states, would not confederate on any other. We have been told that, each state being sovereign, all are equal. So each man is naturally a sovereign over himself, and all men are therefore naturally equal. Can he retain this equality when he becomes a member of civil government? He cannot. As little can a sovereign state, when it becomes a member of a federal government. If New Jersey will not part with her sovereignty, it is vain to talk of government. A new partition of the states is desirable, but evidently and totally impracticable.

Mr. Williamson illustrated the cases by a comparison of the different states to counties of different sizes within the same state; observing, that proportional representation was admitted to be just in the latter case, and could not, therefore, be fairly contested in the former.

The question being about to be put, Mr. Patterson hoped that, as so much depended on it, it might be thought best to postpone the decisions until tomorrow; which was done, *nem. con.*

The committee rose, and the House adjourned.

The debate continued on 11 Jun 1787 [11]:

(Monday, Jun 11)

In the Committee of the Whole. --- The clause concerning the rule of suffrage in the national legislature, postponed on Saturday, was resumed.

Mr. Sherman proposed, that the proportion of suffrage in the first branch should be according to the respective numbers of inhabitants; and that in the second branch, or Senate, each state should have one vote and no more. He said, as the states would remain possessed of certain individual rights, each state ought to be able to protect itself; otherwise, a few large states will rule the rest. The House of Lords in England, he observed, had certain particular rights under the constitution, and hence they have an equal vote with the House of Commons, that they may be able to defend their rights.

Mr. Rutledge proposed, that the proportion of suffrage in the first branch should be according to the quotas of contribution. The justice of this rule, he said, could not be contested. Mr. Butler urged the same idea; adding, that money was power; and that the states ought to have weight in the government in proportion to their wealth.

Mr. King and Mr. Wilson, in order to bring the question to a point, moved, "that the right of suffrage in the first branch of the national legislature ought not to be according to the rule established in the Articles of Confederation, but according to some equitable ratio of representation." The clause, so far as it related to suffrage in the first branch, was postponed, in order to consider this motion.

Mr. Dickinson contended for the actual contributions of the states, as the rule of their representation and suffrage in the first branch. By thus connecting the interests of the states with their duty, the latter were sure to be performed.

Mr. King remarked, that it was uncertain what mode might be used in levying a national revenue; but that it was probable, imposts would be one source of it. If the actual contributions were to be the rule, the non-importing states, as Connecticut and New Jersey, would be in a bad situation, indeed. It might so happen that they would have no representation. This situation of particular states has been always one powerful argument in favor of the five percent impost.

The question being about to be put, Dr. Franklin said, he had thrown his ideas of the matter on a paper; which Mr. Wilson read to the committee, in the words following: ---

"Mr. Chairman: It has given me great pleasure to observe, that till this point – the proportion of representation – came before us, our debates were carried on with great coolness and temper. If any thing of a contrary kind has on this occasion appeared, I hope it will not be repeated; for we are sent here to consult, not to contend, with each other; and declarations of a fixed opinion, and of determined resolution never to change it, neither enlighten nor convince us. Positiveness and warmth on one side naturally beget their like on the other, and tend to create and augment discord and division, in a great concern wherein our harmony and union are extremely necessary to give some weight to our councils, and render them effectual in promoting and securing the common good.

"I must own, that I was originally of the opinion that it would be better if every member of Congress, or our national council, were to consider himself rather as a representative of the whole than as an agent for the interests of a particular state; in which case, the proportion of members for each state would be of less consequence, and it would not be very material whether they voted by states or individually. But as I find this is not to be expected, I now think the number of representatives should bear some proportion to the number of the represented, and that the decisions should be by majority of members, not by the majority of the states. This is objected to from an apprehension that the greater states would then swallow up the smaller. I do not at present clearly see what advantage the greater states could propose to themselves by swallowing up the smaller, and therefore do not apprehend they would attempt it. I recollect that, in the beginning of this century, when the union was proposed of the two kingdoms, England and Scotland, the Scotch patriots were full of fears, that, unless they had an equal number of representatives in Parliament, they should be ruined by the superiority of the English. They finally agreed, however, that the different proportions of importance in the union of the two nations should be attended to, whereby they were to have only forty members in the House of Commons, and only sixteen in the House of Lords – a very great inferiority of numbers. And yet to this day I do not recollect that any thing has been done in the Parliament of Great Britain to the prejudice of Scotland; and whoever looks over the lists of public officers, civil and military, of that nation, will find, I believe, that the North Britons enjoy at least their full proportion of emolument.

"But, sir, in the present mode of voting by states, it is equally in the power of the lesser states to swallow up the greater; and this is mathematically demonstrable. Suppose, for example, that seven smaller states had each three members in the House, and the six larger to have, one with another, six members; and that, upon a question, two members of each smaller state should be in the affirmative, and one in the negative, they would make -- affirmatives, 14; negative, 7; and that all the larger states should be unanimously in the negative, they would make, negatives, 36; in all, affirmatives, 14, negatives 43.

"It is, then, apparent, that the fourteen carry the question against the forty-three, and the minority overpowers the majority, contrary to the common practice of assemblies in all countries and ages.

"The greater states, sir, are naturally as unwilling to have their property left in the disposition of the smaller, as the smaller are to have theirs in the disposition of the greater. An honorable gentleman has, to avoid this difficulty, hinted a proposition of equalizing the states. It appears to me an equitable one, and I should, for my own part, not be against such a measure, if it might be found practicable. Formerly, indeed, when almost every province had a different constitution, -- some with greater, others with fewer, privileges, -- it was of importance to the borderers, when their boundaries were contested, whether, by running the division lines, they were placed on one side or the other. At present, when such differences are done away, it is less material. The interest of a state is made up of the interests of its individual members. If they are not injured, the state is not injured. Small states are more easily and happily governed than large ones. If, therefore, in such an equal division, it should be found necessary to diminish Pennsylvania, I should not be averse to the giving a part of it to New Jersey, and another to Delaware. But as there would probably be considerable difficulties in adjusting such a division, and however equally made at first, it would be continually varying by the augmentation of inhabitants in some states, and their fixed proportion in others, and thence frequently occasion new divisions, I beg leave to propose, for the consideration of the committee, another mode, which appears to me to be as equitable, more easily carried into practice, and more permanent in its nature.

"Let the weakest state say what proportion of money or force it is able and willing to furnish for the general purposes of the Union;

"Let all the others oblige themselves to furnish each an equal proportion;

"The whole of these joint supplies to be absolutely in the disposition of Congress;

"The Congress, in this case, to be composed of an equal number of delegates from each state;

"And their decisions to be by the majority of individual members voting.

"If these joint and equal supplies should, on particular occasions, not be sufficient, let Congress make requisitions on the richer and more powerful states for further aids, to be voluntarily afforded, leaving to each state the right of considering the necessity and utility of the aid desired, and of giving more or less, as it should be found proper.

"This mode is not new. It was formerly practiced with success by the British government with respect to Ireland and the colonies. We sometimes gave even more than they expected, or thought just to accept; and, in the last war, carried on while we were united, they gave us back in five years a million sterling. We should probably have continued in such voluntary contributions, whenever the occasions appeared to require them, for the common good of the empire. It was not till they chose to force us, and to deprive us of the merit and pleasure of voluntary contributions, however, were to be disposed of at the pleasure of a government in which we had no representative. I am, therefore, persuaded, that they will not be refused to one in which the representation shall be equal.

"My learned colleague (Mr. Wilson) has already mentioned, that the present method of voting by states was submitted to originally by Congress under a conviction of its impropriety, inequality, and injustice. This appears in the words of their resolution. It is of the sixth of September, 1774. The words are, ---

" 'Resolved, That, in determining questions in this Congress, each colony or province shall have one vote; the Congress not being possessed of, or at present able to procure, materials for ascertaining the importance of each colony.' "

On the question for agreeing to Mr. King's and Mr. Wilson's motion, it passed in the affirmative.

Massachusetts, Connecticut, Pennsylvania, Virginia, North Carolina, South Carolina, Georgia, aye, 7; New York, New Jersey, Delaware, no, 3; Maryland, divided.

It was then moved by Mr. Rutledge, seconded by Mr. Butler, to add to the words "equitable ratio of representation," at the end of the motion just agreed to, the words "according to the quotas of contribution." On motion of Mr. Wilson, seconded by Mr. Pinckney, this was postponed in order to add, after the words "equitable ratio of representation,", the words following -- "in proportion to the whole number of white and other free citizens and inhabitants of every age, sex, and condition, including those bound to servitude of a term of years, and three fifths of all other persons not comprehended in the foregoing description, except Indians not paying taxes, in each state" -- this being the rule in the act of Congress, agreed to by eleven states, for apportioning quotas of revenue on the states, and requiring a census only every five, seven, or ten years.

Mr. Gerry thought property not the rule of representation. Why, then, should the blacks, who were property in the south, be, in the rule of representation, more than cattle and horses of the north?

On the question, --

Massachusetts, Connecticut, New York, Pennsylvania, Maryland, Virginia, North Carolina, South Carolina, Georgia, aye, 9; New Jersey, Delaware, no, 2.

Mr. Sherman moved, that a question be taken, whether each state shall have one vote in the second branch. Everything, he said, depended on this. The smaller states would never agree to the plan on any other principle than an equality of suffrage in this branch.

Mr. Ellsworth seconded the motion. On the question for allowing each state one vote in the second branch, --

Connecticut, New York, New Jersey, Delaware, Maryland, aye, 5; Massachusetts, Pennsylvania, Virginia, North Carolina, South Carolina, Georgia, no, 6.

Mr. Wilson and Mr. Hamilton moved, that the right of suffrage in the second branch ought to be according to the same rule as in the first branch.

On this question for making the ratio of representation the same in the second as in the first branch, it passed in the affirmative.

Massachusetts, Pennsylvania, Virginia, North Carolina, South Carolina, Georgia, aye, 6; Connecticut, New York, New Jersey, Delaware, Maryland, no, 5.

It is important to follow what happened here. Wilson and Pinckney brought up the agreement that had been reached by "eleven states, for apportioning quotas of revenue on the states". That agreement occurred, not in the Constitutional Convention, but in the debate back on 18 Apr 1783 when Congress was trying to reform the Articles of Confederation. What we have here is a subtle, but important shift in context. In 1783, the debate had centered on how to allocate requisitions, and a three-fifths rule regarding slaves was adopted as a compromise because the delegates had difficulty ascertaining how to assess slaves from a purely economic standpoint. But on 11 Jun 1787, the same three-fifths rule was adopted as a means of allocating representation in Congress. In this case, the three-fifths rule was agreed to, not because of any racial bias, but because the underlying method of allocating representatives was still based on the relative amount of contributions each state could pay in direct taxation; i.e., still an economic argument as it had been before.

On 13 Jun 1787, the committee reported out their findings, consisting of 19 resolutions. The only one that concerns us is the seventh one, based on Randolph's original proposal of 30 May, as modified by debate on 11 Jun [12]:

> "7. Resolved, That the right of suffrage in the first branch of the national legislature ought not to be according to the rule established in the Articles of Confederation, but according to some equitable ratio of representation; namely, in proportion to the whole number of white and other free citizens, and inhabitants of every age, sex, and condition, including those bound to servitude for a term of years, and three fifths of all other persons not comprehended in the foregoing description, except Indians not paying taxes, in each state."

On 15 Jun 1787, Patterson of New Jersey laid before the Convention an alternate plan to that proposed earlier by Randolph. His goal was to establish a system that was more federal than national, aided by several members who thought likewise but for different reasons. The only part of his resolutions that concern our topic is the third one [13]:

> (Friday, June 15)
>
> 3. Resolved, That whenever requisitions shall be necessary, instead of the rule for making requisitions mentioned in the Articles of Confederation, the United States in Congress assembled be authorized to make such requisitions in proportion to the whole number of white and other free citizens and inhabitants, of every age, sex, and condition, including those bound to servitude for a term of years, and three fifths of all other persons not comprehended in the foregoing description, except Indians not paying taxes; that, if

such requisitions be not complied with in the time specified therein, to direct the collection thereof in the non-complying states, and for that purpose to devise and pass acts directing and authorizing the same; -- provided, that none of the powers hereby vested in the United States in Congress assembled shall be exercised without the consent of at least __ states; and in that proportion, if the number of confederated states should hereafter be increased or diminished.

A long debate in committee on Mr. Patterson's recommendations occurred on 19 Jun 1787, which did not touch directly on our subject. In the end, Patterson's proposal was rejected, and the Committee submitted to the entire House the resolutions reported out of committee on 13 Jun 1787. The only two that concern us are the first portion of number three and number seven [14]:

"3. Resolved, That the members of the first branch of the national legislature ought to be elected by the people of the several states, for the term of three years..."

"7. Resolved, That the right of suffrage in the first branch of the national legislature ought not to be according to the rule established in the Articles of Confederation, but according to some equitable ratio of representation; namely, in proportion to the whole number of white and other free citizens, and inhabitants of every age, sex, and condition, including those bound to servitude for a term of years, and three fifths of all other persons not comprehended in the foregoing description, except Indians not paying taxes, in each state."

The basic principle that the members of the first branch of the legislature were to be directly elected by the people was confirmed by a vote taken on 21 Jun 1787 [15]:

It was then moved and seconded to agree to the 1st clause of the 3rd resolution, as reported from the committee, namely: --

"Resolved, That the members of the first branch of the legislature ought to be elected by the people of the several states:"

Yeas: Massachusetts, Connecticut, New York, Pennsylvania, Delaware, Virginia, North Carolina, South Carolina, Georgia, aye, 9; Nay: New Jersey, 1. Divided: Maryland, 1.

The debate on the seventh resolution commenced on 28 and 29 Jun, as follows [16]:

(Thursday, June 28)

It was moved and seconded to amend the 7th resolution reported from the committee, so as to read as follows, namely: --

"Resolved, That the right of suffrage in the first branch of the legislature of the United States ought to be in proportion to the whole number of white and other free citizens and inhabitants, of every age, sex, and description, including those bound to servitude for a term of years, and three fifths of all other person not comprehended in the foregoing description, except Indians not paying taxes, in each state."

It was moved and seconded to erase the word "not" from the first clause of the 7th resolution, so as to read, --

"Resolved, That the right of suffrage in the in the second branch of the legislature of the United States ought to be according to the rule established in the Articles of Confederation."

The determination of the house on the motion for erasing the word "not" from the 1st clause of the 7th resolution was postponed, at the request of the deputies of the state of New York, till tomorrow.

And then the house adjourned till tomorrow, at 11 o'clock, A. M.

(Friday, June 29)

It was moved and seconded to strike out the word "not" out of the 1st clause of the 7th resolution reported from the committee.

On the question to strike it out, it passed in the negative.

Yeas: Connecticut, New York, New Jersey, Delaware, 4. Nays: Massachusetts, Pennsylvania, Virginia, North Carolina, Georgia, 6. Divided: Maryland, 1.

It was then moved and seconded to agree to the first clause of the 7th resolution, as reported from the committee, namely: -- "Resolved, that the right of suffrage in the first branch of the legislature of the United States ought not to be according to the rule established in the Articles of Confederation, but according to some equitable ratio of representation."

On the question to agree, it passed in the affirmative.

Yeas: Massachusetts, Pennsylvania, Virginia, North Carolina, South Carolina, Georgia, 6. Nays: Connecticut, New York, New Jersey, Delaware, 4. Divided, Maryland, 1.

On 2 Jul 1787, a committee was appointed to attempt to resolve the impasse on the 8th resolution and remaining portions of the 7th resolution. Mr. Rutledge also proposed a modification of the 7th resolution on 5 Jul, but it was rejected. On 5 Jul 1787, the committee reported out its recommendation, in two resolutions. Although they do not relate directly to our subject, they caused some debate on it. Only the first of these is relevant, and reads in part [17]:

"1. That, in the first branch of the legislature, each of the states now in the Union shall be allowed one member for every forty thousand inhabitants, of the description reported in the seventh resolution of the Committee of the whole House..."

A debate on our subject did not begin until 6 Jul 1787; here the report referred to is the one provided on 5 Jul, the debate was as follows [18]:

(Friday, July 6)

In Convention. -- Mr. Gouverneur Morris moved to commit so much of the report as relates to "one member for every forty thousand inhabitants." His view was, that they might absolutely fix the number for each state in the first instance; leaving the legislature at liberty to provide for changes in the relative importance of the states, and for the case of new states.

Mr. Wilson seconded the motion; but with a view of leaving the committee under no implied shackles.

Mr. Gorham apprehended great inconvenience from fixing directly the number of representatives to be allowed to each state. He thought the number of inhabitants the true guide; though perhaps some departure might be expedient from the full proportion. The states, also, would vary in their relative extent by separations of parts of the largest states. A part of Virginia is now on the point of a separation. In the province of Maine, a convention is at this time deliberating on a separation from Massachusetts. In such events, the number of representatives ought certainly to be reduced. He hoped to see all the states made small by proper divisions, instead of their becoming formidable, as was apprehended, to the small states. He conceived, that, let the government be modified as it might, there would be a constant tendency in the state governments to encroach upon it; it was of importance, therefore, that the extent of the states should be reduced as much, and as fast, as possible. The stronger the government shall be made in the first instance, the more easily will these divisions be effected; as it will be of less consequence, in the opinion of the states, whether they be of great or small extent.

Mr. Gerry did not think, with his colleague, that the larger states ought to be cut up. This policy has been inculcated by the middling and small states, ungenerously, and contrary to the spirit of the Confederation. Ambitious men will be apt to solicit needless divisions, till the states be reduced to the size of counties. If this policy should still actuate the small states, the large ones could not confederate safely with them; but would be obliged to consult their safety by confederating only with each other. He favored the commitment, and thought that representation ought to be in the combined ratio of numbers of inhabitants and wealth, and not of either singly.

Mr. King wished the clause to be committed, chiefly in order to detach it from the report, with which it had no connection. He thought, also, that the ratio of representation proposed could not be safely fixed, since in a century and a half our computed increase of population would carry the number of representatives to an enormous excess; that the number of inhabitants was not the proper index of ability and wealth; that property was the primary object of society; and that, in fixing a ratio, this ought not to be excluded from the estimate. With regard to new states, he observed, that there was something peculiar in the business, which had not been noticed. The United States were now admitted to be proprietors of the country north-west of the Ohio. Congress, by one of their ordinances, have impoliticly laid it out into ten states, and have made it a fundamental article of compact with those who may become settlers, that, as soon as the number in any one state shall equal that of the smallest of the thirteen original states, it may claim admission into the Union. Delaware does not contain, it is computed, more than thirty-five thousand souls; and, for obvious reasons, will not increase much for a considerable time. It is possible, then, that, if this plan be persisted in by Congress, ten new votes may be added, without a greater addition of inhabitants than are represented by the single vote of Pennsylvania. The plan, as it respects one of the new states, is already irrevocable -- the sale of the lands having commenced, and the purchasers and settlers will immediately become entitled to all the privileges of the compact.

Mr. Butler agreed to the commitment, if the committee were to be left at liberty. He was persuaded that, the more the subject was examined, the less it would appear that the number of inhabitants would be a proper rule of proportion. If there were no other objection, the changeableness of the standard would be sufficient. He concurred with those who thought some balance was necessary between the old and the new states. He contended strenuously, that property was the only just measure of representation. This was the great object of government; the great cause of war; the great means of carrying it on.

Mr. Pinckney saw no good reason for committing. The value of land had been found, on full investigation, to be an impracticable rule. The contributions of revenue, including imports and exports, must be too changeable in their amount; too difficult to be adjusted; and too injurious to the non-commercial states. The number of inhabitants appeared to him the only just and practicable rule. He thought the blacks ought to stand on an equality with the whites; but would agree to the ratio settled by Congress. He contended that Congress had no right, under the Articles of Confederation, to authorize the admission of new states, no such case having been provided for.

Mr. Davy was for committing the clause, in order to get at the merits of the question arising on the report. He seemed to think that wealth or property ought to be represented in the second branch; and numbers in the first branch.

On the motion for committing, as made by Mr. Gouverneur Morris, --

Massachusetts, Connecticut, Pennsylvania, Virginia, North Carolina, South Carolina, Georgia, aye, 7; New York, New Jersey, Delaware, no, 3; Maryland, divided.

So the issue of representation at the ratio of one for every forty thousand, and how the forty thousand were to be determined, was committed, that is, sent to a committee of five (G. Morris, Gorham, Randolph, Rutledge, and King). They had their discussions, and made a report on 9 Jul, 1787, where debate on our subject, although indirect, resumed [19]:

(Monday, July 9)

In Convention - Mr. Daniel Carroll, from Maryland, took his seat.

Mr. Gouverneur Morris delivered a report from the committee of five members, to whom was committed the clause in the report of the committee consisting of a member from each state, stating the proper ratio of representatives in the first branch to be as one to every forty thousand inhabitants, as follows, viz.:

"The committee to whom was referred the first clause of the first proposition reported from the grand committee, beg leave to report:

"That, in the first meeting of the legislature, the first branch thereof consist of fifty-six members, of which number New Hampshire shall have 2, Massachusetts, 7, Rhode Island, 1, Connecticut, 4, New York, 5, New Jersey, 3, Pennsylvania, 8, Delaware, 1, Maryland 4, Virginia, 9, North Carolina, 5, South Carolina, 5, Georgia, 2.

"But, as the present situation of the states may probably alter, as well in point of wealth as in the number of their inhabitants, that the legislature be authorized from time to time to augment the number of representatives. And in case any of the states shall hereinafter be divided, or any two or more states united, or any new states created within the limits of the United States, the legislature shall possess authority to regulate the number of representatives, in any of the foregoing cases, upon the principles of their wealth and number of inhabitants."

Mr. Sherman wished to know on what principles or calculations the report was founded. It did not appear to correspond with any rule of numbers, or of any requisition hitherto adopted by Congress.

Mr. Gorham. Some provision of this sort was necessary in the outset. The number of blacks and whites, with some regard to supposed wealth, was the general guide. The legislature is to make alterations from time to time, as justice and propriety may require. Two objections prevailed against the rule of one member for every forty thousand inhabitants. The first was, that the representation would soon be too numerous; the second, that the Western States, who may have a different interest, might, if admitted on that principle, by degrees outvote the Atlantic. Both these objections are removed. The number will be small in the first instance, and may be continued so. And the Atlantic States, having the government in their own hands, may take care of their own interest, by dealing out the right of representation in safe proportions to the Western States. These were the views of the committee.

Mr. L. Martin wished to know whether the committee were guided in the ratio by the wealth or number of inhabitants of the states, or both; noting its variations from former apportionments by Congress.

Mr. Gouverneur Morris and Mr. Rutledge moved to postpone the first paragraph, relating to the number of members to be allowed each state in the first instance, and take up the second paragraph, authorizing the legislature to alter the number from time to time, according to wealth and inhabitants. The motion was agreed to, *nem. con.*

On the question on the second paragraph, taken without any debate, --

Massachusetts, Connecticut, Pennsylvania, Delaware, Maryland, Virginia, North Carolina, South Carolina, Georgia, aye, 9; New York, New Jersey, no, 2.

Mr. Sherman moved to refer the first part, apportioning the representatives, to a committee of a member of each state.

Mr. Gouverneur Morris seconded the motion, observing that this was the only case in which committees were useful.

Mr. Williamson thought it would be necessary to return to the rule of numbers, but that the Western States stood on a different footing. If their property should be rated as high as that of the Atlantic States, then their representation ought to hold a like proportion; otherwise, if their property was not to be equally rated.

Mr. Gouverneur Morris. The report is little more than a guess. Wealth was not altogether disregarded by the committee. Where it was apparently in favor of one state, whose numbers were superior to the numbers of another by a fraction only, a member extraordinary was allowed to the former, or so vice versa. The committee meant little more than to bring the matter to a point for the consideration of the House.

Mr. Read asked why Georgia was allowed two members, when her inhabitants had stood below that of Delaware.

Mr. Gouverneur Morris. Such is the rapidity of the population of that states, that, before the plan takes effect, it will probably be entitled to two representatives.

Mr. Randolph disliked the report of the committee, but has been unwilling to object to it. He was apprehensive that, as the number was not to be changed till the national legislature should please, a pretext would never be wanting to postpone alterations, and keep the power in the hands of those possessed of it. He was in favor of the commitment to a member from each state.

Mr. Patterson considered the proposed estimate for the future, according to the combined rules of numbers and wealth, as too vague. For this reason New Jersey was against it. He could regard negro slaves in no light but as property. They are no free agents, have no personal liberty, no faculty of acquiring property, but on the contrary are themselves property, and, like other property, entirely a the will of the master. Has a man in Virginia a number of votes in proportion to the number of his slaves? And if negroes are not represented in the states to which they belong, why should they be represented in the general government? What is the true principle of representation? It is an expedient by which an assembly of certain individuals, chosen by the people, is substituted in place of the inconvenient meeting of the people themselves. If such a meeting of the people was actually to take place, would the slaves vote? They would not. Why then should they be represented? He was also against such an indirect encouragement of the slave trade, observing, that Congress, in their act relating to the change of the eighth article of Confederation, had been ashamed to use the term "slaves", and had substituted a description.

Mr. Madison reminded Mr. Patterson that his doctrine of representation, which was, in principle, a genuine one, must forever silence the pretensions of the small states to an equality of votes with the large ones. They ought to vote in the same proportion in which their citizens would do if the people of all the states were collectively met. He suggested, as a proper ground of compromise, that, in the first branch, the states should be represented according to their number of free inhabitants, and, in the second, which had, for one of its primary objects, the guardianship of property, according to the whole number, including slaves.

Mr. Butler urged warmly the justice and necessity of regarding wealth in the apportionment of representation.

Mr. King had always expected that, as the Southern States are the richest, they would not league themselves with the Northern, unless some respect were paid to their superior wealth. If the latter expect those preferential distinctions in commerce, and other advantages which they will derive from the connection, they must not expect to receive them without allowing some advantages in return. Eleven out of thirteen of the states had agreed to consider slaves in the apportionment of taxation, and taxation and representation ought to go together.

On the question for committing the first paragraph of the report to a member from each state, --

Massachusetts, Connecticut, New Jersey, Pennsylvania, Delaware, Maryland, Virginia, North Carolina, Georgia, aye, 9; New York, South Carolina, no, 2.

One again, we see here that slaves were to be counted as part of the formula for representation only on the basis of how much their labor contributed to wealth -- the means of assessing taxation. The committee considered the proportions, and revised it to 65 members in the first branch initially. The Convention then debated the fine points on how some states should have greater or fewer representatives. They agreed to a formula on 10 Jul 1787. The portion of the debate attendant to our subject resumed on 11 Jul 1787 [20]:

(Wednesday, July 11)

In Convention. -- Mr. Randolph's motion, requiring the legislature to take a periodical census, for the purpose of redressing inequalities in the representation, was resumed.

Mr. Sherman was against shackling the legislature too much. We ought to choose wise and good men, and then confide in them.

Mr. Mason. The greater the difficulty we find in fixing a proper rule of representation, the more unwilling ought we to be to throw the task from ourselves on the general legislature. He did not object to the conjectural ratio which was to prevail in the outset; but considered a revision from time to time, according to some permanent and precise standard, as essential to the fair representation required in the first branch. According to the present population of America, the northern part of it had a right to preponderate, and he could not deny it. But he wished it not to preponderate hereafter, when the reason no longer continued. From the nature of man, we may be sure that those who have power in their hands will not give it up, while they can retain it. On the contrary, we know that they will always, when they can, rather increase it. If the Southern States, therefore, should have three fourths of the people of America within their limits, the Northern will hold fast the majority of representatives. One fourth will govern the three fourths. The Southern States will complain; but they may complain from generation to generation without redress. Unless some principle, therefore, which will do justice to them hereafter, shall be inserted into the Constitution, disagreeable as the declaration was to him, he must declare he could neither vote for the system here, nor support it in his state. Strong objections had been drawn from the danger to the Atlantic interests from new Western States. Ought we to sacrifice what we know to be right in itself, lest it should prove favorable to states which are not yet in existence? If the Western States are to be admitted into the Union, as they arise, they must, he would repeat, be treated as equals, and subjected to no degrading discriminations. They will have the same pride, and other passions, which we have; and will either not unite with, or will speedily revolt from, the Union, if they are not in all respects placed on an equal footing with their brethren. It has been said, they will be poor, and unable to make equal contributions to the general treasury. He did not know but that, in time, they would be both more numerous and more wealthy than their Atlantic brethren. The extent and fertility of their soil made this probable; and although Spain might for a time deprive them of the natural outlet for their productions, yet she will, because she must, finally yield to their demands. He urged numbers of inhabitants, though not always a precise standard of wealth, was sufficiently so for every substantial purpose.

Mr. Williamson was for making it a duty of the legislature to do what was right, and not leaving it at liberty to do or not to do it. He moved that Mr. Randolph's propositions be postponed, in order to consider the following: -- "that, in order to ascertain the alterations that may happen in the population and wealth of the several states, a census shall be taken of the free white inhabitants, and three fifths of those of other description, on the first year after this government shall have been adopted, and every __ year thereafter; and that the representation be regulated accordingly."

Mr. Randolph agreed that Mr. Williamson's proposition should stand in place of his. He observed, that the ratio fixed for the first meeting was a mere conjecture; that it placed the power in the hands of that part of America which could not always be entitled to it; that this power would not be voluntarily renounced; and that it was consequently the duty of the Convention to secure its renunciation, when justice might so require, by some constitutional provisions. If equality between great and small states be inadmissible, because in that case unequal numbers of constituents would be represented by equal numbers of votes, was it not equally inadmissible, that a larger and more populous district of America should hereafter have less representation than a smaller and less populous district? If a fair representation of the people be not secured, the injustice of the government will shake it to its foundations. What relates to suffrage is justly stated, by the celebrated Montesquieu, as a fundamental article in republican governments. If the danger suggested by Mr. Gouverneur Morris be real, of advantage being taken of the legislature in pressing moments, it was an additional reason for tying their hands in such a manner that they could not sacrifice their trust to momentary considerations. Congress have pledged the public faith, to new states, that they shall be admitted on equal terms. They never would, nor ought to, accede on any other. The census must be taken under the direction of the general legislature. The states will be too much interested to take an impartial one for themselves.

Mr. Butler and Gen. Pinckney insisted that blacks be included in the rule of representation equally with whites; and for that purpose moved that the words "three fifths" be struck out.

Mr. Gerry thought that three fifths of them was, to say the least, the full proportion that could be admitted.

Mr. Gorham. This ratio was fixed by Congress as a rule of taxation. Then it was urged, by the delegates representing the states having slaves, that the blacks were still more inferior to freemen. At present, when the ratio of representation is to be established, we are assured that they are equal to freemen. The arguments on the former occasion had convinced him that three fifths was pretty near the just proportion, and he should vote according to the same opinion now.

Mr. Butler insisted, that the labor of a slave in South Carolina was as productive and valuable as that of a freeman in Massachusetts; that as wealth was the great means of defense and utility to the nation, they were equally valuable to it with freemen; and that, consequently, an equal representation ought to be allowed for them in a government which was instituted principally for the protection of property, and was itself to be supported by property.

Mr. Mason could not agree to the notion, notwithstanding it was favorable to Virginia, because he thought it unjust. It was certain that he slaves were valuable, as they raised the value of land, increased exports and imports, and, of course, the revenue; would supply the means of feeding and supporting an army; and might, in cases of emergency, become themselves soldiers. As in these important respects they were useful to the community at large, they ought not to be excluded from the estimate of representation. He could not, however, regard them as equal to freemen, and could not vote for them as such. He added, as worthy of remark, that the Southern States have this peculiar species of property over and above the other species of property common to all the states.

Mr. Williamson reminded Mr. Gorham, that, if the Southern States contended for the inferiority of blacks to whites when taxation was in view, the Eastern States, on the same occasion, contended for their equality. He did not, however, either then or now, concur in either extreme, but approved of the ratio of three fifths.

On Mr. Butler's motion, for considering blacks as equal to whites in apportionment of representation, --

Delaware, South Carolina, Georgia, aye, 3; Massachusetts, Connecticut, New Jersey, Pennsylvania, Maryland, Virginia, North Carolina, no, 7; New York, not on the floor.

Mr. Gouverneur Morris said he had several objections to the proposition of Mr. Williamson. In the first place, it fettered the legislature too much. In the second place, it would exclude some states altogether, who would not have a sufficient number to entitle them to a single representation. In the third place, it will not consist with the resolution passed on Saturday last, authorizing the legislature to adjust the representation, from time to time, on the principle of population and wealth; nor with the principles of equity. If slaves were to be considered as inhabitants, not as wealth, then the said resolution would not be pursued; if as wealth, then, why is no other wealth but slaved included? These objections may perhaps be removed by amendments. His great objection was, that the number of inhabitants was not a proper standard of wealth. The amazing difference between the comparative numbers and wealth of different countries rendered all reasoning superfluous on the subject. Numbers might, with greater propriety, be deemed a measure of strength than of wealth; yet the late defense made by Great Britain against her numerous enemies proved, in the clearest manner, that it is entirely fallacious even in this respect.

Mr. King thought there was great force in the objections of Mr. Gouverneur Morris. He would, however, accede to the proposition, for the sake of doing something.

Mr. Rutledge contended for the admission of wealth in the estimate by which representation should be regulated. The Western States will not be able to contribute in proportion to their numbers; they should not therefore be represented in that proportion. The Atlantic States will not concur in such a plan. He moved that, "at the end of -- years after the first meeting of the legislature, and of every --- years thereafter, the legislature shall proportion the representation according to the principles of wealth and population."

Mr. Read thought, the legislature ought not to be too much shackled. It would make the Constitution, like religious creeds, embarrassing to those bound to conform to it, and more likely to produce dissatisfaction than harmony and union.

Mr. Mason objected to Mr. Rutledge's motion, as requiring of the legislature something too indefinite and impracticable, and leaving them a pretext for doing nothing.

Mr. Wilson had himself no objection to leaving the legislature entirely at liberty, but considered wealth as an impracticable rule.

Mr. Gorham. If the Convention, who are comparatively so little biased by local views, are so much perplexed, how can it be expected that the legislature hereafter, under the full bias of those views, will be able to settle a standard? He was convinced, by the arguments of others and his own reflections, that the Convention ought to fix some standard or other.

Mr. Gouverneur Morris. The arguments of others, and his own reflections, had led him to a very different conclusion. If we cannot agree on a rule that will be just at this time, how can we expect to find one that will be just in all times to come? Surely, those who come after us will judge better of things present than we can of things future. He could not persuade himself that numbers would be a just rule at any time. The remarks of Mr. Mason relative to the western country had not changed his opinion on that head. Among other objections, it must be apparent, they would not be able to furnish men equally enlightened, to share in the administration of our common interests. The busy haunts of men, not the remote wilderness, was the proper school of political talents. If the western people get the power into their hands, they will ruin the Atlantic interests. The back members are always most averse to the best measures. He mentioned the case of Pennsylvania formerly. The lower part of the state had the power in the first instance. They kept it in their own hands, and the country was the better for it. Another objection with him, against admitting the blacks into the census, was, that the people of Pennsylvania would revolt at the idea of being put on a footing with slaves. They would reject any plan that was to have such an effect. Two objections had been raised against leaving the adjustment of the representation, from time to time, to the discretion of the legislature. The first was, they would be unwilling to revise it at all. The second, that, by referring to wealth, they would be bound by a rule which, if willing, they would be unable to execute. The first objection distrusts their fidelity. But if their duty, honor, and their oaths, will not bind them, let us not put into their hands our liberty, and all our other great interests; let us have no government at all. In the second place, if these ties will bind them, we need not distrust the practicability of the rule. It was followed in part by the committee in the apportionment of representatives yesterday reported to the House. The best course that could be taken would be to leave the interests of the people to the representatives of the people.

Mr. Madison was not a little surprised to hear this implicit confidence urged by a member who, on all occasions, had inculcated so strongly the political depravity of men, and the necessity of checking one vice and interest by opposing to them another vice and interest. If the representatives of the people would be bound by the ties he had mentioned, what need was there of a Senate? What of a revisionary power? But his reasoning was not only inconsistent with his former reasoning, but with itself. At the same time that he recommended this implicit confidence to the Southern States in the northern majority, he was still more zealous in exhorting all to a jealousy of a western majority. To reconcile the gentleman with himself, it must be imagined that he determined the human character by the points of the compass. The truth was, that all men having power ought to be distrusted to a certain degree. The case of Pennsylvania had been mentioned, where it was admitted that those who were possessed of the power in the original settlement never admitted the new settlements to a due share of it. England was a still more striking example. The power there had long been in the hands of the boroughs -- of the minority -- who had opposed and defeated every reform which had been attempted. Virginia was, in a less degree, another example. With regard to the Western States, he was clear and firm in opinion that no unfavorable distinctions were admissible, either in point of justice or policy. He thought, also, that the hope of contributions to the treasury from them had been much underrated. Future contributions, it seemed to be understood on all hands, would be principally levied on imports and exports. The extent and fertility of the western soil would, for a long time, give to agriculture a preference over manufactures. Trials would be repeated till some articles could be raised from it that would bear a transportation to places where they could be exchanged for imported manufactures. Whenever the Mississippi should be opened up to them (which would, of necessity, be the case as soon as their population would subject them to any considerable share of the public burden,) imposts on their trade could be collected with less expense and greater certainty than on that of the Atlantic States. In the mean time, as their supplies must pass through the Atlantic States, their contributions would be levied in the same manner with those of the Atlantic States. He could not agree that any substantial objection lay against fixing numbers for the perpetual standard of representation. It was said that representation and taxation were to go together; that taxation and wealth ought to go together, that population and wealth were not measures of each other. He admitted that, in different climates, under different forms of government, and in different stages of civilization, the inference was perfectly just. He would admit that, in no situation, numbers of inhabitants were an accurate measure of wealth. He contended, however, that in the United States it was sufficiently so for the object in contemplation. Although their climate varies considerably, yet, as the governments, the laws, and the manners, of all were nearly the same, and the intercourse between different parts perfectly free, population, industry, arts, and the value of labor, would constantly tend to equalize themselves. The value of labor might be considered as the principal criterion of wealth, and the ability to support taxes, and this would find its level in different places, where the intercourse should be easy and free, with as much certainty as the value of money or any other thing. Wherever labor would yield most, people would resort, till the competition should destroy the inequality. Hence it is that the people are constantly swarming from the more to the less populous places -- from Europe to America -- from the northern and middle parts of the United States to the southern and western. They go where land is cheaper, because there labor is dearer. If it be true that the same quantity of produce raised on the banks of the Ohio is of less value than on the Delaware, it is also true that the same labor will raise twice or thrice the quantity in the former, than it will raise in the latter situation.

Col. Mason agreed with Mr. G. Morris, that we ought to leave the interests of the people to the representatives of the people; but the objection was, that the legislature would cease to be the representatives of the people. It would continue so no longer than the states now containing a majority of the people should restrain that majority. As soon as the southern and western population should predominate, which must happen in a few years, the power would be in the hands of the minority, and would never be yielded to the majority, unless provided for by the Constitution.

On the question for postponing Mr. Williamson's motion, in order to consider that of Mr. Rutledge, it passed in the negative, --

Massachusetts, Pennsylvania, Delaware, South Carolina, Georgia, aye, 5; Connecticut, New Jersey, Maryland, Virginia, North Carolina, no, 5.

On the question on the first clause of Mr. Williamson's motion, as to taking a census of the free inhabitants, it passed in the affirmative, --

Massachusetts, Connecticut, New Jersey, Pennsylvania, Virginia, North Carolina, aye, 6; Delaware, Maryland, South Carolina, Georgia, no, 4.

The next clause, as to three fifths of the negroes, being considered, --

Mr. King, being much opposed to fixing numbers as the rule of representation, was particularly so on account of the blacks. He thought the admission of them along with whites at all would excite great discontents among the states with no slaves. He had never said, as to any particular point, that he would in no event acquiesce in a support it; but he would say that, if in any case such a declaration was to be made by him, it would be in this. He remarked that, in the temporary allotment of representatives made by the committee, the Southern States had received more than the number of their white and three fifths of their black inhabitants entitled them to.

Mr. Sherman. South Carolina had not more beyond her proportion than New York and New Hampshire; nor either of them more than was necessary in order to avoid fractions, or reducing them below their proportion. Georgia had more, but the rapid growth of that state seemed to justify it. In general, the allotment might not be just, but, considering all circumstances, he was satisfied with it.

Mr. Gorham supported the propriety of establishing numbers as the rule. He said that in Massachusetts estimates had been taken in the different towns, and that persons had been curious enough to compare these estimates with the respective numbers of people, and it had been found, even including Boston, that the most exact proportion prevailed between numbers and property. He was aware that there might be some weight in what had fallen from his colleague, as to the umbrage which might be taken by the people of the Eastern States. But he recollected that, when the proposition of Congress for changing the eighth article of the Confederation was before legislature of Massachusetts, the only difficulty then was, to satisfy them that the negroes ought not to have been counted equally with the whites, instead of being counted in the ratio of three fifths only.

Mr. Wilson did not well see on what principle the admission of blacks, in the proportion of three fifths, could be explained. Are they admitted as citizens -- then why are they not admitted on an equality with white citizens? Are they admitted as property -- then why is not other property admitted into the computation? There were difficulties, however, which he thought must be overruled by the necessity of compromise. He had some apprehensions, also, from the tendency of the blending of the blacks with the whites, to give disgust to the people of Pennsylvania, as had been intimated by his colleague (Mr. Gouverneur Morris). But he differed from him in thinking numbers of inhabitants so incorrect a measure of wealth. He had seen the western settlements of Pennsylvania, and, on a comparison of them with the city of Philadelphia, could discover little other difference than that property was more unequally divided here than there. Taking the same number in the aggregate, in the two situations, he believed there would be little difference in their wealth and ability to contribute to the public wants.

Mr. Gouverneur Morris was compelled to declare himself reduced to the dilemma of doing injustice to the Southern States, or to human nature, and he must therefore do it to the former; for he could never agree to give such encouragement to the slave trade as would be given by allowing them a representation for their negroes; and he did not believe those states would ever confederate on terms that would deprive them of that trade.

On the question for agreeing to include three fifths of the blacks, --

Connecticut, Virginia, North Carolina, Georgia, aye, 4; Massachusetts, new Jersey, Pennsylvania, Delaware, Maryland, South Carolina, no, 6.

On the question as to taking the census "the first year after the meeting of the legislature," --

Massachusetts, New Jersey, Pennsylvania, Delaware, Virginia, North Carolina, South Carolina, aye, 7; Connecticut, Maryland, Georgia, no, 3.

On filling the blank for the periodical census with fifteen years, -- agreed to, *nem. con.*

Mr. Madison moved to add, after "fifteen years," the words "at least," that the legislature might anticipate when circumstances were likely to render a particular year inconvenient.

On this motion, for adding "at least," it passed in the negative, the states being equally divided.

Massachusetts, Virginia, North Carolina, South Carolina, Georgia, aye, 5; Connecticut, New Jersey, Pennsylvania, Delaware, Maryland, no. 5.

A change in the phraseology of the other clause, so as to read, "and the legislature shall alter or augment the representation accordingly," was agreed to, *nem. con.*

On the question on the whole resolution of Mr. Williamson, as amended, --

Massachusetts, Connecticut, New Jersey, Delaware, Maryland, Virginia, North Carolina, South Carolina, Georgia, no, 9.

So it was rejected unanimously.

Adjourned.

Once again, we see that the debate centered on the most expedient way to allocate representation in Congress, as to whether it should be done by population alone, by an estimate of wealth alone, or by some compromise regarding how to count the slaves, where were technically property for the purposes of taxation. Those opposed to slavery, like Mr. Morris, were in favor of counting slaves as three-fifths because doing so would give the slave-owning states more power in Congress than a full counting; that power would then be used to promote, or at least protect the institution of slavery. This is hardly the sentiment of a racist. Southern states wanted slaves to be counted equally with whites on the same principle. This is evident in the argument between Williamson and Gorham: that the Southern states were engaging in hypocrisy in this regard -- when it came counting people to gauge the amount of taxes to be paid, the Southern states wanted to reduce the black people to low ratios; but when it came to counting for the purposes of representation, they wanted equality. Likewise, the Northern States wanted high ratios because that would increase the Southern taxation, and thus decrease their own. The concept that this was fundamentally a debate on economic terms is reinforced by the type of comments made about the future influence of the western states which did not yet exist.

The debate continued the next day, as follows [21]:

(Thursday, July 12)

In Convention. -- Mr. Gouverneur Morris moved to add, to the clause empowering the legislature to vary the representation according to the principles of wealth and numbers of inhabitants, a proviso, "that taxation shall be in proportion to representation."

Mr. Butler contended, again, that representation should be according to the full number of inhabitants, including all the blacks, admitting the justice of Mr. Gouverneur Morris' motion.

Mr. Mason also admitted the justice of the principle, but was afraid embarrassments might be occasioned to the legislature by it. It might drive the legislature to the plan of requisitions.

Mr. Gouverneur Morris admitted that some objections lay against his motion, but supposed they would be removed by restraining the rule to direct taxation. With regard to indirect taxes on exports and imports, and on consumption, the rule would be inapplicable. Notwithstanding what had been said to the contrary, he was persuaded that the imports and consumption were pretty nearly equal throughout the Union.

Gen. Pinckney liked the idea. He thought it so just that it could not be objected to; but foresaw that, if the revision of the census was left to the discretion of the legislature, it would never be carried into execution. The rule must be fixed, and the execution of it enforced by the Constitution. He was alarmed at what was said, (by Mr. Gouverneur Morris,) yesterday, concerning the negroes. He was now again alarmed at what had been thrown out concerning the taxing of exports. South Carolina has, in one year, exported to the amount of 600,000 sterling, all which was the fruit of the labor of her blacks. Will she be represented in proportion to this amount? She will not. Neither ought she then to be subject to a tax on it. He hoped a clause would be inserted into the system, restraining the legislature from taxing exports.

Mr. Wilson approved the principle, but could not see how it could be carried into execution, unless restrained to direct taxation.

Mr. Gouverneur Morris having so varied his motion by inserting the word "direct," it passed, *nem. con.*, as follows: "provided always that direct taxation ought to be proportioned to representation."

Mr. Davie said it was high time to speak out. He saw that it was meant by some gentlemen to deprive the Southern States of any share of representation for their blacks. He was sure that North Carolina would never confederate on any terms that did not rate them at least as three fifths. If the eastern States meant, therefore to exclude them altogether, the business was at an end.

Dr. Johnson thought that wealth and population were the true, equitable rules of representation; but he conceived that these two principles resolved themselves into one, population being the best measure of wealth. He concluded, therefore, that the number of people ought to be established as the rule, and that all descriptions, including blacks equally with whites, ought to fall within the computation. As various opinions had been expressed on the subject, he would move that a committee might be appointed to take them into consideration, and report them.

Mr. Gouverneur Morris. It had been said that it is high time to speak out. As one member, he would candidly do so. He came here to form a compact for the good of America. He was ready to do so with all the states. He hoped and believed that all would enter into such a compact. If they would not, he was ready to join with any other states that would. But as the compact was to be voluntary, it is in vain for the Eastern States to insist on what the Southern States will never agree to. It is equally vain for the latter to require what the other states can never admit, and he verily believed the people of Pennsylvania will never agree to a representation of negroes. What can be desired by these states more than has already been proposed -- that the legislature shall, from time to time, regulate representation according to wealth and population?

Gen. Pinckney desired that the rule of wealth should be ascertained, and not left to the pleasure of the legislature; and that property in slaves should not be exposed to danger, under a government instituted for the protection of property.

The first clause in the report of the first grand committee was postponed.

Mr. Ellsworth, in order to carry into effect the principle established, moved to add to the last clause adopted by the House the words following: "and that the rule of contribution by direct taxation, for the support of the government of the United States, shall be the number of white inhabitants and three fifths of every other description, in the several states, until some other rule, that shall more accurately ascertain the wealth of the several states, can be devised and adopted by the legislature."

Mr. Butler seconded the motion, in order that it might be committed.

Mr. Randolph was not satisfied with the motion. The danger will be revived, that the ingenuity of the legislature may evade or pervert the rule, so as to perpetuate the power where it shall be lodged in the first instance. He proposed, in lieu of Mr. Ellsworth's motion, "that, in order to ascertain the alterations in representation that may be required, from time to time, by changes in the relative circumstances of the states, a census shall be taken within two years from the first meeting of the general legislature of the United States, and once within the term of every --- years afterwards, of all the inhabitants, in the manner and according to the ratio recommended by Congress, in their resolution of the 18th of April, 1783, (rating the blacks at three fifths of their number,) and that the legislature of the United States shall arrange the representation accordingly." He urged, strenuously, that express security ought to be provided for including slaves in the ratio of representation. He lamented that such a species of property existed; but, as it did exist, the holders of it would require this security. It was perceived that the design was entertained by some of excluding slaves altogether; the legislature, therefore, ought not to be left at liberty.

Mr. Ellsworth withdraws his motion, and seconds that of Mr. Randolph.

Mr. Wilson observed that less umbrage would, perhaps, be taken against an admission of the slaves into the rule of representation, if it should be so expressed as to make them indirectly only an ingredient of the rule, by saying that they should enter into the rule of taxation; and as representation was to be according to taxation, the end would be equally attained. He accordingly moved, and was seconded, so to alter the last clause adopted by the House, that, together with the amendment proposed, the whole should read as follows: "provided always that the representation ought to be proportioned according to direct taxation; and, in order to ascertain the alterations in the direct taxation which may be required, from time to time, by the changes in the relative circumstances of the states, *Resolved*, that a census be taken within two years from the first meeting of the legislature of the United States, and once within the term of every --- years afterwards, of all the inhabitants of the United States, in the manner and according to the ratio recommended by Congress in their resolution of the 18th of April, 1783, and that the legislature of the United States shall proportion the direct taxation accordingly."

Mr. King. Although this amendment varies the aspect somewhat, he had still two powerful objections against tying down the legislature to the rule of numbers, -- first, they were at this time an uncertain index of the relative wealth of the states; secondly, if they were a just index at this time, it cannot be supposed always to continue so. He was far from wishing to retain any unjust advantage whatever in one part of the republic. If justice was not the basis of the connection, it could not be of long duration. He must be shortsighted indeed who does not foresee that, whenever the Southern States shall be more numerous than the Northern, they can and will hold a language that will awe them into justice. If they threaten to separate now in case injury shall be done them, will their threats be less urgent or effectual when force shall back their demands? Even in the intervening period there will be no point of time at which they will not be able to say, Do us justice, or we will separate. He urged the necessity of placing confidence, to a certain degree, in every government; and did not conceive that the proposed confidence, as to a periodical adjustment of the representation, exceeded that degree.

Mr. Pinckney moved to amend Mr. Randolph's motion, so as make "blacks equal to the whites in the ratio of representation." This, he urged, was nothing more than justice. The blacks are the laborers, the peasants, of the Southern States. They are as productive of pecuniary resources as those of the Northern States. They add equally to the wealth, and considering money as the sinew of war, to the strength, of the nation. It will also be politic with regard to the Northern States, as taxation is to keep pace with representation.

Gen. Pinckney moves to insert six years, instead of two, as the period, computing from the first meeting of the legislature, within which the first census should be taken. On this question for inserting "six" years instead of "two," in the proposition of Mr. Wilson, it passed in the affirmative.

Connecticut, New Jersey, Pennsylvania, Maryland, South Carolina, aye, 5; Massachusetts, Virginia, North Carolina, Georgia, no, 4; Delaware, divided.

On the question for filling the blank for the periodical census with "twenty years," it passed in the negative.

Connecticut, New Jersey, Pennsylvania, aye, 3; Massachusetts, Delaware, Maryland, Virginia, North Carolina, South Carolina, Georgia, no, 7.

On the question for ten years, it passed in the affirmative.

Massachusetts, Pennsylvania, Delaware, Maryland, Virginia, North Carolina, South Carolina, Georgia, aye, 8; Connecticut, New Jersey, no, 2.

On Mr. Pinckney's motion, for rating blacks as equal to whites, instead of as three fifths, --

South Carolina, Georgia, aye, 2; Massachusetts, Connecticut, (Dr. Johnson, aye,) New Jersey, Pennsylvania (three against two,) Delaware, Maryland, Virginia, North Carolina, no, 8.

Mr. Randolph's proposition, as varied by Mr. Wilson, being read, for taking the question as a whole, --

Mr. Gerry urged that the principle of it could not be carried into execution, as the states were not to be taxed as states. With regard to taxes on imposts, he conceived they would be more productive where there were no slaves than where there were, the consumption being greater.

Mr. Ellsworth. In case of a poll-tax, there would be no difficulty. But there would probably be none. The sum allotted to a state may be levied without difficulty, according to the plan used by the state in raising its own supplies.

On the question on the whole proposition, as proportioning representation to direct taxation, and both to the white and three fifths of the black inhabitants, and requiring a census within six years, and within every ten years afterwards, --

Connecticut, Pennsylvania, Maryland, Virginia, North Carolina, Georgia, aye, 6; New Jersey, Delaware, no, 2; Massachusetts, South Carolina, divided.

Adjourned.

The debate continued the next day, but this time the focus was on representation in the "second branch", that is, the Senate. However, the debate soon turned again to the degree to which relative wealth should affect representation in Congress, and to what degree the population was an accurate indicator of wealth. In the end, they settled on the method of counting as before, and extended that principle to all new states that might enter the union. Herewith the debate on 13 Jul 1787 [21]:

(Friday, July 13)

In Convention. -- It being moved to postpone the clause in the report of the committee of eleven as to the originating of money bills in the first branch, in order to take up the following, "that in the second branch each state shall have an equal voice," --

Mr. Gerry moved to add, as an amendment to the last clause agreed to be the House, "that from the first meeting of the legislature of the United States till a census shall be taken, all moneys to be raised for supplying the public treasury by direct taxation shall be assessed on the inhabitants of the several states according to the number of their representatives respectively in the first branch." He said this would be as just before as after the census, according to the general principle that taxation and representation ought to go together.

Mr. Williamson feared that New Hampshire will have reason to complain. Three members were allotted to her as a liberal allowance, for this reason, among others -- that she might not suppose any advantage to have been taken of her absence. As she was still absent, and had no opportunity of deciding whether she would choose to retain the number on the condition of her being taxed in proportion to it, he thought the number ought to be reduced from three to two, before the question was taken on Mr. Gerry's motion.

Mr. Read could not approve of the proposition. He had observed, he said, in the committee a backwardness, in some of the members from the large states, to take their full proportion of representatives. He did not then see the motive. He now suspects it was to avoid their due share of taxation. He had no objection to a just and accurate adjustment of representation and taxation to each other.

Mr. Gouverneur Morris and Mr. Madison answered, that the charge itself involved an acquittal; since, notwithstanding the augmentation of the number of members allotted to Massachusetts and Virginia, the motion for proportioning the burdens thereto was made by a member from the former state, and was approved by Mr. Madison, from the latter, who was on the committee. Mr. Gouverneur Morris said, that he thought Pennsylvania had her due share in eight members; and he could not in candor ask for more. Mr. Madison said, that, having always conceived that the difference of interest in the United States lay not between the large and small, but the Northern and Southern States, and finding that he number of members allotted to the Northern States was greatly superior, he should have preferred an addition of two members to the Southern States -- to wit, one to North and one to South Carolina, rather than of one member to Virginia. He liked the present motion, because it tended to moderate the views both of the opponents and advocates for rating very high the negroes.

Mr. Ellsworth hoped the proposition would be withdrawn. It entered too much into detail. The general principle was already sufficiently settled. As fractions cannot be regarded in apportioning the number of representatives, the rule will be unjust, until an actual census shall be made. After that, taxation may be precisely proportioned, according to the principle established, to the number of inhabitants.

Mr. Wilson hoped the motion would not be withdrawn. If it should, it will be made from another quarter. The rule will be as reasonable and just before, as after, a census. As to fractional numbers, the census will not destroy, but ascertain them. And they will have the same effect after, as before, the census; for, as he understands the rule, it is to be adjusted not to the number of inhabitants, but of representatives.

Mr. Sherman opposed the motion. He thought the legislature ought to be left at liberty; in which case they would probably conform to the principles observed by Congress.

Mr. Mason did not know that Virginia would be a loser by the proposed regulation, but had some scruple as to the justice of it. He doubted much whether the conjectural rule which was to precede the census would be as just as it would be rendered by an actual census.

Mr. Ellsworth and Mr. Gerry moved to postpone the motion of Mr. Gerry.

On the question, it passed in the negative.

Connecticut, New Jersey, Delaware, Maryland, aye, 4; Massachusetts, Pennsylvania, Virginia, North Carolina, South Carolina, Georgia, no, 6.

On the question on Mr. Gerry's motion, it passed in the negative, the states being equally divided.

Massachusetts, Pennsylvania, North Carolina, South Carolina, Georgia, aye, 5; Connecticut, New Jersey, Delaware, Maryland, Virginia, no, 5.

Mr. Gerry, finding that the loss of the question had proceeded from an objection, with some, to the proposed assessment of direct taxes on the *inhabitants* of the states, which might restrain the legislature to a poll-tax, moved his proposition again, but so varied as to authorize the assessment on the *states*, which leaves the mode to the legislature, viz.: "that, from the first meeting of the legislature of the United States until a census shall be taken, all moneys for supplying the public treasury by direct taxation shall be raised from the said several states, according to the number of their representatives respectively in the first branch."

On this varied question, it passed in the affirmative.

Massachusetts, Virginia, North Carolina, South Carolina, Georgia, aye, 5; Connecticut, New Jersey, Delaware, Maryland, no, 4; Pennsylvania, divided.

On the motion of Mr. Randolph, the vote of Monday last, authorizing the legislature to adjust, from time to time, the representation upon the principles of wealth and numbers of inhabitants, was reconsidered by common consent, in order to strike out wealth, and adjust the resolution to that requiring periodical revisions according to the number of whites and three fifths of the blacks. The motion was in the words following: --

"But as the present situation of the states may probably alter in the number of their inhabitants, that the legislature of the United States be authorized, from time to time, to apportion the number of representatives; and, in case of the states shall hereafter be divided, or any two or more states united, or new states created within the limits of the United States, the legislature of the United States shall possess authority to regulate the number of representatives, in any of the foregoing cases, upon the principle of their number of inhabitants, according to the provisions hereafter mentioned."

Mr. Gouverneur Morris opposed the alteration, as leaving still an incoherence. If negroes were to be viewed as inhabitants, and the revision was to proceed on the principle of numbers of inhabitants, they ought to be added in their entire number, and not in the proportion of three fifths. If as property, the word *wealth* was right; and striking it out would produce the very inconsistency which it meant to get rid of. The train of business, and the late turn which it had taken, had led him, he said, into deep mediation on it, and he would candidly state the result. A distinction had been set up, and urged, between the Northern and Southern States. He had hitherto considered this doctrine as heretical. He still thought the distinction groundless. He sees, however, that it is persisted in; and the southern gentlemen will not be satisfied unless they see the way open to their gaining a majority in the public councils. The consequence of such a transfer of power from the maritime to the interior and landed interest, will, he foresees, be such an oppression to commerce, that he shall be obliged to vote for the vicious principle of equality in the second branch, in order to provide some defense for the Northern States against it. But, to come more to the point -- either this distinction is fictitious or real; if fictitious, let it be dismissed, and let us proceed with due confidence. If it be real, instead of attempting to blend incompatible things, let us at once take a friendly leave of each other. There can be no end of demands for security, if every particular interest is to be entitled to it. The Eastern States may claim it for their fishery, and for other objects, as the Southern States claim it for their peculiar objects. In this struggle between the two ends of the Union, what part ought the Middle States, in point of policy, to take? To join their eastern brethren, according to his ideas. If the Southern States get the power into their hands, and be joined, as they will be, with the interior country, they will inevitably bring on a war with Spain for the Mississippi. This language is already held. The interior country, having no property nor interest exposed on the sea, will be little affected by such a war. He wished to know what security the Northern and Middle States will have against this danger. It has been said that North Carolina, South Carolina, and Georgia only, will in a little time have a majority of the people of America. They must in that case include the great interior country, and every thing was to be apprehended from their getting the power into their hands.

Mr. Butler. The security the Southern States want is, that their negroes may not be taken from them, which some gentlemen within or without doors have a very good mind to do. It was not supposed that North Carolina, South Carolina, and Georgia, would have more people than all the other states, but many more relatively to the other states than they now have. The people and strength of America are evidently bearing southwardly, and south-westwardly.

Mr. Wilson. If a general declaration would satisfy any gentleman, he had no indisposition to declare his sentiments. Conceiving that all men, wherever placed, have equal rights, and are equally entitled to confidence, he viewed without apprehension the period when a few states should contain the superior number of people. The majority of people, wherever found, ought in all questions to govern the minority. If the interior country should acquire this majority, it will not only have the right, but will avail itself of it, whether we will or no. This jealousy misled the policy of Great Britain with regard to America. The fatal maxims espoused by her were, that the colonies were growing too fast, and that their growth must be stinted in time. What were the consequences? First, enmity on our part, then actual separation. Like consequences will result on the part of the interior settlements, if like jealousy and policy be pursued on ours. Further, if numbers be not a proper rule, why is not some better rule pointed out? No one has yet ventured to attempt it. Congress have never been able to discover a better. No state, as far as he had heard, had suggested any other. In 1783, after elaborate discussion of a measure of wealth, all were satisfied then, as they now are, that the rule of numbers does not differ much from the combined rule of numbers and wealth. Again, he could not agree that property was the sole source or primary object of government or society. The cultivation and improvement of the human mind was the most noble object. With respect to this object, as well as to other personal rights, numbers were surely the natural and precise measure of representation. And with respect to property, they could not vary much from the precise measure. In no point of view, however, could the establishment of numbers, as the rule of representation in the first branch, vary his opinion as to the impropriety of letting a vicious principle into the second branch.

On the question to strike out *wealth*, and the make the change as moved by Mr. Randolph, it passed in the affirmative.

Massachusetts, Connecticut, New Jersey, Pennsylvania, Maryland, Virginia, North Carolina, South Carolina, Georgia, aye, 9; Delaware, divided.

Mr. Read moved to insert, after the word "divided," "or enlarged by addition of territory;" which was agreed to, *nem con.*

Adjourned.

The allocation of votes in the Senate was debated on 14 Jul, resulting in equal representation by states. On 16 Jul, the Convention reviewed the items that had been agreed to in the several previous sessions. The "report" referred to is the one provided by the committee to the House on 9 Jul, containing amended provisions as agreed to between that day and the 16th.

(Monday, July 16)

In Convention -- On the question for agreeing to the whole report, as amended, and including the equality of votes in the second branch, it passed in the affirmative.

Connecticut, New Jersey, Delaware, Maryland, North Carolina (Mr. Spaight, no), aye, 5; Pennsylvania, Virginia, South Carolina, Georgia, no, 4; Massachusetts, divided (Mr. Gerry, Mr. Strong, aye; Mr. King, Mr. Gorham, no).

The whole, thus passed, in the words following, viz.: --

"Resolved, That, in the original formation of the legislature of the United States, the first branch thereof shall consist of sixty-five members, of which number New Hampshire shall send 3, Massachusetts, 8; Rhode Island, 1; Connecticut, 5; New York, 6; New Jersey, 4; Pennsylvania, 8; Delaware, 1; Maryland, 6; Virginia, 10; North Carolina, 5; Georgia, 3. But as the present situation of the states may probably alter in the number of their inhabitants, the legislature of the United States shall be authorized, from time to time, to apportion the number of representatives; and in case any of the states shall hereafter be divided, or enlarged by the addition of new territory, or any two states united, or any new states created within the limits of the United States, the legislature of the United States shall possess authority to regulate the number of representatives, in any of the foregoing cases, upon the principle of their number of inhabitants, according to the provisions hereafter mentioned; provided always, that representation ought to be proportioned according to direct taxation. And in order to ascertain the alteration in the direct taxation, which may be required from time to time by the changes in the relative circumstances of the states, --

Resolved, That a census be taken within six years from the first meeting of the legislature of the United States, and once within the term of every ten years afterwards, of all inhabitants of the United States, in the manner and according to the ratio recommended by Congress in their resolution of the 18th day of April, 1783; and that the legislature of the United States shall proportion the direct taxation accordingly.

Recall that the three-fifths rule is part of the formula agreed to by Congress on 18 Apr 1783, and is therefore incorporated by reference into the Constitution. This provision was reviewed but not altered in the 26 Jul 1787 session, at which time a committee was appointed to generate a draft Constitution based on the agreed-to items. The draft was reported out of committee on 6 Aug 1787. The only portions which concern our subject are Article 4, Section 4 and Article 7, Section 3, as follows [22]; but section 4 of Article 7 is also included because it relates to a later discussion of slavery as an institution:

(Monday, August 6)

(Draft Constitution)

[Art. 4] "Sect. 3. The House of Representatives shall, at its first formation, and until the number of citizens and inhabitants shall be taken in the manner hereinafter described, consist of sixty-five members, of whom three shall be chosen in New Hampshire, eight in Massachusetts, one in Rhode Island and Providence Plantations, five in Connecticut, six in New York, four in New Jersey, eight in Pennsylvania, one in Delaware, six in Maryland, ten in Virginia, five in North Carolina, five in South Carolina, and three in Georgia.

[Art. 4] "Sect. 4. As the proportions of numbers in the different states will alter from time to time; as some of the states may hereafter be divided; as others may be enlarged by addition of territory; as to or more states may be united; as new states will be erected within the limits of the United States, -- the legislature shall, in each of these cases, regulate the number of representatives by the number of inhabitants, according to the provisions hereinafter made, at the rate of one for every forty thousand.

[Art. 7] "Sect. 3. The proportions of direct taxation shall be regulated by the whole number of white and other free citizens and inhabitants, of every sex and condition, including those bound to servitude for a term of years, and three fifths of all other persons not comprehended in the foregoing description, (except Indians not paying taxes;) which number shall, within six years after the first meeting of the legislature, and within the term of every ten years afterwards, be taken in such manner as the said legislature shall direct."

[Art. 7] "Sect. 4. No tax or duty shall be laid by the legislature on articles exported from an state; nor on the migration or importation of such persons as the several states shall think proper to admit; nor shall such migration or importation be prohibited."

There was a short debate on 8 Aug 1787 regarding the two pertinent sections of Article 4 as follows [23]:

(Wednesday, August 8)

Article 4, Section 3 was then taken up.

Gen. Pinckney and Mr. Pinckney moved that the number of representatives allotted to South Carolina be "six."

On the question, --

Delaware, North Carolina, South Carolina, Georgia, aye, 4; New Hampshire, Massachusetts, Connecticut, New Jersey, Pennsylvania, Maryland, Virginia, no, 7.

The third section of Article 4 was then agreed to.

Article 4, Section 4 was then taken up.

Mr. Williamson moved to strike out, "according to the provisions hereinafter made," and to insert the words "according to the rule hereinafter to be provided for direct taxation." -- See article 7, section 3.

On the question for agreeing to Mr. Williamson's amendment, --

New Hampshire, Massachusetts, Connecticut, Pennsylvania, Maryland, Virginia, North Carolina, South Carolina, Georgia, aye, 9; New Jersey, Delaware, no. 2.

Mr. King wished to know what influence the vote just passed was meant to have on the succeeding part of the report, concerning the admission of slaves into the rule of representation. He could not reconcile his mind to the article, if it was to prevent objections to the latter part. The admission of slaves was a most grating circumstance to his mind, and he believed would be so to a great part of the people of America. He had not made a strenuous opposition to it heretofore, because he had hoped that this concession would have produced a readiness, which had not been manifested, to strengthen the general government, and to mark a full confidence in it. The report under consideration had, by the tenor of it, put an end to all these hopes. In two great points, the hands of the legislature were absolutely tied. The importation of slaves could not be prohibited. Exports could not be taxed. Is this reasonable? What are the great objects of the general system? First, defense against foreign invasion; secondly, against internal sedition. Shall all the states, then, be bound to defend each, and shall each be at liberty to introduce a weakness which will render the defense more difficult? Shall one part of the United States be bound to defend another part, and that other part be at liberty, not only to increase its own danger, but to withhold the compensation for the burden? If slaves are to be imported, shall not the exports produced by their labor supply a revenue the better to enable the general government to defend their masters? There was so much inequality and unreasonableness in all this, that the people of the Northern States could never be reconciled to it. No candid man could undertake to justify it to them. He had hoped that some accommodation would have taken place on this subject; that, at least, a time would have been limited for the importation of slaves. He never could agree to let them be imported without limitation, and then be represented in the national legislature. Indeed, he could so little persuade himself of the rectitude of any such a practice, that he was not sure he could assent to it under any circumstances. At all events, either slaves should not be represented, or exports should be taxable.

Mr. Sherman regarded the slave trade as iniquitous; but the point of representation having been settled, after much difficulty and deliberation, he did not think himself bound to make opposition; especially as the present article, as amended, did not preclude any arrangement whatever on that point, in another place of the report.

Mr. Madison objected to one for every forty thousand inhabitants as a perpetual rule. The future increase of population, if the Union should be permanent, will render the number of representatives excessive.

Mr. Gorham. It is not to be supposed that the government will last so long as to produce this effect. Can it be supposed that this vast country, including the western territory, will, one hundred and fifty years hence, remain one nation?

Mr. Ellsworth. If the government should continue so long, alterations may be made in the Constitution, in the manner proposed in a subsequent article.

Mr. Sherman and Mr. Madison moved to insert the words "not exceeding" before the words "one for every forty thousand;" which was agreed to, *nem. con.*

Mr. Gouverneur Morris moved to insert "free" before the word "inhabitants." Much, he said, would depend on this point. He would never concur in upholding domestic slavery. It was a nefarious institution. It was the curse of heaven on the states where it prevailed. Compare the free regions of the Middle States, where a rich and noble cultivation marks the prosperity and happiness of the people, with the misery and poverty which overspread the barren wastes of Virginia, Maryland, and the other states having slaves. Travel through the whole continent, and you behold the prospect continually varying with the appearance and disappearance of slavery. The moment you leave the Eastern States, and enter New York, the effects of the institution become visible. Passing through the Jerseys, and entering Pennsylvania, every criterion of superior improvement witnesses the change. Proceed southwestwardly, and every step you take, through the great regions of slaves, presents a desert increasing with the increasing proportion of these wretched beings. Upon what principle is it that the slaves shall be computed in the representation? Are they men? Then make them citizens, and let them vote. Are they property? Why, then is no other property included? The houses in this city (Philadelphia) are worth more than all the wretched slaves who cover the rice swamps of South Carolina. The admission of slaves into the representation, when fairly explained, comes to this, -- that the inhabitants of Georgia and South Carolina, who goes to the coast of Africa, and, in defiance of the most sacred laws of humanity, tears away his fellow-creatures from their dearest connections, and damns them to the most cruel bondage, shall have more votes, in a government instituted for the protection of the rights of mankind, than the citizen of Pennsylvania or New Jersey, who views, with a laudable horror, no nefarious a practice. He would add, that domestic slavery is the most prominent feature in the aristocratic countenance of the proposed Constitution. The vassalage of the poor has ever been the favorite offspring of aristocracy. And what is the proposed compensation to the Northern States, for a sacrifice of every principle of right, of every impulse of humanity? They are to bind themselves to march their militia for the defense of the Southern States, for their defense against those very slaves of whom they complain. They must supply vessels and seamen, in case of foreign attack. The legislature will have indefinite power to tax them by excises, and duties on imports, both of which will fall heavier on them than on the southern inhabitants; for the bodea tea used by a northern freeman will pay more tax then the whole consumption of the miserable slave, which consists of nothing more than his physical subsistence and the rag that covers his nakedness. On the other side, the Southern States are not to be restrained from importing fresh supplies of wretched Africans, at once to increase the danger of attack and the difficulty of defense; nay, they are to be encouraged to it, by an assurance of having their votes in the national government increased in proportion; and are, at the same time, to have their exports and their slaves exempt from all contributions for the public service. Let it not be said that direct taxation is to be proportional to representation. It is idle to suppose that the general government can stretch its hand directly into the pockets of the people, scattered over so vast a country. They can only do it through the medium of exports, imports, and excises. For what, then, are all the sacrifices to be made? He would sooner submit himself to a tax for paying for all the negroes in the United States, than saddle posterity with such a Constitution.

Mr. Dayton seconded the motion. He did it, he said, that his sentiments on the subject might appear, whatever might be the fate of the amendment.

Mr. Sherman did not regard the admission of the negroes into the ratio of representation as liable to such insuperable objections. It was the ratio of freemen of the Southern States who were, in fact, to be represented according to the taxes paid by them, and the negroes are only included in the estimate of the taxes. This was his idea of the matter.

Mr. Pinckney considered the fisheries, and the western frontier, as more burdensome to the United States than the slaves. He thought this could be demonstrated, if the occasion were a proper one.

Mr. Wilson though the motion premature. An agreement to the clause would be no bar to the object of it.

On the question, on the motion to insert "free" before "inhabitants," --

New Jersey, aye, 1; New Hampshire, Massachusetts, Connecticut, Pennsylvania, Delaware, Maryland, Virginia, North Carolina, South Carolina, Georgia, no, 10.

On the suggestion of Mr. Dickinson, the words, "provided that teach state shall have one representative, at least," were added, *nem. con.*

Article 4, section 4, as amended, was agreed to, *nem. con.*

So, we have at this point, the initial allocation of the House of Representatives among the states, to be modified per the rule for determining direct taxation; which in turn is to be determined by the decennial census, in which the three-fifths rule for slaves was invoked. As the record shows, the three-fifths rule was a compromise reached initially in 1783 when the debate concerned how to fairly assess the relative economic benefit of slaves as compared to free men. Far from implying a racial motive, it was in fact an indirect condemnation of slavery as a viable economic institution. It was all about the money, so to speak; there was no indication that the relative moral value of black people was involved in this assessment.

The debate on 20 Aug 1787 mostly concerned the topic of how to define treason; but two modifications to the Art. 7, Sect. 3 of the 6 Aug 1787 draft were made that day, as follows [24]:

(Monday, August 20)

Article 7, section 3 was taken up. The words "white and others" were struck out, *nem. con.*, as superfluous.

Mr. Ellsworth moved to require the first census to be taken within "three," instead of "six," years from the first meeting of the legislature; and on the question, --

New Hampshire, Massachusetts, Connecticut, New Jersey, Pennsylvania, Delaware, Maryland, Virginia, North Carolina, aye, 9; South Carolina, Georgia, no, 2.

Mr. King asked what was the precise meaning of *direct* taxation. No one answered.

Mr. Gerry moved to add to Article 7, section 3, the following clause: --

"That, from the first meeting of the legislature of the United States until a census shall be taken, all moneys for supplying the public treasury by direct taxation shall be raised from the several states, according to the number of their representatives respectively in the first branch."

Mr. Langdon. This would bear unreasonably hard on New Hampshire, and he must be opposed to it.

Mr. Carroll opposed it. The number of representatives did not admit of a proportion exact enough for a rule of taxation.

Before any question, the House adjourned.

The debate on 21 Aug 1787 mostly concerned other topics, but Article 7, Section 3 was agreed to in that debate, 10 - 1. The debate on Article 7, Section 4 resumed, and the discussion focused on the utility of a tax on exports. They agreed to prohibit a tax on exports. Then the debate turned on the part of Article 7, Section 4 that dealt with prohibition or taxation on slaves, which is not attendant to our subject. It is interesting, though, to observe how the framers of the Constitution treated slavery, as follows [25]:

(Tuesday, August 21)

On the question on Article 7, section 4, as far as to "no tax shall be laid on exports," it passed in the affirmative, --

Massachusetts, Connecticut, Maryland, Virginia (Gen Washington and Mr. Madison, no), North Carolina, South Carolina, Georgia, aye, 7; New Hampshire, New Jersey, Pennsylvania, Delaware, no, 4.

Mr. L. Martin proposed to vary article 7, section 4 so as to allow a prohibition or tax on the importation of slaves. In the first place, as five slaves are to be counted as three freemen, in the apportionment of representatives, such a clause would leave an encouragement to this traffic. In the second place, slaves weakened one part of the Union, which the other parts were bound to protect; the privilege of importing them was therefore unreasonable. And, in the third place, it was inconsistent with the principles of the revolution, and dishonorable to the American character, to have such a feature in the Constitution.

Mr. Rutledge did not see how the importation of slaves could be encouraged by this section. He was not apprehensive of insurrections, and would readily exempt the other states from the obligation to protect the Southern against them. Religion and humanity had nothing to do with this question. Interest alone is the governing principle with nations. The true question at present is, whether the Southern States shall or shall not be parties to the Union. If the Northern States consult their interest, they will not oppose the increase of slaves, which will increase the commodities of which they will become the carriers.

Mr. Ellsworth was for leaving the clause as it stands. Let every state import what it pleases. The morality or wisdom of slavery are considerations belonging to the states themselves. What enriches a part enriches the whole, and the states are the best judges of their particular interest. The old Confederation had not meddled with this point; and he did not see any greater necessity for bringing it within the policy of the new one.

Mr. Pinckney. South Carolina can never receive the plan if it prohibits the slave trade. In every proposed extension of the powers of Congress, that state has expressly and watchfully excepted that of meddling with the importation of negroes. If the states be all left at liberty on this subject, South Carolina may perhaps, by degrees, do of herself what is wished, as Virginia and Maryland have already done.

Adjourned.

(Wednesday, August 22)

In Convention - Article 7, Section 4 was resumed.

Mr. Sherman was for leaving the clause as it stands. He disapproved of the slave trade; yet, as the states were now possessed of the right to import slaves, as the public good did not require it to be taken from them, as a it was expedient to have as few objections as possible to the proposed scheme of government, he thought it best to leave the matter as we find it. He observed, that the abolition of slavery seemed to be going on in the United States, and that the good sense of the several states would probably by degrees complete it. He urged on the Convention the necessity of despatching its business.

Col. Mason. This infernal traffic originated in the avarice of British merchants. The British government constantly checked the attempts of Virginia to put a stop to it. The present question concerns not the importing states alone, but the whole Union. The evil of having slaves was experienced during the late war. Had slaves been treated as they might have been by the enemy, they would have proved dangerous instruments in their hands. But their folly dealt by the slaves as it did the tories. He mentioned the dangerous insurrections of the slaves in Greece and Sicily; and the instructions given by Cromwell, to the commissioners sent to Virginia, to arm the servants and slaves, in case other means of obtaining its submission should fail. Maryland and Virginia, he said, had already prohibited the importation of slaves expressly. North Carolina had done the same in substance. All this would be in vain, if South Carolina and Georgia be at liberty to import. The western people are already calling out for slaves for their new lands, and will fill that country with slaves, if they can be got through South Carolina and Georgia. Slavery discourages arts and manufactures. The poor despise labor when performed by slaves. They prevent the emigration of whites, who really enrich and strengthen a country. They produce the most pernicious effect on manners. Every master of slaves is born a petty tyrant. They bring the judgment of Heaven on a country. As nations cannot be rewarded or punished in the next world, they must be in this. By an inevitable chain of causes and effects, Providence punished national sins by national calamities. He lamented that some of our eastern brethren had, from a lust of gain, embarked in this nefarious traffic. As to the states being in possession of the right to import, this was the case with many other rights, now to be properly given up. He held it essential, in every point of view, that the general government should have power to prevent the increase of slavery.

Mr. Ellsworth, as he had never owned a slave, could not judge of the effects of slavery on character. He said, however, that if it was to be considered in a moral light, we ought to go further, and free those already in the country. As slaves also multiply so fast in Virginia and Maryland, that it is cheaper to raise then import them, whilst in the sickly rice swamps foreign supplies are necessary, if we go no further than is urged, we shall be unjust towards South Carolina and Georgia. Let us not intermeddle. As population increases, poor laborers will be so plenty as to render slaves useless. Slavery, in time, will not be a speck in our country. Provision is already made in Connecticut for abolishing it. And the abolition has already taken place in Massachusetts. As to the danger of foreign influence, that will become a motive to kind treatment of the slaves.

Mr. Pinckney. If slavery be wrong, it is justified by the example of all the world. He cited the case of Greece, Rome, and other ancient states; the sanction given by France, England, Holland, and other modern states. In all ages, one half of mankind have been slaves. If the Southern States were let alone, they will probably of themselves stop importations. He would himself, as a citizen of South Carolina, vote for it. An attempt to take away the right, as proposed, will produce serious objections to the Constitution, which he wished to see adopted.

Gen. Pinckney declared it to be his firm opinion that if himself and all his colleagues were to sign the Constitution, and use their personal influence, it would be of no avail towards obtaining the assent of their constituents. South Carolina and Georgia cannot do without slaves. As to Virginia, she will gain by stopping the importations. Her slaves will rise in value, and she has more than she wants. It would be unequal to require South

Carolina and Georgia to confederate on such unequal terms. He said, the royal assent, before the revolution, had never been refused to South Carolina, as to Virginia. He contended, that the importation of slaves would be for the interest of the whole Union. The more slaves, the more produce to employ the carrying trade; the more consumption also; and the more of this, the more revenue for the common treasury. He admitted it to be reasonable that slaves should be dutied like other imports; but should consider a rejection of the clause as an exclusion of South Carolina from the Union.

Mr. Baldwin had conceived national objects alone to be before the Convention; not such as, like the present, were of a local nature. Georgia was decided on this point. That state has always hitherto supposed a general government to be the pursuit of the central states, who wished to have a vortex for every thing; that her distance would preclude her from equal advantage; and that she could not prudently purchase it by yielding national powers. From this it might be understood in what light she would view an attempt to abridge one of her favorite prerogatives. If left to herself, she may probably put a stop to the evil. As one ground for this conjecture, he took notice of the sect of ----, which he said, was a respectable class of people, who carried their ethics beyond the mere equality of men, extending their humanity to the claims of the whole animal creation.

Mr. Wilson observed that, if South Carolina and Georgia were themselves disposed to get rid of the importation of slaves in a short time, as had been suggested, they would never refuse to unite because the importation might be prohibited. As the section now stands, all articles imported are to be taxed. Slaves alone are exempt. This is, in fact, a bounty on that article.

Mr. Gerry thought we had nothing to do with the conduct of the states as to slaves, but ought to be careful not to give any sanction to it.

Mr. Dickinson considered it as inadmissible, on every principle of honor and safety, that the importation of slaves should be authorized to the states by the Constitution. The true question was, whether the national happiness would be promoted or impeded by the importation; and this question ought to be left to the national government, not to the states particularly interested. If England and France permit slavery slaves are, at the same time, excluded from both those kingdoms. Greece and Rome were made unhappy by their slaves. He could not believe that the Southern States would refuse to confederate on the account apprehended; especially as the power was not likely to be immediately exercised by the general government.

Mr. Williamson stated the law of North Carolina on the subject, to wit, that it did not directly prohibit the importation of slaves. It imposed a duty of £5 on each slave imported from Africa; £10 on each from elsewhere; and £50 on each from a state licensing manumission. He thought the Southern States could not be members of the Union, if the clause should be rejected; and that it was wrong to force any thing down not absolutely necessary, and which any state must disagree to.

Mr. King thought the subject should be considered in a political light only. If two states will not agree to the Constitution, as stated on one side, he could affirm with equal belief, on the other, that great and equal opposition would be experienced from the other states. He remarked on the exemption of slaves from duty, whilst every other import was subjected to it, as an inequality that could not fail to strike the commercial sagacity of the Northern and Middle States.

Mr. Langdon was strenuous for giving the power to the general government. He could not, with a good conscience, leave it with the states, who could then go on with the traffic, without being restrained by the opinions here given, that they will themselves cease to import slaves.

> Gen. Pinckney thought himself bound to declare candidly, that he did not think South Carolina would stop her importations of slaves in any short time; but only stop them occasionally, as she now does. He moved to commit the clause, that slaves might be made liable to an equal tax with other imports; which he thought right, and which would remove one difficulty that had been stated.
>
> Mr. Rutledge. If the Convention thinks that North Carolina, South Carolina, and Georgia, will ever agree to the plan, unless their right to import slaves be untouched, the expectation is in vain. The people of those states will never be such fools as to give up so important an interest. He was strenuous against striking out the section, and seconded the motion of Gen. Pinckney for a commitment.
>
> Mr. Gouverneur Morris wished the whole subject to be committed, including the clauses relating to taxes on exports and to a navigation act. These things may form a bargain among the Northern and Southern States.
>
> Mr. Butler declared, that he never would agree to the power of taxing exports.
>
> Mr. Sherman said it was better to let the Southern States import slaves than to part with them, if they made that a *sine qua non*. He was opposed to a tax on slaves imported, as making the matter worse, because it implied they were *property*. He acknowledged that, if the power of prohibiting the importation should be given to the general government, it would be exercised. He thought it would be its duty to exercise the power.
>
> Mr. Read was for the commitment, provided the clause concerning taxes on exports should also be committed.
>
> Mr. Sherman observed, that that clause had been agreed to, and therefore should not be committed.
>
> Mr. Randolph was for committing, in order that some middle ground might, if possible, be found. He could never agree to the clause as it stands. He would sooner risk the Constitution. He dwelt on the dilemma to which the Constitution as exposed. By agreeing to the clause, it would revolt the Quakers, the Methodists, and many others in the states having no slaves. On the other hand, two states might be lost to the Union. Let us then, he said, try the chance of a commitment.
>
> On the question for committing the remaining part of sections 4 and 5 of Article 7, --
>
> Connecticut, New Jersey, Maryland, Virginia, North Carolina, South Carolina, Georgia, aye, 7; New Hampshire, Pennsylvania, Delaware, no, 3; Massachusetts, absent.

Some of the founders desired abolish slavery while others wanted to at least restrict it and cause it to die off gradually. But, it was evident that at least two states, and possibly a third, would refuse to join the Union if slavery were restricted too much or prohibited. For that reason, slavery was left intact as an institution: the only restrictions on it were a prohibition on importation after 1808, and a duty on importation was permitted. It is important to remember the importance of including all the states into the Union, at the expense of continuing to allow slavery. The main issue at this time was Spain's activity in the west, and its desire to encroach on the American states where it could. Spain was already prohibiting navigation on the Mississippi River, and was unwilling to negotiate. What if the three southern states had refused to join the Union? It is difficult to say; it is possible that they would have remained independent, but they could just as easily fallen prey to either Britain or Spain. In that case, slavery would still have been allowed as it had under Britain; Spain, meanwhile, held most of South America in slavery.

A committee was appointed to compile all the changes made to the 6 Aug 1787 draft, which was reported out in a near-final version on 12 Sep 1787. Article 7, sections 3 and 4 of the 6 Aug draft were placed in Article 1, Section 2 of the final version. A few minor changes to the relevant section were agreed to on 13 Sep 1787, in which the word 'servitude' was changed to 'service', and 'forty' was changed to 'thirty'.

6 Summary

So here you have the true and complete story of how the three-fifths rule came into being. As I mentioned earlier, it was superseded by the 14th Amendment in 1868. The candid reader should now see that the debates that led to the adoption of the "three-fifths" rule were all based on how to fairly judge the economic contribution of slaves relative to freemen. The fact that they concluded that slaves should be rated lower in economic terms proves, if it proves anything, that the founders recognized, at least intuitively, that slavery was not economically competitive in the long run. It is no secret that some of the founders hated the institution of slavery; that others were fond of it since it allowed them to avoid hard work; and that others disliked it but regarded it as a necessary evil in the short term. Each member of the Convention no doubt had their prejudices about other people, including north vs. south as well as black vs. white. But there is no evidence from the historical record that the three-fifths rule came about because of a consensus on the part of the founders that black people were inherently morally inferior to whites. To claim otherwise is evidence of a race-baiting crusade and willful ignorance of historical facts. So now you know the facts, from which you may judge the quality of argument presented by our modern "debaters".

References

[1] Jonathan Elliot, *The Debates in the Several State Conventions on the Adoption of the Federal Constitution as Recommended by the General Convention at Philadelphia in 1787*, Philadelphia: J. B. Lippincott & Co., 1881, Vol. 1, pp. 70-74

[2] ibid., Vol. 5, pp. 63, 64

[3] ibid., Vol. 5, pp. 77-80

[4] ibid., Vol. 1, pp. 93-95

[5] ibid., Vol. 5, p. 127

[6] ibid., Vol. 5, p. 129

[7] ibid., Vol. 5, p. 130

[8] ibid., Vol. 5, pp. 134, 135

[9] ibid., Vol. 5, pp. 135-137

[10] ibid., Vol. 5, pp. 175-178

[11] ibid., Vol. 5, pp. 178-182

[12] ibid., Vol. 5, p. 190

[13] ibid., Vol. 5, p. 192

[14] ibid., Vol. 1, p. 182. It should be noted that the detailed exposition of the committee report of 13 Jun 1787 is not contained in Madison's papers, and is therefore not in Vol. 5 of Elliot. It is contained in the summary section in Elliot's Vol. 1, with the annotation "Paper deposited by President Washington, in the Department of State."

[15] ibid, Vol. 1, p. 184

[16] ibid., Vol. 1, pp. 191, 192; Vol. 5, pp. 253, 259

[17] ibid., Vol. 5, p. 274

[18] ibid., Vol. 5, pp. 280, 281

[19] ibid., Vol. 5, pp. 288-290

[20] ibid., Vol. 5, pp. 294-302

[21] ibid., Vol. 5, pp. 306-309

[22] ibid., Vol. 5, pp. 377, 378

[23] ibid., Vol. 5, pp. 391-394

[24] ibid., Vol. 5, p. 451

[25] ibid., Vol. 5, pp. 457-461

On the General Welfare Clause
(18 May 2011)

Mr. Mike Wallace of Fox News interviewed Representative Ron Paul of Texas on 15 May 2011. In the course of the interview, the topic of the meaning of the "general welfare" clause of the U. S. Constitution came up. Mr. Paul's view was that the Constitution did not grant the government to do anything it wanted under a justification of "general welfare". Mr. Wallace cited the 1937 Supreme Court case "Helvering v. David", which ruled that Social Security was permitted under the powers of Congress called out in Article 1 Section 8 of the U. S. Constitution. By extension, therefore, in Mr. Wallace's view, the Supreme Court has ruled that Congress may pass laws it claims to further the "general welfare". Mr. Wallace did not explain how payments to individuals, that is, laws that promote "individual welfare", can actually be the same as "general welfare".

What is the true meaning of the "general welfare" clause? It appears in two places in the Constitution: a) the Preamble, and b) Article 1, Section 8. The Preamble reads:

> We the people of the United States, in order to form a more perfect union, establish justice, insure domestic tranquility, provide for the common defense, promote the general welfare, and secure the blessings of liberty to ourselves and our posterity, do ordain and establish this Constitution for the United States of America.

Article 1, Section 8 reads: "The Congress shall have power to lay and collect taxes, duties, imposts and excises, to pay the debts and provide for the common defense and general welfare of the United States; but all duties, imposts and excises shall be uniform throughout the United States"; whereupon follows 17 clauses calling out a list of specific enumerated powers granted to Congress.

To see the intent of the founding fathers, it is necessary only to review three passages of the *Federalist Papers*. The first is *Federalist Papers* #23, in which Hamilton refers back to the Articles of Confederation, where the phrase "general welfare" was first used. He is discussing the principle that powers must be granted to governments commensurate with the ends desired, as follows:

> Defective as the present Confederation has been proved to be, this principle appears to have been fully recognized by the framers of it; though they have not made proper or adequate provision for its exercise. Congress have an unlimited discretion to make requisitions of men and money; to govern the army and navy; to direct their operations. As their requisitions are made constitutionally binding upon the States, who are in fact under the most solemn obligations to furnish the supplies required of them, the intention evidently was that the United States should command whatever resources were by them judged requisite to the "common defense and general welfare." It was presumed that a sense of their true interests, and a regard to the dictates of good faith, would be found sufficient pledges for the punctual performance of the duty of the members to the federal head.

It is important to recall that the purpose of the Articles of Confederation was to manage the war effort against Great Britain. Therefore, in the *Federalist Papers* #23, Hamilton asserts that the general welfare consisted of maintaining that war effort. His complaint here is that Congress under the Articles was too weak to force the states to uphold their end of the financial obligation.

The Constitution was formed as a union of the states into a system that is partly national and partly federal. The powers granted to the government were greater than were granted by the Articles, in order to meet the needs of a compact union; i.e., to ensure that the union of the states functioned as a true nation, not as simply a federation. In other words, the government under Constitution would have greater powers to promote the general welfare than the Articles which it replaced. James Madison explained what these powers of "general welfare" are in the *Federalist Papers* #41, as follows:

> Some, who have not denied the necessity of the power of taxation, have grounded a very fierce attack against the Constitution, on the language in which it is defined. It has been urged and echoed, that the power "to lay and collect taxes, duties, imposts, and excises, to

> pay the debts, and provide for the common defense and general welfare of the United States," amounts to an unlimited commission to exercise every power which may be alleged to be necessary for the common defense or general welfare. No stronger proof could be given of the distress under which these writers labor for objections, than their stooping to such a misconstruction.
>
> Had no other enumeration or definition of the powers of the Congress been found in the Constitution, than the general expressions just cited, the authors of the objection might have had some color for it; though it would have been difficult to find a reason for so awkward a form of describing an authority to legislate in all possible cases. A power to destroy the freedom of the press, the trial by jury, or even to regulate the course of descents, or the forms of conveyances, must be very singularly expressed by the terms "to raise money for the general welfare."
>
> But what color can the objection have, when a specification of the objects alluded to by these general terms immediately follows, and is not even separated by a longer pause than a semicolon? If the different parts of the same instrument ought to be so expounded, as to give meaning to every part which will bear it, shall one part of the same sentence be excluded altogether from a share in the meaning; and shall the more doubtful and indefinite terms be retained in their full extent, and the clear and precise expressions be denied any signification whatsoever? For what purpose could the enumeration of particular powers be inserted, if these and all others were meant to be included in the preceding general power? Nothing is more natural nor common than first to use a general phrase, and then to explain and qualify it by a recital of particulars. But the idea of an enumeration of particulars which neither explain nor qualify the general meaning, and can have no other effect than to confound and mislead, is an absurdity, which, as we are reduced to the dilemma of charging either on the authors of the objection or on the authors of the Constitution, we must take the liberty of supposing, had not its origin with the latter.

It is obvious therefore, that the powers conveyed to Congress for the purposes of common defense and general welfare are the enumerated powers listed in the 17 clauses immediately following the main heading of Article 1, Section 8. If you look them up, no where will you find anything resembling the "social programs" currently in force at the federal level.

Last, Hamilton alluded to this principle briefly in the *Federalist Papers* #62, as follows:

> A good government implies two things: first, fidelity to the object of government, which is the happiness of the people; secondly, a knowledge of the means by which that object can be best attained. Some governments are deficient in both these qualities; most governments are deficient in the first. I scruple not to assert, that in American governments too little attention has been paid to the last. The federal Constitution avoids this error; and what merits particular notice, it provides for the last in a mode which increases the security for the first.

Here we see from his last sentence that the U. S. Constitution provides the means, that is, the legitimate powers, by which the happiness of the people is to be secured, which is the object of government. Since all legislative power is vested in the Congress per Article 1, Section 1, it seems that Hamilton is referring to the same list of powers as contained in Article 1, Section 8. He also mentions "knowledge of the means by which that object can be best obtained". He was discussing the Senate in the *Federalist Papers* #62; but here is a case where all of us would do well to examine the powers granted in Article 1, Section 8 so we can see for ourselves the legitimate powers of government conducive to liberty, security, and the general welfare.

Why the House Originates Revenue Bills
(1 Jun 2011)

Article 1, Section 7 of the U. S. Constitution states:

> All bills for raising revenue shall originate in the House of Representatives; but the Senate may propose or concur with amendments as on other bills.

It is instructive to recount the debate in the Constitutional Convention during which this provision was decided. In early July of 1787, the delegates to the Convention were debating many aspects of how the proposed new government would function. On 5 Jul 1787, a committee led by Mr. Gerry reported out its recommendations, one of which stated in part, "that all bills for raising or appropriating money ... shall originate in the first branch of the legislature." The debate on this provision occurred the next day. It turned out that the sentiments expressed by George Mason and Benjamin Franklin convinced the delegates to adopt this provision. Here are the excerpts from James Madison's notes regarding the arguments made by Mason and Franklin [1]. Keep in mind that the "first branch" referred to is the House of Representatives, the members of which are directly elected by the people, and the "second branch" is the Senate, the members of which were originally chosen by the state legislatures. Hence the House represented the people; the Senate represented the states.

> Mr. Mason. The consideration which weighed with the committee was, that the first branch would be the immediate representatives of the people; the second would not. Should the latter have the power of giving away the people's money, they might soon forget the source from whence they received it. We might soon have an aristocracy. He had been much concerned at the principles which had been advanced by some gentlemen, but had the satisfaction to find they did not generally prevail. He was a friend to proportional representation in both branches; but supposed that some points must be yielded for the sake of accommodation.
>
> Dr. Franklin did not mean to go into a justification of the report; but as it had been asked what would be the use of restraining the second branch from meddling with money bills, he could not but remark, that it was always of importance that the people should know who had disposed of their money, and how it had been disposed of. It was a maxim, that those who feel can best judge. This end would, he thought, be best attained, if money affairs were to be confined to the immediate representatives of the people. This was his inducement to concur in the report. As to the danger or difficulty that might arise from a negative in the second branch, where the people would not be proportionally represented, it might easily be got over by declaring that there should be no negative; or, if that will not do, by declaring that there shall be no such branch at all.

The delegates believed that the subject of revenue and taxation should be decided by those in the government who most directly represent the people, as they can be held to account more readily than those representing the states. (However, the members of the Senate are now elected by the people per the 17th Amendment, which was ratified in 1913.) James Madison amplified this concept later in the *Federalist Papers #58*:

> The House of Representatives cannot only refuse, but they alone can propose, the supplies requisite for the support of the government. They, in a word, hold the power of the purse -- that powerful instrument by which we behold, in the history of the British Constitution, an infant and humble representative of the people gradually enlarging the sphere of its activity and importance, and finally reducing, as far as it seems to have wished, all the overgrown prerogatives of the other branches of the government.

It would be novel indeed, if the modern House would refuse to fund something, even though the national debt is so large. It would be novel if the House only raised revenue that was necessary for the support of the government; taxes, deficits, and the total debt would likely be much smaller. But such a great portion of the money raised now goes to spending that is not related to the function of the government per se. The budgetary power does in fact cause Congress to dominate the government, which is as it should be. Unfortunately, the revenue policies have in modern times caused the government to exert undue influence over industry and the people alike.

References

[1] Jonathan Elliot, *Debates on the Adoption of the Federal Constitution in the Convention Held at Philadelphia in 1787; With a Diary of the Debates of the Congress of the Confederation; as reported by James Madison*, Philadelphia: J. B. Lippincott & Co., 1881, Vol. 5, pp. 282-284

The False Claim for a "Living Constitution"
(3 Jun 2011)

There are a significant number of people to buy into the argument that the U. S. Constitution should be a "living document". It is not just some crackpots who believe it; it is embraced by a fair number of educated people, some of them educated in constitutional law. Before I examine a supposed justification for the "living constitution", it is useful to spell out what is meant by that phrase. The underlying philosophy of the "living constitution" sect (for it is a civil religion) is that the U. S. Constitution was a great advancement in the 18th century, but is now obsolete. With the advent of technology and industry that supplanted the agricultural economy of the colonial period, it is necessary, they claim, for the government to expand its powers as it sees fit in order to do good, help the people, to pick economic winners and losers, and to regulate the activities of business and the people for the common good. These expansions of power are justified, they claim, because it is all done for the benefit of the people.

It is pretty obvious that the intent of the founding fathers was to create a limited government with limited specified powers, as stated in Article 1, Section 8 of the Constitution. The main idea was to protect individual liberty as much as possible, consistent with peace and stability. But the advocates for the "living constitution" sometimes attempt to find a justification for the arbitrary-power model of government in the writings of the founding fathers themselves. Mr. Garrett Epps does so in his essay of 1 Jun 2011 [1], titled "Constitutional Myth #2: The Purpose of the Constitution is to Limit Congress". It is true that the Constitution was intended to create a federal government that had viable powers, unlike the Congress under the Articles of Confederation. Congress under the Articles was simply too weak to function as a viable government, and it was obvious that some new form of government was required. That is quite different than saying the Constitution was designed to allow the federal government to anything it wanted. Mr. Epps claims in his article that Alexander Hamilton viewed federal powers as unlimited. To do so, he quotes a section from Hamilton's *Federalist Papers #34*:

> There ought to be a capacity to provide for future contingencies as they may happen, and as these are illimitable, in their nature, it is impossible safely to limit that capacity.

Mr. Epps uses this passage in isolation in an attempt to show that Hamilton regarded the federal government as having arbitrary powers, including one to create more powers, and the power to use them all as it saw fit in the future. There are two fallacies here. The first is that Mr. Epps fails to point out that the *Federalist Papers #34* is part of a long sequence on taxation (numbers 30 through 36) in which Hamilton expends great effort to show that federal and state taxation are compatible, can be efficiently collected, and are devoted to different expenses. The federal expenses that Hamilton had in mind here are mentioned two paragraphs later in the same essay:

> What are the chief sources of expense in every government? What has occasioned that enormous accumulation of debts with which several of the European nations are oppressed? The answer plainly is, wars and rebellions; the support of those institutions which are necessary to guard the body politic against these two most mortal diseases of society. The expenses arising from those institutions which are relative to the mere domestic police of a State, to the support of its legislative, executive, and judicial departments, with their different appendages, and to the encouragement of agriculture and manufactures (which will comprehend almost all the objects of state expenditure), are insignificant in comparison with those which relate to the national defense.

Secondly, Mr. Epps declines to point out that Hamilton had, a few days earlier in the *Federalist Papers #33*, discussed the fact that only specific powers were conferred to the federal government. In his discourse on taxation, Hamilton addresses objections to the "Supremacy Clause" (Article VI). The critics had claimed that this and the power of taxation would be the "pernicious engines by which their local governments would be destroyed and their liberties extinguished". But Hamilton explains:

> If a number of political societies enter into a larger political society, the laws which the latter may enact, pursuant to the powers intrusted to it by its constitution, must necessarily be supreme over those societies, and the individuals of whom they are composed. It would otherwise be a mere treaty, dependent on the good faith of the parties, and not a government, which is only another word for political power and supremacy. But it will not follow from this doctrine that acts of the larger society which are not pursuant to its constitutional powers, but are invasions of the residual authorities of the smaller societies, will become the supreme law of the land. These will be merely acts of usurpation, and will deserve to be treated as such.

It is clear that Hamilton regarded the powers of the federal government to be limited; otherwise, how could he claim that laws contrary to the constitution are acts of usurpation? It is true that we the people have grown lazy and have failed to call acts of usurpation by their real name. The only fix for that is education. I would urge everyone to read the *Federalist Papers*, so as not to be misled by those like Mr. Epps who wish to impose arbitrary government upon you. It is clear that neither Hamilton nor the other founders implicitly advocated the notion of a "living constitution".

References

[1] http://www.theatlantic.com/national/archive/2011/06/constitutional-myth-2-the-purpose-of-the-constitution-is-to-limit-congress/239374/

Phrases from the U. S. Constitution

Note: This essay was originally published 7 Apr 2018, and was later incorporated as Question 25 in the book *Real World Graduation*. It poses a multiple-choice question, followed by an explanation of the correct answer.

The Question

Which of these are phrases found in the Constitution of the United States of America?

a) "... separation of church and state..."
b) "... government shall have the right ..."
c) "... people shall be entitled to general welfare ..."
d) "... right to rest and leisure ..."
e) Both a) and c)

The Answer

This is a trick question. None of the suggested choices appear in the U. S. Constitution.

Answer (a), often cited by atheists, actually comes from a letter sent by Thomas Jefferson to Nehemiah Dodge and others of "a Committee of the Danbury [CT] Baptist Association" on 1 Jan 1802. The second paragraph reads as follows [1]:

> Believing with you that religion is a matter which lies solely between man and his God, that he owes account to none other for his faith or his worship, that the legislative powers of government reach actions only, and not opinions, I contemplate with sovereign reverence that act of the whole American people which declared the their legislature should "make no law respecting an establishment of religion, or prohibiting the free exercise thereof," thus building a wall of separation between church and state. Adhering to this expression of the supreme will of the nation in behalf of the rights of conscience, I shall see with sincere satisfaction the progress of those sentiments which tend to restore to man all his natural rights, convinced he has no natural rights in opposition to his social duties.

It thus informs the Baptist group that the intent of the First Amendment is to prohibit the government from creating a state religion, compelling participation in any religion, compelling belief in any doctrine, or prohibiting belief in any doctrine, or otherwise interfering with private religious activities. Jefferson does not claim that the First Amendment mandates public atheism, as some would have you believe. If it did, why would Jefferson, having taken an oath to uphold the Constitution, write to members of a church?

Answer (b) is incorrect because in the U. S. Constitution, the government was granted powers, whereas rights are simply regarded as intrinsic freedoms belonging to each person. In the American system, only persons have rights; governments can only have powers. The American system is a divided sovereignty, meaning that the federal government has certain powers, and the states have certain powers, but none of either set of powers can interfere with the rights of a citizen.

Answer (c) is incorrect; it is a common misuse of the statement in the Preamble to the Constitution, which reads:

> We the People of the United States, in order to form a more perfect union, establish justice, insure domestic tranquility, provide for the common defense, and promote the general welfare...

In this context, general welfare meant that the government was granted powers to do things that would benefit the people in general (such as building roads, canals, and creating a Post Office); it has nothing to do with providing "welfare" to individuals (which is accomplished only by taking money out of someone else's pocket). The concept of public "welfare", or "safety net", is an entirely different idea, and is not contained the Constitution.

Answer (d) is actually a quote from Article 119 of the 1936 Constitution of the Union of Soviet Socialist Republics [2]. This was nothing more than propaganda. History shows that there was not a moment of rest or leisure under communism, unless you were a member of the Communist Party. Incidentally, Article 122 of the same Constitution guaranteed that "women in the USSR are accorded equal rights with men". In other words, women were equal slaves to the all-seeing, all-knowing, all-directing socialist state.

References

[1] Merrill D. Peterson, ed., *Jefferson: Writings*, New York: Literary Classics of the United States, 1984, p. 510

[2] https://www.departments.bucknell.edu/russian/const/1936toc.html

2
Economics and Finances

Introduction

This chapter contains seven essays that discuss historical financial and economic topics. The purpose of these is to present an accurate history of central banking, paper money, the U. S. national debt, and one of its components (Social Security).

The first essay relates the history of how the Bank of England was started, the underlying rationale for it, and how it affected the British people. It may be summarized as: debt was necessary to fight wars; interest on the debt was paid rigorously, the debt came to be regarded as an asset, and was then used as a basis to issue (or "back") the currency. The Bank of England is Great Britain's central bank, different in structure, but functionally the same as the American central bank, the Federal Reserve, which has accomplished similar results.

The second essay is a history of the financing of the American Revolutionary War, especially the issuing of the "Continental" currency. It covers some of the same elements as the first essay in chapter one, but the emphasis is on the economic and financial effects of the Continentals. Too much money was issued, and as always, the relative value of each unit declined rapidly compared to stable money (in this case, the Spanish Milled Dollar).

The third essay recounts the fiasco of the assignats (paper money) issued by the provisional government during the French Revolution. They came up with a novel way to ensure the value of the money: by confiscating the land owned by the Catholic Church. Of course it failed; there is no practical way for a paper money note to be traced to a plot of land, and they issued far too much currency. But it is interesting to note one difference between the American and French experiences: the French imposed severe penalties for refusing to accept the assignats or trading in any stable money.

The fourth essay contains some basic facts about the steady increase of the national debt between 1929 and 2022, comparing it to the growth of gross domestic product (GDP). It shows that the debt-to-GDP ratio was steady at about 0.6 for most of that time, except for two periods: a) the two-front World War II; and b) the past 15 years or so. The data for the national debt prior to 1929 is contained in the book *The Control and Manipulation of Money*.

The fifth essay presents data on the financial status of Social Security from the start of operations in 1937 to 2022. It includes the tax rates, income limits, growth of the Trust Fund, the nature of the Trust

Fund, and a comparison of returns from Social Security as compared to typical investments. Also, this essay shows why the Social Security system is not actually a Ponzi scheme.

Often a bank is "bailed-out" by the FDIC or the Federal Reserve when it has a liquidity or solvency problem, and the costs thereof are transferred indirectly to the taxpayers. That is accomplished by assessing charges on the participating banks, which in turn are passed on to their customers, who are taxpayers. Essay six describes the difference between the typical "bail-out" and a "bail-in", which occurred in Cyprus in 2013, and may come to the U. S. in the future.

The seventh essay presents a "multiple-guess" question on the nature of U. S. currency, along with an explanation of the correct answer.

The Origin of the Bank of England

Note: This essay is extracted from section 1.12 of the book, *The Control and Manipulation of Money.* I have inserted explanatory notes in square brackets when quoting the older authors.

One of the lessons of history is that national debt tends to benefit the wealthy to the detriment of the common working people. The reason is that the wealthy can afford to invest in government debt and receive the annual interest payments, and are in no hurry to have the debt paid off. Meanwhile, those investments can still be sold on the open market for their current value. In other words, government debt becomes an asset if the holder thereof can find someone to buy it. It is instructive to examine the details by which the first great national debt with regular financing was developed, namely the example of England beginning with the reign of William III (a.k.a. William of Orange, Holland) and Mary II (Stuart) as related by Walker [1]:

> When William of Orange succeeded to the throne of England [1689], Louis XIV [of France], then at the zenith of his power, refused to acknowledge him as a legitimate monarch, and espoused the cause of the exiled Stuart [James II of England]. War, of course, followed. But fighting, in consequence of the invention of gunpowder, and the changes it gradually introduced into warfare, had become an expensive luxury; a game which kings, with their limited and uncertain revenues, could ill afford to play at, particularly for a great length of time. War with one so powerful as the *Grand Monarque* [Louis XIV] could not be safely commenced or successfully prosecuted, while every penny must be extorted from a reluctant and now independent Commons [Parliament], and the taxes immediately assessed on the large land or other property holders of the realm.
>
> Such was the difficulty which King William encountered; but, fortunately for his fame, he was a shrewd financier, as well as an able soldier. Up to this time, England had never had a permanent organized national debt, a national bank, or any regular and reliable system of revenue. Grants and subsidies had been voted from time to time; duties and special taxes had been imposed, but these were not to be counted upon.
>
> The monarch might and did borrow money from time to time, in great emergencies, but on the most disadvantageous terms. The credit of the government was always low, because there was no regularity or system in the public finances. Men had no confidence in the responsibility or punctuality of the government. William changed all this. He borrowed for a specified period, and promised the punctual payment of the interest semi-annually, and the principal when due; and pledged "the public funds" for the fulfillment of his promises. Hence the public securities [government bonds] were called "the funds".
>
> He negotiated loans and issued stocks [government debt obligations]. He granted annuities upon the payment of specific sums. Interest and principal were secured by a pledge of the public funds, or revenues derived from various sources.
>
> This put a new face upon the financial affairs of England: but something further was desirable; viz., an agency by which the national debt could be readily managed, and its semi-annual interest promptly paid.
>
> This was accomplished by the incorporation of a national bank [Bank of England, 1697], consisting of the holders of the public stocks [government debt], to the amount of £1,200,000.
>
> One thing more was wanting; viz., a permanent and sufficient income, to meet not only the interest on the accumulated debt, but the current expenses of the government, already large, and constantly increasing. To effect this, a land-tax was established; small, indeed,

in amount, and upon a fixed valuation, so that it could not be increased with the increasing value of the land.

A system of duties on all imports was also enacted, and an excise upon all home manufactures and products. In short, a system of indirect taxation was adopted, far more general and effective than any which had before existed.

Thus was completed the grand triad of the system of finance, inaugurated by the English Revolution [1688]; viz. -- funding, banking, and indirect taxation. The immediate as well as ultimate, results of the new system are alike remarkable and worthy of our attention.

First, the credit of the government was firmly established. It could borrow more money, and at a lower rate of interest than ever before. Men of small means could now loan money to the government, and with entire confidence. The whole community could be laid under contribution [i.e., payment of taxes].

Second, government was enabled to carry on war by borrowing, instead of imposing taxes. War could be waged with credit, instead of cash. Parliament had only to vote a loan. No expenditure need be stopped for want of funds, while the national credit was unimpaired. This was a great change. Many a war had been abruptly closed for want of funds. There was no such necessity hereafter.

Third, this course removed the fear of immediate and pressing taxation from the rich, because the greater part was now to fall upon the masses of the people, who pay taxes, not in proportion to property, but to consumption [in the form of tariffs and excise taxes]. This was an agreeable consideration to the wealthy classes; and the more so, because, as the public stocks [debt] were multiplied, better opportunities were afforded for investments [in government debt].

Fourth, especially was the new policy acceptable to the aristocracy, who, at that time, even more perhaps than now [1867], monopolized the public offices, and whose revenues and patronage were increased by governmental expenditures.

The American patriot Thomas Paine [2] of *Common Sense* fame and some additional details by Walker [3] give an accounting of how the national debt in Great Britain grew with each war from 1688 (under William III and Mary II) to 1867 (under Victoria), starting with the initial debt (investors in the £1.2 M of government debt administered by the newly formed Bank of England):

a. War vs. France from 1688 to 1697: cost = £20.3 M; total debt in 1697 = £21.5 M

b. War of Spanish Succession, 1702 to 1713: cost = £32.25 M; total debt = £53.75 M

c. Approximately £7.5 M paid off between 1727 and 1739; total debt in 1739 = £46.25 M

d. War of Austrian Succession, 1739 to 1748: cost = £31.75 M; total debt in 1748 = £78.0 M

e. Then came eight years of peace, during which £3.0 M of the debt was repaid; the debt in 1756 was £75.0 M

f. Seven Years War, known in America as the French and Indian War, 1756 to 1763: cost = £72.5 M, total debt in 1763 = £147.5 M

g. Then came peace for twelve years, and in that time £10.5 M was paid off; the debt in 1775 was about £136.0 M

h. The American War [American Revolution], 1775 to 1783: cost = £103 M; total debt in 1783 was £239 M

i. Ten years of peace, and the debt was reduced by £5.0 M; total debt in 1793 was £234 M

j. The Jacobin War, 1793 up to 1796, when Paine wrote: additional debt to that time was £44.0 M; total debt in 1796 was about £278 M

k. The total cost of the Jacobin War that ended in 1802 turned out to be £248 M; and the debt in 1803 was £526 M.

l. Then came the final Napoleonic War, from 1803 to 1815, which cost £339 M; the debt in 1815 was £865 M

m. From 1815 to 1835 a total of £87 M was paid off; and the debt in 1835 was £778 M

n. Then 800,000 slaves were emancipated in the West Indies at a cost of about £22 M; and the debt as of 1867 was about £800 M or so

Paine's great contribution was to notice that each war cost about 50% more than the preceding one. He was correct except for the War of Austrian Succession (£31.75 M vs. his projection of £48 M) and the Jacobin War (£248 M vs. his estimate of £162 M). Walker [4] informs us why repayments were so slow during time of peace:

> Because it was no object with the ruling class to pay off the debt, since the national stocks [national debt] had become the most eligible investments [interest paid to the holders of the debt by the government but actually paid by the people]; so the resources of the nation were squandered upon the court [aristocratic class].

Walker informs us that this convergence of debt and taxation in England resulted in the impoverishment of the working class [5]:

> This is especially apparent in England. What has become of the yeomanry [small independent landowners], once the pride of the country? Their little estates have disappeared; have been swallowed up by the terrible system of taxation to which they have been subjected. The pleasant hedges which still surround the small enclosures, once constituting the freeholds of her yeomanry, may yet be seen in all parts of the country. They are the monuments of an industrious, brave, and independent class of men, now extinct. These lands are indeed tilled by the hands of their descendants, no longer yeomanry, but peasants, almost the paupers of the nation. ...
>
> The economy of a national debt, under the modern financial system, must always impoverish the productive classes. Its entire influence on them is oppressive. It deprives them of their honest reward, by a false currency [i.e., a fiat money], which robs them of a large share of their nominal wages; it imposes upon them, through indirect taxation, an undue proportion of the public burdens, and is in fact, a stupendous enginery for depressing them, though perhaps not so intended. Hitherto we have known little of its effects in the United States. Until the present time we have felt little pressure from public indebtedness and consequent taxation; but the case is now [1866] altered. We have an immense debt, and a larger amount of annual interest than any other people on the face of the earth.

References

[1] Amasa Walker, *The Science of Wealth: A Manual of Political Economy*, Boston, MA: Little, Brown & Co., 1867, pp. 363-365

[2] Thomas Paine, *The Decline and Fall of the English System of Finance*, an essay dated 6 Apr 1797. It was banned in England for over 20 years, so that should tell you something.

[3] op. cit., Amasa Walker, pp. 366, 367

[4] op. cit., Amasa Walker, p. 366

[5] op. cit., Amasa Walker, pp. 369-371

History of the "Continental Currency" During the American Revolution

Note: This essay was published 24 Jan 2022, and is derived from chapter 7 of the book *The Control and Manipulation of Money*. It contains a more complete description of the financial and economic aspects of the Revolution than the essay above, which mostly addressed the military and political aspects of the Revolution. All of the references for the four sections are shown at the end.

1 Preview, 1775-1788

This essay contains a record of the "Continental dollars", issued by Congress to finance the American Revolution. They were denominated in Spanish Milled dollars (nominally 386.7 grains silver), at 6% interest. They were actually bills of credit (bearer bonds) since they bore interest, but they circulated as money. John Adams described them [1-1]:

> The American paper money is nothing but bills of credit, by which the public, the community, promises to pay the possessor a certain sum in a certain limited time. In a country where there is no coin or not enough in circulation, these bills may be emitted to a certain amount, and they will pass at par; but as soon as the quantity exceeds the value of ordinary business of the people, it will depreciate, and continue to fall in its value, in proportion to the augmentation of its quantity.

There was in the 13 colonies in 1775 a total of about $12,000,000 in circulation; about $7,000,000 of it was in the form of paper money previously issued by the colonies and about $5,000,000 in gold and silver, mostly in silver Spanish Milled Dollars (SM$). The colonial paper money was denominated in pounds sterling; each pound contained 20 shillings and each shilling contained 12 pence, same as in England, except the definitions of the colonial pounds differed from the English definition. The English pound sterling was at that time 1,858.062 grains at 0.925 pure, which is 1,718.7018 grains pure. The colonial pound in Georgia and South Carolina was 1,547 grains; in Virginia, Massachusetts, Rhode Island, Connecticut, and New Hampshire as 1,289 grains; in New Jersey, Delaware, Pennsylvania, and Maryland as 1,031.25 grains; in New York and North Carolina as 966 grains of silver. The total of these colonial paper issues came to an equivalent of SM$7,000,000.

The French *livre tournois*, hereafter called simply a *livre*, consisted of 20 *sous*, each *sou* consisting of 12 *deniers*. In 1726, the French government fixed the denomination at 740 *livres*, 9 *sous* per 8 troy ounces (1 mark) of pure gold, or 92.5562 *livres* per troy ounce of gold. Also, eight troy ounces of silver contained 51 *livres*, 2 *sous* and 3 *deniers*, or 6.389 *livres* per troy ounce of silver. A troy ounce consists of 480 grains, so one *livre* equaled 5.186 grains of gold or 75.129 grains of silver. The ratio of gold to silver in French coinage was therefore one to 14.487. Using the 386.7 grains of silver as the nominal reckoned value of a Spanish milled dollar, the French *livre* was worth 0.194 Spanish milled dollars. But compared to the official Spanish standard, in which the milled dollar contained 394.46 grains of silver, the French *livre* was worth 0.190 Spanish milled dollars. In the following, the former (reckoned) values are used for conversion.

The Dutch *guilder*, or *gulder*, also called a *florin*, consisted of 0.60561 grams of fine gold, or 9.615 grams of fine silver. There are 15.4323 grains per gram (31.103 grams per troy ounce), so the gold *guilder* contained 9.345 grains of fine gold or 148.38 grains of fine silver. Using the reckoned value of the Spanish milled dollar of 386.7 grains of silver, the *guilder* was worth 0.38 milled dollars. The *guilder* was thus worth 1.97 French *livres* at 75.129 grains of silver. However, the French typically valued the Dutch *guilder* at twice the value of a French *livre* [1-1], and that conversion is used here (*guilder* = 0.388 Spanish milled dollar).

The core problem in fighting the war was that Congress had no authority to collect taxes; it could only requisition the States. Only South Carolina came close to meeting its obligations throughout the war. The issuance of Continentals was the only means Congress had to finance the war; but of course it was a paper mill built on a promise of future redemption. It is important to remember that between one-third and one-half of the population was loyal to the Crown, about 20,000 joined the British army, and other loyalists did the best they could to discredit the use of the Continentals as a way to disrupt the patriotic cause [1-2].

The amount issued by date is based on Schuckers [1-3], the depreciation schedule per Elliot [1-4], and the alternate claims of over-issue are per Schuckers [1-5] and Gouge [1-6], both of whom quote Philadelphia merchant Pelatiah Webster. Webster's original depreciation data only indicates the month, and they are recorded here as at the end of the month. Major events of the Revolution are shown for historical context.

It is important to remember that although Congress issued "Continentals", each State also issued its own paper money throughout the war until 1783. Jefferson estimated the total amount of paper issued by the States was about $200,000,000 [1-7]. The total emissions for the States are shown on 31 Dec for each year, as there are no records of the exact dates of emissions.

The nomenclature SM $1.0 ~ C $1.25 means that one Spanish milled dollar traded for $1.25 in Continentals. It turns out that more was issued than was authorized by Congress, according to both Schuckers and Gouge.

2 History, 1775-1788

5 Mar 1770: The Boston Massacre.

16 Dec 1773: The Boston Tea Party.

1 Jun 1774: Port of Boston closed by the British.

6 Aug 1774: The Quartering and Regulating Acts are enforced in Boston.

14 Oct 1774: The First Continental Congress issued a Declaration of Rights opposing various acts of Parliament dating back to 1767.

1 Jan 1775: The population of the States at this time was estimated [2-1] as: MA, 352,000; NH: 200,000 (discovered in 1782 to be only 82,000); RI: 58,000; CT: 202,000; NY: 238,000; NJ: 138,000; PA: 341,000; DE: 37,000; MD: 174,000; VA: 300,000; NC: 181,000; SC: 93,000; GA: 27,000; slaves in the Southern States, 500,000; for a total of 2,743,000 It was on this basis that the requisitions were allocated to the States.

1 Feb 1775: The 'Minutemen' was established in Massachusetts, they were people who formed themselves into a militia to defend the colony.

19 Apr 1775: Battles of Lexington and Concord, MA.

10 May 1775: First session of the Second Continental Congress (hereafter called Congress).

17 Jun 1775: Battles of Bunker Hill and Breed's Hill, Boston, MA.

22 Jun 1775: Congress authorized $2,000,000 in Continentals to be issued. They contained the inscription [2-2]:

CONTINENTAL CURRENCY

No. _________ Dollars

This Bill entitles the bearer to receive ______ Spanish milled dollars, or the value thereof in gold or silver, according to the resolution of Congress, held at Philadelphia, on the 10th of May, A.D. 1775.

3 Jul 1775: George Washington took command of the Continental Army at Boston.

25 Jul 1775: Congress authorized $1,000,000 in Continentals to be issued; total = $3,000,000.

~15 Aug 1775: Rhode Island is the first to make the Continental legal tender. The other colonies followed suit shortly thereafter [2-3]. The long-term consequences were, as the currency depreciated (after 1777), that people began to buy property rather than hold onto the currency. Some wealthy people sold off property at what they believed to be good prices, only to find later that the money they received was worthless. Others ran up large debts, knowing they would be able to pay off the debts easily with a small amount of real money as the Continentals depreciated.

12 Nov 1775: Surrender of Montreal to American General Montgomery.

29 Nov 1775: Congress authorized $3,000,000 in Continentals to be issued; total = $6,000,000.

31 Dec 1775: Battle of Quebec. During 1775, the States had issued paper money [2-4]: Massachusetts ($483,500 estimated), Rhode Island ($200,000), Connecticut ($500,000), New York ($112,500), Pennsylvania ($420,000), Delaware ($80,000), Maryland ($535,111), Virginia ($875,000), and South Carolina ($4,182,365 estimated).

8 Jan 1776: Thomas Paine published 'Common Sense'.

11 Jan 1776: Congress passed a resolution against anyone who refused to accept the Continentals as a legal tender, or accepted them at less than face value [2-5]:

> Whereas, it appears to this Congress that several evil disposed persons, in order to obstruct and defeat the efforts of the United Colonies, in defense of their just rights, have attempted to depreciate the bills of credit emitted by the authority of this Congress. Resolved, therefore, that any person who shall hereafter be so lost to all virtue and regard for his country, as to refuse to receive said bills in payment, or obstruct and discourage the currency or circulation thereof, and shall be duly convicted by the committee of the city, county, or district, or in case of appeal from their decision, by the assembly, convention, council, or committee of safety of the colony where he shall reside, such person shall be deemed, published, and treated as an enemy of his country and precluded from all trade or intercourse with the inhabitants of these Colonies.

17 Feb 1776: Congress authorized $4,000,000 in Continentals to be issued; total = $10,000,000.

27 Feb 1776: Battle of Moore's Creek, NC.

4-17 Mar 1776: Battle of Boston; British evacuate Boston for the remainder of the war.

27 May 1776: Congress authorized $5,000,000 in Continentals to be issued; total = $15,000,000.

5-14 Jun 1776: The Americans retreated from Canada, abandoning any further efforts to bring Canada into the war.

12 Jun 1776: The 'Declaration of the Rights of Man' (George Mason and James Madison) was passed as a resolution in the Virginia Legislature.

28 Jun 1776: Battle of Sullivan's Island, SC.

4 Jul 1776: Declaration of Independence was formally adopted by Congress (having been read and approved 2 Jul 1776).

12 Jul 1776: Congress proposed the Articles of Confederation.

13 Aug 1776: Congress authorized $5,000,000 in Continentals to be issued; total = $20,000,000.

27-29 Aug 1776: Battle of Long Island, NY.

15, 16 Sep 1776: Battle of Manhattan, NY.

3 Oct 1776: Congress established a loan office, seeking a loan of $5,000,000 at 4%, and paying 0.125% commission to those who sold the loan certificates [2-6]. The loan certificates were payable to the bearer, and passed as money. They added to the general depreciation of the money.

11-13 Oct 1776: Battle of Valcour Island (Lake Champlain, NY).

28 Oct 1776: Battle of White Plains, NY.

20 Nov 1776: Evacuation of Fort Lee, NY.

28 Nov - 12 Dec 1776: The Continental Army was defeated and retreated through New Jersey to Pennsylvania.

23 Dec 1776: Congress authorized a loan from France for up to £2,000,000; a net loan was subsequently obtained for 935,570 *livres* (SM$181,500) from Farmers General of France. [2-7]

26-29 Dec 1776: Battle of Trenton, NJ.

28 Dec 1776: Congress authorized $5,000,000 in Continentals to be issued; total = $25,000,000.

31 Dec 1776: During 1776, the States had issued paper money [2-8]: Massachusetts ($483,500 est.), Rhode Island ($300,000), Connecticut ($366,300), New York ($637,500), New Jersey ($133,000), Pennsylvania ($227,000), Maryland ($415,111), Virginia ($1,500,000), and South Carolina ($4,182,365 estimated).

3 Jan 1777: Battle of Princeton, NJ.

7 Jan 1777: Battles of Elizabethtown, NJ and Newark, NJ.

14 Jan 1777: Congress imitated a prior resolution adopted in Rhode Island, making the Continentals a legal tender. It also adopted a resolution asking the States to stop issuing State currency in favor of Congress alone. The resolution reads, in part [2-9]:

> Resolved, That all bills of credit, emitted by authority of Congress, ought to pass current in all payments, trade, and dealings, in these states, and be deemed in value equal to the same nominal sums in Spanish milled dollars; and that whoever shall offer, ask, or receive more in the said bills for any gold or silver coins, bullion, or any other species of money whatsoever, than the nominal sum or amount thereof in Spanish milled dollars, or more, in the said bills, for any lands, houses, goods, or commodities whatsoever, than the same could be purchased at of the same person or persons in gold, silver, or any other species of money whatsoever; or shall offer to sell any goods or commodities for gold or silver coins, or any other species of money whatsoever, and refuse to sell the same for the said continental bills; every such a person ought to be deemed an enemy to the liberties of these United States, and to forfeit the value of the money so exchanged, or house, land, or commodity so sold or offered for sale. And it is recommended to the legislatures of the respective states, to enact laws inflicting such forfeitures and other penalties on offenders as aforesaid, as will prevent such pernicious practices.

31 Jan 1777: SM $1.0 ~ C $1.25.

26 Feb 1777: Congress authorized $5,000,000 in Continentals to be issued; total = $30,000,000.

28 Feb 1777: SM $1.0 ~ C $1.50.

31 Mar 1777: SM $1.0 ~ C $2.00.

27 Apr 1777: Battle of Ridgefield, CT.

30 Apr 1777: SM $1.0 ~ C $2.25.

20 May 1777: Congress authorized $5,000,000 in Continentals to be issued; total = $35,000,000.

31 May 1777: SM $1.0 ~ C $2.25.

30 Jun 1777: SM $1.0 ~ C $2.25.

31 Jul 1777: SM $1.0 ~ C $3.00.

4-7 Jul 1777: Battle of Hubbardton, NY.

6 Aug 1777: Battle of Oriskany, NY.

15 Aug 1777: Congress authorized $1,000,000 in Continentals to be issued; total = $36,000,000.

16 Aug 1777: Battle of Bennington, NY.

31 Aug 1777: SM $1.0 ~ C $3.00.

11 Sep 1777: Battle of Brandywine Creek, PA.

19 Sep 1777: First Battle of Freeman's Farm, NY.

30 Sep 1777: SM $1.0 ~ C $3.00.

4 Oct 1777: Battle of Germantown, PA.

7 Oct 1777: Second Battle of Freemen's Farm (commonly known as the Battle of Saratoga). This defeat marked the end of the British attempt to split the colonies in two by controlling the Hudson River.

31 Oct 1777: SM $1.0 ~ C $3.00

7 Nov 1777: Congress authorized $1,000,000 in Continentals to be issued; total = $37,000,000.

22 Nov 1777: Congress urged the states to impose wage and price controls in an effort to support or stabilize the purchasing power of the Continentals. Schuckers [2-10] relates:

> The second of the system of laws for supporting the value, or more properly the purchasing power of the bills [Continentals], were those for the limitation of prices. ... If prices could be kept down, the trouble would be prevented, anybody could see that. Why not limit prices, then? This idea seems to have originated in New England; and Congress, impressed with a belief that limitations would be effective in sustaining the bills, seized upon the New England idea, and recommended it to the states (November 22nd, 1777) for their immediate adoption, and renewed it in respect of various details during the ensuing two years. Apply the regulations, said Congress in substance, to the prices of labor, to manufactures, internal produce and imported commodities, to the charges of innkeepers and to land and water carriage: limit the number of retailers in the counties, and make them take out licenses to observe laws made for their regulation; let such persons as have no licenses be restrained from purchasing greater quantities of clothing and provisions than are necessary for family use and upon offenders against these laws let such penalties be inflicted as will brand them with indelible infamy!

But price limits had the opposite effect. Prices increased because of the depreciation as a matter of economics, regardless of the admonitions and threats from Congress [2-11].

30 Nov 1777: SM $1.0 ~ C $3.00.

3 Dec 1777: Congress authorized $1,000,000 in Continentals to be issued; total = $38,000,000. Congress also authorized a loan from France for £2,000,000; a net loan was subsequently obtained for SM$3,267,000 (18,000,000 *livres*) [2-12]

19 Dec 1777: Beginning of the winter at Valley Forge.

31 Dec 1777: SM $1.0 ~ C $4.00. During 1777, the States had issued paper money [2-13]: Massachusetts ($483,500 estimated), Rhode Island ($15,000), Connecticut ($17,500), Pennsylvania ($532,000), Delaware ($66,500), Virginia ($2,700,000), and South Carolina ($4,182,365 estimated).

8 Jan 1778: Congress authorized $1,000,000 in Continentals to be issued; total = $39,000,000.

22 Jan 1778: Congress authorized $2,000,000 in Continentals to be issued; total = $41,000,000.

31 Jan 1778: SM $1.0 ~ C $4.00.

6 Feb 1778: The Americans negotiated an alliance with France. Louis XVI agreed to loan Congress 18,000,000 *livres* (SM$3,492,000) to be paid in various installments. France agreed to recognize American independence, and to provide military support. The Americans agreed to conclude peace with Great Britain only if independence was recognized, and if France was a party to the treaty.

16 Feb 1778: Congress authorized $2,000,000 in Continentals to be issued; total = $43,000,000.

28 Feb 1778: France loaned Congress 750,000 *livres* (SM$145,000) (cf. 6 Feb 1778); SM $1.0 ~ C $5.00.

5 Mar 1778: Congress authorized $2,000,000 in Continentals to be issued; total = $45,000,000.

31 Mar 1778: SM $1.0 ~ C $5.00.

4 Apr 1778: Congress authorized $1,000,000 in Continentals to be issued; total = $46,000,000.

11 Apr 1778: Congress authorized $5,000,000 in Continentals to be issued; total = $51,000,000.

18 Apr 1778: Congress authorized $500,000 in Continentals to be issued; total = $51,500,000.

30 Apr 1778: SM $1.0 ~ C $6.00.

15 May 1778: Congress was unable to pay the army regularly, and when it did was in depreciated money. To compensate, Congress authorized half-pay for seven years to all army officers, and $80 for enlisted men, to be paid at the end of the war [2-14].

19 May 1778: France loaned Congress 750,000 *livres* (SM$145,000) (cf. 6 Feb 1778).

22 May 1778: Congress authorized $5,000,000 in Continentals to be issued; total = $56,500,000.

31 May 1778: SM $1.0 ~ C $5.00.

8 Jun 1778: Congress imposed an export embargo on livestock, corn, wheat, beef, and pork, and asked the States to enforce it until 15 Nov 1778. The purpose was to ensure adequate supplies would be available for the army [2-15].

20 Jun 1778: Congress authorized $5,000,000 in Continentals to be issued; total = $61,500,000.

28 Jun 1778: Battle of Monmouth, NJ.

30 Jun 1778: SM $1.0 ~ C $4.00.

4-7 Jul 1778: Massacre at Wyoming Valley, PA by the British and their Indian allies.

9 Jul 1778: Eight States (NH, MA, RI, CT, NY, PA, VA, and SC) ratified the Articles of Confederation.

20 Jul 1778: The American army was in place at White Plains, NY while the British Northern army occupied New York City. The war in the North was a stalemate until the end.

21 Jul 1778: North Carolina ratified the Articles of Confederation.

24 Jul 1778: Georgia ratified the Articles of Confederation

30 Jul 1778: Congress authorized $5,000,000 in Continentals to be issued; total = $66,500,000.

31 Jul 1778: SM $1.0 ~ C $4.00.

3 Aug 1778: France loaned Congress 750,000 *livres* (SM$145,000) (cf. 6 Feb 1778).

29 Aug 1778: Battle of Butts Hill, RI.

31 Aug 1778: SM $1.0 ~ C $5.00.

5 Sep 1778: Congress authorized $5,000,000 in Continentals to be issued; total = $71,500,000.

6 Sep 1778: The British burned New Bedford and Fair Haven, CT

26 Sep 1778: Congress authorized $10,000,000 in Continentals to be issued; total = $81,500,000.

30 Sep 1778: SM $1.0 ~ C $5.00.

8 Oct 1778: Congress passed a resolution encouraging that all price limitations be removed, seeing that it had not worked as intended. But the States continued the practice for another three years [2-16].

31 Oct 1778: SM $1.0 ~ C $5.00.

1 Nov 1778: France loaned Congress 750,000 *livres* (SM$145,000) (cf. 6 Feb 1778).

4 Nov 1778: Congress authorized $10,000,000 in Continentals to be issued; total = $91,500,000.

10 Nov 1778: Massacre at Cherry Valley, NY by the British and their Indian allies.

26 Nov 1778: New Jersey ratified the Articles of Confederation.

30 Nov 1778: SM $1.0 ~ C $6.00.

14 Dec 1778: Congress authorized $10,000,000 in Continentals to be issued; total = $101,500,000.

31 Dec 1778: SM $1.0 ~ C $6.00. During 1778, the States had issued paper money [2-17]: Massachusetts ($483,500 estimated), Virginia ($2,700,000), North Carolina ($2,125,000), and South Carolina ($4,182,365 estimated). The total amount of coin received and disbursed by the Treasury in 1779 came to $78,666 [2-18].

1 Jan 1779: The issues of Continentals from 20 May 1777 and 11 Apr 1778 had become so thoroughly counterfeited by the British that Congress called them in to be burned, but were still legal for payment of taxes until 1 Jun 1779 (later extended to 1 Jan 1780) [2-19]. The total amount of Continentals issued so far was $101,500,000 [2-20].

5 Jan 1779: Congress asked the States for $15,000,000 for 1779 to be used as a sinking fund for the loans and Continentals. None would be paid [2-21].

9 Jan 1779 ff: The British invaded Georgia from Florida and pillaged the countryside.

31 Jan 1779: SM $1.0 ~ C $8.00 (average).

3 Feb 1779: Congress authorized $5,000,160 in Continentals to be issued; total = $106,500,160.

12 Feb 1779: Delaware ratified the Articles of Confederation.

14 Feb 1779: Battle of Kettle Creek, GA.

19 Feb 1779: Congress authorized $5,000,160 in Continentals to be issued; total = $111,500,320.

24 Feb 1779: The Americans captured the British army at Vincennes and Detroit. This ended the British attempt to take the Northwest Territories (now the States of Wisconsin, Michigan, Indiana, and Illinois).

28 Feb 1779: SM $1.0 ~ C $10.00.

31 Mar 1779: SM $1.0 ~ C $10.50 (average)

1 Apr 1779: Congress authorized $5,000,160 in Continentals to be issued; total = $116,500,480.

28 Apr 1779 ff: A war of total destruction was waged by the British throughout Georgia and South Carolina, except Charleston (since there were many loyalists there).

30 Apr 1779: SM $1.0 ~ C $16.10 (average).

5 May 1779: Congress authorized $10,000,100 in Continentals to be issued; total = $126,500,580. Delaware ratified the Articles of Confederation, making twelve of the thirteen. Only Maryland held out.

7 May 1779: Congress authorized $50,000,100 in Continentals to be issued; total = $176,500,680.

21 May 1779: Congress requisitioned $45,000,000 from the States, owing to the depreciation of the Continentals (valued at about SM$0.04). None would be paid [2-22].

30 May 1779: SM $1.0 ~ C $23.50 (average).

31 May - 2 Jun 1779: The British captured Stony Point, NY and Verplanck's Point, NY. The Americans now had to go around the mountains to get between New York and New Jersey.

4 Jun 1779: Congress authorized $10,000,100 in Continentals to be issued; total = $186,500,780.

10 Jun 1779: France loaned Congress 250,000 *livres* (SM$48,500) (cf. 6 Feb 1778).

30 Jun 1779: SM $1.0 ~ C $20.00 (average).

5 - 11 Jul 1779: The British burned New Haven, Fairfield, and Green Farms, CT.

17 Jul 1779: Congress authorized $15,000,280 in Continentals to be issued; total = $201,501,060.

31 Jul 1779: SM $1.0 ~ C $19.00 (average).

17 Aug 1779: George Washington wrote to a distant cousin, Lund Washington, who was managing Mount Vernon during the war, to give advice on accepting the depreciating Continentals in payment of debts owed to him. He will accept the Continentals on recent debts since they were contracted when they were already depreciated, but will not accept them for old debts contracted before they were emitted, or when they traded at par. He wrote [2-23]:

> Some time ago (but how long I cannot remember) you applied to me to know if you should receive payment of General Mercer's bonds; and after this, of the bond due from the deceased Mr. Mercer's estate to me; and was, after animadverting a little upon the subject; authorized to do so; of course I presume the money has been received. I have since considered the matter in every point of view my judgment enables me to place it, and am resolved to receive no more old debts; such I mean as were contracted and ought to have been paid before the War at the present nominal value of the money, unless compelled to it, or it is the practice of others to do it. Neither justice, reason, nor policy requires it. The law, undoubtedly, was well designed; it was intended to stamp a value and give a free circulation to the paper bills of credit; but it never was nor could be intended to make a man take a shilling or sixpence in the pound for a just debt, which he is well able to pay, thereby involving himself in ruin. I am as willing now as I ever was to take paper money for every kind of debt, and at its present depreciated value for those debts which have

been contracted since the money became so; but I will not in future receive the nominal sum for such old debts as come under the above description, except as before excepted.

29 Aug 1779: Battle of Newtown, NY (now Elmira).

31 Aug 1779: SM $1.0 ~ C $20.00.

1 Sep 1779: Congress passed a resolution that no more than $200,000,000 in Continentals should be in circulation at any time [2-24]. It is unlikely that this restraint was observed.

13 Sep 1779: Congress issued an address to the public explaining the current state of the finances [2-25]. A total of $159,948,880 in Continentals had been issued and in circulation, $7,545,196 had been borrowed from France before Mar 1778 with interest payable in France, $26,188,909 had been borrowed since then, with interest payable in America; and other amounts borrowed abroad were estimated at 4,000,000. But only $3,027,560 had been received in taxes. Thus the sum of loans received and interest due, less taxes paid came to $36,761,665. Part of the long address to the States reads [2-26, 2-27]:

> Exclusive of the great and ordinary expenses incident to the war the depreciation of the currency has so swelled the price of every necessary article, and of consequence made such additions to the usual amount of expenditures, that very considerable supplies must be immediately provided by loans and taxes; and we unanimously declare it to be essential to the welfare of these States, that the taxes already called for be paid into the continental treasury by the time recommended for that purpose.
>
> The ability of the United States must depend on two things; first the success of the present revolution; and secondly, on the sufficiency of the natural wealth, value, and resources of the country.
>
> That the time has been when honest men might, without being chargeable with timidity, have doubted the success of the present revolution, we admit; but that period has passed. The independence of America is now fixed as fate, and the petulant efforts of Britain to break it down are as vain and fruitless as the raging of the waves which beat against their cliffs.
>
> Let it be remembered that paper money is the only kind of money which cannot 'make itself wings and fly away'. It remains with us, it will not forsake us, it is always ready and at hand for the purpose of commerce or taxes, and every industrious man can find it.
>
> Whether, admitting the ability and political capacity of the United States to redeem their bills, there is any reason to apprehend a wanton violation of the public faith?
>
> It is with great regret and reluctance that we can prevail upon ourselves to take the least notice of a question which involves in it a doubt so injurious to the honor and dignity of America. The enemy, aware that the strength of America lay in the union of her citizens, and the wisdom and integrity of those whom they committed the direction of their affairs, have taken unwearied pains to disunite and alarm the people, to depreciate the abilities and virtues of their rulers, and to impair the confidence reposed in them by their constituents.
>
> Hence has proceeded the notable discovery that as the congress made the money they also can destroy it; and that it will exist no longer than they find it convenient to permit it.
>
> You surely are convinced that it is no more in their power to annihilate your money than your independence, and that any act of theirs for either of those purposes would be null and void. We should pay an ill compliment to the understanding and honor of every true American, were we to adduce many arguments to show the baseness or bad policy of violating our national faith, or omitting to pursue the measures necessary to preserve it. A bankrupt, faithless republic, would be a novelty in the political world, and appear among respectable nations like a common prostitute among chaste and respectable matrons.

16 Sep 1779: France loaned Congress 250,000 *livres* (SM$48,500) (cf. 6 Feb 1778).

17 Sep 1779: Congress authorized $15,000,360 in Continentals to be issued; total = $216,501,420.

28 Sep 1779: Congress authorized a loan from Spain for SM$5,000,000; a net loan was subsequently obtained for SM$174,017 [2-28].

30 Sep 1779: SM $1.0 ~ C $24.00 (average).

4 Oct 1779: France loaned Congress 250,000 *livres* (SM$48,500) (cf. 6 Feb 1778).

9 Oct 1779: Battle of Savannah, GA.

14 Oct 1779: Congress authorized $5,000,180 in Continentals to be issued; total = $221,501,600.

26 Oct 1779: Congress authorized a loan from France for SM$10,000,000; a loan was obtained for SM$1,815,000 (10,000,000 *livres*). Congress also authorized a loan from Holland for SM$10,000,000, and loans were eventually obtained: SM$2,000,000 on 14 Sep 1782; SM$800,000 on 1 Feb 1785; SM$400,000 on 11 Oct 1787; and SM$400,000 on 2 Jul 1788 [2-29].

31 Oct 1779: SM $1.0 ~ C $30.00.

17 Nov 1779: Congress authorized $10,050,540 in Continentals to be issued; total = $231,552,140.

19 Nov 1779: Congress asked the States to limit prices based on 1774 prices [2-30]: a) wages of common labor, tradesmen, and mechanics to be limited to 20 times the rate in 1774; b) domestically produced items limited in price to 20 times the 1774 price; c) but items of military use to be exempt from price controls.

29 Nov 1779: Congress authorized $10,000,140 in Continentals to be issued; total = $241,552,280. (Schuckers has $241,552,780; it is not clear where the $500 discrepancy is.) However, Alexander Hamilton, in his report of 1790, says that a total of $357,476,541 of "old emission" had been made from 1776 to 1781, and an additional $2,070,486 in 'new emission' (1780 and 1781) [2-31]. The 'new emission' of Continentals was authorized 18 Mar 1780. It is not clear how this discrepancy arose unless Hamilton's figures include the "indents" (loan certificates).

30 Nov 1779: SM $1.0 ~ C $38.50 (average).

~15 Dec 1779: Congress was unable to obtain any money. The Continentals had depreciated so much that no one would loan metal money against them for a promise to pay in paper. Although Congress used legal tender laws and price controls, the over-issue of Continentals destroyed the nation's credit and commerce. The people simply lost confidence in the Continentals and they began to go out of circulation.

21 Dec 1779: France loaned Congress 250,000 *livres* (SM$48,500) (cf. 6 Feb 1778).

31 Dec 1779: SM $1.0 ~ C $41.50 (average). During 1779, the States had issued paper money [2-32]: Massachusetts ($483,500 estimated), Rhode Island ($133,000), Virginia ($2,500,000), North Carolina ($1,125,000), and South Carolina ($4,182,365 estimated). The amount of coin received and disbursed by the Treasury came to $73,000 for all of 1779 [2-33].

~15 Jan 1780: This marked the beginning of a large influx of hard money: a) English procurements for its army; b) French assistance and payments to its soldiers in the States; and c) loans from foreign nations.

31 Jan 1780: SM $1.0 ~ C $42.50 (average).

25 Feb 1779: Congress, instead of making requisitions for money, asked that the States make in-kind contributions to be delivered as requested by the military [2-34]: a) 330,000,000 pounds of beef; b) 455,000 gallons of rum; c) 123,000 barrels of flour; d) 695,000 bushels of corn; e) 53,000 bushels of salt; f) 9,000 tons of hay; g) 7,000 hogsheads of tobacco; and h) 52,000 bushels of rice. The costs were to be tabulated in Spanish Milled Dollars and Congress would settle accounts with the States later.

29 Feb 1780: France loaned Congress 750,000 *livres* (SM$145,000) (cf. 6 Feb 1778); SM $1.0 ~ C $50.00 (average).

29 Feb 1779: General Greene wrote to Joseph Reed, President of the Supreme Executive Council of Pennsylvania [2-35]:

> Our provisions are in a manner gone. We have not a ton of hay at command, nor magazines to draw from. Money is extremely scarce, and worth little when we get it. We have been so poor for a fortnight that we could not forward the public dispatches for want of cash to support the expresses.

~ 1 Mar 1780: Now that the Continentals had become so depreciated that they no longer circulated because no one would accept them, gold and silver replaced them. As Schuckers relates [2-36]:

> And it is a curious illustration of the laws which govern paper money, that as excessive issues had exiled the cash of the country from its accustomed place in the business of the people, it began to flow back as the paper money approached the period of its mortality. As this daily less capably performed the office of the instrument of exchange, gold and silver more certainly and amply flowed in to supply its place.

18 Mar 1780: Congress issued a report recognizing the depreciation of the Continentals, and proposing a method to redeem them. The idea was that the separate States may have better credit than did Congress. The resolution announced a plan for redemption and the issuing of new bills [2-37]:

> These United States having been driven into this just and necessary war at the time when no regular civil governments were established of sufficient energy to enforce the collection of taxes or to provide funds for the redemption of such bills of credit as their necessities obliged them to issue; and before the powers of Europe were sufficiently convinced of the justice of their cause or of the probable event of the controversy to afford them aid or credit, in consequence of which their bills increasing in quantity beyond the sum necessary for the purpose of a circulating medium and wanting at the same time specific funds to rest on for their redemption they have seen them daily sink in value notwithstanding every effort that has been made to support the same: insomuch that they are now passed by common consent in most parts of these United States at least thirty-nine fortieths below their nominal value and still remain in a state of depreciation whereby the community suffers great injustice, the public finances are deranged, and the necessary dispositions for defense of the country are much impeded and perplexed; and whereas, effectually to remedy these evils for which purpose the United States are now becoming competent, their independence being well assured, their civil governments established and vigorous, and the spirit of their citizens ardent for exertion, it is necessary speedily to reduce the quantity in circulation, and to establish and appropriate such funds that shall ensure the punctual redemption of the bills.

It then directs the States to send in taxes already levied on 7 Oct 1779 and 23 Feb 1780 but not paid. It continues:

> That silver and gold be receivable in payment of the said quotas at the rate of one Spanish milled dollar in lieu of forty dollars of the bills now in circulation.
>
> That the said bills as paid in except for the months of January and February past, which may be necessary for the discharge of past contracts, be not reissued but destroyed.
>
> That as fast as the said bills shall be brought in and be destroyed, and funds shall be established as hereafter mentioned for other bills, other bills not to exceed on any account one twentieth part of the nominal sum of the bills brought in to be destroyed.
>
> That the bills which shall be issued be redeemable in specie within six years after the present, and bear an interest at the rate of five per centum per annum to be paid also in specie at the redemption of the bills or at the election of the holder annually.

Congress thus announced that the Continentals were to be discounted as 40:1 and destroyed; to be replaced when funding permitted by new bills (the "new issue") at the rate of 20:1; and the new bills would bear interest at 5%. The 40:1 provision signaled the end of the relevance of the Continental.

31 Mar 1780: SM $1.0 ~ C $62.50 (average).

18 Apr 1780: Congress passed a resolution calling for the redemption of the Continentals at the value they had in Spanish milled dollars at the time of issue [2-38]:

> That Congress will as soon as may be, make such provision for discharging or continuing the loans that have been made to these United States, or loan office certificates, as that the holders of them shall sustain no loss thereon by any depreciation of the bills loaned subsequent to the respective dates of the said certificates.

30 Apr 1780: SM $1.0 ~ C $60.00.

12 May 1780: The Americans surrendered Charleston, SC to the British.

23 May 1780: France loaned Congress 750,000 *livres* (SM$145,000) (cf. 6 Feb 1778).

29 May 1780: Battle of Waxhaws, SC.

31 May 1780: SM $1.0 ~ C $60.00.

Jun - Oct 1780: A guerilla war was conducted by the Americans under Williams, Sumter, Pickens, and Marion in the South. At the same time, the British under Tarleton waged a reign of terror throughout the Carolinas, which lasted until Jun 1782.

6 Jun 1780: Battle of Elizabethtown, NJ.

21 Jun 1780: France loaned Congress 750,000 *livres* (SM$145,000) (cf. 6 Feb 1778).

28 Jun 1780: Congress published the schedule of redemption of the Continentals [2-39]:

> Resolved, that the principal of all loans which have been made to these United States shall finally be discharged by paying the full current value of the bills when loaned; which payment shall be made in Spanish milled dollars, or the current exchange thereof in other money at the time of payment.
>
> That the value of the bills, when loaned, shall be ascertained for the purposes above mentioned (cf. 18 Apr 1780) by computing thereon a progressive rate of depreciation, commencing with the first day of September, 1777, and continuing to the 18th of March, 1780, in geometrical progression and proportion of the time, from period to period, as hereafter stated, assuming the depreciation at the several periods to be as follows: On the first day of March, 1778, one dollar and three quarters of a dollar of the said bills for one Spanish milled dollar; on the first of September 1778, as four of the former for one of the latter; on the 1st day of March 1779, as eighteen of the former for one of the latter; and on the 18th day of March, 1780, as forty of the former for one of the latter." Thus the latter Continental issues were redeemed for 2.5 cents on the dollar.

30 Jun 1780: SM $1.0 ~ C $60.00.

10 Jul 1780: The first contingent of French troops landed in Newport, RI to aid the American cause.

11 Jul 1780: Congress fixed the redemption schedule of Continental currency and bills of credit at 40 to 1. Its reckoned value was about 65 to 1 at this time.

12 Jul 1780: Battle of Cross Roads, SC.

17 Jul 1780: The Bank of Pennsylvania was established by Robert Morris and other Philadelphia merchants, to aid in supplying provisions to the army [2-40]. Its initial capital was PA £315,000 and British sterling £150,000 in bills of exchange provided by the Treasury.

29 Jul 1780: The Treasury, pursuant to the directive of 28 Jun 1780, published a day-by-day depreciation schedule [2-41] for the Continentals from 1 Sep 1777 (at par) to 18 Mar 1780 (SM $1.0 ~ C $40.00)

31 Jul 1780: SM $1.0 ~ C $62.50 (average).

16 Aug 1780: Battle of Camden, SC.

18 Aug 1780: Battle of Fishing Creek, SC.

20 Aug 1780: Battle of Musgrave's Mills, SC.

26 Aug 1780: Congress again appealed to the States to pay the requisitions.

31 Aug 1780: SM $1.0 ~ C $70.00 (average).

15 Sep 1780: Congress asked MA, NH, CT, NJ, PA, and DE to supply 3,000 head of cattle to support the army [2-42].

22-25 Sep 1780: American General Benedict Arnold attempted to hand West Point over to the British; the plot is detected and he escaped to the British lines.

28 Sep 1780: Battle of Black Mingo, SC.

30 Sep 1780: SM $1.0 ~ C $75.00.

5 Oct 1780: France loaned Congress 750,000 *livres* (SM$145,000) (cf. 6 Feb 1778).

7 Oct 1780: Battle of King's Mountain, SC.

31 Oct 1780: SM $1.0 ~ C $77.50 (average).

20 Nov 1780: Battle of Blackstock Hill, SC.

27 Nov 1780: France loaned Congress 1,000,000 *livres* (SM$194,000) (cf. 6 Feb 1778).

30 Nov 1780: SM $1.0 ~ C $90.00 (average)

31 Dec 1780: SM $1.0 ~ C $100.00; Elliot [2-43] states that $891,326 of new emission was issued in 1780. During 1780, the States had issued paper money [2-44]: Massachusetts ($483,500 estimated), Rhode Island ($66,600), Connecticut ($632,700), New Jersey ($600,000), Pennsylvania ($1,516,000), Virginia ($30,666,000), North Carolina ($3,600,000), and South Carolina ($4,182,365 estimated).

1 Jan 1781: A mutiny was staged by most of the army in PA, complaining about not being paid, shortages of provisions, and not being released after three years per their original enlistments. It was resolved peacefully although British spies tried to instigate a full revolt. The British spies were caught and hanged [2-45].

15 Jan 1781: Congress requisitioned $879,342 in coin from the States [2-46], to be paid immediately for current expenses. None was ever paid.

17 Jan 1781: Battle of The Cowpens, SC.

31 Jan 1781: SM $1.0 ~ C $100.00.

15 Feb 1781: France loaned Congress 750,000 *livres* (SM$145,000) (cf. 6 Feb 1778).

21 Feb 1781: Robert Morris was appointed Superintendent of the Finances. He reformed the entire system, and organized the Treasury. Not only did he eliminate the corruption and incompetence, but went directly to military commanders to find out what was needed; and even issued his own promissory notes against his credit when necessary to supply the army. Schuckers writes [2-47]:

> But in a word, arms and ammunition, pay of troops and subsistence stores, were supplied upon the private resources of Robert Morris. He bore upon his broad and ample shoulders, to the close of the war, almost the whole pecuniary burdens it entailed, and through its most critical and important period he was its vital stay and support. It is no figure of speech to aver that in his field of public duty he rendered services not less valuable than and splendid than those even of Washington; though it is necessary to state that he was reimbursed for all his advances.

28 Feb 1781: SM $1.0 ~ C $110.00 (average).

1 Mar 1781: Maryland finally ratified the Articles of Confederation; it then went into effect.

31 Mar 1781: SM $1.0 ~ C $127.50 (average).

18 Apr 1781: A Committee in Congress reported that the debt was SM$24,057,577 in specie, and that SM$19,507,457 would be needed for 1782. But in fact the details of the national domestic debt were so confused that no accurate figure has ever been devised. The foreign debt was about SM$6,000,000 with annual interest due of SM$360,000 [2-48].

23 Apr 1781: The British surrendered Fort Watson, SC to the Americans.

25 Apr 1781: Battle of Hobkirk's Hill, SC.

30 Apr 1781: SM $1.0 ~ C $167.50 (average).

10-15 May 1781: The British gradually evacuated Camden, Orangeburg, Fort Motte, Nelson's Ferry and Fort Granby (all in SC).

15 May 1781: France loaned Congress 750,000 *livres* (SM$145,000) (cf. 6 Feb 1778).

26 May 1781: The Bank of North America was established. It issued bank notes, which were payable on demand, and were accepted by Congress in payment of taxes. The initial capital was SM$400,000, but the actual amount of specie held was SM$40,000 [2-49].

31 May 1781: SM $1.0 ~ C $350.00 (average, 200:1 to 500:1). The Continental currency was abolished as circulating money.

5 Jun 1781: The British surrendered Augusta GA to Americans.

29 Jun 1781: The British abandoned Ninety-Six, SC.

6 Jul 1781: Battle of Green Springs, VA. General Greene and Lafayette pressured British General Cornwallis to evacuate to Yorktown, VA.

1 Aug 1781: France loaned Congress 1,000,000 *livres* (SM$194,000) (cf. 6 Feb 1778).

15 Aug 1781: France loaned Congress 750,000 *livres* (SM$145,000) (cf. 6 Feb 1778).

29 Aug - 21 Sep 1781: General George Washington secretly moved the Continental Army from White Plains, NY to Yorktown, VA.

8 Sep 1781: Battle of Eutaw Springs, SC.

20 Sep 1781: The Board of Treasury was abolished due to the inefficiency of its operation [2-50].

6-19 Oct 1781: Battle of Yorktown, VA; Lord Cornwallis surrendered, and this ended the war for practical purposes, except for some battles in Georgia lasting until Jun 1782.

30 Oct 1781: Congress requisitioned SM$8,000,000 from the States, payable in quarterly payments. But only SM$420,031 had been received by Aug 1782 [2-51].

5 Nov 1781: France guaranteed a 10,000,000 *livres* (SM$1,940,000) loan to Congress from Holland (cf. 6 Feb 1778).

15 Nov 1781: France loaned Congress 750,000 *livres* (SM$145,000) (cf. 6 Feb 1778).

31 Dec 1781: During 1781, the States had issued paper money [2-52]: Massachusetts ($483,500 estimated), New York ($411,250), New Jersey ($800,000), Pennsylvania ($1,330,000), Virginia ($87,500,000), North Carolina ($26,250,000), and South Carolina ($4,182,365 estimated). Meanwhile, $1,179,249 of new emission had been issued in 1781 by Congress, and the total of "new emission" was $2,070,485 [2-53].

7 Jan 1782: The Bank of North America began operations in Philadelphia. The capital consisted of SM$70,000 in hard money from individuals and SM$254,000 from Congress, using proceeds from one of the foreign loans. Robert Morris, head of the Bank, used some employees to deter people from redeeming the notes issued by the Bank, and they soon traded at par with the Spanish dollar.

27 Feb 1782: The Parliament of Great Britain passed a resolution declaring that the war in America was over.

1 Apr 1782: France loaned Congress 1,500,000 *livres* (SM$291,000) (cf. 6 Feb 1778).

4 Apr 1782: Trade in hard money was common among the people by this time (probably since early 1780) since a great deal had been brought in by the British but hoarded until the Continentals were withdrawn. Thomas Paine wrote in the Pennsylvania Packet of 4 Apr 1782 [2-54]:

> The progress and revolution of our domestic circumstances are as extraordinary as the Revolution itself. We began with paper, and we end with gold and silver.

17 May 1782: Robert Morris, superintendent of finances, wrote to Congress explaining the financial situation [2-55]:

> The habitual inattention of the States has reduced us to the brink of ruin, and I cannot see a probability of relief from any of them. I rather perceive a disposition to take money from the public treasury, than to place any in it. A variety of causes prevents the collection of taxes, and delays the payment of them, even after they are collected. In many States they are not laid. ... The public departments are now absolutely at a stand, for the want of money, and many things already commenced I must desist from. This cannot be wondered at, when it is considered, that near five months of the present year have elapsed without my having received anything on account of its expenditures, except the trifling sum of five thousand, five hundred dollars, and that sum, calculating on the expenses of eight millions annually, is about one-fourth of what is necessary to support us for a single day.

1 Jul 1782: France loaned Congress 1,500,000 *livres* (SM$291,000) (cf. 6 Feb 1778).

5 Jul 1782: France loaned Congress 3,000,000 *livres* (SM$582,000) (cf. 6 Feb 1778).

11 Jul 1782: The British surrendered Savannah, GA; this ended the war militarily.

16 Jul 1782: Benjamin Franklin negotiated a contract with France, documenting the loans that France had made or guaranteed, along with a repayment schedule [2-56]. Per the 1778 treaty, Louis XVI of France loaned Congress 18,000,000 *livres* (SM$3,492,000) at 5% interest, although interest was waived until the peace treaty with Britain. The loans and guarantees were as follows:

a. 1778: 750,000 *livres* (SM$145,500) on 4 occasions: 28 Feb, 19 May, 3 Aug, and 1 Nov 1778.

b. 1779: 250,000 *livres* (SM$48,500) on 4 occasions: 10 Jun, 15 Sep, 4 Oct, and 21 Dec 1779, plus 1,000,000 *livres* (SM$194,000) on 27 Nov 1779.

c. 1780: 750,000 *livres* (SM$145,000) on 4 occasions: 29 Feb, 23 May, 21 Jun, and 5 Oct 1780.

d. 1781: 750,000 *livres* (SM$145,000) on 4 occasions: 15 Feb, 15 May, 15 Aug, and 15 Nov 1780; plus 1,000,000 *livres* (SM$194,000) on 1 Aug 1780.

e. 1781: France guaranteed a loan of 10,000,000 *livres* (SM$1,940,000) from Holland on 5 Nov 1781.

f. 1782: 1,500,000 *livres* (SM$291,000) on 2 occasions: 10 Apr and 1 Jul 1782, plus 3,000,000 *livres* (SM$582,000) on 5 Jul 1782.

4 Sep 1782: Congress requisitioned SM$1,200,000 from the States [2-57], but did not require it be paid directly to Congress. The States were to use the revenue to pay down loan office certificates and other U. S. debt payable in their own States.

14 Sep 1782: Congress authorized a loan from France for SM$4,000,000; a net loan was obtained for SM$1,089,000 (6,000,000 *livres*) [2-58].

16 Oct 1782: Congress requisitioned another SM$2,000,000 from the States [2-59].

31 Dec 1782: The States did not issue any of their own paper money in 1782 [2-60].

1 Jan 1783: The financial condition was as follows [2-61, 2-62]: Total foreign debt = SM$7,885,085; domestic debt = SM$34,115,290; arrears due on both foreign and domestic debt = SM$2,415,956, excluding approximately SM$20,000,000 in debts contracted by the several States during the war. The State debts were later absorbed by the United States under the Constitution at SM$21,500,000.

20 Jan 1783: Britain, France, Spain, and the U. S. signed the preliminary articles of the Treaty of Paris that would end the Revolutionary War.

23 Jan 1783: Congress ratified the agreement with France made on 16 Jul 1782.

5 Feb 1783: Congress passed a resolution in which officers received one month's pay in notes [2-63]; private soldiers received one month's pay which was delivered in weekly installments of 50 cents each. The total for this one month's pay was SM$256,232.86.

21 Feb 1783: France loaned 600,000 *livres* (SM$116,400) to Congress, but Louis XVI made it clear that he was unwilling to loan any more since America's credit was so bad (but see 15 Apr 1783).

18 Mar 1783: General Washington wrote an appeal to the President of Congress and its members on behalf of the "Patriot Army." In it he recounted the Newburgh circular, his address on it, and the favorable response he received from the officers; he reiterated the army's long sufferings; he noted the obligation of Congress to treat the army justly; he reminded them of previous assurances given by Congress; and finally he urged Congress not to leave the army in want and destitution, as it would always be remembered as a sign of Congress' ingratitude for services rendered by the army [2-64]. He also recommended that men who had been promised half pay for life would be better served by full pay for a fixed number of years.

22 Mar 1783: Congress agreed to a resolution per General Washington's suggestion on payment to the army [2-65]. It modified the pay provision for soldiers from half-pay for life to full pay for five years at once, known as the commutation. The lump sum was to be paid by issuing certificates bearing 6% interest. This was a good bargain for the government, as it would reduce the total outlay, since most soldiers would likely live more than ten years. It would also benefit the soldiers, who, having left their farms and occupations, would find a lump sum handy in getting back on their feet. But the public was opposed to it, angry that such a large amount was to be paid at once, since their wages were small in comparison. The public had forgotten the sacrifices made by the army, and became occupied with their own problems.

15 Apr 1783: Congress ratified the peace treaty with Great Britain, formally ending the war. France loaned 6,000,000 *livres* (SM$1,164,000) to Congress [2-66]. This was the last Louis XVI could do.

18 Apr 1783: Congress passed a resolution [2-67] to recommend to the States that Congress be given a power to levy duties for a period of 25 years on certain imported items in order to raise revenues to pay the debts of the war. The items on which duties were to be paid amounted to between 1.1% to 26.6% on rum and other liquors, wines, tea, pepper, sugar, molasses, cocoa, and coffee; in addition to a 5% duty on all other items. It was estimated at this time that the import duties would bring about SM$1,000,000 annually to Congress. The resolution also recommended that a standing annual requisition of SM$1,500,000 be apportioned to the various States according to population (New Hampshire: SM$52,708; Massachusetts: SM$224,427; Delaware: SM$22,443; Maryland: SM$141,517; Rhode Island: SM$ 32,318; Virginia: SM$256,487; Connecticut: SM$132,091; North Carolina: SM$109,006; New York: SM$128,243; South Carolina: SM$96,183; New Jersey: SM$83,358; Georgia: SM$16,030; and Pennsylvania: SM$205,189). It was sent to the States on 26 Apr 1783 with an address by James Madison, Alexander Hamilton, and Oliver Ellsworth in which they outlined the need for revenue, as the current debt amounted to SM$42,000,325 (including SM$5,000,000 for the commutation) with an annual interest due of SM$2,415,956. Congress remained helpless in the meantime, since all thirteen States would have to ratify this amendment to the Articles before the revenue could be collected.

2 Jun 1783: The Continental Army received immediate discharge furloughs [2-68]. But Congress was unable to pay the three months salary that had been promised in Apr 1783. Instead, the soldiers received paper notes bearing 6% interest; the cash value was estimated at 10% of face value. The soldiers of the Continental Army, who had defeated the British Empire, dispersed peacefully and went home with no money in their pockets.

3 Sep 1783: British negotiators signed the Treaty of Paris, ending the Revolutionary War. The terms of the treaty included the following provisions: a) loyalists were to be compensated for loss of property suffered during the war; b) British creditors holding private debt were to be paid in full; c) there would be no persecution of loyalists; d) opportunity would be provided for loyalists to recover estates lost during the war; e) private debts owed to loyalists would be paid in sterling; and f) Britain would give up forts in the western New York and the Ohio Valley. But Congress had no power to force any of the States to observe any of these provisions.

At the return of peace, trade between the States and England resumed, as there was still considerable demand for English products. However, since the Continental currency had collapsed, the Americans had to pay for imports in hard money. The war had left many areas ruined. In the south, the farms had not recovered enough to resume trading in indigo, rice or tobacco. The same problem prevailed in the middle States, and they were unable to pay as they normally would, by exporting wheat and furs. The New England States fell on hard times because shipping had become unprofitable owing to the Navigation Acts. Many in the States were living off the land, and resorted to barter to obtain what they needed. Many demagogues claimed that the remedy was cheap paper money, and some States began to issue worthless paper in order to give the illusion of prosperity.

Although not perceived as such at the time, the treaty ending the war began the most crucial period in the history of America [2-69]. The American States were surrounded on the south and west by Spanish lands, and on the north by Canada, which was still a British colony. The big risk was that the States now had no common enemy, and without some sort of unifying force, would degenerate into thirteen petty republics bickering among themselves. They were also vulnerable to encroachment by the larger and more organized European powers.

3 Nov 1783: The Continental Army was formally disbanded [2-70], even though the British still occupied New York City. The main problem was that Congress could no longer afford to maintain the army; in fact, it owed considerable back pay to the soldiers. Many soldiers begin to think they would never get paid, and there was widespread dissension and distrust of Congress. Many members of the army from Pennsylvania, Maryland, Delaware, and Virginia had been previously furloughed on 26 May, 11 Jun, 9 Aug, and 26 Sep 1783.

31 Dec 1783: Of the SM$8,000,000 that had been requisitioned 30 Oct 1781, only SM$1,486,155 had been paid [2-71]. During 1781, the States had issued paper money [2-72]: Massachusetts ($483,500 est.), New Jersey ($85,000), Pennsylvania ($300,000), North Carolina ($100,000), and South Carolina ($4,182,365 estimated).

1 Jan 1784: Thomas Jefferson estimated the national debt to be about SM$68,000,000; about SM$8,000,000 was due from foreign loans; SM$36,500,000 represented the debts of the several States incurred during the war, and the rest was due to individuals or to States. Congress had made many requisitions to the States during the war, and the current status was [2-73, 2-74]:

a. Of the 19 May 1779 requisition for SM$45,000,000, none had been paid.

b. Of the 30 Oct 1781 requisition for SM$8,000,000, States had paid as follows: New Hampshire: $3,000 of $373,598; Massachusetts: $247,677 of $1,307,596; Rhode Island: $67,848 of $216,684; Connecticut: $131,578 of $747,196; New York: $39,064 of $373,598; Pennsylvania: $346,633 of $1,120,794; Delaware: zero of $112,085; Maryland: $89,302 of $933,996; Virginia: $115,104 of $1,307,594; North Carolina: zero of $622,677; South Carolina: $344,302 of $373,598; Georgia: zero of $24,905.

c. States were credited with having paid the SM$1,200,000 requisition of 4 Sep 1782.

d. Of the 16 Oct 1782 requisition for SM$2,000,000, none had been paid.

5 Feb 1784: John Adams was able to get a loan from moneylenders in Holland [2-75] for 2,000,000 guilders (SM$1,176,000) at 6% interest.

5 Apr 1784: Thomas Jefferson, as head of a finance committee in Congress, delivered a report [2-76] on the finances of the Confederacy. The expenses for 1784 were estimated as: a) SM$457,525 for public services; b) SM$442,648 for interest on foreign debt; c) SM$3,580,030 for interest on domestic debt; and d) SM$1,000,000 debts contracted but still unpaid from 1782 and 1783, which totaled to about SM$5,480,203. This figure was not practical as a revenue target. Jefferson proposed that the States be given credit for the SM$1,200,000 that had been requisitioned on 4 Sep 1782 (included in the SM$3,580,030 number), since it had given the States leeway to use it to pay interest due on certificates issued by the States and other liquidated debts. He then recommended that a new requisition

be ordered that would get the States up to three-fourths of the original SM$8,000,000 that had been requisitioned on 30 Oct 1781. He calculated the apportionment, deducting for some receipts that had been made, and requested a requisition for 1784 of SM$4,577,591. This would be enough to meet the current needs. It was voted down by Congress, probably realizing the demands on the States were too great.

28 May 1784: Congress established a Board of Treasury to manage the finances, although it did not go into operation until 25 Jan 1785 [2-77].

3 Jun 1784: Congress passed an act specifying how accounts were to be settled with the States: a) Supplies that the States had furnished were to be assessed at their value in specie, plus 6% interest from the date they were provided; b) depreciation of the Continentals was accounted for; c) creditors of the U. S. were given certificates bearing 6% interest; d) old certificates issued by the Army officers could be exchanged for new ones [2-78].

17 Aug 1784: Robert Morris, superintendent of finances, informed French officials that the U. S. would default on its interest payment on the 10,000,000 *livre* loan from Holland that France had guaranteed (cf. 5 Nov 1781) [2-79]. He also informed the French officials that no interest could be paid on the direct loans from France. These defaults ruined American credit.

25 Jan 1785: The Board of Treasury went into operation, with John Lewis Gervais, Samuel Osgood, and Walter Livingston appointed to manage the finances.

6 Jul 1785: Congress defined the U. S. dollar as 375.64 grains of fine silver [2-80], and adopted a decimal system for smaller amounts (mills, pennies, nickels, dimes, quarters, and half-dollars). A mill is a tenth of a penny.

13-14 Jul 1785: A committee in Congress led by James Monroe introduced a motion [2-81] to amend the Articles of Confederation to grant Congress the power to regulate foreign commerce, levy import duties, send and receive ambassadors, enter treaties and alliances, and establish courts for trial of piracy, if eleven States were agreeable. Monroe's committee had concluded that granting such a power was desirable: a) a tax on foreign goods would aid domestic manufacturers; b) Congress would be able to deal reciprocally with foreign powers, such that America would not always be at a disadvantage; c) it would allow uniform commercial rules among the States; and d) it would prepare the way for the establishment of a navy to protect commerce. Richard Henry Lee of Virginia led the opposition to it, noting that granting powers to Congress would: a) endanger liberty; b) may tempt Congress to expands its powers even further; and c) increase the risk of undue foreign influence upon Congress if powers affecting foreign nations were concentrated in Congress. He also argued that the interests of the northern and southern States were different. Lee feared that the northern States would use their numerical advantage to vote themselves benefits in the carrying trade that would serve to impoverish the southern States (since it had no shipping industry). Congress took no action on it, preferring to leave propositions for amending the Articles to the several State legislatures.

13 Sep 1785: The charter of the Bank of North America was revoked by the State of Pennsylvania. This was revenge for the bank's opposition to issuing additional paper money, as many in Pennsylvania continued to believe that paper was the source of wealth. The Bank continued operations, since it had a second charter issued by Congress [2-82].

27 Sep 1785: Congress requisitioned SM$3,000,000 from the States; none of it would ever be paid. Estimated expenses for 1785 totaled SM$404,553 for military and civil department; SM$440,252 for interest on the foreign debt, and SM$743,054 for interest on the domestic debt. Also, interest on certificates issued to the soldiers was SM$289,423, and the actual expenses for 1784 had exceeded that years' estimate by SM$1,141,551 [2-83]. Tax evasion was the common default position:

> Were States ever so able to bear taxation more disinclined to do their duty in this regard? Everywhere did individuals seek to evade the payment of taxes; not because they were too poor to pay, for the sums asked were small compared with the resources of the people, but rather from habit, and because evasion of the duty was so general.

1 Feb 1786: Of the four requisitions upon the States since 30 Oct 1781, totaling SM$15,670,987, only a total of SM$2,450,803 had been paid by the States [2-84]. Congress decided to allow holders of the unpaid certificates issued by Congress should present them to the loan offices in the States where they were issued, to be turned in for new ones after being assessed as to their current value in specie [2-85].

15 Feb 1786: The minimum anticipated expenses for 1787 associated with payment of interest on foreign loans and other foreign obligations was SM$577,307, including: a) interest on loans from France, SM$240,741; b) interest on certificates to foreign officers payable in France, SM$22,370; c) interest on a loan from Spain (to Mar 1787), SM$48,596; and d) interest on a loan from Holland (to Jun 1787), SM$265,600. The total receipts since 1781 amounted to SM$2,457,987: a) from requisitions made between 1 Nov 1781 and 1 Nov 1784, SM$2,025,089; b) from requisitions made between 1 Nov 1784 and 1 Jan 1786, SM$432,898 [2-86].

8 Aug 1786: Congress established a coinage standard, per the decimal system organized in Jul 1785 [2-87]. A dollar was defined as 375.64 grains of pure silver, or 24.6268 grains of pure gold. The fineness of the coinage was to be 11/12 (0.91666 fine). The ratio of gold to silver was thus 15.253 to one. It also specified two gold coins, one of ten dollars (Eagle) containing 246.268 grains of fine gold, and the other of five dollars (Half Eagle) containing 123.34 grains of fine gold. However, only the copper coins were actually minted.

23 Aug 1786: Congress authorized the issue of certificates, called 'indents', for payment of accrued interest on loan-office certificates and other debts. But these did not pay the debt or help the creditors, since there was very little coming in from the requisitions made on the States [2-88].

18 Sep 1786: Congress ordered the States to pay the requisitions in specie, declining to accept any type of paper money, including the Continentals. Meanwhile, the notes issued by the Bank of North America circulated at par; the bank had good credit because it had demonstrated its ability to redeem on demand. Its cash account was $5,957,000 Mexican dollars [2-89].

19 Sep 1986 to 1 Mar 1787: Shays' Rebellion began, which was a revolt led by Daniel Shays in Vermont, Massachusetts, New York, and New Hampshire, over the decline in value of the paper money, high taxes, and foreclosures. This rebellion and the continuing inability of Congress to raise money led to the calling of the Constitutional Convention.

20 Sep 1786: Congress refuses to accept the Continentals in payment of taxes or even postage stamps. This marked the formal end of the Continental paper money [2-90].

17 Oct 1786: Congress asked the States for a requisition of SM$3,777,062, of which SM$1,606,632 to be in 'indents', and SM$2,170,430 in specie. Congress was now allowing people to pay part of their taxes in 'indents' instead of money. The annual interest on the domestic debt was at this time SM$1,606,560 [2-91].

31 Dec 1786: Congress had received approximately only SM$500,000 requisitioned from the States in the past two years [2-92]; Congress was delinquent on its interest payments.

1 Mar 1787: End of Shays' rebellion (cf. 19 Sep 1786).

25 May 1787: The Constitutional Convention began in Philadelphia.

17 Sep 1787: Proposed Constitution sent to the States for ratification.

22 May 1788: A committee of Congress reported that there had been a great deal of negligence and fraud in the handling of the government's accounts during the war, and in resolving accounts between Congress and the States. Some time was allowed to straighten out the accounts, but was never satisfactorily accomplished [2-93].

21 Jun 1788: New Hampshire became the ninth State to ratify the Constitution, and it went into effect (excluding Virginia, New York, North Carolina, and Rhode Island, since they had not yet ratified it).

30 Sep 1788: A committee in Congress issued a report on the finances concerning revenues remitted to Congress from the tax receivers between Nov 1784 and 21 Apr 1788. Between Nov 1784 and 21 Apr 1785, only SM$143,648 had been remitted, and from 21 Apr 1785 to 21 Apr 1788, only SM$996,448 was remitted. The rest that was obtained by Congress [2-94] for this period consisted of SM$1,881,139 in 'indents' (certificates of interest) and a fairly small amount from sale of public land.

Note (cf. 13 Sep 1779): Elliot [2-95] cites Jefferson's claim that the C $50,000,000 authorized on 14 Jan 1779 was C $24,447,620 for new emission, the rest to replace mutilated bills. Schuckers [2-96] shows this as C $25,552,780, but as an addition to the C $50,000,000. Schuckers also cites an additional C $10,000,000 to replace counterfeit bills, but he does not cite the date. Admittedly, none of these are consistent; Schuckers gives the total of issued Continentals as C $359,547,126.

3 Data, 1775-1788

Figure 3-1 shows the accumulated amount of Continentals issued along with the value of the Continental with respect to the Spanish Milled Dollar. The solid curve (accumulated emissions) is read on the left scale and the dashed curve (relative value) is read on the right. At the end, in May 1781, the Continental dollar had depreciated to the point where it traded for two-tenths of a penny as seen at lower right.

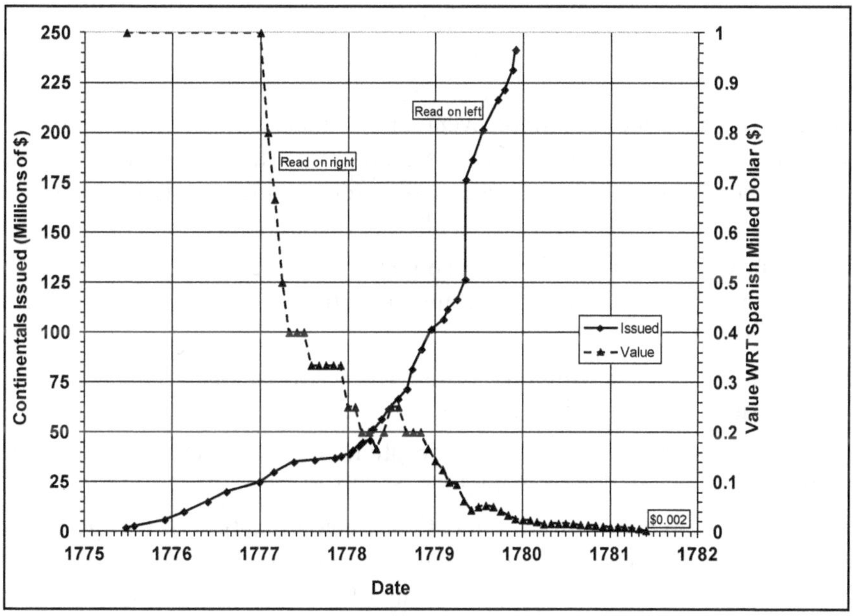

Figure 3-1: Continentals Issued and Value With Respect to the Spanish Milled Dollar

4 Summary, 1775-1788

So ends the history of the Continental paper money. There are some important lessons to be learned from this history. First, the Continentals were essentially fiat paper money, backed only by a promise of future redemption at interest. The history showed that such a promise could not be kept for the same reason the Continentals were issued in the first place: Congress, which claimed to have the power to direct the Revolution, did not have the power to raise a single penny in taxes. Without a reliable revenue stream, Congress had no choice but to risk depreciation, continue borrowing, and default; confident that the slack would be eventually be taken up by patriotism. They were correct in that estimation as it turned out, but a great many people lost everything they had worked for, and many took great losses by accepting the depreciating Continentals at face value. In fairness to Congress, there probably was no other way to finance the Revolution, and the Continentals succeeded long enough to get the Americans through the early parts of the war in the North.

Secondly, the British engaged in a great deal of counterfeiting of the Continentals, hoping it would drive the Americans into despair and end the revolt. As Bolles [4-1] put it:

> Many in Great Britain and elsewhere believed, that, if Continental paper money could be destroyed, the Americans would be obliged to submit, from lack of funds to maintain their cause. This is why the British Government promoted so extensively the business of counterfeiting. But General Clinton wrote truthfully, in January 1780, "Every day teaches me the futility of calculations founded on its failure." Great Britain had not yet fathomed that depth of American patriotism, what the people were willing to suffer to acquire independence; nor had the mother-country reckoned accurately the aid which France was to bestow.

Third, price controls do not work, as no one will sell for money that is declining in value unless he can elevate the price. If an official price is below the price of production, or below the price that commands a reasonable profit, that item will not be produced at all. In that case, one of two things will happen. Either there will exist shortages (which is what governments claim they are trying to prevent), or the government itself will have to take up production.

Fourth, a fiat paper money must be made a legal tender because that is the only way to ensure that it will be accepted at all if there is competing money of better quality (cf. 14 Jan 1777). The fines and forfeitures had little effect as once again economic reality superseded the desires of Congress.

Fifth, as soon as the public realized the money was depreciating, they began to buy real property and increase their debts, knowing that it can be paid off easily in depreciated money later [4-2]. They also are tempted to engage in speculation.

Sixth, the depreciated Continentals were eventually withdrawn from circulation, starting in 1782. They were still accepted in payment of taxes, and were exchanged for bills of the new emission, and were exchanged for other money [4-3]. They were eventually redeemed for a small fraction of their face value (cf. 28 Jun 1780) and became obsolete; they were collected up and burned.

Seventh, Gresham's law was in full force. The paper circulated while the people hoarded the good money of gold and silver; when the paper depreciated to virtually nothing, the gold and silver went back into circulation (cf. 4 Apr 1782).

Eighth, the persecutions of those who refused the depreciating money failed to restore its value; they depreciated anyway because people realized the true declining value [4-4].

Ninth, there was a considerable amount of corruption and incompetence in handling the public finances; Bolles writes, summarizing the report of 30 Sep 1788 [4-5]:

> The remainder of the report is, for the most part, a continuation of the dismal story. Extraordinary negligence, wastefulness, disorder, and corruption marked the early years of the government; even in the darkest periods through which the country has since passed, it may be questioned whether a greater lack of system or moral rectitude has prevailed.

Last, despite the inconveniences and moral hazard of the Continentals, it did serve to finance the revolution; there was no other way. Schuckers notes [4-6]:

> When, therefore, the Second Continental Congress - an immortal body! - addressed itself to a consideration of the finances, almost immediately upon its meeting, May 10th, 1775, nothing was more natural and probable than a prompt resort to paper money. First, it provided for the creation of an army. Having done this, and entirely conscious that a supply of cash [specie or coin] ... the members of the Congress being entirely aware, then that the supply of cash was inadequate even for the current and ordinary business of the colonists, immediately betook themselves to bills of credit...

Brough summarizes its utility in retrospect [4-7]:

> Notwithstanding all the difficulties attending the use of this money (i.e., Continentals), it rendered considerable service to the colonists, and was generally admitted, even by its opponents, to have done excellent service during the revolutionary war. Thomas Paine said of it (in a letter to Abbe Raynal), 'Every stone in the bridge that has carried us over seems to have a claim on our esteem. But this was the cornerstone, and its usefulness cannot be forgotten'.

Former Treasury Secretary Gallatin commented in 1831 on paper money and the necessity thereof during the Revolution [4-8]:

> The general objections to a paper issued by government, have already been stated at large. Yet it must be admitted, that there may be times when every other consideration must yield to the superior necessity of saving or defending a country. If there ever was a time, or a cause which justified a resort to that measure, it was the war for independence. It would be doing gross injustice to the authors of the revolution and founder of that independence, to confound them with those governments, which from ambitious view have, without necessity, inflicted that calamity on their subjects. The old Congress, as the name purports, were only an assembly of plenipotentiaries, delegated by the several colonies or states. They could only recommend, and had not the power to lay taxes; the country was comparatively poor; extraordinary exertions were necessary to resist the formidable power of Great Britain; those exertions were made, and absorbed all the local resources; the paper money carried the United States through the most arduous and perilous stages of the war; and, though operating as a most unequal tax, it cannot be denied that it saved the country. ... It is to be hoped that a similar state of things will not again occur; but at all events, the issue of a government paper ought to be kept in reserve for extraordinary exigencies.

References

[1-1] Henry Phillips, Elisha Reynolds Potter, *Historical Sketches of the Paper Currency of the American Colonies: Pt. D Ser. Continental Paper Money*, Roxbury, MA: W. Elliot Woodward, (1866), p. 16, quoting *Adams' Works*, Vol. 7, p. 296

[1-2] J. W. Schuckers, *A Brief Account of the Finances and Paper Money of the Revolutionary War*, NY: Sanford J. Durst Numismatic Publications, 1978, pp. 103, 104 (originally published 1874 by John Campbell & Son, Philadelphia)

[1-3] op. cit., Schuckers, p. 125. Schuckers here is quoting a report issued by Joseph Nourse, Register of the Treasury to the House of Representatives, 30 Jan 1828.

[1-4] Jonathan Elliot, *The Funding System of the United States and Great Britain*, Washington, DC: Blair & Rives, 1845, p. 9. Elliot reproduces here a set of statistics published by Pelatiah Webster of Philadelphia, who tracked the depreciation through the existence of the Continentals.

[1-5] op. cit., Schuckers, pp. 110, 111

[1-6] William Gouge, *A Short History of Paper Money and Banking In the United States*, Philadelphia: T. W. Ustick, 1833, Part 2, p. 25. Gouge quotes an "estimate by the Register of the Treasury in 1790".

[1-7] op. cit., Schuckers, pp. 20, 21

[2-1] op. cit., Schuckers, p. 13

[2-2] op. cit., Phillips and Potter, p. 25

[2-3] op. cit., Schuckers, pp. 28, 29

[2-4] op. cit., Schuckers, p. 127

[2-5] op. cit., Phillips and Potter, p. 41

[2-6] op. cit., Schuckers, pp. 18, 19

[2-7] Annual Report of the Secretary of the Treasury on the State of the Finances for the Year 1876, Washington, DC: Government Printing Office, 1876, Table M, pp. 24, 25. This section of this report recounts the loans and debts incurred during the Revolution. Schuckers, p. 107 has the 23

Dec 1776 loan from the Farmers-General at 1,000,000 l. (SM$194,000), and has the 28 Sep 1779 loan from Spain at SM$150,000.
[2-8] op. cit., Schuckers, p. 127
[2-9] Albert S. Bolles, *A Financial History of the United States*, NY: Augustus M. Kelley (1969), Vol. 1, pp. 175, 176 (originally published 1884 by D. Appleton & Co., NY)
[2-10] op. cit., Schuckers, pp. 32-34
[2-11] op. cit., Bolles, Vol. 1, pp. 165-173
[2-12] Annual Report of the Secretary of the Treasury on the State of the Finances for the Year 1876, Washington, DC: Government Printing Office, 1876, Table M, pp. 24, 25. This section of this report recounts the loans and debts incurred during the Revolution. Schuckers, p. 107 has the 23 Dec 1776 loan from the Farmers-General at 1,000,000 l. (SM$194,000), and has the 28 Sep 1779 loan from Spain at SM$150,000.
[2-13] op. cit., Schuckers, p. 127
[2-14] op. cit., Schuckers, pp. 74, 75
[2-15] op. cit., Schuckers, p. 37
[2-16] op. cit., Bolles, Vol. 1, p. 169
[2-17] op. cit., Schuckers, p. 127
[2-18] op. cit., J. W. Schuckers, p. 48
[2-19] op. cit., Phillips and Potter, pp. 100-102
[2-20] op. cit., Schuckers, p. 48
[2-21] op. cit., Schuckers, pp. 52, 56
[2-22] op. cit., J. W. Schuckers, pp. 52, 56
[2-23] John C. Fitzpatrick, editor, *The Writings of Washington from the Original Manuscript Sources*, Washington, DC: United States Printing Office, 1937, Vol. 16, pp. 123, 124
[2-24] Jonathan Elliot, *The Funding System of the United States and Great Britain*, Washington, DC: Blair and Rives, (1845), p. 11.
[2-25] op. cit., Schuckers, p. 58
[2-26] op. cit., Phillips and Potter, pp. 137-143
[2-27] op. cit., Bolles, Vol. 1, p. 83
[2-28] Annual Report of the Secretary of the Treasury on the State of the Finances for the Year 1876, Washington, DC: Government Printing Office, 1876, Table M, pp. 24, 25. This section of this report recounts the loans and debts incurred during the Revolution. Schuckers, p. 107 has the 23 Dec 1776 loan from the Farmers-General at 1,000,000 l. (SM$194,000), and has the 28 Sep 1779 loan from Spain at SM$150,000.
[2-29] Annual Report of the Secretary of the Treasury on the State of the Finances for the Year 1876, Washington, DC: Government Printing Office, 1876, Table M, pp. 24, 25. This section of this report recounts the loans and debts incurred during the Revolution. Schuckers, p. 107 has the 23 Dec 1776 loan from the Farmers-General at 1,000,000 l. (SM$194,000), and has the 28 Sep 1779 loan from Spain at SM$150,000.
[2-30] op. cit., Phillips and Potter, pp. 149-151
[2-31] op. cit., Elliot, p. 11. There is a note on the same page calling out Senate Document 229, 25 Feb 1843 (27th Congress) as citing these same figures. However, the Senate document only cites the total amount of Continentals issued ($242,100,176) and the amount redeemed ($168,280,219.12).
[2-32] op. cit., Schuckers, p. 127
[2-33] op. cit., Schuckers, p. 48
[2-34] op. cit., Schuckers, p. 62
[2-35] op. cit., Schuckers, p. 62
[2-36] op. cit., Schuckers, p. 84
[2-37] op. cit., Phillips and Potter, pp. 151-153, 160
[2-38] op. cit., Phillips and Potter, p. 210
[2-39] op. cit., Phillips and Potter, pp. 210, 211

[2-40] op. cit., Schuckers, p. 78
[2-41] op. cit., Phillips and Potter, pp. 211-217
[2-42] op. cit., Schuckers, p. 63
[2-43] op. cit., Elliot, p. 11.
[2-44] op. cit., Schuckers, p. 127
[2-45] op. cit., Schuckers, pp. 81, 82
[2-46] op. cit., Schuckers, p. 86
[2-47] op. cit., Schuckers, pp. 92, 96, 97
[2-48] op. cit., Bolles, Vol. 1, p. 272
[2-49] op. cit., Bolles, Vol. 1, pp. 273, 274
[2-50] op. cit., Bolles, Vol. 1, p. 306
[2-51] op. cit., Bolles, Vol. 1, pp. 307, 320
[2-52] op. cit., Schuckers, p. 127
[2-53] op. cit., Elliot, p. 11
[2-54] op. cit., Bolles, Vol. 1, p. 326
[2-55] op. cit., Bolles, Vol. 1, p. 310
[2-56] *The Secret Journal of the Acts and Proceedings of Congress*, Boston, MA: Thomas B. Wait, 1821, Vol. 3, pp. 281-289
[2-57] op. cit., Bolles, Vol. 1, p. 313
[2-58] Annual Report of the Secretary of the Treasury on the State of the Finances for the Year 1876, Washington, DC: Government Printing Office, 1876, Table M, pp. 24, 25. This section of this report recounts the loans and debts incurred during the Revolution. Schuckers, p. 107 has the 23 Dec 1776 loan from the Farmers-General at 1,000,000 l. (SM$194,000), and has the 28 Sep 1779 loan from Spain at SM$150,000.
[2-59] op. cit., Bolles, Vol. 1, p. 314
[2-60] op. cit., Schuckers, p. 127
[2-61] op. cit., Schuckers, pp. 107-109
[2-62] op. cit., Bolles, Vol. 1, p. 317
[2-63] George Bancroft, *History of the United States of America from the Discovery of the Continent*, NY: D. Appleton & Company, 1888, Vol. 6, p. 62
[2-64] op. cit., Fitzpatrick, Vol. 26, pp. 229-232
[2-65] Gaillard Hunt, ed., *Journals of the Continental Congress*, Washington, DC: U. S. Government Printing Office, 1922, Vol. 24, pp. 206-210
[2-66] op. cit., Bolles, Vol. 1, p. 244
[2-67] op. cit., Hunt, ed., Vol. 24, pp. 256-261
[2-68] op. cit., Bancroft, Vol. 6, pp. 82, 83
[2-69] John Fiske, *John Fiske's Historical Writings*, NY: Houghton, Mifflin and Company, 1901, Vol. 12, pp. 65-69, 194-198
[2-70] op. cit., Bancroft, Vol. 6, p. 105
[2-71] op. cit., Albert S. Bolles, Vol. 1, p. 322
[2-72] op. cit., Schuckers, p. 127
[2-73] op. cit., Hunt, ed., Vol. 26, pp. 297-310
[2-74] op. cit., Bolles, Vol. 1, p. 322
[2-75] op. cit., Bolles, Vol. 1, p. 257
[2-76] op. cit., Hunt, Vol. 26, pp. 185-198. See also Bolles, Vol. 1, p. 321
[2-77] op. cit., Bolles, Vol. 1, p. 333
[2-78] op. cit., Bolles, Vol. 1, p. 327
[2-79] op. cit., Bancroft, Vol. 6, pp. 123, 124
[2-80] op. cit., Bolles, Vol. 1, pp. 341, 342
[2-81] op. cit., Bancroft, Vol. 6, pp. 140-147
[2-82] op. cit., Bolles, Vol. 1, pp. 345, 346

[2-83] op. cit., Bolles, Vol. 1, pp. 348, 349
[2-84] op. cit., Bolles, Vol. 1, p. 348
[2-85] op. cit., Bolles, Vol. 1, pp. 338, 339
[2-86] op. cit., Hunt, Vol. 30, pp. 70-76
[2-87] op. cit., Bolles, Vol. 1, pp. 341, 342
[2-88] op. cit., Bolles, Vol. 1, pp. 346, 347
[2-89] op. cit., Bolles, Vol. 1, pp. 344, 345
[2-90] op. cit., Bolles, Vol. 1, pp. 344, 345
[2-91] op. cit., Bolles, Vol. 1, p. 350
[2-92] op. cit., Bancroft, Vol. 6, pp. 140-147
[2-93] op. cit., Bolles, Vol. 1, pp. 338, 339
[2-94] op. cit., Bolles, Vol. 1, p. 357
[2-95] op. cit., Elliot, pp. 6, 7 Elliot reproduces here a set of statistics published by Pelatiah Webster of Philadelphia, who tracked the depreciation through the existence of the Continentals.
[2-96] op. cit., Schuckers, p. 110

[4-1] op. cit., Bolles, Vol. 1, pp. 151, 152
[4-2] op. cit., Schuckers, pp. 29, 30
[4-3] op. cit., Bolles, Vol. 1, p. 287
[4-4] op. cit., Schuckers, pp. 26-28
[4-5] op. cit., Bolles, Vol. 1, p. 358
[4-6] op. cit., Schuckers, p. 11
[4-7] William Brough, *The Natural Law of Money*, NY: Greenwood Press, 1969, p. 87 (originally published by G. P. Putnam's Sons, 1896)
[4-8] Albert Gallatin, *Considerations on the Currency and Banking System of the United States*, Philadelphia, PA: Carey & Lea, 1831, p. 86

History of the Assignats of the French Revolution

This essay was originally published 13 Dec 2021, and is derived from section 3.2 of the book *The Control and Manipulation of Money*.

The history of the assignats, issued during the French Revolution, was documented by White [1], Dillaye [2], and von Sybel [3]. Before describing the details of the monetary fiasco of the French Revolution, it is important to have a cast of characters. They are:

Bergasse: Nicholas Bergasse, a member of the Estates-General as representing the nobility; member of the National Assembly.

Bonaparte: Napoleon Bonaparte, an army officer who became dictator of France after he seized power at the end of the Revolution. His reign consisted of twenty years of war and starvation for the French people.

Brillat-Savarin: Jean Anthelme Brillat-Savarin, a member of the Estates-General and member of the National Assembly.

de Cazales: Jacques Antoine Marie de Cazales, a member of the Constituent Assembly.

Du Pont: Pierre Samuel du Pont de Nemours, initially supported the French Revolution, President of the National Assembly; personally defended Louis XVI and was scheduled for execution but was spared by the death of Robespierre; his son founded the E. I. du Pont de Nemours Company in the U. S.

Jacobins: a political club founded by Robespierre (Society of the Jacobins, Friends of Freedom and equality), the group that instigated the Revolution and presided over the Reign of Terror.

Louis XVI: King of France (Bourbon dynasty).

Marie Antoinette: Wife of King Louis XVI, sister of Austrian Emperor Joseph I.

Marat: Jean-Paul Marat, journalist and primary propagandist for the Jacobins.

Maury: Jean-Sifrein Maury, a member of the Estates-General 1789 representing the clergy; member of the National Assembly until he fled France in Oct 1791, appointed cardinal in 1794.

Mirabeau: Honore Gabriel Riqueti, Count of Mirabeau: a member of the French aristocracy who was a leader of the Revolution in its early stages; member of the Estates-General (representing the nobility) from 5 May 1789 to 9 Jul 1789; member of the Constituent Assembly from 9 Jul 1789 to 2 Apr 1791.

Montesquieu: Charles-Louis de Secondat, Baron de la Brede et de Montesquieu, historian and political philosopher; author of *The Spirit of the Laws*.

Necker: Jacques Necker, a Swiss banker, served as Director-General of the Treasury from 29 Jun 1777 to 19 May 1781, Controller-General of the Finances from 25 Aug 1788 to 11 Jul 1789, and Chief Minister to the king from 29 Jul 1789 to 3 Sep 1790.

Robespierre: Maximilien Francois Marie Isidore de Robespierre, a leader of the Jacobin conspiracy to overthrow the French monarchy; member of the Estates-General from 6 May 1789 to 16 Jun 1789; member of the National Assembly from 17 Jun 1789 to 9 Jul 1789; member of the National Constituent Assembly from 9 Jul 1789 to 30 Sep 1791; President of the National Constituent Assembly from 22 Aug 1793 to 7 Sep 1793 and 4 Jun 1794 to 19 Jun 1794; President of the Jacobin Club from 31 Mar 1790 to 3 Jun 1790 and 7 Aug 1793 to 28 Aug 1793; member of the Committee of Public Safety from 25 Mar 1793 to 27 Jul 1794; led the Reign of Terror; guillotined 28 Jul 1794.

Talleyrand: Charles-Maurice de Talleyrand-Perigord, a member of the Estates-General (representing the clergy) from 12 Apr 1789 to 9 Jul 1789; member of the Constituent Assembly from 9 Jul 1789 to 30 Sep 1791; fled France in Sep 1792, was later Foreign Minister under Napoleon.

France had been both poor and bankrupt for some years by the late 1780's due to the irresponsibility of the government. For example, in 1787, the revenues were 351 M *livres*, but the expenses were 555 M; leaving a one-year deficit of 198 M *livres* [4]. The immediate problem was that France was in desperate financial condition early in 1789; it had a large national debt and little ability to raise taxes to cover the current budget deficit. The Catholic Church at this time was held in low regard by the leaders of the government. It owned between 25% and 35% of the land in France; the value of the lands was estimated at 2,000,000,000 livres. The Church's annual income was about 160,000,000 livres (100,000,000 in tithes, and 60,000,000 from income on the land); and paid a tax of 3,000,000 or 4,000,000 livres [5]. They were also derelict in providing for the poor, as was their alleged purpose. Necker had proposed an income tax at a 25% rate, but the measure failed.

Another cause of the Revolution was the inherent unfairness of the tax system [6]. The poor paid a large fraction of the taxes in the form of a poll tax and excise taxes on necessities. Worse than that, tyrannical means were used by the government to collect the taxes, and it was well known among the people that much of the money went to pay for frivolous expenses at the King's court.

King Louis XVI called a special session of the Estates-General (later called the National Assembly) on 5 May 1789 to discuss the nation's finances. The idea came to some of the members of the National Assembly that they could create prosperity by creating money. Since the nation was so deep in debt that it had no credit, borrowing or stealing from the Church seemed to be the only way to keep the government in operation. Talleyrand was the first to propose confiscation of the property of the Church (cf. 10 Oct 1789) and issue paper money against it in order to pay off the enormous debts that had been run up by the government [7]. Necker, the Minister of Finance, and others (such as Bergasse) who understood money opposed it. But the notion of prosperity through paper money became popular, aided by the propaganda of Marat. The National Assembly then entered into debate on how to issue paper money, to be secured by confiscating the property of the Catholic Church.

French money was denominated in *livre tournois*, commonly called a livre, which was defined as 75.1283 grains of silver, and thus were reckoned to be 0.194 Spanish milled dollars (using the actual amount of silver in the typical Spanish coin). No 1-livre coins were in use at this time; the actual coins were a gold coin called a *Louis d'or*, equal to 24 *livres*, a gold coin of 48 livres called a double Louis d'or, and a half Louis d'or worth 12 livres, and a silver coin called an *ecu*, worth 6 *livres*. There were also fractional ecus at valued at 3.0, 1.5, and 0.75 *livres*. In the following "1.0 livre = A xxx" is used to denote the number of assignats equaling the value of a livre. At this time, the livre was also called a franc, although technically the franc had not been used since 1641. I have retained the units in the references, even when francs are called out prior to 1795. The franc was formally redefined in 1795; 1 franc = 1.0125 livre.

Herewith is the sad story of the depreciation of money during the French Revolution. Keep in mind as you read this, those who led the Revolution were the "enlightened" people, the ones who had read Voltaire (Francois-Marie Arouet) and Rousseau, who knew everything there was to know about how to create a "just" society. These were the "progressives" of their era. I would encourage you to pay close attention to what they did once they gained power.

5 May 1789: Louis XVI called the Estates-General into session to discuss the terrible financial condition of France. It consisted of 1,145 members: 270 of the nobility, 291 representing the clergy, and 584 representing the people (also called the Third Estate) [8]. In the months that followed, the Third Estate argued against the privileges of the nobility, that the remainder of the feudal system in France should be abolished, and established a National Constituent Assembly. Eventually the nobility and clergy joined with them.

9 Jul 1789: The National Constituent Assembly convened.

14 Jul 1789: Riots in Paris and storming of the Bastille that began the French Revolution. It was a civil war begun by socialist revolutionaries who sought to destroy the old order and bring "justice and equality" to France. This was the beginning of the immigration of the nobility and wealthy people out of France [9].

27 Aug 1789: The National Assembly adopted The Declaration of the Rights of Man [10], having been debated since 4 Aug 1790.

12 Oct 1789: Talleyrand proposed issuing a new paper currency to be secured by a mortgage on lands owned by the Catholic Church [11]. Issuing a new paper currency was the only means available for the National Assembly to fund the Revolution. The idea was that they would be issued to those who had loaned the government money, and they would use them to buy the Church land if they desired, and if not, to use them as bonds, to pay taxes, and to use as circulating money [12, 13].

2 Nov 1789: The lands of the Catholic Church were confiscated [14]. The Church had accumulated the land over the previous 1,500 years; it consisted of between 25 and 33% of all the land in France, and was valued at about 2,000,000,000 livres. The goal was to issue paper money (assignats) so that middle-class people could buy the land; thus gaining their support for the Revolution. White [15] described the objectives:

> It was urged, then, that the issue of four hundred millions of paper, (not in the shape of interest-bearing bonds, as had at first been proposed, but in notes small as well as large), would give the treasury something to pay out immediately, and relieve the national necessity; that, having been put into circulation, this paper money would stimulate business; that it would give to all capitalists, large or small, the means for buying from the nation the ecclesiastical real estate; and that from the proceeds of this real estate the nation would pay its debts and also obtain new funds for new necessities. Never was theory more seductive both to financiers and statesmen.

19 Dec 1789: The National Assembly finalized the plan for issuing the paper money, called assignats, and authorized 400,000,000 to be issued [16].

17 Apr 1790: The National Assembly issued 400,000,000 livres in assignats. They were to be used to purchase the church lands, but also to be used as circulating currency [17, 18], and the portion received for the land was to pay the current expenses of the government. The circulating portion was secured by the confiscated land formerly owned by the Catholic Church, and bore interest at 3%. The basic claim was that the assignats had the same virtue as metal money, in that it represented something tangible, namely the land, and therefore, the paper assignats would not suffer the same fate as the paper issues of John Law in the 1720's. The assignats thus were proclaimed to have true value, competitive with gold and silver. Louis XVI encouraged the public to begin using it. A few of the clergy opposed it, mostly on the basis of the theft of the Church lands, and some in the National Assembly opposed it, especially Necker, Maury, Cazales, and Bergasse.

27 Aug 1790: By this time, the assignats received by the government had already been spent, and the national finances were as bad as ever [19]. A report by Montesquieu recommended an additional issue of assignats. He recognized the risks, but thought it was necessary to save France.

Early Sep 1790: The government now needed money again. Mirabeau knew the dangers of paper money, but went along with it, believing it was the best way to get the people to buy the Church lands, and noting that the first issue had served to improve credit [20]. He advocated in the National Assembly for one additional issue of assignats, enough to cover the entire national debt (at that time was 2,400,000,000 livres). Brillat-Savarin and du Pont de Nemours correctly noted the inconsistencies in Mirabeau's argument, but they were disregarded. Necker opposed it, but was unsuccessful; he resigned and left France. Talleyrand gave a speech opposing the new issue; it ended with [21]:

> You can, indeed, arrange it so that the people shall be forced to take a thousand livres in paper for a thousand livres in specie [i.e., specie he had lent to the government]; but you can never arrange it so that a man shall be obliged to give a thousand livres in specie [i.e., in his possession] for a thousand livres in paper -- in that fact is embedded the entire question; and on account of that fact the whole system fails.

29 Sep 1790: The National Assembly issued 800,000,000 livres in assignats; total = 1,200,000,000 livres. The law also specified that no more than 1,200,000,000 should ever be issued, and when assignats were paid into the treasury for purchase of land, they were to be burned [22]. But when 160,000,000 livres were received in payment for the former Church lands, they were not burned; they were re-issued. Also, this limitation was ignored when the government found it convenient (cf. 19 Jun 1791). At the same time the National Assembly started funding various "public works projects" that increased the national debt.

~15 Nov 1790: The National Assembly passed a law specifying a coinage standard; the standard money was silver, and the ratio of silver to gold was changed from 15.5:1 to 14.5:1 [23]. But the public decided to keep the silver coins, and it became necessary to issue another 100,000,000 assignats in small denominations that could be used for small transactions or change.

27 Nov 1790: The National Assembly passed a law requiring every member of the clergy to swear an oath to the Revolution; failure to do so would result in a loss of their position and their income. Most of them refused on the date called for, 4 Jan 1791 [24].

Jan 1791: Coin became very scarce, as people begin to recognize the depreciation of the assignats [25]. The propaganda of the day was to claim that the value of metal coins was rising, instead of the true cause, which was that the assignats were declining in value. This was nothing more than Gresham's Law in action: an inferior currency, when accepted, drives the superior one out of circulation.

~Feb 1791: The beginning of the decline in industry and manufacturing, since the businessmen could not calculate accurately with the depreciating assignats; this led to a general decline in the prospects for labor, and businessmen added to their prices to compensate for ambiguity about the value of the assignat. Also the markets were now saturated because the initial issue had over-stimulated business. Meanwhile, many wealthy and powerful people were making large profits from speculation, betting on the value of assignats, instead of investing. At this point 1.0 livre was between A 1.06 and A 1.11 [26, 27], but the discount on foreign exchange was closer to 1.0 livre = A 1.30. High tariffs on imports did not affect the state of industry in France; it continued to decline. White explains [28]:

> But what the bigotry of Louis XIV [in revoking the Edict of Nantes] and the shiftlessness of Louis XV could not do in nearly a century, was accomplished by this tampering with the currency in a few months.

Early Jun 1791: The 1,200,000,000 of assignats had been spent by the government: 108,000,000 to pay down the debt, 416,000,000 to pay overdue interest, and 476,000,000 to pay the current expenses [29].

19 Jun 1791: The National Assembly issued 600,000,000 livres in assignats, total = 1,800,000,000 livres [30, 31]. There was virtually no opposition to it in the National Assembly, as France had now adopted a scheme of permanent inflation by paper money; it was widely believed among the government leadership that officially-issued fiat money led automatically to prosperity.

~ Aug 1791: Growth of corruption among the legislators, being influenced and bribed by speculators in the national debt instruments [32] and debtors who had a vested interest in seeing the assignats depreciate. The speculators could sell at a profit in nominal terms, and the debtors could repay in amounts far less than they had borrowed.

3 Sep 1791: The New Constitution was adopted.

30 Sep 1791: The Constituent Assembly was abolished and replaced by the National Legislative Assembly.

~ Oct 1791: The assignat had depreciated about 20%: 1.0 livre ~ A 1.2 [33].

17 Dec 1791: The 800,000,000 assignats issued in Jun 1791 were all spent: 472,000,000 toward the pre-existing debt, and 128,000,000 for administration, but the Constituent Assembly had also run up another 800,000,000 in new debt [34]. The Legislative Assembly issued 300,000,000 in assignats, total = 2,100,000,000 livres.

1 Jan 1792: The assignat had depreciated about 32%: 1.0 livre ~ A 1.32 [35, 36].

1 Feb 1792: 1.0 livre ~ A 1.66 [37].

1 Mar 1792: 1.0 livre ~ A 1.88 [38].

~1 Apr - 1 Sep 1792: The other nations of Europe begin preparations to invade France, to prevent the spread of the Revolution.

20 Apr 1792: France declared war on Prussia and Austria.

30 Apr 1792: The Legislative Assembly issued 300,000,000 in assignats, total = 2,400,000,000 livres [39]. White explains the economic condition of the working people at this point [40]:

> This [the new issue of assignats] was hailed by many as a measure in the interests of the poorer classes of people, but the result was that it injured them most of all. Henceforward, until the end of this history, capital was quietly taken from labor and locked up in all the ways that financial ingenuity could devise. All that saved thousands of laborers in France from starvation was that they were drafted off into the army and sent to be killed on foreign battlefields.

Jun-Aug 1792: There were food riots in Paris; the king and royal family were imprisoned; and the Revolutionary Commune took power.

31 Jul 1792: A finance report from the Assembly stated that 2,400,000,000 assignats had been issued, and that the worth of the national lands exceeded that value. The government then decided to issue another 300,000,000; total = 2,700,000,000 livres [41].

20 Sep 1792: The French were defeated at Valmy.

21 Sep 1792: The National Convention replaced the Legislative Assembly; the monarchy is abolished.

Oct 1792: Beginning of forgeries of the assignats by other nations in Europe, especially, Belgium, Switzerland, and England [42], then exported to France. Some of them were so good that only an expert could tell the real ones from the fake ones.

~ 1 Nov 1792: 1.0 livre ~ A 1.75 [43].

7 Nov 1792: The National Convention recommended that Louis XVI be tried before the Convention for treason.

14 Dec 1792: By this time, 600,000,000 assignats had been destroyed, but 700,000,000 replaced them; total = 2,800,000,000 livres [44].

21 Jan 1793: Louis XVI was executed.

9 Feb 1793: The National Assembly issued a decree that the estates of those who had fled France were to be confiscated [45, 46]. This was used, in the same way as the Church lands, to justify further issues of assignats. New issues of assignats were subsequently made in most months of 1792.

31 Jan 1793: The National Convention issued 200,000,000 assignats; total = 3,000,000,000 livres [47].

28 Feb 1793: Prices had become so high that even people who could find employment could not afford to live. Marat suggested that the problem could be solved by robbing the stores [48, 49]. So, a large number of people in Paris began rioting and looting about 200 shops on 28 Feb 1793. The mob was paid off with a bribe of 7,000,000 francs.

Feb 1793: The Reign of Terror began, led by the Committee on Public Safety. There were riots in Paris over high prices, and many executions, including those who refused to accept the assignats.

11 Apr 1793: The National Convention passed a law prohibiting the purchase of silver or gold under penalty of six years imprisonment [50].

3 May 1793: The Assembly enacted price controls on grains; but the prices set were too low, and the farmers could not afford to sell. So they held back their crops, producing a food shortage [51].

22 Jun 1793: The National Convention passed the Forced Loan decree [52], which amounted to a progressive income tax. It was levied on all married men with incomes above 10,000 francs, and all unmarried men with incomes above 6,000 francs. It was estimated to bring in 1,000,000,000 francs, but only brought in 200,000,000 francs; so later the National Convention extended it down to people with incomes of 1,000 francs. It was fixed at 10% for incomes of 1,000 francs, and at 50% for those with incomes above 9,000 francs.

31 Jul 1793: The National Convention authorized another issue of 2,000,000,000 assignats [53].

1 Aug 1793: Legislation was passed prohibiting trading in coin. Those caught selling silver or gold, or pricing in assignats and specie differently, received six years in prison; for refusing to accept assignats as legal tender, was fined 3,000 francs for a first offense and for a second offense to pay 6,000 francs and be imprisoned for 20 years [54].

10 Aug - 7 Sep 1793: General robbery of the people by the government [55]. On 29 Aug alone, about 3,000 wealthy people's homes were searched and robbed by the Committee of Surveillance (the Revolutionary secret police), and about 2,000 of these were subsequently arrested and executed. The government, led by Robespierre, organized a conspiracy to murder a large number of people who were in prison on political charges; about 15,000 were murdered. 1 livre = 1.66 [56].

8 Sep 1793: The penalties for violating the 1 Aug 1793 currency law were increased to death and confiscation of property. Also, informers were given rewards for turning in violators, thus France became a nation of spies and informers [57].

~15 Sep 1793: 1.0 livre ~ A 3.35 [58].

29 Sep 1793: The National Convention passed the Law of the Maximum, which imposed price controls on all food. The price was calculated as the sum of four components [59]: a) the basic price to be set at 1.33 of its price in 1790; b) an allowance for transportation; c) wholesale profit fixed at 5%; and d) retail profit fixed at 10%. This amounted to less than the cost of production, so naturally they were either evaded, or farmers didn't bother to bring items to markets, which led to severe shortages. The government found it necessary to issue ration papers that would allow people to buy at the official price, if there was any to be had. Farmers could not afford to sell at the official prices, and to relieve the food shortages, the government sent out the military to confiscate entire crops. The law proved to be difficult to enforce. Nonetheless, many businesses were ruined by losses, and the ones that stayed in business charged high prices for risking their lives: the penalty for violating the Law of the Maximum was death. The enforcement mechanism depended on a network of spies. Sometimes violators were let off with the destruction of their homes.

16 Oct 1793: Marie Antoinette was executed; by this time, another 3,000,000,000 assignats had been issued, although only 1,200,000,000 entered into circulation; total = 4,200,000,000 livres [60].

13 Nov 1793: All transactions in silver and gold were prohibited under penalty of death [61].

~15 Dec 1793: 1.0 livre ~ A 2.0 [62]. This temporary increase in value was promoted by optimism due to French victories.

1 Jan 1794: The number of assignats in circulation was 5,536,000,000 livres; the value of lands confiscated from the nobility and the church, held as security for them, was estimated at 15,000,000,000 livres [63].

15 May 1794: The National Convention passed a law specifying the death penalty upon anyone who inquired before a transaction was to be made as to what form of money was to be used [64].

4 Jun 1794: Robespierre was elected a President of the National Convention, and afterwards thousands were executed by the decree of the Revolutionary Tribunal.

28 Jul 1794: Robespierre was executed, which ended the Reign of Terror.

8 Dec 1794: The law that had expelled the nobility and clergy was repealed, and their lands were to be restored [65]. They returned to France in the early part of 1795, hoping to restore a limited monarchy.

23 Dec 1794: The Law of the Maximum was repealed [66].

31 Dec 1794: The total number of assignats in circulation = 7,000,000,000 livres [67].

1 Apr 1795: 1.0 livre = A 9.9 [68].

1 May 1795: Approximately 12,000,000,000 counterfeit assignats were in circulation [69]; 1.0 livre = A 12.4 [70].

31 May 1795: An additional 3,000,000,000 assignats were issued, total = 10,000,000,000 livres [71]; 1.0 livre ~ A 14.2 [73]; see 1 May 1795 for amount of counterfeits.

~ 1 Jun 1795: 1.0 livre ~ A 18.29 to A 20.85 [73, 74].

1 Jul 1795: 1.0 livre = A 33.66 [75].

31 Jul 1795: An additional 4,000,000,000 assignats were issued, total = 14,000,000,000 [76]. Throughout the next 18 months, prices went up at the same rate as the depreciation, but wages remained stagnant. Wages actually had fallen since so many businesses had closed up due to the difficulty of dealing in paper money, and the laws necessary to enforce them. There was now a large labor surplus available to be drafted into the army [77].

1 Aug 1795: 1.0 livre ~ A 33.33 to A 36.8 [78, 79, 80].

15 Aug 1795: The franc was defined as a coin of 5 grams of silver at 90% pure, which is 4.5 grams = 69.44 grains pure silver.

22 Aug 1795: A Constitutional Convention adopted a constitution for a new government, to be run by a body called The Directory. By this time another 21,000,000,000 assignats had been issued; the total is now 35,000,000,000 in circulation [81].

1 Sep 1795: 1.0 livre ~ A 40.0 to A 48.0 [82, 83].

13 Sep 1795: Napoleon massacred the royalists in a street battle in Paris, and took power as dictator [84].

1 Oct 1795: 1.0 livre = A 50.2 [85].

1 Nov 1795: 1.0 livre = A 104.0 to A 107.8 [86, 87].

2 Nov 1795: Beginning of the Directory. The first item of business was to print more assignats. The problem was that the printers could only make 60 to 70 million per day, while the government was spending 80 to 90 million per day [88]. The second item of business was to exact a forced loan from the remaining wealthy citizens; it didn't work, since the assignat was now valued at less than 1/100th of a livre [89].

1 Dec 1795: 1.0 livre = A 122.0 to A 149.0 [90, 91].

1 Feb 1796: 1.0 livre = A 222.4 to A 288.0 [92, 93]. At this point, the assignat was virtually worthless, but most of it was in the hands of the working people. Those who could afford to had previously invested their money in real estate and other objects of tangible lasting value. Von Sybel [94] tells us:

> Commerce had sunk to mere usurious gambling, since everyone had before his eyes the daily fall in the value of the assignats, and thus the consequent rise in the price of wares; even those, therefore, who had no thought of gain, but only wished to avoid loss, bought up as large stores of every kind of goods as they could in any way obtain. As ready money had been rendered very rare by the Emigration, the requisitions, and the unfavorable balance of trade ever since 1789; and as the rate of interest had risen in the wealthiest Departments to 12 per cent and in Paris to 30 percent -- there was virtually no banking

business at all. The dealers in old stores had taken the place of money dealers, and advanced, not ready money, as formerly, upon pledges, but vice versa, exchanged the falling assignats for furniture, clothes, watches, rings, books, and provisions, at, of course, their own usurious prices. It is easy to understand the difficulty under such circumstances of providing for the people, in the midst of scarcity, when every possessor of property was endeavoring to invest his capital in stores of goods, and thereby withdrawing the latter for a long time from circulation. Before the end of the year [1796] the paper money was in the hands of the proletaries [workers], the officials, and the small rentiers [small farmers], whose property was not large enough to invest in stores of goods or national lands.

18 Feb 1796: The assignats were now valued at 1.0 livre = A 600 [95]. They were exchanged for a new paper currency called the mandat, claimed to be "as good as gold", at 30 assignats for one mandat. The plates and paper for printing the assignats were destroyed. White [96] cites 40,000,000,000 in assignats had been in circulation; now exchanged for 1,333,000,000 mandats.

~ Mar 1796: 1 livre = M 2.85 = A 85.5 [97].

~ May 1796: 1 livre ~ M 6.66 = A 199.8 [98].

16 Jul 1796: The Directory issued a decree stating that all the paper money, assignats and mandats, should be accepted at their real value compared to silver or gold, and that trade could commence in whatever currency the parties agreed to [99]. This was the practical end of the legal tender status of both paper issues; the mandats depreciated further to 1 livre = M 50.0 = A 1500.0

~ Aug 1796: 1 livre ~ M 50.0 = A 1,500.0; about 2,500,000,000 mandats were in circulation [100].

14 Feb 1797: The Directory formally decreed that assignats and mandats were no longer legal tender, the plates and paper for printing mandats were to be destroyed as were the assignat machines previously, and that taxes could be temporarily paid to the government in both paper currencies at 100:1 [101].

May 1797: The assignats and mandats still in circulation are both are worthless; the Directory formally proclaimed that the 21,000,000,000 of assignats are of no value and should be discarded [102].

30 Sep 1797: The Directory ordered that two-thirds of the national debt was to be paid in bonds that could be used to buy the confiscated Church lands, and the remaining third was to remain on the books to be paid in some future unknown way. These bonds soon depreciated to 3% of their face value, same as the assignats and mandats had [103]. This was the end of the paper money experiment, and it took forty years to recover from it. Metal money came out of the hoards, and came in from foreign nations in the course of trade as it was required.

1798: Arbitrary government by the Directory, etc.

10 Nov 1799: Napoleon assumed power "to save the Republic". Of course, that is patently false. There was no working "republic" to save; all Napoleon did impose a personal dictatorship to replace the dictatorship run by socialist crusaders that had replaced an irresponsible aristocratic oligarchy. Whereupon France pursued the same moronic policies as Louis XIV had done: useless wars, poverty, and the ruin of France.

So ends the story of the assignats and mandats, paper money supposedly "secured" by the real estate confiscated from the Church. The 'assignats' were doomed at the start. Such a system of "backing" by land, or redemption, was a pure fantasy: if one was in possession of a certain amount of assignats, how exactly would he cash them in for land? The paper notes did not each describe a section of land, nor was any of the land marked out as being assigned to a particular note. There was no practical way for a person to actually obtain the land that supposedly backed the paper, and the entire system was sold to the public with propaganda. It turned out to be a particularly viscous fiction; the assignats depreciated greatly, and the promises of rainbows and unicorns soon turned into the reality of prisons and the guillotine as the government attempted to maintain the value of the assignats by force.

We should not relegate this episode to obscurity as the work of fanatics. It is instructive to us because it indicates what happens when governments get desperate. It is easy to see the tyrannical acts perpetuated under the guise of "liberty, equality, and fraternity" (the slogan of the French Revolution). First was the outright confiscation of the property of the Church that had been accumulated over the previous 1,500 years. It is true that the Church had become corrupt and had deviated from its true mission, but if the Church lands were to be secularized, surely a more equitable method could have been used. Second was the persecution of the old aristocracy and the Church officials simply because they did not agree with the Revolution. But the persecutions did not stop with the nobility; how can it, if the goal is power? The paper assignats were issued as a means to gain public support for the Revolution; the claim that they were issued against and secured by the confiscated Church lands was some combination of fantasy, ignorance, or knowing and deliberate lying. There was no way to redeem them; they were no better than the paper issued by John Law only 70 years earlier. Once the assignats began to fail, the lies and persecutions began: a) wage and price controls that led to shortages; b) false claim that gold and silver were becoming more valuable, when in fact it was the paper that was depreciating; c) collapse of business since the depreciation had destroyed the principle of accurate accounting; d) prohibitions on trading in gold and silver, or even asking what form of money was to be used in a transactions; e) riots out of desperation due to shortages, high prices, and stagnant wages; f) open robbery of the people by the government; g) capital punishment for minor (but necessary) offenses; h) confiscation of property owned even by the poor and middle class; and finally, i) collapse of the system followed by 20 years of starvation and warfare under a new dictator. France has still not fully recovered from this fiasco.

It is worse than that. This entire episode was led by the foremost modern thinkers of their time. Our modern "progressives" have adapted the Jacobin slogan of "liberty, equality, and fraternity" to "liberal, equity, and united"; but make no mistake, they will pursue the same basic tactics. It won't be necessary to break out the guillotine because the progressives will pursue a gentler, kinder brand of tyranny: they will be content with "mandatory re-education" and bankrupting their opponents with legal bills.

The continuing issue of the assignats violated a basic principle of paper money, as pointed out by von Sybel [104]:

> Wherever a great quantity of paper money is suddenly issued, we invariably see a rapid increase of trade. The great quantity of the circulating medium sets in motion all the energies of commerce and manufactures; capital for investment is more easily found than usual, and trade perpetually receives fresh nutriment. If this paper represents real credit, founded upon order and legal security, from which it can derive a firm and lasting value, such a moment may be the starting point of a great and widely extended prosperity; as for instance, the most splendid improvements in English agriculture were undoubtedly owing to the emancipation of the country banks. If, on the contrary, the new paper is of precarious value, as was clearly seen to be the case with the French assignats as early as February 1791, it can have no lastingly beneficial fruits. For the moment, perhaps, business receives an impulse all; the more violent, because everyone endeavors to invest his doubtful paper in buildings, machines and goods— which under all circumstances retain some intrinsic value. Such a movement was witnessed in France in 1791, and from every quarter there came satisfactory reports of the activity of manufactures. The commercial excitement, and, in an equal degree, the commercial danger, were enhanced by one particular circumstance. The exchange with foreign countries had been for some years unfavorable to France. Since the year 1783 the country imported more than it exported; then came Necker's wholesale purchases of corn, and lastly the utter derangement of commercial relations by the Revolution, which every where prostrated the home production, and rendered it necessary to give orders in foreign countries. France had, therefore, to make more payments than it received, and consequently to bear the expenses of those payments, and to lose in the exchange. The loss in the spring of 1791 was from 9 to 11 percent. Here too the assignats exercised an influence; for as, at this period, they stood at 4

> to 6 percent discount, and the foreign merchant had to be paid in silver, the total loss to the French exchange was 15 percent.

Dillaye gave several false reasons as to why the assignats depreciated so quickly (opposition by the clergy and counterfeiting), but he was correct on two points, first, the excessive amount, and secondly [105]:

> Want of title to the land dedicated as security for the redemption of the assignat; it having been confiscated from clergy and nobility, without any forms of law, by a government purely revolutionary, and before that government had acquired any single element of that stability and permanence essential to sovereignty.

Or, to put it simply, illegitimate is as illegitimate does, which is the collectivist way.

References

[1] Andrew Dickson White, *Fiat Money Inflation in France*, NY: Irvington-on-Hudson, The Foundation for Economic Education, 1959. It was originally given as lectures to members of Congress on 12 Apr 1876, and later revised by the author and published in 1912.
[2] Stephen D. Dillaye, *Assignats and Mandats: A True History*, Philadelphia, Henry Carey Baird & Co., 1877
[3] Heinrich von Sybel, *History of the French Revolution*, London: John Murray, 1867
[4] op. cit., von Sybel, Vol. 1, p. 47
[5] op. cit., von Sybel, Vol. 1, pp. 142-145; he also states in Vol. 1, pp. 510, 511 that sales of the Church lands had brought in 1,800,000,000 livres as of Feb 1792 (but recall that the assignat was depreciated to 1.6 at this time), and the value of the remaining part was less than 350,000,000. The 2,000,000,000 livre valuation is given by op. cit., White, p. 28.
[6] op. cit., von Sybel, Vol. 1, pp. 43-45, 255-257
[7] op. cit., von Sybel, Vol. 1, pp. 141-146
[8] op. cit., Dillaye, p. 10
[9] op. cit., Dillaye, p. 14
[10] op. cit., von Sybel, Vol. 1, pp. 87-95
[11] op. cit., von Sybel, Vol. 1, p. 144
[12] op. cit., von Sybel, Vol. 1, p. 167
[13] op. cit., White, p. 28
[14] op. cit., von Sybel, Vol. 1, pp. 146, 147, 169
[15] op. cit., White, p. 28. See also op. cit., von Sybel, Vol. 1, pp. 146, 147
[16] op. cit., Dillaye, pp. 15, 16
[17] op. cit., von Sybel, Vol. 1, p. 167
[18] op. cit., White, pp. 31, 32
[19] op. cit., von Sybel, Vol. 1, p. 252
[20] op. cit., White, pp. 37-40
[21] op. cit., White, p. 43; quoting an appendix in Thiers' *History of the French Revolution*
[22] op. cit., White, pp. 46, 47, 113
[23] op. cit., White, pp. 49, 50
[24] op. cit., Dillaye, p. 20
[25] op. cit., White, p. 56
[26] op. cit., von Sybel, Vol. 1, pp. 281, 282
[27] op. cit., White, pp. 55-62
[28] op. cit., White, p. 55
[29] op. cit., von Sybel, Vol. 1, p. 264
[30] op. cit., von Sybel, Vol. 1, pp. 265, 266; see also op. cit., Dillaye, p. 19
[31] op. cit., White, p. 113

[32] op. cit., Dillaye, p. 35
[33] op. cit., White, p. 66
[34] op. cit., von Sybel, Vol. 1, p. 393
[35] op. cit., White, pp. 68, 69; see also op. cit., von Sybel, Vol. 1, pp. 510, 511
[36] op. cit., von Sybel, Vol. 1, pp. 510, 511
[37] op. cit., White, p. 68
[38] op. cit., White, p. 68
[39] op. cit., White, p. 114
[40] op. cit., White, p. 68
[41] op. cit., White, 68, 69
[42] op. cit., Dillaye, pp. 32, 33
[43] op. cit., White, p. 71
[44] op. cit., White, pp. 69, 114
[45] op. cit., von Sybel, Vol. 1, pp. 417, 418
[46] op. cit., White, p. 69
[47] op. cit., White, p. 114
[48] op. cit., White, pp. 72, 73
[49] op. cit., von Sybel, Vol. 1, pp. 418-421
[50] Francis A. Walker, *Money*, NY: Henry Holt and Company, 1891, p. 344
[51] op. cit., White, pp. 75, 76, 114
[52] op. cit., White, pp. 73, 74
[53] op. cit., White, p. 75
[54] op. cit., White, pp. 78, 79, 114
[55] op. cit., von Sybel, Vol. 2, pp. 47-91
[56] op. cit., von Sybel, Vol. 2, p. 89
[57] op. cit., White, p. 79
[58] op. cit., White, p. 71
[59] op. cit., White, pp. 76-79
[60] op. cit., White, pp. 83, 84, 115
[61] op. cit., White, p. 79
[62] op. cit., White, p. 71
[63] op. cit., Dillaye, p. 29
[64] op. cit., White, p. 79
[65] op. cit., Dillaye, pp. 38, 39
[66] op. cit., Dillaye, pp. 38, 39
[67] op. cit., White, p. 115
[68] op. cit., Walker, p. 345, quoting M. Bresson's *History Financiere de la France*, Vol. 2, p. 225
[69] op. cit., Dillaye, p. 69
[70] op. cit., Walker, p. 345
[71] op. cit., White, p. 87
[72] op. cit., von Sybel, Vol. 4, p. 330
[73] op. cit., von Sybel, Vol. 4, p. 333
[74] op. cit., Walker, p. 345
[75] op. cit., Walker, p. 345
[76] op. cit., White, p. 115
[77] op. cit., White, p. 89
[78] op. cit., von Sybel, Vol. 4, p. 336
[79] op. cit., Walker, p. 345
[80] op. cit., White, p. 88
[81] op. cit., White, p. 115
[82] op. cit., White, p. 88

[83] op. cit., Walker, p. 345
[84] op. cit., Dillaye, pp. 41-43
[85] op. cit., Walker, p. 345
[86] op. cit., White, p. 88
[87] op. cit., Walker, p. 345
[88] op. cit., White, pp. 91, 92
[89] op. cit., White, pp. 95, 96
[90] op. cit., White, p. 88
[91] op. cit., Walker, p. 345
[92] op. cit., White, p. 88, 89
[93] op. cit., Walker, p. 345
[94] op. cit., von Sybel, Vol. 4, pp. 334, 335
[95] op. cit., White, p. 93
[96] op. cit., White, pp. 92, 93, 116
[97] op. cit., White, p. 96
[98] op. cit., White, p. 96
[99] op. cit., White, pp. 98, 99, 104
[100] op. cit., White, p. 116
[101] op. cit., White, p. 99
[102] op. cit., White, p. 99
[103] op. cit., White, p. 99
[104] op. cit., von Sybel, Vol. 1, pp. 281, 282
[105] op. cit., Dillaye, p. 43

Facts Concerning the National Debt

Note: This essay was originally published 26 Jun 2011; it has been updated to 2022, using revised official data (as of 26 Mar 2023) from the federal government as indicated.

There is a great deal of talk these days about the large national debt and the large annual deficits that have created the debt over many years. I thought this would be an opportune time to summarize the simple historical facts about the debt, so you will not be led astray by claims made by advocates for various budget and tax policies being floated in Washington. There are some who continue to claim, contrary to facts, that there was a $5 trillion surplus at the end of the Clinton administration. The fact is that the total national debt at the end of the Clinton administration (FY 2000) was about $5.7 trillion (debt, not surplus); the total debt increased about $1.4 trillion in those eight years.

Figures 1 and 2 illustrate the same data. They are based on official numbers from the Department of the Treasury [1] and revised numbers from the Bureau of Economic Analysis at the Department of Commerce [2]. They show the growth of the national debt from 1929 to the fiscal year ending on 30 Sep 2022, the gross domestic product (GDP) (a measure of the total value of goods and services produced in the nation), and the debt-to-GDP ratio. The GDP data applies to calendar years but the national debt figures are for fiscal years; the two are not time-aligned, but are close enough for a general assessment. Keep in mind however, that the growth of the GDP in the late 1940's, early 1970's to early 1980's, and in 2021 and 2022 are largely a result of high monetary inflation.

FY (ending)	National Debt ($B)	U. S. GDP ($B)	Debt/GDP	FY (ending)	National Debt ($B)	U. S. GDP ($B)	Debt/GDP	FY (ending)	National Debt ($B)	U. S. GDP ($B)	Debt/GDP
1929	16.9	104.6	0.16	1961	288.9	562.2	0.51	1992	4,177.0	6,342.0	0.66
1930	16.1	92.2	0.17	1962	298.2	603.9	0.49	1993	4,535.7	6,667.0	0.68
1931	16.8	77.4	0.22	1963	305.8	637.5	0.48	1994	4,800.2	7,085.0	0.68
1932	19.4	59.5	0.33	1964	311.7	684.5	0.46	1995	4,988.7	7,414.0	0.67
1933	22.5	57.2	0.39	1965	317.2	742.3	0.43	1996	5,323.2	7,838.0	0.68
1934	27.0	66.8	0.40	1966	329.3	813.4	0.40	1997	5,502.4	8,332.0	0.66
1935	28.7	74.2	0.39	1967	344.7	860.0	0.40	1998	5,614.2	8,793.0	0.64
1936	33.7	84.8	0.40	1968	358.0	940.7	0.38	1999	5,776.1	9,353.0	0.62
1937	36.4	93.0	0.39	1969	368.2	1,017.6	0.36	2000	5,662.2	9,951.0	0.57
1938	37.1	87.4	0.42	1970	389.2	1,073.3	0.36	2001	5,943.4	10,286.0	0.58
1939	40.4	93.4	0.43	1971	424.1	1,164.9	0.36	2002	6,405.7	10,642.0	0.60
1940	42.9	102.9	0.42	1972	448.5	1,279.1	0.35	2003	6,998.0	11,142.0	0.63
1941	48.9	129.3	0.38	1973	469.1	1,425.4	0.33	2004	7,596.1	11,867.0	0.64
1942	72.4	166.0	0.44	1974	492.7	1,545.2	0.32	2005	8,170.4	12,638.0	0.65
1943	136.6	203.1	0.67	1975	576.6	1,684.9	0.34	2006	8,680.2	13,398.0	0.65
1944	201.0	224.4	0.90	1976	653.5	1,873.4	0.35	2007	9,229.2	14,061.0	0.66
1945	258.6	228.0	1.13	1977	718.9	2,081.8	0.35	2008	10,699.8	14,369.0	0.74
1946	269.4	227.5	1.18	1978	789.2	2,351.6	0.34	2009	12,311.3	14,119.0	0.87
1947	258.2	249.6	1.03	1979	845.1	2,627.3	0.32	2010	14,025.2	14,964.0	0.94
1948	252.2	274.5	0.92	1980	930.2	2,857.3	0.33	2011	15,222.9	15,518.0	0.98
1949	252.7	272.5	0.93	1981	1,028.7	3,207.0	0.32	2012	16,432.7	16,155.0	1.02
1950	257.3	299.8	0.86	1982	1,197.1	3,343.8	0.36	2013	17,156.1	16,692.0	1.03
1951	255.2	346.9	0.74	1983	1,410.7	3,634.0	0.39	2014	18,141.4	17,393.0	1.04
1952	259.1	367.3	0.71	1984	1,663.0	4,037.6	0.41	2015	18,922.2	18,036.0	1.05
1953	266.0	389.2	0.68	1985	1,945.9	4,339.0	0.45	2016	19,976.8	18,569.0	1.08
1954	271.2	390.5	0.69	1986	2,214.8	4,579.6	0.48	2017	20,492.7	19,477.3	1.05
1955	274.3	425.5	0.64	1987	2,431.7	4,855.2	0.50	2018	21,974.1	20,533.1	1.07
1956	272.7	449.4	0.61	1988	2,684.4	5,236.4	0.51	2019	23,201.4	21,381.0	1.09
1957	270.5	474.0	0.57	1989	2,953.0	5,641.6	0.52	2020	27,747.8	21,060.5	1.32
1958	276.3	481.2	0.57	1990	3,364.8	5,963.1	0.56	2021	29,617.2	23,315.1	1.27
1959	284.7	521.7	0.55	1991	3,801.7	6,158.1	0.62	2022	31,419.7	25,464.5	1.23
1960	286.3	542.4	0.53								

Figure 1: U. S. National Debt, GDP, and Debt/GDP Ratio 1929-2022 [1, 2]

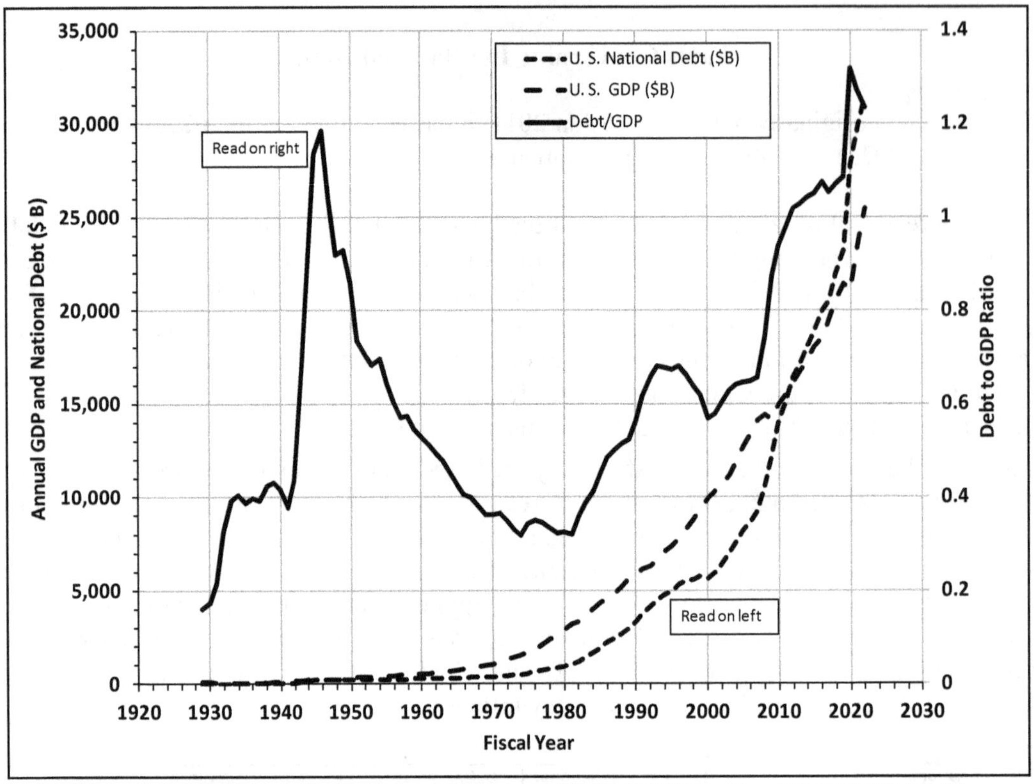

Figure 2: U. S. National Debt, GDP, and Debt/GDP Ratio, 1929-2022 [1, 2]

It is easy to see that debt/GDP ratio was very high during World War II, and has now returned to slightly above that level (which is an indicator of a serious financial problem). It also shows that debt has grown faster than GDP in the past decade or so (especially during the Wuhan virus of 2020), even though monetary inflation tends to artificially improve the GDP.

References

[1] https://fred.stlouisfed.org/series/GFDEBTN/

[2] U. S. Bureau of Economic Analysis, Table 1.1.5 Gross Domestic Product; (NIPA Tables) https://apps.bea.gov/iTable

The Financial Status of Social Security

This essay addresses the financial status of the "Social Security Trust Fund", originally published 15 May 2014 and updated here to Dec 2022. The Social Security Trust Fund is a short name for the "Federal Old Age and Survivors Trust Fund" (42 U. S. C. Sec. 401). The Social Security program was sold to the public in 1935 as an insurance program by which contributions made during one's working lifetime would be used pay benefits in retirement. The goal was to reduce poverty among the elderly, estimated at around 50% in the 1930's. Payments into the system are accomplished by direct withholding of a fixed percentage of income. Initially some occupations were exempt from Social Security taxes (known as FICA taxes) but now nearly all workers are required to contribute to it.

1 Revenues and Expenditures 1937 - 2022

Figures 1-1 and 1-2 show the revenues collected by withholding against the expenditures made by the Social Security Administration (SSA) between 1937 and 1977 (Figure 1-1) an 1977 and 2022 (Figure 1-2) per the SSA website [1-1]. Nearly all the expenditures are in the form of payments to beneficiaries; the cost of administering the system has decreased steadily over time: in 1957, it was about 2.2% of expenditures, by 2013, was down to 0.74% of expenditures. Note that the solid line in Figure 1-1 (revenues) tracks closely with the dashed line (expenditures); and that the system was mostly in balance throughout this initial forty-year period. For years in which the revenues exceeded expenditures (indicated by the thin dashed line), the excess was carried over into an account called the "Social Security Trust Fund". By law, these assets cannot be invested in marketable securities; they are restricted only to instruments backed directly by the "full faith and credit of the United States"; i.e., Treasury bonds.

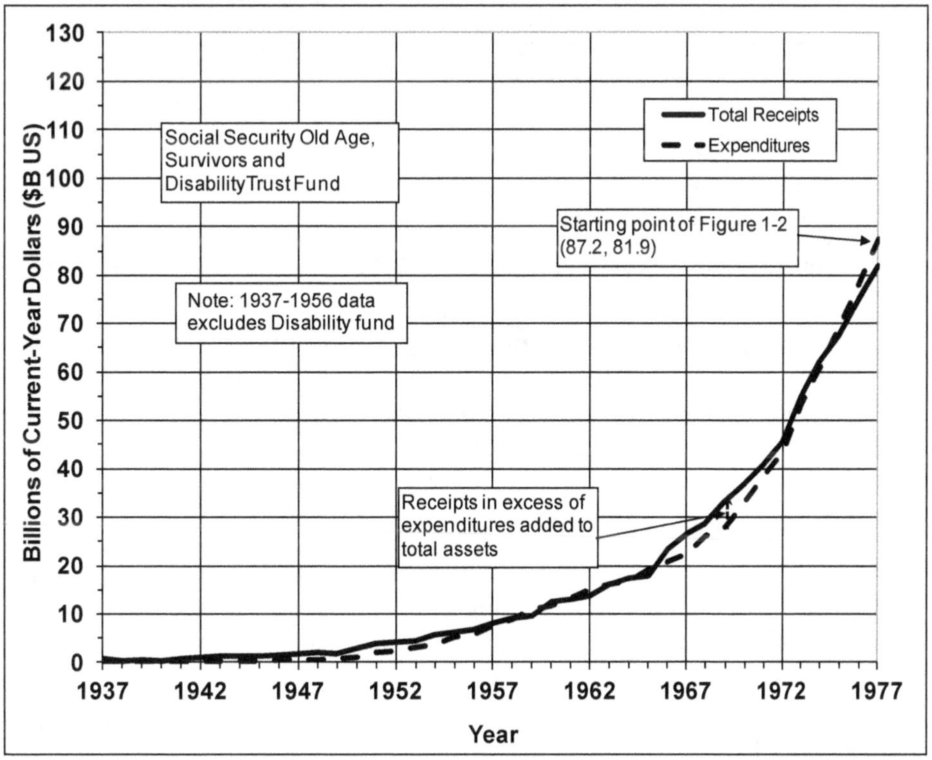

Figure 1-1: Social Security Revenues and Expenditures, 1937-1977

Figure 1-2 shows exactly the same data, but for the years 1977 to 2022 from the same dataset [1-1]. Because of the enormous increase in the FICA tax rates, the growth of population, the number of workers included in the system, and the general depreciation of the currency, it is necessary to show the Y-axis of this chart in units ten times that shown in Figure 1-1. The end point of Figure 1-1 and starting point of Figure 1-2 are the same dollar value as shown by the respective notes. Starting in 1985, due to the "Social Security Amendments of 1983" [1-2], much more revenue was collected than was necessary to pay benefits, as shown by the large divergence between the two lines. The thin dashed line shows an example of the growth from year to year of the assets in the Trust Fund. The idea of the reform bill was that large surpluses would be built up during the years when the "Baby Boom" generation was working, such that adequate assets would exist when that large generation began retirement in about 2011. Again, the excess of revenue over current expenses were invested in Treasury notes and added to the assets in the Trust Fund.

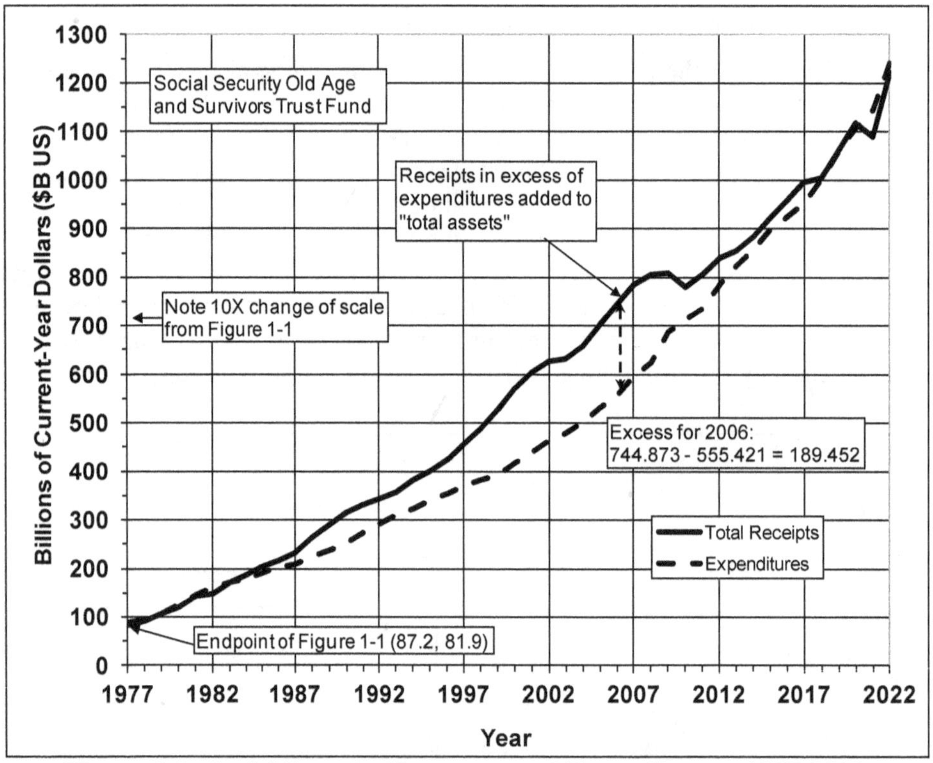

Figure 1-2: Social Security Revenues and Expenditures, 1977-2022

Figure 1-2 shows an example for the year 2006: the excess of revenues over expenditures was $189.452 B. This amount was added to the assets of the overall Trust Fund.

2 Growth of the Trust Fund 1937 - 2022

It is difficult to see from Figures 1-1 and 1-2 the actual growth of assets in the Trust Fund. Again, based on data from the SSA website [1-1, 1-2], Figures 2-1 and 2-2 indicate the financial status of the Trust Fund for the intervals 1937 to 1977 and 1977 to 2022 respectively.

Figure 2-1 shows that the total accumulated assets of the Trust Fund came to $32.49 B in 1977. The total accumulated assets in 1977 were fairly small since the program revenues and expenses were closely aligned between 1937 and 1977.

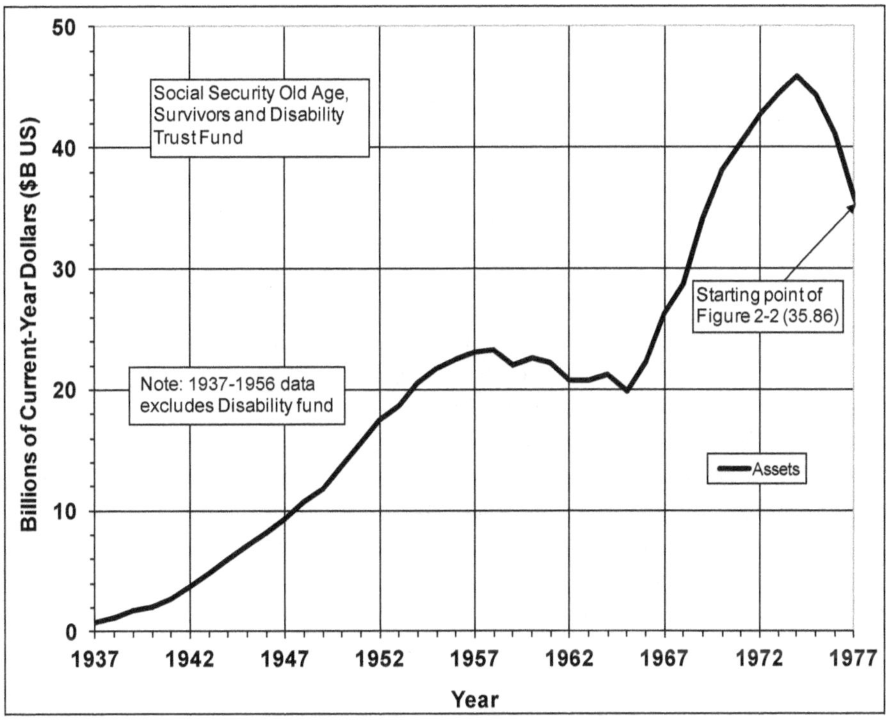

Figure 2-1: Social Security Trust Fund Assets, 1937 - 1977

Figure 2-2 shows the same data as Figure 2-1 but for 1977 to 2022; notice that the Y-axis is now 100X that of Figure 2-1 for the same reasons as stated before. Recalling the example from Figure 1-2 for the year 2006, it is seen that the growth of the Trust Fund was the same $189.452 billion. By 2022, the total accumulated Trust Fund amounted to $2.829 trillion (a trillion is a thousand billion).

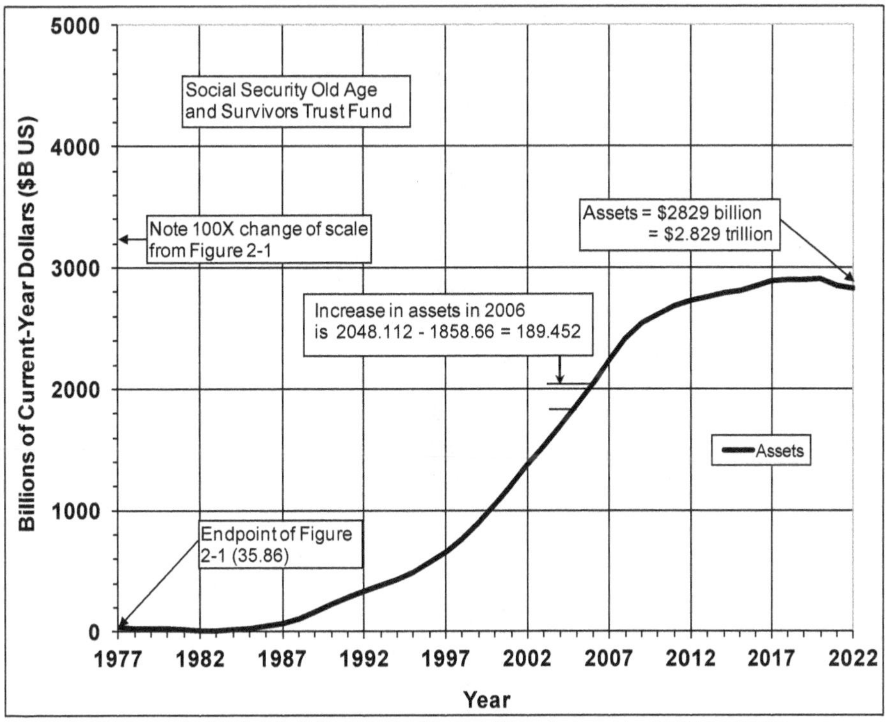

Figure 2-2: Social Security Trust Fund Assets, 1977 - 2022

3 The True Nature of the Trust Fund

Social Security Old Age Insurance does not function like real insurance. There is no contract between the worker and the SSA which legally obligates the SSA to actually pay benefits, as would be the case in a traditional annuity. Likewise, the Social Security Trust Fund is not a trust fund in the usual sense: it contains no actual assets to be distributed to the claimants. The reason is simple: although the "Trust Fund" holds "assets" in the form of Treasury notes, they can only be used to pay claimants if the SSA takes them to the Treasury Department and demands payment. Since the federal government is the payer in general, and Treasury notes are its debt, the notes in the SSA "Trust Fund" are actually liabilities, not assets. They are "assets" to the SSA, but not to the actual payer; hence the Social Security "Trust Fund" is nothing more than an accounting fiction. When current-year revenues exceed current-year expenditures (which occurred in 2021 as seen on Figure 1-2), the SSA must demand redemption of the Treasury notes from the Treasury Department. The Treasury Department, having no assets of its own, will have no choice but to go to Congress. Congress can then do any or all of these options: a) cut benefits to match the current revenues; b) raise taxes to make up for the shortfall; c) order the Treasury to create and sell more bonds and use that money to pay SSA who can then pay the claimants; or d) order the Federal Reserve to print the amount of currency necessary based on its procurement of Treasury bonds, credit it to the SSA so that the SSA can pay the claimants. Option a) cannot happen because Congress would have to explain why benefits are being cut with such a large pool of "assets" with which to pay them. Option b) is the honest choice, and for that reason alone is out of reach for the ruling elite. Option c) will increase the national debt, and option d) will increase monetary inflation.

So what is the true nature of the "Trust Fund"? It is a record of the largest theft-by-diversion in the history of mankind. Those payroll taxes were paid by the workers under the false notion that the revenue would be used to secure future Social Security benefits. No such thing happened: Congress spent all the excess revenue on other general budget items, and simply gave the SSA IOUs in the form of Treasury notes, falsely calling it a "Trust Fund". The Office of Management and Budget notes [3-1]:

> These [Trust Fund] balances are available to finance future benefit payments and other Trust Fund expenditures – but only in a bookkeeping sense. These funds are not set up to be pension funds, like the funds of private pension plans. They do not consist of real economic assets that can be drawn down in the future to fund benefits. Instead, they are claims on the Treasury that, when redeemed, will have to be financed by raising taxes, borrowing from the public, or reducing benefits or other expenditures. The existence of large Trust Fund balances, therefore, does not, by itself, have any impact on the Government's ability to pay benefits.

Pay careful attention to that last sentence: it is an artful way of explaining that the SSA's ability to pay Social Security benefits is independent of the size of the "Trust Fund" because the "Trust Fund" does not contain any real marketable assets, as would be the case in a true pension fund.

4 The True Purpose of 1983 Amendments

The true purpose of the 1983 Amendments is now clear. President Ronald Reagan, who had served eight years as Governor of California, and had been educated as an economist, knew or should have known that Congress cannot resist spending more than it receives. He also knew or should have known that even an honest government cannot save money the way people do: what could the SSA have done with the excess revenue -- pile up mountains of cash in the basement of some office building? There is nothing else a government can do except spend it, which is why governments must always be restricted to collecting the revenue they need for the current year, and nothing more. The true purpose of the 1983 Amendments was to establish a means of raising extra revenue for Congress to spend without having to raise income or any other federal taxes. They could and did falsely claim that the revenue was to be used to make Social Security more secure. They then spent the money on other things, leaving Social Security in exactly the same place financially as it was before.

Figure 2-2 showed that the "assets" in the Trust Fund in 1999 amounted to $896 billion. We need look no further for proof of a diversion than the statement in President Bill "Perjurer-in-Chief" Clinton's 2000 Budget proposal [4-1]:

> In his State of the Union address, the President unveiled his proposal to save Social Security by using some of the projected budget surplus to strengthen the system and by investing a portion of the surplus in equities to raise the rate of return. These actions will substantially improve the program's fiscal position, strengthening it until mid-century. It will require tough choices and a bipartisan approach to fix Social Security and to reach the President's overall goal of saving the Trust Fund at least until 2075. During this year, the President will work with Congress to restore the system to fiscal health, and to address his other priorities including protections for the elderly at high risk of poverty.
>
> **Devote 62 percent of the budget surplus for the next 15 years to Social Security**: The Administration proposes to set aside 62 percent of the projected unified budget surplus of the next 15 years for Social Security. This amounts to more than $2.7 trillion in additional resources available to meet Social Security benefit obligations.

There never was a budget surplus. There was never going to be a budget surplus. The plan and result was to spend everything and lull the working taxpayers into a false sense of security by maintaining the illusion of a Trust Fund.

5 Why Social Security is Not a Ponzi Scheme

Some analysts and economists have claimed that the Social Security system is nothing more than a Ponzi scheme. I believe I can show that there are enough differences between the two to demonstrate that this claim is incorrect.

Let's begin by reviewing what Ponzi scheme is. It was named for Carlo Ponzi, a Boston businessman who talked people into investing in a plan to earn a profit through arbitrage of international reply coupons (IRC). An IRC is an international agreement by which nations agree to deliver mail from other nations within their postal system. Ponzi's plan was to take advantage of the difference in postal rates among the various nations participating in the IRC treaty. His plan fell through with great losses because the overhead on each transaction was too high. Ponzi's plan started as a legitimate enterprise, but he turned it into a fraud when he started realizing losses. He then diverted money provided by new investors by using it to pay off the original investors, and of course he took a cut for himself. In honor of Mr. Ponzi, any investment plan in which early investors are paid off with funds provided by new investors instead of profits is now called a Ponzi scheme. Instead of earning money by wise investing, the fund managers camouflage their losses by sending out false financial statements. When necessary, they make payments to the original investors by robbing the newer investors. This continues until the management runs out of new investors, or the operators steal everything they can. Normally, Ponzi schemes attract investors by claiming to have invented some secret stock market advantage, or by claiming to have discovered some hidden trading tactic that is always profitable. With that background in mind, here are five reasons why Social Security is not a Ponzi scheme.

1. "Investing" in a Ponzi scheme is voluntary, "investing" in Social Security is not. If you are working, whether for wages or in business for yourself, you are inducted into the system except for some very narrow exceptions (usually involving employment by a religious institution).

2. A Ponzi scheme, although fraudulent, is ultimately subject to Securities regulation, thus incurring a legal obligation to conduct the business honestly (although they have no intention of doing so). Social Security is not subject to any Securities regulation; the Social Security Administration is under no legal obligation to pay benefits: it operates solely on the whim of Congress. The whole thing could be abolished tomorrow if Congress chose to do so.

3. Because a Ponzi scheme is set up to be nominally subject to regulation, an investor can demand to get his money back at any time. However, no one can get their Social Security "investment" back until they meet age or disability requirements set by Congress.

4. A Ponzi scheme is based on attracting a small number of wealthy people to invest in it; thus it robs the rich when it fails. Social Security is based on forcing a large number of poor and middle class people to participate; thus it will rob the poor and middle class when it fails.

5. Ponzi scheme managers send out false financial statements to give the illusion that it is solvent in the short run. The Social Security Administration publishes honest financial statements that prove that it is insolvent in the long run.

6 History of How Social Security Has Been Funded

Having reviewed the false and hypocritical notion of a viable Social Security Trust Fund, we turn now to a historical review of how the program has been funded since it was established in 1935. It is not administered, as has been shown, as a traditional Ponzi scheme. The Social Security system has always been funded as a regressive payroll tax. That is, it is financed entirely by a straight percentage of income, no deductions, no exclusions, and no exemptions. It is regressive in the sense that the poor and the middle class pay the same fraction of their income, meaning that the burden upon the poor is greater in relative terms than the burden on the middle class. A tax rate of say 5% represents a different number of dollars per paycheck to the poor and the middle class. Suppose a working poor person earns $20,000 per year (about $385 per week), and a middle class person earns $50,000 per year (about $960 per week). If the tax rate on both is 5%, the poor person pays about $20.00 per week in Social Security taxes, whereas the middle class person pays about $48.00. So, the middle class person pays a lot more; but, the $20.00 paid by the poor is more important to him insofar as providing necessities for his family than the $48.00 paid by the middle class person. Thus the economists say that this type of tax is regressive upon the poor.

Figure 6-1 provides a historical view of the tax rates and maximum income to which the tax applied, in then-year dollars [6-1, 6-2]. The various dashed lines (tax rates) are read on the left, the solid line (income) on the right. The tax rates are broken out into two sections: Old Age Survivors (OAS), which is for retirement benefits, and Disability Insurance (DI). The DI tax and benefit was not created until 1956.

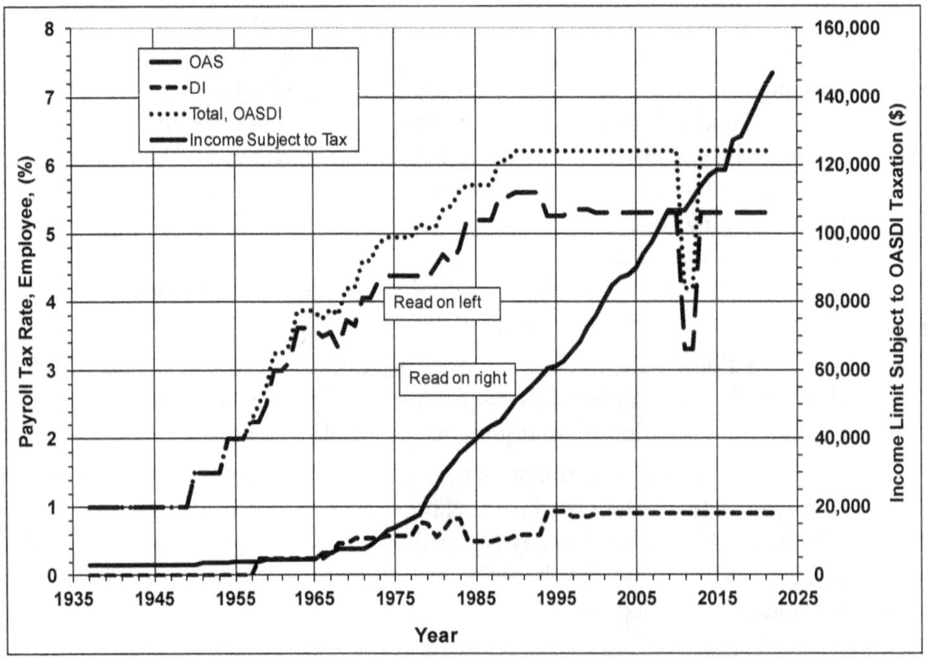

Figure 6-1: Tax Rates and Income Subject to Social Security Taxation, 1937-2022

There is one important point to make about the left scale of Figure 6-1: this scale is labeled "Tax Rate, Employees". But an equal tax rate is additionally paid by the employers. That means the total tax rate on incomes is double the tax rates shown on the left scale. In 2014, the total tax rate for OASDI is 12.4%. There is nothing on Figure 6-1 that should be surprising to even the casual observer. You can see the typical progression of tax rates as well as the increasing maximum income level to which Social Security taxes are levied. The increase in the tax rate is due to the general expansion of the program; first to help the elderly poor, then to help the elderly middle class, and now as a general middle-class generic benefit. It is always the same with government programs: the goal is to expand it until everyone believes they are benefiting from it. Then it becomes politically impossible to curtail it, as people will believe they are being short-changed if the program is reduced.

But there is another tangible benefit to the government from programs like Social Security: if everyone depends on it during their retirement, the government controls their lives. People tend to do what the government tells them if their income depends on the government. You can see a dip in the tax rates for 2011 and 2012. This was done as a temporary measure to put more money in people's pockets, in hope that it would help the economy come out of the 2008 recession. It didn't work, as evidenced by the fact the nation was still in a recession in 2014.

Note that I have omitted thus far any discussion about what is paid by the wealthy. That is because Social Security was envisioned as a program for the poor, then it became a program for the middle class. Therefore, since the poor and the middle class are the main beneficiaries, it was thought prudent (probably correctly), that taxes should be levied only on incomes up through the upper middle class levels; incomes above a certain amount are exempt because the maximum benefit paid corresponds only to incomes up to the middle class levels. So, there has never been a Social Security tax that was levied on all income. Besides, the wealthy have the means and contacts to make sure their tax burden is reduced to the maximum extent politically possible. Normally that comes in the form of special deductions and allowances, but in the case of a payroll tax, it comes in the form of a limit on the income subject to the tax.

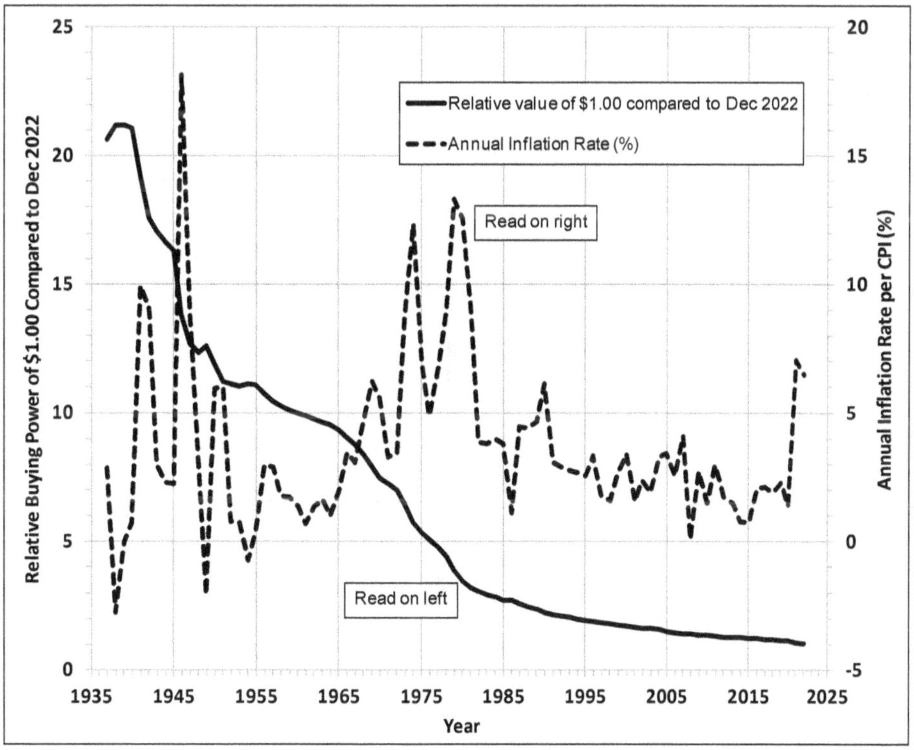

Figure 6-2: Relative Buying Power of $1.00 and Annual Inflation Since 1937

Some have exaggerated the growth in the income subject to taxation, claiming that the tax was miniscule compared to modern times. But in fact the growth in the level of income subject to taxation is an artifact of the high inflation rates we have had since the Federal Reserve gained power. In 1937, (the first year of taxation), the maximum amount subject to taxation was only \$3,000; but keep in mind that \$3,000 then went a lot further than the same amount now. In order to see a more accurate picture of the growth in taxable income levels, it is necessary to account for the effect of inflation. That can be done by normalizing the income levels to given year as a baseline by adjusting per the annual inflation rate. We chose to do so by normalizing the buying power of \$1.00 to the value of a 2022 dollar, as shown on Figure 6-2, by applying the cumulative inflation rates for each year [6-3]. It is easy to identify the periods of high inflation (1941-1948, 1968-1982, 2021, and 2022) and low inflation (1952 - 1967, 1982-1987, and 1991-2020). For example, one dollar in 1988 had the same buying power as \$2.46 in 2022; a dollar in 1949 would buy what \$12.57 would buy in 2022; and a dollar in 1939 would buy what \$21.22 would buy in 2022.

The next step is to compare the actual median income levels with the amounts subject to taxation [6-4]. Wage data is available only back to 1967, and is shown on Figure 6-3. The dashed curve shows again the amount of income that is subject to Social Security taxation; the solid curve is the median household income. It is easy to see that the levels subject to taxation were once approximately correlated with median income (assuming the trend from the 1930's was about the same as in the early 1960's), but is now in excess of twice the median income. Taxes have been going up steadily since the mid-1970's, measured in both the tax rate and the amount of income subject to the tax. No surprises there. Next we will consider the return obtained in the form of benefits for each generation of workers.

There is a third important point about the tax rates shown back on Figure 6-1. Financial advisors routinely explain that it is necessary for a worker to save and invest about 15% of his income throughout his working years, in order to have enough for retirement. Recalling that the true tax rate is double what is shown on the left of Figure 6-1, it is easy to see that many people are already paying 12.4% into Social Security. But how many believe they can retire on Social Security benefits alone?

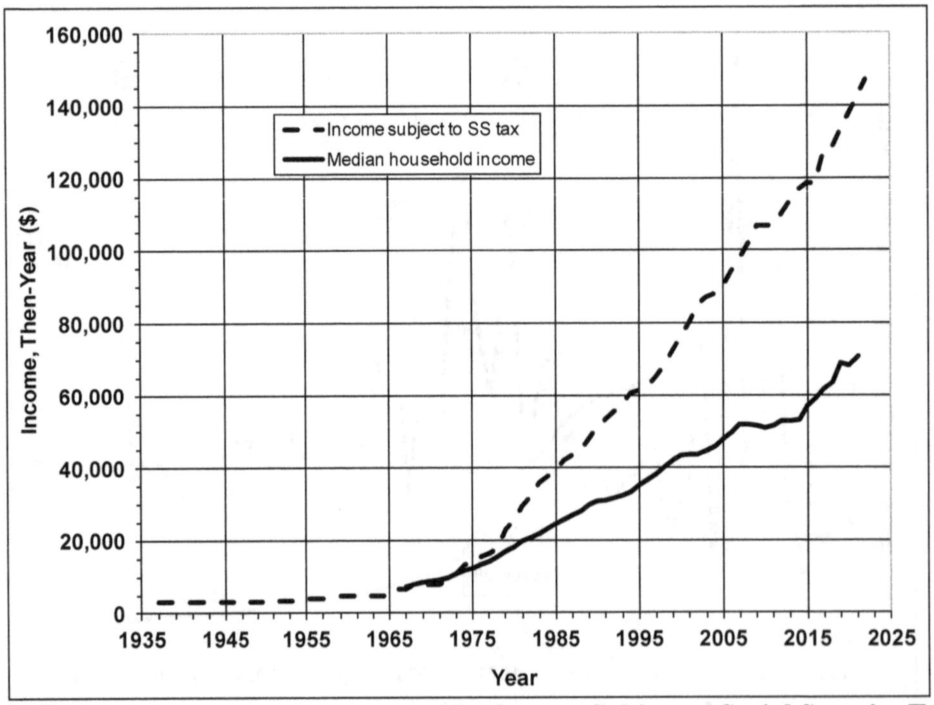

Figure 6-3: Comparison of Median Income and Income Subject to Social Security Taxation

7 The True Rate of Return on Social Security Contributions

We have seen that the total tax rate for OASD (12.4%, divided equally between employer and worker) approximates the savings rate for retirement as recommended by most financial planners (15%). It is important to evaluate which method of retirement financing offers the greatest benefit to the worker. To do so, it is necessary to evaluate the return on investment for Social Security vs. other retirement methods, such as 401(k) and Individual Retirement Accounts (IRA). Is the average worker better off paying into and collecting from Social Security, or would he be better off to invest and save on his own?

Fortunately, the Social Security Administration has conducted a study by Clingman et al [7-1] that answers the question for the Social Security system. In their analysis, the SSA calculated the real rates of return for Social Security benefits as a function of income level and year of birth, assuming a worker retired at the nominal retirement age. It included a range of income levels from very low income to very high income, which is important because the benefits paid out are higher relative to income for low-income workers. The real rate of return is the interest rate necessary upon the taxes paid in order to finance the Social Security benefits received; i.e., it is the average annual rate of return necessary to finance the typical benefit received. The main assumptions underlying the calculations, all reasonable, are:

a. Includes the amount of payroll taxes paid from start of work to retirement

b. Workers enter the workforce at age 21 and retire at 65, and receive benefits according to their life expectancy

c. Workers are assumed to earn at some fixed percentage of the average wage index for their entire careers (Median = 100%, Low = 25%; Very Low = 25%)

d. For married couples, assumes there is neither death nor divorce prior to receiving benefits

e. Families are assumed to include two children

f. Takes into account the longer life spans (and hence increased time of benefit payment) of women

Figure 7-1 shows the results of the SSA study for median income earners. On the left side is the rate of return under the present benefit schedule. However, that is somewhat misleading, since the SSA program will begin to pay out more in benefits than it collects in revenue beginning in 2021. The right side shows the rate of return if current tax rates remain unaltered, and the SSA system is forced to cut benefits in order to remain solvent. But, it also assumes that the fictional "Trust Fund" is repaid such that the real reduction in benefits does not begin until 2033. Therefore, the right side values are somewhat optimistic, since there is no evidence that the $2.829 trillion in "Trust Fund" "assets" that were "borrowed" ("stolen and spent") by Congress will actually be repaid out of general revenues over the long term, given the budget pressures that future Congresses will face.

There are several important features of the curves on Figure 7-1. First, the people who contributed the earliest, and began collecting benefits the earliest, have the highest rate of return. Although not shown here, workers with low and very low income levels have higher rates of return (Very Low is about 50% higher; Low is about 20% higher). The optimistic chart on the left shows the rates of return leveling out beginning with those born around 1960; the right charts shows the rates of return steadily decreasing. This behavior is due to two factors. First, the early participants paid a much lower tax rate and received relatively higher benefits, affordable at that time because the ratio of workers paying taxes to those collecting benefits was large. The second reason is that those born later spend most of their working lives paying high Social Security tax rates; the rate of return would be even lower if not for the fact that life spans have increased in the past several decades, and consequently benefits are paid over a longer period.

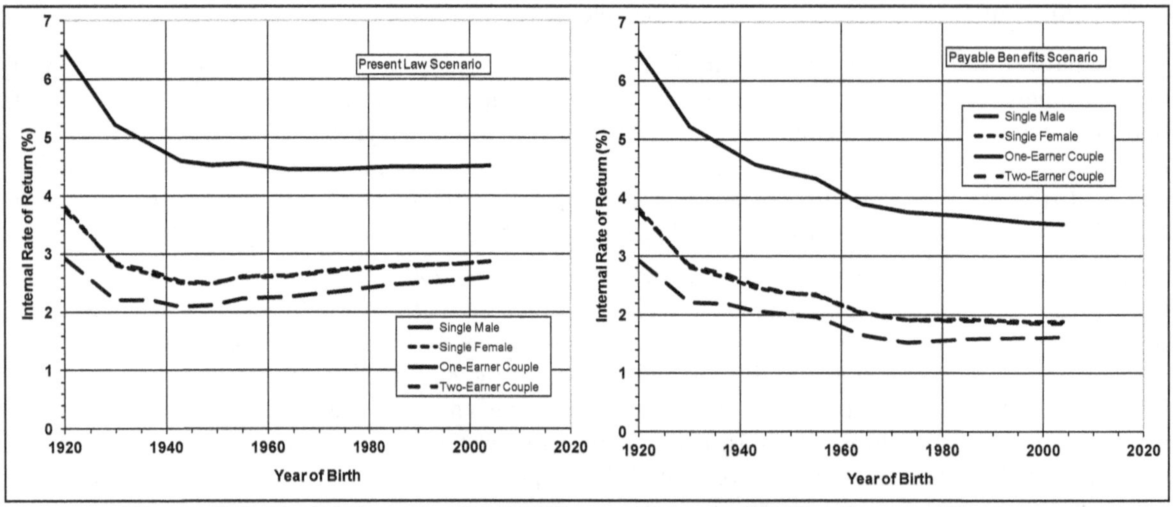

Figure 7-1: Social Security OASDI Rate of Return, Median Income Workers

Secondly, not every type of worker receives the same general rate of return. Figure 7-1 shows that single males fare the worst in rate of return, and single-earner couples fare the best. Single females and two-earner families are about the same. The females obtain a better rate of return than their male counterparts mostly owing to longer life spans. The two-earner families fare worse than a single-earner family because benefits are not paid as individuals (as would be the case with an individual retirement account); the benefits are paid jointly to husband and wife, not commensurate with their actual tax contributions.

The rates of return shown on Figure 7-1 are much worse than what is typically achieved by investing in stocks and bonds over the long run. Gay [7-2] has calculated that annualized total return above inflation from the stock market at about 6.6%, going back to 1926. Lind [7-3] has used historical data to project annualized rates of return of 2.3% for Treasury notes, 4.8% for U. S. aggregate bonds; 7.2% for international stocks; 8.2% for small-cap stocks, and 7.4% for S&P 500 investments. Brightman [7-4] has used historical data to show that the annualized returns on a 60/40 mix of stocks and bonds averaged 7.6% for the period between 1871 and 2010. Certainly all of these calculations involve simplifying assumptions, and there of course no guarantees that the next century will function the same as the past. But considering that there have been some bad economic times in the past century, it is reasonable to conclude that in the long run (which is the only one that matters for retirement planning), private investment offers a much better rate of return than a pay-as-you-go government system like Social Security.

References

[1-1] http://www.ssa.gov/oact/STATS/table4a3.html
[1-2] http://www.ssa.gov/history/1983amend.html

[3-1] U. S. Government Printing Office, *Budget of the United States Government, FY 2000 Budget, Analytical Perspectives*, p. 337; https://www.gpo.gov/fdsys/pkg/BUDGET-2000-PER/pdf/BUDGET-2000-PER.pdf

[4-1] U. S. Government Printing Office, *Budget of the United States Government, Fiscal Year 2000*, p. 41; https://fraser.stlouisfed.org/docs/publications/usbudget/BUDGET-2000-BUD.pdf

[6-1] U. S. Social Security Administration, https://www.ssa.gov/OACT/progData/taxRates.html
[6-2] U. S. Social Security Administration, https://www.ssa.gov/OACT/COLA/cbb.html

[6-3] Bureau of Labor Statistics, BLS Beta Lab, Series CUUR0000SA0 (All items in US city average, all urban consumers, not seasonally adjusted), https://beta.bls.gov/dataQuery/find?removeAll=1&q=CUUR0000SA0

[6-4] United States Census Bureau, median income data (per mean of middle fifth), Table H-3, all races; https://www.census.gov/data/tables/time-series/demo/income-poverty/historical-income-households.html

[7-1] M. Clingman, K. Burkhalter, C. Chaplain, "Internal Real Rates of Return Under the OASDI Program for Hypothetical Workers", Social Security Administration, Office of Chief Actuary, Baltimore MD, March 2013

[7-2] C. Gay, "Is the 7% Return for Stocks Extinct?", US News and World Report, 8 Aug 2012; http://money.usnews.com/money/personal-finance/mutual-funds/articles/2012/08/08/is-the-7-percent-return-for-stocks-extinct

[7-3] M. E. Lind, "Q and A" Estimating Long Term Market Returns", Charles Schwab, 22 May 2014; http://www.schwab.com/public/schwab/nn/articles/Q-and-A-Estimating-Long-Term-Market-Returns

[7-4] C. J. Brightman, "Expected Return", 2012; https://www.researchaffiliates.com/Production%20content%20library/IWM_Jan_Feb_2012_Expected_Return.pdf

On Bail-outs and Bail-ins

(25 Jan 2014)

Are you tired of seeing the government rescuing wealthy bankers from their errors with your tax money? Are you tired of watching banks creating questionable securities, then making large profits by selling them to unsuspecting customers based on risk ratings that were bought and paid for by the banks who created the suspect securities? Meanwhile, when the bad securities crashed, the bankers took your tax money from the government to continue and expand their gambling racket. Are you tired of watching your friends and neighbors lose their houses and jobs while the politically well-connected bankers are compensated and rewarded for failure? In short, are you tired of seeing these Wall Street losers line up to take bailouts to save them from their own incompetence while the taxpayers take the loss? Well cheer up chumps, in addition to future recurring bail-outs, there will come a day when you will be "invited" to "participate" in a "bail-in". Here's how the scam will work.

When you make a deposit at a bank, you receive in return a demand deposit in the form of either a savings account or checking account entry. Likewise, when you purchase a certificate of deposit, you receive a document, which is, like the savings and checking accounts, a receipt showing that the bank owes you the deposited amount upon presentation of a claim. In other words, the bank does not sequester the money you deposited; it simply issues you a future right to a certain amount of money in the future, namely, the amount you deposited in one of the account types. You are actually lending those assets to the bank, and the bank may do with it as it pleases. The bank is merely obligated to fulfill its promise return it to you upon demand, and likewise with all other depositors. The bank therefore keeps a small amount of cash on hand to disburse to its depositors from day to day; the rest is loaned out at a profit to the bank. Yes it's true: banks make their profits by lending out something they do not actually own: your deposit. But that is the foundation of a beneficial credit system, and it works so long as the system naintains the confidence of the people.

But what if the bank engages in shady real-estate transactions, or lends money to people who refuse to pay back, or who cannot pay back; or if the bank over-extends itself through highly leveraged investments that decline in value? There may come a time when the bank's cash flow is insufficient to meet the daily demands by its depositors; in that case, it will have to obtain more capital to cover those losses and make good on its promises to the depositors. But what if it cannot raise the required capital? Remember, banks do not make money by risking their money; only by risking yours. The CEO of the bank is not going to pony up $300 million of his own money to cover the depositors: he will inform the government that a bailout is needed. If enough banks make the same mistakes, and the entire cartel becomes insolvent, then they get a very large bailout because they can claim that the entire financial system will collapse. So it becomes an extension of the old rubric, which goes: "If you owe the bank $100 and can't pay, you have a problem. If you owe the bank $1,000,000 and can't pay, the bank has a problem". To which we now add, "If the banks owe $1,000,000,000,000 and can't pay, then the taxpayers have a problem." Hence the need for the government to bail out the bankers; the funds to do so are either created by the central bank (the Federal Reserve in the U. S.), or an insurance fund maintained by the banks (the Federal Deposit Insurance Corporation in the U. S.), and the repayment is made by future tax increases to pay off the new debt created by the central bank. A bail-out is when the bank is rescued by some external entity acting on behalf of the government.

A bail-in is different. A bail-in is when bankers are rescued by internal entities, which is to say, the depositors. A bail-in is accomplished by getting the government to allow the banks to refuse to honor claims by depositors, or prevent risk of capital loss to the bank by depositors demanding their own property back. The bankers are unable to understand the colossal nerve of depositors, demanding to exercise their rights, formerly issued by the bank, to retrieve their own property on demand. To the bankers, you are nothing more than an ingrate if you still insist that the bank uphold its end of the deal. A bail-in is manifested by "capital controls" (not on the banks since they do not risk their capital), but on its depositors. It comes in the form of limitations upon depositors on how much can be withdrawn per day or week; a prohibition on the cashing of checks, limitations on how much currency can taken out of the country, limitations on overall volume of transactions, etc. It matters not that a depositor needs money to pay for groceries or the mortgage: what matters is that the bank, by exercising a bail-in, gets to keep their money as long as it needs to, thus avoiding default, until it can coerce, bribe, or intimidate a government or other banks to give it a bail-out. Now banks do not have the legal power to invoke a bail-in unilaterally: it has thus far required a conspiracy with the government to transfer such a power to the bank; for which consideration, the politicians are of course rewarded with favorable loan terms or even forgiveness of existing loans. A bail-in generally does not permit the banks to pilfer the contents of "safe deposit" boxes, but it would be naive to exclude such a future possibility.

Lest you think this is all idle speculation, be advised that it already happened in Cyprus in 2013. When the Cypriot national banks got into trouble, it negotiated a bailout with the IMF and other European central banks, but the deal was contingent upon the government of Cyprus to allow a bail-in binding on depositors. So, in March of 2013, Cypriot depositors were saddled with the following restrictions on their own property [1, 2], some of which were still in effect as of Jan 2014:

a. Withdrawals limited to 300 Euros per day
b. Cashing of checks prohibited
c. Persons exiting Cyprus could take no more than 1,000 Euros with them
d. Payments or transfers to foreign accounts limited to 5,000 Euros per month
e. A 9.9% tax levied on depositors with balances greater than 100,000 Euros, and a 6.75% tax on deposits less than 100,000 Euros

What happened when the government imposed these violations of rights upon its own citizens in order to save the incompetent and/or corrupt bankers? Did the people reach for the pitchforks and torches and descend upon the bankers and politicians? No; they patiently waited in long lines like sheep; they raised no protest at the violation of their rights; they did not question the merits of the government's actions against them. You may be sure that this quiet acquiescence did not go unnoticed by the bankers and their political cronies. When U. S. banks get in trouble again, as they are sure to do, it will create the perfect excuse for the government to restrict most cash transactions, allow the banks to prosper without risk, and track your every economic move electronically.

References

[1] BBC News Europe, "Cyprus eases some bank restrictions after bailout", 29 Mar 2013, http://www.bbc.co.uk/news/world-europe-21978286

[2] Edward Harrison, "Cyprus' Bank Deposit Bail-In", 16 Mar 2013, http://www.nakedcapitalism.com/2013/03/cyprus-bank-deposit-bail-in.html

The Nature of U. S. Currency

Note: This essay was originally published 28 Jul 2018, and was later incorporated as Question 41 in the book *Real World Graduation*. It poses a multiple-choice question, followed by an explanation of the correct answer.

The Question

The basic currency unit of the United States is called the dollar. The word "dollar" is a modification of the word "taler", which is a nickname for "thaler", which was the name of a coin minted by the Dutch which contained one ounce of 0.999 pure silver. The U. S. dollar was originally devised in 1786 to imitate the thaler, and defined it as a coin containing 375.64 grains of pure silver. There are 480 grains in a troy ounce, so the dollar consisted 0.7825 troy ounces of silver. There are 31.103 grams per troy ounce, and therefore the dollar was 24.3406 grams of pure silver. Silver was traditionally regarded as 1/15th the value of gold, hence the dollar, although defined in silver, was equivalent to 25.052 grains or 1.622 grams or 0.0521 troy oz. of gold.

In 1834, the U. S. government decided to reduce the weight of gold in the gold coinage, so it altered the value of silver to be 1/16th of the value of gold, thus one dollar was devalued to 1.521 grams of gold. This put the dollar implicitly on a gold standard, although coins of both types circulated (and the dollar remained at 0.7825 ounces of silver).

In 1900, the dollar was formally converted to a gold standard, in which one dollar was worth 23.195 grains (which is 0.0483 troy ounces or 1.503 grams), of pure gold. The dollar was thus valued at 20.694 dollars per troy ounce.

In 1934, the dollar was devalued to $35 dollars per troy ounce of gold (13.71 grains or 0.02857 troy ounces or 0.8886 grams).

In modern times, dollars are issued as paper Federal Reserve Notes by a consortium of private banks acting as a central bank, called the Federal Reserve Bank. The dollar is backed by the "full faith and credit of the United States Government". Therefore, the paper dollar, while itself is nothing more than paper and ink, is simply a representation of real value. How is the "full faith and credit of the United States Government" manifested when redeeming the paper dollars (in other words, for what things of value may paper dollars be exchanged at any Federal Reserve Bank)?

a) Gold, at the rate of 1/16th troy ounce per dollar

b) Silver, at the rate of 0.7825 troy ounces per dollar

c) Stock in the Federal Reserve Banks

d) Land held in trust by the Government, mostly in the western states

e) The citizen may choose either gold at 0.02857 ounces per dollar per the 1934 gold standard, or silver at 0.7825 ounces per dollar per the revised 1834 silver standard.

The Answer

This is a trick question; none of the answers are true. Since 1933, the U. S. dollar has been what is known as a "fiat currency", which is paper currency that has no value in and of itself, and cannot be traded in for anything else of value. Former Chairman of the Federal Reserve Alan Greenspan confirmed in testimony before Congress in 2004 that the U.S. dollar is in fact such a fiat currency [1]:

> We have statutorily gone into a fiat money standard, and as a consequence of that it is inevitable that the authority, which is the producer of the money supply, will have inordinate power.

The "producer of the money supply" that Greenspan referred to is the Federal Reserve. If you attempt to trade your "Federal Reserve Note" so-called "dollars" into something of value at any bank, you will receive a vacant stare from the teller before she bursts out laughing, because Federal Reserve Notes are not redeemable for anything of actual value. Examples of "actual value" would be a commodity such as gold, silver, oil, land, or other items of value which would normally provide security for a paper currency.

The federal government routinely sells U. S. Treasury bonds that are denominated in Federal Reserve "dollars". The Treasury Bonds and the Federal Reserve Notes are backed by the "full faith and credit" of the U. S. Government. How can this be? If the dollars are not secured by commodities held by the government in trust, how would the federal government pay off a large holder of U. S. Treasury bonds if the holder will not be satisfied by more slips of worthless (Federal Reserve) paper? The holder of the bonds will be compensated through Congress' unlimited ability to levy a tax. In other words, the federal government does not have enough gold to pay the bond holder, but you and all the other taxpayers do, because you have sufficient wealth (future earnings and savings) that can be taxed. The federal government does not hold stocks in profitable corporations that have actual value to pay the bond holder, but you and all the other taxpayers do. So, if the time should come when creditors lose faith in the Federal Reserve Notes and Treasury Bonds, and begin to demand actual payment in commodities for money lent, Congress will pay them by taxing all U. S. citizens as much as is required to pay the bond. The federal government will never give up title to the land in the western states, because that would constitute a loss of stature and sovereignty. The politicians will never allow the bonds to go into default, because that would constitute for them a loss of prestige. As usual, the taxpayers will pay the charges, plus interest, for the excesses of the Federal Reserve and the enabling politicians. Incidentally, the Federal Reserve is not an agency of the federal government; it is a consortium of private banks. It is called the Federal Reserve to give the illusion that you, the citizen, have a say through your representatives in Congress as to how the nation's finances are handled. In fact, there is no control of the Federal Reserve by Congress except for the occasional confirmation of an appointment made by the President. The most recent example is the confirmation on 23 Jan 2018 of Jerome H. Powell as the Chairman of the Board of Directors of the Federal Reserve System.

The important point here is that the Federal Reserve is a leading member of the international banking cartel, and it does what is best for the cartel, not for the American people. It's claimed duty is to supervise the banking system, manage the money supply to prevent recessions, stabilize the value of the dollar, increase the general standard of living, and at the same time, to maximize employment [2]. Those last four are mutually contradictory objectives. The Federal Reserve has in reality become a means to institutionalize inflation, which is a hidden tax on all working people, to finance the excesses of the federal government. It does so as an indirect, but independent servant of Congress: it buys up all the debt that Congress, through its spending excesses, directs the Treasury to issue, but that cannot be sold to the wary public.

References

[1] Alan Greenspan, Chairman of the Federal Reserve, in testimony before Congress, 11 Feb 2004
[2] *The Federal Reserve System: Purposes and Functions*, Washington DC: Board of Governors of the Federal Reserve, 1963, pp. 1-15

3
Recent Issues

Introduction

This chapter contains 15 essays on recent issues in America, arranged in approximate chronological order.

The first addresses "lessons learned" from the famous gun-running operation engineered by the Bureau of Alcohol, Tobacco, Firearms, and Explosives (BATFE) known as "Fast and Furious". It was working great until there was a big problem, and then it fell apart.

The second is an extended discussion on "gun control", describing the various categories of arguments used by the proponents thereof, and why they are all either false or misleading. It should be pointed out that the common phrase "gun violence" in itself is misleading: it should be called "people violence using guns as a tool". It is falsely called "gun violence" because the advocates for "gun control" do not want you to realize that the weapon is the human mind; the gun is only a tool. Many people are attacked by knives and baseball bats, but no one talks about "knife control" or "baseball bat control". Gun control is all about power, not public safety.

The third essay gives an example of the inconsistency and illogic of "gun control" as applied to a group of people who are victimized by violent attacks.

The fourth essay is a commentary on the prospect for "immigration reform" as proposed by prominent members of Congress in 2013. The problem with their proposal was that it offered too little to the illegal immigrants, and that is why it was never enacted. The same situation prevails today.

The fifth essay addresses the politics of dependency as a consequence of the modern "welfare" system. It quotes at length from a book written in the 1880's that addressed the same problem Great Britain had in the early 1800's with their "Poor Laws". There is nothing new under the sun; people are people, and the failed policies of the past will fail again.

The sixth essay recounts the IRS scandal from 2010 to 2013, in which certain IRS employees used their power to deny tax-exempt status to certain groups based on their name or political affiliation. It was a search-and-suppress operation, designed to limit the ability of certain groups to educate the public on issues of national interest.

The seventh essay recounts Secretary Hillary Clinton's email scandal, in which she had classified data on unauthorized servers, and destroyed all of it even after being served with a subpoena; more importantly, it describes why Hillary Clinton can never be prosecuted for this or anything else.

The eighth essay describes the opposite case with Donald Trump; it cites his two real crimes, and why it is likely he will be hounded into the grave by the judicial system. The indictment handed down in New York 30 Mar 2023 is just the beginning.

The ninth and tenth essays describe why the "Black Lives Matter" movement and ANTIFA are likely to fail in the long run. The causes of their probable respective failures are different.

The eleventh essay is a translation of President Joe Biden's Inaugural Address from 20 Jan 2021, clarified to indicate what I suspected to be the true objective of his policies (which turned out to be accurate).

The twelfth essay is a comment on President Biden's open border policy, suggesting a rationale that goes beyond the usual incompetence and incoherence of his administration.

The thirteenth essay describes the recent appropriation by Congress for 87,000 new IRS employees, using the IRS' documents to show that collecting additional revenue is only a minor objective, and suggests a method to address the problem.

The fourteenth essay contains the speech before Congress by Ukrainian President Volodymyr Zelenskyy, supplemented with an Americanized version that could be given (for example) by any resident of Texas.

Last, a short essay describes the one thing that all politicians (as distinguished from true statesmen) are afraid of.

Operation "Fast and Furious"

Note: This is a combination of two essays titled "What We've Learned from Operation Fast and Furious", Parts 1 and 2, issued 4 Dec 2011 and 29 Jan 2012. They have been combined here. Also, a few references have been added, and the initial accusation that Dennis K. Burke would run for Governor of Arizona has been deleted.

The U. S. Congress and the Department of Justice have launched "investigations" into the "Operation Fast and Furious" program designed and implemented by the Bureau of Alcohol, Tobacco, Firearms, and Explosives (BAFTE). This program was initiated by BAFTE field agents in Arizona; its purpose was to supply and then trace weapons smuggled to the Mexican drug cartels so that they could be exposed and arrested. At least, that's what BATFE officials want you to believe, according to a recent article by Dennis Wagner [1].

But before we get to lessons learned, it is necessary to review the salient points of the program as cited by Mr. Wagner. The facts appear to be as follows:

a. The BATFE leadership knowingly and willfully allowed "straw buyers" to buy firearms at dealer shops in America, and then knowingly and willfully allowed them to be smuggled into Mexico.

b. Mexico, a sovereign nation, has strict gun control (only certain government employees are allowed to own guns). This strict gun control partly explains why Mexico is a pathologically corrupt feudal state, in which the average citizen is little more than a serf, lorded over by a caste of petty dictators and their favorites. The serfs are kept in line by local gangsters (the federal police) equipped with guns, badges, and uniforms. That is a discussion for another time. The important point is that the BATFE leadership permitted guns to be transferred to Mexico in violation of Mexico's domestic laws.

c. The BATFE leadership knew that the smuggled guns were being sold in Mexico (in violation of Mexico's laws) to members of drug cartels who are waging a guerilla war against the Mexican government, and that they constituted a partial source of firepower for the drug cartels.

d. The BATFE leadership knew that a great number of Mexican police and citizens were being murdered by the drug cartels; it is reasonable to assume that at least some small fraction of that firepower came from the guns that BATFE knew were smuggled in under its auspices.

e. The BATFE leadership knew that the plan was devised by the local BATFE office in Phoenix, and although it was coordinated with the Department of Justice, it apparently was never coordinated with the Department of State.

f. The BATFE leadership knew that the Mexican government was kept in the dark about the entire operation; at the same time, the Mexican government was asking for U. S. aid to try and reduce the availability of weapons by the cartels.

g. The BATFE leadership knew that some BATFE agents were opposed to the operation and had protested to their superiors; official policy was to ignore those objections.

h. The BATFE leadership knew that some of the BATFE-coordinated smuggled guns were recovered at crime scenes in Mexico and traced back to the U. S. The BAFTE leadership also knew that the vast majority of weapons used by the cartels come from Asia and South America, not the U.S. But they also knew and supported false claims that most of the weapons used by the cartels came from America. They knew that these false statistics were being used by politicians in America as an excuse to further erode the Second Amendment rights of U. S. citizens.

The first thing we've learned from Operation Fast and Furious is that none of the foregoing is a problem for a federal agency. What about the BATFE allowing straw buyers to commit felony purchases from legitimate gun dealers? Not a problem. What about the BATFE allowing those buyers to smuggle weapons into Mexico in violation of Mexico's laws? Not a problem. What about the BATFE providing material assistance to drug cartels who were attempting to undermine the legitimate government of Mexico, thus conducting a secret foreign policy of aiding factions actively engaged in a revolution against a friendly government? Not a problem. What about the BATFE standing by as a great number of Mexican citizens were killed and injured by the drug cartels partly being armed indirectly by the BATFE itself? Not a problem. What about the BATFE knowingly supporting propaganda efforts to subvert the Second Amendment to the U. S. Constitution which each member of the BATFE took an oath to uphold as a condition of employment? Not a problem.

But then, on 14 Dec 2010, a Border Patrol agent named Brian Terry was killed in a shootout with some Mexican drug dealers. The BATFE assisted in the subsequent investigation and discovered that Agent Terry had been killed with one of the firearms that had been smuggled into Mexico under Operation Fast and Furious. Now the BATFE leadership had a VERY BIG PROBLEM. Why? The problem was that a member of the U. S. Border Patrol was killed. HE WAS A FEDERAL EMPLOYEE JUST LIKE BATFE EMPLOYEES -- HE WAS ONE OF THEM.

That was when the dam broke. The members of the BATFE who opposed the operation, along with some Department of Justice employees who had similar misgivings, leaked the story to the press. Of course, the upper echelon of the Justice Department and BATFE denied everything. But over time, little by little, some of the truth has come out. Congress and the Department of Justice have begun to "investigate" the operation. Some personnel changes were in order: U. S. Attorney Dennis K. Burke, who gave the BATFE legal cover for Fast and Furious, resigned in Aug 2011 as public knowledge of the scandal unfolded. Acting BATFE Director Kenneth Melson was promoted to a post as senior advisor in the Justice Department's forensic division. Special Agent William D. Newell, who was in charge of the Fast and Furious operation in Arizona, was promoted to Country Attaché for Mexico.

We have learned several other things too. First, a federal agency can commit an unlimited number of felonies without having to take responsibility. Secondly, a federal agency can hire or instigate others to commit felonies under its supervision without accountability. Third, the BATFE does have some sense of moral outrage, but only if a federal employee is killed; not when regular Mexicans or non-federal employee American citizens are killed. Fourth, brilliant exercises like "Fast and Furious" are a just cause for raises and promotions all around. As for those "investigations", it is likely that nothing more will ever be revealed.

Mr. Dennis Wagner of *The Arizona Republic* once again performed a valuable public service in his 29 Jan 2012 article [2] regarding "Operation Fast and Furious". It was a follow-up to the 27 Nov 2011 article.

In the 29 Jan 2012 article, Mr. Wagner recounted the career of Dennis K. Burke, who was the U. S. Attorney for the state of Arizona throughout the entire period that "Operation Fast and Furious" was being conducted by the BATFE. Apparently Mr. Burke knew about the Operation early on. Prior to becoming U. S. Attorney, Mr. Burke served as a law clerk for a justice on the Arizona Supreme Court, and as a staff lawyer on the U. S. Senate Judiciary Committee. During that time, he was influential in drafting what eventually became the Violent Crime Control and Law Enforcement Act of 1994 (which banned possession of certain semiautomatic rifles and magazines). He later worked with Rahm Emmanuel in the Clinton administration on firearms issues, including discussions on extending background check requirements under the Brady Handgun Violence Protection Act through the use of executive orders. Mr. Wagner cited a 1997 article published in the *Arizona Business Gazette*, in which Mr. Burke said that gun control was his most fulfilling accomplishment in government service. Just what we need: government officials devoted to and proud of, their role in the destruction of the rights of citizens.

President Obama nominated Mr. Burke for U. S. Attorney for Arizona in 2009; it is not known if Mr. Burke's sterling citizen disarmament record influenced the selection or not. Suffice to say, it was a fortuitous choice for Mr. Obama.

Mr. Wagner's article laid out a very important timeline. The gun battle leading to the death of Border Patrol Agent Brian Terry occurred on 14 Dec 2010. The BATFE investigated the incident, and as a result, Mr. Wagner's article states: "Within hours, Burke was notified that two guns found at the scene were linked to Fast and Furious". Then some BATFE agents leaked details to Congress, followed by Senator Grassley's letter 27 Jan 2011 [3] in which he accurately stated BATFE's actions, followed by Mr. Burke's claim to the Department of Justice that Mr. Grassley's accusations were "categorical falsehoods".

Now this is a very important point. Mr. Burke was notified "within hours" after the investigation that two guns found at the scene were part of the Operation, but how would the investigating BATFE agents know that? They could only have known by comparing the make, model, and serial number of guns found at the scene to the same data for all guns involved in the Operation. How else could they have known? If the comparison only took a short time, BATFE must have had pretty accurate records. If so, the identity of the "straw purchasers" and the selling dealer must also have been known, since that data is written both on the bills of sale and on the BATFE form to be retained by dealers for all sales. In the notification to Mr. Burke, BATFE's proof thereof would have been unassailable since serial numbers are unique to each firearm.

Why then would Mr. Burke in several internal emails [4] denounce Senator Grassley as promoting "categorical falsehoods", claim that members of Mr. Grassley's staff were "stooges for the gun lobby", and criticize the BATFE for not denying the reports about the guns in question? I leave that to your imagination. He also claimed that Senator Grassley's letter was an attempt to "distract from the incredible success in dismantling [Southwest Border] gun trafficking operations". Let me get this straight. The BATFE engineered a gun smuggling ring in order to ... dismantle gun trafficking?

But the most important thing we've learned in all this is: if you, as an American citizen, exercise your rights under the Constitution, and own anything more powerful than a single-shot pea-shooter, this problem is your fault. At least that's what BATFE officials want you to believe.

References

[1] Dennis Wagner, "Behind the fall of gun probe", *The Arizona Republic*, 27 Nov 2011, p. 1

[2] Dennis Wagner, "Firearm scandal, political fall", *The Arizona Republic*, 29 Jan 2012, p. 1

[3] https://www.grassley.senate.gov/imo/media/doc/Judiciary-01-27-11-letter-to-ATF-SW-Border-strategy.pdf

[4] https://www.politico.com/story/2011/12/docs-top-officials-sent-false-fast-and-furious-denials-069680

The Practical Aspects of Gun Control

Note: This essay is a compilation of essays that were originally published as an 8-part series between 20 Jan 2013 and 25 May 2013. A few minor portions have been edited, and it includes two new sections: a) on the treatment of former slaves after the Civil War; and b) a comment on the mentally ill.

1 The Cultural Aspect
2 The Historical Aspect
3 The Moral Aspect
4 The Technological Aspect
5 The Statistical Aspect
6 The Political Aspect

In the original essay on this topic [1], which addressed the massacre at Sandy Hook Elementary, I was clear in my opinion that the way to reduce mass shootings is to lock up the dangerous people in appropriate mental institutions, not to impose regulations on the 150 million citizens who exercise their rights. This essay considers the practical aspects of "gun control".

1 The Cultural Aspect

The advocates for disarmament of the American people are constantly misinforming us with claims that other advanced nations have adopted "sensible" laws regarding gun ownership, and that we Americans should "get modern", join up with "civilized society", and either abolish the Second Amendment or neuter it with regulations. But these same disarmament advocates fail to point out (knowingly or not) that the real issue regarding the Second Amendment is not what kind of guns should be available; it is ultimately about the degree of individual freedom that the citizen possesses and how it is to be preserved; to what extent the people should passively trust any government (with its enormous powers); and whether in fact, any government is willing or capable of fulfilling its promises in times of emergency. The debate is not about guns per se, just as the First Amendment is not about the color of ink or the scheduling of talk shows.

The so-called American "gun culture" is nothing more than a by-product of the American "freedom culture". The advocates for disarmament claim that other nations and societies have "progressed" to the point that privately-owned arms are now unnecessary, and that the Second Amendment is an interesting but useless anachronism. It is in fact the other way around: many other nations and societies have "regressed" to the point that the individual freedom is being abolished in the face of bureaucratic tyranny. The nations of Europe were the first to develop the concept of individual liberty, but now most of them have abandoned it; a few illustrations should suffice to show that these so-called "progressive" nations are not worthy of emulation when it comes to firearm restrictions. These same restrictions are symptoms of a larger problem, namely, the degradation of the importance of the individual.

The once free and vigorous Germans have fallen furthest. It was the Germanic peoples that infused the subjects of the Roman Empire with the notion of individual freedom, so foreign to Roman understanding. And so it was for many centuries, until the gradual encroachment of the state under the influence of the Prussians. The Germans were prepared for the scientific prescription of tyranny outlined by their fellow countryman Karl Marx in the 1870's. Only the scientific German mind could conceive of Marxism, the foundation of the modern systematic totalitarian systems of Fascism and Communism. For some reason, the Germans have gradually combined traditional duty with modern blind obedience. It was no surprise that the German people embraced Hitler when he said in 1933 [2]:

> "Our aim is to draw from the midst of the people a class of leaders which shall be as hard as steel. When in this way the people have been rightly trained through its political leadership, then the social spirit will come to its own, for he who thinks only in terms of economics will never be able to think and act truly socially."

Or Hitler again in 1935 [3]:

> "The question of fallibility or infallibility [of the government] is not under discussion; the individual has as little right to question the action of the political leaders as the soldier to question the orders of his military superiors."

The past few centuries of history shows that the average German will do anything that anyone with a government ID tells them to do -- "Tote that barge" -- "Lift that bale" -- "Round up those Protestants" -- "March those Jewish children into that gas chamber." Never a hint of protest, or questioning of authority; they have become so suppressed in their thinking that they no longer believe there is any legitimate need for self-defense; they implicitly trust all government employees. They are willing to have all means of resistance licensed and registered. They will not object to the universal weapon confiscation that Hitler implemented, simply because the government says they must. It is true that the people of Germany collectively own about 5 million firearms, subject to some of the strictest control in existence; each firearm must be licensed, and a justification for the license must be stated. Self-defense is not a valid reason.

The German mindset is nothing new. The German Confederation (1815-1866) was a full police state, complete with censorship, arbitrary searches, internal passports, no right to trial by jury, and no right to bear arms [4]. The German Empire (1866-1918) continued in much the same manner, complete with persecution of Catholics and protection of the anti-Semite National Socialists [5]. Even after the First World War, a civil service bureaucracy with a strong tradition of exercising absolute authority, and which retained all its traditional privileges, continued to dominate the German people [6].

The Germans have had their Frederick William, their Bismarck, and their Hitler; another one will arise sooner or later, and there will be no domestic resistance to him. Tyrants do not tolerate competition. When that new German tyrant emerges, he will find it a simple matter to seize absolute control by seizing all the guns; it will be easy because the registration and licensing requirements will point him to all the potential sources of resistance.

The British once had a long tradition of individual freedom, but has eroded since the Second World War. Apparently the British have fallen prey to the notion that guns are only for evil. They have lost their original notion of human dignity and the right to self defense; they are no longer a model useful to America. For some reason, the British no longer read Blackstone [7]:

> Both the life and limbs of a man are of such high value, in the estimation of the law of England, that it pardons even homicide if committed *se defendendo*, or in order to preserve them. For whatever is done by a man, to save either life or members, is looked upon as done upon the highest necessity and compulsion.

They no longer read even Hobbes. Here was a man who advocated the absolute divine right of kings, believed one was guilty until proven innocent, and endorsed the punishment of groups for the crimes of individuals; and yet recognized the immutable right of self-defense, both for oneself and for others [8]:

> Whensoever a man transferreth his right, or renounceth it, it is either in consideration of some right reciprocally transferred to himself, or for some other good he hopeth for thereby. For it is a voluntary act: and of the voluntary acts of every man, the object is some good to himself. And therefore there be some rights which no man can be understood by any words, or other signs, to have abandoned or transferred. As first a man cannot lay down the right of resisting them that assault him by force to take away his life, because he cannot be understood to aim thereby at any good to himself. The same may be said of wounds, and chains, and imprisonment, both because there is no benefit consequent to such patience, as there is to the patience of suffering another to

> be wounded or imprisoned, as also because a man cannot tell when he seeth men proceed against him by violence whether they intend his death or not.

The modern British have even forgotten John Locke, who extends defense to both liberty and property [9]:

> The state of war is a state of enmity and destruction; and therefore declaring by word or action, not a passionate and hasty, but a sedate settled design, upon another man's life, puts him in a state of war with him against whom he has declared such an intention, and so has exposed his life to the other's power to be taken away from him, or anyone that joins with him in his defense, and espouses his quarrel: it being reasonable and just I should have a right to destroy that which threatens me with destruction. ... For I have reason to conclude, that he who would get me into his power without my consent, would use me as he pleased, when he got me there, and destroy me too when he had a fancy to it: for nobody can desire to have me in his absolute power, unless it be to compel me by force to that, which is against the right of my freedom, i.e., to make me a slave. To be free from such force is the only security of my preservation: and reason bids me look on him, as an enemy to my preservation, who would take away that freedom, which is the fence to it: so that he who makes an attempt to enslave me, thereby puts himself into a state of war with me. ... This makes it lawful for a man to kill a thief, who has not in the least hurt him, nor declared any design upon his life, any further than by the use of force, so as to get him into his power, as to take away his money, or what he pleases from him: because in using force, where he has no right, to get me into his power, let his pretense be what it will, I have no reason to suppose, that he, who would take away my liberty, would not when he had me in his power, take away everything else. And therefore it is lawful for me to treat him, as one who has put himself into a state of war with me, i.e., kill him if I can, for to that hazard does he justly expose himself, whoever introduces a state of war, and is aggressor in it.

Britain has produced some of the best moral and legal minds in history, being the first to properly understand liberty and defense, yet the modern British subject cannot legally practice self-defense for themselves or their family, nor to defend their property, nor to preserve any liberty. While it is possible to obtain a Firearms or Shotgun Certificate, allowing one to own a gun, self-defense cannot be legally cited as the reason for wanting one.

Perhaps the Parliament decided that they should have a clean, tidy kingdom, and should not have to tolerate the Queen's innocent subjects going about defending themselves from her criminal subjects. Having adopted this notion that self-defense being obsolete -- regarded now as too messy, too violent -- Parliament decided it is better to disarm the innocent than to have this kind of inconvenience. Better the peaceful subject tolerate any indignity or violence than to resist. Parliament accordingly passed a series of laws disarming the people in response to a school shooting there, knowing full well that no law prohibiting self-defense will affect them personally any more than laws affect the Queen or the criminals. So the modern law-abiding British gave up all their guns (except for an occasional two-shot hunting shotgun) for Queen, country, and public safety; the only problem being that it has not made the subjects safe, since the criminal subjects do not care about the innocent or the law or the Queen. The same policies will be continued under King Charles III.

The French and most other European governments (except for the Czech Republic and Switzerland) have imposed similar restrictions on the people's ability to keep arms: requiring licenses and "justifications", and imposing limits on the number of cartridges that can be purchased annually.

The Chinese are certainly no model for America. Their entire history is one of enslavement by one warlord or another. There is neither a history of, nor a desire for, freedom as understood in the West. The Communists, simply the largest and most successful warlords, are now permitting a little economic freedom, but will never tolerate true political freedom, or any notion of the importance of the individual. They will certainly never permit the notion of self-defense to catch on, nor permit the tools thereof to be possessed freely by the people; it would be the end of their reign.

The Japanese have a similar tradition of allowing themselves to be suppressed by arbitrary government power; it was only in 1945 they accepted the concept that the emperor was not a god. All guns are prohibited to the people, although the Yakuza (Japanese mafia) is not inconvenienced at all. That makes perfect sense to the powerful: sometimes the Yakuza works for the government, sometimes the government works for the Yakuza; but the taxpaying Japanese people are always at the mercy of both.

The people of India have a history similar to the Chinese, except they have been pushed around by tribal leaders and colonial masters rather than warlords.

Nothing need be said about the people of Africa: it is the only continent where slavery is still practiced, by blacks enslaving blacks, and sometimes Arabs enslaving blacks. This is the place where the notion of individual life and liberty is so suppressed that they are willing to watch two million of their children die of malaria every year because some bureaucrat at the UN outlawed DDT. It is the place where the large massacres are most recent (Rwanda, Sudan, Zimbabwe) and in which children are fighters in the numerous tribal and civil wars.

The "rights of persons" is talked about in many places, but America is one of the few places left where those rights are taken seriously enough that the people retain the power to enforce them if necessary. America inherited these concepts from the British, who have now largely abandoned them. Only a small fraction of the American people believe that self-defense is evil, or that government can always be trusted so long as the people have the power to vote. Granted, the American politicians have made some progress in weakening these sentiments by increasing dependence on government programs. But for now, the American culture, generally speaking, still embraces not only the notion of liberty, but recognizes the need for arms in the hands of the people to protect it.

2 The Historical Aspect

We shall now review gun control, or as it is more properly called, citizen disarmament, in its historical context. It is no secret that governments always lust for more power, and the one clear path to power is to make the people defenseless. A few examples will show that an unarmed population is ripe for any brand of tyranny the powerful care to dish out, not to mention the professional criminal element.

2.1 Examples from World History

2.1.1 The Roman Empire

The correct name of the "Roman Empire" was "The Senate and People of Rome". The fact is that the people never mattered too much; and after a while, neither did the Senators as the emperors increased their powers. The empire declined gradually from many causes, most of them related to exorbitant taxes: so bad in fact, that although Italy has the best farmland in Europe, the empire ultimately had to import food because the farmers were literally taxed off their land. The people were always unarmed, and always subject to the caprices of the higher ranks. But things became much worse for the people once the Germanic tribes began to encroach on the territory. Consider the words of the historian de Sismondi, regarding the results of domestic civil wars and the subsequent attitudes of the barbarians upon entering Italy in the middle of the third century AD [10]:

> Ninety-two years of nearly incessant civil war taught the world on what a frail and unstable foundation of virtue of the Antonines had reared the felicity of the empire. The people took no share whatever of these intestine wars; the sovereignty had passed into the hands of the legions, and they disposed of it at their leisure; while the cities, indifferent to the claims of the pretenders, having neither garrisons, fortifications, nor armed population, awaited the decision of the legions without a thought of resistance. Yet their helpless and despicable neutrality did not save them from the ferocity or rapacity of the combatants, who wanted other enemies than soldiers, richer plunder than that of a camp; and the slightest mark of favor shown by a city to one pretender to

> the empire, was avenged by his successful competitor by military executions, and often by the sale of the whole body of the citizens as slaves. ...
>
> In all their invasions, the barbarians preserved the recollection of the long terrors and the long resentment with which the Romans had inspired them. Their hatred was still too fresh and fervent to allow them to show any pity to the vanquished foes. Till then they had seen nothing of the Romans but their soldiers; but when they suddenly penetrated into the midst of these magnificent and populous cities, at first they feared that they should be crushed by a multitude so superior to their own; but, when they saw and understood the cowardice of the enervated masses, their fear changed into the deepest scorn. Their cruelty was in proportion to these two sentiments, and their object was rather destruction than conquest. The population, which had been thinned by the operation of wealth and luxury, was now further reduced by that of poverty. The human species seemed to vanish before the sword of the barbarians. Sometimes they massacred all the inhabitants of a town; sometimes they sent them into slavery, far from the country of their birth.

2.1.2 The Frankish Empire under Charlemagne, Louis I, and Charles II (the Bald)

The famous Charlemagne (whom the French regard as Charles I, one of their greatest kings) presided over a system of continuous foreign warfare and increasing domestic poverty and serfdom. He engaged in no less than 53 military campaigns during his reign (768-814), mostly against the Saxons and Slavs [11]. Meanwhile, the main domestic feature of his reign was internal disintegration as evidenced by the growth of servitude and the expansion of overt slavery. These trends came about because the small freeholders were ruined by the wars; the politically-connected nobility deprived freemen of inheritances through court intrigue; and some people voluntarily became serfs in return for protection, since the disarmed population could no longer defend their rights or property [12].

The domestic situation became slightly better under the just Louis I (814-843), but very much worse under the corrupt and incompetent Charles II (843-877). The general trends of the empire included a growing irresponsibility of the nobility, interested now only in their wealth and power, continual degradation of the once-free farmers, overall weakness, both morally and spiritually, and exposure of the unarmed people to every evil, foreign and domestic alike. The consequences of these trends came to their fruition during the invasions of the Danes beginning in 841, as explained by de Sismondi [13]:

> In the year 841, Oscar, duke of the Northmen or Danes, ascended the Seine as far as Rouen, took and pillaged that great city, to which he set fire on the 14th of May, and continued to lay waste and plunder the banks of the Seine during a fortnight. Not an individual appeared to resist him. The inhabitants of the country were confounded in one common state of degradation and servitude with the cattle, which aided them in their labors; those of the towns were vexed, oppressed, unprotected; all were disarmed; all had lost the requisite determination, as well as physical strength, to defend their lives as well as the slender remnant of property which the nobles had left them. ... The progress of cowardice and debasement among the sons of Charlemagne's soldiers, -- among the French, in whom courage seems generated by the very air they breathe, -- is one of the most remarkable phenomena, but also one of the best attested, of the age we are contemplating: it proves to what a degree slavery can annihilate every virtue, and what a nation may become in which one caste arrogates to itself the exclusive privilege of bearing arms. ... Another division, leaving their boats at Rouen, had advanced by land as far as Beauvais, and had spread desolation throughout the adjacent country. The Danes passed two hundred and eighty-seven days in the country lying on the Seine; and when they quitted it, with their ships laden with the spoil of France, it was not to return home, but to transfer the scene of their depredations to Bordeaux. Yet, we do not hear what either Lothaire or Charles the Bald were doing during this period; nor why those nobles who had reserved to themselves the exclusive right of bearing arms, could not draw a sword in defense of their country. Those ambitious chiefs, who had destroyed at once the power of the king and of the people, seemed now to rival each other only in abject pusillanimity.

2.1.3 The Byzantine Empire

The risk of civilian disarmament is not limited to foreign invasion. The Byzantine Empire, oriental successor to the Eastern Roman Empire, likewise continued the old tradition of rendering the population unarmed and defenseless. By the twelfth century the empire came to be dominated by a military aristocracy, which preyed upon the people as it wished, as described by Ostrogorsky [14]:

> The military were the ruling class in the state and they lived off the rest of the population. ... Military service had become the only lucrative profession. The people were crushed by intolerable burdens. The state increased its demands for taxation, and the last straw was provided by the usual extortions of the tax-collectors, who now included a number of foreigners to the great resentment of the taxpayers. In the cities a great many sold their freedom in order to find protection in the service of some powerful lord, a practice by no means unusual in Byzantium. ... But the whole trend of the times, with the growth of the great estates, and the overburdening and impoverishment of the lower classes, made it inevitable that ever wider strata of the population were bartering their freedom to become, if not slaves, then at least serfs.

2.1.4 France during the Hundred Years War

People are often forced to fend for themselves when the government either turns out to be derelict in its duty, or becomes part of the criminal element itself. Guizot, quoting the contemporary chronicler William of Nangis, writes of conditions in France between 1350 and 1390 [15]:

> "There was not", he says, "in Anjou, in Touraine, in Beauce, near Orleans and up to the approaches in Paris, any corner of the country which was free from plunderers and robbers. They were so numerous everywhere, either in little forts occupied by them or in the villages and country-places, that peasants and tradesfolks could not travel but at great expense and great peril. The very guards told off to defend cultivators and travelers took part most shamefully in harassing and despoiling them. It was the same in Burgundy and the neighboring countries. Some knights who called themselves friends of the king and of the king's majesty, and whose names I am not minded to set down here, kept in their service brigands who were quite as bad. What is far more strange is that when those folks went into the cities, Paris or elsewhere, everybody knew them and pointed them out, but none durst lay a hand upon them."

2.1.5 England under Henry VII and Henry VIII

The risk of consolidation of power is evident in the history of the first two Tudor kings of England, Henry VII (1485-1509) and Henry VIII (1509-1547). The social structure of feudalism was rapidly declining, and Henry VII enforced the Statute of Livery and Maintenance in order to reduce the nobility, as cited by Green and Finlason [16, 17]:

> The introduction of gunpowder had ruined feudalism. The mounted and heavily-armed knight gave way to the meaner footman. Fortresses which had been impregnable against the attacks of the Middle Ages crumbled before the new artillery. Although gunpowder had been in use as early as Crecy, it was not until the accession of the House of Lancaster that it was really brought into effective employment as a military resource. But the revolution in warfare was immediate. ... Broken as was the strength of the baronage [from the civil wars of 1453-1485] there still remained lords whom the new monarch [Henry VII] watched with jealous solicitude. Their power lay in the hosts of disorderly retainers who swarmed around their houses, ready to furnish a force in case of revolt, while in peace they became centers of outrage and defiance to the law. Edward [V] had ordered the dissolution of military households in his Statute of Liveries, and the Statue was enforced by Henry with the utmost severity.

Here we see Henry VII suppressing the organized bands of nobles who had caused the civil unrest during the War of the Roses and afterward. But to concentrate power in one place did not work out too well; we see that within 40 years under Henry VIII, the unarmed people became subject to the worst tyranny in England's history as described by Green [18]:

> The ten years which follow the fall of Wolsey [1531] are among the most momentous in our history. The New Monarchy at last realized its power, and the work for which Wolsey had paved the way was carried out with a terrible thoroughness. The one great institution which could still offer resistance to the royal will was struck down. The Church became a mere instrument of the central despotism. The people learned their helplessness in rebellions easily suppressed and avenged with ruthless severity. A reign of terror, organized with consummate skill, held England panic-stricken at Henry's feet. The noblest heads rolled on the block. Virtue and learning could not save Thomas More: royal descent could not save Lady Salisbury. The putting away of one queen, the execution of another, taught England that nothing was too high for Henry's "courage" or too sacred for his "appetite". Parliament assembled only to sanction acts of unscrupulous tyranny, or to build up by its own statutes the great fabric of absolute rule. All the constitutional safeguards of English freedom were swept away. Arbitrary taxation, arbitrary legislation, arbitrary imprisonment were powers claimed without dispute and unsparingly exercised by the Crown.

In the space of a few pages, the great historians de Sismondi, Ostrogorsky, Guizot, and Green demonstrate that an unarmed population is regarded with contempt by foreigners and domestic tyrants alike. All the other honest historians have reached like conclusions. These are but a few instances where history shows the risk of disarmament -- I mean risk to the people, not to the government; governments are never disarmed. It should not be necessary to add to these the more recent examples: a) the policy of universal starvation-and-gulag under Lenin and Stalin in Russia; b) the same under the Kim regimes in North Korea; c) the massacre of the Jews by Hitler; d) the massacre of the Armenians by the Turks; e) the general massacre of his fellow Cambodians by Pol Pot; f) the garden-variety tyrannies of Pinochet in Chile, Amin in Uganda, Mussolini in Italy, Franco in Spain, and Castro in Cuba; g) the massacre of the recently-disarmed Tutsi's by the Hutu's in Rwanda (as the American administration under Clinton stood by and watched); and last but not least, h) Mao Zedong [Tse-tung] of China. Together, these regimes murdered about 200 million of their own people in the 20th century alone. Why would we expect any better behavior from governments in the 21st century?

2.1.6 Conclusion

When disarmed, people are executed, massacred, and sold into slavery according to the whims of the armed. We in America may have little fear of an invasion by Canada or Mexico, but be certain that every domestic government contains the possibility of tyranny, and there is of course no need to mention the deeds of criminals who take the same opportunity whenever offered. We shall see a similar case of tyranny in America as enacted by the southern Democrats against the newly-freed slaves. But first, it is necessary to address the right to bear arms in the context of American history and in so doing, uncover the true purpose of the Second Amendment to the U. S. Constitution.

2.2 American History

Three very important things must be kept in mind in the course of analyzing the Second Amendment. First, the original Constitution as ratified did not contain a Bill of Rights, nor did it provide any powers to disarm the people. Second, the first eight Amendments to the Constitution apply to individuals, but, contrary to the claims of some, do not *grant* any rights: they *recognize* rights that already existed and cite these as express limitations of the powers of the new federal government. Third, the phrase "well-regulated" in the Second Amendment has two different meanings, neither of which has anything to do with the legitimacy of private arms.

2.2.1 The Powers of the People Aside from the Constitution

To gain a true understanding of whether the people are to be armed, we need look no further than the comments made by Hamilton, Madison, and Jay in *The Federalist Papers* [19]. Keep in mind that *The Federalist Papers* were written during the ratification period as a means to explain the Constitution to the voters of New York; clearly the amendments were not in existence. Let us examine then the sentiments of the founding generation on the subject of an armed population, referencing the Constitution prior to the adoption of the Second Amendment.

Hamilton advocates a "select" militia in *The Federalist Papers #29*, and then shows it cannot be a danger to liberty given that the people in general are fully armed:

> The attention of the government ought particularly to be directed to the formation of a select corps of moderate extent, upon such principles as will really fit them for service in case of need. By thus circumscribing the plan, it will be possible to have an excellent body of well-trained militia ready to take the field whenever the defense of the State shall require it. This will not only lessen the call for military establishments, but if circumstances should at any time oblige the government to form an army of any magnitude, that army can never be formidable while there is a large body of citizens, little, if at all, inferior to them in the discipline and use of arms, who stand ready to defend their own rights and those of their fellow-citizens.

Thus Hamilton recognizes the right of the people to defend against the government and its select militia should the need arise; clearly the people must be armed in order to have that power.

Madison lays out in the *Federalist Papers* #46 a scenario in which the federal government became tyrannical, and how the people would be expected to respond:

> To these [the army of the federal government] would be opposed a militia amounting to near half a million of citizens with arms in their hands, officered by men chosen from among themselves, fighting for their common liberties, and united and conducted by government [states] possessing their affections and confidence. It may well be doubted whether a militia thus circumstanced could ever be conquered by such a proportion of regular troops. Those who are best acquainted with the last successful resistance of this country against the British will be most inclined to deny the possibility of it. Besides the advantage of being armed, which the Americans possess over the people of almost every other nation, the existence of subordinate governments, to which the people are attached, and by which the militia officers are chosen, forms a barrier against the enterprises of ambition, more insurmountable than any which a simple government of any form can admit of. Notwithstanding the military establishments in the several kingdoms of Europe, which are carried as far as the public resources will bear, the governments are afraid to trust the people with arms. ... Let us not insult the free and gallant citizens of America with the suspicion, that they would be less able to defend the rights of which they would be in actual possession, than the debased subjects of arbitrary power would be to rescue theirs from the hands of their oppressors.

It is important to note that the population of the thirteen states at the time of writing was about 3 million or so; the half-million referenced by Madison would constitute about 15 to 20% of the total population, a far higher ratio than the numbers of any standing army. The existing right to possess arms by the people is, as Madison contends, the remedy for a tyrannical government.

It is inconceivable that the original Constitution would recognize the legitimate right of the people not only to be armed, but to take up arms against a domestic tyranny, but then be amended during the first years of operation to remove that right. It is quite the contrary: the Bill of Rights exists because the anti-Federalist faction, ever wary of encroachment by governments, demanded a Bill of Rights so as to clarify the limits of governmental power. Madison was initially opposed to a bill of rights, agreeing with Hamilton that it would cause confusion. As Hamilton put it in *The Federalist Papers #84*:

> I go further and affirm that bills of rights, in the sense and to the extent in which they are contended for, are not only unnecessary in the proposed Constitution, but would even be dangerous. They would contain various exceptions to powers not granted; and, on this very account, would afford a colorable pretext to claim more than were granted. For why declare that things shall not be done which there is no power to do?

2.2.2 The Bill of Rights Limits Powers

The main contention between the Federalists and anti-Federalists was that the anti-Federalists demanded a bill of rights to ensure that those basic guarantees were clear as a limitation on the power of the government. Madison changed his mind about a Bill of Rights once the ninth necessary state ratified it, and many state ratification documents came to Congress with recommendations that a Bill of Rights be added to it. He was one of the people in the First Congress who actively promoted amendments to the Constitution. In his speech before Congress on 8 Jun 1789, Madison laid out the case for a bill of rights, and then indicated his means of proving they were limitations on the power of the government [20]:

> There have been objections of various kinds made against the constitution: Some were levelled against its structure, because the president was without a council; because the senate, which is a legislative body, had judicial powers in trials of impeachments; and because the powers of that body were compounded in other respects, in a manner that did not correspond with a particular theory; because it grants more power than is supposed to be necessary for every good purpose; and controls the ordinary powers of the state governments. I know some respectable characters who opposed this government on these grounds; but I believe that the great mass of the people who opposed it disliked it because it did not contain effectual provision against those encroachments on particular rights, and those safeguards which they have been long accustomed to have interposed between them and the magistrate who exercised the sovereign power: nor ought we to consider them safe, while a great number of our fellow citizens think these securities necessary.
>
> It has been a fortunate thing that the objection to the government has been made on the ground I stated; because it will be practicable on that ground to obviate the objection, so far as to satisfy the public mind that their liberties will be perpetual, and this without endangering any part of the constitution, which is considered as essential to the existence of the government by those who promoted its adoption.
>
> The amendments which have occurred to me, proper to be recommended by congress to the state legislatures, are these:

Madison then pointed out specific places in the text of the existing Constitution where specific changes to the language were to be made. After discussing the preamble, mode of election and apportionment, and compensation to representatives, he then began on the rights of the people:

> Fourthly. That in article 1st, section 9, between clauses 3 and 4, be inserted these clauses, to wit, The civil rights of none shall be abridged on account of religious belief or worship, nor shall any national religion be established, nor shall the full and equal rights of conscience be in any manner, or on any pretext infringed.
>
> The people shall not be restrained from peaceably assembling and consulting for their common good; nor from applying to the legislature by petitions, or remonstrances for redress of their grievances.
>
> The right of the people to keep and bear arms shall not be infringed; a well armed, and well regulated militia being the best security of a free country: but no person religiously scrupulous of bearing arms, shall be compelled to render military service in person.

Note that the insertion of the guarantees of freedom of the press, religion, assembly, and keeping and bearing arms are all to be located in the same place in the Constitution on equal terms. Note also that the principle of being armed precedes the statement about militias. The intent of what we now know as the bill of rights was to insert these provisions into Article 1, Section 9 of the Constitution, but was probably put into the familiar form as a matter of readability. It is this Section 9 which lists all the powers *denied* to the federal government. It is clear then, that far from granting any rights, the Second Amendment, just as with the other portions of the Bill of Rights, recognizes pre-existing rights and expressly denies the government any power to negate any of them.

But that is not all. The expert jurist St. George Tucker, who wrote the interpretation of the Constitution as used in most law schools for at least one hundred years, applied this same logic even in light of the Second Amendment as actually adopted [21]:

> "A well regulated militia being necessary to the security of a free state, the right of the people to keep, and bear arms, shall not be infringed."
>
> This may be considered as the true palladium of liberty. ... The right of self defense is the first law of nature: in most governments it has been the study of rulers to confine this right within the narrowest limits possible. Wherever standing armies are kept up, and the right of the people to keep and bear arms is, under any color or pretext whatsoever, prohibited, liberty, if not already annihilated, is on the brink of destruction. In England, the people have been disarmed, generally, under the specious pretext of preserving game: a never failing lure to bring over the landed aristocracy to support any measure, under that mask, though calculated for very different purposes. True it is, their bill of rights seems at first view to counteract this policy: but the right of bearing arms is confined to protestants, and the words suitable to their condition and degree, have been interpreted to authorize the prohibition of keeping a gun or other engine of destruction of game to any farmer or inferior tradesman, or other person not qualified to kill game. So that not one man in five hundred can keep a gun in his house without being subjected to a penalty.

2.2.3 The Meaning of "Well-Regulated"

General Washington made numerous comments and complaints regarding difficulties with the militia in the early stages of the Revolution. He wrote to William Livingston, Governor of New Jersey, on 24 Jan 1777 [22]:

> Sir: The irregular and disjointed state of the militia of this province makes it necessary to inform you, that, unless a law is immediately passed by your legislature, to reduce them to some order, and oblige them to turn out, in a different manner from what they have hitherto done, we shall bring very few into the field, and even those few will render little or no service.

He wrote a similar letter to the Pennsylvania Council of Safety five days later [23]. Washington requested aid from Governor Jonathan Trumbull (a colonial governor who sided with the Americans) on 6 Mar 1777 [24]:

> Sir: I flatter myself, that I should never again be under the necessity of trespassing upon the public spirit of your state, by calling upon her for another supply of militia; but, such has been the unaccountable delay in the recruiting of the Continental Battalion, chiefly owing to the long time that unhappily elapsed before the officers were appointed, that I see no prospect of keeping the field till the new levies can be brought into it, but by a reinforcement of militia. For want of proper laws in the southern governments, their militia were never well regulated; and since the late troubles, in which the old government were unhinged, and new ones not yet firmly established, the people have adopted a mode of thinking and acting for themselves. It is owing to this, that when a summons is issued for militia, those only turn out that please, and they for what time they please, by which means they sometimes set off for their homes in a few days after they join the army.

After New Jersey passed a law establishing the rules for calling out militia, Washington wrote again to Livingston on 5 Apr 1777 [25]:

> As you must certainly be best acquainted with the circumstances of your own state, I entirely acquiesce with any mode which you may think most expedient in regard to calling out your militia at this time.

During this time, and at other times thereafter, Washington noted that the militia was not reliable in the early part of the war, as he mentions in a letter to the President of Congress on 26 Mar 1777 [26]:

> For want of proper coercive powers, from disaffection, and other causes, the militia of this state are not to be depended upon. They are drawn out with difficulty; and at a most enormous expense, as their acts will show; they come, you can scarce tell how, they go, you hardly know when. In the same predicament are those of Pennsylvania. Numbers from this state have joined the enemy, and many more are disposed to do so ...

This is not to imply that Washington held the militia in low regard; he commended their conduct numerous times [27]. The salient point to be made from these passages, given the general difficulties of acquiring sufficient troops (and money) to prosecute the war, that the phrase "well-regulated" in the Second Amendment has nothing to do with "regulation" of who may and may not possess arms; it does not even refer to training per se. It refers to a set of laws by which the militia, when called into service, will actually show up for duty. The Second Amendment, in its militia capacity, simply allows the federal government to call upon the armed people for duty, should a national emergency require it.

The phrase "well-regulated" had other meanings during the colonial period, often used as a euphemism for "disciplined" or "practiced". While it is impossible to know if Madison had that connotation in mind when he wrote the text of the Second Amendment, it certainly fits the notion of a militia requiring little training when called into service. Hamilton, as General Washington's aide during the war, was certainly familiar with the concept of readiness: he illustrates this "disciplined" and "practiced" notion in *The Federalist Papers #29*:

> To oblige the great body of yeomanry, and of other classes of citizens, to be under arms for the purpose of going through military exercises and evolutions, as often as might be necessary to acquire a degree of perfection which would entitle them to the character of a well-regulated militia, would be a real grievance to the people, and a serious public inconvenience.

2.2.4 Conclusion

Neither the text of the Constitution nor the Second Amendment grants any powers to prohibit the right of the people to possess arms; given that the purpose of arms was for defense of self and liberty, it may be safely concluded that the arms in question are those equal in nature to the professional armies and the "select" militia.

Only the most casual thinker could believe that the National Guard is the "militia" referred to in the Second Amendment. There are several reasons why it could not be so. First, the militia was expected to provide their own arms; but the members of the National Guard are supplied arms by the government, and are to be turned into the government when their duty is over. Secondly, the militia is to be commanded by officers chosen at the state level; but the National Guard is under the plenary authority of the President; the state only asks the President to call them out. Third, the Second Amendment refers to the "people" which everywhere else in the Constitution means individuals; it is inconceivable that Madison would use the word "people" here if he meant specific military organizations controlled by the federal government.

As to whether the Second Amendment curtails only the federal powers, but leaves the states open to impose any restrictions they please, it is necessary that only three things be observed. First, the first eight amendments define pre-existing liberties of the people. Second, they exist to clarify limitations on the power of government. Third, according to Article 6 of the Constitution, all state officers are required to support the federal Constitution by oath or affirmation. It is illogical to suppose that the officers of state governments, having taken an oath to support the federal Constitution that recognizes limitations on powers due to the liberties of the people, should have powers at the state level to circumvent those liberties. But I further recognize that there is no end of arrogance among the power-mad at either state or federal levels.

3 The Moral Aspect

In considering the moral aspect of citizen disarmament, commonly called "gun control", it is helpful to return once again to English jurist William Blackstone [28]:

> In these several articles consist the rights, or, as they are frequently termed, the liberties of Englishmen: liberties, more generally talked of than thoroughly understood; and yet highly necessary to be perfectly known and considered by every man of rank or property, lest his ignorance of the points whereon they are founded should hurry him into faction and licentiousness on the one hand, or a pusillanimous indifference and criminal submission on the other. And we have seen that these rights consist, primarily, in the free enjoyment of personal security, of personal liberty, and of private property. So long as these remain inviolate, the subject is perfectly free; for every species of compulsive tyranny and oppression must act in opposition to one or the other of these rights, having no other object upon which it can possibly be employed. To preserve them from violation, it is necessary that the constitution of parliament be supported in its full vigor; and limits, certainly known, be set to the royal prerogative. And, lastly, to vindicate these rights when actually violated or attacked, the subjects of England are entitled, in the first place, to the regular administration and free course of justice in the courts of law; next, to the right of petitioning the king and parliament for redress of grievances; and lastly, to the right of having and using arms for self-preservation and defense. And all these rights and liberties it is our birthright to enjoy entire; unless where the laws of our country have laid them under necessary restraints. Restraints in themselves so gentle and moderate, as will appear upon further inquiry, that no man of sense of probity would wish to see them slackened. For all of us have in our choice to do every good thing that a good man would desire to do; and are restrained from nothing, but what would be pernicious either to ourselves or to our fellow-citizens.

So it is that every citizen is to be aware of his rights to life, liberty, and property, and at the risk of being both a coward and traitor to freedom and posterity, be prepared with arms to defend those freedoms should the government fail to perform its duties to preserve them. But what about those "necessary restraints" that Mr. Blackstone refers to -- doesn't "gun control" fall under the category of "gentle and moderate" restrictions conducive to the happiness of the people? No. Gun control is quite the opposite: it is the means by which you, the citizen, are turned into a helpless dependent subject because it removes the ultimate restraint upon the power of governments and criminals alike. It is the means by which you, the citizen, are convinced that your life, liberty, and property are not worth fighting for; and you should leave that to the professionals, since you might get hurt and not be able to pay taxes. It is the means by which your moral compass is forced to always point toward the government, begging them to save you; or maybe worse, subordinate yourself to the whims of some gang of professional criminals.

Is it moral to leave people defenseless in situations where the police are not available or cannot be of use, such as Hurricane Katrina, Hurricane Sandy, the LA riots after the O. J. Simpson verdict, or the many riots that took place in the 1960's, including most major cities? The police have not signed up to protect you from everything. The police generally do a fine job, but their task is to investigate crimes after they have occurred, make arrests in accordance with the evidence, and thus bring the suspect into the justice system. The judicial system may limit the future actions of criminals, but has no effect on the crime that is about to happen. You, as a moral agent, are responsible for your own safety. In fact, the police are not legally obligated to protect you from anything, or even to show up when they are called, especially in those unusual times when the number of calls greatly exceeds the capacity of the system to respond. Is it moral on your part to demand that the police risk their lives to defend yours? The police do not sign up for responding to large-scale civil breakdown. Many of the police in New Orleans fled to Baton Rouge during Hurricane Katrina; LAPD was ordered to stand down during the LA riots. Rightfully so -- they have families to look out for, which supersedes your needs and demands. What if the attack on New York City on 11 Sep 2001 had been a larger, more general attack in which the normal governance had broken down? The criminals would have gone berserk, as they are always looking for an excuse. History shows that you will be on your own. The National Guard troops were in their barracks by sundown during the LA riots; in the aftermath of Hurricane Katrina they actually disarmed the citizens, leaving them easy prey for the gangs.

Politicians are always protected by bodyguards with high-capacity weapons -- this is more than hypocrisy; it is immorality of the highest order: no moral government would permit its employees to arrogate an exemption for themselves while requiring the common people to go about unarmed. Recall that all legislative authority is vested in the Congress; consider now the words of James Madison in *The Federalist Papers* #57:

> I will add, as a fifth circumstance in the situation of the House of Representatives, restraining them from oppressive measures, that they can make no law which will not have its full operation on themselves and their friends, as well as the great mass of society. This has always been deemed one of the strongest bonds by which human policy can connect the rulers and people together. It creates between them that communion of interests and sympathy of sentiments of which few governments have furnished examples; but without which every government degenerates into tyranny. If it be asked what is to restrain the House of Representatives from making legal discriminations in favor of themselves and a particular class of the society? I answer: the genius of the whole system; the nature of just and constitutional laws, and the manly spirit which actuates the people of America -- a spirit which nourishes freedom, and in return is nourished by it.

The same principle applies at the state and local government levels. How can a just government exempt itself from its own laws? But yet it is evident that "We the People" have failed to enforce this dictum upon our politicians; we see at every turn numerous exemptions to the laws created for the benefit of politicians, bureaucrats and their associates. It is especially evident in the gun laws: our (allegedly) morally-superior government employees parade the streets with taxpayer-paid (supposedly) morally-superior bodyguards, while the people are forced by law to remain defenseless at all times and in all places.

Vice President Joe Biden (now President) took the time in 2013 to look down his nose and lecture us lowlifes that we only need a double-barrel shotgun for self-defense, even at home. I wonder what type of weapons, containing how many rounds, and of what type, his Secret Service detail carries with them when protecting him, even in his home.

Senator Joe Manchin (D-WV) released a video in 2013 claiming "that no one is going to take my guns away". He's right -- no one is going to take his guns away because he is a member of the (allegedly) morally-superior ruling elite. He will have access to all the guns and ammunition he wants for the rest of his life, and so will all his friends and family for all of their lives. It will be interesting to see what Senator Manchin thinks of you and your rights in the upcoming disarmament votes in Congress.

When the government is armed and the people are not, one has tyranny; when the people are armed and the government is not, one has anarchy; in America, both are armed, wary of each other, and each side is able to suppress the worst instincts of the other. But our modern politicians do not like the idea of any challenges to their quest for arbitrary power.

Criminals know two things: a) they will always be able to get a gun, no matter what the law is; and b) they are likely to get shot by their intended victims if those intended victims have guns. It is evident that criminals always favor gun control for the same reasons the politicians do: it has no effect upon their livelihood and makes their job easier. Conversely, armed people don't have to take any crap from criminals or from governments. It is immoral to be afraid of criminals, but yet that is what our government demands. The reason they demand it is simple: the government needs the existence of large criminal networks to justify part of its existence, and it also helps keep the people in fear.

We commonly hear arguments that "one doesn't need a semi-automatic rifle" since the Second Amendment was written during a time when only muzzle-loading muskets were available. But exactly the same argument could be made about radio, TV talk shows, and internet sites, since only newspapers and handbills existed when the First Amendment was written. I would be curious to know, given their self-appointed superior moral righteousness, what part of the First Amendment is the mainstream media willing to give up in order to reduce the incidence of libel, defamation of character, and slander?

"We the People" would do well to recall the words of Alexander Hamilton in *The Federalist Papers* #78:

> There is no position which depends on clearer principles that that every act of a delegated authority, contrary to the tenor of the commission under which it is exercised, is void. No legislative act, therefore, contrary to the Constitution can be valid. To deny this would be to affirm that the deputy is greater than his principal; that the servant is above his master; that the representatives of the people are superior to the people themselves; that men acting by virtue of powers may do not only what their powers do not authorize, but what they forbid.

The U. S. Constitution clearly states that the right the people to keep and bear arms shall not be infringed; and every state and local officer swears an oath to also uphold the federal Constitution. Under what pretended morality do they claim power to do what is prohibited by their oath? Or carve out exemptions to the laws for themselves? Or tell us that we are not morally suitable to possess the tools necessary to take care of ourselves should the need arise?

4 The Technological Aspect

Some prominent members of the media are opposed to the Second Amendment on the grounds that modern guns (so they claim) are too dangerous; that the Second Amendment logically only applies to muzzle-loading single shot muskets of the type commonly in use at the time of the adoption of the Constitution. What they seem unable to understand (or are unwilling to admit they understand) is that the modern semi-automatic pistol or rifle is nothing more than the 21st century equivalent of the Brown Bess musket, just as the daily newspaper, radio, TV, and the internet are nothing more than 21st century equivalents of the weekly newspaper and the handbill. If the members of the media claim it is logical for gun owners to be limited to 10-round magazines, it is equally logical that TV news shows be limited to 10 minutes per day and newspapers to 10 pages. If the citizens are to be limited on a logical basis to purchasing one gun per month, there is no reason why *The New York Times* cannot logically be limited to publishing one day per month, and the TV networks likewise limited to broadcasting once per month. If we are to have logical background checks on anyone who seeks to buy a gun, there is no logical reason why we should not impose background checks on every reporter, editor, publisher, writer, broadcaster, advertiser, and producer. If gun owners are to be logically forced to put trigger locks on their guns, and keep ammunition stored separately in their own homes in order to prevent "accidental discharge", there is no logical reason why a government employee cannot be deployed to lock down all newspaper, radio, and TV productions until the intended material is reviewed in order to prevent "accidental disclosure of inconvenient facts". In short, if the rights of the people are to be denied simply due to the advance of technology, it is evident that every right could logically be so limited. This may be a good way for the people to obtain a more "responsible" media: demand a plan to regulate it the same as the Second Amendment. Let us see if our illustrious First Amendment advocates are willing to be restricted to the same extent as the Second Amendment advocates they are so quick to demonize.

But that is not the only technological aspect to be considered. If we look back at the long development of the firearm, we see a steady progression in its improvements [29]. Here is a quick summary of the advance of firearms technology:

1249: The first description of gunpowder in Europe (which we would now call blackpowder).
1346: Cannon were used by the English at the Battle of Crecy.
1381: The first cannon that could be deployed by a single person (town of Augsburg).

1418: Mortars were used at the Battle of Cherbourg.
1460: The first matchlock rifle was invented.
1586: The first paper cartridges were invented.
1610: The first magazine-fed rifle was invented.
1690: The first "revolving" pistol was invented (the barrels revolved instead of the cylinder).
1730: The first breech-loading rifles were invented.
1774: The percussion cap method of ignition was invented (i.e., first use of self-priming cartridges).
1830: The double-barrel sporting shotgun was in popular use.
1835: The modern 6-shot revolver was invented.
1840: The combined self-priming cartridge was invented.
1845: The first magazine-fed pistol was invented.
1860: The lever-action rifle was invented.
1862: The belt-fed rapid-fire gun was invented (by Gattling)
1866: Gun-cotton (which we now call gunpowder or smokeless powder) was invented.
1884: The first full-automatic belt-fed machine gun was invented.
1885: The first semi-automatic rifle with detachable magazine was invented (Mannlicher).
1886: The first bolt-action rifle with a detachable magazine was invented.
1895: The automatic repeating rifle (full-automatic machine gun) was invented.
1902: The semi-automatic shotgun was invented.
1918: The hand-held full-automatic machine gun (Thompson) was invented.

It is not necessary to go any further. All the common firearms now in production are simply improvements and variations on these; including those for greater safety or for a variety of calibers. The famous AK-47, M-1, M-14, and M-16 semi- and selective-fire types were not invented until the middle decades of the 20th century. The important thing to remember is that all the guns that are now so feared by governments are based on technology that is over one hundred years old; comparable to being afraid of telephones, washing machines, and toasters. Secondly, anyone with a machine shop capable of 1920's accuracy and tolerances can build as many machine-guns (and all lesser types) as necessary. If drug dealers can build ocean-going submarines to smuggle cocaine into the U. S., it does not take much imagination to see that a similar thing can be done with clandestine production of guns and ammunition, should the government attempt to regulate the current legal ones out of existence.

5 The Statistical Aspect

It has been said that a good statistician can take any three numbers and justify whatever conclusion he is being paid to come up with. We will consider some of the statistics concerning citizen disarmament, but first, let us consider a few elements of basic logic.

Consider two families, both with young children. They live in houses next door to each other. One home has a bathtub and the other does not. How much more likely is it that a child in the home containing a bathtub will "drown in a bathtub in their home", compared to the children living in the house without the bathtub? It is evident that the children living in the house with no bathtub have zero chance of drowning in a bathtub in their home, since there are none. Therefore, statistically speaking, children in homes with bathtubs are infinitely more likely to drown in a bathtub than the neighbor children, although drowning in bathtubs is fairly rare.

The School Bus Information Clearinghouse [30] reports that in the U. S., 6 children per year are killed in school bus accidents, while another 29 children per year are killed either getting on or off a school bus, or are killed accidentally while waiting for a school bus. When you consider how many children are riding school busses every day, it is evident that they are pretty safe. But consider the children who are home schooled, or who walk to school: they never take a school bus. Therefore, the children who ride school busses, although deaths are exceeding rare, are in a statistical sense infinitely more likely to be killed in school bus accidents than those who do not ride them.

If a person has an automobile accident, is it more or less likely that the accident will have occurred within 25 miles from home, or more than 25 miles from home? I am certain that it is the former: accidents are not called "deliberates"; they are most likely to occur wherever the typical person is most of the time relative to their home. Since most people do not drive more than 25 miles from home on a typical day, most car accidents should occur near home than away from it. Accidents in the home occur in a very familiar place.

I'm a mental midget who went to public schools, and even I could figure those out. But our illustrious gun-control fanatics are always seeking to convince us that guns in the hands of the citizens are an abnormality in "civilized" society; that they cause suicides; that they cause crime in general; and are to be greatly dreaded, and then prohibited. These fanatics seek to impose their quest for power by repeating weak claims that can be neither proven nor disproven; by pretending that correlation equals causation; sometimes by simply lying. Let us consider a few examples.

5.1 Regarding Suicide and Presence of Guns

The advocates for gun control pretend that a high rate of gun ownership leads to a high rate of suicide. It is easy to determine factually whether such a claim proves cause-and-effect, or if gun ownership and suicides are even correlated. Figures for gun ownership rates and the suicide rates are readily available for many nations [31, 32]. The data (from 2007) is presented as number of guns per 100 persons (which is easily converted to number of guns per 100,000) to match the suicide rate data in number per 100,000. Now, if guns cause suicide, or make suicide more likely, then we should find high suicide rates in nations with high gun ownership rates. It is obvious that not all suicides are the result of gunshot wounds, but suffice to say, even if guns only make suicide easier, then the same proposition would have to hold: one would expect high suicide rates in nations with high gun ownership rates, and vice-versa. The results for a sample of 37 nations are shown on Figure 5.1-1.

Here I have shown gun ownership and suicide rates for 37 nations, sorted by continent. For each continent, I have chosen the ones with the highest gun ownership rate with a corresponding number from the same continent with the lowest ownership rate. Those values can be seen in the second column. For example, Switzerland, Finland, Serbia, Cyprus, Sweden, Norway, and France have the highest gun ownership rates in Europe, counterbalanced by Poland, the Netherlands, Scotland, Hungary, England, Slovakia, and Portugal having the lowest gun ownership rates of the 37 nations in Europe. The fourth column indicates the number of guns per 100,000 residents. The fifth shows the suicide rate per 100,000. Next, the sixth and seventh columns show the rank of gun ownership and rank of suicides for this data. The eighth column is the ratio of gun presence to suicides (i.e., the overall number of suicides per gun); note how small the numbers are. To make this data more readable, I have multiplied them by a factor of one million, as shown in the second-to-last column. The last column indicates the rank of suicides per gun for this set of 37 nations. There was insufficient data for Africa.

Consider the top five nations and bottom five nations for gun presence and their respective suicide rates as shown in columns 6 (gun ownership rank for this dataset) and 7 (suicide rate rank for this dataset). The U. S. is first in gun ownership rate, 13th in suicide rate. Likewise, Switzerland is second and 20th; Finland is third and 7th; Serbia is fourth and 6th; and Cyprus is fifth and 32nd. On the other hand, South Korea is 33rd in gun ownership, but ranks first in suicide rate. Likewise, China is 27th in gun ownership rate, 2nd in suicides; Hungary is 24th and third; Japan is 36th and 4th; and Russia is 18th and fifth. In other words, some nations have high gun rates and high suicide rates (Finland and Serbia); some have high gun rates and low suicide rates (U. S. and Cyprus); some have low gun rates and low suicide rates (Tajikistan and Philippines), and some have low gun rates and high suicide rates (Japan and Poland), and the others fall somewhere in between as expected. If the claims of the gun-control advocates were true, one would expect that the rate of gun possession in general would lead to higher rates of suicide in general. But the large dispersion in the data proves that gun presence and suicide rates are not correlated.

In fact, if I were corrupt like our gun-control fanatics, I could use the preceding facts to make the false assertion that guns prevent suicide. Of course such a proposition is false - no rational person could believe it. But enough dummies would believe it if I had the means to get the media to repeat it a hundred billion times. Congress would then pass a law requiring depressed persons to prove they owned guns.

Continent	Gun ownership rank (continent)	Nation	Guns per 100,000	Suicides per 100,000	Gun ownership rank (this data)	Suicide rate rank (this data)	Raw suicides per gun	Suicides per gun x 1 million	Rank, suicides per gun
North America	1	U. S.	88800	12.0	1	13	0.0001351	135.1	34
	2	Canada	30800	11.5	10	18	0.0003734	373.4	28
	3	Mexico	15000	4.0	15	30	0.0002667	266.7	30
South/ Central America	1	Uruguay	31800	15.8	9	8	0.0004969	496.9	22
	2	Panama	21700	5.5	12	28	0.0002535	253.5	31
	3	Peru	18800	0.9	13	36	0.0000479	47.9	37
	4	Paraguay	17000	3.6	14	31	0.0002118	211.8	33
	17	El Salvador	5800	8.0	23	25	0.0013793	1379.3	15
	18	Dom. Rep.	5100	2.3	26	34	0.0004510	451.0	24
	19	Cuba	4800	12.3	28	12	0.0025625	2562.5	10
	20	Ecuador	1300	7.1	31	26	0.0054615	5461.5	6
Europe	1	Switzerland	45700	11.1	2	20	0.0002429	242.9	32
	2	Finland	45300	16.8	3	7	0.0003709	370.9	29
	3	Serbia	37800	19.5	4	6	0.0005159	515.9	21
	4	Cyprus	36400	3.6	5	32	0.0000989	98.9	35
	5	Sweden	31600	11.9	6	14	0.0003766	376.6	27
	6	Norway	31300	11.9	7	15	0.0003802	380.2	26
	7	France	31200	15.0	8	10	0.0004808	480.8	23
	29	Portugal	8500	11.5	19	19	0.0013529	1352.9	16
	30	Slovakia	8300	9.9	20	21	0.0011928	1192.8	17
	31	England	6200	11.8	22	16	0.0019032	1903.2	14
	32	Hungary	5500	21.7	24	3	0.0039455	3945.5	8
	33	Scotland	5500	11.8	25	17	0.0021455	2145.5	13
	34	Netherlands	3900	8.5	30	24	0.0021795	2179.5	12
	35	Poland	1300	15.4	32	9	0.0118462	11846.2	4
Asia	1	Pakistan	11600	0.9	16	37	0.0000759	75.9	36
	2	Russia	8900	21.4	18	5	0.0024045	2404.5	11
	3	Georgia	7300	4.3	21	29	0.0005890	589.0	19
	4	China	4900	22.0	27	2	0.0044898	4489.8	7
	5	Philippines	4700	2.1	29	35	0.0004468	446.8	25
	24	South Korea	1100	31.7	33	1	0.0288182	28818.2	2
	25	Tajikistan	1000	2.6	34	33	0.0026000	2600.0	9
	26	Kyrgyzstan	900	8.8	35	23	0.0097778	9777.8	5
	27	Japan	600	21.7	36	4	0.0361667	36166.7	1
	28	Singapore	500	7.0	37	27	0.0140000	14000.0	3
Australia/ NZ	1	New Zealand	22600	13.2	11	11	0.0005841	584.1	20
	2	Australia	15000	9.7	17	22	0.0006467	646.7	18

Figure 5.1-1: Gun Ownership and Suicide Rates for 37 Nations.

The second-to-last column in Figure 5.1-1 shows the number of suicides per gun (magnified by a million to make the numbers easier - the real rate of suicides per gun are shown in the third-from-right column). There is again a wide dispersion in the data, from a low of 47.9 in Peru to a high of 36,166 in Japan. This suggests, although does not prove, that suicide in nations like Japan involves means other than gunshot wounds; but may indicate a high correlation of immediate access to guns as a factor in places like Peru. Are you going to give up your rights because of the behavior of people in Peru? The last column on the right shows the suicide rank with respect to suicides per gun. The five nations with the least correlation of suicides per gun are Peru, Pakistan, Cyprus, the U. S., and Paraguay.

It must be observed that the gun rate is the overall number of guns per unit population; it says nothing about how often guns are used in suicides. The data for suicide method is shown in Figure 5.1-2, based on data assembled by the World Health Organization [33] and researchers in Taiwan [34].

		Suicide Method by Percentage, Men					Suicide Method by Percentage, Women					
	Source	All Pois-onings	Hanging	Drowning	Firearms	Falls & other	All Pois-onings	Hanging	Drowning	Firearms	Falls & other	Note
U. S.	Ref [33]	7.4	20.4	0.9	60.6	10.7	31.5	16.9	2.1	35.7	13.9	
Canada	Ref [33]	10.6	44.4	2.3	21.6	21.0	39.3	36.8	4.0	3.8	20.6	
Mexico	Ref [33]	6.2	68.8	0.5	20.5	4.0	28.4	51.3	0.7	13.4	6.2	
Uruguay	Ref [33]	3.0	41.1	2.7	47.8	5.3	10.5	27.5	9.1	35.7	17.1	
Panama	Ref [33]	19.7	63.5	0.0	11.9	5.0	49.2	44.1	0.0	2.2	4.4	
Peru	Ref [33]	56.9	14.1	3.3	11.8	13.8	84.8	7.3	2.4	1.2	4.2	
Paraguay	Ref [33]	16.0	42.9	1.6	30.4	9.1	41.0	27.1	1.9	21.5	8.5	
El Salvador	Ref [33]	86.6	8.4	0.3	3.8	0.8	95.1	3.2	0.0	1.4	0.4	
Dom. Rep.	Ref [33]	24.9	42.8	2.5	20.2	9.6	42.7	31.9	3.6	8.4	13.2	
Cuba	Ref [33]	10.6	76.8	0.6	3.4	8.6	21.8	27.4	1.3	0.7	48.8	
Ecuador	Ref [33]	33.8	41.3	1.6	19.2	4.1	66.6	23.9	0.8	5.3	3.4	
Switzerland	Ref [33]	13.9	27.3	3.0	33.5	22.4	38.5	19.1	10.1	3.4	28.6	
Finland	Ref [33]	17.8	33.1	3.5	26.7	18.8	49.7	20.3	10.6	2.6	16.8	
Serbia	Ref [33]	4.5	57.6	3.3	20.1	14.5	14.0	57.2	7.9	5.2	15.7	
Cyprus		No data										
Sweden	Ref [33]	16.3	39.4	5.3	17.1	22.0	43.0	25.1	12.4	0.9	18.5	
Norway	Ref [33]	11.3	37.9	4.6	27.1	19.0	33.8	32.3	13.5	2.0	18.4	
France	Ref [33]	9.6	48.9	3.9	22.1	15.5	28.3	29.2	12.4	4.1	25.9	
Portugal	Ref [33]	16.4	52.2	4.3	11.1	16.0	32.7	31.2	11.6	3.2	21.2	
Slovenia	Ref [33]	4.3	64.7	2.5	11.8	16.7	11.7	53.1	12.2	1.2	21.8	
England	Ref [33]	15.1	55.2	2.4	3.5	23.7	41.4	35.9	4.7	0.6	17.6	
Hungary	Ref [33]	11.6	70.3	1.4	4.0	12.7	35.1	43.4	4.5	0.6	16.4	
Scotland	Ref [33]	15.1	55.2	2.4	3.5	23.7	41.4	35.9	4.7	0.6	17.6	
Netherlands	Ref [33]	13.1	47.9	6.6	4.4	28.0	25.8	33.6	11.0	0.6	29.0	
Poland	Ref [33]	2.1	91.2	0.5	1.1	5.2	8.7	77.6	3.0	0.2	10.5	
Pakistan	Ref [34]	26.0	40.0		15.0	10.0	26.0	40.0		15.0	10.0	1
Russia		No data										
Georgia	Ref [33]	7.9	53.2	0.9	3.2	34.8	8.6	50.8	0.8	0.8	39.1	
China	Ref [34]	69.0	20.0	5.0			69.0	20.0	5.0			
Philipinnes		No data										
South Korea	Ref [33]	37.9	39.2	3.2	0.4	19.3	43.6	26.0	3.8	0.1	26.6	
Tajikistan		No data										
Kyrgyzstan		No data										
Japan	Ref [33]	3.8	68.7	2.6	0.2	24.6	7.2	59.9	7.8	0.0	25.2	
Singapore	Ref [34]	5.9	16.6			72.4	5.9	16.6			72.4	2
Australia	Ref [33]	9.1	45.4	1.3	11.5	32.7	27.2	36.4	3.9	2.6	29.9	
New Zealand	Ref [33]	7.4	48.4	1.9	11.2	31.1	20.1	42.5	4.4	2.2	30.7	
1. Source data did not distinguish between sexes; assumed to be equal.												
2. Jumping from high places is the chosen method for 72.4% of suicides in Singapore.												

Figure 5.1-2: Suicide Method by Percentage for 37 Nations

The results in Figure 5.1-2 show that the expectation from Figure 5.1-1 is about right: even in nations with fairly widespread gun ownership, hanging and poisoning are the most common methods of suicide. Gunshot wounds are the chosen method for more than 40% of suicides only in the U. S. and Uruguay. Even in nations with fairly high gun rates, such as Finland, Sweden, Serbia, and Norway, hanging is the method of choice. Even in Peru, which had the lowest ratio of suicides per gun, only 12% of suicides were by gunshot wound. This suggests, although does not prove, that the presence of guns does not affect the suicide method in general. This data does not address the question about the suicide method chosen for those with ready access to guns in their homes. I would expect that people who choose to commit suicide would choose to do so by the fastest method rather than poisoning themselves with arsenic over a six-month period. The important point is that the widespread availability of guns in a society does not increase the general suicide rate (Figure 5.1-1), nor does it affect the method of suicide in a significant manner (Figure 5.1-2).

5.2 Regarding "Violent Crime and Household Risk"

Those who advocate for gun control often claim they do so in the interest of public safety, meaning the potential reduction in violent crime or safety in the home. To justify the attack on your rights they will often cite crime statistics, and claim that their particular disarmament measure will reduce crime by a certain amount. Then, when their favorite gun control measure has been in effect for ten or twenty years, and the crime rates have nonetheless gone up, they will still claim victory for disarmament on the curious and improvable notion that "the rise in crime would have been higher without the gun control we so heroically imposed". A more important justification for gun control in recent times is "to keep the children safe", especially since the massacre by gunfire at the Sandy Hook gun-free school zone. I will only say in regard to that shooting -- if the politicians and bureaucrats are dumb enough to establish lax security, it is best not to advertise it; at least keep the crazies guessing about it. We cannot expect politicians and bureaucrats to admit their mistakes, nor do I accuse them of respecting the Constitution. So we are left with an examination into the statistics of the situation to see for ourselves if gun control is justified or not.

When speaking of crime and the associated statistics, it is wise to remember that there are three types of violent crimes: a) the ones committed by professional criminals as part of their livelihood, b) ones committed by typically non-violent criminals who find it necessary on occasion to perform a deed of violence; and c) the ones committed by those who are normally regular citizens, but decide to commit a violent crime motivated under transient conditions of jealousy, anger, hatred, or greed.

As to the first class of criminals, like the various ethnic mafias, and certain gangs like MS-13 or the Aryan Brotherhood, it should be recognized that no amount of gun control will have any effect on them. Guns are a necessary implement of their trade, and will be obtained by them no matter what. If a person makes a living as an auto mechanic, he naturally has wrenches and screwdrivers as they are the tools of his trade. Likewise with IT engineers with their computers and salesmen with their telephones. No professional criminal will ever be deprived of the use of guns, as they are the most expedient means for conducting their business. Their victims are usually other professional criminals, and the causes for the crime are a violation of long-standing rules of the organization or encroachment by outsiders on traditional rights to commit other crimes (such as labor union control, loan-sharking, prostitution, gambling, etc.).

As for the second class of criminals, including the common street drug dealer, burglars, con men, car thieves, and so on: they do not use guns in the course of normal business, but have occasion to do so at various times. Some are always armed as a matter of self-protection; but all of them have ready access to guns regardless of gun control when they are needed. They can be obtained from other professional criminals, especially ones of the first class, who will never be disarmed. (Sometimes the BATFE provides arms to already fully-armed Mexican drug cartels.) This class of criminals generally use guns when violence is necessary, since it is the most expedient and effective method. This class of criminals also usually preys on others of their class, usually over gang colors or in battles to determine drug-dealing territory.

Then there is the last and smallest class of criminals: the wife who found her husband was cheating with her best friend; the embezzler who was discovered by his boss; a murder for retribution; a murder for the insurance payout; or the occasional mental incompetent who thinks he is a cartoon character and proceeds to shoot people in a theater.

Figure 5.3-1 shows a selection of data [35] for gun ownership rates vs. homicide rates for various nations, similar to what was shown earlier on suicide rates. Again, the data shows no correlation between gun ownership rates and murder rates. There are nations with very low gun ownership rates and correspondingly low murder rates (Japan, Singapore, Poland, and China). There are no nations among the top ten in gun ownership rates that were also in the top ten in murder rates; the closest correlation of that nature occurs with Uruguay (#9 in gun ownership rate, #11 in murder rate). Others in the top ten in gun ownership have very low murder rates under 2.2 per 100,000 (Canada, Finland, Serbia, Cyprus, Switzerland, Sweden, Norway, and France); the only exception was the U. S. (first in gun ownership, 14th in murder rate at 4.8 per 100,000). The most interesting statistics comes from nations with moderate to low gun ownership rates, but very high murder rates (Mexico, El Salvador, Dominican Republic, Ecuador, and Kyrgyzstan). The others in this data fall somewhere between these extremes; once again the dispersion in the data demonstrates that gun ownership rates are unrelated to murder rates; if anything, high gun ownership by the general public may prevent the murder rates from approaching truly pathological levels as in El Salvador, Mexico, and Panama.

Continent	Gun ownership rank (continent)	Nation	Guns per 100,000	Murders per 100,000	Gun ownership rank (this data)	Murder rate rank (this data)	Raw murders per gun	Murders per gun x 1 million	Rank, murders per gun
North America	1	U. S.	88800	4.8	1	14	0.0000541	54.1	28
	2	Canada	30800	1.6	10	20	0.0000519	51.9	29
	3	Mexico	15000	22.7	15	3	0.0015133	1513.3	7
South/ Central America	1	Uruguay	31800	5.9	9	11	0.0001855	185.5	24
	2	Panama	21700	21.6	12	4	0.0009954	995.4	11
	3	Peru	18800	10.3	13	8	0.0005479	547.9	18
	4	Paraguay	17000	11.5	14	7	0.0006765	676.5	13
	17	El Salvador	5800	69.2	23	1	0.0119310	11931.0	2
	18	Dom. Rep.	5100	25.0	26	2	0.0049020	4902.0	4
	19	Cuba	4800	5.0	28	13	0.0010417	1041.7	10
	20	Ecuador	1300	12.7	31	6	0.0097692	9769.2	3
Europe	1	Switzerland	45700	0.7	2	34	0.0000153	15.3	37
	2	Finland	45300	2.2	3	17	0.0000486	48.6	30
	3	Serbia	37800	1.2	4	23	0.0000317	31.7	34
	4	Cyprus	36400	1.7	5	19	0.0000467	46.7	31
	5	Sweden	31600	1.0	6	31	0.0000316	31.6	35
	6	Norway	31300	0.6	7	35	0.0000192	19.2	36
	7	France	31200	1.1	8	28	0.0000353	35.3	33
	29	Portugal	8500	1.2	19	26	0.0001412	141.2	26
	30	Slovakia	8300	1.5	20	21	0.0001807	180.7	25
	31	England	6200	1.2	22	24	0.0001935	193.5	23
	32	Hungary	5500	1.3	24	22	0.0002364	236.4	20
	33	Scotland	5500	1.2	25	25	0.0002182	218.2	21
	34	Netherlands	3900	1.1	30	29	0.0002821	282.1	19
	35	Poland	1300	1.1	32	27	0.0008462	846.2	12
Asia	1	Pakistan	11600	7.8	16	10	0.0006724	672.4	14
	2	Russia	8900	10.2	18	9	0.0011461	1146.1	9
	3	Georgia	7300	4.3	21	15	0.0005890	589.0	17
	4	China	4900	1.0	27	30	0.0002041	204.1	22
	5	Philippines	4700	5.4	29	12	0.0011489	1148.9	8
	24	South Korea	1100	2.6	33	16	0.0023636	2363.6	5
	25	Tajikistan	1000	2.1	34	18	0.0021000	2100.0	6
	26	Kyrgyzstan	900	20.1	35	5	0.0223333	22333.3	1
	27	Japan	600	0.4	36	36	0.0006667	666.7	15
	28	Singapore	500	0.3	37	37	0.0006000	600.0	16
Australia/ NZ	1	New Zealand	22600	0.9	11	33	0.0000398	39.8	32
	2	Australia	15000	1.0	17	32	0.0000667	66.7	27

Figure 5.3-1: Gun Ownership and Homicide Rates for Selected Nations

It is important in this debate to keep in mind who is doing the killing and who is doing the dying. If professional criminals are killing other professional criminals, a net good to society results, and we should wish the murder rate to be higher than it is. The reverse applies if innocent people are dying. Figure 5.3-2 shows some data on what type of people are doing the dying. As shown here, a very high percentage of the homicide victims in large U. S. cities have long prior arrest records. I will not make the Democratic Party assumption that an arrest equals a conviction, nor do I assume that the prior arrests were for violent crimes; but suffice to say, these victims were more likely to be criminals themselves than not. Most homicides are committed either with guns or knives, and most homicides occur in the large cities. I will not make the Democratic Party assumption that "large city" equals "black people". The racist sentiments of the Democratic Party are adequately refuted by the homicide data on Figure 5.3-1: of the top ten nations in murder rate (within this data set), none have a sizeable black population. The crime of murder is not confined to any one race in particular; it is confined to criminals in general.

Homicide Data, General Reference [43]			
City	Years	% of Murder Victims with Prior Arrests	Reference
Milwaukee	2011	77	[36]
New Orleans	2011	64	[37]
Baltimore	2007	91	[38]
Philadelphia	2011	62	[39]
Newark	2009, 2010	85	[40]
Chicago	2003-2011	77	[41]
New York City	2012	70	[42]

Figure 5.3-2: Arrest Status of Homicide Victims in the U. S.

Let's pursue this idea of criminals killing criminals a little further, and examine how it fits into the overall homicide rates in the U. S. Figure 5.3-3 shows an extract from the FBI Uniform Crime Report [44]; it cites the totals for homicides by weapon type for several recent years. It is easy to see that rifles, including the much-maligned AK-47, AR-15, and other semi-automatic types, accounted for a very small portion of gun-related homicides. In fact, for the year 2011, the total number of homicides committed by rifles constitutes less than 4% of all homicides by firearm, and about 2.5% of all homicides regardless of weapon. Secondly, the overall homicide rate is generally decreasing as shown in the second-to-last row, where it has declined from 4.96 per 100,000 in 2007 to 4.06 in 2011, a drop of about 20% or so. Third, the fraction of total homicides committed with guns and knives is about 80% of the total, which has remained fairly constant over time.

FBI UCR Expanded Homicide Data Table 8 [44] Murder Victims by Weapon, 2007-2011					
Weapons	**2007**	**2008**	**2009**	**2010**	**2011**
Total	**14,916**	**14,224**	**13,752**	**13,164**	**12,664**
Total firearms:	10,129	9,528	9,199	8,874	8,583
Handguns	7,398	6,800	6,501	6,115	6,220
Rifles	453	380	351	367	323
Shotguns	457	442	423	366	356
Other guns	116	81	96	93	97
Firearms, type not stated	1,705	1,825	1,828	1,933	1,587
Knives or cutting instruments	1,817	1,888	1,836	1,732	1,694
Blunt objects (clubs, hammers, etc.)	647	603	623	549	496
Personal weapons (hands, fists, feet, etc.)[1]	869	875	817	769	728
Poison	10	9	7	11	5
Explosives	1	11	2	4	12
Fire	131	85	98	78	75
Narcotics	52	34	52	45	29
Drowning	12	16	8	10	15
Strangulation	134	89	122	122	85
Asphyxiation	109	87	84	98	89
Other weapons or weapons not stated	1,005	999	904	872	853
[1] Pushed is included in personal weapons.					
Population (millions)	301.580	304.375	307.007	309.330	311.587
Total murder rate per 100,000	4.95	4.67	4.48	4.26	4.06
Gun & knife murder rate per 100,000	3.96	3.75	3.59	3.43	3.30

Figure 5.3-3: FBI UCR Homicide Data for US, 2007-2011

Now let's consider the relevant homicide rate, defined as cases where the victim was not himself a professional criminal. Since most professional criminals are killed (by other criminals) with knives and guns, we can adjust the data in Figure 5.3-3. To obtain the relevant number of homicides, we can subtract from the total homicides committed by guns and knives the fraction in which the victims are criminals. Again, I am not assuming that all victims with arrest records are the same type of professional criminal as the perpetrator, nor am I assuming that the statistics for the big cities are the same as other areas. But, such an analysis is useful to establish the relevance of crime statistics instead of the sensational one used to justify degrading your rights. Figure 5.3-4 shows how the murder rate for 2011 would be altered if only relevant crimes were included, that is, if varying fractions of criminal victims were subtracted from the total. The line marked "50% excl" means that half of the homicides committed with guns and knives were subtracted from the total, on the supposition that half of those victims were criminals themselves. Again, we do not know the actual percentages, but a figure of half of all murders committed with guns and knives could conceivably be correct, given the statistics in Figure 5.3-3.

It is easy to see from Figure 5.3-4 that the *relevant* murder rate (cases in which the victim was not a criminal himself) is far less than the officially stated one: if the trend of the "60% excl" line is correct (60% of victims killed with knives and guns were themselves criminals), the murder rate for 2011 falls from 4.05 to 2.05, a reduction of nearly half. This proves that all we have to do to cut the murder rate in half is to get the professional criminals to stop killing each other. But they can never do that -- after all, we're talking about their livelihood. Yet, the professional politicians, ever anxious to protect and defend their criminal pets, are fond of using the actions of professional criminals to justify taking your Second Amendment rights away. But killing the Second Amendment is not about reducing crime, as we will see shortly.

One last statistical topic commands our attention. What about the "household risk" of owning a gun? Won't the children find it and accidentally shoot themselves? The same thing applies to common household cleaning products -- won't children find them and poison themselves? Shall we have trigger locks on Windex and Mr. Clean, or perhaps require a background check to purchase Comet and Formula 409? It is the duty of parents to manage their household risk in every respect, which includes power tools, cleaning agents, guns, electric outlets, kitchen knives, medicines, and even bathtubs. If the parents are derelict or incompetent, it is unlikely that any law will help; certainly not a law that reduces your rights.

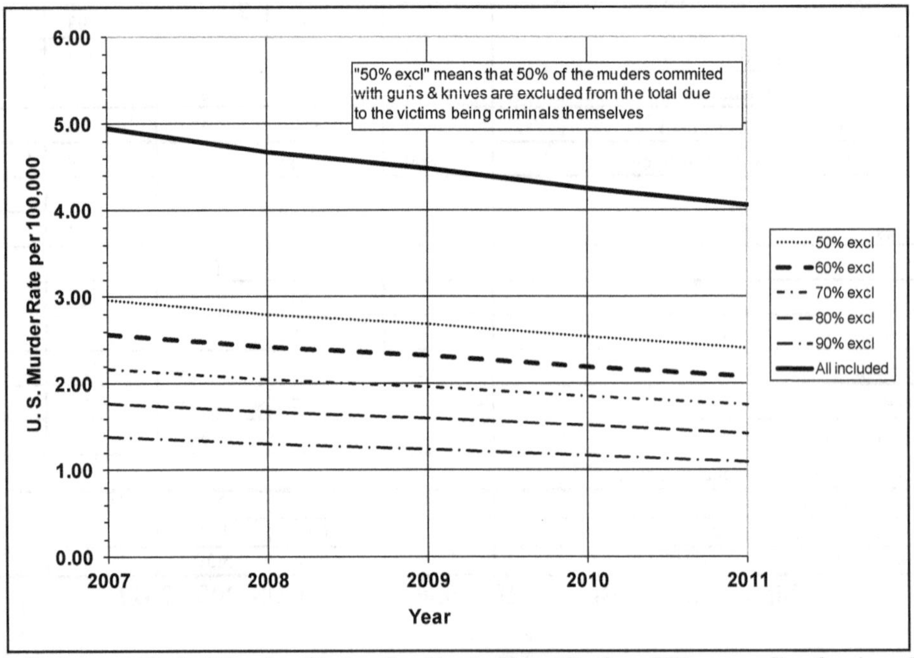

Figure 5.3-4: Relevant U. S. Murder Rates (by Excluding Victims Who Are Professional Criminals)

We are sometimes deluged with claims such as "you are 43 times more likely to shoot a family member with your gun as you are to shoot a burglar". It turns out that that particular statement was proven false some years ago. But let's suppose it was true. It would prove, if it proved anything, that the very low murder rate with guns (in which neither perpetrator nor victim was a professional criminal) is still 43 times lower than the incidence of burglars being shot; it excludes the hundreds of thousands of cases in which burglars are deterred by looking down the wrong end of the barrel; it also proves that burglary is therefore pretty rare in armed societies. It is rare because burglars do not like to be shot. The point is that being armed (if you choose to do so) offers a greater general protection against external threats than the increased risk at home; otherwise, responsible people (the vast majority) would not do it. Not every household should be ordered to possess firearms; but those who wish to do so should not be prevented or inconvenienced.

6 The Political Aspect

We have seen thus far that gun control does not have any positive benefits: it certainly does not reduce crime, nor affect suicide rates. It is a well-known fact that the places in America with the strictest gun control suffer from the highest crime rates. So why do so many politicians continue to introduce and vote for legislation that restricts the keeping and bearing of arms by the citizens? Note that I singled out, as they do, the citizens; there are exactly zero gun-control laws on the books that negatively affect the arms possessed by government and its employees. I believe there are two classes of gun-control advocates at the political level. First is the wishful thinker who actually believes that regulation of liberty and property will lead to a "safe and just" society. The second is the more obvious: these are the ones who seek absolute power over the people. Both agree that more government is the solution to man's problems in modern society, conveniently forgetting that governments are staffed by men with the same inclinations, faults, ambitions, and criminal tendencies in about the same proportion as society in general.

The first category of gun control advocates are an odd lot to be sure. These are the one who believe out of blind confidence in their fellow man (for there is no evidence to support it) that the death rates from accidents, crimes, and suicides can be made arbitrarily low if only the rate of gun ownership can be made arbitrarily low. They believe without reason or facts that the primary cause of untimely death and injury is you, the citizen, exercising your rights. They believe that with suitably strict regulation, the evil within men that leads to crimes will be suddenly expunged, and we will, by simple rule of law, enter into a period of peace, harmony, and happiness; primarily because they have confidence that everyone else (including the current gun-owning future/potential criminals) are just as benevolent deep down as they are; the problem is not the evil motivation of men, only the hardware they possess. I do not need to point out that this type of thinker is divorced from reality, and even worse, is willing to reject all the contrary evidence in order to maintain their self-imposed fictions. The British have been disarmed within the past twenty years; but the streets of that nation are not safer than before. A British soldier was fatally stabbed and nearly beheaded on a London street in broad daylight by two fanatics who were happy to explain it all to the camera while holding the bloody axes and knives in their hands. The people of Chicago, Detroit, and Los Angeles have been disarmed within living memory, but those places are likewise more dangerous than they were prior to the 1960's. I am doubtful that anything can be done about this first class of gun control advocates; with contrary facts in plain view, they persist in seeking to "educate" the people about the virtues of disarmament. They are wildly successful because most members of the popular media and most famous celebrities agree with this basic (false) notion about the inherent goodness of men; hence the ubiquity of their propaganda campaigns. Repeat a big enough lie often enough and pretty soon it becomes part of the mechanical subconscious, especially among the young.

Now before we get to the second type of advocate, it is important to understand the common attributes of all gun control laws [45]. The common characteristics are:

a. Manufacturing, sale, and importation of firearms and ammunition, or parts thereof, to be performed only by enterprises or individuals licensed by the government.
b. The principal components of all firearms must be labeled with a serial number.
c. Only persons of a certain age, who are of sound mind, and have not been convicted of crimes are eligible to own firearms.
d. Records of all sales and transfers are to be maintained by the licensed dealers and manufacturers, including name and address of the recipient and the serial number of firearm
e. Government organizations at all levels are exempt from all provisions.

It is not necessary to analyze them any further, for all the desired power and ultimate disarmament flows from these few provisions. Once these general conditions are in place, it is a simple matter to further alter the regulations: impose taxes on possession; require licenses for ownership of guns and ammunition (not only manufacturers); make people liable for the actions of others; make them liable to surprise inspections; restrict the nature and type that may be possessed; regulate ammunition; restrict the types of persons who may buy and sell; and even cancel licenses as necessary to make gun and ammunition ownership impossible. Then the government has all the power.

But what is the underlying motive for governments to enhance their arbitrary power by obtaining a monopoly on personal arms? There are probably three general reasons, given, as shown previously, that gun control leads if anything to more dangerous conditions for the people. First is the desire or belief that regulation of every aspect of everyone's lives will lead to a perfect society; in this respect the politicians are infected with the same delusions as the first class, which also infected Lenin, Stalin, and Mao. A second reason is that the government would have both the means and the motive to purge the nation of "undesirables", same as Hitler in Germany, Stalin in Russia, the military dictators in Guatemala, the Ottomans in Turkey, Pol Pot in Cambodia, and the temporary internment of American citizens of Japanese descent by Franklin Roosevelt in the U. S. A third possible reason is that governments want power for the sake of power such that their jobs are made easier and less dangerous, as they will have nothing to fear from the people. This would allow the government to have a monopoly on the commission of crimes with no possibility of retribution or prosecution. It also makes life easier for the criminal element, who would become the natural allies of the government.

Licensing leads invariably to registration, and registration leads to confiscation as soon as the political conditions are right. Once the government knows who has what types of firearms and ammunition, it is a simple matter to target those people for taxation, restriction, and eventual confiscation (or as former U. S. Attorney General Eric Holder put it, "mandatory gun buy-backs"). In America, the politicians are proud to point out that the federal gun control laws prohibit the establishment of a registry of gun owners. But there is a fallacy to this argument, namely, that although it is technically prohibited, there is no penalty associated with violating it, and, lacking specific definitions and penalties, no one can be prosecuted. If a secret federal registration of gun owners exists in America and is uncovered, the worst that can happen to the government employees is a month-long taxpayer-paid administrative leave/vacation during the "investigation" followed by raises and promotions. The goal of all gun control, historically considered, is the disarmament of the people; the most efficient path to disarmament is registration and confiscation under the rubric of "public safety". History has shown that it takes only a few sensational crimes, as in Great Britain, Australia, and the U. S. to get the politicians babbling about "public safety".

The politicians in America are likely to use the recent United Nations "Arms Trade Treaty" [46] to implement a de facto registration of gun owners in America. They can claim deniability by saying they did not realize the treaty could be used as an excuse by the bureaucracy to supersede the Second Amendment to the Constitution. This treaty protects and defends the same entities that have been responsible for at least 200 million mass murders by governments; but restricts you, the individual, from possessing tools necessary to defend yourself. The U. N. accuses you, the individual, of being the cause of worldwide mass murder.

If the police chiefs, mayors, governors, members of Congress, and the President wish to claim that public safety demands that your Second Amendment rights be restricted, let them first swear under penalty of perjury that they have permanently disarmed the ethnic mafias, the Cripps, the Bloods, Mara Salvatrucha (MS-13), the Hell's Angels and all the other professional criminal gangs, and further let them swear under penalty of perjury they have disarmed all non-affiliated criminals. Let them swear under penalty of perjury that no criminal will ever acquire arms. Let them swear that no officer of the law will ever commit a crime. Let them swear that all their bodyguards are disarmed. They will never do any of these, since they know that disarming the criminals is impossible, and are afraid to make promises about the conduct of government employees. They will however accuse you of making unreasonable demands. Secondly, they will not do it because if all the aforementioned persons were disarmed (an impossibility, but for sake of argument), the only guns left would be in the hands of normal citizens, which are not a threat to public peace or safety. Their refusal only proves that they respect the criminals more than they respect your rights.

That is not the end of their hypocrisy. Once the police chiefs and the mayors get the gun control laws they desire passed, surely they will then disarm the police, right? After all, with gun control in place, the job of the police officer will be perfectly safe, right? And the same goes for the state and federal officers, right? It is easy to see this hypocrisy: no government ever disarms itself, it only disarms the people.

I shall repeat once again the basic principles of the U. S. Constitution and its allocation of legitimate powers, as explained by Hamilton and Madison. First, no legitimate government can exempt itself from the laws as stated in *The Federalist Papers* #57:

> I will add, as a fifth circumstance in the situation of the House of representatives, restraining them from oppressive measures, that they can make no law which will not have its full operation on themselves and their friends, as well as on the great mass of society. This has always been deemed one of the strongest bonds by which human policy can connect the rulers and the people together. It creates between them that communion of interests and sympathies of sentiments of which few governments have furnished examples; but without which every government degenerates into tyranny. If it be asked what is to restrain the House of Representatives from making legal discriminations in favor of themselves and a particular class of society? I answer: the genius of the whole system; the nature of just and constitutional laws; and above all, the vigilant, manly spirit which actuates the people of America -- a spirit which nourishes freedom, and in return is nourished by it.
>
> If this spirit shall ever be so far debased as to tolerate a law not obligatory on the legislature, as well as on the people, the people will be prepared to tolerate anything but liberty.

Repeating again: secondly, the American people have a legitimate right to resist tyranny per *The Federalist Papers* #28:

> If the representatives of the people betray their constituents, there is then no resource left but in the exertion of that original right of self defense which is paramount to all positive forms of government, and which against the usurpations of the national rulers, may be exerted with infinitely better prospect of success against those of the rulers of an individual State....
>
> The obstacles to usurpation and the facilities of resistance increase with the increased extent of the state, provided the citizens understand their rights and are disposed to defend them. The natural strength of the people in a large community, in proportion to the artificial strength of the government, is greater than in a small, and of course more competent to a struggle with the attempts of the government to establish a tyranny....

American politicians have long used their power against black people in America [47]. When black people were enslaved in the South, they were routinely denied the right to keep and bear arms, thus ensuring that the institution of slavery would remain largely unchallenged. But the (Democrat) politicians in the South were likewise undeterred when formal slavery was abolished after the Civil War. No sooner had the fighting stopped when the Democrats in the South began passing "Jim Crow" laws, designed to keep the black people defenseless. One of the favorite techniques was to pass laws designed to prohibit the sale of less expensive guns, the only ones the black people could afford. Another tactic was to make gun ownership by members of the (Democrat) Ku Klux Klan easy, but nearly impossible for black people. A third tactic was to allow the police to choose who could own guns and who could not -- guess who the Democrats in the South decided were not good enough? But this last tactic was not used solely the South; New York City used the same scheme under its "Sullivan Law" to disarm the Italian immigrants.

I think I have shown that there is no practical formula for "gun control", as it magnifies the powers of the criminal element and the government alike at the expense of the liberties of the people.

References

[1] Edward D. Duvall, “Retard Control, Not Gun Control”, 26 Dec 2012; included here as an Appendix.

[2] Norman H. Baynes, *Hitler's Speeches*, London: Oxford University Press, 1942, Vol. 1, p. 482. The occasion was a speech at the *Fuhrertagung*, 19-20 Jun 1933

[3] ibid., Vol. 1, p. 447. The occasion was a speech at the *Nuremberg Parteitag*, 18 Sep 1935.

[4] Ernest F. Henderson, *A Short History of Germany*, New York: Macmillan Co., 1906, Vol. II, pp. 335-339, 344, 345

[5] Carlton J. H. Hayes, *Contemporary Europe Since 1870*, New York, Macmillan Co., 1953, pp. 139-141

[6] Hajo Holborn, *A History of Modern Germany, 1840-1945*, Princeton, NJ: Princeton University Press, 1969, p. 555

[7] William Blackstone, *Commentaries on the Laws of England*, Book 1, Chapter 1, Section 2 (1765)

[8] Thomas Hobbes, *Leviathan*, chapter 14 (1651)

[9] John Locke, *The Second Treatise of Government*, (1689), sections 16 - 18

[10] J. C. L. de Sismondi, *A History of the Fall of the Roman Empire*, London: Longman, Rees, Orme, Brown, Green & Longman, and John Taylor, 1834 , Vol. 1, pp. 37 - 40

[11] Francois P. G. Guizot, *The History of France*, New York: John B. Alden, 1885, Vol. 1, p. 168

[12] J. C. L. de Sismondi, *A History of the Fall of the Roman Empire*, London: Longman, Rees, Orme, Brown, Green & Longman, and John Taylor, 1834 , Vol. 2, pp. 82, 83, 100, 101

[13] ibid., Vol. 2, pp. 134, 137 - 139

[14] George Ostrogorsky, *History of the Byzantine State*, New Brunswick, NJ: Rutgers University Press, Revised Edition, 1969, pp. 393, 394

[15] Francois P. G. Guizot, *The History of France*, New York: John B. Alden, 1885, Vol. 2, pp. 153, 154

[16] John Richard Green, *A Short History of the English People*, New York: American Book Company, 1880, p. 301

[17] W. F. Finlason, *Reeves' History of the English Law*, London: Reeves and Turner, 1869, Vol. 2, p. 444; Vol. 3, p. 196

[18] John Richard Green, *A Short History of the English People*, New York: American Book Company, 1880, pp. 331, 332

[19] *The Federalist Papers* are a series of newspaper essays published by Alexander Hamilton, James Madison, and John Jay between 27 Oct 1787 and 28 May 1788. Their purpose was to explain the Constitution to the voters of New York State and encourage them to urge their representatives to ratify it. *The Federalist Papers* may be downloaded for free at https://fremontvalleybooks.com and https://edduvall.com.

[20] Jack N. Rakove, ed., *Madison: Writings*, New York: The Library of America, 1999, pp. 441, 442

[21] St. George Tucker, *View of the Constitution of the United States*, Indianapolis, IN: Liberty Fund, 1999, pp. 238, 239. (First published in 1803)

[22] John C. Fitzpatrick, editor, *The Writings of Washington*, Washington, United States Printing Office, (1932) Vol. 7, pp. 56, 57

[23] ibid., Vol. 7, p. 79
[24] ibid., Vol. 7, pp. 253, 254
[25] ibid., Vol. 7, p. 363
[26] ibid., Vol. 7, p. 319
[27] ibid., Letter to the President of Congress, 5 Jan 1777 (Vol. 6, pp. 467-471); to the Pennsylvania Council of Safety, 12 Jan 1777 (Vol. 6, pp. 504, 505); in General Orders, 5 Sep 1777 (Vol. 9, p. 182); to Brig. General Samuel Holden Parson, 10 and 11 Jul 1779 (Vol. 15, pp. 396, 407); to the President of Congress, 13 Jul 1779 (Vol. 15, p. 419); to James Bowdoin, 14 Jun 1780 (Vol. 19, pp. 8 - 10); in General Orders, 16 Jun 1780 (Vol. 19, p. 17); in General Orders, 22 Jun 1780 (Vol. 19, pp. 54, 55); to the President of Congress, 25 Jun 1780 (Vol., 19, p. 65); in General Orders, 20 Oct 1781 (Vol. 23, pp. 243 - 248). This last one came the day after the victory at Yorktown.
[28] William Blackstone, *Commentary on the Laws of England*, 1765, Book 1, Chap. 1, pp. 144, 145
[29] W. W. Greener, *The Gun and Its Development*, London: Cassell and Company, Ltd., 1910
[30] www.schoolbusinfo.org
[31] Small Arms Survey 2007 Part 2 (http:/ / www.smallarmssurvey.org/ files/ sas/ publications/ year_b_pdf/ 2007/ 2007SAS_English_press_kit/2007SASCh2_summary_en. pdf); summarized on wikipedia at http://en.wikipedia.org/w/index.php?oldid=547789057
[32] http://en.wikipedia.org/w/index.php?oldid=547795916
[33] V. Ajdacic-Gross, M. G. Weiss, M. Ring, U. Hepp, M. Bopp, F. Gutzwiller, W. Rossler, "Methods of Suicide: International Suicide Patterns Derived from the WHO Mortality Database", Bulletin of the World Health Organization, Vol. 86, No. 9, Sep 2008, pp. 657-736; available at: https://www.ncbi.nlm.nih.gov/pmc/journals/522/
[34] K. Chein-Chang Wu, Ying-Yeh Chen, P. S. F. Yip, "Suicide Methods in Asia: Implications in Suicide Prevention", International Journal of Environmental Research and Public Health, 2012, No. 9.
[35] Derived from a 2010 study by the United Nations Office of Drugs and Crime; available at: http://en.wikipedia.org/w/index.php?oldid=548495123
[36] 2011 Milwaukee Homicide Review Commission Report, available at: http://city.milwaukee.gov/ImageLibrary/Groups/cityHRC/reports/2011Reportv6.pdf
[37] *New Orleans Times-Picayune*, 1 Jan 2012, available at: http://www.nola.com/crime/index.ssf/2012/01/nopd_release_of_murder_victims.html
[38] *USA Today*, 31 Aug 2007
[39] Philadelphia Police Department Murder and Shooting Analysis, p. 9, available at: https://www.phillypolice.com/assets/crime-maps-stats/PPD-Homicide-Analysis-2011-vs-2012.pdf
[40] Newark Star-Ledger, 24 Oct 2011, see also: https://www.politifact.com/factchecks/2011/oct/24/cory-booker/cory-booker-says-newark-shooting-victims-have-high/
[41] Chicago Police Department, 2011 Murder Analysis Report, p. 41, available at: https://home.chicagopolice.org/wp-content/uploads/2014/12/2011-Murder-Report.pdf
[42] *The New York Times*, 28 Dec 2012
[43] *World News Daily*, 4 Mar 2013 http://www.wnd.com/2013/03/most-murder-victims-in-big-cities-have-criminal-record/
[44] FBI Uniform Crime Report, Crime in the U. S., 2011, Table 8, available at: http://www.fbi.gov/about-us/cjis/ucr/crime-in-the-u.s/2011/crime-in-the-u.s.-2011/tables/expanded-homicide-data-table-8
[45] Jay Simkin, Aaron Zelman, *"Gun Control": Gateway to Tyranny*, Milwaukee, WI: Jews for the Preservation of Firearms Ownership, 1993, pp. 84 - 93
[46 http://www.un.org/disarmament/ATT/
[47] http://www.old-yankee.com/rkba/racial_laws.html

Appendix: "Retard Control, Not Gun Control"
(26 Dec 2012)

We have now just passed one of the darkest Christmas seasons in memory, after so many small children were murdered by a clinical retard at an elementary school in Newtown, CT. The tiny bodies were not even cold when our Marxist politicians, ever alert to exploit a tragedy, took to the airwaves to demand that all the other citizens give up their Second Amendment rights because of the action of a single retard. President Obama has since commissioned a task force to develop new and innovative ways to disarm the people; their report is due sometime in Jan 2013.

When I use the word "retard", I am not referring to those who have below-average IQ; I am referring to those who have been recognized as clinically insane by competent mental health authorities - the people that pose a clear danger to themselves and others.

Most of the recent mass shooters, including Retard Jared Loughner of Tucson AZ fame, Retard James Holmes of Aurora CO fame, and the latest one, Retard Adam Lanza of Newtown CT fame, were all profoundly mentally ill. In fact, the Christmas Eve shooter of Webster NY, Retard William Spengler, had previously served 17 years in prison for murdering his grandmother. All were known to be retards by the local health officials -- why was nothing done to intervene? Is this how our illustrious government seeks to protect us -- by failing in its duty while taking away the rights of the people?

I suspect that the government prefers to let these retards walk free until they commit some horrific crime; it keeps the rest of the people nervous and fearful. History shows that people who are afraid are more willing to give up their liberties if they can be convinced that doing so will ensure their safety. What better way for the politicians and the bureaucrats to kill two birds with one stone: implement some gun control to reduce the Second Amendment guarantee while assuring the weak-minded that we will have a safer nation because of it? It is typical for that type of politician, already suitably divorced from reality, to actually believe they can eliminate evil by passing laws to regulate inanimate objects. The real problem, as far as these shootings are concerned, is that we no longer have a viable mechanism to commit these retards to institutions, where they can either be treated as they require by expert medical practitioners and restored to mental health, or comforted and cared for in a place where they can only hurt each other. It is unfortunate that some will fall into the latter category; but that is how it is. Or maybe our illustrious politicians would prefer small children being killed in their schools by retards on the loose, either by shooting, by burning the building down, or running them down with a pickup truck.

The National Rifle Association released a statement recommending, among other things, that perhaps instead of giving up liberty, we should have armed guards in the schools. I am not convinced that it is the ultimate answer, but suffice to say that our Marxist politicians immediately rejected the idea and castigated the NRA for being "tone deaf". The mainstream media of course neglected to mention that there are about 130,000 elementary and high schools in America and about a third of them have had armed guards for decades. They will never mention it; doing so would only remind the voters that armed guards in the public schools are necessary only in cities where the Democratic Party has established their brand of paradise: Boston, Providence, New York, Philadelphia, Newark, Baltimore, Washington DC, Buffalo, Cleveland, Toledo, Gary, Chicago, Detroit, Kansas City, and St. Louis. It is odd indeed that the Marxist politicians would criticize the NRA for recommending something that the Democrats have been doing for decades. But this omission makes perfect sense when you recall that the goal is not public safety -- if it were, we would be committing dangerous retards to institutions where they belong. The goal is to disarm the people.

It is not just the opportunistic politicians joining the gun-control/disarmament bandwagon. Now Dr. Fareed Zakaria (commentator for CNN and political advisor to Mr. Obama) also desires to solve the retard problem by essentially killing off the Second Amendment. In his 23 Dec 2012 article [A-1], *Evidence Overwhelming: Loose Guns Laws to Blame*, Dr. Zakaria cites reductions in homicides in other nations after gun prohibition, ridicules existing gun laws in the U. S. as being too lenient, then concludes: "Instead, why not have the government do something much simpler and that has proved successful: limit access to guns." He is referring, as stated earlier in the column, to banning all semi-automatic and automatic firearms, as was done in Great Britain, Japan, and Australia. That brings up an important topic. Dr. Zakaria is a native of India; India has draconian gun prohibition laws which are a holdover from the British colonial regime. If India is such a free and safe society, why did Dr. Zakaria emigrate to the U. S., so full of gun owners? He must have thought there was greater freedom here. He was right. What he fails to realize is that freedom exists here but not in India partly because the people are armed. As the famous Indian activist Mahatma Ghandi wrote [A-2]:

> Among the many misdeeds of the British rule in India, history will look upon the Act depriving a whole nation of arms, as the blackest.

Apparently Dr. Zakaria disagrees with Mr. Ghandi and would like to turn the American people into the suppressed subjects that the Indian people were when ruled by Her Majesty Queen Victoria. If His Lordship Viceroy and Governor-General Dr. Zakaria won't believe Mr. Ghandi, perhaps he will believe a leader of his adopted nation, Senator (later Vice President) Hubert H. Humphrey [A-3]:

> Certainly one of the chief guarantees of freedom under any government, no matter how popular and respected, is the right of citizens to keep and bear arms. This is not to say that firearms should not be very carefully used, and that definite safety rules of precaution should not be taught and enforced. But the right of citizens to bear arms is just one more guarantee against arbitrary government, one more safeguard against the tyranny which now appears remote in America, but which historically has proved to be always possible.

This is the basic fact that His Lord Highness Fareed and other like-minded Marxists deliberately ignore, hoping you will not notice. Only an armed population has a reasonable chance of remaining free, given the usual long-term trend of every government toward absolute power. This pattern is true throughout history, no matter the form or construction of the government. We shall see in the coming weeks ever more shrill demands by the Marxist element for you, the citizen, to give up your right to be armed; which is in essence, a demand that you give up your long-term prospects for freedom. We shall see who in Washington, if any, are willing to oppose them.

The best answer to the random shootings is retard control, not gun control. If and when the government finds a backbone and takes action to ensure that retards are placed in their proper environment (where they can get real treatment), we will have fewer tragedies like the Newtown incident.

References

[A-1] *The Arizona Republic*, 23 Dec 2012, p. B10

[A-2] Cited by Abhijeet Singh, "Colonial Roots of Gun Control", Mahatma Ghandi, *An Autobiography OR The Story of My Experiments With Truth*, p. 238; http://abhijeetsingh.com

[A-3] *Guns* magazine, Feb 1960, p. 4; https://gunsmagazine.com/classic-issues/guns-magazine-1960-classic-editions/

Dealing with Anti-Gay Activists

Note: This essay was originally published 16 Mar 2019, and was later incorporated as Question 74 of the book *Real World Graduation*. It poses a multiple-choice question, followed by an explanation of the correct answer.

The Question

A certain homosexual man is consistently being harassed and intimidated by people who are opposed to the "gay lifestyle". He has been assaulted several times (requiring hospitalization), lives in fear for his life, and is thinking of buying a gun for self-defense. However, it is illegal to own, possess, or carry a gun in his city. The city is economically distressed, and he is unable to sell his house and move away. What should he do?

a) File complaints with the police, and depend on them for protection.

b) Turn "straight".

c) Get a gang of gays together, go out and administer a beating one of his assailants; that will send a message to his abusers and solve the problem.

d) Hire some lawyers and attempt to sue his antagonists for harassment and violations of his civil rights.

e) A combination of a) and d).

The Answer

This is a trick question. All of the answers are wrong.

Answer a) is wrong because the police are not legally required to provide protection to anyone. The police are far too busy answering calls to spend much time protecting one person or a group. (They are not legally required to respond to a call for help, either.)

Answer b) might work, it might not, but why should a person change their personal habits because someone doesn't like them?

Answer c) is wrong, even if it were possible, because the gays would then be committing the same crime as their harassers.

Answer d) is wrong because it is too late for paper shuffling by lawyers.

The homosexual's opinion of the value of his own life is far more important than the opinion of some "legislator" who passed laws to prohibit gun ownership (in effect, outlawing self defense). The homosexual should get a gun regardless of how many laws he violates. If even 20% of gays armed themselves, and if even two or three of their abusers turned up dead or in the operating rooms, there will soon be far fewer incidents, because people who are offended by the gay lifestyle are not offended enough to die over it.

In fact, this is how Jim Crow ended. Contrary to some political views, Jim Crow was not abolished because some legislators passed some "equal voting rights" laws, or ended legal segregation. Those laws were passed in the 1960's, after Jim Crow was already on his deathbed, so to speak. Jim Crow was nearly dead because black people got guns and started shooting back at the Klan; the Klan was offended by black people asserting their right to life and liberty, but not offended enough to die over it.

Gun control does not work and those who favor it know it. Here's the proof. Require any police chief, Mayor, Governor, President, or legislator who favors gun control to sign the following statement:

> "I do hereby solemnly swear under penalty of perjury that the gun control laws in effect during my tenure in office guarantee that no member of any criminal gang had, has, or will have, any access to any firearm at any time for any reason."

No official will ever sign such a statement because they know full well that "gun control" has no effect on the criminal element. It certainly has no effect on the government employees (who are generally exempted). It only affects the citizens, making them weaker and both the government and the criminals stronger. Care to guess why the government and criminals both favor gun control?

This is a general principle: your life and safety, and that of your family and your property take precedence over the whims of all politicians, the regulations of all bureaucrats, all the laws. If you are any type of patriot, and you need a gun to defend yourself, your family, and your property, then get one, no matter who in the government doesn't like it or what the law is.

The Prospects for Immigration Reform

Note: This essay was written 17 Aug 2013, when the "gang of eight" Senators was contemplating a "comprehensive immigration reform" bill. That bill never came to anything, and the immigration problem continued to fester until the Trump administration, which began to defend the border. The border was subsequently erased for practical purposes by the Biden administration. A later essay (The Open-Border Policy Rationale) describes my opinion on Biden's motives. However, the basic principles of immigration are as valid now as they were in 2013. In the original essay, I recommended repealing NAFTA. President Trump accomplished that, and it was replaced by the USMCA treaty. I do not know if that new treaty affected immigration or not; but Mr. Trump's actions to secure the border certainly made a big difference. I also recommended in the original that those here illegally should remain since they weren't leaving anyway; I now think it is time to round them up and send them home.

The Congress of the United States is currently (Aug 2013) considering a bill to "reform" our immigration system. The "reform" bill is based on a set of recommendations made by eight Senators (Democrats Bennet (CO), Durbin (IL), Menendez (FL), and Schumer (NY); Republicans Flake (AZ), Graham (SC), McCain (AZ), and Rubio (FL)). These illustrious gentlemen have assured us many times that they desire only to fix our broken immigration system, provide legal standing to everyone, and enhance our future prosperity. The core of the problem, which has existed since at least the Carter administration (1977-1981) and probably before that, is that a great many foreigners have either entered the U. S. in violation of the immigration laws, or have entered legally but remained in the U. S. after their visas have expired. So the appropriate answer to this problem, as the honorable gentlemen propose, is to change the law to accommodate the lawbreakers; all 10, 20, 30, or 40 million of them, depending on whose number you believe. (No one knows the real number except the ruling elite, and they aren't saying.)

Let's consider the provisions of the proposed legislation. It sets up an administrative system which is tasked with implementing the following changes under 8 general categories:

1. Persons in the country illegally shall be required to:
   a. Register their presence with the federal government;
   b. Undergo a background check; and
   c. Obtain a work permit.
   d. When these are accomplished, they may remain in the U. S. and continue working and collecting social welfare benefits.
2. After registration and obtaining the work permit, persons now here illegally shall:
   a. Pay a fine;
   b. Be required to pay income taxes;
   c. Be required to learn English;
   d. Be required to wait ten years before applying for a green card (which would grant them permanent legal residence, in addition to the permanent legal residence conferred by the work permit).
3. After "going to the back of the line" and waiting for everyone else that came to this country legally has been served, the persons now here illegally, having gone through the above process, shall be eligible to apply for citizenship.
4. A nationwide e-verify employment system shall be implemented (such that only persons in the country legally can be employed).
5. 750 miles of fencing along the border shall be constructed;
6. 20,000 new Border Patrol agents are to be hired;
7. Surveillance of the border with Mexico shall be increased.

8. These reforms are to be fully funded, and the Department of Homeland Security (DHS) shall not be able to change the provisions thereof.

We all know that the opinions of regular Americans do not matter. Even casting aside what the American people want, there are two big problem areas with this legislation. First, the vast majority of persons now here illegally probably will not sign up for it on the grounds that it would deprive them of advantages they already enjoy. Secondly, every pro-illegal alien activist group will do everything they can to prevent people from signing up for it on the grounds that it offers too little.

Let's look at it from the standpoint of a typical person here illegally. How many persons in this category are subjected to a background check? None -- they can live and work freely undetected and have been doing so for upwards of 25 years. How many persons in this category are being audited by the IRS? None -- they do not pay income taxes nor do they file any forms. How many persons in this category are standing in line at the Motor Vehicle Bureau? None -- they are not required to register their cars, nor get licenses, nor are they inconvenienced by the expense of obtaining car insurance. How many in this category are deprived of health care? None -- they are not inconvenienced by the expense of health insurance, yet obtain free health care at every hospital. How many persons in this category have to stand idly by while their children grow up deprived of an education? None -- all children are eligible for public education regardless of their legal status or that of their parents. Why would a person in this category volunteer to learn English, which is to them a foreign language? Why would they sign up to be investigated? Why would they sign up to pay a fine they currently do not have to pay? Why would they sign up to pay taxes from which they are currently exempt? Why would they volunteer to stand in line at the Motor Vehicle Bureau? Should this offer become law, I believe the vast majority of the people now here illegally will view it as nothing more than a series of unwarranted demands. Our ruling elite seem to have forgotten that most of the people here illegally are proud of their heritage and are proud to be citizens of their native countries. They may not be willing to trade that in for a promise of a future green card; they likely will become resentful about being pressured to Americanize. They have demonstrated their preference by failing generally to assimilate into American society.

Let's look at it from the standpoint of the National Council of "Ku Klux" la Raza "The Race" (working motto: "Por la Raza, todo. Por los otros, nada", which in translation means: "For us, everything. For the lowlife yankee gringos, nothing") [1]. While this proposed legislation caves in to a great many of the traditional demands made by the pro-illegal alien activists and the Council, the activist groups probably have four main issues with it. First, it does not grant automatic first-class citizenship status (with preferential voting and candidacy rights) to persons now here illegally. Second, it does not require Americans to learn Spanish. Third, it does not grant the activist groups any legal regulatory powers over American citizens. Fourth, it does not directly cede any territory to Mexico. The first and second will certainly come to pass in due time, but not fast enough for the activists. The third will probably occur as part of the implementing regulations, but it is not guaranteed. The fourth is unlikely to occur, since no federal government official wants to preside over a loss of territory, and thus a loss of power. Bottom line, this proposal simply does not give the illegal aliens enough.

Why would our ruling elite put forth a proposal contrary to the wishes of most Americans in such a way that it is likely to be rejected even by the very people it is intended to benefit? It turns out that the two factions of the ruling elite have different motives. The Democratic faction has four objectives. First, it is desperate to obtain greater tax revenue. Second, it wants a steady supply of uneducated people that can be cheaply employed as maids and servants in their mansions, as well as a healthy supply of cheap labor for their corporate friends. Third, they expect to find a way to confer citizenship quickly, and expect that the new citizens will vote Democratic as have most new citizens of the past. Fourth, they desire these new residents/citizens to apply for more social welfare benefits, thus transferring control of their lives to the government. The Republican faction has more modest goals. It too wants to expand the tax base. It also wants cheap labor for its corporate cronies. But it also hopes that the newly minted citizens, being largely of the Catholic faith, will side with them on the abortion debate. It also expects (contrary to the Marxist view held by the Democrats) that the new residents will use their new-found property rights as Americans to establish independent small businesses and help the economy grow.

The important point for us Americans to remember is that we should not blame the people now here illegally as if this situation were entirely their fault. We were born in America with all its benefits. Most of the people now here illegally were born in countries that are pathologically corrupt wastelands; lorded over by a merciless armed Marxist plutocracy; the common person having no prospect of obtaining any type of civil or property rights. Second, the traditional peasant farmer was once able to support his family with his relatively primitive agricultural methods. But no matter how uneducated he may be, he is still smart enough (smarter than our ruling elite) to recognize that he cannot compete with American and Canadian mechanized agriculture; he was in essence forced off his land because the former customers for his small surplus can buy much cheaper now due to the North American Free Trade Agreement (NAFTA). Illegal immigration increased dramatically after the passage of NAFTA. This immigration-reform proposal is nothing more than a big-government/big-corporation band-aid that pretends to fix an immigration problem caused by NAFTA, another big-government/big-corporation idea. So the ruling elite parties on.

There are other shortcomings in the bill as well, considered from the American viewpoint. Most of the people now here illegally overstayed their visa, which the Border Patrol does not enforce. There is no provision for expanding the Immigration and Customs Enforcement (ICE), which does have jurisdiction over visas. The 750 miles of fence is but a small fraction of the border with Mexico, and there is no guarantee that even these 750 miles will be contiguous, or will be constructed in high-traffic crossing areas, or will be monitored.

The nationwide e-verify program is a nullity on its face. It is already illegal to hire people who are not legal residents; they simply make day-to-day contracts for cash. Nothing will change with a nationwide e-verify, except it will be an exceedingly useful tool for the IRS to use against American citizens. Last but not least, Congress can restrict the legal discretion of DHS all they want, but DHS will ignore the law as they please -- what will Congress do about it, de-fund DHS?

The proper legislative course of action is:

a. Repeal NAFTA

b. Grant permanent legal status to all persons now here illegally without prejudice since they aren't leaving anyway, regardless of the law

c. Militarize the border with Mexico commensurate with border infractions

d. Fully fund ICE to enforce the visa laws

e. Prohibit permanently application for U. S. citizenship to all persons now here illegally

f. Reduce annual immigration quotas from all nations commensurate with the number of persons now here illegally holding citizenship of that respective nation; increase immigration quotas from nations whose citizens have thus far obeyed our immigration laws. This policy shall continue for 100 years.

References

[1] The National Council of La Raza gave an award to Jose Angel Gutierrez in 1994; who famously stated in 1969: "We have got to eliminate the gringo, and what I mean by that is if the worst comes to the worst, we have got to kill him." cf. https://nationalcenter.org/ncppr/2012/07/11/national-council-of-la-raza/

The Politics of Dependency

Note: This essay was published 19 Apr 2014. It is still relevant now, same as the reference cited was valid in the 1800's. The UK statistical records have been updated since the original essay, and the new figures are shown below. Overall, the conclusion is the same.

The topic of this essay is the policy that seeks to reduce poverty. But before addressing the modern particulars, first consider an extended passage from a book by the 19th century American economist Francis A. Walker [1]. I have indicated in square brackets some explanatory notes, mostly related to the calculation of dates. It is very important to recall as you read this, that Dr. Walker was a white person talking about other white people. In his 1884 book he writes [2]:

> **The Impotent vs. the Able-bodied Poor**. The relief of the impotent poor, whether by private or public charity, is, so far as political economy is concerned with it, a question relating to the consumption of wealth. It is so much a matter of course, under our modern civilization, that the very young and the very old, the crippled and deformed, who are unable to earn their own maintenance, shall not be allowed to starve, that the matter of relief to these classes becomes one of administrative detail, that does not require even to be alluded to in an elementary treatise on economics.
>
> The experience of that country from which we derive our law and much of our administrative machinery [Great Britain], is, however, so instructive as to the influence for mischief upon the entire laboring population and upon the future production of wealth which may be wrought by ill-considered provisions for the distribution of alms to the able-bodied poor, as to make it worthwhile briefly to recite that experience here; and thereupon to define the limits outside of which the consumption of wealth for this purpose becomes prejudicial to production.
>
> We shall get at our subject most directly by inquiring why it is that the laborer works at all. Clearly that he may eat. If he may eat without it, he will not work. The neglect or contempt of this very obvious truth by the British Parliament, during the latter part of the eighteenth and the earlier part of the nineteenth century, brought the working classes of the kingdom almost to the verge of ruin, created a vast body of hopeless and hereditary pauperism, and engendered vices in the industrial system which have been productive of evil down to the present day.
>
> **Establishment of the English Pauper System**. By the act of the 43rd year of Queen Elizabeth's reign [1601], every person in the kingdom was given a legal right to public relief, if required; but voluntary pauperism was severely dealt with, and the able-bodied compelled to work.
>
> The principle of requiring the able-bodied poor to work continued for generations to be fundamental in the English pauper system; and for the better enforcement of this requisition parishes or unions of parishes were, by an act of 9th George I. [1722], authorized to build workhouses, residences in which might be made a condition of relief. Moreover, from the days of Elizabeth to that of George III, the spirit which actuated the poor laws was jealous and severe. Doubtless in that administration unnecessary harshness was sometimes practiced; but, on the whole, the effect on the working classes was wholesome, for it was made undesirable to become a pauper.
>
> **Removal of the Workhouse Test**. On the accession of George III [1760], a different theory came to direct legislation relating to poor relief, and a widely different temper of administration began to prevail. Six successive acts, passed in the first years of George III, intimated the changed spirit in which pauperism was thereafter to be dealt with. In the 22nd year of that reign [1781], the act known as Gilbert's act gave a fuller expression to this spirit. By the act the workhouse was no longer to be used as a test of voluntary pauperism:
>
> The 32nd section provided "That where there shall be in any parish, township, or place, any poor person or persons, who shall be able and willing to work but who cannot get employment, the guardian of the poor of such parish, etc., on application made to him by or on behalf of such poor

person, is required to agree for the labor of any such poor person or persons at any work or employment suited to his or her strength and capacity, in any parish or place near the place of his or her residence, and to maintain, or cause such person or persons to be properly maintained, lodged and provided for, until such employment shall be procured, and during the time of such work, and to *receive the money to be earned by such work or labor, and apply it in such maintenance as far as the same will go, and make up the deficiency, if any*."

By the repeal of the workhouse test, and by the additional most injudicious provision which we have placed in italics, a deadly blow was struck at the manhood and self-sufficiency of the working classes of England.

The Logical Outcome. By 1832 the false and vicious principle on which Gilbert's act was based had been carried logically out to its limits in almost universal pauperism. The condition of the person who threw himself flat upon public charity was better than that of the laborer who struggled on to preserve his manhood in self-support. The drone was better clothed, better lodged, and better fed than the worker.

All the incidents of this bad system were unnecessarily bad. The allowance for each additional child was so much out of proportion to the allowance for adults, that the more numerous a man's children the better his condition, and thus the rapid increase of an already pauperized population was encouraged; while the allowance in the case of illegitimate children was even greater than for those born in wedlock. "It may be safely affirmed," said the Poor Law Commissioners of 1831, "that the virtue of female chastity does not exist among the lower orders of England, except to a certain degree among domestic servants, who know that they hold their situations by that tenure and are more prudent in consequence."

Such may be the effects of foolish laws. The legislator may think it hard that his power for good is so closely restricted; but he has no reason to complain of any limits upon his power for evil. On the contrary, it would almost seem that there could be no nation, of any race of men, which a few laws respecting industry, trade and finance, passed by country squires or labor demagogues in defiance of economic principles, could not transform within half a generation into a nation of beasts.

Poor Law Reform. We have seen what a system the English squirearchy substituted for the economic law that he that would eat must work. The natural effects of this system were wrought speedily and effectually. The disposition to labor was cut up by the roots; all restraints upon increase of population disappeared under a premium of births; self-respect and social decency vanished before a prize for bastardy. The amount expended in the relief and maintenance of the poor had risen, in 1832, to £7,000,000.

In this exigency, which, in truth, constituted one of the gravest crises of English history, Parliament, by the Poor Law Amendment Act (4th and 5th, William IV) [1833 and 1834], returned to the principle of the act of Elizabeth. The workhouse test was restored; allowances in relief were abolished; paid overseers were appointed, and a central system was created for the due supervision of the system; illegitimacy was discouraged by punishing the father, instead of rewarding the mother; and the law of pauper settlement was modified so as to facilitate the migration of laborers in search of employment.

By this great legislative reform the burden of pauperism, in spite of the continuing effects of the old, evil system, was reduced in three years, by an average amount, the kingdom over, of forty-five percent.

The Principle that Should Govern Poor Relief. The moral of this episode in the industrial history of England is easily drawn. It is of the highest economic consequence that pauperism shall not be made inviting; but that, on the contrary, the laborer shall be stimulated to the utmost possible exertions to achieve self-support, only accepting relief as an alternative to actual starvation. It is not, to this end, necessary that any brutality of administration shall deter the worthy poor who

> have no other resource; but it should be the prime object of legislation on this subject to make the situation of the pauper less agreeable than of the independent laborer, and that, by no small interval.
>
> "All", says Mr. George W. Hastings [3], "who have administered the Poor Law, must know the fatal readiness with which those hovering on the brink of pauperism believe they cannot earn a living, and the marvelous way in which, if the test be firmly applied, the means of subsistence will be found somehow."

The white people of England between the 1780's and the 1830's showed that if you subsidize dependency, you get more of it. If you reward illegitimacy and the breakdown of the family, you get more of it. If you treat the idle better than the worker, you get more idle people, and a great deal of resentment from those who work and pay taxes to support the idle. It turns out that the people of America, white and black alike, have demonstrated the exact same behavior in the last fifty years as the English did over a similar interval. Ambition to work is generally down; illegitimacy and poverty are generally up among all the races in America. But this problem cannot get the attention it deserves because those heavily invested in the current system will not allow a discussion of it. Consider the similarity of Walker's conclusions with the remarks of Congressman Paul Ryan (R-WI), on 12 Mar 2014:

> We have got this tailspin of culture, in our inner cities in particular, of men not working and just generations of men not even thinking about working or learning to value the culture of work.

To which Her Most High Indignancy Congresswoman Barbara Lee (D-CA) commented:

> Let's be clear, when Mr. Ryan says 'inner city', when he says 'culture', these are simply code words for what he really means: 'black'.

She also called Representative Ryan's statement a "thinly veiled racial attack". By calling Ryan's statement "a racial attack", Her Imperial Righteousness Congresswoman Lee is implying that blacks and whites are somehow different; that black people do not want the same things as white people, and behave differently than white people. That sentiment is foreign to true civil rights advocates, but typical for narrow-minded race-baiting bigots. How can Congress correct the problem if one faction of Congress calls the other side racists just for stating the obvious? But enough said about politicians. What about the £7,000,000 that Dr. Walker mentioned, and how does it relate to America today?

The data from two websites reveal the following statistics:

a. Nominal GDP in England in 1832 was £35,210,000,000 measured in 2013 £ [4].
b. The price deflator from 2013 to 1832 is 81.07 [5]
c. The GDP in England in 1832 £ is therefore £35,210,000,000/81.07 = £310,965,000

The fraction of GDP devoted to poor relief in 1832 England is the £7,000,000 Walker referred to divided by £310,965,000, or 2.22% of GDP, which Walker called a "grave crisis".

The U. S. 2013 federal budget [6] contains the following entries under the category "Welfare" (all figures are in $ billions US).

a. Family and Children:	269.8
b. Unemployment:	53.2
c. Workers Compensation	8.0
d. Housing:	53.9

for a total of $384.9 billion US. This excludes $366.6 billion for "Vendor payments for health care (Welfare)". I have excluded the latter figure since the payments for poor relief in England likely did not include any medical expenses.

Using only the $384.9 billion figure, and the 2013 GDP of the U. S. [7] as $15,684.8 billion US, it is seen that the $384.9 B represents 2.45% of GDP; even worse than the ratio under the English system. If the medical costs of welfare were included, the total comes to 4.79% of GDP.

So where does it end? It doesn't. We will have more of the same (dependency and resentment) because the race-baiting politicians want it that way.

References

[1] Francis A. Walker (1840-1897); economist and statistician, officer in the Union Army in the Civil War; chief of the Bureau of Statistics 1869-1870, Superintendent of the 1870 Census, President of the Massachusetts Institute of Technology 1881-1897.

[2] Francis A. Walker, *Political Economy*, NY: Henry Holt and Co., 1884, pp. 356 -361

[3] George W. Hastings (1825-1917), English Liberal politician, Member of Parliament from East Worcestershire 1880-1892. He was expelled from the House of Commons for fraud.

[4] https://ourworldindata.org/grapher/total-gdp-in-the-uk-since-1270

[5] http://www.measuringworth.com/ukcompare/

[6] http://www.usgovernmentspending.com/federal_budget_detail_fy10bs12014n_4010#usgs302

[7] https://www.tradingeconomics.com/united-states/gdp

A Review of the IRS Scandal

Note: This essay was published 29 Jun 2014. It was a review of the scandal at the IRS involving the targeting of various conservative groups to delay tax-exempt status as a way of interfering in the 2010 and 2012 elections.

We have all heard the reports about how the Internal Revenue Service (IRS) selectively targeted organizations by delaying their applications for 501(c)(4) tax-exempt status over the course of two federal election cycles (2010 and 2012). Singling out certain groups was important to the current administration, since the 21 Jan 2010 Citizens United ruling by the Supreme Court prohibited limitations on political spending by nonprofit groups. After that ruling, a great many "Tea Party" and other pro-freedom groups applied for tax-exempt status to enable them to raise funds and use part of those to inform the public about issues of importance in the upcoming elections.

The method of identifying which groups were to be delayed or denied was based on their names ("Tea Party", "9/12", etc.), or their views on the Bill or Rights or Constitution, or their views on the federal budget and spending in general. The ever-efficient IRS even created a spreadsheet called "Be On the Look Out" for (BOLO) as a way to establish targeting keywords that would trigger "closer scrutiny". None of the 501 applications were denied outright during the period from March 2010 to April of 2012. Instead, the IRS non-profit review offices delayed approval of applications in several creative ways:

a. By demanding information that could not exist ("What books are your members reading");
b. By asking whether any of their members intended to run for elective office;
c. By demanding a list of donors, the amounts donated, and how the donations were spent;
d. By demanding copies of all web pages, blog posts, and brochures ever used by the organization;
e. By demanding copies of all emails sent or received by organization members.

The IRS Tax Exempt review division also illegally leaked donor lists of some organizations to their opponents, audited those who had donated to the "Tea Party" groups, and in some cases, urged other government entities (FBI, ATF, OSHA) to illegally investigate or harass the applicants. Finally, complaints about the abuse of power at the IRS became so distracting that the Treasury Department Inspector General was forced to look into it. He released a report [1] detailing the basics of the IRS activities, along with a list of nine recommendations. In summary, he concluded:

> The IRS used inappropriate criteria that identified for review Tea Party and other organizations applying for tax-exempt status based upon their names or policy positions instead of indications of potential political campaign intervention. Ineffective management: 1) allowed inappropriate criteria to be developed and stay in place for more than 18 months, 2) resulted in substantial delays in processing certain applications, and 3) allowed unnecessary information request to be issued.

President Richard "I am not a crook" Nixon was nearly impeached for merely asking the IRS to attack his opponents. President Bill "Perjurer in Chief" Clinton successfully used the IRS to harass his opponents. It appears that the Obama administration did the same thing, and when caught, has responded to this series of events by denial, obfuscation, and changing the subject, same as usual. Numerous IRS officials delayed informing Congress of what they knew as the internal investigation proceeded. One of them, Deputy Commissioner for Enforcement and Services Steven T. Miller, falsely stated on 15 May 2012 that the abuses were the work of two rogue agents in Cincinnati; but as it turned out, was being orchestrated from Washington the whole time, probably by Lois G. Lerner, Director of IRS Tax Exempt and Government Entities Division [2]. We will probably never know who Lois Lerner was taking orders from, whether it was President "leading with his behind" Obama, his staff, the Department of Justice, the Treasury Department, or the upper echelon of the Democratic Party. In August of 2012, Congress issued a subpoena for all emails to and from Lois G. Lerner for the period 1 Jan 2009 to 2 Aug 2013. After 18 months, on 13 Jun 2014, the IRS finally admitted that it would not comply with the subpoena because

Lerner's computer hard drive crashed on 13 Jun 2011, and the emails prior to that date are irretrievably lost. Three days later, the IRS admitted that it also no longer had subpoenaed emails from six other IRS employees in Lerner's division because their hard drives also crashed. Meanwhile, Attorney General Eric Holder has refused to open an investigation into the abuse of power.

We the People have a right to evaluate the conduct of our government agencies. To do so, we need only review the statements made by the principals involved. On 14 May 2013, President Barack "I lied, period" Obama called the reports of IRS abuse "intolerable and inexcusable". Lois G. Lerner testified under oath before Congress on 22 May 2013:

> My professional career has been devoted to fulfilling responsibilities of the agencies for which I have worked, and I am very proud of the work I have done in government. ... I have not done anything wrong. I have not broken any laws, I have not violated any IRS rules or regulations, and I have not provided false information to this or any other congressional committee.

On 24 Jul 2013, President "leading with his behind" Obama said the entire episode was nothing more than a "phony scandal"; on 2 Feb 2014, he told interviewer Bill O'Reilly that there "was not a smidgen of corruption" at the IRS.

There is only one conclusion. Lois Lerner faithfully fulfilled her responsibilities to implement administration policies, and therefore did nothing wrong, and did not commit perjury before Congress. It is a "phony scandal" because the correct intended policy was actually enacted by the IRS; the corruption is intolerable and inexcusable only because Lois Lerner and her accomplices were dumb enough to get caught. Fortunately, they were able to get the most damaging evidence destroyed in time (remember, this started in March of 2010).

They're all Lerner's now. We do not need a special prosecutor to establish it. When IRS Commissioner Douglas H. Shulman-Lerner told Congress on 22 May 2012 that "there is absolutely no targeting", he was correct because the IRS was not singling out certain disapproved non-Democratic groups, it was harassing and delaying applications from all of them. When IRS Commissioner John Koskinen-Lerner said on 26 Jun 2014 that a special prosecutor would be "a monumental waste of taxpayer money"; he is correct because it will not be able to find anything. All the other Lerner's, their supporters, and the usual Democratic minions in the media will run out the clock until Obama pardons them on his last day in office.

All things considered, this was another successful operation by the IRS: raises and promotions all around and more power, as usual.

References

[1] Michael E. McKenney, Acting Deputy Inspector General for Audit, U. S. Treasury Department, "Inappropriate Criteria Were Used to Identify Tax-Exempt Applications for Review", Reference Number 2013-10-053, 14 May 2013

[2] Staff Report, Committee on Oversight and Government Reform, U. S. House of Representatives, "Lois Lerner's Involvement in the IRS Targeting of Tax-Exempt organizations", 11 Mar 2014, pp. 3-5

Why Hillary Clinton Cannot Be Indicted

Note: This is a compilation of 3 essays that were published 8 Mar 2016, 1 Jul 2016, and 6 Nov 2016. Some of my predictions were fairly accurate (the 1 Jul 2016 essay nearly predicted James Comey's comments on 5 Jul 2016). But I was wrong about the last prediction: the last essay was published 2 days before Donald Trump was elected as the 45th President, defeating Hillary Clinton. A funny thing happened on the way to the coronation....

(8 Mar 2016)

The U. S. State Department, having dragged its feet as long as it could, has finally released all the emails from former Secretary of State Hillary Clinton's private, unauthorized email server. All total, over 2,000 of those emails are classified, some at very high levels of secrecy. Mrs. Clinton has consistently claimed that "none of them were marked classified at the time". That proves, if it proves anything, that Mrs. Clinton is either completely irresponsible or a moron. It is obvious even to casual thinkers that emails to and from the U. S. Secretary of State are of great interest to our nation's enemies. It also seems logical that those emails could have been intercepted at many places on the internet without a need to attack her server directly. One would think that a person in their right mind holding a highly sensitive office like Secretary of State would make the appropriate application and assume all their emails should be protected by a classified server -- but not Mrs. Clinton.

After Mrs. Clinton had her staff attempt to delete the emails off her server, and after the whole matter came to light, the FBI was tasked with recovering those emails (she thought were gone), and to examine whether any laws had been broken. There are some who believe that Mrs. Clinton could be indicted at least for gross negligence. But I suspect that will never happen. FBI Director James Comey testified before Congress on 1 Mar 2016. He was asked by Congressman Steve Chabot when he thought the investigation would be wrapped up one way or the other. Director Comey's response was:

> I can't, congressman, as you know we don't talk about our investigations. What I can assure you is that I am very close personally to that investigation to ensure that we have the resources we need, including people and technology, and that it's done the way the FBI tries to do all of its work: independently, competently and promptly. That's our goal, and I'm confident that it's being done that way, but I can't give you any more details beyond that.

It is strange indeed that the FBI Director would have a personal hand in the "investigation". I hope I am proven wrong, but I suspect Mr. Comey is directly involved in order to ensure that all the evidence is collected up and destroyed, exactly the way Mrs. Clinton wanted it; just the way President Barack "I lied, period" Obama ordered it. The FBI is certainly thorough; once they are done, there won't be proof that Hillary Clinton ever worked at the State Department. That kind of thoroughness takes time.

Mrs. Clinton cannot be indicted: she is too high on the political food chain to be inconvenienced by having to take responsibility for her actions. Like I said, I hope I am proven wrong, but it seems in these modern times that "taking responsibility" is only for the little people.

(1 Jul 2016)

Since my last essay as to why Hillary Clinton cannot be indicted, a few interesting things have happened. First, President Barack "I lied, period" Obama stated on Fox News Sunday's 10 Apr 2016 episode:

> I do not talk to the Attorney General about pending investigations. I do not talk to the FBI directors about impending investigations. We have a strict line and have always maintained it. I guarantee it. I guarantee that there is no political influence in any investigation conducted by the Jus-

tice Department, or the FBI; not just in this case, but in any case. Full stop. Period. Nobody gets treated differently when it comes to the Justice Department because nobody is above the law.

There are several problems here. Obama said "impending" investigations, not "active" ones. He did not claim that no one on his staff (such as the President's Counsel) discusses investigations with the DoJ or FBI. Every time Obama says "period", you know he's lying, like the time he said you could keep your doctor and your health plan, "period". If there really is no political interference, surely there would be no need to assure the public about it.

Second, Obama endorsed Clinton on 9 Jun 2016. Now ask yourself, when was the last time any political figure endorsed another, if there was even a 1/100th of 1% chance that the latter could have legal problems? Never -- that isn't how politicians operate. He endorsed her because he knows she will not have any legal problems because he and his staff have taken steps to make sure of it.

Third, Bill Clinton met secretly with Attorney General Loretta Lynch at the Phoenix airport on 27 Jun 2016. He went out of his way to wait for her private plane, then requested access (which was granted), and they spoke for about 30 minutes. Of course, it was all about golf and grandchildren, if you are naive and gullible enough to believe it. The respective security details prevented anyone from taking pictures on the tarmac (a public place), and it was discovered only by local Phoenix reporter Christopher Sign (KNXV-TV) based on tips from his local contacts. What political figure, or lawyer, or government official would be dumb enough to meet secretly with the spouse of a person being investigated by their department? Ms. Lynch is not dumb. Today she stated that she would "accept" (not "act upon") the FBI's recommendation regarding Hillary Clinton. What was the plan before? Are we to believe that the fix was in before, but now that she met with Bill Clinton, she will go along with a criminal indictment if the FBI recommends it?

Here is what I believe will happen. As I said in my previous (8 Mar 2016), all the evidence against Hillary is being collected up to be destroyed or permanently sealed just the way Hillary wanted it. But the FBI report will state that she "or her staff" had "accidentally or inadvertently" committed some "errors of judgment" that would normally amount to "technicality-type" misdemeanors, but in view of her "outstanding public service", and "to avoid a political crisis", no charges will be recommended. So Lynch will be off the hook. Hillary, knowing the evidence is safely hidden or destroyed, will then pretend to issue an apology for some "inerrant carelessness by her staff". She will do her best to keep from bursting out laughing. Then the whole thing goes away.

That is how things work in banana republics, and that is how our federal government works when high-ranking political figures like Barack "leading with his behind" Obama, Bill "Perjurer in Chief" Clinton, Loretta Lynch, and Hillary "irredeemably deplorable" Clinton are involved. The one thing we do not know is how deep the corruption has pervaded the rank-and-file of the FBI and Justice Department.

(6 Nov 2016)

I shall mention a few other things in this, my third essay on why Hillary Clinton cannot be indicted. In my second one (1 Jul 16), I predicted that the FBI would issue a report making all sorts of excuses for Clinton. On 5 Jul 2016, FBI Director James Comey held a press conference, outlining all the sordid details of the email situation, and then claiming that no prosecutor would pursue the case as a criminal matter because "intent" was lacking, although some classified data was certainly exposed on unclassified computer systems. He did not explain why the FBI was making a recommendation, since the FBI normally assembles facts and leaves the decision to the prosecutor's office as to whether an indictment should be handed down. But I can see his point: since the fix was in from the start, he was merely saving Attorney General Loretta Lynch the inconvenience of having to address the issue directly. The Democrats praised James Comey for his fine public service and outstanding integrity.

Then came the issue with Anthony Weiner. Mr. Weiner, as you may recall, was forced to resign as Congressman over allegations that he sent emails with explicit sexual content to an underage girl. Mr.

Weiner is the estranged husband of Huma Abedin, Hillary Clinton's long-time aide and confidante at both the Department of State and the Clinton Foundation. The FBI had been investigating that case when they discovered emails to and from Hillary Clinton on Huma Abedin's laptop, which she shared with Mr. Weiner. The FBI then had a problem: what if this laptop contained copies of emails that the FBI had promised to destroy in order to protect Clinton, or even worse, contained new ones they had not previously known about? Mr. Comey had to conduct a search into those emails, but also had to notify Congress that he was doing so, having previously promised to keep Congress abreast of any new developments. That letter went to Congress on 28 Oct 2016.

The Democrats condemned Mr. Comey; Minority Leader Nancy Pelosi even said that Mr. Comey's qualifications were now suspect; he was now an ally of Mr. Trump; a Republican toady hired by a Republican, a force for evil trying to inject the FBI into an election; Adolf Hitler's second cousin (or words to that effect).

But, to the FBI's relief, the emails found on Ms. Adedin's laptop were duplicates or purely personal; it was an easy matter to dispose of them along with the previous batches before any of them leaked out. Today (6 Nov 2016), Mr. Comey sent a letter to Congress in which he stated the email investigation of Clinton was now closed, and the latest investigation did not change his conclusion as stated on 5 Jul 2016.

The Democrats now regard Mr. Comey as a fine public servant worthy of the highest approbation from patriotic Americans everywhere. So the fix continues, like it would in any other place run by the Chicago mafia. The FBI certainly has done its part in getting Hillary "Irredeemably deplorable" Clinton elected President.

Donald Trump's Two Crimes

Note: This essay was published 11 Jan 2020, just after the first impeachment of Donald Trump, and just prior to China's release of the Wuhan virus. It cites two examples of Donald Trump's real problem: he is not a charter member of the ruling elite.

The House of Representatives impeached President Trump on 18 Dec 2019 in the form of two articles:

> Article 1: Using the powers of his high office, President Trump solicited the interference of a foreign government, Ukraine, in the 2020 United States Presidential election. He did so through a scheme or course of conduct that included soliciting the Government of Ukraine to publicly announce investigations that would benefit his reelection, harm the election prospects of a political opponent, and influence the 2020 United States Presidential election to his advantage. President Trump also sought to pressure the Government of Ukraine to take these steps by conditioning official United States Government acts of significant value to Ukraine on its public announcement of the investigations. President Trump engaged in this scheme or course of conduct for corrupt purposes in pursuit of personal political benefit. In so doing, President Trump used the powers of the Presidency in a manner that compromised the national security of the United States and undermined the integrity of the United States democratic process. He thus ignored and injured the interests of the Nation.
>
> Article 2: The Constitution provides that the House of Representatives "shall have the sole Power of Impeachment" and that the President "shall be removed from Office on Impeachment for, and Conviction of, Treason, Bribery, or other high Crimes and Misdemeanors". In his conduct of the office of President of the United States and in violation of his constitutional oath faithfully to execute the office of President of the United States and, to the best of his ability, preserve, protect, and defend the Constitution of the United States, and in violation of his constitutional duty to take care that the laws be faithfully executed --- Donald J. Trump has directed the unprecedented, categorical, and indiscriminate defiance of subpoenas issued by the House of Representatives pursuant to its "sole Power of Impeachment". President Trump has abused the powers of the Presidency in a manner offensive to, and subversive of, the Constitution, in that:
>
> The House of Representatives has engaged in an impeachment inquiry focused on President Trump's corrupt solicitation of the Government of Ukraine to interfere in the 2020 United States Presidential election. As part of this impeachment inquiry, the Committees undertaking the investigation served subpoenas seeking documents and testimony deemed vital to the inquiry from various Executive Branch agencies and offices, and current and former officials.
>
> In response, without lawful cause or excuse, President Trump directed Executive Branch agencies, offices, and officials not to comply with those subpoenas. President Trump thus interposed the powers of the Presidency against the lawful subpoenas of the House of representatives, and assumed to himself functions and judgments necessary to the exercise of the "sole Power of Impeachment" vested by the Constitution in the House of Representatives.

The first article claims that there was a quid pro quo in regards to releasing foreign aid to Ukraine; the second states that Trump has prevented Congress from exercising its powers of supervision and oversight.

The first article is false for two reasons. The first is: if any taxpayer money is sent to any foreign government, especially one known to be as corrupt as Ukraine, there should be a quid pro quo. Why would any logical taxpayer want a President to send money to a foreign government without getting something in return? Are we American taxpayers a bunch of dimwitted Santa Clauses -- we give money away to people known to be crooks? Secondly, Joe Biden had already bragged on video that he intimidated and blackmailed the Ukrainian government into terminating an investigation into his son's (Hunter Biden) employment with a Ukrainian energy firm. Now put this in perspective: suppose Mr. Biden wins the Democratic nomination, and then goes on to defeat Mr. Trump in the 2020 election. Do you, a citizen, want a President Biden that can be blackmailed by Ukraine in order to cover for his son? Keep in mind that if Ukraine has dirt on either Biden, it has already been speedily transmitted to Russia. Do you want Putin giving orders to President Biden? Trump had a perfectly legitimate reason to ask the Ukrainians to either clear Biden or expose any crimes in order to ensure that Americans do not inadvertently find themselves voting for a crook.

The second article is also false. There is no provision in the Constitution that guarantees that Congress can have any Executive branch document it wants. Taken to its extreme logical progression, the Democrats are claiming that the Presidential veto power is unconstitutional. Also, subpoenas are routinely arbitrated by a petition to the courts, but the Democrats in Congress made no attempt to do so. If the Democrats were sincere about seeing all Executive documents, surely they would have impeached President Obama for declaring Executive Privilege regarding the entire "Fast and Furious" gun-running scheme (providing guns to the Mexican drug cartels).

But Donald Trump has committed two crimes which can never be forgiven nor forgotten nor excused by the ruling elite:

Crime 1: Donald Trump asked "Why?"

a. Why is the US supporting NATO when the other members of NATO, much closer to the assumed Russian threat, do not support it commensurately? If the French would not help us get the Germans out of France in WW II, why would we assume the Western Europeans would help us get the Russians out of Western Europe now?

b. Why do the Western Europeans and the US foreign policy bureaucrats believe Russia would or could invade Western Europe in the first place?

c. Why is America attempting to cure the ills of the open sewer known as the Middle East? Why are we spending blood and treasure attempting to provide the virtues of democratic institutions on a group of people who believe that "freedom" means of the ability to kill your neighbor because he attends a different mosque? Why are we trying to guarantee free and fair elections in Baghdad, when we can't seem to have one in Chicago?

d. Why is America allowing 30 million illegal immigrants into American without knowing who they are, where they are, or what they are doing? Why is the American taxpayer being expected to pay the living expenses of illegal immigrants?

Crime 2: Donald Trump asked "How?"

a. How does the continued presence of American troops in Europe, the Middle East, and Asia benefit the American people?

b. How are illegal immigrants improving the lives of Americans who are struggling along paycheck to paycheck as it is?

c. How has the ruling elite served the American people these last 40 years, given the general decline in wages and opportunity, combined with a decline in the quality of the education system?

d. How has the American citizen benefitted from trade deals with China in which the Chinese get to steal everything they can, force technology transfers, and export to the US cheap crap made of Chinesium by undercutting American workers?

Those are Donald Trump's real crimes, and that is why he will be pursued by the ruling elite for the rest of his life, even after he leaves office.

References

[1] *Articles of Impeachment Against Donald John Trump*, House Resolution 755, 116th Congress, First Session, 18 Dec 2019.

How "Black Lives Matter" Will Fail
(28 Jun 2020)

The peaceful riots that began in Minneapolis with the death of George Floyd have spread across the nation in the 35 days since, having begun as peaceful protests by "Black Lives Matter" (BLM) against alleged institutional racism in the Minneapolis Police Department. They have now evolved into full-fledged destruction of property and an attempt to erase American culture. The violence was partly the result of opportunists seeking to take a five-finger discount at retail stores, but more importantly, the subversive activities of the street army known as ANTIFA. ANTIFA is a separate problem; they capitalized on the George Floyd incident as an excuse to make trouble. Black Lives Matter has problems of its own that will ultimately cause it to fail as a movement.

The real problem with police misconduct is that it is often covered up and papered over. There are some cases, such as the one involving Michael Brown (Ferguson, MO) or Fred Gray (Baltimore, MD) that do require some investigation before an evaluation of misconduct can occur. But in the case of George Floyd (Minneapolis, MN), nearly the entire engagement was caught on video. Any non-government employee caught on video doing the same thing to Mr. Floyd would have been arrested for murder within the hour. But, given that it was committed by a government employee in uniform, the natural inclination of the "oversight" board and "internal affairs" would be to cover it up and make excuses as necessary to justify the conduct of the police. The real problem is not that misconduct is widespread or racial; the problem is that misconduct is excused and covered up when it does happen. A similar incident was caught on video in the case of Eric Garner (New York, NY), and although a prohibited hold was utilized by the officer which at minimum contributed to Mr. Garner's demise, the officer received the usual raise and promotion.

"Black Lives Matter" is a Marxist activist group that uses police incidents as a means to gain attention, donations, and political power, which they use to intimidate politicians and (they hope) the general population. Given that true misconduct is rare, the incident concerning George Floyd in Minneapolis on 25 May 2020 gave BLM their best opportunity in years.

BLM has developed an extensive propaganda system. It is based on the false narrative that every police department consists of 100% white racist cops who spend their entire shift shooting and lynching black people. The true fact is that between 10 and 20 unarmed black people are killed by police every year; BLM conveniently ignores the other fact that between 4,000 and 5,000 black people are killed by other black people (mostly in battles over which gang gets to sell crack on which street corners).

BLM claims to desire radical changes in how police departments are operated, but history shows that if any of their recommendations are adopted, the big losers will be black people, not the wealthy activists. The goal for the leaders of BLM is the acquisition of power over society in general, in order to dictate the rules for a new societal order. The new social order will consist of guilt by association based on race and economic status.

The BLM movement contains the seed of its own destruction. It is already evident that not a single leader of BLM cares about real black people. The leadership of BLM never explains how a police department staffed by 60% black officers is racist against blacks. If BLM actually cared about the lives of black people, or their prosperity, or equality, they would start asking some very hard questions of the people (Democrats) who have been running America's largest cities for 50 years. Here are some sample questions BLM could ask, but never will:

1. Why are the public schools so bad in minority neighborhoods?
2. Why is the local economy in minority neighborhoods so bad that young black men see drug dealing as the path to prosperity?
3. Why are the occasional and relatively rare incidents of police misconduct so regularly excused and covered up?

4. Why is it that in minority neighborhoods, the streets are dirty, the potholes aren't filled, the streetlights aren't timed correctly, and the city workers can't get the grass cut on the city-owned property?

5. Why are local government policies designed specifically to weaken the black family, one of the two institutions (along with Christianity) that preserved black people during the two previous Democratic Party attacks (slavery and Jim Crow)?

The reason BLM will never ask these questions is because they already know the answer: the goal of the Democratic Party, even when local offices are held by black Democrats, is to suppress black people. The fact that BLM cares nothing about actual black people will become obvious sooner or later, when the public finds out that the money donated to BLM is turned over to PACs to run political ads on behalf of Democratic candidates at all levels. The goal once again, is to acquire political power and ultimately (if successful) to impose Marxism on America. I am reasonably confident that the general public will tire of being called racists and reject BLM's basic claim that all whites, Asians, Jews, and Hispanics are racist. Mostly likely most black Americans will reject the BLM-inspired changes that will cause their quality of life to decline.

The Nature of ANTIFA
(14 Jul 2020)

The mainstream news may have you believe otherwise, but ANTIFA is nothing more than the usual subversive Marxist street army, similar in makeup and tactics used by street gangs employed by dictators throughout history. In other words, its name is the exact opposite of what it actually is: it is in fact the fascist street army promoting a totalitarian governing philosophy on behalf of the Democratic Party. ANTIFA has recently come to the forefront as sponsors of the "mostly peaceful protests" that occurred after the death of George Floyd in Minneapolis.

Given the public antics of ANTIFA, it is not difficult to assess the characteristics of their leadership and followers:

a. Mostly wealthy and upper-middle class white people, some of whom possess advanced degrees from Ivy League schools. Some of them are the sons and daughters of the ruling elite.

b. Mostly financed by powerful global Foundations with the goal of applying pressure from below to convince the public that safety can be gained only by granting the elites more power.

c. Mostly arrogant enough to embrace the ideology of tyranny; in other words, the belief they can create paradise on earth if only they had sufficient control.

d. Mostly ignorant enough to believe that street violence can intimidate the general public into accepting a socialist political and economic system.

e. Mostly homosexual.

f. Mostly atheist.

g. Mostly useful morons; easily brainwashed and easily led.

h. Mostly chant their invectives in English since they cannot pronounce the original German.

i. Mostly pansies that will run home crying to their Mommies as soon as someone stands up to them.

Currently ANTIFA is mostly tolerated by the Mayors and Governors of our largest states, because said so-called leaders are either on the same payroll as ANTIFA or too afraid to object. What we have here is a large number of wimps occupying positions of local leadership. Unfortunately, we cannot count on those leaders when we need them. It would be most helpful if these creampuff local leaders ordered the respective cupcake Chiefs of Police to track down the members of ANTIFA and make arrests, so that the fruitcake prosecutors could take them to court. Don't count on it. In the end, as always, the people will either put up with this problem, or it will die out when the bad weather comes, or the people will deal with it directly. My prediction is that the general public will tire of watching these mental midgets try to destroy our culture and institutions. They will put some pressure on the creampuff local leaders who will pretend to take some action (maybe even a harrrrumph or two in a finely worded speech). But most likely someone (not within the government) will find out how to identify the ANTIFA members. Once the ANTIFA nitwits are publicly exposed, the movement will collapse as the members scamper like rats back to their Trust Fund estates.

The Biden Inaugural Address, Translated
(20 Jan 2021)

Joseph R. "Wimpy" Biden, Jr. was sworn in today as America's 46th President, and gave his inaugural address on the Capitol. It's the usual patronizing garbage we have come to expect from all politicians. He was joined at the Capitol by many dignitaries: President Bill "Perjurer in Chief" Clinton, former Secretary of State Hillary "Irredeemably deplorable" Clinton, President Barack "Leading with my behind" Obama, and President George W. "Woodrow Wilson" Bush, to name a few. The big tech titans were not present, but of course were happy that they got their guy elected, no matter what it took. Mark "Junior High" Zuckerberg, Jack "Censorship is good" Dorsey, and Jeff "I own that, too" Bezos were celebrating in their penthouses. Comrades Vice President Kamala "Smirky" Harris and Alexandria "Binkie" Ocasio-Cortez (America's tallest toddler) were also celebrating the start of the new revolution. But it important not to take Mr. Biden's words at face value; they must be translated according to the policies of the Democratic Party, which is now in control of the entire federal government. I have provided below the complete transcript, clarifying in square brackets Mr. Biden's actual intent, given his previous announcements and plans, and the various known objectives of the Democratic Party. Replace the original words in quotes with the words in the square brackets.

President Biden:

Chief Justice Roberts, Vice President Harris, Speaker Pelosi, Leader Schumer, Leader McConnell, Vice President Pence, distinguished "guests" ["members of the Establishment"], and my "fellow Americans" ["soon-to-be serfs"].

This is "America's" ["China's"] day. This is "democracy's" ["Russia's"] day; a day of history and hope; of renewal and resolve. Through a crucible for the ages America has been tested anew and America has risen to the challenge. Today, we celebrate the triumph not of a candidate, but of a "cause" ["socialist revolution"], the cause of "democracy" ["Marxism"]. The will of the people has been "heard" ["rejected"] and the will of the people has been "heeded" ["ignored"]. We have learned again that "democracy" ["incompetence"] is "precious" ["essential"]. "Democracy" ["corruption"] is "fragile" ["useful"]. And at this hour, my "friends" ["serfs"], "democracy" ["tyranny"] has prevailed.

So now, on this hallowed ground where just days ago "violence" ["ANTIFA"] sought to shake this Capitol's very foundation, we come together as one "nation" [Party"], under "God" ["humanism"], "indivisible" ["divided"], to carry out the peaceful transfer of power as we have for more than two centuries. We look ahead in our uniquely American way - restless, bold, optimistic - and set our sights on the nation we know "we can be and we must be" ["must be fundamentally changed"]. I thank my predecessors of both parties for their presence here. I thank them from the bottom of my heart. You know the resilience of our Constitution and the strength of our "nation" ["Party"]. As does President Carter, who I spoke to last night but who cannot be with us today, but whom we salute for his lifetime of service.

I have just taken the sacred oath each of these patriots took - an oath first sworn by George Washington. But the American story depends not on any one of us, not on some of us, but on all of us. On "We the People" who seek a more perfect Union. This is a "great" ["crappy"] nation and "we" ["Constitution-embracers"] are a "good" ["bad"] people. Over the centuries through storm and strife, in peace and in war, we have come so far. But we still have far to go. We will press forward with speed and urgency, for we have much to "do" ["destroy"] in this "winter" ["dawn"] of "peril" ["confusion"] and "possibility" ["chaos"]. Much to repair ["demonize"], much to "restore" ["investigate"], much to heal ["attack"], much to "build" ["ruin"], and much to "gain" ["steal"].

Few periods in our nation's history have been more challenging or difficult than the one we're in now. A once-in-a-century virus silently stalks the country. It's taken as many lives in one year as America lost in all of World War II. Millions of jobs have been lost. Hundreds of thousands of businesses closed. A cry for racial "justice" ["retribution"] some "400" ["20"] years in the making moves us. The dream of justice for "all" ["some"] will be deferred no longer. A cry for "survival" ["more funding"] comes from the "planet itself" ["climate hoaxers"]. A cry that can't be any more desperate or any more clear. And now, a rise in political "extremism" ["revolution"], "white" ["Harvard-educated"] "supremacy" ["dominance"], "domestic terrorism" ["socialism"] that we must "confront" ["accept"] and we will "defeat" ["support"].

To "overcome" ["obtain"] these "challenges" ["objectives"] - to "restore" ["eliminate"] the "soul" ["liberties"] and to "secure" ["cancel"] the future of America - requires more than words. It requires that most "elusive" ["common"] of things in a "democracy" ["revolution"]: Unity ["Control"]. "Unity" ["Power"]. In another January in Washington, on New Year's Day 1863, Abraham Lincoln signed the Emancipation Proclamation. When he put pen to paper, the President said, "If my name ever goes down into history it will be for this act and my whole soul is in it." My whole soul is in it. Today, on this January day, my whole soul is in this: "Bringing" ["Separating"] America "together" [into tribes"]. "Uniting" ["Dividing"] our people. And "uniting" [dividing"] "our nation" ["the spoils"]. I "ask" ["demand"] every "American" ["Democrat"] to join me in this cause. Uniting to "fight" ["aid"] the "common foes" ["ANTIFA and BLM street armies"] we "face" ["embrace"]: Anger, resentment, hatred. Extremism, lawlessness, violence. Disease, joblessness, hopelessness. With "unity" ["division"] we can do "great" ["insidious"] things, "important" ["destructive"] things. We can "right wrongs" ["abolish rights"]. We can put people to work in "good jobs" ["labor camps"]. We can "teach" ["indoctrinate"] our children in "safe" ["dangerous"] schools. We can "overcome" ["perpetuate"] this deadly virus. We can "reward" ["denigrate"] work, "rebuild" ["reduce"] the middle class, and make health care "secure" ["precarious"] for "all" ["those who oppose my regime"]. We can deliver racial "justice" ["preferences"].

We can make America, once again, the leading force for "good" ["useless wars"] in the world. I know speaking of unity can sound to some like a foolish fantasy. I know the forces that divide us are deep and they are real. But I also know they are not new. Our history has been a constant struggle between the "American" ["false"] "ideal" ["notion"] that we are all created equal and the harsh, ugly reality that "racism" ["work"], nativism ["self-reliance"], "fear" ["integrity"], and "demonization" ["religion"] have long "torn us apart" ["prevented victory for the Party"]. The battle is perennial. Victory is never assured. Through the Civil War, the Great Depression, World War, 9/11, through struggle, sacrifice, and setbacks, our "better angels" ["basic moral principles"] have always prevailed. In each of these moments, enough of "us" ["them"] "came together" ["stood up"] to "carry all of us forward" ["deter tyranny"]. "And" ["But"], we can "do so" ["defeat them"] now.

"History" ["Delusion"], "faith" ["atheism"], and "reason" ["propaganda"] show the way, the way of unity ["socialist conformity"]. We can see "each other" ["those who embrace the Constitution"] not as "adversaries" ["competitors"] but as "neighbors" ["enemies"]. We can treat "each other" ["those who believe in the Constitution"] with "dignity" ["hatred"] and "respect" ["persecution"]. We can "join" ["enlist"] forces, "stop" ["increase"] the shouting, and "lower" ["elevate"] the temperature. For without "unity" ["division"], there is no "peace" ["revolution"], only "bitterness" ["freedom"] and "fury" ["liberty"]. No progress, only exhausting outrage. No "nation" ["balkanization"], only a state of "chaos" ["stability"]. This is our historic moment of crisis and challenge, and "unity" ["brute force"] is the path forward. And, we must meet this moment as the United "States" ["Party"] of "America" [Socialism"]. If we do that, I guarantee you, we will not fail. We have never, ever, ever failed in "America" ["utopias"] when we have "acted" ["conspired"] together. And so today, at this time and in this place, let us start afresh. All of us. Let us "listen" ["obey"] "to one another" ["the Party"]. "Hear" ["Destroy"] "one another" ["all conservatives"]. "See" ["Censor"] "one another" ["all conservatives"]. "Show respect" ["Demonize"] "to one another" ["all conservatives"]. Politics "need not" ["must"] be a raging fire destroying "everything in its path" ["the Party's enemies"]. Every disagreement "doesn't have to" ["must"] be a cause for total war. And, we must "reject" ["firmly establish"] a culture in which "facts themselves are" ["propaganda itself is"] "manipulated" ["promoted"] and even "manufactured" ["forced"].

My fellow "Americans" ["Establishment elites"], we have to "be different than" ["continue"] this. America has to "be better than" ["adopt"] this. And, I believe America "is better than" ["can be forced to adopt"] this. Just look around. Here we stand, in the shadow of a Capitol dome that was completed amid the Civil War, when the Union itself hung in the balance. Yet we endured and we prevailed. Here we stand looking out to the great Mall where Dr. King spoke of his dream. Here we stand, where 108 years ago at another inaugural, thousands of protestors tried to block brave women from marching for the right to vote. Today, we mark the swearing-in of the first woman in American history elected to national office - Vice President Kamala Harris. Don't tell me things can't change. Here we stand across the Potomac from Arlington National Cemetery, where heroes who gave the last full measure of devotion rest in eternal peace. And here we stand, just days after a "riotous" ["non Party"] mob thought they could use "violence" ["a protest"] to "silence" ["object to"] the "will of the people" ["questionable subversion of an election"], to stop the work of "our democracy" ["the Party"], and to drive us from this sacred ground. That did not happen. It will never happen. Not today. Not tomorrow. Not ever.

To all those who supported our campaign I am "humbled" ["grateful"] "by" ["for"] the "faith" ["crimes"] you have "placed in" ["committed for"] us. To all those who did not support us, let me say this: "Hear me out as we move forward" ["you will be investigated and audited"]. Take a measure of me and my heart. And if you still disagree, "so be it" ["you'll be bankrupt and in jail"]. That's "democracy" ["socialism"]. That's "America" ["rule by the Party"]. The right to dissent peaceably, "within the guardrails of our Republic" ["so long as I permit it"], "is perhaps" ["will be"] our nation's "greatest" ["most obvious"] "strength" ["initiative"]. Yet hear me clearly: Disagreement must not "lead to disunion" ["be permitted"]. And I pledge this to you: I will be a President for all "Americans" ["loyal Party members and the Establishment"]. I will "fight as hard for" ["attack and punish"] those who did not support me "as for" ["and reward"] those who did. Many centuries ago, Saint Augustine, a saint of my church, wrote that a people was a multitude defined by the common objects of their love. What are the common objects we "love" ["accept"] that define us as "Americans" ["robots"]? I think I know. "Opportunity" [Obedience"], "security" ["silencing"], "liberty" ["imprisonment"], "dignity" ["bankruptcy"], "respect" ["ridicule"], "honor" ["demonization"]. And, yes, "the truth" ["propaganda"].

Recent weeks and months have taught us a painful lesson. There is truth and there are lies. Lies told for power and for profit. And each of us has a duty and responsibility, as citizens, as Americans, and especially as leaders - leaders who have pledged to "honor" ["disregard"] our Constitution and "protect" ["sacrifice"] our nation - to defend the truth and to defeat the lies. I understand that many Americans view the future with some fear and trepidation. I understand they worry about their jobs, about taking care of their families, about what comes next. I get it. But the answer is not to turn inward, to retreat into competing factions, distrusting those who don't look like you do, or worship the way you do, or don't get their news from the same sources you do. We must "end" ["promote"] this "uncivil" ["civil"] war that pits red against blue, rural versus urban, "conservative" ["patriot"] versus "liberal" ["subversive"]. We can do this if we open our souls instead of hardening our hearts. If "we" ["the other side will"] show a little tolerance and humility. If "we're" ["they're"] willing to "stand" ["cooperate"] in "the other person's shoes" ["the Party's objectives"] "just for a moment" ["permanently"]. Because here is the thing about life: There is no accounting for what fate will deal you. There are some days when we need a hand. There are other days when we're called on to lend one. That is how we must be with one another. And, if we are this way, our country will be "stronger" ["regimented"], more "prosperous" [dangerous"], more ready for the "future" ["conquest"].

My fellow Americans, in the work ahead of us, we will need each other. We will need all our strength to persevere through this dark winter. We are entering what may well be the toughest and deadliest period of the virus. We must "set aside" ["focus on"] the politics and "finally face" ["stumble through"] this pandemic as one nation. I promise you this: as the Bible says weeping may endure for a night but joy cometh in the morning. We will get through this, together.

The world is watching today. So here is my message to those beyond our borders: America has been tested and we have come out stronger for it. We will repair our alliances and "engage with" ["concede to"] the world once again. Not to meet yesterday's challenges, but today's and tomorrow's. We will lead not merely by the example of our power but by the power of our example. We will be a strong and trusted partner for "peace" ["negotiations"], "progress" ["concessions"], and "security" ["weakness"]. We have been through so much in this nation. And, in my first act as President, I would like to ask you to join me in a moment of silent prayer to remember all those we lost this past year to the pandemic. To those 400,000 fellow Americans - mothers and fathers, husbands and wives, sons and daughters, friends, neighbors, and co-workers. We will honor them by becoming the people and nation we know we can and should be. Let us say a silent prayer for those who lost their lives, for those they left behind, and for our country. Amen.

This is a time of testing. We "face" ["lead"] an attack on democracy and on truth. A raging virus. Growing inequity. The sting of systemic racism. A climate in crisis. America's role in the world. Any one of these would be enough to challenge us in profound ways. But the fact is we face them all at once, presenting this nation with the gravest of responsibilities. Now we must step up. All of us. It is a time for boldness, for there is so much to do. And, this is certain. We will be judged, you and I, for how we resolve the cascading crises of our era. Will we rise to the occasion? Will we master this rare and difficult hour? Will we meet our obligations and pass along a new and better world for our children? I believe we must and I believe we will. And when we do, we will write the next chapter in the American story. It's a story that might sound something like a song that means a lot to me. It's called "American Anthem" and there is one verse stands out for me:

> "The work and prayers of centuries have brought us to this day
> What shall be our legacy? What will our children say?...
> Let me know in my heart When my days are through
> America, America,
> I gave my best to you."

Let us add our own work and prayers to the unfolding story of our nation. If we do this then when our days are through our children and our children's children will say of us they gave their best. They did their duty. They healed a broken land. My fellow Americans, I close today where I began, with a sacred oath.

Before "God" ["Marx"] and all of you I give you my word. I will always "level with" ["lie to"] "you" ["those who oppose the Party"]. I will "defend" ["abolish"] the Constitution. I will defend our "democracy" ["socialist revolution"]. I will "defend" ["hate"] America. I will give my all in your service thinking "not" ["only"] of power, "but" ["and"] of "possibilities" ["greater power"]. "Not" [Certainly"] of personal interest, "but" ["out"] of the public "good" ["coffers"]. And together, we shall write an American story of "hope" ["pessimism"], not "fear" ["confidence"]: of unity, not division; of "light" ["power"], not "darkness" ["freedom"]; an "American" ["socialist"] story of "decency and dignity" ["decay and discrimination"]; of "love and of healing" ["hatred and revenge"]; of "greatness and of goodness" ["mediocrity and stalemate"]. May this be the story that guides us, the story that inspires us; the story that tells ages yet to come that we answered the call of history. We met the moment.

That democracy and hope, truth and justice, "did not die" ["croaked"] on our watch "but thrived" ["completely"]. That our "America" ["revolution"] secured "liberty" ["control"] at home and stood "once again" ["for the first time"] as "an beacon" ["an example"] to "the world" ["socialists everywhere"]. That is what we owe our forebears, one another, and generations to follow. So, with purpose and resolve we turn to the tasks of our time: sustained by faith, driven by conviction; and, devoted to one another and to this country we "love" ["hate"] with all our hearts. May "God" ["Mao"] "bless" ["curse"] America and may "God" ["President Xi"] protect our "troops" ["socialist comrades"].

Thank you, "America" ["chumps"].

The Open-Border Policy Rationale
(25 Jul 2022)

There was a recent convocation of the ruling elite in Aspen, CO. During the presentations, Trymaine Lee, a correspondent from MSNBC, interviewed U. S. Secretary of Homeland Security Alejandro Majorkas on 21 Jul 2022, and part of it went like this:

> Trymaine Lee: "Is the border safe now? I was watching a news channel and they were talking about an invasion that was happening."
>
> (Audience laughs)
>
> Alejandro Majorkas: "The border is secure; the border we are working to make more secure. That has been a historic challenge."

Majorkas' claim may seem quite a surprise, first, since about 3 million illegal aliens (that we know of) have already crossed into the U. S. in the past year. All these people are being let in; we don't know who they are, where they are, or what they intend to do (besides getting free benefits paid for by U. S. taxpayers). The second major point is that illegal alien immigration was much less under the Trump administration. The U. S. is in fact being invaded, and (finally) a few State Governors have found the backbone to state the obvious.

When Majorkas said "the border is secure", what he really meant was "the border policy is secure". The Biden administration has at various times issued several lies to justify the open border. The first one was that the people of Central America must be allowed to come here because we (Americans) have induced so much climate change that we are driving them out of their traditional occupations. The second lie was that the white people of America are so racist that we owe the indigenous people of Central America an equal opportunity to come here as historical compensation. The third lie was that opening the border will facilitate trade, and thus promote prosperity for all, i.e., the globalist argument. The fourth lie was that unlimited immigration is good because immigrants create jobs, or take jobs that Americans won't do, or immigrants have special skills that Americans don't have; in other words, foreigners are simply better people than Americans. The good news is that Vice President Kamala "Smirky" Harris (the "border czar") has promised to find the "root cause".

But the real question remains: if illegal immigration was almost zero during the last part of the Trump administration, what is the purpose of the completely open-border policy under the Biden administration? Some conservative commentators have noted that we are generally importing poverty, social dependence, and ignorance; and that large immigration means that the American taxpayer gets to pay for other nations' socialist incompetence. Some have observed that many of the illegal aliens come here with no intention of assimilating into American culture, and the result of unrestricted immigration is that Americans end up tolerating any movement that dilutes western civilization. Some have also claimed that this is a ploy to import as many ignorant people as possible because the Democratic Party leadership, relying on historical trends, is confident that the invaders will all vote for Democrats as soon as they get voting rights, with citizenship or without. In other words, the former illegal immigrants will partly cancel out the votes of those who still believe in the Constitution and the legitimate control of borders. Those are probably all correct to some extent. I will now suggest a reason that I have not heard mentioned elsewhere.

All this talk about China taking over Taiwan is a diversion: the real goal is the strategic encirclement of the U. S. Taiwan can be blockaded at any time; that requires only a sufficient Chinese navy and a convenient pretext. Pretexts are easy for Communists, and they have built the navy. Taiwan is small potatoes: China could gain world domination if it could acquire control of Central America. It seems to me that President Joe "Wimpy" Biden, either a wholly-owned subsidiary of the Chinese Communist Party or under blackmail pressure, has been ordered to de-populate El Salvador, Guatemala, Honduras, Nicaragua, Panama, and Ecuador. (I exclude Costa Rica because it is relatively prosperous and has abolished its military.) It will be much easier for China to establish colonies in empty places than to deal with people who may prefer their traditional nations. Keep in mind that China is a long way from the western hemisphere, and it probably can only transport an army of 100,000 or 200,000 troops in a reasonable amount of time. It will not be practical to transport the heavy weapons necessary for a real battle. A small, lightly-armed land force could conquer Central America quickly if: a) it is mostly empty; b) the remaining people are unarmed; and c) the local governments and military establishments are corrupt. The last two were accomplished decades ago.

Consider the basic arithmetic as shown in the table. The totals lead to an average population density of about 275 people per square mile (about the same as our major cities and suburbs, such as Philadelphia, New York, Boston, etc.). If 4 million per year are resettled in the U. S. over the next seven years, the total population will be reduced by 28 million, and the net remaining will be 18 million or so. The average population density would then be about 105 per sq. mile (roughly the same as Iowa, Kentucky, and eastern Oklahoma). Since most would remain in the cities, the population density in the rural areas would be significantly lower. The Chinese could export 10,000,000 people to Central America reasonably quickly if camouflaged carefully enough, and thereby establish solid, durable colonies.

Nation	Population	Area (sq. miles)
Guatemala	18,576,000	42,042
El Salvador	6,550,000	8,260
Honduras	10,225,000	43,277
Nicaragua	6,784,000	45,678
Panama	4,453,000	29,761
Total	**46,588,000**	**169,018**

Chinese control of Central America would give it enormous advantages. First, it could establish military bases in these (former) nations (plus Cuba), and form an alliance with Mexico, America's sometime enemy. (Recall that Mexico sided with Germany in both World Wars.) Secondly, it would have full control of the Panama Canal: not just the operation of the canal itself, but all the approaches to it. Third, the Caribbean Sea and the Gulf of Mexico would come under full Chinese surveillance and intimidation. Fourth, China would gain indirect control over the U. S. ports at Corpus Christi, Galveston, Houston, New Orleans, Mobile, Pensacola, Tampa, and Miami. Fifth, China would have direct leverage over all the Caribbean island nations, including islands populated by British nationals. Britain has foreign policy control and defense obligations on its' Caribbean dependencies: Anguilla, Bermuda, the British Virgin Islands, the Cayman Islands, Montserrat, and Turks and Caicos. If the U. S. was unwilling to assist Britain in defending these islands (or sides with China as the ruling elite prefers), a breach would occur between the U. S. and our greatest ally.

Majorkas was right if you accept the fact that he is always lying. The open border is not causing an "invasion"; it is facilitating an "evacuation" for the benefit of Communist China.

Fourscore and Seven (Thousand New IRS Agents)
(21 Nov 2022)

Congress passed on 12 Aug 2022 and President Biden signed into law on 16 Aug 2022 the "Inflation Reduction Act". Part of this law provides $80,000,000,000 to the IRS to fund modernization and increased tax enforcement. Those who voted for this bill did so (if they read it) expect to obtain additional revenues as follows [1]: a) $181,000,000,000 from improved tax enforcement; b) $74,000,000,000 from a 1% excise tax on stock buybacks; c) $222,000,000,000 from a 15% corporate minimum rate on companies with $1,000,000,000 in revenue; and d) $53,000,000,000 from an extension of the limitation on excess business losses. These values total to $530,000,000,000 over ten years. If so, these projections admit that it will cost 15 cents to obtain each additional dollar, which is a very high 15% collection expense ratio. For comparison, the IRS' current annual expenditure for FY 2021 [2] was $13,700,000,000, and its collections in FY 2021 were [3] $4,900,000,000,000, which represents a collection expense ratio of 0.27%. That difference alone should convince you that this is not about additional revenue.

Part of the $80,000,000,000 is to be devoted to hiring 87,000 new IRS employees, but the type of employees was left to IRS discretion. According to the IRS [4], it has already hired 4,000 new customer service employees to help answer the phone and assist taxpayers with questions, and it plans to hire another 1,000 before 1 Jan 2023. According to another IRS statement [5], the IRS is developing a plan on how to spend the remainder of the $80,000,000,000. Commissioner Rettig also sent a letter to members of the Senate [6], stating in part:

> These resources are absolutely not about increasing audit scrutiny on small businesses or middle-income Americans. As we've been planning, our investment of these enforcement resources is designed around the Department of the Treasury's directive that audit rates will not rise relative to recent years for households making under $400,000. Other resources will be invested in employees and IT systems that will allow us to better serve all taxpayers, including small businesses and middle-income taxpayers. Enhanced IT systems and taxpayer service will actually mean that honest taxpayers will be better able to comply with the tax laws, resulting in a lower likelihood of being audited and a reduced burden on them.

Notice that the Commissioner cited Treasury Secretary Janet Yellen's directive to maintain the audit rate on persons making less than $400,000 annually to the historical norm. Notice that Secretary Yellen did not instruct Mr. Rettig to ensure that the audits are non-partisan; she only instructed him to ensure the overall rate is within historical norms. We can have high confidence that, since Lois Lerner is the patron saint of the IRS, the audit rate for non-Democrats is going to be increased dramatically. It is worse than that: Secretary Yellen does not require Commissioner Rettig to prove that the overall audit rates are within historical norms; it is merely a directive. This legislation gives the IRS a lot more power; but power does not confer confidence in the institution, which is the IRS' real problem.

How can a corrupt politically-motivated government agency be reformed? There are three things that seem like good ideas, but are impractical. First, the IRS cannot be abolished so long as the government requires revenue, and every government requires revenue to carry out its legitimate functions. Second, individuals will be subject to audits so long as our tax code is based on the income tax (personal and businesses). No one in Congress is going to vote to repeal the individual income tax, so audits of individuals will continue indefinitely. Third, the IRS is not going to give up any of its powers; in fact it will likely petition Congress for an expansion of its powers. Any plan to promote the public's confidence in the IRS must operate under these constraints. The best that can be hoped for is to ensure that those who are examining our returns for compliance and auditing regular taxpayers are themselves paying their taxes. In other words, it is necessary that all IRS employees be audited for tax law compliance. It will not guarantee that IRS audits of regular taxpayers are non-partisan, but at least we can have confidence that the partisans in the IRS are subject to the same scrutiny.

However, audits of IRS employees must be conducted a little differently than IRS audits of regular taxpayers. We cannot have a situation in which one IRS employee "audits" another IRS employee, as the opportunity for evasion and cheating is too great (remember the core problem here). The audits are not intended to be punitive; they are designed solely to ensure public confidence that those who enforce the law are equally subject to it. An IRS audit system should be set up along these guidelines.

1. Every IRS employee (save for a few, such as the janitorial staff, who have no contact with taxpayers or with tax forms), shall be audited every three years, and said audits shall cover the past three tax years. About 57,000 audits will be required each year, since the number of IRS employees will be about 185,000 after all the new hires are brought on.

2. The auditors shall not be current or former IRS employees, and shall have no first-degree relatives (siblings, aunts, uncles, cousins, or children) who are currently employed by the IRS.

3. Any IRS employee subject to such audits found to be in arrears on tax payments (excluding extensions and other allowances per the current law, same as other taxpayers) shall be permitted an appeal. Said appeal shall be finalized within 30 days of the initial audit findings. If the appeal shows that the IRS employee is in fact delinquent on their taxes, they shall be dismissed with prejudice (ineligible for future employment) within 24 hours. There shall be no managerial discretion permitted regarding dismissal. Payments on delinquent taxes shall follow the current guidelines per the existing law, same as all other taxpayers.

4. The statistics of the audit shall be published annually, noting how many audits were conducted, how many were found in compliance, how many were not, and the locations in which those dismissed resided (by State and county only).

References

[1] Analyses as cited in: https://en.wikipedia.org/wiki/Inflation_Reduction_Act_of_2022

[2] https://www.irs.gov/statistics/irs-budget-and-workforce

[3] FY 2022 IRS Agency Financial Report, (Form 5456), available at: https://www.irs.gov/pub/irs-pdf/p5456.pdf

[4] https://www.irs.gov/newsroom/irs-quickly-moves-forward-with-taxpayer-service-improvements-4000-hired-to-provide-more-help-to-people-during-2023-tax-season-on-phones

[5] https://www.taxpayeradvocate.irs.gov/news/tas-tax-tip-what-the-inflation-reduction-act-means-for-you/

[6] Commissioner Rettig to Members of the United States Senate, 4 Aug 2022; available at: https://www.irs.gov/pub/irs-utl/commissioners-letter-to-the-senate.pdf

President Zelenskyy's Speech Before Congress, Americanized
(4 Jan 2023)

Introduction

Ukrainian President Volodymyr Zelenskyy delivered a speech before Congress 22 Dec 2022 [1]. In **Part 1**, you will find the verbatim speech as given by President Zelenskyy. The Members of Congress (with a few exceptions) slapped their flippers vigorously and frequently before Mr. Zelenskyy. **Part 2** is an Americanized rendition of his speech that could be given before Congress by any resident of Texas, which would naturally address our southern border instead of Ukraine's eastern border. I will leave to you to assess how the speech in **Part 2** would be received.

Part 1

PRESIDENT VOLODYMYR ZELENSKYY'S SPEECH BEFORE CONGRESS, 22 DEC 2022

Dear Americans!

In all states, cities and communities. All who value freedom and justice. Appreciates the same as Ukrainians — in all our cities, in every family. May my words of respect and gratitude be heard by every American heart today!

Madam vice president, I thank you for your efforts in helping Ukraine!

Madam speaker, you bravely visited Ukraine during a full-scale war! Thank you!

It is a great honor and privilege to be here!

Dear members of Congress, from both parties who were also in Kyiv! Dear members of Congress and senators, from both parties, who will still visit Ukraine, I am sure in it, in the future! Dear representatives of our Diaspora who are present here and are present throughout the country! Dear journalists! It is an honor to be in the Congress of the United States of America and to address you and all Americans.

Despite all obstacles and gloomy scenarios, Ukraine did not fall. Ukraine is alive and fighting.

And this gives me a good reason to share with you our first joint victory — we defeated Russia in the battle for the world's opinion. We have no fear. And no one in the world should have it.

The Ukrainians won, and this gives us the courage that the world admires. The Americans won, and therefore you managed to unite the global community in defense of freedom and international law. The Europeans have won — that's why Europe is now stronger and more independent than at any time in its history. Russian tyranny has lost its grip on us and will never again influence our thoughts. But we must do everything to ensure that the countries of the global south also achieve such a victory.

I know: the Russians can also have a chance for freedom only when they defeat the Kremlin in their thoughts. But the battle is still going on. And we must defeat the Kremlin on the battlefield. This is a battle not only for land, for one or another part of Europe. This is a battle not only for the life, freedom and safety of Ukrainians or any other people that Russia seeks to conquer. This is a battle for what kind of world our children and grandchildren and their children and grandchildren will live in. It will determine whether it will be a democracy — for Ukrainians and for Americans, for everyone.

This battle cannot be frozen or postponed. It cannot be ignored, hoping that the ocean or something else will protect itself. From the United States to China, from Europe to Latin America, from Africa to Australia, the world is too interconnected, too interdependent for any one person to remain aloof and safe while this battle rages on. Our two nations are allies in this battle. And next year is a crucial time in it. The time when Ukrainian courage and American determination must guarantee the future of our freedom with you. Freedoms of people who stand for their values.

Ladies and Gentlemen! Americans!

Yesterday, before going here to Washington, I was on the front line in our Bakhmut. In our fortress in the east of Ukraine, in the Donbas, which Russian military and mercenaries have been storming continuously since May. Attacks every day and every night. But Bakhmut stands. Even last year, 70.000 people lived there. Now there are only a few civilians left there. There is no place that is not covered with blood. There is not an hour when the terrible roar of artillery does not sound. There, one trench can change hands several times a day after bloody battles, sometimes hand-to-hand. But the Ukrainian Donbas stands. The Russian army is using everything it can against Bakhmut and our other beautiful cities. The advantage of the occupiers in artillery is very noticeable. They have many times more shells than we have. They use many times more missiles and aircraft than we have ever had. But our defence forces are standing. And we are all proud of them.

Russian tactics are primitive. They burn everything in front of them. They drove thugs to the front. They are sending convicts to war. They threw everything against us just as another tyranny once threw everything against the free world in the Battle of the Promontory. Just as brave American soldiers resisted and fought back against Hitler's forces against all odds during Christmas 1944, brave Ukrainian soldiers are doing the same to Putin's forces this Christmas. Ukraine stands and will never surrender!

This is the front line: a tyranny that knows no shortage of brutality against the lives of free people. We need your help not just to stand in such battles but to turn it around. To win on the battlefield. We have artillery. Yes. Thank you. Is it enough? Frankly, no. For Bakhmut to be not only a fortress that repels the attacks of the Russian army but for the Russian army to retreat completely, more guns and shells are needed. In this case, as in the battle of Saratoga, the struggle for Bakhmut will change the course of our war for independence and freedom.

If your *Patriots* stop Russian terror against our cities, it will enable Ukrainian patriots to work to protect our freedom fully. If Russia does not reach our cities with artillery, it tries to destroy them with missiles. Moreover, Russia found an accomplice in this genocidal policy. This is Iran. Iran's killer drones, which are heading to Russia by the hundreds, have become a threat to our critical infrastructure. So one terrorist finds another. And it's only a matter of time before they hit your other allies if we don't stop them now. We have to do it!

I believe that there should not be any taboos between us in the Alliance. Ukraine has never asked and is not asking for American soldiers to fight on our land instead of us. I assure you that Ukrainian soldiers are perfectly capable of piloting American tanks and planes by themselves. Financial aid is also critically important. And I would like to thank you both for the financial packages you have already given us and those you may decide on. Your money is not charity. It is an investment in global security and democracy that we treat most responsibly.

Russia can stop this aggression if it wants to. But you can hasten our victory, I know it. And it will prove to any potential aggressor that no one will be able to violate the borders of another nation, commit atrocities and reign over people against their will. It is naive to expect steps towards peace from Russia, which likes to be a terrorist state. Russians are still poisoned by the Kremlin.

Restoring the international legal order is our joint task. We need peace. Ukraine has already made relevant proposals, and I just discussed them with President Biden — our formula for peace. 10 points that can and must be implemented for the sake of our common security, guaranteed for decades to come. And the summit that can be held — I am happy to note today that president Biden has supported our initiative. Each of you, ladies and gentlemen, can contribute to its implementation. That America's leadership remains unchallenged, bicameral, and bipartisan.

You can increase sanctions in such a way as to make Russia feel how destructive its aggression is. It is in your power to help us bring to justice all those who unleashed this unprovoked and illegal war. Let's do it! Let the terrorist state be responsible for terror and aggression and compensate all the damages caused by the war.

Let the world see that the United States is here!

Ladies and Gentlemen. Americans.

In two days, we will celebrate Christmas. Maybe, candlelit. Not because it is more romantic. But because there will be no electricity. Millions won't have neither heating nor running water. All of this will be the result of Russian missile and drone attacks on our energy infrastructure. But we do not complain.

We do not judge and compare whose life is easier. Your well-being is the product of your national security -- the result of your struggle for independence and your many victories. We, Ukrainians, will also go through our war of independence and freedom with dignity and success.

We'll celebrate Christmas -- and even if there is no electricity, the light of our faith in ourselves will not be put out. If Russian missiles attack us -- we'll do our best to protect ourselves. If they attack us with Iranian drones and our people will have to go to bomb shelters on Christmas Eve -- Ukrainians will still sit down at a holiday table and cheer up each other. And we don't have to know everyone's wish as we know that all of us, millions of Ukrainians, wish the same -- victory. Only victory.

We already built strong Ukraine -- with strong people, strong army, and strong institutions. Together with you. We develop strong security guarantees for our country and for entire Europe and the world. Together with you. And also -- together with you -- we'll put in place everyone, who will defy freedom. This will be the basis to protect democracy in Europe and the world over.

Now, on this special Christmas time, I want to thank you. All of you. I thank every American family, which cherishes the warmth of its home and wishes the same warmth to other people. I thank President Biden and both parties at the Senate and the House -- for your invaluable assistance. I thank your cities and your citizens, who supported Ukraine this year, who hosted our people, who waved our national flags, who acted to help us. Thank you all. From everyone, who is now at the frontline. From everyone, who is awaiting victory.

Standing here today, I recall the words of the President Franklin Delano Roosevelt, which are so good for this moment: "The American People in their righteous might will win through to absolute victory." The Ukrainian people will win, too. Absolutely. I know that everything depends on us. On Ukrainian Armed Forces. Yet, so much depends on the world. So much in the world depends on you.

When I was in Bakhmut yesterday, our heroes gave me the flag. The battle flag. The flag of those who defend Ukraine, Europe and the world at the cost of their lives. They asked me to bring this flag to the U.S. Congress -- to members of the House of Representatives and senators, whose decisions can save millions of people. So, let these decisions be taken.

Let this flag stay with you, ladies and gentlemen. This flag is a symbol of our victory in this war. We stand, we fight and we will win. Because we are united. Ukraine, America and the entire free world. May God protect our brave troops and citizens. May God forever bless the United States of America.

Merry Christmas and a happy victorious new year.

****

Part 2:

Here is the same speech that could be delivered by a resident of Texas. I have indicated in **bold** any changes from the speech made by President Zelenskyy.

AN AMERICANIZED VERSION OF PRESIDENT ZELENSKYY'S SPEECH TO CONGRESS

Dear **Ruling Elite**!

In all states, cities and communities. All who **denigrate** freedom and justice. Appreciates the same as **Globalists** — in all our **universities**, in every **bureaucracy**. May my words of **ridicule** and **contempt** be heard by every **federal derelict** today!

Madam vice president, I **reject** you for your efforts in helping **Mexico**!

Madam speaker, you **quietly** visited **San Diego before** the full-scale **invasion**! **Big deal**!

It is **truly disturbing that I have** to be here!

Dear members of the **ruling elite**, from both parties who were **never** in **Texas**! Dear members of Congress and senators, from both parties, who will **never** visit **the border**, I am sure in it, in the future! Dear **participants** of **the invasion** who are present here and are present throughout the country! Dear **propagandists**! It is **a disgrace** to be in the Congress of the United States of America and to address you and all Americans.

Despite all **law** and **common sense**, **Congress will** not **act**. **Congress** is **asleep** and **failing**.

And this gives me a good reason to share with you **your** first joint victory — **you** defeated **America** in the battle for the world's opinion. **Americans** have **great** fear. **But** no **invader** in the world should have it.

The **Mexican cartels** won, and this gives **them** the courage that the world admires. The **administration** won, and therefore you managed to **aid** the **bureaucracy** in **destruction** of **American sovereignty**. The **Americans** have **lost** — that's why **America** is now **weaker** and **less** independent than at any time in its history. **Administrative** tyranny has **tightened** its grip on us and will never again **improve** our **situation**. **And you will** do everything to ensure that the **enemies** of the **United States** also achieve such a victory.

I know: the **cartels** can also have a chance for **domination** only when they defeat the **Americans with** their **actions**. But the battle is still going on. And we must defeat the **cartels** on the battlefield. This is a battle not only for land, for one or another part of **America**. This is a battle not only for the life, freedom and safety of **Texans** or any other people that **Mexico** seeks to conquer. This is a battle for what kind of **America** our children and grandchildren and their children and grandchildren will live in. It will determine whether it will be a democracy — for **Texans** and for Americans, for everyone.

This battle cannot be frozen or postponed. It cannot be ignored, hoping that the **river** or something else will protect itself. From the United States to **Canada**, from **Brownsville** to **International Falls**, from **Miami** to **Seattle**, the **nation** is too interconnected, too interdependent for any **federal employee** to remain aloof and **disinterested** while this **invasion** rages on. **Your** two **factions** are allies in this battle. And next year is a crucial time in it. The time when **Democratic subversives** and **Republican cowards will ensure** the **decline** of our freedoms **by invaders**. Freedoms of **citizens** who **hoped** for **your assistance**.

Ladies and Gentlemen! **Politicians**!

Yesterday, before going here to Washington, I was on the front line in **El Paso**. In our **city** in the **west** of **Texas**, in the **desert**, which **Mexican** military and **cartels** have been storming continuously since **Feb 2021**. **Invasions** every day and every night. **And America is overrun**. **Just** last year, **3,500,000** people **invaded us**. Now there are only a few **Americans unaffected** there. There is no place that is not covered with **illegal immigrants**. There is not an hour when **their insatiable demands for benefits** does not sound. There, one **ranch** can change hands several times a day after bloody **encounters**, sometimes hand-to-hand. But the **Texas territory** stands. The **cartel** army is using everything it can against **El Paso** and our other beautiful cities. The advantage of the **invaders** in **propaganda** is very noticeable. They have many times more **allies** than we have. They use many times more **lawsuits** and **speeches** than we have ever had. **And** our **Border Patrol is struggling**. **But you** are all **critical** of them.

Cartel tactics are primitive. They burn everything in front of them. They **hide criminals in** the **crowds**. They are sending **young women** to **slavery**. They **throw** everything against us just as another tyranny once threw everything against the **United States** in the **Mariel Boatlift**. Just as brave American soldiers resisted and fought back against Hitler's forces against all odds during Christmas 1944, **Texas National Guardsmen** are **attempting** the same to **cartel** forces this Christmas. **Texas** stands and will never surrender!

This is the front line: a tyranny that knows no shortage of brutality against the lives of free people. We need your help not just to stand in such battles but to turn it around. To win on the **border**. We have **surveillance**. Yes. Thank you. Is it enough? Frankly, no. For **Texas** to be not only a **State** that repels the **invasion** of the **cartel** army but for the **cartel** army to retreat completely, more **guts** and **sense** are needed. In this case, as in the battle of **San Jacinto**, the struggle for **Texas** will change the course of our **battle** for **sovereignty** and **stability**.

Since your policies promote cartel terror against our cities, it **generally aids foreign criminals** to work to **destroy** our freedom fully. If **Mexico** does not reach our cities with **invaders**, it tries to destroy them with **drugs**. Moreover, **Mexico** found an accomplice in this genocidal policy. This is **China**. **China's** killer **fentanyl drug**, which **is** heading to **America** by the **ton**, have become a threat to our **young people**. So one **criminal helps** another. And it's only a matter of time before they hit our **older people** if we don't stop them now. **But you won't** do it!

I believe that there should not be any **misunderstanding** between us in the **debate**. **Texas** has **repeatedly** asked **but** is not **receiving any federal support** to fight **for the freedom taken from** us. I assure you that **Texas citizens** are perfectly capable of **catching Mexican coyotes** and **invaders** by **ourselves**. **Public awareness** is also critically important. **But** I would like to **remind** you both **of** the **constant demonization** you have **consistently** given us and **media personnel allied with you**. Your **criticism** is not **warranted**. It is an **indication of media conspiracy** and **hypocrisy** that we **reject** most **vigorously**.

Congress can stop this **invasion** if it wants to. But you **will** hasten our **defeat**, I know it. And it will prove to any potential aggressor that **everyone** will be able to violate the borders of **this** nation, commit atrocities and reign over **Americans** against their will. It is naive to expect steps towards **border security** from **Biden, who likes to be an anti-American fanatic**. **Congress is** still **intimidated** by the **globalists**.

Restoring the international legal **border** is our joint task. We need **borders**. **Texans have** already made relevant proposals, and **we have recommended** them **to** President Biden — our formula for **stability**. **One objective** that can and must be implemented for the sake of our common security, guaranteed for decades to come. **It's** the **step** that **won't** be **taken** — I am **sad** to note today that President Biden has **rejected all** initiative. Each of you, **cupcakes** and **creampuffs**, **won't** contribute to its implementation. That America's leadership remains **indifferent, weak**, and **cowardly**.

You **will divert attention** in such a way as to make **Mexico** feel how **beneficial** its **invasion** is. It is in your power to help us bring to justice all those who unleashed this **invited but** illegal **invasion**. **You'll fake** it! Let the **Mexican cartels** be **rewarded** for **crime** and **slavery** and **appreciate** all the **advantages reaped** by the **invasion**.

Let the world see that the United States is **destroying itself**!

Democrats and **Republicans.** **Politicians**.

In two days, we will celebrate Christmas. **Nervous**, **uneasy**. **Certainly** because it is **less comfortable**. **And** because there will be no **confidence**. **Texans will** have neither **peace** nor **public safety**. All of this will be the result of **cartel drug** and **crime** invasions on our **civil** infrastructure. But we **complain in vain**.

We do not judge and compare whose life is easier. Your well-being is the product of your **political manipulations** -- the result of your struggle for **power** and your many **cronies**. We, **Texans**, will **naturally** go through your invasion of **drugs** and **criminals** with **resentment** and **resignation**.

We'll celebrate Christmas -- and **given that** there is no **border**, the **lack** of our **confidence** in **Congress** will **only** be **declining further**. If **cartel gangsters** attack us -- we'll do our best to protect ourselves. If they **inundate** us with **foreign enemies** and our people will have **to hide in our basements** on Christmas Eve -- **Texans** will still sit down at a holiday table and cheer up each other. And we don't have to know everyone's wish as we know that all of us, millions of **Texans**, wish the same -- **borders**. Only **borders**.

We already built strong **Texas** -- with strong people, strong **economy**, and strong institutions. **But without** you. We develop strong **economic freedom** for our **State** and for entire **America** and the world. **But without** you. **But unfortunately** -- **thanks to** you -- **you'll** put in place **illegals**, who will **eradicate** freedom. This will be the basis to **destroy civilization** in **Texas** and the **other States**.

Now, on this special Christmas time, **we have** to **reject** you. All of you. I **reject** every **Congressional politician**, which cherishes the **security** of its home **but denies** the same **security** to other people I **reject** President Biden and both parties at the Senate and the House -- for your **negligent policies**. I **reject** your **attitude** and your **condescension**, who **ignored Texas** this year, who **ridiculed** our people, who **laughed off our requests**, who **failed** to help us. **Curse** you all. From **Texas**, who is now at the frontline. From everyone, who is awaiting **action**.

Standing here today, I recall the words of the **President James Earl Carter [2]**, which are so good for this moment: **"The gap between our citizens and our government has never been so wide."** The **American** people will **lose, continuously**. Absolutely. I know that everything depends on us. On **Texas National Guard.** Yet, so much depends on the **Congress**. So much in the **States** depends on you.

When I was in **El Paso** yesterday, our **citizens** gave me the **message**. The **political message**. The **message** of those who defend **El Paso, Texas**, and the **nation** at the cost of their **freedom**. They asked me to bring this **message** to the U.S. Congress -- to members of the House of Representatives and senators, whose decisions can **stop** millions of **invaders**. So, let these decisions be taken.

Let this **message** stay with you, **wimps** and **weasels**. This **message** is a **reminder** of **your incompetence** in this **invasion**. **You cower, you lie** and we will **lose**. Because we are **forgotten**. **El Paso, Texas** and the entire **American people**. May God protect our **Border Patrol** and citizens. May God forever bless the United States of America.

Merry Christmas and **another disastrous incompetent** new year.

References

[1] This transcript per: https://www.msn.com/en-us/news/world/full-text-read-ukraine-president-volodymyr-zelensky-s-address-to-congress/ar-AA15yZvm

[2] The text from President Carter is from his speech of 15 Jul 1979, in which he presented his energy policy in five points. The first four points were all good ideas, as relevant now as they were then, although the fifth point was useless and counterproductive. It is often referred to as the "Malaise Speech".

What Politicians Fear Most

Note: This essay was originally published 28 May 2018, and was later incorporated as Question 32 in the book *Real World Graduation.*

The Question

What charge will cause the greatest amount of fear, anger, and resentment among politicians?

a) Flip-flopper
b) Liar
c) Crook
d) Ideologue
e) They are equally afraid of all of the above.

The Answer

This is a trick question. All of the answers are false.

Answer a) is false because it implies that what he stood for before mattered, and what he stands for now matters, the question being why did he change his mind? "Flip-flopping" is the euphemism that one politician uses against a second one when the second one appears to have changed his policy or views on a certain issue. Politicians usually do not change their mind on policy. They simply appear to be "flip-flopping" because they were actually pandering to different groups. All it means is that he got caught telling opposite stories to different groups of interested citizens on the same subject. No politician cares if you can't keep his opinions straight: you are not a member of the ruling elite. Therefore, it doesn't matter if you think he's changing his mind as necessary to please the audience in front of him.

Answer b) is wrong because being caught in a lie implies that people are paying attention to what was said, even if it is false. Every politician demands to be heard, even if not believed. Politicians now believe that politics is war, and the methods used in war (mainly deception), are all a normal part of the process. No politician cares if you believe him or not: you are not a member of the ruling elite; therefore, it doesn't matter if you think he's a liar.

Answer c) is wrong because it implies that what a politicians does, and whether it is legal or not, is important to the politician. It is rare for a politician to be prosecuted for anything, except for making the political class look bad by engaging in the kind of overt corruption that everyone understands. A politician that stuffs cash in his suit coat pockets in the course of taking bribes is certainly in legal trouble because he is acting like a member of the Mafia. But there will be no legal trouble at all if the same cash is deposited in his campaign fund, or in his "Foundation", or "Initiative", or a trust fund, or one of his political action committee funds, where it may be drawn out as desired, all legal. Generally, prosecutors are not interested in prosecuting their friends and allies in government service. No experienced politician is afraid of being prosecuted. You are not a member of the ruling elite; therefore, it doesn't matter if you think he's a crook.

Answer d) is wrong because it implies that politicians take governing philosophy seriously one way or the other. Each politician accuses others of differing viewpoints as "ideologues", implying that the other guy is some sort of extremist. But each politician also regards each citizen as an extremist if they don't agree with the politician's views. No politician cares if you like his view of the legitimate role of government: you are not a member of the ruling elite; therefore, it doesn't matter if you think he's a power-mad crusader.

The correct answer to this question is "being regarded as irrelevant". Politics is the business of acquiring, using, and abusing power. A politician who is regarded as irrelevant can neither gain power, nor use power to change society, nor abuse power for his own benefit. That is their real fear; that is the one thing they are resentful about, and is the one thing that will cause them to explode in anger.

But it is not just the politicians who fear irrelevance; the bureaucrats fear it even more. That is why the bureaucrats are always hard at work creating more regulations and eliminating your rights. The objective is to gain the necessary power to control conditions so as to make you dependent upon the government, while ensuring that they never have to be concerned about losing their jobs.

4
Looking Ahead

Introduction

The first three chapters related the activities of people throughout history, some good, some bad, some indifferent. Each of them had their unique historical consequences, and in some of the latter cases, the consequences are yet to be experienced. But all had one thing in common: the actions and consequences all occur in time. This chapter contains two essays that look ahead; they are the most important ones.

The first addresses the differences between two important religions, Islam and Humanism, and contrasts them further with Christianity. The objective is simply to summarize the attributes of each.

The second one describes a great number of actions usually ascribed to Christianity, but are in fact either obsolete, irrelevant, phony, or fraudulent. The objective is to state clearly the means of salvation without getting bogged down by tradition or distracted by claims made by activists.

The Differences Between Islam, Humanism, and Christianity

Note: This essay was first published 28 Jan 2007, and this version has been edited to include Humanism as a religion. Although this goes into some detail on the differences between Islam, Humanism, and Christianity, it is equally applicable to all other religions besides Islam and Humanism.

Islam has gotten a great deal of attention these past few years after the attacks on New York and Washington as engineered by al Qaeda; the religion of humanism has now been engrained in most U. S. schools and even some churches. These two religions are the enemies of freedom, and a comparison between them and Christianity is summarized as follows.

1 Salvation

a. In Islam, the believer is commanded to perform works on behalf of Allah in order to obtain salvation; man does all the work. The achieving of salvation is consistent with the prejudices and viewpoints of man. It requires doing things that gain the approbation of Allah, which are to be rewarded in eternity accordingly. The Moslem's salvation is always in doubt, since it depends solely on the arbitrary will of Allah. The Moslem must "hope" for salvation.

b. In Humanism, there is no "god" and no concept of eternity. Therefore, man is his own god, and "salvation" is rejected in favor of "progress". The goal is to live according to the rules of ethics and morality, neither of which are absolutes; both are arbitrary as determined by the individual. Among the fundamental notions of humanist progress are: a) only science and nature provide any satisfaction; b) that all cultures and traditions are equal; c) that man will progress to perfection; and d) that mankind will live best under a system of universal economic and political equality enforced by a world government staffed by experts.

c. In Christianity, the believer recognizes that he is a sinner, cannot redeem himself before God, cannot attain God's approbation, and therefore requires God's grace for salvation. In Christianity, God has already done all the work for individual salvation. The Christian achieves salvation by believing that the second Member of the Trinity (thus God Himself) came to earth as the God-man Jesus Christ, who took upon Himself the penalty for all sins as our substitute. As a result, God the Father is satisfied with the substitutionary work of Christ in the cross, and believers are thus reconciled to Him. God did all the work in salvation; man only has to believe that God, in His mercy, did as He promised. Salvation is permanent; Christians have "confidence" of salvation after faith. All sins are forgiven except one: the failure to accept God's plan for salvation by faith in Christ. Salvation in Christianity appears too good to be true, which proves it is the work of God, not of man.

2 Rituals

a. In Islam, the believer is commanded to worship and satisfy Allah by specific rituals. Moslems are required to pray to Allah while facing toward Mecca five times daily. Normally the prayers consist of chants based on verses from the Islamic holy book, the Q'uran. In order to obtain a place in paradise, the Moslem is required to perform certain other duties on behalf of Allah, among which are:

> 1. Giving a certain portion of their income to the local mosque, such that the money can be distributed to the poor, or used to finance the spread of Islam.
>
> 2. Visiting the holy places of Islam at Mecca at least once in their lives. During this pilgrimage, the Moslem is commanded to wear special clothing when near the Kaaba (a holy building), to walk around the Kaaba seven times, and to revere a small holy black stone set into one wall of the Kaaba.

3. Fasting during one month of the year (Ramadan).
4. Appending "peace be upon him" whenever the Prophet Mohammed is mentioned.

b. In Humanism, the believer's task is participate in meetings and demonstrations, and to finance and support the promotion of the latest fad established by the humanist thinkers. Among the latest fads are one-world government, economic socialism, critical race theory, arbitrary changing of sexes and species, and man-made climate change.

c. Christianity has only one required ritual, known as the Communion. It is not a good deed to please God; it is a memorial to the work of Jesus Christ on the cross. It consists of eating bread and drinking wine (or grape juice) to symbolize in remembrance that Christ gave his body and endured spiritual death on our behalf. It is true that many Christian churches and denominations have invented rituals (such as water baptism and the Catholic Mass), but these were intended only as teaching aids. They are not required as part of Christianity.

3 Evangelism

a. In Islam, the doctrine is spread by persuasion, intimidation, or conquest as necessary. The Moslem is required, if called, to wage war (jihad) on other nations and peoples in order to spread Islam. The Moslem is allowed to use any type of cruelty and tyranny in the course of this action. History shows that ultimately the victims are given a choice to either adopt Islam or be executed. These religious wars can be commanded by the religious leaders for any offense, real or pretended. In Islam, Allah needs and demands the services of man to implement the plan of Allah.

b. In Humanism, the doctrine is spread by attacking its main enemy, Christianity. The tactics include: a) ridicule; b) indoctrination of children; c) large-scale propaganda; d) overt persecution; e) demonization; f) capitalization on "crises" (real and imagined) and engineered social chaos to gain power; g) frivolous lawsuits; and h) false accusations of racism, sexism, homophobia, misogyny, or whatever other emotional vitriol that is useful for denigrating Christianity.

c. Christianity includes an institution known as missionary work, in which people preach the gospel (good news) of Christ's work to those who have not heard it, in order that they may believe and receive salvation. In Christianity, the plan of God proceeds regardless of any opposition by men. The spread of the gospel is through the grace of God, and does not depend on military action for its success. Because salvation is by faith alone, "forced conversions" are illogical. However, the medieval Catholic Church did in fact distort the gospel, and did try to forcibly convert unbelievers. Such practices are contrary to Christianity. In Christianity, religious wars are commanded only by fools (which admittedly were common during the medieval era).

4 Sacred Places

a. In Islam, the believer is commanded to respect holy places, and to pilgrimage to them on a regular basis. Islam contains many holy places, especially the holy cities of Mecca and Medina, where the Prophet Mohammed lived. Each Moslem nation likewise contains a few holy cities, each of which contains various sacred artifacts to commemorate famous Moslems of the past.

b. In Humanism, the only sacred place is the mind of man.

c. In Christianity, there are no places that are ordained as "holy" or sacred, not even the places where Jesus was born, died, and was resurrected. Christ's kingdom is not of this world, and so there is no need for any sacred places on earth. It is true that some Christian sects have considered the city of Bethlehem and the location of Jesus' crucifixion sacred, but is only as a historical reminder, not as part of Christianity. The only thing considered sacred in Christianity is the Word of God (but the physical book is not regarded as a "sacred" or "holy" object).

5 Good Works

a. In Islam, the believer's salvation is contingent on the quality and volume of acts and good works performed by the believer in Allah's interest. Regardless of what works the Moslem performs on behalf of Allah, his entrance into paradise is contingent upon Allah accepting his works and sacrifices.

b. In Humanism, there are three categories of good works: a) activities consistent with their own arbitrary moral and ethical judgment; b) whatever actions advance the cause of the humanist philosophy; and c) actions that leave a legacy for their successors and family.

c. In Christianity, God has promised that whoever believes in the work of Jesus Christ has eternal salvation, and no good works are required. Once a person has expressed faith in Christ, the believer can never lose his salvation no matter how many sins he commits. God cannot revoke salvation, for to do so would be conceding that His work is of lesser power than the sins of men. God cannot renege on a promise of salvation by faith; otherwise He would not be God. Therefore, no "good works" are required for salvation, but actions that turn out for the good are a result of living the Christian way of life. However, Christians realize that they cannot change the world in general; the inherent evil of mankind continues to be what it is.

6 Entrance (or Free Will)

a. In an Islamic system, each person is grafted into the system at birth. A Moslem is automatically inducted in the religion of Islam at birth if he is born in a Moslem nation. There is no choice in the matter. Anyone born a Moslem who converts to another religion or who rejects Islam is liable for the death penalty. Historical events, and even events in the believer's life, are considered to be pre-ordained by Allah; free will in Islam is only narrowly defined because most events are "the will of Allah".

b. In Humanism, the system is naturally attractive to people because it relieves them of responsibility to a superior power. Because it is so easy and natural, some effort is required by the individual to reject it.

c. In Christianity, a person is free to accept or reject Christianity per their own free will; there is no automatic induction by birth or heritage or infant baptism. A person can become a Christian only by faith, and faith is voluntary. Renunciation of faith is also voluntary, although it has no practical effect (since a believer cannot lose his salvation).

7 Instruction

a. In Islam, the believer is expected to study and obey the mandates of the Q'uran as written by the Prophet Mohammed, his immediate successors, and the scholarly commentators. These are taught by those who have become experts in the Q'uran. The instruction mainly consists of becoming familiar with the required rituals, the requirements and exactions of the Islamic Law, the mandate to spread Islam by any means necessary, and how to obtain Allah's favor in eternity. Everything in the Q'uran is regarded as equally applicable to all times and places.

b. In Humanism, instruction is acquired as the believer sees fit, devoted to learning the wisdom of the great philosophers and teachers of the past, and to improve upon those using: a) the latest scientific discoveries and theories; and b) philosophical innovations. The personal objectives are: a) to become an expert in desired areas of interest; and b) to pass that knowledge on to the next generation. The overall objective is to eventually make man a perfect creature in a perfect world. Since there is no concept of life after death, all instruction is devoted to improving the lot of man on earth.

c. In Christianity, instruction is accomplished by those who are knowledgeable in the original Biblical scriptures, and can provide an accurate interpretation of them, recognizing: a) the Biblical scriptures are revelation from God; b) that they must be interpreted according to the customs that prevailed when written; and c) not all of the Biblical scripture is applicable in the present time, since human history is divided into specific eras. In Christianity, the Bible is examined by Christian theologians to determine God's intent. The goal is to learn the way that God wants us to think and live so that the believer may maximize happiness and contentment in temporal life and obtain rewards in eternity.

8 Images and Statues

a. In Islam, images and statues of the Prophet Mohammed and Allah are prohibited because the Prophet was afraid that Moslems would start to worship the images and statues (as they had done for centuries before the Prophet founded Islam). In Islam, superstition is introduced into worship as a result of great learning and insight.

b. In Humanism, images and statues are generally in the form of institutions such as United Nations or the various organizations that promote the humanist philosophy. Occasionally a statue of the earth goddess Gaia is shown respect if it can be used to establish a middle ground between humanism and theistic religions.

c. In Christianity, images and statues are permitted as learning aids with the understanding that the worship of images and statues is another example of idolatry. It is true that some Christian sects of the past introduced worship of images, statues, institutions, and the veneration of relics, but those were all a distortion of Christianity. In Christianity, superstition is introduced into worship only out of ignorance.

9 Relation to Politics

a. Islam was founded as a means to convince the warring Arab tribes to abandon their individual idols and unite under Allah under the guidance of the Prophet Mohammed. To do so, Islam had to become a religion with political objectives. Since the goal is to conquer the entire earth and establish a world-wide paradise in Allah's name, the text of the Q'uran may be interpreted by the Islamic theologians as necessary to meet the immediate needs of political and religious leaders. Allah requires and demands a monopoly on the faith of the people. No other faith or religion can be tolerated or allowed to co-exist.

b. Humanism is an inherently political religion. Humanism advances its theories and doctrines through the use of political power to establish laws that encourage or require the public conform to the philosophy, even if they otherwise reject it. Humanist philosophy is based on the concept of "no absolutes", but once the humanist philosophers devise a claim, it becomes an absolute to be imposed on everyone else by political mean. The objective is to establish humanism as a one-world social, political, and economic system governed by a small number of morally superior elites; this central objective requires the accumulation of political power.

c. Christianity is neither political nor a religion; it is a relationship with God. It exists and expands regardless of the political climate. The principles of Christianity as applied to politics rejects world-government because flawed mankind cannot create paradise. Christianity coexists with all other faiths, even ones hostile to Christianity. Because of free will, there cannot be a "Christian" nation, only one that is based on Christian principles (although all other faiths are tolerated). It is true that some nations have mandated Christianity and persecuted others, but that is a distortion of Christianity.

Ninety-Four Things You Don't Have To Do
(22 Jan 2012)

It seems that there is some confusion about what it takes to make it into heaven after death. Many people do not believe there is a God. You'll be pleased to know that the devil believes in God - the devil has actually seen God. Many people have come to believe that Christianity involves becoming some kind of obnoxious do-gooder, always going around interfering in other people's business. Rather than getting bogged down in irrelevant details, I will simply tell you what Christianity is, and how to obtain salvation; and, for clarity, I will list some of the things you **DON'T** have to do to attain salvation.

Your soul will exist forever. The question at hand is -- where will it exist, in heaven or in the hell? Heaven and hell are real, your sins and failures are real, and the fact that God must reject you is real, unless you accept His remedy.

Salvation occurs by faith alone in Christ alone: that Jesus Christ, the God-man, came to earth and was judged by God the Father for our sins, as a substitute for the judgment that we rightfully deserved. Jesus Christ performed all the work necessary to obtain forgiveness of our sins; all we have to do for salvation accept the work of Jesus on our behalf. As it says in the Word of God:

> **John 3:16:** For God so loved the world that he gave his one and only Son, that whoever believes in Him shall not perish but have eternal life.
>
> **Acts 4:12**: Salvation is found in no one else, for there is no other name under heaven given to men by which we must be saved.

The mechanics are simple: simply tell God the Father in your own words that you believe in the work of Christ (having paid the penalty for sin), and that you are trusting Jesus Christ as your Savior. That's it. Now you may think to yourself, "That is too good to be true", or "That is too simple". Of course it's too good to be true, if you compare it to some system that a person would create. But this is God's plan, a perfect plan: salvation is yours by faith alone. Don't be fooled: nothing else is required; and once you have believed in Christ for salvation, you will be in heaven for eternity after death.

You do not need to "do" anything for salvation: God has already done all the work. And so, as promised, here is a partial list of all the things you do not have to do or any other things you have to believe. Believe only in Jesus Christ.

You do not have to 1) become emotional over any sins, or 2) confess any sins in public, or 3) make a promise to do good, or 4) get baptized, or 5) feel sorry for sins, or 6) "commit your life to Jesus", or 7) change your evil ways, or 8) repent of your sins, or 9) do penance, or 10) get the "second blessing", or 11) speak in "tongues", or 12) get "the Ghost", or 13) receive communion, or 14) wait for the Rapture, or 15) invite Christ anywhere, or 16) go on crusades against unbelievers, or 17) make Jesus "Lord", or 18) answer an "altar call".

You do not have to 1) revere the Pope or a Patriarch, or 2) trust the Vatican, or 3) say the Hail Mary, or 4) say prayers to any saints, or 5) sponsor a novena, or 6) pay an indulgence, or 7) go to Mass, or 8) believe in the "relics of the True Cross", or 9) believe or reject purgatory, or 10) say the rosary, or 11) have reverence for the Shroud of Turin, or 12) obtain confirmation or sacraments, 13) or abstain from your favorite foods during Lent, or 14) venerate the remains of saints, or 15) light any candles, or 16) make the sign of the cross, or 17) pray to statues, or 18) sprinkle yourself with perfumed "holy water".

You don't have to 1) listen to fire-and-brimstone sermons, or 2) get along with your mother-in-law, or 3) sing hymns of praise, or 4) give to the poor, or 5) aid those in prison, or 6) visit the sick, or 7) be fruitful and multiply, or 8) rest on Sunday, or 9) pray for the dead, or 10) have faith in a priesthood, or 11) attend revival meetings, or 12) "love everyone".

You don't have to 1) oppose abortion, or 2) march for social justice, or 3) oppose those who march for social justice, or 4) support tax increases so others can help the poor, or 5) vote for a Republican, or 6) oppose those who vote for Republicans, or 7) support Israel, or 8) oppose the teaching of evolution, or 9) promote prayer in the public schools, or 10) embrace prophetic politics.

You don't have to 1) respect the "science" of Mary Eddy Baker, or 2) respect John Smith's golden tablets, or 3) respect Islam, or 4) respect any other religion, or 5) perform a pilgrimage to Jerusalem or Bethlehem, or 6) look down on "the heathen", or 7) support the "social gospel", or 8) engage in wishful thinking, or 9) the trust the infallibility of church leaders, or 10) have confidence in man, or 11) have faith in man's miracles, or 12) claim "cleanliness", or 13) believe in faith-healing, or 14) love all creation, or 15) wish "peace and goodwill to all", or 16) trust in the brotherhood of man, or 17) have hope in an institution.

You don't have to 1) adopt the simple life of the Amish, or 2) buy "sacred" music (especially that crummy "Christian Rock"), or 3) celebrate Christmas, or 4) pay tithes, or 5) try for sinless perfection, or 6) give drunken bums a few bucks, or 7) build an altar, or 8) give a wave offering, or 9) gain the affection of God, or 10) clean stained-glass windows, or 11) handle snakes, or 12) celebrate Easter, or 13) travel to shrines, or 14) contribute to a "building fund", or 15) be a nice person, or 16) visit a sacred place, or 17) worship at the Church of the Holy Sepulchre, or 18) search for the "Holy Grail", or 19) visit cathedrals.

In other words, you don't have to do any of the numerous phony actions and or adopt any of the phony beliefs that have become associated with Christianity throughout the centuries. I suppose there are many others, but these ninety-four came readily to mind.

So, now that you know that all the outward so-called manifestations of Christianity are either fake or irrelevant, focus on the one thing that matters: faith in Jesus Christ.

www.ingramcontent.com/pod-product-compliance
Lightning Source LLC
Chambersburg PA
CBHW080911170426
43201CB00017B/2282